NICHOLAS II
Tsar to Saint

by

TONY ABBOTT

ILLUSTRATED
203 IMAGES
(inc. 148 PHOTOGRAPHS, 25 PRINTS, 30 DRAWINGS)
PHOTO CREDITS APPEAR IN THE APPENDICES

New Angle Publishing

Copyright © Tony Abbott 2023
Printed in the United Kingdom
First Published 2023

INDEPENDENT PUBLISHING NETWORK
ISBN 978-1-80068-965-7
Paperback Edition (colour on white paper)

CONTENTS

CHAP		PAGE
Copyright		vi
Acknowledgements		vii
Conventions		viii
Introduction		ix
Foreword		xii
Dedication		xiv

PART I

01 THE ROYAL MARRIAGE (1)
   Maria Feodorovna 9
   Schleswig & Holstein 11
   Betrothal 12
   The court of Nicholas II 21
   Expectations for Russia 26

02 THE CORONATION (33)
   The ceremony 34
   The Khodynka Field tragedy 40
   The French ambassador's ball 48

03 PALACES, BALLS AND FABERGÉ (55)
   Seclusion of palace life 64
   Girls at the palace 68
   The grand ball 73
   Peter Carl Faberge 83

04 THE CULT OF MYSTICISM (87)
   The turn of the century 87
   Mystics and mayhem 91
   Phantom pregnancy 102
   The drugs legacy 106

05 INDUSTRIALISATION & WAR (109)
   The financial crisis 110
   The Siberian Railway 1891-1916 112
   War with Japan 1904-1905 115

CHAP		PAGE
06	ARRIVAL OF AN HEIR (119)	
	The royal disease	123
07	THE FIRST REVOLUTION 1905 (129)	
	Bloody Sunday	130
	The state dumas	136
08	RASPUTIN (145)	
	Arrival at the Imperial Court	151
	Meeting the Imperial Family...........................	155
	Rasputin investigated	159
09	SECLUSION AT TSARSKOE SELO (169)	
	A new norm at Alexander Palace	169
	A world of cameras	177
10	THE IMPERIAL YACHT STANDART (189)	
	The royal visits	194
	The alliances	212
	Royal romances	223
	The Standart Fabergé egg	227
	Standart photographs	228
11	MAD MONKS AND HYPNOTISM (231)	
	Rasputin returns from pilgrimage (1911)	238
	Proof of haemophilia	244
	Spala 1912 – Rasputin returns again	247
	The science of hypnotism	252
12	WAR IN EUROPE (257)	
	The war from the palace	264
	Nurses at the palace	270
	Fabergé red cross portraits egg	278
	Russian Jewish soldiers on the western front .	279
	Indifference to the Keiser	281
13	RASPUTIN IS DONE FOR (285)	
	Rasputin at the helm	286
	The murder of Rasputin	290

CHAP			PAGE
14	REVOLUTION & ABDICATION	(301)	
	The February Revolution 1917		302
	Final words on weak willidness		308
	Abdication of a dynasty		319
15	HOUSE ARREST	(333)	
	Home to prison		333
	Exile in Siberia		339
	Journey to Ekaterinburg		349
16	THE END OF DAYS	(357)	
	Civil war		360
	House of special purpose		366
	Execution of a Dynasty		376

PART II

17	THE AFTERMATH	(389)	
18	PLOTS & SCHEMING	(401)	
	British Intelligence in Russia		401
	Talks of rescues and executions		405
	The Lockhart plot		416
19	THE GREAT ESCAPE	(419)	
	The band of royal women		422
	Leaving Mother Russia		426
	The end in exile		434
20	THE OFFICIAL INVESTIGATIONS	(439)	
	The Sokolov investigation		442
	Sokolov's cargo leaves Russia		448
	The Gajda investigation		453
21	THE SEARCH FOR THE REMAINS	(461)	
	The last tango in Paris		461
	Recovering the relics		465
	Discovering the graves		469

CHAP			PAGE
22	THE ROAD TO SAINTHOOD	(475)	
	Mrs Kulikovska		478
	The interminable debate		486

APPENDICES   (497)

    A. Movements under house arrest 497
        Key dates, Durations
    B. Birthdays 497
    C. Executions 498
        Perm, Ipatiev House, Alapayevsk
        Peter and Paul fortress, Elsewhere
        Survived, Executioners
    D. Timeline 501
    E. Photographs, prints, drawings 509
    F. Further reading 515
    G. List of Names 517

INDEX OF NAMES   (525)

The Russian Imperial Family 1896 – 1918
L to R : Olga, Marie, Nicholas, Alexandra, Anastasia, Alexei, Tatiana

COPYRIGHT

The composition of words and images in this book have been lovingly crafted and presented in a unique style that aims to be enjoyable and educational. The editorial and moral rights and copyright of this creation belong to the author and no part of it may be reproduced or used in any form without written permission from the copyright owner except for the reasonable use of quotations in a review and for sales promotions.

Some images are in copyright and permission has been granted by their respective owners for this publication. Most images are in the public domain. Some images have had minor editing of levels, contrast etc. and some have been mildly restored or coloured. Any attribution due is listed in the appendices in the list of photographs. Even public domain images can by copyrighted if they are noticeably different to the original, such as with restoration and colouring.

The numerous quotations included in this book are mostly from books that are in the public domain from diaries and memoirs. These can be used wherein desired by any third party for any purpose.

Every effort was made to research thoroughly and to verify the information contained herein; a lot of research didn't make it simply because it could not be verified. While it is always the intention to portray accurate information there will inevitably be a margin of error due to the historical nature, especially for events that have several contending versions. In the many instances of duality, the method has been to present competing accounts and invite the reader to consider the likeliest option.

The author assumes no responsibility for errors, or other inaccuracies, omissions, or any other inconsistencies herein. And lastly, for the benefit of any Yussoupoffs remaining – 'All references made to characters dead or alive are purely intentional.'

New Angle Publishing

Nicholas II Tsar to Saint
INDEPENDENT PUBLISHING NETWORK

All content herein artistic and moral belong to the author
email@tonyabbott.co.uk

ACKNOWLEDGEMENTS

A very grateful and big 'thank you' to the lady overseeing *The Last Tsar – Blood and Revolution* exhibition at the Science Museum in London, for a most helpful and informative conversation and whose interpretation of the newly discovered Romanov photographs greatly helped me to visualise this work. Thanks also to those secretaries, editors, archivists and good people that took the time to help me, from Bonhams to Get Archive LLC and those individuals that made the completion of this work become a reality.

John Jukes, Brisbane, Australia, beta reader (Fiverr as Jukes92)
Cover artist, Rose Miller
The Science Museum, London
The Queen's Gallery Buckingham Palace
The Royal Collection Trust, UK
State Archive of the Russian Federation
State Hermitage Museum, St Petersburg
Beinecke Rare Book and Manuscript Library at Yale University

Online Archives:
Internet Archive	Gutenberg Project
Library of Congress	Get Archive LLC
JSTOR digital library	Wikipedia
Wikimedia Commons	British Library

Zlatoust City History Museum, Russia
Tyne & Wear Archives & Museums, UK
Penn Museum Archives, US
Bonhams, London
The Siberian Times (Online)
Tretyakov Gallery, Moscow
Getty Open Content Program
Encyclopaedia Britannica, Inc
Romanov100 (Website)
stevemorse.org (online Julian to Gregorian converter)

CONVENTIONS

Gregorian and Julian calendars:

The wide use of dates is intended to provide a sense of immersion in the progression of the story. It may be that for one chapter we conclude it at 1918 but for the next for another topic we are back to 1896. It has been impossible to completely avoid moving forward and backwards in time but it's restricted as far as possible and in the main the story is presented in a sequential date order.

Old Russia used the Julian calendar and on 14 February 1918 a new Russia moved in line with the Gregorian calendar. Whereas the Julian year started in Easter the Gregorian year starts on 1 January. They are 12 days apart in the 19th Century and 13 days apart in the 20th Century.

It's possible for a Gregorian date in 1918 to be equivalent to a Julian date in 1917. This causes confusion when researching as it's not always clear which system has been used and discrepancies are commonplace in Russian source material. The Gregorian is preferred in this book but in some instances the Julian exists for clarity (e.g. diary dates). Julian dates are denoted by (J) and Gregorian dates are denoted by (G), all other dates should be taken as Gregorian. Some dates simply cannot be determined and in this case the date has been used as found and assumed to be Gregorian.

Patronymics:

Royal names are chosen and don't always follow a strict format. The Russian middle name is derived from the father's first name known as a 'patronym' and a surname is the family name, e.g. Romanov. Suffixes –vich, –ovsky mean *son of* and suffixes –eva, –evna, –ova, –ovna mean *daughter of*. They can take slightly different form depending on the origin, like Polish or Slavic. The use of V and FF are interchangeable such as in *Romanov* or *Romanoff*. Similarly, Y is a common Slavic addition, e.g. *Ekaterinburg* and *Yekaterinburg* or *Feodorovna* and *Fyodorovna*.

Names like Friedrich (Frederick) and Fyodor (Theodore) are sometimes not distinctly differentiated, as there is no Russian equivalent for the German name Friedrich. A patronym from a saint is often used such as the Romanov patron Our Lady of Saint Theodore – i.e. Feodorovna.

With half of the Russian royal bloodline being German in origin, the females took their name from the so-called Feodorovskaya Icon of the Mother of God; e.g. Alexandra Feodorovna, Maria Feodorovna. There is no right or wrong way other than when converters took on Orthodox names they tended to avoid obvious German names. In Maria Feodorovna's case, taking her father's patronym would have made her Maria Christianova, a lovely name, but an obvious Christian one too.

INTRODUCTION

The Romanov ruling dynasty lasted from 1613 when it first established power, until 1917 with the forced abdication of Tsar Nicholas II. Over three centuries, eighteen Romanovs had sat on the Russian throne. This work tells the story of the last ruling family and the intimacy they shared through the good times and the hardships of a modernising country that they were unsuited and unable to adapt to. They were not blameless either, their careless abandonment of the machinations of government and a lack of awareness of the world around them saw to their demise and the end of the monarchy in Russia, as well as the dissemination of the Romanov family.

This work coincided with exhibitions in London that marked the centenary of the deaths of Nicholas II and members of the immediate Russian royal family and their aides. These visually striking displays were a moving experience for this author and gifted the inspiration to begin writing. At Buckingham Palace; the *Russia, Royalty & the Romanovs* exhibition was compelling. At the entrance to the gallery hung full length oil on canvas portraits of the Emperor and Empress of Russia painted in 1914 and on loan from the Tsarskoe Selo State Museum and Heritage Site and the two Imperial Fabergé eggs (the Mosaic egg and the Colonnade egg) from the Royal Collection were the highlight of the exhibition. Equally enthralling, in a separate gallery at Buckingham Palace, was the exhibition of *Roger Fenton's Photographs of the Crimea*; a collection of 360 photographs. It was the first time that a war had been fully documented with photographs; each one very moving considering they contain no depictions of combat or scenes of the effects of war itself.

Another two Imperial Fabergé eggs were on display at the Science Museum exhibition, *The Last Tsar – Blood and Revolution*; two of the last ever made, in honour of contributions made during World War I. The Red Cross Portraits egg (1915) to honour Tsarina Alexandra and her daughters (see *page 278*), and the Steel Military egg (1916) in recognition of Tsar Nicholas II's efforts at the western front.

These treasures were brought together to reflect the truly magnificent opulence and craftsmanship of a remarkable time in Russian history and to mark the anniversary of a significant event that changed its future. Galleries were crammed with objet d'art at which visitors stood and observed for ages, dazzled by the exhibits and intently reading the little labels and plaques for further information. It gave a real sense of living in the moment; looking at the photographs, the clothes, the personal objects that had represented a connection to their world. The way to experience history is to try and be were people once stood, to visualise what they might have once seen and to experience their feelings and emotions, as far as one can conceptualise it.

There are already so many books about Nicholas II so is another really necessary and what can possibly be left that hasn't been said? One soon comes to the realisation whilst researching, that the Romanov story is one of multiple theories with alternate endings and intrigue and mischief at every turn. Just when you think you've nailed something down, another thing appears requiring a complete rethink. There is often no right or wrong way and frequently the reader is asked to consider the likeliest scenario; an absolute fact in one version may just be hearsay in another. Only Russian history provides different dates with each version and it can be a fruitless enterprise trying to establish the true or likely scenario.

By way of an example about typical discrepancies consider the death of Soviet official Filipp Goloshchekin, stated in the book (page 244) by Russian author Victor Alexandrov, *The End of the Romanovs* (1966) as having been shot in 1939, but Wikipedia gives the date of his execution as 28 October 1941. A more extreme example would be the death of Pyotr Ermakov given by Victor Alexandrov as having been shot in 1939 (page 244) but Wikipedia says that he died of cancer on 22 May 1952. Then there's the Tsar's chief executioner Yakov Yurovsky, who according to Victor Alexandrov was reported by the Moscow press as having died in 1962 whereas Wikipedia states that it was 2 August 1938. These discrepancies are from one paragraph alone on page 244.

Furthermore, Victor Alexandrov criticises on page 197 a contemporary work, *The Last Days of the Romanovs* written by Pavel Bykov, calling it confused. He says, *"They* [Communist Party veterans] *can hardly have been convinced by 'The Last Days of the Romanovs' in which P. M. Bykov's account of Vassili Yakovlev and his mission is extremely confused. We wonder if Bykov himself believed his account!"* There were a lot of authors calling in to question the accounts of other authors during the 1920s and 1930s when there was an unprecedented number of memoirs written.

It would appear that Victor Alexandrov et al would pluck out dates from nowhere when the research could not establish the fact. Presumably he picked the likeliest fact and we therefore lean towards Victor Alexandrov in this example for no better reason than he was Russian, got published, and was closer in time to the events, leaving us with his version of the facts.

In the 1920s aside from World War I, it's hard to think of a topic that was more popular than the Russian Revolution 1917 and the fate of the Romanovs. The multitude of conflicting accounts meant that an exorbitant effort went in to researching the source material for this book to arrive at the likeliest versions. The many works on the Romanovs pretty much cover the same ground and websites tend to be consistently consistent using the quill of the age; copy & paste. Here and there though, a work does break the mould and it's a pleasure to read something offering a new perspective and boldly presenting new theories for serious consideration, like this book.

For this work I wanted no exposure to recent works and very little has come from modern authors. I trust that you will come to agree the final product brings a unique perspective to the table every bit as meticulously researched and accurate as any existing telling of this story thus far. Of course, many books were obligatory reading such as the works of Nikolai Sokolov and the challenging *The File on the Tsar* by Summers & Mangold which both needed to be scanned for their revelations. By not attempting to reword the work of others, an unfortunate trend of the age with AI, freedom was exercised to trespass in to well established theories that would otherwise preclude further interpretation of the established or accepted facts; even the highly respected Nikolai Sokolov was fair game and open to criticism.

Summers & Mangold had stretched the established theories and their work should be better regarded today than it is, especially against the works of profiteers like the priest Iliodor and Prince Felix Yussoupoff, whose accounts are the source of many established theories but in reality border on historical fiction. The depiction of Nicholas II's character has suffered greatly because of these distortions and this book while exploring the good and bad sides of his character cannot determine with absoluteness the answer to the pertinent question of whether he was a good or bad person.

His character is usually assumed from the many letters (published in 1929) between him and his wife Alexandra and where he sits in Russian history is best left to historians but for this work the greater emphasis is placed on memoirs peculiar to the period between 1920 and 1938 which often fill the gaps. The many authors of that period and those since were limited by secrecy until the opening of the Russian State Archives in 1991 which added another dimension to the understanding of what had happened back in the day. For example, the correct date of Rasputin's birth was known only when the first researcher visited the archives and came across the date in a secret police file (*see page 145*).

It was an age when people communicated with letters and kept diaries, activities all too distant in our modern lives. Photography was the in thing thanks to Kodak and images of the Romanovs are being discovered all the time. There's a pleasantness to images of those long departed and in reading the words they had set the time aside to write; their thoughts and experiences recorded for posterity. What other way 'cept procreation is there to preserve the memories of human existence.

Yet another book on Nicholas II might not be an attractive nomination for a Pulitzer award but perhaps it succeeds in bringing excitement to a well rested tale, part biography, part historical textbook; it would be too easy to think of it as a collection of quotes and fillers. But it achieves so much more, with every image and text chosen carefully to draw the reader in to the story. Should you find yourself looking deeply in to a photograph for a while, then the goal has been achieved and you have become truly mesmerised.

FOREWORD

Nicholas II is best known as the last ruler of the era of Russian Tsars and Emperors and in particular for the fall of the Romanov Imperial dynasty that claimed descendancy from Augustus Caesar. The name 'Romanov' gives homage to the Roman Empire with the title of Tsar meaning 'Caesar' – *The house of Roman Caesars*. The title of Keiser also derives from Caesar. Such a powerful seat is always for the occupier to protect by strengthening autocracy, succession after succession, acquiring more wealth and power for the next ruler that comes along.

Like the Roman Empire, Russia over-relied on slave labour, over-spent on the military and was rife with government corruption. Russia also suffered a string of military losses and created the political instability to collapse their realm. These were the similarities between Rome and Russia and demonstrate that great empires follow the Rome model and spurt in and out of existence affected by small concerns that grow in to big problems.

For want of a nail the Kingdom was lost, the proverb goes. Benjamin Franklin used it in his almanac of 1758, published under the pseudonym 'Poor Richard', to illustrate the importance of being vigilant of seemingly unimportant events that can lead to problematic issues. For Nicholas II this was in neglecting the affairs of state and ignoring the plight of the peasants and workers which festered and morphed in to rebellion then revolution.

Although relatively short and seemingly straightforward, Nicholas II's reign was rather complicated. What other ruler had experienced two wars, constant industrial striking, two revolutions and closed three parliaments (Dumas). In terms of industry and religion he strengthened the country but is mostly described for his weakness in leading the people, the government, the military and therefore the country and empire, which culminated in ruin.

Romanov history could fill volumes but within these limited pages the events that significantly affected Nicholas II's reign are presented as the story of the last tsar and emperor of Russia from the time he became tsar to his canonisation. It's also the story of a royal family that fought desperately to carve out a separate reality who in many respects just wanted to be left alone. One gets the impression that they would have been well suited living on a farm with just the animals and each other to contend with.

It's also a humble love story with five children at the centre that will not fail to connect emotionally with the reader. The family stands juxtaposed with the cruelty and barbarity happening outside of the palace gates where people knew the reality of starvation and torture and slaughter and felt the cruelty of the regime that was led and orchestrated by the autocrat within the gates who seemingly had no care for the unfurling travesty.

The problems facing Russia at the turn of the twentieth century showed why a monarch was necessary; Church, military, government, parliament, workers, and nobles all revolved around the monarch. If that monarch is not interested in keeping things together or incapable of doing so, the snakes of the Gorgon eat each other until the head is consumed which is what was allowed to happened with bloody wars and a civil war that attracted the foreign intervention of a few hundred thousand troops waring in the Russian interior for years. It happened in the absence of solid dynastic leadership.

Following the February Revolution 1917 when the royal family were put under house arrest, orderly chaos turned in to a fiasco. Was there really any need for thousands of politicians to be assassinated and thousands of citizens to be executed and for the royal family to be murdered in such an undignified way – all because a few Jews rebelled against an oppressive regime. Some might call it justified vengeance but surely the one does not vindicate the other. Change is a necessary component for evolution and with Nicholas II opposing reforms things eventually reached a boiling point and the inevitable happened, except that one murderous regime was replaced by another. The internal struggle could have been so different and been sorted out amicably, as there were endless opportunities to do so but none were taken. Sophie Buxhoeveden (lady in waiting to Empress Alexandra) in her book described succinctly the many foreign officials that were circling Ipatiev House (the place of house arrest and execution) but not doing much to press for the release of the royal prisoners therein.

"Unfortunately, all foreign Governments were then so much occupied with their own affairs that all of them lost the opportune moment when the more important ones could, each in turn, have saved the Emperor and his family."

You are invited on this literary journey to employ your imagination. At times you might believe a conclusion is reached but for that to be true you need to have read every book ever written about Nicholas II. Do consider the accepted versions given here alongside any alternatives or arguments put forward and make your own path to the likeliest truth. I trust you will enjoy this work much as I did creating it. Please be seated, get comfortable and advance through these pages with imagination ready and expectations high.

TONY ABBOTT, 17 July 2023

"With the lapse of time the historian can keep aloof from political contamination and give the true its rightful place."
— VICTOR ALEXANDROV, The End of The Romanovs

This work is dedicated to the Romanov children
who through their short lives showed pure love
and exemplified the beauty of the human soul

Olga

Tatiana

Marie

Anastasia

Alexei

Stavka, 1 September 1915 – LTR: General Pustovoitenko, Nicholas II, General Alekseev

PART I

CHAPTER I
The Royal Marriage

IN 1894, the 26 year old Nicholas Alexandrovich Romanov inherited the Russian throne and married Queen Victoria's favourite granddaughter Alix. Together they ruled over 150 million subjects across 8,660,000 square miles covering one sixth of the world's land surface. Finding comfort in their mutual solitude they gradually withdrew from court life to their palaces, preferring their children and countryside residence in Tsarskoe Selo, on the outskirts of St Petersburg. In having distanced themselves they triggered a chain of events that would lead to their demise and a tragic end for the Russian empire.

Queen Victoria of the United Kingdom of Great Britain and Ireland had nine children with her consort Prince Albert. As a result of her efforts to marry them in to royal families across the European continent she became known as the grandmother of Europe and was therefore one of the first to be informed about the engagement of her granddaughter Alix to the heir apparent of the Russian throne, the Tsarevich Nicholas. The welcomed news was brought to her by granddaughter Elizabeth (aka Ella, Alix's sister) who was very excited to be the one making the announcement.

> *"Friday 20th April 1894. Ella came in, much agitated to say that Alicky and Nicky were engaged, begging they might come in. Saw them both. Alicky had tears in her eyes, but looked very bright & I kissed them both."*
> — QUEEN VICTORIA, diary

CHAPTER I

Queen Victoria with her grandchildren, February 1879
top: Victoria, Elizabeth *bottom*: Irene, Alix

Queen Victoria's husband Prince Albert was diagnosed with typhoid fever (*page 277*) and consequently died on 14 December 1861. He passed away in the Blue Room at Windsor Castle in the presence of the Queen and five of their nine children. Then after, Queen Victoria's relationship with her daughters became oppressive as she withdrew in to her depression and the distance she put between herself and them would be mirrored somewhat between Alix and her children in years to come.

Alix's mother was Princess Alice, Queen Victoria's second daughter and third child who had married in to a German royal family in 1862, to the Grand Duke Friedrich Wilhelm Ludwig Karl of Hesse and by Rhine. Prince Friedrich and Princess Alice had seven children during their eleven year marriage. On their tenth wedding anniversary their daughter Alix was born, a Princess of Hesse and by Rhine. Hesse was a grand duchy in western Germany that existed from 1806 as Hesse-Darmstadt and from 1816 as Hesse. Darmstadt was the capital of Hesse lasting until the end of the German Empire in November 1918.

Alix lost her brother Friedrich when she was just one year old in 1873. Her other brother Ernest was chasing him when Friedrich fell twenty feet out of a window and died from internal bleeding that same evening. Friedrich had died suddenly from his injuries because he suffered from haemophilia, a disease that first occurred in the family with Queen Victoria. Four years later in 1877 her father became King Ludwig IV and one year after that the household was struck with diphtheria which claimed the lives of mother Alice and sister Marie.

Two of Queen Victoria's daughters, Alice and Beatrice, were carriers of the disease and it was fully affected in her fourth son Leopold who was 30 years old when he too died suddenly on the following morning due to his haemophilia after a fall that caused fatal internal bleeding. Alice had passed the disease to her children Friedrich, Alix and Irene whereas Beatrice, the youngest of Queen Victoria's children had passed it to her daughter Ena and younger son Leopold who survived for thirty-three years with the disease and died from a knee operation. Ena married the Spanish King Alfonso XIII and she passed the disease to two of their five sons, Alfonso and Gonzalo. Alfonso the Prince of Asturias and heir apparent died at 31 from internal bleeding after a car accident and Gonzalo died at 19 from severe abdominal bleeding, also caused in a car accident but because as a haemophiliac he could not be operated on and subsequently died two days later.

Alix was just six years old in 1878 and had lost three members of her immediate family (mother Alice, older brother Friedrich, younger sister Marie). She had been so close to her sister Marie they were described as inseparable and her death caused irreparable damage to Alix's mental health. Alice had been the first of Queen Victoria's children to die and her children were brought to the Isle of Wight and raised at Osborne House. Alix was a beautiful and happy girl but her family losses were devastating and she became withdrawn with a depression that would never leave her and a sadness that was etched on her face so that she was rarely ever known to genuinely smile outside of her immediate family. A member of the Russian court would describe it once, that she always looked as if she were about to burst in to tears at any moment.

The children at Osborne House had their own nurse who prepared personal monthly reports for Queen Victoria. The children's relationship with their grandmother was said to have been a loving one, in contrast with the distance she had placed between herself and her own children since Prince Albert's passing. Alix was said to be the favourite grandchild and considered to be a future queen of England. She was therefore raised in a predictably austere English manner and prepared for future royal duties.

In June 1884 when Alix was 12 years old, she visited Russia for the first time to attend the wedding of her sister Princess Elizabeth of Hesse and by Rhine to the Grand Duke Sergei Alexandrovich of Russia, a brother to Emperor Alexander III and uncle to the 16 year old Tsarevich Nicholas, whom she met for the first time. Alix returned to St Petersburg in the winter of 1889 to visit Elizabeth and enjoyed ice skating with Nicholas and his family. During that blissful six weeks Nicholas and Alix came upon the realisation that love was blossoming between them.

As a young woman Alix became renowned as one of the most beautiful of eligible princesses in Europe. When she returned from St Petersburg her first cousin Prince Albert Victor, Duke of Clarence and Avondale (son of Edward VII and therefore also her first cousin,) became enamoured with her and pursued her well in to 1890 with a passion. He proposed but was rejected because by then Alix was already in love with Nicholas of Russia.

Princess Alice of Great Britain 1861 and a young Alix (5 years old) 1877

That same year in 1890, Prince Albert Victor fell in love with Princess Hélène of Orléans, a daughter of Prince Philippe the Count of Paris and deposed pretender to the throne of France. Queen Victoria was opposed to the match because Hélène was a Catholic and Prince Philippe would not give his consent thereby vetoing a marriage. Queen Victoria looked to Mary of Teck; the only daughter of Queen Victoria's first cousin Princess Mary Adelaide of Cambridge and her Austrian husband Francis von Hohenstein, Duke of Teck. But Prince Albert Victor died unexpectedly at 28 years old from influenza during the pandemic of 1889-1892 and Queen Victoria arranged for Mary of Teck to marry another of her grandsons, the Prince of Wales and future King George V of England.

Nicholas' mother, the Russian Empress Maria Feodorovna, had also expressed a wish for her son to marry Hélène in a pressing move to dissuade him from pursuing Alix, whom she considered to be of low ranking. But she did not know that Nicholas had already professed his love for Alix after they had last met a second time in St Petersburg when he recorded in his diary the desire to marry her.

> *"My dream is to one day marry Alix. I have loved her for a long time, and still deeper and stronger since 1889, when she spent six weeks in St. Petersburg. For a long time, I resisted my feeling that my dream will come true."* — NICHOLAS ALEXANDROVICH, 1890

Alix viewed things slightly differently believing Nicholas had not given her the fullest attention. He appeared distant and disinterested in pursuing her. Queen Victoria subsequently plied her matchmaking skill with the Russian court enquiring on suitors subtly hinting at Nicholas but she was told that he was being prepared for royal life and his first duty was to serve a term in the army and that any interest he may have afforded Alix was purely an infatuation that would pass. Maria Feodorovna viewed the approach with suspicion whereas the Emperor was too busy dealing with his son's obsession over a certain ballerina, Mathilde Feliksovna Kschessinska.

Nicholas was 22 years old and starting to grow his signature beard, Mathilde was 18 years old and already a successful ballerina. She was of Polish descent and the most famous in the Mariinsky Ballet (formerly the Imperial Russian Ballet). Young officers with ballerinas was not uncommon and his infatuation was recorded in his diary, having first met Mathilde at a minor ball when his father invited her to his table. At the next ball he found himself seated next to her and several balls later, the fact that they were always seated together was reported to Alexander III who forbade Nicholas to continue the association. It has been suggested that she was Alexander III's mistress but she would have been of an exceptionally young age for that relationship and therefore it was highly unlikely. Nicholas had grown stubborn behind his new beard and military appointment to the Life Guard Hussars, so in 1890 the Emperor dealt with the ensuing romance by sending him and his sibling brother George on a voyage around the world aboard a Russian battleship from which they would be fortunate to return alive.

CHAPTER I

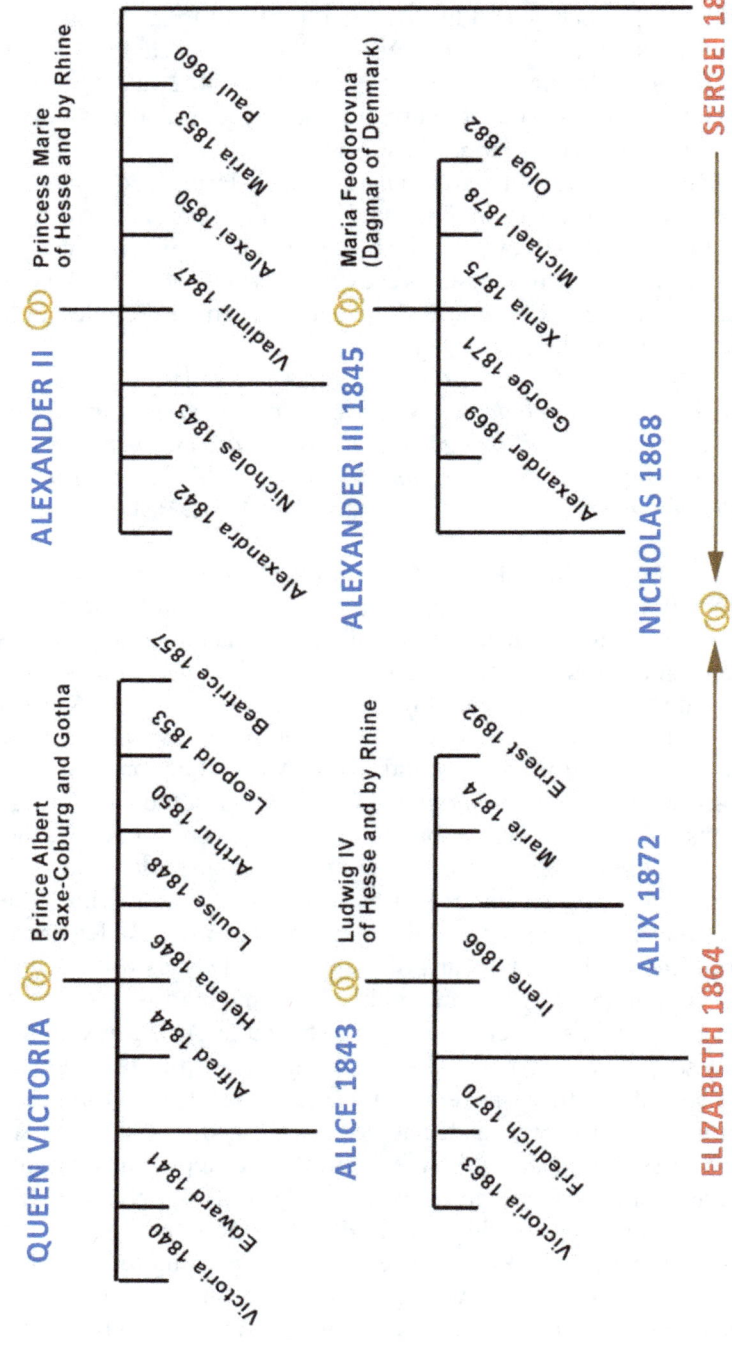

Nicholas' infatuation with Mathilde meant that separation had become necessary but the obvious question is whether the real reason was that Mathilde fell pregnant. It wasn't until 1955 that parts of her memoirs were discovered in a Russian vault. Written many years after the affair they put to rest a rumour that she had taken his virginity and produced an illegitimate child; she was pregnant but lost it when a horse drawn sleigh overturned. According to an article in the Mirror online on 22 December 2017 titled 'The last tsar's secret love child', Mathilde wrote: *"It was said afterwards that I had children with the Heir, but it was not true. I often wished that I had."* Nicholas was therefore, expected to remove this from his mind.

During the voyage, brother George (the prince of Greece and Denmark) caught tuberculosis and by the time they reached India was in such a bad state that he needed to return home. They continued to Ceylon where he met with his cousin Alexander in whom he confided about the 'senseless trip', not taking his separation well. On 11 May 1891 he visited Nagasaki and got a dragon tattoo on his right forearm and then visited Kyoto, the former capital of Japan up until 1868. During an excursion trip to the port town of Ōtsu on lake Biwa, the largest lake in Japan (670 square metres), Nicholas first visited the treasures at the Miidera Temple situated at the foot of Mount Hiei to the northeast of Kyoto, then returning to Ōtsu Nicholas took a jinrikisha ride through the streets, (a Japanese rickshaw believed to have originated in Japan in 1868 during the Meiji period and lasting well in to the 1920s).

Suddenly from out of nowhere he was attacked despite the route being lined with policemen. The would-be assassin was Tsuda Sanzo, a 36 year old Japanese policeman of the Shiga Prefecture security team that had been assigned to protect the route. Tsuda (the surname, i.e. family name, comes first in the Japanese convention) was a descendant of a samurai line that was abolished in 1868, a year after Emperor Meiji (known as Meiji the Great) became the first monarch of the Empire of Japan. He ran towards Nicholas wielding his sabre at Nicholas' head. Nicholas reacted instinctively just managing to avoid a fatal blow but receiving slight injuries to the temple and the back of the head. His forehead was left with a permanent scar to remind him of the incident which was attributed to the headaches he suffered from thereafter for the rest of his life. If not for George whose reflexive pummelling of Tsuda with a bamboo cane fended off the attacker, Nicholas would surely have been killed, with some credit due to the jinrikisha pullers who also helped to disarm Tsuda. It turned out the wounds were superficial, if at first concerning because of the amount of blood emanating. He received first aid in a local kimono shop and was then taken to the Shiga Prefecture Office to be assessed by a doctor. Nicholas' hatred of Japan had been moulded at that time, and he refused to be treated by Japanese doctors, returning to Kyoto and soon after going to Kobe to board his ship.

CHAPTER I

Emperor Meiji was struck with dishonour by the assassination attempt and took the fastest train to Kyoto and on to Kobe to express his apology to Nicholas in person. It was a political incident which some thought may have involved the Japanese government to some degree. With his ship and five accompanying Russian warships at Kobe, a retaliation by Russia would have been disastrous considering Japan had no fleet to talk about. But Nicholas was gracious and accepted the apology. His wounds were looked at by naval doctors and the Japan tour was cut short (*more about the injuries on page 480*). Nicholas went straight to Vladivostok to lay the first stone for the eastern terminus that began the huge construction project of the Siberian Railway and after that significant event he was back in St Petersburg wasting no time in throwing himself once more in to the throes of the very fit and youthful ballerina Mathilde Kschessinska.

In 1892 when Alix had made her second trip to St Petersburg to visit her sister Ella and formed the impression that Nicholas was not as impressed with her, the reason was that on the outbound leg of his voyage Nicholas visited Germany and became infatuated with Princess Margaret of Prussia, the sister of Keiser Wilhelm II. It was the libido of youth and he went on to rise in the ranks moving from one Hussar regiment to another, moving to the famed Preobrazhensky Life-Guards Regiment and in due course having advanced to the rank of Colonel in both Hussar regiments. He realised that military life and the outdoors held a great attraction for him and it was a lifestyle choice that would remain throughout his life.

When Mathilde's memoirs were published in the 1960s she stated that their affair had lasted from 1890 to April 1894 when Nicholas became engaged to Alix. It has been suggested that Mathilde continued to see Nicholas after he was married, a possibility that was investigated by the author Coryne Hall in her biography of Mathilde called *Imperial Dancer*, published in 2006. She found that these insinuations were ill founded and that Nicholas was entirely faithful to his wife.

Mathilde continued her royal affairs with two Romanov grand dukes that she was seeing at the same time which produced a child. She was never romantically connected to Nicholas again despite having said that she wished their relationship could have continued, suggesting pressure from the Imperial Court. But by no means was it the end for Mathilde, on the death of Emperor Alexander III in 1894, Nicholas kept a back seat interest in her career and she was given a palace on the Neva as well as being given charge of the Imperial Ballet. Over her dancing career she attained much success playing major roles in Swan Lake, The Nutcracker, Giselle and many others and was awarded the rare status of *Prima ballerina assoluta*. In later years she opened a ballet school with one of her students being the very talented Dame Margot Fonteyn whom Mathilde taught to dance. How Nicholas' life might have been with the hyperenergetic Mathilde at his side.

Maria Feodorovna

Maria Feodorovna was a daughter of the King and Queen of Denmark, sister of the heir apparent Frederick of Denmark, sister of the King of Greece, sister of Queen Alexandra of England, wife of the Emperor of Russia and mother of the heir apparent to the Russian throne.

Princess Dagmar of Denmark, 1875.
Always trendy and keenly interested in world affairs

Siblings:

- ❖ Frederick VIII King of Denmark 1906-1912
- ❖ George I King of Greece 1863-1913
- ❖ Alexandra of Denmark consort of Edward VII (Effectively Queen of England 1901 to 1910)
- ❖ Princess Thyra of Denmark spouse of the exiled heir to the kingdom of Hanover Ernest Augustus. Deprived of the thrones of Hanover upon its annexation by Prussia.

CHAPTER I

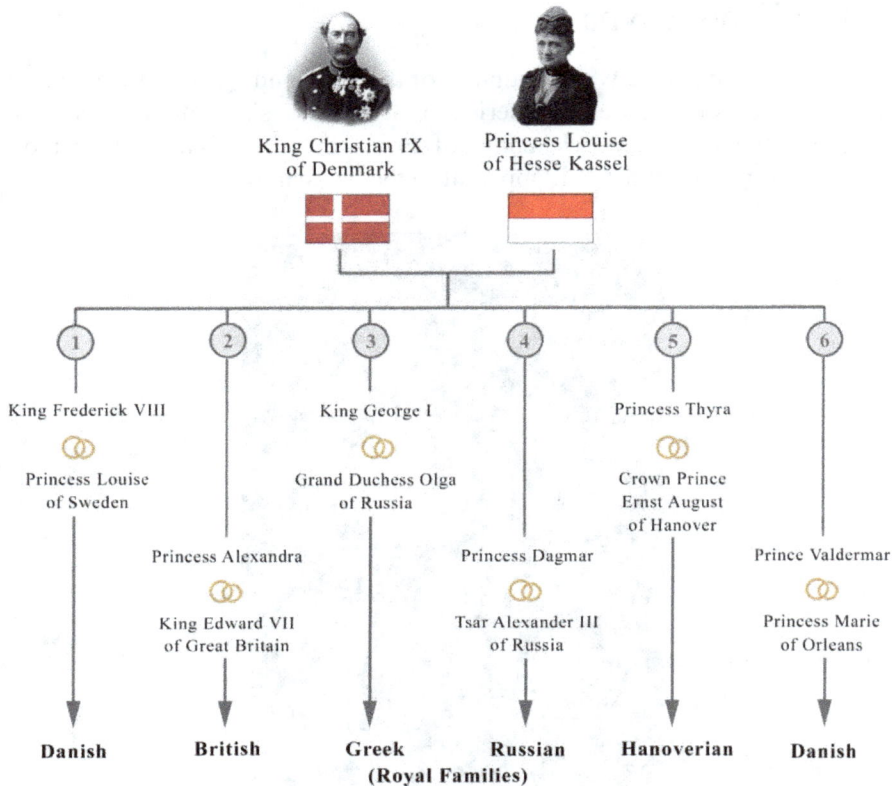

Maria Feodorovna was highly intelligent, composed, charming and good looking with deep piercing eyes and a gravelly voice. She put family and charity at the heart of her life and the public adored her, she was even idolised. In their youth the Danish sisters became trend setters, always looking glamorous in their stylish outfits. Dagmar carried elegance and wore expensive and trying designs, one of her favourite designers was the Parisian house of Worth. It was noted that she was the best dressed woman in Europe.

As well as Queen Victoria forming marital connections across Europe, Queen Louise of Denmark was also connecting her children to Great Britain, Russia, Greece, Sweden and Norway, becoming known as the mother-in-law of Europe. Princess Dagmar of Denmark on her conversion to the Russian Orthodox Church changed her name to Maria Feodorovna, before marrying the then Tsarevich Alexander of Russia in 1866. When her husband Emperor Alexander III died in 1894 she became known by the title Dowager or Dowager Empress, bestowed to high ranking royal widows which carries a slightly higher status at official functions than a consort (the companion of a reigning monarch).

Schleswig and Holstein

Dagmar (Maria Feodorovna) held anti-German sentiment for all of her life. It was due to the Prussian annexation of Danish territories in 1864 known as the Second Schleswig War (aka Prusso-Danish War). Her hatred of Germany was shared by her sister Alexandra who after her marriage to Edward VII of Great Britain was shielded from diplomatic affairs for this reason. It was not until 1914 that their warnings about Germany were realised, when England and Russia came together against Germany in war.

Strange it was that the Danish sisters married German husbands; Maria Feodorovna to Alexander of Russia who was half German on account of his mother and grandmother being German, and Alexandra to Edward of Saxe-Coburg and Gotha lineage. Indeed, the Danish and Russian houses were 50% German, as might be expected for dynastic gene diversification purposes, but in comparison, Queen Victoria and Prince Albert of Great Britain were 100% of German stock.

The German hatred can be attributed to the Danish war with Prussia when Christian IX was blamed for losing it and humiliating the country. When the war started Dagmar was 17 and Alexandra 20 and their mother was openly and passionately anti-German which she passed on to her children. Queen Louise witnessed the unnecessary mass slaughter of many Danish people with the Danish sisters undoubtedly seeing the Prussian brutality at first hand for themselves.

The war was fought over two southern Danish provinces, Schleswig and Holstein, neither having any meaningful representation in the Danish parliament. Christian IX was addressing the matter of representation in the constitution, which he signed on 18 November 1863, but it only applied to Schleswig. This was because Schleswig on the Danish border held more importance for Denmark, being the seat of many of the heraldic ancestors and where the ruling houses of Denmark came from. The people of Holstein were on the Prussian border and themselves felt more Prussian than Danish but their exclusion by Christian IX led to an accusation of a contravention of the London Protocol 1852; the peace agreement that existed whereby the German Confederation had returned Schleswig and Holstein to Denmark on condition they be regarded equally.

Prussia and Austria argued that when Schleswig had been included in the Danish constitution but not Holstein, it had been a violation of the peace protocol. Christian IX then acted without government approval and offered Holstein up and proposed an alliance with Prussia in exchange for Denmark retaining control of Schleswig. Prussian Prime Minister Otto von Bismarck rejected the proposal as not only did Bismarck feel justified in taking action on behalf of Holstein, a previous member of the German Confederation, but also relished the opportunity to start a war with Denmark.

CHAPTER I

The manner in which Denmark was so convincingly and badly beaten was seen as a national disgrace. Both provinces had been lost and the Danish borders pushed back by 200 kilometres. Danish land was reduced by 40% and the country's population diminished by a third. Following the creation of the German Empire in 1871, Holstein remained German and a referendum was held on Schleswig resulting in the south wanting to remain in Germany and the north voting for Denmark, forming the border between Denmark and Germany that has remained uncontested ever since.

Betrothal

Notwithstanding Maria Feodorovna's prejudice against Germany, it's hard to see any reason why the pairing of Nicholas and Alix could have been anything less than perfect considering their impeccable lineage; he the son of an Emperor and she the granddaughter of an Empress. Both were young, good looking and the most desirable prince and princess in Europe, and rather unnecessarily so, they happened to be in love with each other. In addition, they were connected through family ties; Nicholas' mother and Alix's auntie by marriage were Danish sisters. But quite evidently these credentials held no sway and both families openly opposed a marriage.

Queen Victoria saw Russia as a dangerous throne to occupy and once remarked of Alexander III that he was a sovereign whom she did not look upon as a gentleman. She envisaged greater things for Alix and enlisted Alix's sister Victoria of Hesse and by Rhine to persuade a marriage to Prince Albert Victor, with the ultimate aim of luring her back to England. But as discussed, Alix was only interested in Nicholas and Prince Albert Victor died unexpectedly. Empress Maria Feodorovna saw Alix as the offspring of a lowly German family and as a princess of Denmark was opposed to everything German. She was holding out for the best match for her son and favoured Princess Elena of Montenegro (the future queen of Italy). But, in a similar vein to Alix, Nicholas stubbornly refused to consider anyone else, compelling his mother to engage Alexander III to withhold his approval, a requirement for any marriage in the royal household.

The alternative for Queen Victoria on Albert Victor's passing was a union for Alix to a lowly German or Slavic prince, therefore she came to see the benefit of pairing Alix with Nicholas but Maria Feodorovna had already dismissed the notion when Queen Victoria had enquired for suitors hinting at Nicholas. The obstacle to a marriage was on the Russian side entirely and aside from Maria Feodorovna's reservations, Alix was a devout Lutheran and could not occupy a royal position without first aligning herself with the Russian Orthodox Church which she was unwilling to consider.

Nicholas tried to convince her that conversion was necessary, saying that his mother had converted before her marriage and that her sister Elizabeth, although not required to do so, had also converted in preparation for her wedding ten years earlier in June 1884 to Nicholas' uncle Sergei. Elizabeth was approving of the pairing from the very beginning having facilitated their courtship in St Petersburg and got on favourably with Nicholas, always spurring him past his shyness to chase Alix. Nicholas meanwhile continued to argue the benefits of Russian Orthodoxy over other Christian religions, a pointless argument to have with a devout Lutheran and this pressure Alix naturally repelled.

Alexander III's health suddenly took a turn for the worse due to an old injury which caused a kidney disease. What had not been realised until 1894 was that his condition of fulminating nephritis was linked to a rail crash that happened six years earlier. There had been no cause for concern back then because he walked away from the crash unscathed. He was a big man and notoriously strong; he could bend an iron rod with his hands and crush a silver coin in the palm of his hand. In October 1888 the family were returning from Livadia to St Petersburg on the Imperial train when it derailed near the Borki station at Kharkov in Ukraine, causing twenty-three deaths. The royal family survived unscathed but were trapped in the carriage under a collapsed section of the roof. Alexander III held it up on his shoulders allowing them to escape and this is when the damage was done internally.

CHAPTER I

Transport Secretary Sergey Witte did the investigation in to the crash and concluded the train had been travelling too fast. For his thoroughness he was appointed to Director of State Railways (later he would become Prime Minister). In Witte's memoirs he corroborates the amazing feat of Alexander III's remarkable strength. His health condition now caught up with him and got worse day by day. Nicholas seemed only concerned with Alix and begged his father for permission to marry her until a seriously deteriorating Alexander III relented.

Nicholas immediately set out for Coburg on 14 April 1894 to represent the family on 19 April 1894 for the wedding of Alix's brother Ernest to Princess Victoria Melita of Edinburgh (Alix's cousin). They were first cousins; Ernest the son of Princess Alice and Victoria Melita the daughter of Prince Alfred, Duke of Edinburgh. Victoria Melita's mother the Grand Duchess Maria Alexandrovna, was a daughter of Alexander II of Russia and the only Romanov to have married (1874) in to the British royal family.

Empress Maria Feodorovna with Emperor Alexander III of Russia, King of Poland and Grand Duke of Finland.

THE ROYAL MARRIAGE

By 1894 Nicholas had pretty much sorted out his head following the world voyage and his romantic dilemmas and wanted to pick up where he had left off with Alix but in Coburg he was shy around her and unable to find any words. The idea of revealing his true emotions chilled him yet he could truly feel his heart flutter in her presence. Wilhelm II was already the Keiser while his cousins Nicholas of Russia and George of England were not yet on their thrones.

He persuaded Alix that converting to Russian Orthodoxy didn't mean denouncing Lutheranism and that in any case it was her royal duty to do so and marry in to the Russian dynasty for the sake of stability in Europe. Alix was hard to convince so with all patience having left him Wilhelm II called for Nicholas, presented him with a fresh uniform, and told him to stop dithering and propose to Alix posthaste, which Nicholas duly did that evening, whereupon Alix dutifully accepted his unwavering proposal.

Unfortunately, the newly betrothed risked stealing the limelight from the newlyweds, Ernest and Victoria, and the engagement was therefore announced on 20 April, the day after the event they were attending. One can almost feel their excitement and surmise how the couple must have been instructed to wait at least until after the Coburg wedding concluded before making an announcement and their eagerness must have been glowing.

Nicholas remained in Coburg for two weeks and promised Alix to see her again in June of that year when he was due to visit their mutual cousin in England, George, Duke of Cornwall and York (later George V) for the christening of George's son Edward, Prince of Wales; the boy that would one day inherit the British throne briefly in 1936 as Edward VIII. Edward was a nephew to both Alix and Nicholas and they were also his godparents. Back in Russia Nicholas found his father in seriously declining health; there were no transplants or dialysis back then and his inevitable death was feared so he was moved for rest, to the peaceful and pleasant surroundings of the Livadia Palace in Crimea.

As the time neared for Nicholas to head off to England he was advised that it was not prudent to leave at such a time when his father was so close to death. But he would have none of it and on 3 June 1894 boarded the Polar Star and sailed off to see Alix with a flurry of expectations, arriving at Walton-on-Thames to greet an equally excited Alix. Their destination was Windsor to visit Queen Victoria, along the way making brief visits to Sandringham in Norfolk, the official residence of the Prince of Wales and Marlborough House on the Mall, the London residence of the Prince and Princess of Wales.

Nicholas had visited Marlborough House on the previous year for the wedding of the prince and princess of Wales but Alix had declined that invitation. On that occasion he toured the sights such as Westminster Abbey but this time he was extremely surprised and delighted to be unchaperoned

CHAPTER I

with Alix. Queen Victoria had seen to it that the usually prescribed etiquette in such proceedings was disregarded so that the betrothed could be afforded the maximum time alone together, such was Queen Victoria's enthusiasm to progress the marriage. Nicholas noted his sentiment in his diary on 11 July 1894 as he departed on the Imperial Yacht Polar Star, *"A sad day, parting, after more than a month of blissful existence!"*

1894 was revealing itself as the best year of their lives so far and they started planning a wedding for the spring of 1895. But their fortunes were to change direction affected by world events and the family affairs that over shadowed them. When Nicholas returned to Russia he found his father's health fast deteriorating and Maria Feodorovna was now more accepting of Alix for a quick marriage extending an invitation for her to come to Livadia Palace as a matter of urgency.

Nicholas and Alix official engagement photograph, November 1894

Alix left England in the autumn of 1894 arriving at the Russian court to find Alexander III in excruciating pain. He was insistent on receiving her in his full Imperial regalia which he did on 21 October 1894. Alix was just 22 years old, could speak hardly any Russian and poor French, but her youthful looks and calming nature made a good impression on him, not so much on Maria Feodorovna who kept her guard in reserving her judgement.

Alexander III had little confidence in the abilities of court physician Dr Girsh and sent him and other medical practitioners away. Only Father John of Kronstadt remained at his bedside performing shamanistic healing rituals; it was the first time that Nicholas and Alix were exposed to mysticism. Within ten days of Alix's arrival the Emperor Alexander III passed away, on 1 November 1894 aged 49 years old. According to Orthodox tradition no time was wasted in making the funeral arrangements; the procession was on 13 November and the burial service on 19 November.

As the heir apparent, Nicholas immediately became Tsar and Emperor Nicholas II which was confirmed to him around two hours after the death of his father. He was utterly distraught as he had worshipped his father and perhaps had some trepidations about picking up the mantle. Fortunately for Nicholas his cousin Grand Duke Alexander Mikhailovich was with him at Livadia to share in his bereavement.

"I saw tears in his blue eyes. He took me by the arm and led me downstairs to his room. We embraced and cried together. He could not collect his thoughts. He knew that he was Emperor now, and the weight of this terrifying thought crushed him."
— ALEXANDER MIKHAILOVICH

Much telling of the first ten minutes when Nicholas learned that his father had died suggests that he wasn't prepared for tsardom and neither did he wish to be the tsar. The source is entirely from Alexander Mikhailovich's diary published in his memoirs *Once a Grand Duke*, in New York in 1932, thirty-eight years after the event. Whatever Nicholas said in those intimate few minutes can be considered as emotional babble at best and cannot be accepted as verbatim. The purpose of memoirs is often to illuminate the past with a best-selling version of the facts, as the many examples will demonstrate throughout this book.

As Nicholas stepped out on to the porch that evening there were dark clouds overhead, an ominous storm raged through the night that lasted for two weeks. From the lawn of Livadia Palace could be heard the Russian Black Sea Fleet from their base at Sevastopol, firing seventy one volleys of gun salutes marking the death of Emperor Alexander III. And on that lawn the Romanov family had gathered to commit their allegiance to the new Emperor Nicholas II.

CHAPTER I

In the morning the first thing Nicholas did was to receive his fiancée in to the Russian Orthodox Church and by decree proclaimed her the Grand Duchess Alexandra Feodorovna. She wanted the name 'Ekaterina' but Nicholas preferred 'Alexandra' so that they could be a second Nicholas and Alexandra like his great grandparents Nicholas I and his wife Alexandra Feodorovna. Although Alix became Alexandra, she would continue to be called Alix by her family and by Nicholas. The new emperor was impatient and determined to get married straight away instead of waiting for the planned spring wedding.

Nicholas was advised that his father's funeral should precede the wedding and that it should take place at the Peter and Paul Cathedral in St Petersburg where the previous Romanov tsars were laid to rest. Alexandra was a huge support to him as her father had died just two years earlier which had almost destroyed her. With his resolve strengthened Nicholas insisted that the wedding would follow his father's funeral service and so it happened on 26 November 1894, at the Grand Church of the Winter Palace in St Petersburg. It was unfortunate for Alexandra of whom it was said had arrived in Russia behind a coffin, which was taken as a bad omen.

"Every hour that passes, I bless the Lord from the bottom of my soul for the happiness which He has granted me. My love and admiration for Alix continually grows. There are no words capable of describing the bliss it is to be living together." — NICHOLAS II

The Imperial wedding of Nicholas and Alexandra painted by Ilija Repin, in the Chapel at the Winter Palace on 26 November 1894

This is the diary entry that Nicholas made on his wedding day:

> *"The day of my wedding! Everyone had coffee together, and then went off to dress: I put on the Hussar uniform and at 11.30 drove with Misha to the Winter Palace. The whole Nevsky was lined with troops waiting for Mama to drive past with Alix. While she was being dressed in the Malachite Hall, we all waited in the Arabian room. At ten to one the procession set off for the big church, from where I returned a married man! In the Malachite Hall, we were presented with a huge silver swan from the family. After changing, Alix sat with me in a carriage harnessed in the Russian manner with a postilion, and we rose to the Kazan cathedral. There were so many people on the streets, it was almost impossible to pass!*
>
> *"On our arrival at the Anichkov we were met by a guard of honour. Mama was waiting for us in our rooms with the bread and salt. We sat the whole evening answering telegrams. We dined at 8 o'clock and went to bed early as she had a bad headache!"*

Note: In the previous passage, Misha is Nicholas' brother and Mikhail. Nevsky is the name of an avenue. The bread and salt is a traditional gesture that represents hospitality to welcome a guest. Salt was expensive and salt tax wasn't completely abolished until the end of the 19th century. At weddings the bride and groom feed a piece of bread dipped in salt to each other to symbolise that they will share whatever happens in life together. Anichkov is a palace, where Nevsky Prospect and the Fontanka River meet.

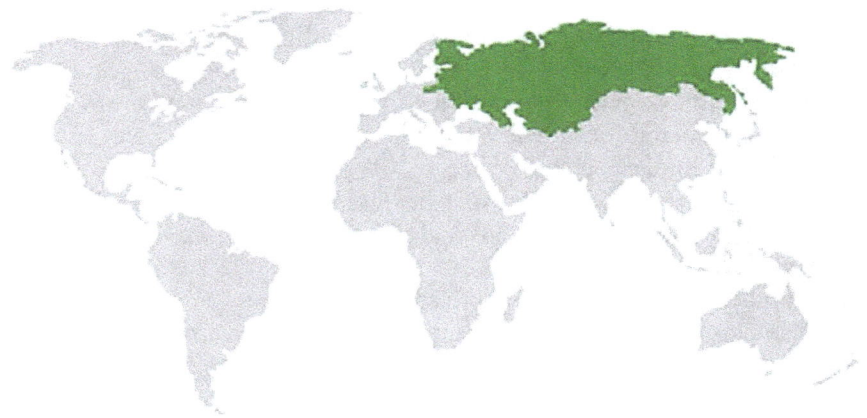

The Russian Empire in the 1890s

Before the wedding Nicholas had tutors brought in to teach his fiancée the Russian language and she was also schooled in Russian Orthodoxy. Her chosen patronymic name 'Feodorovna' was derived in part from her father

CHAPTER I

Ludwig IV whose first name was Friedrich and equally it applied to the Romanov patron whose patronym had been traditionally used by tsarinas. On her wedding day Alix, the Grand Duchess became the Tsarina and one of the richest women in the world. She was yet to be crowned and on her coronation would become Empress Alexandra Feodorovna, one of the most powerful women on the planet.

The royal wedding took place in the Imperial Chapel of the Winter Palace on 26 November 1894, illuminated throughout by the tall windows and elegant candlelit chandeliers. The service involved many Russian traditions, the salient ones were the holding of candles and the crowning. They were met at the entrance by the priest Palladius, the Metropolitan Bishop of St Petersburg and Ladoga and received lit candles which they held throughout the ceremony while the scriptures were being read. In the second part of the service the bride and groom were crowned. The placing of crowns is the important part in Russian Orthodox marriages and rings are usually exchanged on the engagement ceremony.

Traditionally the couple stand on a rose-coloured fabric and the priest places the crowns on their heads, or nominated guests can hold the crowns over the heads. They share a cup of wine then walk behind the priest as he moves three times around the central lectern or altar to symbolise the journey the couple will take through their married life. When the priest has said the benediction he removes the crowns and at that very moment the bride and groom are officially married. Before leaving the church the newlyweds take a bite from a Russian traditional bread dipped in salt, the partner that has made the biggest bite will be the head of that household.

No photographs exist of Alexandra in her wedding dress but she was possibly the only one wearing white and not obliged to exhibit deference to Alexander III, with Nicholas wearing a black band on the sleeve of his Hussar uniform. General Ellis reported to Queen Victoria on how a shadow of sadness seemed to hang over the whole ceremony. Alix's sister Elizabeth attended with the Prince and Princess of Wales in representation of Queen Victoria for the wedding. Ella sent her grandmother detailed sketches of Alexandra's wedding dress with vivid descriptions and which are the only depictions left to posterity.

Another witness at the magnificent spectacle was Danish artist Laurits Tuxen, a painter for the Danish court. He was commissioned separately by Maria Feodorovna and Queen Victoria to paint the scene. Tuxen visited the Winter Palace on 24 November 1894 to sketch out the Chapel. On the actual wedding day he found himself unexpectedly placed in the choir and immediately took advantage of this error by placing himself on the steps of the pulpit fortuitously having secured the best possible vantage point. It took sixteen months to complete both works and his autobiography, *En Malers Arbejde*, recounts the experience in detail.

Imperial brides traditionally wore dresses incorporating silver or gold and magnificent diadems and tiaras from the Romanov jewellery collection. The Tuxen paintings show aides holding the crowns above their heads, the Metropolitan holds up the wedding rings as they stand before him holding their lit candles. Alexandra wears a specially made tiara and male guests hold her train; it was so heavy that it took five chambermaids to carry it when she walked. Alexandra's Boucheron pearl and diamond tiara was gifted to her by Nicholas on their engagement, he purchased it in London during the summer of 1894; it was a treasured jewellery piece that Alexandra would wear throughout her life on formal occasions and for portraits.

It was the greatest day of their lives so far and for Nicholas it would remain above all others including his coronation day and arguably the births of his children as his life ambition was to marry Alix. She stood next to him in her full magnificence under a diamond studded tiara and coronet sitting on a wreath of orange blossom. The Romanov nuptial coronet was made in 1840 from precious stones taken from the possessions of Catherine II (the Great) and sat slightly behind the tiara. In the centre was placed the famed 13-carat Pink Diamond, made for Empress Elizabeth Alexeievna, consort to Alexander I. (i.e. the headpiece was a combination of two crowns.)

Alexandra stood in a glorious sparkling silver thread gown and a gold-embroidered mantle lined with ermine and held with a diamond clasp that had been made for Catherine II. The lace veil that lay across the back of her mantle had once been worn by her mother Princess Alice, and her sisters Elizabeth, Victoria and Irene. She was a marvel glorified with diamond cherry earrings and three banded bracelets and a necklace made of diamonds threaded on silk adorning her slender neck.

The Court of Nicholas II

When the new tsar and tsarina took up at the Grand Court in St Petersburg she was 22 and he was 26 years old. Not even the granddaughter of Queen Victoria was prepared for it. They were the absolute rulers of an enormous empire with over 150 million subjects. Russia's navy was not as mighty as the British, nor did it rule over as many subjects by comparison with the British Empire who controlled 240 million subjects, but their union certainly moved both empires closer. Initially they resided at the Anichkov Palace but Nicholas didn't like the fortress styled building and moved to the Winter Palace, the official royal residence since Peter the Great founded St Petersburg in 1703. Following the assassination of Alexander II on 13 March 1881 (J) the sheer size of the Winter Palace had been judged a security risk and Alexander III had been moved to the smaller. more manageable Gatchina Palace where Maria Feodorovna was still residing.

CHAPTER I

As soon as Nicholas and Alexandra were settled in to the Winter Palace, the focus turned to preparations for their coronation. It was a testing time for Alexandra who believed that Nicholas' role should not be dictated by his mother. Alexandra noted in her diary that it was all happening so fast and even her wedding had felt like an extension of the funeral. She was not at all pleased that it had been cut to a bare minimum out of respect for the death of the previous emperor and with Maria Feodorovna calling the shots it was harder to get a foot in the door. But Nicholas was not going to upset his mother in mourning and in any case, the responsibility for the coronation preparations fell to the Dowager and not the Tsarina.

When Nicholas became tsar in 1894 his cousin George was not yet the king of England. Photos of the two men are often admired for their physical similarity on account of their mothers being Danish sisters. George's first cousin Keiser Wilhelm II however, had been the Prussian king and German Emperor since 1888. Coincidentally, in years to come Nicholas II and Wilhelm II abdicated within a year; Nicholas II ending the House of Romanov after 304 years and Wilhelm II ending the House of Hohenzollern after 400 years. These three cousins Nicholas, Wilhelm and George, were instrumental in bringing about World War I, mainly it's said, attributable to Wilhelm II for his tactless foreign policy and insulting behaviour. But they certainly got on reasonably well because in 1910 the Keiser was in England for the funeral of Edward VII and in 1913 just months before World War I started, both Nicholas II and George V attended the wedding of Wilhelm II's daughter, Princess Victoria Louise of Prussia, in Berlin.

The three cousins ruled the three major empires of the world. If they are seen as relations then that family ruled the largest empire in world history. Nicholas would rule through a period of great social and political unrest in which his own beliefs in strict authoritarianism would prove to be unsuited in a rapidly changing and modernising world. The other two cousins viewed Russia as a backward society; whilst Britain and Germany were industrialising, Russia was farming. But in reality Russian industry had grown much faster than was credited and was outperforming England and Germany in industrial growth and ore production.

In terms of ideology the cousins each had their religion; Christian, Lutheran, Orthodox. Only the Russian seat saw itself as a literal link between God and the people. In this ideology, an autocrat soon becomes delusional believing they are themselves divine. The first line of the tsar's official title was *By the Grace of God Emperor and Autocrat of All the Russias*. The archaic Slavic title of 'Tsar' (meaning Caesar) signified complete power over the country and its subjects – politically, legally and spiritually. The tsar was regarded so close to God that in the Russian coronation a new tsar crowns himself, there being no other that is more worthy to do it.

The Russian court was incredibly opulent and much more formal and intolerant than the British system. Queen Victoria described it as being over the top, but it was none-the-less the court that Nicholas inherited from his forebears. On the questionnaire for the first Russian census conducted in 1897, Nicholas gave his occupation as 'Owner of Russia'. He was therefore rather obstinate in claiming his right to assert godlike rule but he was not as prepared for it as he might have believed and his claim to a divine right did not mean he was suited to it. His grandfather Alexander II when he was the heir apparent was well prepared to rule from 1855 and was credited for being the greatest reformer since Peter the Great, becoming known as Alexander the Liberator for the reforms he introduced that enabled the emancipation of Russian serfs in 1861. He was the wise ruler that sold Alaska to the US in 1867 because he realised that it couldn't be defended and who fought wars that gave Bulgaria, Montenegro, Romania and Serbia their independence. And yet despite reforms and freedoms there was always opposition to his autocratic rule. He was in the process of taking measures against anarchistic threats when he was assassinated in 1881.

His son Alexander III, on the other hand, wasn't as sympathetic or open to reforms and ruled with an iron fist. He kept out of external wars while building a brutal interior and ended up with the same anarchistic disorders that had faced his father. Alexander III's legacy was one of confusion yet Tsar Nicholas II and Tsarina Alexandra strongly believed in this model of autocracy and in their divine and incontestable right to rule with absolute power. Alexander III had not been the eldest son and therefore was not originally the heir apparent and received the schooling of a grand duke. When his brother Nicholas died in 1865 and he became the heir apparent, there was still sixteen years before he would take the throne in March 1881, giving him ample time to prepare for it.

Nicholas II, unlike his father Alexander III, had been the heir apparent from the day he was born and still he was not prepared when his time came to rule. He was bullied by his father who thought his disposition too feeble to mould in to a viable ruler and therefore gave him hardly any schooling at all outside of the academics. He did not trust Nicholas to determine the future of a dynasty that had ruled since the first Mikhail Romanov in 1613 nor did he believe his son took the responsibilities of ruling an empire seriously, for someone who was destined one day to be the richest and most powerful ruler in the world. He perhaps saw in his other sons Alexander, George, and Mikhail, the qualities more preferable for a dynastic ruler.

Nicholas' mild manners, his attentiveness to others, his soft demeanour, unobtrusiveness and idiosyncrasies were irritable features to his father. Nicholas would laugh at comedy plays and shed tears in theatre dramas unconcerned by who saw him. Nicholas' sister Olga Alexandrovna, before she died in 1960 wrote the foreword in a biography about her called *The Last Grand*

CHAPTER I

Duchess, published posthumously in New York (1964). She thought that he was 'unfit' for the role, *"Even at that time I felt instinctively that sensitivity and kindness on their own were not enough for a sovereign to have.*

Nicholas II reviewing the morning periodicals

In the presence of his father Nicholas remained silent, showed no emotion and offered no opinion. He called his father by his title *Emperor* and not *Papa* which was traditional and was more at ease around his *Mama*. His father never took him in to his confidence nor introduced him to the operations of the government and was very openly critical of him. Alexander II had introduced reforms that Alexander III deemed too liberal and had produced counter-reforms. Nicholas had the option to revisit his grandfather's vision to undo his father's counter-reforms, and continue on the path to a constitutional monarchy, but he was not clear on the direction to take, not having been prepared politically one way or the other. His wife Alexandra played the decisive role in promoting her belief that they should pass to their successor a more secure and incontestable autocracy than ever before.

Nicholas decided to blindly continue his father's legacy in re-asserting and strengthening the monarchy by brutally crushing the anarchistic activity and opposition that he too faced and which served only to pave the way for a future revolution. Once, the Transport Minister Sergey Witte requested that Alexander III appoint the Tsarevich Nicholas as the Chairman of the Committee of the Siberian Railway construction project. Alexander III told him that Nicholas was too young for such a responsibility and asked Witte, "*Have you ever spoken to His Imperial Highness the Grand Duke Tsarevich?*" When Witte replied that he had, Alexander III continued, "*Don't tell me you never noticed that the grand duke is a dunce!*" Nicholas II retained all of his father's advisors, demonstrating his disregard for political or diplomatic counselling with his lack of interest in seeking out those best suited to advise him. His ministers, given the time, would come to regard him in the same low esteem with which his father had bestowed.

From *The Memoirs of Count Witte*, chapter III (page 207), The Czar's Attempts At Reform, published in 1921:

> "*While his august father was still reigning, Nicholas gave proof of sincere sympathy for the lot of the peasant. Thus in 1893, in his capacity of chairman of the Committee on the Siberian Railroad, he sided with me in my efforts to encourage migration of landless peasants to Siberia, which measure was opposed by the landowners.*"

> "*When Nicholas ascended the throne, I thought that he would inaugurate an era marked by a policy of fairness and intelligent care for the peasant, in keeping with the admirable traditions of his grandfather, the Emperor* Liberator. *But my hopes were to be shattered. It soon became apparent that the young Emperor had fallen under the sway of powers inimical to the interests of the peasantry.*"

The preceding phrases help in understanding how Nicholas regarded his subjects and what sort of person he was at that time and how ministers thought of him. Much is documented about the wickedness of his regime and how uncaring he was, which was a major factor in the investigation by the Orthodox Church in relation to his canonisation after the end of his life. But it's difficult to grasp where he was at in his humanity because he was a man of extremes; he loved wildlife yet his favourite sport was hunting.

Having served three successive Emperors, Witte from his memoirs tried desperately to alleviate the hardships of the peasantry using his influence in the Tsar's service. In his view Nicholas was lacking empathy towards those that Nicholas referred to as 'people of lesser birth'. Witte tried desperately to present the plight of the poor and ethnic groups like the Jewish communities but he was never able to get it successfully across to Nicholas.

There are two ways to look at it. One is that Nicholas was inept and too weak to be heard in the sea of powerful ministers and the other way to see it, is that he was so obstinate that he did not value procuring advice holding the belief that he always knew best. He was said to arrive at meetings and sit quietly without hardly any participation from him. Other accounts give him more credit saying that when he chaired board meetings for the Siberian Railway Committee he would sit for hours not knowing what to say but no member ever reported that he looked tired or disinterested. He was attentive and well-mannered and there can be no doubting these were traits that got him through the administrative side of his duties.

It's been something of a mystery to historians, if he was so weak, in determining the extent of his involvement in a regime that was so brutal. Was Nicholas a good man or a bad one. Was he easily manipulated or was he so headstrong that no one could reason with him. Some accounts say that he was neither weak nor cruel and that history has recorded only those events that were outside of his direct control whose failures have been attributed to weaknesses in his placid character.

Accepting his ignorance in regime matters is to excuse his role in the pogroms that were the cause of so many deaths perpetrated in his name. It isn't that simple, that Nicholas failed to prevent atrocities because he was weak-willed – he was after all, the emperor. Rather, it has more to do with being complicit with the Russian psyche for racism and ethnic cleansing, which were not ideas that Nicholas disapproved of but instead supported and encouraged as evidenced in his side notes. In this regard he played an active role in sanctioning the cruelty of the pogroms.

The inherent hatred of Jews was passed to him by his father's tutor Pobiedonostsev who instructed him on autocracy and nationalism and told Nicholas to model himself on Peter the Great and promoted expansionism. It was Pobiedonostsev that helped to indoctrinate the belief that Nicholas had inherited incontestable powers from God and that his duty was to expel the inferior stock from Russia's social stratification.

Expectations For Russia

When Nicholas became Tsar he inherited Minister of Finance Sergey Witte, and Imperial Russian Governing Senate member and future Minister of the Interior Pyotr Durnovo, both men had been loyal ministers for Alexander III and met after his death to share their grief. Durnovo asked Witte what he thought of the new tsar. Witte told him that although inexperienced Nicholas was intelligent and he was impressed by his good manners and that he believed the future looked promising. Durnovo gave a disagreeable glance and revealed his view on the matter:

"Well, Sergey, I am afraid you are mistaken about our young Emperor. I know him better, and let me tell you that his reign has many misfortunes in store for us. Mark my words Nicholas II will prove a modernised version of Paul I."

1890 had been a pivotal year for Germany, Keiser Wilhelm II dismissed Chancellor Otto von Bismarck and consequently his top secret Reinsurance Treaty with Russia, in place since 8 June 1887 following the collapse of the German-Austrian-Russian Dreikaiserbund, was not renewed. The treaty had addressed the joint spheres of interest between the three countries whereby if one became militarily involved with a separate power the other two would remain neutral; unless Germany attacked France or Russia attacked Hungary, otherwise it stood as a stabilising force in Europe.

When the treaty was not renewed, an alliance between Russia and France formed (Franco-Russo alliance 1891-1917) largely based on the foreign debt owed to France to finance Russian industrialisation. By 1894 when royal marriages and engagements were happening in Coburg, Germany was feeling the gradual encirclement from the joint efforts of the major powers in Europe and politicians were interpreting the fluctuating liaisons, or new treaties, as a sign that a war was looming that would be on a scale never seen before.

Russia was not pleased when the Anglo-Japan alliance (1902-1923) was formed to safe guard their mutual interests in China and Korea against Russian aggression. Germany hoped to ally with England who it saw as one and the same people in origin, calling England the motherland. England in turn shared this view of a common ancestry and not least because the British royal house was German. Before World War I the German population in England was second only to the Irish but unlike them, German communities were popular with the English and accepted.

Germany also tried to ally with Russia by promising not to attack them while they were in disputes in the East with Japan, whereas England was assisting Japan by providing intelligence during the Russo-Japanese War (1904-1905). In April 1904 Britain made an alliance with France known as the *Entente Cordiale* in which either country if attacked by Germany would assist the other. It meant France was no longer Britain's main enemy on the continent. France in turn was Russia's only ally in Europe but signed an Entente with Japan in June 1907 to secure French Indochina for itself.

Also in 1907, France, Russia and Britain were brought together under the *Triple Entente*, a merger of the existing Anglo-Franco alliance and Russo-Franco alliance. Thus, in Europe there existed two dominating powers, the *Triple Entente* (England, France, Russia) and the *Triple Alliance* between Germany, Austria-Hungary and Italy. The predicted looming war was just on the horizon.

CHAPTER I

The multitude of marriages between royal houses during these times reflected the uncertainty in Europe, as with classical times when families formed bonds in marriage to avert or strengthen military conquests. The wedding at Coburg in 1894 between Prince Ernest and Princess Melita of Edinburgh, brought together the courts of Germany, England and Russia at a critical time in world politics and basically demanded the joint attendance of Queen Victoria, Keiser Wilhelm II and Tsarevich Nicholas. These three empires symbolised the possibility for a peaceful Europe, an investment of royal genes that was hoped would calm the waves of suspicion and introduce stability. But it was rather late in the day for all that, and the age of neo-classical expansionism that had started with Napoleon, then Britain, then Russia and now Germany, concluded in World War I. Nevertheless, the wedding of Nicholas and Alexandra in 1894 was seen as 'hopeful'.

When Edward VII ascended the British throne in 1901 his first ambition was to strengthen British colonial interests and the sphere of influence in Europe. Wilhelm II at first thought this promising for fresh negotiations but Edward VII hated Wilhelm II and his alliance with France. Wilhelm II turned to Nicholas II, reminding him what had happened in Europe a few decades earlier when Britain and France had allied to meet Russia on the battlefields of Crimea during 1853-1856.

In spite of most commentaries portraying Wilhelm II as a bungler that triggered World War I with German aggression, he appears to be the only one making efforts to avoid a confrontation and perhaps this is a travesty of the adage attributed to Winston Churchill that *"History is written by victors."* According to Victoria of Hesse and by Rhine, Wilhelm II had worked so hard to convince Alix that she could not refuse Nicholas in a desperate bid to secure peace in Europe. Wilhelm II saw the possibility of a new playing field between Germany, Russia and Britain with their marriage. Witte made reference in his memoirs to an excerpt in The Times entitled 'Royal Personages at Coburg' which summarised the hopes of the day:

> *"The fact that the Russian Heir Apparent proposes to marry a German Princess closely related to the Queen of England and to the Emperor of Germany is not an incident which should* [only] *be chronicled in the Court Circular. The peace of the World depends in no small degree on the relations between England, Russia and Germany and anything which tends to increase the cordiality of these relations cannot fail."*

While political leaders had looked to the prospect of a peaceful future and Nicholas was being swept away by a ballerina, Alix had remained unwanted by the house of Romanov and remained unpersuaded to return to England. Germany didn't care where she went, as long as she went, to strengthen foreign ties. In her home town, Count Osten-Sacken, the Russian Ambassador in Berlin, described the Hessian sentiment:

"When the Heir Apparent went to Darmstadt I was ordered to join him there. The first day after my arrival in Darmstadt I had a talk with the old Ober-Hoffmarschalh with whom I was on friendly terms at the time when I was attached to the court. The conversation *turned upon the Princess. 'When I left Darmstadt,' I said, 'Princess Alix was a little girl. Tell me frankly, what do you think of her, now that she is grown up?' The old courtier rose, examined all the doors to make sure that no one was eavesdropping and said: 'What a piece of good luck it is for Hesse-Darmstadt that you are taking her away!' "*
— COUNT OSTEN-SACKEN

Nicholas and Alexandra, 1896

CHAPTER I

Mentioned earlier, the assertion that Nicholas did not want to be tsar comes from Alexander Mikhailovich's book but there was in fact a rumour that he planned to renounce the throne as Grand Duke Konstantin Pavlovich (second son of Emperor Paul I) had done in 1823. The British politics magazine *The Spectator* reported on 27 October 1894, just three months after the engagement announcement, that Nicholas was 'disinclined to accept the throne'. If rumours have some foundation in truth then perhaps genuinely he did not wish to be tsar. Or was it just that in his immaturity Nicholas talked loosely about it which had leaked, much in the same way someone might say "I don't know why I should bother", which would be forgivable considering the huge weight that was descending on him.

At the funeral of Alexander III the Prince of Wales equerry Major-General Arthur Ellis stated that every attention was now 'microscopically' centred on the smallest act of the young emperor. When the coffin entered the Kremlin Nicholas should have walked alone in the procession but instead he invited the Prince of Wales (later George V) to walk with him, and for this deviation it was reported in *The Times* newspaper that knowing all eyes would be upon them, Nicholas used the opportunity to provide the world with evidence of the strong ties existing between Russia and England. At the coronation in 1896 reporters would note that Alexandra looked the more confident and Nicholas somewhat subdued and during the celebrations The *Queen: The Lady's Magazine* identified Alexandra as the more assured.

During the period between the wedding and the coronation the royal couple stayed at the Anichkov and Gatchina Palaces and during summer at Peterhof Palace. Alexandra would have been counting down the months to the coronation and described it as an unbelievable experience. She immersed herself in it completely and thereafter it became her primary role and a matter of state interest to fulfil her duty to produce an heir. If at first Alexandra was the more confident, this changed as all eyes fell upon her to perform her duty and the whole country waited for news of a pregnancy.

Nicholas and Alexandra shared a reclusive nature in wanting respite from the affairs of state and while they were in the early years of marriage a certain level of privacy was afforded to them. Each time Alexandra fell pregnant a weight lifted from her shoulders as it was incontrovertible proof of her fertility. Under the laws for succession the baby was required to be a boy and having four daughters in succession placed a mental strain on them that came to dominate the first ten years of their marriage.

Alexandra's pregnancies and a miscarriage were publicly announced. She was swamped by court obstetricians with the latest medical equipment and methods as she kept trying for a son with all the hopes placed upon her by an empire but as time moved on so too did speculation and rumours circulated that God did not favour them and that it was down to the curse on Nicholas II's reign.

Religious superstitions had not gone well for previous rulers who were prone to having their seat challenged or being overthrown. The Rurikid dynasty died out in the mid-13th century and the tribes of the Rus began a period of instability with several imposters known as the false Dmitris claiming to be rightful Rurikid heirs. Even Poland marched on Moscow and put a king on the throne in 1610. Eventually a Russian with the appropriate lineage surfaced and was crowned in 1613 as Mikhail I, the first king of the Romanov dynasty. The Russian Empire continued to expand for 305 years at a rate of 55 square miles a day (20,000 square miles a year).

In 1797 Tsar Paul I established the Pauline Laws in which were stated that priority in the order of succession to the Russian throne belonged only to male members of the Romanov dynasty, no matter how distant. It was his reaction to previous rulers Catherine I and Elizabeth I that had seized the throne by overthrowing weak male monarchs. Note in the coming chapters as we move in to World War I how Nicholas becomes weaker while Alexandra gains control and power. If the Pauline law had not existed then the circumstances would have been ripe for Alexandra to seize the throne, if not for the love story that existed between them.

Maria Feodorovna (R) in mourning with sister Queen Alexandra (L)

CHAPTER I

THE ROMANOV DYNASTY

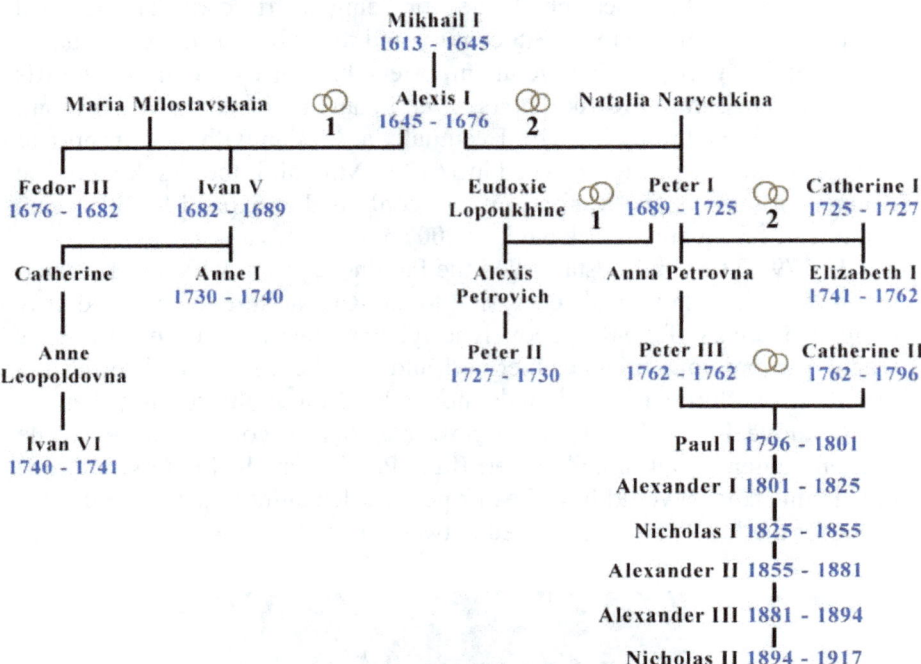

HOW THE ROYAL COUSINS ARE CONNECTED

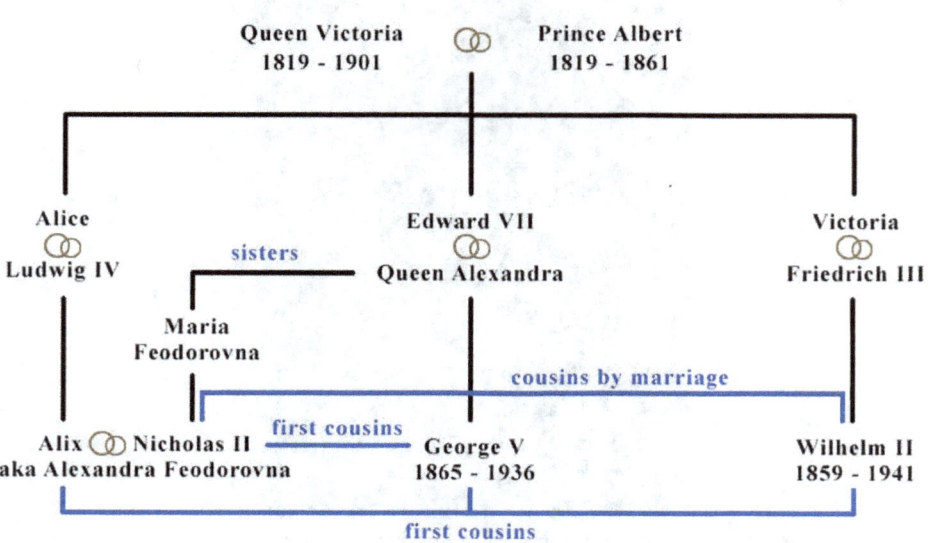

CHAPTER II
The Coronation

THE coronation of Nicholas II was a lavish affair that took place on 26 May 1896 (G), by which time first child Olga was six months old. Although St Petersburg was the capital of Russia, traditionally coronations were held in the 15th Century Cathedral of the Dormition (previously the Uspensky Cathedral,) situated inside the Moscow Kremlin. Pomp and ceremony no longer existed in most of Europe but the Russian coronation was a Byzantine ritual laid down fifteen hundred years earlier and certainly no ruler before Nicholas II had claimed by virtue of birth-right such absolute power for himself and the coronation therefore demanded an extravagance fitting for the modern world stage. Even France declared the Russian coronation day a school holiday. From 8.00 am when Nicholas got out of bed, he noted in his diary:

> *"the weather was fortunately wondrous,"* and also, *"All this happened in the Assumption Cathedral, although it seems like a real dream."*

— *1896 Coronation period (Gregorian dates)*:

- ❖ 18 May Nicholas' birthday / start of celebrations
- ❖ 19 May Nicholas & Alexandra arrive in Moscow
- ❖ 23 May Move to Petrovsky Palace
- ❖ 26 May Coronation Day (14 May (J))
- ❖ 30 May Khodynka tragedy
- ❖ 6 June Alexandra's birthday
- ❖ 7 June End of celebrations / Imperial manifesto published thanking the inhabitants of Moscow

CHAPTER II

The Ceremony

Not wanting to burden the state treasury Nicholas paid for almost the entire coronation from his own purse amounting to around 900,000 rubles. The celebrations lasted for twenty days starting on Nicholas' birthday and lasting until the day following Alexandra's birthday. Events included pageantry, galas, parades, balls, concerts and other grand spectacles. On the second day of the opening celebrations Nicholas and Alexandra went to Moscow, a week before the coronation as was the custom. They arrived at Petrovsky Palace just outside Moscow for rest and preparations and then attended a ceremonial procession to the Kremlin. On the morning of the coronation day Nicholas officially entered the city gate on a white horse.

Nicholas II entering the Moscow gate, print 1896

Coronation Day began with the traditional procession through the streets of Moscow with church bells ringing out. In St Petersburg it was the same, every church was packed and bells rang out all over the city. Nicholas rode in to the city leading several cavalry squadrons amid a roar of cheers, then came the carriage of Maria Feodorovna and even louder cheering was heard and then Alexandra's carriage came but the cheering faded. It was described as an ominous silence on account of her being German which accordingly had reduced her to tears. Onlookers observed that the cheers for the Tsar and Tsarina were muted by comparison with those for the Empress Dowager in sympathy for her widowhood. In Russia mourning happens over two years and the Empress Dowager was still in mourning for her husband.

Representing Queen Victoria at the coronation was Alexandra's uncle Prince Arthur, Duke of Connaught and Strathearn and his wife Duchess Louise Margaret, formerly a Princess of Prussia, wearing Queen Victoria's Turkish diamonds. Also from Alexandra's side of the family were the representatives of Hesse headed by her brother Grand Duke Ernest Ludwig. In his record of the event (*page 39*) Ernest provides vivid details and describes how Nicholas took communion at the altar like a priest. This was a change in the traditional ceremony, made by Nicholas to proclaim that as God's representative he was on par with the priests. Up until then only priests could take communion together at the altar. The priests did not like it but the Church did not split from the state until 1917 so they had no choice but to honour the Tsar's wishes, or rather his demands. He made several changes and embellished the ceremony with much symbolism in an already traditional event that was brimming with ceremonial pomposity.

Nicholas II taking communion at the alter with the priests.
Brian Ludbrook collection

The above print is part of the wonderful coronation souvenir album expertly crafted by the Ministry of the Imperial Court and given as a commemorative gift to the foreign delegations. It's an impressive work of historical importance with attractive borders and lavish decoration, full of vignettes, photographs and drawings. Prince Arthur and the other British dignitaries received copies. One given to Colonel Waters, Prince Arthur's attaché, was donated to the British Museum Library (now British Library).

CHAPTER II

The Hessian delegation 1896 – Alexandra's brother Ernest is seated centre

The coronation was the grandest ever held in Russia and quite possibly in world history but was fated to be the last. The celebration preparations were the responsibility of the Minister of the Imperial Court, a position established in 1826 to oversee the separate ministerial offices that operated the royal court; in 1896 this was Count Illarion Vorontsov-Dashkov. Alexander III had made him Full General of Cavalry in charge of the Hussar regiment of the Leub Guard (1867-74) and would lead Russian forces in the early months of World War I. For his work in planning the coronation he was awarded the Knight of St Andrew on Coronation Day 26 May 1896. Peter the Great picked up the idea of honorary awards in Europe introducing this first and highest order of chivalry 'For Faith and Loyalty' in 1698.

Sent by the pioneering French Lumière brothers for the coronation were Belgian cinematographer Camille Cerf and his teenage assistant Francis Doublier. In 1895 the Cinématographe was invented by the Lumières. It was the first film camera and where the word 'cinema' comes from. They made the first ever motion film 'La Sortie des ouvriers de l'usine Lumière', a short film of the workers leaving the Lumière factory in Lyon at the end of a shift. Just a year later the French embassy had secured for them a special platform inside the Kremlin to accommodate the delicate camera and its crew. Camille Cerf made a 1 hour 33 minute recording on 35mm film capturing the coronation procession which became the first documentary and full length film ever made.

THE CORONATION

For their wedding eighteen months earlier, Nicholas had waited for Alexandra at the church wearing his Colonel's uniform of the Hussars. For the coronation they arrived together and were greeted at the cathedral entrance by the Metropolitan Sergius of Moscow. He greeted them with a blessing and addressed them with a speech which started, *"Thou art entering this ancient and holy temple in order to lay upon thyself a kingly crown and to accept sacred anointment . . ."* The coronation ceremony was a sacred anointment rite to cement the fact that the Tsar was being blessed by God as the head of the church. Nicholas II was to become the conduit to God for 150 million people. However, the ceremonial planners had overlooked the actual date; the 13th monarch would be crowned on the 13th day of the month (of the Julian calendar), some believing that to be another bad omen for the reign.

The priest led them inside where two thrones stood in the centre of the floor on a raised platform. They ascended the fifteen steps and took their places, then read aloud the Orthodox religious creed. Dignitaries brought the Imperial regalia on red velvet cushions with gold trim. The golden sceptre, the chain of the order of the Holy Apostle Andrew, the sword and the orb of the Empire, and the Imperial cloak were presented to Nicholas.

The Russian Imperial Crown

On a red cushion a dignitary brought the Imperial crown, a Romanov heirloom fashioned by Catherine the Great's court jeweller in 1762. Twenty of the largest diamonds in the world were embedded around its central headband and the four circlets on the sides of the crown embellished with

CHAPTER II

thirty-eight roseate pearls. The Byzantine cross on the crown made from eleven large diamonds was supported by a huge uncut ruby adorned by five enormous jewels on the central band. The Metropolitan offered the great Imperial crown to Nicholas, which he graciously took and placed upon his own head. He received the sceptre in his right hand and the orb with his left. As he looked out from the throne he was at that moment the richest and most powerful person that had ever existed on the planet.

Emperor Nicholas II crowns wife Tsarina Alexandra his Empress, 1896

"A people that venerates the Tsar thereby pleases God, for the Tsar is a dispensation from God." — HIERARCH PHILARET OF MOSCOW, 1800s

As soon as Nicholas was crowned Emperor, Alexandra knelt before him. The Metropolitan dipped a gold wand in to myrrh and anointed the Emperor by touching his brow, eyes, nose and mouth, chest and hands. He took the wafer that was offered him, and at that moment became the Supreme Head of the Orthodox Church. The Metropolitan then touched the

Tsarina's brow anointing her with religious responsibility. The Emperor momentarily removed his crown and touched it to Alexandra's forehead to symbolise their joint responsibility. Another dignitary offered the Imperial tiara from a red tasselled cushion, it was a much smaller coronet that had been made from scratch for the occasion and taken nine months to make, with its 2000 flawless diamonds set in gold. Emperor Nicholas II then very deliberately placed the coronet upon Alexandra's head proclaiming her to be his Empress of Russia.

Instantly the bells of the cathedral set off a carillon of bell-ringing echoing out across the city announcing that the rites had been concluded and there existed a newly enthroned Imperial couple. During the ceremony, Nicholas' brother Mikhail and uncles Vladimir, Sergei, and Pavel had been responsible for placing the gold-brocaded Imperial mantle on his shoulders and securing it with an emerald studded diamond clasp. Then they placed a diamond chain around the collar of the Order of St Andrew but Vladimir missed a catch and it fell to the floor which was interpreted yet again, by some witnesses, as one more ill omen for the reign.

> *"The coronation in Moscow was the most splendid ceremony I have ever seen. It was almost eastern in style and lasted 10 days. In Moscow, the cathedral was full of images of saints on a gold background, and all the priests wore golden vestments decorated with embroidery and precious stones. In all the ceremonies, there was a deep mystical meaning and Byzantine traditions.*
>
> *"The Anointed Emperor and Empress became God's Anointed ones. The Emperor, like a priest, receives communion at the altar. After that, in front of the throne, he takes off the crown from his head, kneels down and prays aloud with a wonderful prayer for his people. Then they say a prayer for the emperor, and he rises, and at that moment he is the only non-kneeling person in the entire Russian Empire."*
>
> — ERNEST LUDWIG of Hesse and by Rhine

After the five hour service a new Emperor and Empress descended the Red Staircase to Cathedral Square and became immersed in a sea of 300,000 well-wishers that clamoured for a glimpse of them. The Imperial couple first bowed to the crowd, once in front of them, once to their right and once to their left. The coronation procession then began and they visited the sacred icons of the Archangels Cathedral and the Annunciation Cathedral, their proximity of which can be seen in the Red Staircase print (*next page*).

A coronation banquet followed and in the evening they opened a court ball and glided across the marble floor of the Kremlin palace, where guests danced through the entire night. They danced in the palace grounds and in the streets outside flunkeys distributed ten thousand meals in the courtyard with each person receiving a half-pound of meat, a pound of bread, sausages, preserves and a bottle of beer.

In addition to the Tsar's contribution, public finance was arranged by Dashkov who had increased the budget immediately that Nicholas ascended the throne by increasing the finances awarded for the Ministry of the Court. Alexander III had been a thrifty ruler with his hands firmly on the Imperial Council whose job it was to restrict spending and ratify budgets. How it worked in practice was that the court was granted whatever it requested and Dashkov having no restrictions placed upon him requested a healthy amount from the Minister of Finance which the Imperial Council had to approve.

The Red Staircase (aka Red Porch) Lithograph acquired by coronation guest Zelia Nuttall and gifted by her to the Penn Museum, Philadelphia.

The Khodynka Field Tragedy

Four days in to the coronation celebrations on 30 May (G), Nicholas and Alexandra were scheduled to attend an event at Khodynka Field near Petrovsky Park, a couple of miles northwest of Moscow. An open air public event to celebrate the coronation of a tsar had taken place there since the time of Peter the Great in 1682. In between coronations it was used for military training exercises and was criss-crossed with pits, trenches and other obstacles. To prepare for the coronation crowds wood was used to fill the pits and trenches were covered over with planking alongside which 150 stalls were erected for the distribution of free commemorative bundles.

Each bundle contained a little bread and sausage, a slice of gingerbread cake, sweets, nuts, dried fruit and an enamelled cup emblazoned with the Imperial seal, all wrapped in a kerchief with an image of the Emperor and Empress on one side and the Kremlin on the other. The gingerbread cake had the Imperial monogram and the year 1896 baked on it. There were other stalls provided for water and 30,000 gallons of beer for everyone to receive a free celebratory drink.

One side of the coronation commemorative embossed kerchief handed out to visitors at the Khodynka Field celebration and used to wrap and distribute the traditional gifts from a new monarch to the people; in this case an enamelled steel cup (10.5cm high), some sausage, cakes and sweets. After the tragedy at Khodynka the enamelled cup became known as the sorrow or blood cup symbolising the awful tragedy.

CHAPTER II

Above: Gingerbread cake also described as egg biscuit with the coronation year baked on it.

Below: Commemorative enamelled steel cup. One side bearing the Tsar's monogram in Cyrillic letters topped with the Imperial crown. The reverse side with the double-headed Imperial Eagle of the Romanov dynasty, also surmounted by the Imperial crown.

Near the field is the Petrovsky Palace built by Catherine the Great as a stop-over on journeys between St Petersburg and Moscow. Catherine the Great spent just fourteen days there but successive monarchs used it as a last stop to rest and prepare before entering the city for their coronation. On 30 May, Nicholas and Alexandra arrived at Petrovsky Palace in good time before they were expected to appear on a large pavilion that had been built on the field for them and their VIP guests. From the pavilion the Imperial couple could see and be seen and wave to the excited crowds. 400,000 people had been expected based on numbers from the coronations of Alexander III and Alexander II. People came from all over, many arriving on the previous evening and camping for the night. 1,800 police were put on crowd control duty and water stations were placed at intervals to cope with the extremely hot weather that spring.

Dawn came and people started arriving that had walked through the night from Moscow; they were hungry and asking for food and water when the stalls were setting up, before they were ready to open for 10.00 am. A rumour began that each commemorative cup contained a gold coin. Fearing there might not be enough to go around, people headed for the stalls which created an even larger commotion on the field. In the confusion people tripped on uneven surfaces, many were already severely dehydrated and collapsed under the sweltering heat. In the developing stampede hundreds fell through the flimsy pit coverings and as they crammed in to the gaps between the stalls some fell head first in to inadequately covered trenches. Around twenty people fell in to a well to their deaths. The screams from the field were heard by workers a mile and a half away.

> "Till this day, thank God, everything has been going quite smoothly, but today a grave sin has befallen. The crowd who spent the night in the Khodynskoye Pole [meadow] pending the giving out of a dinner and a mug, pressed upon the wooden constructions, and there was a terrible jam, and it's dreadful to add, about 1300 people were trampled down!" — NICHOLAS II, diary

Camille Cerf and his cameraman Francis Doublier were covering the event for their coronation documentary and captured the pit hoardings as they gave way. Unfortunately there is no film today because the police had questioned their motives, regarding the novelty of filming with some suspicion. The camera crew were detained and eventually released but their camera was never returned.

Tamara Karsavina was a prima ballerina, publishing her autobiography, Theatre Street, in 1931. On half a page she describes her father, brother Lev and their maid Annoushka heading out for Khodynka Field. Karsavina was the only one of the coronation ballet troupe that contracted mumps and had

CHAPTER II

been quarantined for two weeks in a Moscow hospital. In her misery and her loneliness she watched the illuminations and fireworks from her hospital window. Her parents had travelled to Moscow and her mother was permitted to visit her. One morning she brought terrible news of the disaster, she had not felt strong enough to attend the event but father, brother and maid headed out there; how fortunate for them that they had been delayed in getting there.

> Page 66: "*The streets were thick with people streaming to Khodynka. ... They tried to make their way as quickly as they could, manoeuvring through the crowds. Whenever Lev saw a couple walking he swiftly bolted in between, with a polite 'Pardon me.' In the breach thus formed rushed Father, and behind him Annoushka, whose back received all the cuffs. Before they reached their destination they met with several stretchers. Sobbing groups appeared coming from Khodynka. ... Deep ditches on both sides of the ground had been covered with planks, along which people advanced towards the distribution point. All went well for some time, but as the crowd became thicker the planks gave way in several places and people fell into the ditch. The pressure from the back being great, others fell on top and buried those underneath. Mother said that on her way to me she had met several carts loaded with bodies. According to rumour tens of thousands perished.*"
> — TAMARA KARSAVINA, prima ballerina

Strange it is that photographs of Khodynka field show only a flat open field strong enough to take horses and military parades. That noted, 1,389 people were trampled to death or suffocated and a further 1,300 were injured; a tragedy that tainted the whole coronation. Can any organised event be recalled when so many people had died. The numbers used here are from Nicholas' diary as every account typically gives a different number for the deaths. The British Embassy first reported 700 dead and 500 injured then revised it to just under 3,000 deaths. Historian author Orlando Figes in his book *A People's Tragedy: The Russian Revolution, 1891-1924* stated that, "*Within minutes 1,400 people had been killed and 600 wounded.*" In the book *Nicholas II Prisoner of the Purple* (1936) the author claimed 5,000 people were crushed to death. Pavel Bykov in *The Last Days of Tsar Nicholas* stated that the number was 2,000.

Throughout the day corpses were being removed from the field to holding areas, then taken to the Vagankovsky Cemetery outside of Moscow. Many of the dead were not identified by the authorities and the injured filled the surrounding hospitals. An estimated 500,000 people had turned up, 25% over what had been anticipated. The quantity of water was insufficient, and the tragedy of Khodynka is an example cited even today in training courses on crowd management. Stalls had been positioned too closely together to allow people to move freely and flimsy wood coverings were significant hazards that contributed to the disaster. Organisers even continued with the celebrations so that by the end of the day 1,400 people had died, people having continued with the celebrations seemingly unaffected by everything.

Between 1.00 pm and 2.00 pm Nicholas and Alexandra took the short walk from Petrovsky Palace to the pavilion. From the veranda they waved to the cheering crowd as celebrated musician and composer Vasily Safonov conducted a cantata and they greeted the VIP guests. At least five British representatives were in attendance; The Duke and Duchess of Connaught, Bishop Mandell Creighton, Sir Nicholas O'Conor, and the Field Marshall Francis Grenfell (the future Governor of Malta,) who said, "*It was a crowd as large as that of three Derby days.*"

Some accounts say that bodies were still being cleared and stored under the pavilion for removal later whilst the orchestra played and Nicholas waved to the crowd. One account said the festivities had not been cancelled because Russia was a barbarous country where human life seemed of little account. The (London) Evening News reported that when Nicholas departed the field, he stopped by a cart carrying corpses and alighted from his carriage to lift the tarpaulin. He looked at the corpse as tears rolled down his pale cheeks. When someone from the crowd on seeing the Emperor shouted "*Hurrah*" Nicholas shook his head sadly in shame and Alexandra covered her face with a handkerchief in deference.

The pavilion at Khodynka Field. Petrovsky Palace is seen in the background.
30 May 1896

CHAPTER II

Who was to blame for the Khodynka disaster? Many could have been accused; the planners, heads of security, the Minister of the Imperial Court Count Vorontsov-Dashkov, and the man in charge on the field that day, the Grand Duke Sergei Alexandrovich, General-Governor of Moscow and an uncle to Nicholas II. The investigation turned to Dashkov, being the person that was responsible. However, Maria Feodorovna stepped in and Nicholas appointed a commission of inquiry headed by Count Konstantin Ivanovich Palen, a Grand Marshal of the Court and former Minister of Justice. It was carried out under the auspice of the Minister of Justice Nikolai Muraviev (1894 to 1905) and quickly found the Grand Duke Sergei Alexandrovich culpable with his many opponents then calling for his dismissal.

Nicholas' uncles encircled him saying that the blame could not be attributed to a high ranking member of the royal family as that would be disastrous for them all. Uncles Vladimir and Paul threatened to leave the court if Sergei was removed. It should be appreciated that Sergei was not officially responsible for organising the festivities and if anyone had to be singled out then it should have been the head of police who was responsible for the marshalling of the crowds.

Grand Duke Sergei Alexandrovich did not suffer as a result of the investigation but soon afterwards was promoted to commander of the troops of the Moscow district. It ruined his reputation and he was henceforth referred to as the 'Duke of Khodynka'. Some years later at yet another public tragedy known as Bloody Sunday the militant organisation of the Socialist Revolutionary Party would pronounce the death sentence on him in January 1905 for his part in using armed soldiers to disperse crowds. But before that could take place he was assassinated in February 1905 by Ivan Kalyaev a poet who was hanged for the murder towards the end of that same year.

No one was ever held responsible for the Khodynka tragedy, only the Moscow Chief of Police Alexander Vlasovsky and his assistant were dismissed, for shoddy policing and failure to provide safety arrangements and security measures. It's a wonder why the initial investigation was steered away from Dashkov because it was his ultimate responsibility to plan the coronation. Unsurprisingly, after the celebrations Dashkov was appointed to the State Council and sent away from the court. He later suffered a mental breakdown in 1905 and was removed from command in September 1915. He died four months later and perhaps had always carried a guilt which piece by piece had consumed him.

As part of the pre-coronation scheduled events, a strange example of ineptitude by the court organisers is given for 22 May 1986 (G), three days after Nicholas and Alexandra arrived in Moscow and the day before they headed for the Petrovsky Palace near Khodynka Field. The royal entourage arrived at the Trinity Lavra of St Sergius monastery, the spiritual centre of the Russian Orthodox Church situated about 44 miles north-east of Moscow.

But there was no one there to greet them; the organisers had forgotten to notify the rector, one of the most significant men in the Russian Orthodox Church since the Theological Academy had moved there from Moscow in 1814. It was an unexpected and embarrassing royal visit.

A visit to the Trinity Lavra of St Sergius monastery, 22 May 1986.
Nicholas II (centre) with his wife on his left and mother on his right.

Another example was on 29 May (G) at a visit to the Imperial Bolshoi Theatre in Moscow (Bolshoi means big in Russian). A selection of acts from old and new operas were being performed and a new one called *Pearl* featured Mathilde Kschessinska dancing the part of the yellow pearl. After her affair with Nicholas they had not met again in private but he often watched her performances. Maria Feodorovna had asked Dashkov to replace her for the performance but Mathilde complained to Nicholas' uncle Grand Duke Vladimir Alexandrovich and her name went back on the coronation programme. To Alexandra's embarrassment Mathilde made her appearance on the stage and a shocked Alexandra made her disapproval clear by leaving the theatre before the performance ended.

Maria Feodorovna, a much more experienced and astute observer advised Nicholas to cancel all of his remaining appointments and address the Khodynka tragedy head on but he unwisely continued with the celebrations as if nothing had happened. When full details of the tragedy were disclosed the cover story given was that Nicholas had been unsuspecting of any issue at

Khodynka as he had not been informed of what had occurred there a few hours prior to his arrival. In the aftermath of the disaster there was much discussion over how Nicholas and Alexandra had reacted and why they hadn't taken the lead and cancelled the celebrations that day. At least the Khodynka event should have been stopped, people thought, and Nicholas should have acknowledged the deaths of so many. Had Nicholas done so then his reign may well have started out much smoother and taken a different path as the people would have been more sympathetic to him.

The French Ambassador's Ball

In the early evening on the day of the Khodynka tragedy, the Imperial couple visited the Kremlin and lit an electric illumination of Ivan the Great and then Alexandra lit the towers and walls of the Kremlin with 200,000 electric lights painting the illusion that it was outlined with Jewels. The rest of the city bathed in hundreds of thousands of colourful lamps and Chinese lanterns strung across from house to house illuminating the jet black sky. After that they dined with Maria Feodorovna and a little later attended a ball held by the French ambassador Montebello, where they had another dinner and danced until 2.00 am, an invitation that the wiser Dowager had declined.

Illuminated Moscow Kremlin for the coronation of Nicholas II, May 1896

Opinion was divided on whether Nicholas and Alexandra had been affected by the deaths at Khodynka that day. Some believed Nicholas was uncaring and others that the Imperial couple were deeply troubled and their presence at the French Ambassador's ball was due to political pressure from their advisers and the extended family who pointed out that non-attendance would be seen as an insult by France, Russia's only strong European ally.

Sergey Witte, the then Minister of Finance, suggested that the ball be cancelled in view of the tragedy and according to him it was Nicholas' uncles, Grand Dukes Vladimir, Alexis, Sergei and Paul that pressed Nicholas to attend the ball for diplomatic reasons. However, Pavel Bykov, in his book *The Last Days of Tsar Nicholas* states that Nicholas was questioning why the French ball should be cancelled. Not long in to the ball, as Nicholas and Alexandra took to the floor to open the dance, the Grand Dukes Nicholas, Michael, George and Alexander walked out in protest that he had decided to remain at the ball unaffected by the tragic events of that day.

"I know for a fact that neither of them wanted to go. It was done under great pressure from his advisers . . . Nicky's ministers insisted that he must go as a gesture of friendship to France."
— GRAND DUCHESS OLGA ALEXANDROVNA

"In view of the terrible expense, the French ambassador begged the Imperial couple to attend." — COUNTESS MARIE KLEINMICHEL

Countess Marie Kleinmichel was a famous grand dame who married a Colonel of the Preobrazhensky regiment and whose brother Fedor was a Lieutenant General and hero of the Russo-Turko wars and who was killed later in the Russo-Japanese War (1904). She was even a friend of Keiser Wilhelm II. She held masquerade costume balls at her mansion in the north of St Petersburg where the high society gathered and therefore she had a finger on the social pulse as her salon was where the real gossip was circulating. In the quote above from Countess Kleinmichel her use of the word 'begged' is interesting because it suggests that Nicholas and Alexandra had expressed reservations about attending the French ambassador's ball and perhaps had at first decided not to attend contrary to the accounts that Nicholas was uncaring and unaffected by the Khodynka tragedy.

An interesting story about Countess Kleinmichel that shows what remarkable ingenuity she possessed and how she managed to survive the hurly burly for so many years, would happen in the October Revolution 1917. To avoid the rioters she displayed a plaque on her door reading '*No entry. The building belongs to the Petrograd Soviet. Countess Kleinmichel is imprisoned in the Peter and Paul Fortress.*' It worked, no one entered, and she created the delay to pack her belongings and escape Russia.

CHAPTER II

"All high society Petersburg gathers here, all foreign diplomats, noble persons coming from abroad, etc., attracted both by the amiable and friendly cordiality of the reception, and by the prospect of an interesting conversation with the hostess of the house and visitors to her salon." — LEON TROTSKY (referring to Kleinmichel's salons)

Some accounts mitigate Nicholas' decision to attend the ball with slight comments like *their faces were evidently pale* or *they didn't want to be there*. The famous Russian historian Alexander Bokhanov explains in one of his books why it was impossible for the Tsar to refuse the invitation. British Bishop Mandell Creighton, one of the British contingent on the Khodynka pavilion, was of the opinion that the Imperial couple had decided to attend the ball because of the expectations which dictated that they lay aside any personal feelings and they were simply prisoners of etiquette and tradition. In other accounts the following diary extract is used to demonstrate that Nicholas was uncaring because it implies that by omitting to mention the tragedy that day at Khodynka in itself is evidence that it was not on his mind.

"Dinner at Mama's at 8. Went to the ball at Montebello's. It was very nicely arranged, but the heat was unbearable. After dinner, left at 2."
— NICHOLAS II, diary 1896

This is unfair and is used out of context because Nicholas did mention Khodynka elsewhere in his diary. It should be noted that Nicholas kept his diaries in timetable fashion, probably for his own future recollections and not as a definitive account for the scrutiny of future historians. How likely was it that he would have been unaffected by the deaths of 1,400 people that day and not mention it in his diary. Likewise, the theories of contemporaries are not evidence. One aide stated, *"When Nicholas heard of the catastrophe he did not display the slightest sign of emotion and did not even cancel a ball for that evening."* Of course some sense can be derived from these tidbits of hearsay but it is important to appreciate that where Nicholas stood on this matter may never be truly understood.

Although his diary is not wholly indicative of his thoughts, his public response to Khodynka was and earned him the label of 'Nicholas the Bloody'. The newspapers saw his handling of the tragedy as a sign that he did not know how to take control of important matters. The conversation at dinner that evening with his mother, could only have been about Khodynka and she surely pressed him not to attend the ball. The Chinese Ambassador Extraordinary to the coronation Li Hung-Chan, who was at the ball in his yellow mandarin robes and peacock feather, commented that a Chinese emperor would not have attended the ball following such a tragedy and surmised that Russian statesmen were inexperienced and unskilled.

The French, knowing a thing or two about grand balls, had made a huge effort in transporting many items from Paris which had included 200,000 flowers prepared and sent at the very last moment to look at their best. The plates for the dinner were brought from the Garde-meuble National in Paris (the body responsible for the administration of all furniture and objects for French royal residences). Nicholas and Alexandra turned up in splendid dress and greeted the Ambassador Gustave Lannes de Montebello. The ball was opened by their Imperial majesties dancing a quadrille.

Of course Nicholas had known about the deaths at Khodynka when he stood waving from the pavilion, he was the Emperor after all. He recorded in his diary that he had been told about 10.30 am, that's thirty minutes after the deaths began and three hours before he stood on the pavilion. He also wrote on how moved and distraught he was. What outraged Moscow society was that they perceived him to be indifferent and that was taken to be highly disrespectful to the victims and their families. The Moscow reporter Vladimir Alekseevich Gilyarovsky, considered to be the most reliable source on the Khodynka Field tragedy, noted one headline waiting at his office for the press: '*This means trouble! This reign will bring no good!*'

On 31 May 1896, the day following the Khodynka tragedy, the Imperial couple finally responded by visiting the wounded in the hospital wards. Still they received criticism for having only spent half a day to grab headlines. The truth was they did a lot more than that and hardly needed to be out grabbing headlines considering they were already at the centre of attention on a global level. At 2.00 pm they visited the Old St Catherine hospital and toured the wards. The following day, 1 June at 3.00 pm, they visited the St Mary hospital where the second largest group of injured were being treated.

> "*I was extremely upset at seeing in the hospital all these poor wounded and semi-crushed people, and almost each one of them had lost a family member. It was absolutely heart-wrenching. But at the same time they were so sensible and dignified in their simplicity that they caused a desire to get down on one's knees before them. They were so moving, not blaming anyone except themselves.*
>
> "*They said that they themselves were to blame, and that they regretted having upset the Tsar by this! They were as dignified as always, and one can take pride in realising that one belongs to such a great and wonderful people. Other classes should follow their example, instead of devouring one another and, most of all, with their cruelty inciting people's minds to such a state as I have never yet seen in all my thirty years in Russia.*" — MARIA FEODOROVNA

Nicholas declared that the state would bury the dead and that he would personally pay 1000 rubles to each of the families. One report was that the families didn't receive anything and another that they did get the money but from the government and not the Tsar's own pocket as purported. Official palace releases portrayed Nicholas as the victim of Khodynka; the story was that an unfortunate tragedy had over-shadowed the coronation. It served him well at the time because there were many British visitors in Moscow for the coronation who sympathised more for Nicholas than for the victims, so the propaganda had worked.

It was tactless and when the full story reached people it served only to alienate him further. It was a mistake not having dismissed the Grand Duke Sergei Alexandrovich for the blunder during a time when terrorist activity was escalating against the government and the dissident Leon Trotsky was beginning Marxist political activity directly undermining the regime and which ultimately led to the First Revolution 1905. At the start of his reign, irreparable damage to the perception of the monarchy had been done. The final day of coronation celebrations must have come as a great relief.

"Having changed clothes, we went to the station. and said goodbye to Mom; she went to Gatchina, and we immediately went in the opposite direction along Moscow-Brest. got to St Odintsovo, from where the carriages drove to Ilyinsky. An indescribable joy to get to this nice quiet place! And the main consolation is to know that all these celebrations and ceremonies are over!" — NICHOLAS II

The Imperial couple descending the Red Staircase

THE CORONATION

On 9 June 1896 in connection with the coronation celebrations funded by Nicholas, the 16th and final All-Russia Exhibition was opened in Nizhny Novgorod (approx. 270 miles east of Moscow,) a suburb of Kanavino on the west bank of the Oka River. A newly created city was built adjoining the fair containing 120 impressive pavilions displaying industrial achievements and decorative arts which aimed to rival the other great fairs being held in Europe that year. Two great masts made from Siberian forest trees were erected at the complex entrance and a sturdy rope tied between them from which was hung the Imperial Standard to flutter overhead. The weather was glorious on the opening day, except that the air was as stifling hot as it had been at Khodynka. Men in full uniform or top-buttoned suits and women in full dresses and feathered hats waited for Nicholas and Alexandra to arrive.

All of a sudden at 11.00 am just before the Imperial couple were due, a tremendous storm descended upon the venue. Clouds that appeared in the distance came upon them fast and turned in to a thunderstorm. People ran for cover and looked on as much of the exhibition was destroyed, including the marvellous entrance masts torn down under thunder, lightning and hail that also shook buildings and smashed windows. In a testament to Russian perseverance, within twenty-four hours most of the complex was restored and the Imperial couple attended the opening ceremony the next day on 10 June 1896. But with the Imperial Standard having been brought down people could not help but reconcile it as yet another bad omen for the reign.

The first Russian automobile designed by Evgeniy Yakovlev and Pyotr Freze, revealed at the Nizhny Novgorod exhibition 1896. Taken by Russian photographer Maxim Petrovich Dmitriev (d. 1948).

CHAPTER II

The Fabergé Imperial Coronation Egg at the Musée des Arts Décoratifs in Paris. Nicholas gave this egg to Alexandra in 1897. The shell is of gold embellished with a translucent yellow enamel and overlaid with black enamelled double-headed eagles. Inside the white velvet-lined egg is an exquisitely detailed miniature 18th-century golden carriage replica of a coach once owned by Catherine the Great and used in Nicholas and Alexandra's coronation procession in 1896. Nicholas gifted an egg each year for Easter, to his wife and mother.

CHAPTER III
Palaces, Balls and Fabergé

THERE are plenty of royal palaces in Russian cities and several famous ones that sit not far from St Petersburg, near the town of Tsarskoe Selo, the present day Pushkin. Their construction are attributable to an age when Russia was seeking to equal the architectural magnificence of the Palace of Versailles. Peter the Great (Peter I – Pyotr Alekséyevich) was the ruler that elevated the title of Tsar to Emperor and was looking at the bigger picture with Russian expansionism and ambitious building projects that still survive as a testament to the Romanov dynasty who were responsible for the grand Russian palaces. It is very fortunate that many of them remain to the present day considering the many decades of soviet rule.

CATHERINE PALACE

Peter the Great acquired some land and a manor house at Tsarskoe Selo in 1717 for his second wife Catherine I (Marta Helena Skavronsky). She ruled Russia for two years after her husband's death and having no heir of her own, she recognised as her successor the grandson of her husband's first wife Eudoxia. He was the last male Romanov and became Peter II (Pyotr

CHAPTER III

Alexeyevich) on her death. The land was valued for its high ground, indeed its first name was 'Saari Moith' meaning a high place in Finnish. This land that operated as a farmstead was acquired when Peter the Great was building St Petersburg and required suburban residences not far from the new capital. It was renamed to Tsarskoe Selo meaning 'the place of the tsars' and Catherine I chose the spot where to build a grand palace. When her husband informed her that he needed a nearby summer residence, he perhaps had not intended for such a grand enterprise.

What started out as a manor house greatly improved over the following seven successions until Catherine II (aka Catherine the Great – originally Sophie Frederike Auguste, princess of Anhalt-Zerbst, Germany,) came to the throne in 1762. She developed it in the French Rococo style and lavished it with a rich art collection. There is sometimes confusion over which Tsarina Catherine was responsible for this palace and the true answer is that Catherine I built it and Catherine II made it what it became, the majestic palace that today is a UNESCO World Heritage site.

ALEXANDER PALACE

Towards the end of the reign of Catherine II, in 1792 she began building Alexander Palace in Tsarskoe Selo, a stone's throw from Catherine Palace. It was intended as a wedding present for her grandson Alexander Pavlovich the future Tsar Alexander I. As such it was much smaller than the Catherine Palace but functional and similarly designed by Italian architects, albeit in the slightly differing Baroque style, being a mite less flamboyant than the Rococo. Her favourite grandson whom the palace was named after did use it but preferred to stay at the Catherine Palace and gave over Alexander Palace to his brother, who would succeed him as Nicholas I in 1825 from which time the palace took over as the official summer residence of the tsars.

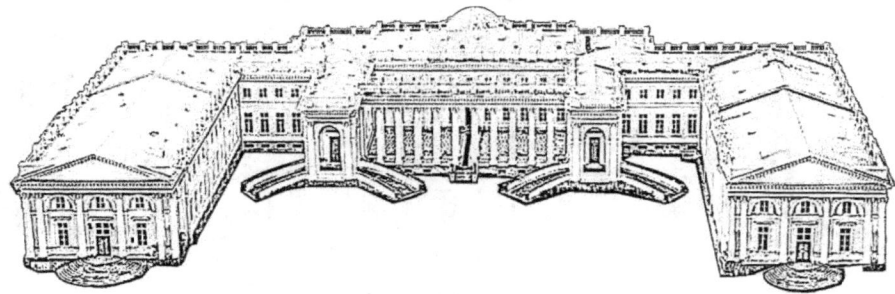

Alexander Palace is a beautiful neo-classical building on the outside, replete with Corinthian columns and an impressive neoclassical portico. Not so impressive on the inside, not having the grandeur and opulence of other palaces, albeit with its pickled-oak parquet floors and homely interior. Here

Russia's first telegraph apparatus was installed for Nicholas I's study in 1843, linking the palace with St Petersburg. Nicholas II was born here and spent a lot of his childhood in the right wing. Later Maria Feodorovna preferred to stay at Alexander Palace when visiting her son, using the same room she'd shared with her husband Alexander III. But her visits lessened as the estrangement with Alexandra became more apparent and developed.

The architect Roman Meltser was commissioned by Nicholas II and Alexandra to design new halls, studies and private rooms in the French Art Nouveau style which they favoured. One of the best examples is the Maple Room where the family would gather for activities. Alexandra adorned her favourite areas with religious icons, books and with personal mementoes of Queen Victoria that she kept in the Pallisander Room. She had a sub-ground chapel built and Nicholas II had his own private pool lined with cobalt and turquoise tiling.

This great construction by Italian architect Giacomo Quarenghi, the foremost practitioner of the neoclassical in Russia, has changed little since it was built despite its many uses. Following the departure of the royal family the Art Nouveau interiors were preserved. It was turned in to a museum to show people the opulence of tsardom which, as it turned out, was a failure and actually created sympathy for the murdered royal family and was therefore repurposed by the early 1930s.

When World War II came a lot of the interior was removed before the palace became Gestapo headquarters but inevitably much of historic value was lost when the palace was set ablaze on their eventual retreat. After the war the restoration of the valued interiors began but it turned out to destroy more than it salvaged. It was not until 1996 that the World Monuments Fund awarded a grant for the restoration and a new museum was created in the right wing, the former living space of the Imperial Family, by the Tsarskoe Selo State Museum and Heritage Site. In 2015 the palace closed for major restoration work to bring back the rooms of the Imperial couple and the new museum has been opened since August 2021.

GATCHINA PALACE

The Great Gatchina Palace stands on a hill next to Lake Serebryany just seventeen miles southwest of Tsarskoe Selo and twenty-eight miles from the centre of St Petersburg. Gatchina Manor once stood there until the owner Prince Boris Kurakin sold it to Catherine the Great in 1765. She gifted it to Count Grigori Grigoryevich Orlov, the man responsible for overthrowing her husband Peter III in 1762, opening the way for her to sit on the throne. Construction on the palace took between 1766 and 1781 and how fortunate it was that Orlov died two years after its completion and Catherine bought it from Orlov's inheritors and gifted yet another palace, to her son Paul I.

CHAPTER III

THE GATCHINA FABERGÉ EGG

Nicholas II presented this egg to his mother for Easter 1901. Inside is a miniature gold replica of the Gatchina Palace. Fabergé's workmaster, Mikhail Perkhin, portrayed such meticulous detail that cannons, a flag and a statue of Paul I can be discerned. The technique involves the application of multiple layers of translucent enamel over guilloche (i.e. mechanically engraved gold) on the shell of the egg.

Owned and kept by Walters Art Museum, Baltimore, Maryland, USA

The classical architecture looks like a medieval castle but unlike a castle it has an ornate interior in the Russian style. Designed by the Italian architect Antonio Rinaldi who used Park limestone mined from the local village at Patritsy for the exterior and Pudost stone for the vestibule and the parapet above the cornice. Paul I made so many additions and improvements that it was almost rebuilt and it's thanks to him the palace is as it stands today; although the Ministry of the Imperial Court for Nicholas I did apply some major landscaping about the exterior. It was a museum since 1917 and in 1990 was classified as a UNESCO World Heritage Site.

Nicholas II out hunting in Spala, 1875 – He also loved shooting at Gatchina

Perhaps hunting became Nicholas II's favourite pastime in his middle age but during his youth spent at Gatchina after the Imperial Family settled there for their better security, he was more attentive to shooting, cycling, lawn tennis, swimming and learned to skate and play ice hockey. The garden in winter was flooded and turned in to a skating surface on which Alexander III liked to glide his huge mass and have fun with the children. When the Imperial Family stayed at Anichkov Palace the gardens were also converted for ice skating. The practice faded away when Alexandra's poor legs had prevented her skating but Nicholas did take several opportunities to skate when visiting his mother at Anichkov Palace after his coronation, playing hockey with Xenia's husband Sandro. In later years he was more ingratiated by long walks with his dogs, the chopping of logs and shovelling snow.

CHAPTER III

ANICHKOV PALACE

Construction was commissioned by Elizabeth I and it's one of the oldest palaces of the many in St Petersburg. Standing on the Nevsky Prospekt street it takes its name from the nearby Anichkov Bridge spanning the Fontanka River. The first wooden bridge was constructed in 1716 by Peter the Great who named it after his engineer Mikhail Anichkov. The wood was replaced with stone some decades later and totally rebuilt in 1908 in pink granite with three arched spans decorated with mermaids and seahorses and giant prancing horses on the four corner pylons. From the slightly humped back bridge can be seen several other palaces of St Petersburg. The new palace was therefore sited near the bridge for strategic reasons.

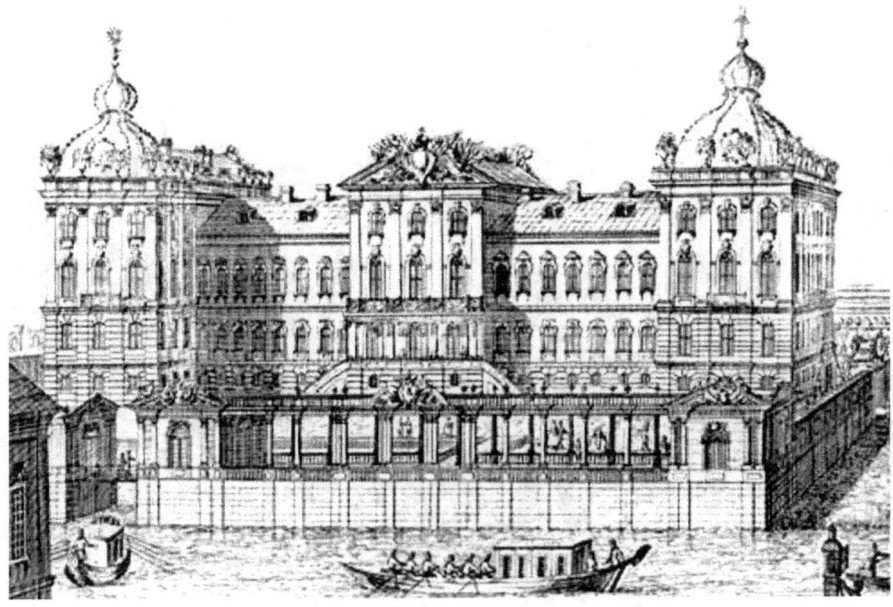

Anichkov Palace, St Petersburg

Anichkov Palace was built by Elizabeth I between 1741 and 1754 and gifted to her lover and unofficial spouse Count Aleksey Razumovsky. While Russian architect Mikhail Zemtsov designed the building, it was the Italian designer Francesco Bartolomeo Rastrelli that complemented it in the Petrine baroque style leaving yet another magnificent palace when Elizabeth I died in 1762. On Razumovsky's death in 1771 Catherine II bought the palace from the Razumovsky estate and commissioned Russian Ivan Starov, Chief Architect of the Commission of the stone construction of St Petersburg and Moscow, to restyle the façade in the Neoclassical design, strictly removing the existing baroque exterior.

When the work was completed in 1776 Catherine II gifted the palace in its entirety to the military leader Prince Grigory Aleksandrovich Potemkin. He retained Starov for a further two years to refashion the various floors and wings. Potemkin was of course Catherine II's lover, well known for his love of women and the exuberances of life. After the romance faded he went on to have long lasting affairs with five of his nieces. When he died in 1791 the palace reverted to the crown and became an increasingly popular residence.

Alexander I (Nicholas II's great great grandfather) made some major structural alterations before passing it to his sister Elena Pavlovna. During the reign of Alexander II much of the remaining neoclassical design was deemed not in line with Rastrelli's original style and the palace front was remodelled. Nicholas II and Alexandra lived here after their wedding and became accustomed to the smaller more comfy living space until they moved, in part because they were sharing the palace with Maria Feodorovna, to the much larger and unhospitable Winter Palace. Still Nicholas II would return for tea with his mother and to play hockey while family occasions were often celebrated here like the wedding in 1914 between Irina, the only daughter of Grand Duchess Xenia Alexandrovna, to Felix Yussoupoff.

PETERHOF PALACE

Peterhof Palace, near St Petersburg

Peterhof, meaning Peter's Court, is a suburb of the old capital located 18 miles west of St Petersburg. It sits on the shore of the Gulf of Finland to greet visitors from Europe coming by sea. The original Monplaisir Palace was built between 1714 and 1721 as Peter the Great's summer residence. It has fulfilled that purpose for all the succeeding tsars each having added their modifications to it. His daughter, the great palace builder Elizabeth I again used Italian architect Francesco Bartolomeo Rastrelli, to add a new floor, a new wing, a small domed church and upgraded the decor in the baroque style. It is essentially the largest of a cluster of smaller palaces with a French garden encompassing 600 acres, sometimes called 'The Russian Versailles'.

WINTER PALACE

Winter Palace, St Petersburg

The Winter Palace stands at the heart of the old capital city of St Petersburg on Palace Square with its northern side looking over the River Neva. The first Winter Palace was a wooden house built in 1708 and was relocated in 1711 by Peter the Great to make room for a second palace made from stone. Tsarina Anne I commissioned the Italian architect Francesco Bartolomeo Rastrelli in 1732 to extend it, which he did by demolishing the neighbouring properties and the Apraksin Palace to make way for the third Winter Palace. In 1754 under Elizabeth I, Rastrelli designed a fourth Winter Palace which was almost completed in 1762 when she died and Catherine II took over, removed Rastrelli and had the baroque interior refurbished in the neoclassical style.

During the late 1780s she entrusted architect Giacomo Quarenghi (prior to his commission to design Alexander Palace,) and Ivan Starov, the architect she had used to refurbish Anichkov Palace, to add several state rooms to the north side looking over the River Neva. However, in 1837 fire destroyed the interiors after which Nicholas I restored them and used the opportunity for architect Alexander Briullov to upgrade the styling.

The palace had grown too big to effectively protect the Imperial Family, and when a bomb went off in the palace and another bomb was used in the assassination of Alexander II in 1881, the decision was made to move the official residence to Gatchina Palace. The last official Imperial function held there was the fantastic ball of 1903 (*page 78*). It became the seat of the Provisional Government in 1917 and during the October Revolution of the same year Bolsheviks stormed the palace to symbolise their victory. The Bolsheviks used the building as a museum of the Revolution and today the building functions as the world famous State Hermitage Museum.

LIVADIA PALACE

Livadia Palace, Crimea

Livadia is a settlement on the southern coast of Crimea two miles west of Yalta. The palace was built in the Neoclassical architectural style with white Crimean limestone with the arched portico in Italian white carrara marble. It has 60 hectares of gardens and woods. From the 1860s it served as the Imperial summer residence of Alexander II and Alexander III. In 1910 Nicholas II demolished it to rebuild a more luxurious one designed by Yalta architect Nikolay Krasnov. 2,500 builders worked day and night to complete the work in just 17 months. The most renowned event was the grand ball for Grand Duchess Olga Nikolaevna's sixteenth birthday just a month after the new palace was completed. It was later used by the Soviets as a sanatorium and today functions as yet another palace museum. Nearby is the Moorish Dulber Palace on the outskirts of Yalta, the name in the Crimean Tatar language means 'beautiful', a home to members of the Romanov family.

CHAPTER III

Seclusion of Palace Life

From the start of their marriage, it was evident that the Tsar and Tsarina were in love, and there were high expectations to produce an heir. People saw it as a restorative process following the damage done by Alexander III's regime but almost instantly the dye was cast in public opinion following the Khodynka tragedy and the scandal over attending the French Ambassador's ball. They responded by retreating further in to their palaces, of which there were plenty within which to hide away. Their innocence placed them in a world apart from the reality of state affairs, a system that had a grip far stronger than the event horizon they were placing around their ignorance of what it meant to be Imperial rulers. The sheer number of palatial residences available was staggering, many times over what any ruler on the planet had ever known.

In St Petersburg the Winter Palace was their official residence and Nicholas and Alexandra had to eventually move in and try to make it their family home despite their wish for a smaller place such as Anichkov or Gatchina. In due course they found reason to move away from the Winter Palace, which would remain as one of the largest and most opulent former royal residences in Europe with its 117 staircases, 1,500 rooms and three million artworks. Peterhof Palace just a small distance to the west was a summer residence, overly opulent intended as a showcase to the world and not a place one could hide away in. To the south in the suburbs at Tsarskoe Selo there was a nice selection of family residences; Alexander Palace, Catherine Palace and even Gatchina which Nicholas used for hunting days. Whilst Gatchina was the residence of Maria Feodorovna, Nicholas made some landscaping improvements to the estate and essentially considered it his own property anyway, as indeed everything was.

After the coronation things became less demanding because they were starting a family and were allowed to settle in at the Winter Palace at their own pace. They appreciated that they had just been through what would doubtlessly be the busiest time in their lives and now that the formalities had passed Alexandra was instrumental in arranging their seclusion which involved restricting visits from the state ministers, the extended family and especially her mother-in-law. But it was not that simple and following the coronation the Imperial couple had a full schedule before them of state visits to foreign courts as was the custom for new monarchs and she realised that the formalities were far from over.

The first visit was to the Viennese court to see Emperor Franz Josef where they also met Austrian Empress Elizabeth who travelled to Vienna to meet them. After a brief interlude in Crimea they visited the German Emperor and then continued on to Copenhagen for a stay with Nicholas' grandparents the King and Queen of Denmark. From Copenhagen they boarded the

Imperial Yacht Standart for her maiden voyage and sailed to St Abb's Head on the shoulder of Scotland's east coast where they were transported to Balmoral to meet Queen Victoria, returning by rail through Scotland and England to Portsmouth. Standart then sailed to France and finally they took the train to Darmstadt, the capital of Hesse in Prussia, to visit Alexandra's father Ludwig IV (*See chapter 10*).

To Alexandra it must have seemed like only yesterday that she had left Darmstadt to marry the Russian tsarevich and now she had returned to Hesse as the most powerful woman in the world. She was exhilarated to see the people turn out to see the Imperial Family, unlike the wall of rejection she had experienced so far from the Russian people. On their return from the great voyage on 29 October 1896, Alexandra developed a number of health complaints and it was feared she may have suffered a miscarriage. In fact she was two months pregnant with Tatiana and it's one reason why she was feeling unwell. Ever since her childhood she'd suffered from sciatica and headaches at which the mildest occurrence Nicholas felt obliged to attend to her needs. It turned out that she used her health complications as an excuse to withdraw increasingly from court life by feigning illness, not because it was a deliberate act, but in part due to her mental state.

She was constantly in prayer for a son but alas was to have four daughters in succession. Given the many months that she was pregnant and having several infants around her, it's not surprising that she would spend as much time as possible at home, masking her desire for seclusion. But life as a high ranking royal meant wholehearted commitment to public engagements and servants were the customary way to look after any children; wet nurses and nannies being respectable surrogates for royal children.

One minute the Imperial couple had been planning their wedding when all of a sudden Nicholas was promoted to Tsar and eighteen stressful months later became Emperor. A state funeral, a royal wedding, a coronation, a voyage around the world and two children, had all happened before the middle of 1897. During the next five years their focus was placed on the pregnancies and locking themselves behind the curtains of the Winter Palace. Maria Feodorovna recognised their seclusion because her mother Louise, Queen of Denmark, had been very much of that disposition, having kept herself within palace walls for much of her life. Maria Feodorovna believed that Alexandra was lazy and neglectful of her duty and that she was interfering with Nicholas' duty to rule the country as he ought to.

In and around 1904-1905 due to increasing public unrest, for the same security reasons that Maria Feodorovna and her husband had once had to leave the Winter Palace and relocate to Gatchina, the Imperial Family moved out of the Winter Palace to the much smaller and safer Alexander Palace in Tsarskoe Selo. Once there, it began the next chapter in their lives and their seclusion turned in to reclusion as the moat around their lives was

CHAPTER III

bolstered with tighter security. Maria Feodorovna tried to talk to them about respecting the burden of their royal duty but they were so tight that she could not come between them. Eventually she saw the way the monarchy was headed and gave up, retreating to her Gatchina Palace.

1901, Nicholas and Alexandra with daughters
Olga, Tatiana, Marie and new born Anastasia

- ❖ 1895 Olga (15 November – Alexander Palace)
- ❖ 1897 Tatiana (10 June – Peterhof Palace)
- ❖ 1899 Marie (26 June – Peterhof Palace)
- ❖ 1901 Anastasia (18 June – Peterhof Palace)
- ❖ 1904 Alexei (12 August (J) – Peterhof Palace)

While Alexandra might have won the battle to keep her husband at home, Nicholas was weighing the options, his natural tendency to make final decisions was at odds with his wife's decisiveness and the wall of uncles that he faced which some said were the true rulers of the Romanov dynasty. His father had considered him to be weak and the uncles, perhaps protective to some extent, felt their duty was to step up and relieve the Tsar of some of the burden, in matters that they believed he was unsuited to deal with. But Nicholas had one redeeming aspect to his character that worked for him, he was stubborn and often stuck to his guns.

Nicholas' choice of advisors was always questionable, having made no changes after his father's death and in trusting his wife during World War I to make willy-nilly ministerial appointments in the government. In shunning his most loyal advisors in Sergey Witte and Pyotr Stolypin it revealed that he saw little or no benefit from experienced counsel, preferring to lead from the heart than rule with the head. For example, Prince Vasily Alexandrovich Dolgorukov of the Horse Guards was first an adviser to Nicholas then a Marshal of the Imperial Court from 1914 to 1917. Dolgorukov was far too young to advise a tsar but he was the son-in-law of Pavel Benckendorff a Marshal of the Imperial Court, and Nicholas respected his loyalty. In this regard Nicholas had been right in the latter; during the final days when the Imperial Family's demise came on the horizon, Dolgorukov was one of those few that decided to stay with the royal family and share their fate.

Sergey Witte, (the Transport Secretary who had risen to be Transport Minister and had requested Nicholas be appointed as Chairman of the Committee of the Siberian Railway,) said that Nicholas' actions were entirely dependent upon the character of his counsellors, most of whom were bad. Alexander Mossolov, the Court Chancellor from 1900, said that the Tsar loathed making a decision in the presence of others. His shyness was obvious and he developed a method of agreeing with everyone and then after they had left, he would politely send them word of his observation or decision, often reversing any agreement that had supposedly been reached. It was described as 'double unfacedness', what in modern terms might be called snidey or two-faced. Nikolai Momyakov the President of the third Duma said of him, *"He doesn't lie, but he doesn't tell the truth either."*

Nicholas' complex personality has puzzled historians because he was polite and respectful and at the same time indecisive and obstinate, he was well educated and well read but at the same time naïve and lowbrow. To match his gentle disposition and devotion to his family, the memoirs of his contemporaries and historians have attributed the flaws in his character to his wife somewhat unfairly. It started out with Alexandra making entries in his diary, according to one source, *"She meddled in everything."* She told Nicholas from the start, *"Invisibly, I wear the trousers and, oh how I yearn to prove it to these idiots."* The idiots she referred to were the ministers.

CHAPTER III

Girls at the Palace

The first two daughters were affectionally known as the big pair and the second two as the little pair. They called themselves collectively OTMA, using the first letter from each of their names. If there was one word to describe each their nature perhaps it might be: O–shy; T-disciplined; M-unselfish; and A–amusing. The big pair often shared a room and dressed alike and the little pair did likewise and also stuck together.

Nicholas II and his daughters on the beach of the Lower Dacha in Peterhof

OLGA although quite shy, was strong minded and hot tempered with an ear for music. She received much attention from suitors far and wide but was determined to marry a Russian to stay in Russia. She was timid, at the same time often left an effect on others. She loved everything, writing, painting, playing piano and took her responsibility as the eldest sibling seriously.

TATIANA looked most like her mother and like her was deeply religious. She was her mother's favourite and is often seen closest to her in photographs. She was the sensible one, very sociable and liked keeping order. Her sisters called her the Governess! She too liked to paint and played the piano.

MARIE was stubborn like her father and they are often seen sharing a private moment together. She was always looking to help her parents and was completely at ease with everyone. She had a particular talent for drawing and like her big sisters liked to paint and play the piano. She was heavier built than the others and commentators have often regarded her as the prettiest of the sisters.

ANASTASIA was the mischievous one and Marie would at times apologise for her when she played a prank on someone. She would climb trees and refuse to come down unless told to do so by her father. She made the whole family laugh and was the obvious prankster in the family. She kept a King Charles Spaniel dog that she always carried around with her, called Jemmy.

At the birth of Olga, Nicholas reputedly said *"We are grateful she was a daughter, if she was a boy she would have belonged to the people, being a girl she belongs to us."* When Olga was one year old in 1896 the family visited Queen Victoria at Balmoral. It was the last time Alexandra would see her grandmother and did not attend her funeral in 1901 on account of being pregnant with her fourth child.

The sisters always spoke Russian between themselves and their father, English to their mother, and French to Swiss born Pierre Gilliard the French language tutor from 1905 and his wife the former Alexandra Tegleva who was Anastasia's nurse. For many years Alexandra was nervous to speak Russian fearing that she would make some unforgivable mistake, especially in years to come when she was a nurse from 1914 assisting with surgeries. She also struggled with French, the official language of the Russian court.

According to some accounts she spoke Russian with a noticeable English accent but according to Captain Nikolai Sablin, *"Alexandra spoke good Russian, although with a noticeable German accent."* And of course she spoke English and German fluently. The children had a German tutor Frau Schneider, and an English language tutor Charles Sydney Gibbes, but the tutors, including French tutor Pierre Gilliard, were never able to get the girls to take language studies seriously. English and Russian being their fluent languages, French and German did not hold much appeal for them.

The girls' only experience of foreign countries had been in short visits to Darmstadt and once to England. They would play in the palace, and around the grounds, and talk by the marble bridge in the Catherine Park. The bridge is one of the most recognisable features in Tsarskoe Selo, built in the 1770s inspired by the bridges in English parks and of course designed in the Russian tradition by Italian architect Andrea Palladio; this type of bridge being known as a Palladian. The girls hardly saw life outside of the palace gates and the public described them as being kept in their gilded cage. They seldom saw other children and other young girls were never asked to the palace.

CHAPTER III

Alexandra standing on the famed bridge in the grounds of Alexander Palace

Their peaceful life at Alexander Palace distanced them from the harsh realities of the peasants and estranged them from the generals, diplomats and politicians. The one time busy comings and goings at the Russian court became vestiges of the past century. Much of the nobility and senior staff were no longer invited to yearly functions such as banquets or balls. Some were even insulted by it. The yearly calendar centred more around the salons of hosts like the Countess Marie Kleinmichel and no longer could many boast that they had heard something 'from the horse's mouth'.

Nicholas and Alexandra believed they had achieved their idyll within their quiet reclusion. It was some years since they had ice skated together and strolled along the banks of the River Neva before they were married. Yet their love would never diminish and they assiduously avoided upsetting each other. From the very beginning of their life together they behaved like newlyweds. They would take walks across the tidy and spotlessly kept grounds at Alexander Park and find peace on the little bridge where Nicholas would smoke one of his long cigarettes from a supply the Sultan of Turkey sent him each year, while Alexandra looked out over the peaceful stream.

In the mornings and late evenings Nicholas worked in his official study. He once remarked "*I never go to bed until the last piece of paper has disappeared from my desk.*" In the afternoons when he had finished with his papers, if he wasn't with Alexandra because she felt unwell, he would take a brisk walk on the grounds, to be with the black swans at the pond. In the evenings the family would sit outside watching the light fade over the park. Their life at home was perfectly ideal for them.

Such was the life they had carved out that they never appreciated the thin membrane separating the institutional autocracy from the workings of government. In later years they were forced to place the country under a tighter grip as those around them allowed it to slip in to anarchy. But here in Tsarskoe Selo at this time, they were happy enough to leave the running of things to the uncles. Each one depended on staff who often sought favours which they would approach Nicholas to grant. Nicholas' stubbornness meant that on the rare occasion when he would deny a request it put him at odds with that uncle. Once Nicholas had said "no" then that was the end of the matter, to that uncle's frustration.

Nikolai Nikolaevich (uncle to Nicholas II) was a tall man, at 6" feet 7' inches and towered over Nicholas by a full twelve inches. That was not the only reason Nicholas was intimidated by him; it was his wild eyes and bellowing voice that made people shiver in his presence. He thought of himself as a Field Marshall. Uncle Alexei Alexandrovich on the other hand loved the sea and was a General-Admiral in the Imperial Russian Navy. Both men Nicholas would be forced to remove in the future. The senior uncle of the family was Vladimir Alexandrovich of Russia, Commander of the Imperial Guards, with a keen interest in the arts.

Much of Nicholas' character that has been examined in biographies has to do with his failed management of the people at his disposal and that his problems started when he himself began to take control of things such as running the military in times of war. But that is to ignore the deputisation of his uncles and the delegation of power he afforded the future Dumas. He had tried leaving the actual administration to the officers, ministers, and officials which had not turned out well. The first lesson in misplaced trust was at Khodynka when his uncle and brother-in-law, Sergei Alexandrovich, in situ as the Governor-General of Moscow, was promoted following the disaster instead of being held accountable for his part and made to accept his share of the responsibility for the failing.

From 1898 to 1904 the children's nanny was a nurse from Ireland called Margaretta Eagar. In her memoirs *Six years at the Russian Court* she tells of her first impression on arriving at the Russian court, "*There are Rembrandts and Fabergé eggs everywhere,*" And she recalls how when she was learning Russian the girls, particularly the big pair, would copy her Limerick accent, "*This arises of course, from their very sheltered lives.*"

Sometimes their cousins would visit or there would be an occasional outing for tea at aunt Olga's or aunt Xenia's. Alexandra was devoted to Nicholas's two sisters, the Grand Duchesses Olga and Xenia. The children's favourite was aunt Olga who visited often and held Sunday parties at her town house. Sometimes aunt Olga would take them to St Petersburg, usually at weekends during the winter months.

Olga, Mikhail and Xenia, siblings of Nicholas II

Alexandra had seen how her peers had no idea of how the lesser classes lived and was determined to bring up her girls to be able to look after themselves. They each received a little pocket money which they needed to manage so that they had to save to buy things. They had nice clothes but often these were hand-me-downs from the big pair to the little pair after a little stitch-work here and there. Alexandra, her ladies in waiting and her daughters all wore corsets, which she insisted upon, advising them that not to wear a corset was behaving promiscuous.

Up until 1898 Alexandra used no maids nor governesses and few members of the court were retained from Alexander III's staff. The girls made their beds and repaired their own clothes. She wanted to raise them in a normal way and delayed passing them to a wet-nurse or a teacher for as long as possible. She saw to their initial education personally, teaching spelling and instructing them how to pray. When Pierre Gilliard began tutoring the children in 1905, to his surprise Alexandra attended his classes.

"I have preserved a vivid recollection of the great interest which the Tsarina, a mother with a high sense of duty, took in the education and training of her children. Instead of the cold and haughty Empress of which I had heard so much, I had been amazed to find myself in the presence of a woman wholly devoted to her maternal obligations."
— PIERRE GILLIARD

The children joined their parents for meals and were taught impeccable manners. They would gather around the table rather informally and without attendants. Some people were appalled to learn that the Empress of Russia had breastfed her children and that she was tutoring them personally, and the blame was ascribed to the austere Englishness that had been ingrained in her while she was growing up on the Isle of Wight.

The Grand Ball

The fitting tribute for a palace was the Russian ball modelled on the French penchant for social gatherings with festivities that included dancing and feasting. The ball became a rite in the Russian way of life mainly among the nobility for those that were of sufficient status to be connected in some way to the host but sometimes the poor were invited to extend relationships or as a gesture of acknowledgement, as Catherine I was renowned for doing. To really get a grip on Russian conformities it should be appreciated how the ball was entwined within the social circuit. If Russian high society is measured by the Romanov dynasty and their magnificent palaces, then its cultural exuberance is exhibited in the grand Imperial balls.

The ball is thought of as a dancing event but that was the icing on the cake and there was far more to a Grand Ball than that. It entailed dining and socialising and the dance was the part which came at the end in the final few hours. The Grand Ball could last for days, its aim to socialise and assemble people in the most lavish surroundings for courtship, commerce, diplomacy and so on. Behind the doors, guests were invited to experience paradise and indulge in the social pleasures of the day, leaving the brutal hardships of life outside in that other world. Dinners had the most exotic fruits and culinary delights with ingredients imported from around the world. The balls were a display of the latest dances, music and costumes. In simple terms the ball was a lavish dinner and dance requiring formal attire and the strictest adherence to etiquette and it was the Russian essence of a civilised society.

Balls were brought to Russia by Peter the Great who went on a tour of the European courts returning with contemporary ideas and vestiges of their culture. He instituted many changes in the Russian court starting by changing his title from Tsar to Emperor and moving the court from Moscow to the new capital St Petersburg. He introduced French as the official language of the court, banned traditional Russian dress and beards at court, and for the first time in Russian history permitted women to attend court. In 1718 he began replicating the balls from Vienna and had placed a marker in history; there was, 'everything up to now' and 'everything from here on'.

The name came from the French word 'bal' (e.g. Bal masqué - masked ball) and this activity became the prototype for gatherings all across Russia

CHAPTER III

albeit less extravagant than Imperial balls. The ball season lasted from Christmas to Shrove Tuesday in the Russian Orthodox calendar. When one was invited to an Imperial ball it was compulsory to attend and refusal was not permitted unless it was for a serious health reason. This was the level of importance given to the Imperial ball to elevate Russian aristocracy to the acceptable level of standing for a civilised society. Guests were brought together mainly for pleasure and amusement but also to form business connections or for diplomacy. Public balls on the other hand were informal events and were therefore optional to attend. The great ball of 1903 had been an Imperial ball whereas the tricentenary ball held in 1913 was a public ball. Although there were some notable balls after 1913, that great public ball on the eve of World War I marked the end of an era for the ball in Russia.

Peter the Great's consort Catherine (later Catherine I from 1725,) had been a maid at court and his mistress. They married secretly because of her low status, in the autumn of 1707. In 1712 they renewed vows and married officially. It took place in a little chapel at the Menzikoff Palace (Situated on the embankment of Vasilyevsky Island, St Petersburg). After the ceremony the attendees returned to the Tsar's home in sleighs, each pulled by six horses and accompanied by a band of music. They had a splendid feast and in the evening there was a grand ball. These were not the first balls in Russia but they were the first Imperial balls to rival the European courts.

The first ball has been attributed in one account to have been for the wedding of the first of the False Dmitris to Marina Mniszech the daughter of a Polish nobleman. She was a wife to all three of the Dmitri pretenders. The name comes from the Greek and means 'devoted' or 'dedicated to' Demeter the Greek goddess of agriculture. The time of the False Dmitris is referred to as the 'Times of Troubles'. Dmitri I claimed to be Ivan the Terrible's son and was installed on the Russian throne on 21 July 1605 by the Rurikids, the ruling dynasty of the Rus. Dmitri I and Marina were Polish, she wore a Polish wedding dress and Dmitri I wore the armour of a Polish hussar when they married in November 1605. Marina's coronation followed on 8 May 1606 and just eleven days later Dmitri I was assassinated, his body cremated and his ashes loaded in to a cannon and fired back to Poland.

Marina and her father Jerzy Mniszech were imprisoned but their lives were spared and they were sent back to Poland in July 1608. Jerzy helped to arrange his daughter's second marriage to False Dmitry II who was killed in December 1610, leaving her with a son Ivan Dmitriyevich born in January 1611. She then found a protector in Ivan Zarutsky, who backed her claim to the throne, making him Dmitry III. There is a Dmitri IV mentioned but some accounts insist that Dmitris III and IV were the same. In any case, Zarutsky had helped in raising the army for Dmitry II for which he earned the title of Boyar. Boyars wielded considerable power through their military support of the Rus. But Jerzy died in May 1613 and without him, in 1614, having failed to gather support for a Cossack uprising, Marina, Zarutsky and her son were captured on 26 July 1613 by the new Tsar Mikhail, the first Romanov ruler. Zarutsky and the boy were publicly hanged and Marina was strangled in prison soon after, although her fate cannot be proven.

The myth goes, that following her son's execution Marina placed a curse on the Romanov dynasty. She warned that as they had killed a tsarevich (i.e. her son) at Ipatiev so the Romanov line would also end with the death of a tsarevich at Ipatiev. "*You began with the death of a tsarevich* [Marina's son at the Ipatiev monastery] *and you will end with the death of a tsarevich!* [Alexei at Ipatiev House]" For this reason Marina carries the nickname 'Marinka the Witch'. The story whether myth or true, did come to pass.

Since Peter the Great made the changes that allowed women at court, throughout the next century four rulers would become Empresses; Catherine I, Anna Ivanovna, Elizabeth I, and Catherine II (also known as the Great). Because of Peter the Great's marriage to Catherine (his second wife) he found it difficult to find suitable pairings equal in rank for his daughters. The French court told him that the antecedents of Catherine were considered unacceptable to the Bourbons of France for the future King Louis XV. Peter the Great therefore searched wider afield for suitors, notably in Holstein-Gottorp. Of their twelve children only two girls Elizabeth and Anna survived to adulthood. Peter the Great had not envisaged such snobbery and as it turned out the first woman to sit on the Russian throne was the daughter of his former maid and second wife, Elizabeth I of Russia.

When Elizabeth I was 17 in 1727 she had lost her fiancé and both parents. The lowly circumstances of her birth were challenged by opponents who stated that she had no claim to the throne on account of her illegitimate birth. Regardless, at thirty-three years old she was placed at the head of a great empire albeit with little political experience and without a consort. She took the court by storm and elevated court balls to the next level. The ball was her obsession and they became renowned as the most extravagant social events ever held. These took place at the Winter and Anichkov palaces in winter and at the Peterhof and Catherine palaces in the summer.

Elizabeth I's exuberance for the workings of the Russian court came to define it. One delicacy at dinners was pineapple, indigenous to South America. Having travelled half way around the world they would bruise on the last leg from the port to the palace in St Petersburg, so Elizabeth had the roads resurfaced. Some of the entertainments cost anywhere between 10,000 and 100,000 rubles which was not extraordinary by her standards and perhaps only a handful of people in Russia could afford to spend like that.

Coronation balls were the most delightfully sumptuous of all, held at the Granatov Palace in Moscow. The most striking aspect was the display of fine clothing which advertised one's wealth and social standing. Men beamed with pride in their military uniforms and rank while ladies rivalled with each other over their appearance, wearing the most expensive dresses made from silks and lace and fabrics imported from China and France. The rules of the ball deemed merchants to offer their wares first to Elizabeth I. Once an item had been selected by her it could not then be offered again to anyone else as it was forbidden to wear the same clothes or style as the Empress; she reportedly owned 15,000 dresses and several thousand pairs of shoes, changing her attire several times a day and never known to have worn the same dress twice.

So it was Elizabeth I that introduced the rules that governed the ball and which evolved as the Russian ball distinct from the French ball. Fans were an essential accessory and depending on whether one was displayed or not, opened or closed or waved, it was a signal to potential suitors of their interest or unavailability, to approach or not to approach. As these rules developed they made for interesting spectacles. It was not advisable to look better than the Empress, for example no one could wear the same hairstyle. As she got older Elizabeth I became increasingly jealous of the beauty of other women. On one occasion when some paint got stuck in her hair and she had no option but to cut a chunk of it away, she compelled every female guest at her next ball to cut away the same chunk of their hair. Some young girls were said to have been in tears having to prepare for that ball, being obliged to attend.

The most domineering aspect of her character came out with the introduction of the masked or masquerade ball, held on 1 January during the Slavic festival of Maslenitsa to begin the ball season, always the eighth week before Easter in the Russian Orthodox calendar. During the season she held two standard balls a week; a large one up to 800 guests of court members, merchants and low nobility and a smaller one for higher ranking nobles. It could be anyone behind the mask from an official to the Empress herself. Around 1742 the masked ball was elevated to the famous metamorphoses balls, of which Elizabeth I reportedly held eight of them for her coronation. Guests dressed as the opposite sex. Most male guests detested the obligation to attend let alone having to endure the ridiculous, even respected military officers were to be seen pulling their tights up and loosening corsets to the amusement of the women who watched on and sniggered not so discreetly behind the courtesy of their male uniforms. Dresses remained the only attire until the early 20th century when Coco Chanel designed suits and blazers for women, spelling the end for the corset.

A ball started with a line dance, then the high-ranking couples danced minuets. The popular dances were the Polonaise, Kadril and the Mazurka was the ultimate challenge for 19th century dancers which in places had to be danced impromptu giving a freedom unlike other dances. According to Parisian dance master Henri Cellarius, *"Of all the new dances which have been introduced into our ball-rooms, there is none whose character is more marked with vigour, spirit and originality than the Mazurka."*

PALACES, BALLS AND FABERGÉ

Above: Dinner and dancing in the Concert Hall of the Winter Palace, May 1873, on the occasion of the 14-day state visit of King Nasir al din Shah of Persia, the first Persian to be photographed. He was assassinated in 1896.
Below: King Nasir al din Shah and Tsar Alexander II sit in the middle ground watching the dancing. Paintings by Hungarian artist Mihály Zichy.

CHAPTER III

The ball became the status event for noble weddings, the Imperial ball being a mark of enlightened society and the coronation ball the height of Russian splendour without rival. The coronation ball of Alexander II took place in 1856 in the Kremlin's Alexander Hall which was a significant year in Russian history marking the end of the Crimean War (1853-1856). Even Queen Victoria held a series of celebratory balls in her newly built ballroom at Buckingham Palace, Britain having joined with the French in 1854 against Russia. But Russia's defeat on 30 March 1856 cast a shadow over the coronation in September 1856, the defeat had been a humiliation and it was realised that Russia was not a major power and that it had to modernise.

On 23 May 1883 the coronation ball of Alexander III began when the Emperor in his uniform of the Semyonovsky Lifeguards Regiment with Empress Maria Feodorovna in white satin, entered the Alexander Hall to greet 2,500 guests and the orchestra opened with a polonaise. 2,200 of the guests attended a midnight supper in the St George and Vladimir Halls that lasted until 2.00 am. The coronation of Nicholas II had been no different with balls marking the historic event but unfortunately the ball held by the French ambassador in honour of the Franco-Russo Alliance is notable for all the wrong reasons and associated with the Khodynka tragedy that was an indicator of the troubles that were to come for the Imperial couple.

The 1903 season was marked by an especially beautiful costume ball at the Winter Palace when 390 hosts and guests attended in costumes of the period of Peter the Great's father, the Tsar Alexei I. It was the greatest of all the Russian balls. Nicholas dressed as Alexei I and Alexandra as his first wife and consort Maria Miloslayskaya. The 17th Century boyar costumes were designed by Sergey Solomko who went to great length in researching the accuracy of the designs, recreating them in authentic fabrics, some are on display at the Hermitage Museum in St Petersburg. Carl Faberge selected the jewellery adorning the costumes which were studded with diamonds, emeralds and pearls. Alexandra's brocade gown had a huge emerald at the front and her crown was studded with emeralds and diamonds.

Alexandra was reminded of court etiquette at such occasions. Unlike other European courts an already crowned dowager empress outranked a new empress consort and the Dowager Empress Maria Feodorovna was therefore more senior than the Empress Alexandra Feodorovna; a pill that she found hard to swallow - Nicholas entered the ballroom with his mother on his arm and his wife walking behind them.

At the dining table Alexandra could not bend her head to eat because her headdress was so heavy. Each guest had their photographic portrait taken and there was even one of the whole Romanov family gathered on the grand staircase for a single portrait, probably the only time this was ever done. Grand Duchess Xenia's husband Alexander Mikhailovich put it succinctly, *"it was the last spectacular ball in the history of the empire."*

It had been the most expensive ball ever held in Russia, spanning three days. On 11 February 1903 there was a concert and a dinner and dance. Day two was given over to rest. The costume ball was on day three from 10.00 pm until 1.00 am.

Alexandra Feodorovna dressed as Maria Miloslavskaya, 1903

A famine had stalked the countryside between 1891-1892 and in 1893 the Salvation Army denounced the '*sickening scenes of want, starvation and utter misery*'. By 1903 the country was heading for a depression, so people questioned such an elaborate event as this grand ball. They wondered why the 290th anniversary of the Romanov dynasty meant anything at all when

CHAPTER III

the tricentenary was just a decade away. But the Romanovs were giving a different message of changing times and looking towards a prosperous future. Even so, in 1913 when similar issues still existed, the last and largest public grand ball was held to mark the Romanov tricentenary.

The 1913 ball celebrated all the great Romanov rulers. The dynasty that had achieved such greatness, whose emperors had become behemoths with great power to wage war at will. But in 1913 it wasn't the Russian Emperor but the German Keiser that was the dominant monarch in Europe. In the preparations for the national celebration the Imperial Family moved to the Winter Palace on 19 February 1913. Alexandra hated being back there, it was a reminder of the first years after her marriage, such a large house with nowhere to hide. It was a huge place lacking in homely comforts which she found unnerving in stark contrast with her beloved Alexander Palace.

The significance for Alexandra was that it was just four months since the stay at Spala when her son had nearly died and which had completely drained her to the point that she was in a wheelchair. At one ball held during the tricentenary celebrations her lady in waiting Sophie Buxhoeveden had to take her away before she fainted. The 1913 ball was held on 21 February 1913 (J), a public holiday signifying the day in 1613 when Muscovites had gathered in Red Square to confirm Mikhail Romanov as the first Tsar by acclamation, and Boyars, Nobility, and Cossacks swore their allegiance.

The day of the tricentenary ball started with a 21-gun salute from the Peter and Paul Fortress, followed with a choral Te Deum in the packed out Cathedral of Our Lady of Kazan in St Petersburg. This was done in every church throughout Russia. Seats at the cathedral were reserved for the royal family, government ministers, Duma members, the military and foreign dignitaries, 4,000 in all. Never had the cathedral been so magnificent, with flags hanging across the 56 granite Corinthian columns, and hundreds of candles giving up their incense with an almost unnoticeable collective flicker illuminating the interior. Mikhail Rodzianko tells an interesting story in his book *The Reign of Rasputin*. When he arrived at the church an apologetic Baron Fersen told him that a peasant was occupying one of the seats reserved for members of the Duma and was refusing to move.

> "... *it was Rasputin. He was dressed in a magnificent Russian tunic of crimson silk, patent-leather top boots, black cloth trousers and a peasant's overcoat. Over his dress he wore a pectoral cross on a finely wrought chain. I drew quite close to him and said in an impressive whisper : 'What are you doing here?' He shot an insolent look at me and replied : 'What's that to do with you?'*

> " '*If you address me as thou [hast], I will drag you from the Cathedral by the beard. Don't you know I am the President of the Duma?'*

"... Probably I must have looked rather formidable, for Rasputin suddenly began to squirm and asked : 'What do you want with me ?' 'Clear out at once, you vile heretic, there is no place for you in this sacred house' 'I was invited here at the wish of persons more highly placed than you,' Rasputin answered insolently, and pulled out an invitation card. 'You are a notorious swindler, no one can believe your words. Clear out at once, this is no place for you.' "
— MIKHAIL RODZIANKO, Duma President

Rasputin fell on his knees and began to pray, Rodzianko nudged him saying that if he didn't go he would call Baron Fersen, the sergeant at arms, and have him kicked out. Rasputin got to his feet and walked to the western doors where his coat was handed to him and he was placed in a car and taken away. Rasputin maintained that he had a personal invite from the Tsar. He vanished in to a Russia that was struggling with mounting strikes (170,000 Russian workers were on strike, that would become 1.5 million by 1914) and commonplace assassinations, the impact of which was yet to materialise in the final chapter of the Romanov dynasty.

The grand fanfare was a fatefully false perception of the mood of the times. While the people revelled in the moment, the nobility couldn't see past it. When Alexandra attended the church service she saw only those people there cheering for the Tsar. She told a lady-in-waiting, *"What cowards those State Ministers are, constantly frightening the Emperor with threats of revolution and here, you see it yourself, we need merely to show ourselves and at once their hearts are ours."* It revealed the chasm of ignorance between the Russian aristocracy and the Russian people.

Nicholas noted nothing in his diary about the opening day of the tricentenary celebrations. The following evening the Imperial Family went to the Mariinsky Imperial Theatre. It was almost a carbon copy of the coronation opera at the Bolshoi on 29 May 1896 (G). On the program was the tragic opera *A Life for the Tsar* by M.I. Glinka. Alexandra became pale with shivers and left the theatre. In Act II, Nicholas watched his ex-lover ballerina Mathilde Kschessinska, dance the mazurka with Anna Pavlova. Exactly as it had happened seventeen years earlier.

It was on the third day of festivities, Saturday 23 February 1913 (J), that a Gala Ball was given by the aristocracy in honour of the Tsar. It was held at the nearby Assembly Hall on Mikhailovskaya Street, not as great as the ball of 1903 but remarkable in that it was the last of the Grand Russian balls. Olga Nikolaevna recorded it as her first ball in an Imperial official capacity. In one account the big pair danced all evening, in another account Tatiana could not attend for she had contracted typhoid fever. Everyone of note attended, notably a young Princess Irina Alexandrovna showing off her suitor for the first time, Prince Felix Yussoupoff.

CHAPTER III

Alexandra predictably wasn't feeling up to greeting the arriving guests, leaving Maria Feodorovna to receive all the attention at the baisemain; the procedure for greeting at formal occasions for guests to declare their arrival and congratulate their Majesties. First a guest meets the Emperor, men bow their head and women make a curtsey, then they shake hands. Next the guest greets the Dowager Empress with a bow or curtsey, she extends her hand and the guest kisses it. Next in line would be the Empress.

Nicholas received the guests in the lower corridor where the dinner was arranged for them. The orchestra opened with music from the polonaise dances from the opera *A Life For The Tsar* to which Nicholas opened the dance with the wife of the St Petersburg District Marshal and Alexandra danced with the District Marshal. It had been a very tiring day for the entire Imperial Family on their leaving at 11.00 pm.

Russian deck of playing cards designed by Dondorf of Frankfurt

In preparation for the tricentenary celebrations, back in 1911 a commemorative Russian style deck of cards was designed by Dondorf, a card game maker in Frankfurt. They used the 100 or so photographs from the Album of the Costume Ball at the Winter Palace from 1903, and matched the picture cards to some of the nobles. The deck was so popular that throughout Soviet times they remained the standard Russian playing cards. Succeeding generations may not have been aware that the characters were in fact real people representing their past Romanov Imperial rulers.

The Tricentenary celebrations ended on Sunday, the fourth day. People partied joyfully in the streets whilst the Imperial Family returned discretely to Tsarskoe Selo so that Alexandra could nurse Tatiana's typhoid fever. It had been a resolute success, with the only notable remark being Alexandra's absence in the formalities and her avoidance of the ballerina Mathilde. Some were a little upset that the Tsar hadn't put on the grandest of Imperial balls but in retrospect that would have been disrespectful to the nobles that had arranged the great tricentenary costume ball, which turned out to be the greatest Russian Ball of them all; how could the Tsar have bettered that.

Peter Carl Faberge

The words 'palaces & Fabergé' sit together as comfortably as 'strawberries & cream'. Gustav Faberge founded Fabergé (with an accented e) in 1842 in St Petersburg. His son Peter pictured right, was a goldsmith that carried the company through its period of prestige, perhaps the No.1 jeweller in the world. After the October Revolution 1917 their workshops were closed and Peter fled to Switzerland where he died in 1920.

In 1913 Easter came early, the great feast of Paskha broke the Lent and the yearly Fabergé delivery came on Easter weekend, the bill was always issued about two or three weeks later. The eggs were delivered to Nicholas personally on Good Friday, 21 March. That year the bill was for 46,000 rubles, not such an extravagance for the richest leader in the world, and who remains today in the top number of richest people that have ever lived, with an estimated inflation-adjusted net worth of between £2.4 to 3.2 billion. For Nicholas, buying a Fabergé egg would have been like going to the shop for a carton of milk. Nicholas' final Fabergé bill was issued on 25 April 1917 addressed to Mr Romanov, Nikolai Alexandrovich, but of course the eggs never found him as by then he was terminally indisposed.

CHAPTER III

THE WINTER EGG (1913)

The Winter egg was presented to Maria Feodorovna on Easter Sunday, the most expensive egg yet produced at 24,700 roubles. Designed by Alma Pihl one of two female designers at Fabergé who came from a distinguished family of Finnish jewellers. It was skilfully made by her uncle, master Albert Holmstrom. The thinly carved shell is engraved on the interior to give the impression of fine ice crystals and the rose-diamond frosted exterior is engraved with set platinum motifs. Inside stands a platinum basket of wood anemones with intricately carved white quartz stems and stamens on gold wire with nephrite carved leaves.

LTR: The Winter egg and the Tricentenary egg. - 1913

THE TRICENTENARY EGG (1913)

The Tricentenary Egg had a purchase price of 21,300 rubles. Its shell surface of white enamel is applied with chased gold forming wreaths, crowns and eagles, adorned with ivory miniatures of the eighteen Romanov rulers and set under rock crystal within rose-cut diamond surrounds. The portraits are painted in watercolours in exquisite detail. The interior houses a blue steel globe of the world with two depictions showing the boundaries of the Russian Empire in 1613 and 1913.

Image: Alexandra and Maria Feodorovna kept their eggs in wooden showcases with bronze fittings. Only once were the public allowed to view them. It was for a charity exhibition sponsored by Alexandra in March 1902 at the mansion of Baron von Dervis in St Petersburg; the first ever exhibition of Fabergé art works. Alexandra provided all of her seven eggs, housed in this display cabinet.

CHAPTER III

> ## FABERGÉ EGGS DURING THE 1904-1905 WAR
>
> Imperial Eggs were not made in 1904 and 1905 because of the outbreak of the Russo-Japanese War in January 1904 and the political unrest in Russia during 1905, as the Tsar deemed it inappropriate to lavish such expenses for gifts. Indeed The Red Cross with Resurrection Triptych egg, was one of the least expensive of all, yet it's one of the most striking.
>
> *"During the war years, eggs were either not made at all, or were very modest and inexpensive."* - François Birbaum, Fabergé's chief designer, memoirs. Each egg took a dedicated team a year to make, usually done in secret. The only stipulation was that there had to be a surprise inside, being that it was an Easter egg 'surprise'.
>
> Seven Fabergé Easter eggs are missing presumed lost or in the hands of secret collectors. They all once belonged to Maria Feodorovna for the years: 1886, 1888, 1889, 1897, 1902, 1903 and 1909. One of her eggs, the Third Imperial Egg (1887), was also missing but turned up in an American antiques hall in 2010 and was purchased for $13,302. The anonymous buyer discovered in 2014 that it was an Imperial Egg worth $33 million.

In 1882 the head of the House of Fabergé Peter Carl Faberge had taken over his father's Goldsmith, Silversmith and jewellery business. 107 years later in 1989 Unilever bought Fabergé Inc (including Elizabeth Arden) for US $1.55 billion, having on the previous month acquired the Calvin Klein Cosmetics Company for US $376 million.

A month after that wonderful Easter, in May 1913, the Imperial Family embarked on a Pilgrimage retracing the journey of the first Romanov tsar from Kostroma the place of his birth to the throne in Moscow, where he was crowned. It further reinforced their belief that the people were wholly behind them. All along the journey people came to greet them, many reaching out hoping to touch the Tsar. On the rivers people swam out to them and on the paths workmen fell to their knees and kissed the Emperor's shadow as he passed them. What more validity did Nicholas and Alexandra need to prove that they were truly adored by the people.

CHAPTER IV
The Cult of Mysticism

AT the turn of the 20th century Alexandra Feodorovna was not well liked by the people and the pressure from having to produce an heir forced her to sink deeper in to a negative mental state. She focused on her ailments and distanced herself from her daughters, the extended family and her state duties.

The Turn of the Century

A letter from Queen Victoria to Nicholas II, following the birth of third daughter Marie:

> *"I am so thankful that dear Alicky has recovered so well, but I regret the 3rd girl for the country."* — QUEEN VICTORIA, 14 July 1899

Alexandra sent a letter to her close friend Princess Marie Bariatinsky on New Year's Eve 1900, two weeks before Queen Victoria died, closing with these words (she is referring to not having had a son):

> *"What sorrows, this last year brought us, what endless anxieties, what worries and losses – God grant the new year may be a calmer and happier one for the whole of dear Russia."*
> — ALEXANDRA FEODOROVNA

An entry made in the diary of her sister-in-law Xenia on 5 June 1901 (J) following the birth of fourth daughter Anastasia:

> *"Alix feels splendid – but my God! What a disappointment ... a fourth girl! They have named her Anastasia. Mama sent me a telegram about it, and writes, 'Alix has again given birth to a daughter!'"*
> — XENIA ALEXANDROVNA

CHAPTER IV

The affection people had for Maria Feodorovna was in contrast to the resentment they showed towards Alexandra Feodorovna but she was more drastically compared to her sister-in-law Xenia, a somewhat proficient male producing machine, which increased the pressure to produce an heir.

Age in 1901:- *Alexandra*: 29 / *Xenia*: 26

Date father died:-
Alexandra: 13 March 1892 / *Xenia*: 1 November 1894

Engagement:-
Alexandra: 20 April 1894 / *Xenia*: 12 January 1894

Marriage:-
Alexandra: 26 November 1894 / *Xenia*: 6 August 1894

Children in 1901:-
Alexandra: 4 daughters, son to come in 1904/ *Xenia*: 1 daughter, 3 sons and pregnant with 4th son. Another son to come in 1907

During the years between 1897 to 1905 the Imperial Family moved around residences and were not always at the Winter Palace. They stayed mostly at Gatchina Palace or the Winter Palace and from 1900 revived the ancient custom of spending Easter in Moscow. In the summer they moved between the Peterhof and Alexander palaces and took a cruise to the coast of Finland. In autumn they stayed at Livadia in Crimea then journeyed to Copenhagen to visit Nicholas' grandparents. In winter they stayed at the hunting grounds of Spala in Poland. At least every two years they travelled abroad. It was the same every year, a schedule laid down by Alexander III and rigidly followed by Nicholas II.

Up until 1841 the only railway in Russia was between St Petersburg and Tsarskoe Selo. But now the Imperial train offered uninterrupted travel as far as Hesse in Germany. Up until 1896 the yacht Derzhava facilitated excursions in the Baltic Sea and the yacht Livadia in the Black Sea. The Polar Star was used for longer voyages. The yacht Standart was requested by Alexander III not long before he died and was commissioned at sea around three months after the coronation in 1896. It was the largest Imperial or private yacht in the world and could go anywhere, rendering the other yachts obsolete in terms of ferrying the Imperial Family.

The turn of the century was a time of European travel by train and with the golden age of sea liners in full swing the well to do were packing their portmanteaus and travelling the world and the European houses were also able to regularly leave the confinement of their palaces and move freely. The German Emperor went to Britain, King George V to Germany, the

Russian Emperor travelled to France and Italy, princesses, queens and empresses went to Germany and Denmark. Nicholas had sailed to Dunkirk for a state visit in 1896 and returned there in 1901. And this was just how the royalty liked to express their freedom. Never before had so many important people moved in such numbers so openly across Europe.

The state visit of King Chulalongkorn of Siam (Thailand) with his four eldest sons at Alexander Palace during his first grand tour in 1897. *Front row*: Maria Feodorovna with daughter Olga Alexandrovna and son Nicholas II. King Chulalongkorn had 116 consorts and concubines and produced 33 sons and 44 daughters.

Not only royals were getting around but a cultural mesh had established of writers, artists, philosophers, revolutionaries, mediums, faith healers and all sorts of talented people interspersing throughout the world. For example, in London the Bolshevik revolutionaries were gathering, including Vladimir Lenin, to plan the Russian Revolution, in a bar at the Angel in the borough of Islington. The renowned Madame Blavatsky travelled extensively, as far as America to establish the Theosophical Society. The ornithologist Allan Hume travelled throughout India and founded the Indian National Congress,

CHAPTER IV

then returned to London and founded the South London Botanical Institute. Nicholas II went on a world cruise. There are numerous examples because travel back then was the popular in thing to experience.

The strange sciences or non-scientific, what today might be described as the supernatural, saw a resurgence in the second half of the 19th Century. The primary destinations were India and China where seekers looked for enlightenment in the teachings of mystics. For example, ornithologist Allan Hume became a chela (student) of the Tibetan spiritual gurus. He developed an interest in theosophy around 1879 and followed the movement founded by Madame Blavatsky and in 1880 his wife and daughter were initiated in to the Theosophical Society. Finally in 1894 he left India for England. That's a lot of travelling and a lot of mysticism for an ornithologist.

Generally the medieval era was an age of superstitions, magicians and witches. It was replaced with the Renaissance which spread throughout Europe from Florence, Venice and Milan. The Renaissance revived classical architecture and arts and created the styles of the baroque and neoclassical. Scientific experimentation and technology replaced superstitious beliefs based on ignorance. From the mid-19th Century in the Modern Era, there was an acceptance of an existential connection with a godly intelligence on a spiritual plane. This connection to a God together with occultist knowledge saw the rise of spiritualism as a new science that ushered in people like Madame Blavatsky and Allan Hume, and Aleister Crowley who in 1905 made the obligatory trip to India and China then returned to England and founded an esoteric order.

Mysticism and occultism dealt with the pressing questions of the time but offered no satisfying answers. The vulnerable and weak-willed as well as those searching for reassurances were readily disposed to believe the magicians' performances. What in the 1870s held fascination and the need to explain the meaning of spiritualist metaphysics, in the new century became a varied landscape of diverse practices whereas Indian and Chinese mystics had been enlightened for centuries but without having a need to commercialise the mysteries.

Madame Blavatsky was a regular visitor to Allan Hume's Rothney Castle in Shimla, India, the place where his bird collecting staff that worked across India brought their specimens for him to classify. In 1874 he transferred 82,000 specimens of 258 types of birds to the British Museum and gave up ornithology. At a dinner party Blavatsky asked Mrs Hume if there was anything she wished for. She talked about a lost brooch from her late mother. That evening Blavatsky directed them to a spot in the garden where they found the brooch. According to the Christian missionary in India John Murdoch, Mrs Hume had given the brooch to her daughter who gave it to a man she met. Blavatsky found the man in Bombay and bought the brooch which she allegedly planted in the garden.

This was why mystics were called tricksters by unbelievers. Russia was one step behind that and had not lost medieval superstitions. In every house there was and possibly still is today, an icon of the Virgin Mary high on the wall facing the front door. When entering and leaving the house, and before and after a meal, one must salute the icon image. A priest is called when a baby has been born to offer it up to the icon image and gives it a Christian name at that moment. After forty days the official Christening takes place in the church. Some may even say that Nicholas II was among the most superstitious Russians that lived.

Mystics and Mayhem

Although Madame Blavatsky (Helena Petrovna Blavatsky, 1831-1891) was Russian she fulfilled most of her achievements abroad. As one of the first proponents of mysticism in Europe she was active in the early 1870s, well before the court of Nicholas II. She was a cousin to Sergey Witte, the government minister mentioned extensively thus far, and therefore he mentions her in his memoirs. Blavatsky was the eldest daughter of Witte's maternal aunt and he recounts seeing her at brief interludes when he was a boy.

Helena Blavatsky married the governor of the Russian province of Erivan. Shortly after, she stowed on an English ship to Constantinople where she entered the circus and worked with horses. She met an aspiring Italian bass opera singer Giovanni Mitrovich who fell in love with her. He took her with him on his 1867 tour through the opera houses in Hungary and Venice where she was utilised as a singer. Mitrovich had at least one affair and Blavatsky left him and had several short lived marriages, without first having divorced her legal Russian husband. She turned up in India and met ornithologist Allan Hume, whom she formed a like-minded partnership of theosophical interests with. Next thing, she was giving piano concerts in London and Paris and became the manager of the royal choir for King Milan of Serbia. This part of her life being over she returned to her husband in Tiflis, Russia, (today Georgia) and this is when Witte saw her for the first time, (he was born in Tiflis in 1849).

At Witte's house near St Petersburg Blavatsky conducted spiritual séances. Among the guests were Count Vorontsov-Dashkov, (future Minister of the Court of Nicholas II). Her séances lasted for an evening or all night sometimes. She never discussed her occult knowledge in the presence of Witte who was sceptical about such matters even as a boy but all her knowledge had come from Allan Hume and India. Mitrovich coincidentally turned up for an operatic performance in Tiflis and resumed a relationship with Blavatsky. Amid the scandalous affair they slipped away to Kiev and later turned up in Odessa where coincidentally Witte's family had resettled at that time.

CHAPTER IV

They opened a series of high street shops and when that didn't work boarded a ship for Cairo where Mitrovich had secured some work. But the ship sank off the African coast and he drowned saving Blavatsky. Now penniless, she found her way to America in 1875 and founded the New York Theosophical Society, then travelled again to establish the Theosophical Society in England. The next stop was a return to India to study occult sciences and thereafter to Paris where she fell ill and died.

From Count Witte's memoirs it can be seen that he also knew a great deal about a certain Philippe Anthelme Nizier from Lyon, better known as Master Philippe. On 6 October 1877 Philippe married Jeanne Julie Landar, a patient that he had once healed. Their daughter married a doctor and Philippe then himself began to practice as a quack and ventured in to fortune telling and other unconventional practices. In October 1884 he published the paper *Principles of Hygiene applicable in Pregnancy, Childbirth and Infancy* at the University of Cincinnati, Ohio, for which he obtained an honorary Doctorate of Medicine. In May 1886 the Royal Academy of Rome conferred on him the title of Honorary Doctor of Medicine.

Philippe was the son of Joseph Philippe, a French butcher in Lyon, and Marie Vachot, and he became one of the most impressive thaumaturges and healers of the 19th century. The 'wonder' started a few months before he was born when his mother visited the effigy representing the venerated Jean-Baptiste-Marie Vianney (1786 – 1859), a Catholic idol representing the parish of Ars (Curé d'Ars). While his mother prayed to Saint Vianney it was revealed to her that a son with a heavenly spirit would be born to her.

From a young age Philippe was known for his strange powers and did not enter medicine in the traditional way but leaned towards groups that practiced alternative methods, therefore achieving a doctorate in France was out of the question. The French medical society said of him *"he performs occult medicine and is a veritable charlatan."* But in Italy he found support from influential people like the Montenegrin sisters, a country that was less pedantic on the means of obtaining a medical qualification.

The Montenegrin sisters were daughters of Nicholas I of Montenegro (king 1910-1918), a minor Slavic principality in southeastern Europe on the Adriatic Sea. Ousted in 1916 by the occupation of Austria-Hungary he fled to Italy where his daughter Elena was the queen and then in 1918 when his throne was deposed he exiled to France. Montenegro has some of the most rugged terrain and barren soil in Europe and because it also has no natural resources Montenegro's sole export were the king's many children, earning him the nickname of the father-in-law of Europe. Once, a visitor told him that he regretted the country had no exports and the king replied, *"Ah, but you forget my daughters,"* of which there were nine; two died young (Marija, Sofie), two queen consorts (Zorka, Elena), one married a prince (Anna), two married a duke (Milica, Anastasia), two remained unmarried (Ksenia, Vjera).

– *The Montenegrin sisters*:

- ❖ Princess Ljubica Petrović- Njegoš of Montenegro (b. 1864) became Zorka Karađorđević of Serbia
- ❖ Princess Milica of Montenegro became Grand Duchess Militza Nikolaevna Romanova of Russia (b. 1866)
- ❖ Princess Anastasia of Montenegro became Grand Duchess Anastasia Nikolaevna Romanova of Russia (b. 1868)
- ❖ Princess Marija Petrović-Njegoš of Battenberg (b. 1874) Died two months after her sixteenth birthday
- ❖ Princess Jelena of Montenegro became Queen consort Elena of Italy (b. 1873)
- ❖ Princess Anna Petrović-Njegoš of Battenberg (b. 1874)
- ❖ Princess Sofia Petrović-Njegoš of Montenegro (b. 1876) Died shortly after birth (2 May – 14 June)
- ❖ Princess Ksenja Petrović-Njegoš of Montenegro (b. 1881)
- ❖ Princess Vjera Petrović-Njegoš of Montenegro (b. 1887)

Quite distinct from the German and Russian lines, the House of Petrović-Njegoš was a dynasty of ruling Christian celibate bishops dating from the early sixteenth century. Succession passed from uncle to nephew on account of their celibacy and they were the reigning family from 1696 to 1918 when Montenegro was annexed by the emergent Kingdom of Serbs, Croats and Slovenes (Yugoslavia from 1929). Montenegro joined World War I on 28 July 1914 on the side of the *Triple Entente.*

To maintain good relations, not that he needed to, Alexander III saw to it that four of the Montenegrin sisters (Milica, Anastasia, Jelena, and Anna,) received Russian schooling until the age of eighteen at the Smolny Institute, a finishing school in St Petersburg for aristocratic girls decreed by Catherine the Great. Arrangements were also made for Milica and Anastasia to marry second rate Russian nobles and they were provided with sizeable dowries.

Alexander III took an interest in Montenegro for no better reason than he viewed Jelena as the prime candidate for a betrothal to his son Nicholas. Jelena was shy and stubborn like Nicholas but nothing would come of it because Nicholas chose a different shy and stubborn woman in Alix of Hesse and by Rhine. Therefore, having been rejected in 1895 Jelena was taken to Venice for the International Art Exhibition and presented to the king and queen of Italy, and in turn to Prince Victor Emmanuel. Jelena and Victor married on 24 October 1896 and Victor ascended the Italian throne on 29 July 1900, following his father's assassination, They ruled Italy together until 1946.

CHAPTER IV

In 1889 Milica of Montenegro married Grand Duke Pavel Nikolaevich of Russia, (a cousin of Nicholas II). and Anastasia of Montenegro married his brother Peter Nikolaevich on her second marriage in 1907. The sisters became better acquainted with the Russian nobility through their marriages and eventually made best friends with the Empress Alexandra Feodorovna.

The Montenegrin sisters Milica and Anastasia, 1890s

Ljubica was the eldest of the Montenegrin dozen (9 daughters, 3 sons). She received schooling in the Montenegrin capital Cetinje (today Podgorica) and from her Swiss tutor Mrs Naikom. How unfortunate that she only lived for just over twenty-five years and died in childbirth with her fifth child who also died with her. Anna was described as unusually beautiful and vivacious, and for a number of years was the oldest living princess in Europe and the last surviving Battenberg before the family anglicised it to Mountbatten.

Sisters Ksenja and Vjera ('faith' in the Slavic language), like Ljubica had the benefit of Swiss tutors. In 1898, the sisters and brother Danilo went to Italy to visit their recently wedded sister Elena, cementing the strong link between the two countries. The Montenegrins flittered between Montenegro, Italy and Paris, keeping up with news and trends. They were not unnoticed in aristocratic circles and continued much as they had before their marriages.

In Paris Princess Milica became an honorary doctor in alchemy (the forerunner of chemistry). With her husband Pavel Nikolaevich and her sister Anastasia they were introduced to the scene of metaphysics, remedies and mysticism in Paris. Through their Russian husbands they ensured another link between the cultural centre of the West and the bohemian East of Europe. There were plenty of high ranking Russian travellers sojourning at Compiègne, immersed in the decorative arts and dabbling with mysticism.

Much earlier during 1874/1875 Philippe applied no less than five times for the authority to practice as a doctor but was denounced so in 1883 he went ahead regardless, healing at his home in Lyon. But without a licence he was again denounced by the doctors of Lyon, in 1877. During this time he met Mathilde Theuriet who became one of his followers and in turn she introduced him to her future husband and occultist Gérard Anaclet Vincent Encausse. It was rather fortuitous for Philippe because Encausse opened up a world of occultists outside of Lyon, introducing Philippe to many of them in Paris where they would come to regard him as a miracle worker and award him the respectful title of 'Master Philippe' in due course.

Encausse eventually became a student of Philippe's and was involved in founding a school of Magnetism in Paris in 1893. He had obtained his Doctor of Medicine degree from the University of Paris in 1894 and was a practicing physician and hypnotist using the pseudonym *Papus* to publish several books. He invited Philippe to open a school in Lyon, and on 26 March 1895 Philippe became the Director of the School of Magnetism and Massage of Lyon. And back in Paris Papus was sufficiently established for the Montenegrin sisters to become familiar with him.

In due course the Montenegrin sisters Militza and Anastasia also found Philippe and insisted that he accompany them to Cannes to meet Militza's husband Grand Duke Pavel Nikolaevich. The Montenegrins became devotees of Philippe, visiting him regularly in Lyon which did not go unnoticed. The whole district knew of Philippe's royal visitors. A woman who kept a tobacco shop opposite the lodgings stated in a police report that she was amazed at the standing of people she saw coming and going, and pointed out the tall, thin man with two fine ladies that she had seen call several times. Grand Duke Vladimir Alexandrovich and other nobles followed with visits to Philippe's practice during 1900.

Philippe was favourably accepted outside of France. Through the Montenegrin connection, he would eventually meet the Kings and Queens of Italy and England, and the emperors of Austria, Germany, and Russia. Capitalising on his fame he accepted an invitation in September 1900 from Grand Duke Vladimir Alexandrovich to visit Russia. He left France with his daughter on 29 December 1900, his reputation preceding him, and stayed in Russia for two months at the accommodation of the grand duke. During his time there he performed séances and healings, electrifying audiences.

CHAPTER IV

In 1901 Nicholas and Alexandra received state visits from Italy and France and that same year they visited Nicholas' grandfather Christian IX in Denmark and Prince Henry of Prussia at Kiel. On 12 September 1901 Nicholas II was a guest of the German Emperor Wilhelm II for naval manoeuvres at Danzig. From there the Imperial Yacht Standart sailed to Dunkirk arriving on 18 September 1901 for a three day return visit to see Émile Loubet, the President of France.

The state visit to France had been in 1896 following the coronation, when crowds had flocked Paris to see them. This time their trip to France was more of an indulgence. They were taken on the Presidential train about fifty miles northeast of Paris to Compiègne, taking in a visit to the Palace of Versailles along the way. They stayed in the beautiful rooms of Napoleon I and Marie Louise at the Château de Compiègne. Marie Louise became pregnant immediately after marrying Napoleon I, who had divorced his first wife Josephine after fourteen years for not providing an heir. Alexandra perhaps shared an affinity with Louise who must have known that failure to produce an heir would have sealed her fate but perhaps also Alexandra felt more aligned with Josephine's failure.

A lithograph from a painting by Pavel Piasetsky of the Standart arriving at the French port of Dunkirk 18 September 1901. The artist was a friend of Nicholas II and accompanied him aboard the Standart for this voyage abroad.

On the following day they attended military manoeuvres in Reims, about 40 miles to the south of Compiègne. There they visited the cathedral famed for being the place where French kings were traditionally crowned.

THE CULT OF MYSTICISM

Day three was a more relaxing affair which included a leisurely walk in a lovely park, a simple pleasure they both appreciated above all others.

Nicholas and Alexandra taking a stroll, print painted by Pavel Piasetsky

"It was a peaceful day for us. In the morning we walked to the nearby sections of the park. We were walking the entire time in front of the guards and a string of watchmen. It is unimaginable what precautions they took everywhere here. At 11.00 am <u>our friend</u> showed up. At 7:00 pm there was a big dinner with educated people of lesser birth and a show. Everything was over at 11:00 pm."
— NICHOLAS II, 19 September 1901

The 'Our friend' from the quote above refers to Master Philippe. He had asked Militza to arrange an audience with the Tsar and she had informed him that Nicholas and Alexandra would be pleased to see him. He was presented to the Imperial couple at the Château de Compiègne by Grand Duke Nikolai Nikolaevich (Nicholas' great uncle who married Anastasia of Montenegro in 1907 at age 51, ten years her senior). Militza had previously sent Papus to Alexandra to assist with her endeavours for a son but that had not worked out so Papus had left the Russian court. Militza hoped that Philippe could resolve their anguish and help them with a fruitful outcome.

At their meeting, Philippe took the opportunity to discuss the matter of his medical certification issue hoping to enlist his royal connection to progress his cause in France. Mysticism was doing the rounds in every salon in Paris and St Petersburg. It was the cult of the age emanating from the hubbub of modernity in Paris. Mostly salons were full of inquisitive women

CHAPTER IV

but some men also attended. They gathered to participate in séances and learn about spiritualism. It was not too far out of the ordinary, for the times, for Nicholas to ask President Loubet to grant Philippe a doctor of medicine degree. Loubet evaded such a ridiculous request.

Philippe had an uncanny reputation for predicting the future and strengthened his hand by announcing to the Imperial couple that a son would be born to them in 1904 and also that a great military defeat and a revolution would follow. They were enchanted by Philippe and asked him to visit them in Russia at his earliest convenience.

Philippe took them at their word and no sooner had the Imperial Family returned from their voyage than he was calling at the court. A house in Tsarskoe Selo was prepared for him where he secretly lived and performed séances for the Imperial couple, the grand dukes and the Montenegrin sisters. Nicholas and Alexandra saw him once or twice a week, at which meetings he experimented with hypnosis and necromancy and conducted nocturnal séances. He prepared concoctions for Alexandra to ingest and lessen her ails and to aid in the prospect for the conception of a male heir; that is to say, he was practising sorcery.

> *"You know, when Witte was President of the council and Minister of Finance he was very much mixed up in the affairs of the famous Philippe, Rasputin's predecessor."*— MAURICE PALÉOLOGUE

The Montenegrin sisters were Alexandra's only friends in Russia and through them Philippe pressed for validity determined to secure a medical doctorate. Militza approached Pyotr Rachkovsky, an Okhrana policeman in Paris, demanding Philippe be given his medical diploma. But that's not how things were done, not even in the less than decadent part of Paris. Nicholas too, looked to cut corners in awarding a doctorate but Russian ministers insisted that Philippe had to pass exams like everyone else. Accordingly, Philippe attended an interview at a hospital on 8 November 1901. He sat before a jury of medical professors and began a séance asking that the panel call out bed numbers from the hospital wards whereupon he proceeded to tell them what was wrong with those patients and attempted to heal them from his chair.

After the interview demonstration the professors went to the wards and confirmed what Philippe had said, and that's how he received his Doctor of Medicine title. In another account from the memoirs of French Ambassador Maurice Paléologue, *"Wine [was] applied to the War Minister, General Kuropatkin, to have Philippe appointed medical officer on the Reserve, and he was also authorised to wear the uniform of a civil general!"* Either way in 1901 Philippe had secured his doctorate from the Medical Military Academy, receiving a military doctor's uniform and the rank of General, but nevertheless, these medical credentials were not recognised in France.

Alexandra's close friendship with the Montenegrin sisters was down to their mutual fascination with mysticism. Alexandra and Nicholas would travel out to spend time with them at the Dulber Palace in Yalta where Militza and her husband lived or they went to their winter residence at the Konstantin Palace in Strelna just outside of St Petersburg that overlooked the shore of the Gulf of Finland. At Dulber Palace they could while away a long weekend immersed in mysticism. Some accounts say that it was where Nicholas attended his first séance and where he partook in drug taking. Given how much Nicholas enjoyed to smoke, it's not a far stretch to accept that he would have taken whatever drug may have been prepared for him, but this would be to presume he had not already delved with drugs when Philippe had stayed in Tsarskoe Selo for those two months. In memoirs of the Head of the Chancellery of the Imperial Ministry Alexander Mossolov, he attributes the arrival of Rasputin around this time to the mystics at the palace; Sund, Badmayev, Papus, Philippe, and these are just a few of the many mystics that descended on the court at this time.

> "*Sometimes the Montenegrin ladies would come and shut themselves up with the Empress in her apartments in Livadia. There were table turnings and consultations of spirits; <u>dead Tsars</u> answered the call of the mediums. The Emperor himself was said to have taken part in the séances, which were carried on by two foreign occultists named Papus and Philippe. This seems to have been the first manifestation of this tendency to a morbid mysticism, which later on enabled Rasputin to gain a footing at Court.*" — ALEXANDER MOSSOLOV

The reference to *dead tsars* from the quote above refers to Philippe invoking the spirit of Alexander III at the séance when Nicholas would ask questions relating to the affairs of state and the spirit would proffer advice. In years to come, in 1905, Nicholas arranged for Papus to conduct a séance at Alexander Palace at which he asked the spirit of his father if he should meet the demands of the revolutionaries and the spirit of Alexander III told him to crush the revolution without hesitation.

When Philippe was taking on the role of faith healer he would not actually touch his patient unlike the Russian practice of healing by the laying of hands. Instead he professed that a healthy mind maintained a healthy body and told Alexandra and Nicholas to look to providence and strive for spirituality. This they did by adopting a very costly campaign throughout 1902/03 refurbishing churches and advancing the canonisation of religious nominees, notably the Elder Seraphim which Nicholas progressed on the date of Seraphim's birth, 19 July, by asking the Holy Synod to conclude the glorification of the revered elder. Nicholas thereafter kept a portrait icon of Seraphim in his study.

CHAPTER IV

Philippe approved of their religious devotion of which he had helped to promote to fanaticism. Enhancing their spirituality could be seen as a way to unify them with the existing Church as opposed to mysticism which pulled them away from it. Mysticism was never a religion but spiritualism was a common belief whereby communication with that which is beyond life can be offered through a medium or a priest, except that the former connects with a spirit, not a god. In promoting spiritualism over mysticism the connotation was that by performing good deeds the Imperial couple might be rewarded with a son.

They developed a conviction that their fortunes had changed and certainly there was a remarkable turnaround in Alexandra's energies from this time. Papus was back at the court and less approving of their religious obsession even though his opinion was contrary to Philippe's strategy. Perhaps Papus, a bona fide medical practitioner, saw through the mysticism. But Papus had revisited the court to no avail having fallen out of favour long ago and his advice to the Imperial couple expressing concern over Philippe and later Rasputin was ignored. The Imperial couple would not entertain any negativity and desperately prayed for a son, believing divine intervention would visit them. Their fertility was not in question but after a fourth daughter was born at Peterhof on 18 June 1901, it started to look as though they really were lacking divine approval, notwithstanding Philippe's prediction that a son was yet to arrive in 1904.

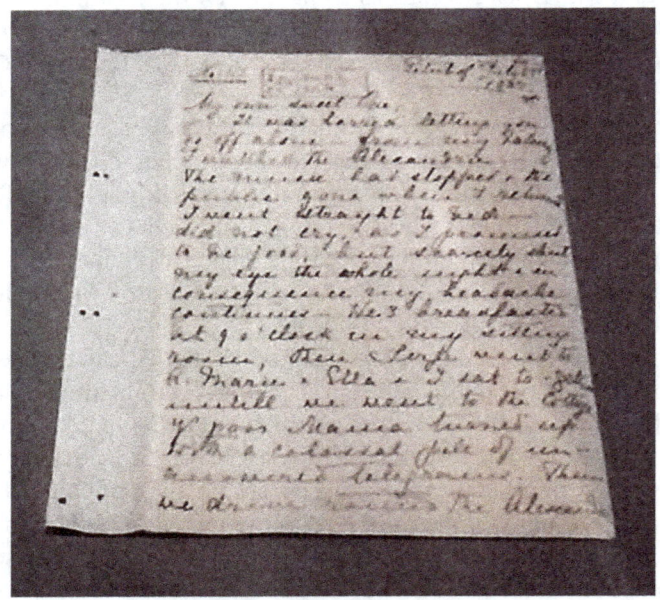

Letter from Alexandra to Ella on display at the Blood & Revolution exhibition in London 2019, on loan from the State Archive of the Russian Federation.

Both Nicholas' mother and Alexandra's sister Elizabeth were most unapproving of '*their friend*' but Nicholas was not receptive and neither listened to his mother's warnings nor cared for Ella's. Nicholas' mother thought Alexandra incapable of seeing sense and not worth the aggravation of trying to persuade her against mysticism. However, she was constantly warned by others and it seems that by mid 1902 these persistent warnings were getting on her nerves which she evidenced in a letter to Nicholas on 23 July 1902 informing him that her sister Ella had:-

"... *assailed me about Our Friend. I remained very quiet and gave dull answers. She has heard many unfavourable things about Him and that He is not to be trusted. I said that we did everything openly and that in our positions there never can be anything hidden, as we live under the eyes of the whole world."*
— ALEXANDRA FEODOROVNA (transcript of image on previous page)

Master Philippe de Lyon

Nicholas became quite attached to Philippe and sought his opinion from time to time whereas Alexandra saw him as the tonic that brought her the reassurances her doctors could not. The hold of mysticism at the Russian court was much talked about at the French court, a fact confirmed in 1902 by Baron Alphonse (the head of the Rothschild banking family in France,) in person to Sergey Witte. He warned Witte that great events in history were always preceded by the prevalence of a bizarre mysticism at the court of the ruler, of which there were many examples to support the theory. Things got worse, at one point a procurator of the Holy Synod Prince A. D. Obolensky, complained to Witte about the interference of the Montenegrin sisters in the affairs of the Holy Synod!

Maria Feodorovna resorted to the court adjutant General Hesse (Head of the Court Police,) asking him to investigate Philippe's charlatan ways as it was reported that he had twice been prosecuted in France for unorthodox or illegal practice. Hesse asked Pyotr Rachkovsky in Paris (the same head of the Okhrana that had been approached by the Montenegrin sisters,) to provide a profile. The discreet investigation was duly carried out and the not so favourable report was passed back to Maria Feodorovna. She presented it to Nicholas to warn him about Philippe's past deeds, providing the evidence of two prosecutions. But Philippes's leverage on Nicholas was enough to protect him and Nicholas' preoccupation with the occultism that had taken root at the court shocked even Maria Feodorovna when he removed Rachkovsky from his post for having produced the damning report.

Phantom Pregnancy

It's not known exactly when in 1902 Alexandra started to develop symptoms of pregnancy but whenever it was, Philippe told her that she was pregnant with a son, revising his earlier prediction by two years. He would not allow her doctors to examine her until late on in the faux pregnancy despite their insistence that she was not pregnant.

Sister Ella had been right to express her concern to Alexandra in July 1902 about Philippe because in early August she was vomiting and having worse headaches than usual. According to Witte she should have been way in to her pregnancy because, *"Everyone noticed that she had grown considerably stouter. She began to wear loose garments and ceased to appear at court functions. Everyone was sure that Her Majesty was pregnant ..."* So it was an increasing mystery to those around her that she was not actually showing. Even stranger, the palace released the news that she was pregnant. All the while in the streets people listened out for cannon shots from the Petropavlovsky Fortress that would announce the arrival of an Imperial heir.

There is a wide debate around what is termed Alexandra's phantom pregnancy that doesn't present the possibility that she was indeed pregnant. When a baby did not come rumours quickly circulated. Some speculated that Alexandra gave birth to another girl and it had to be hidden away, or it was said the baby was so disfigured and grotesque that it was taken out of the city and disposed of; one story was even that Rasputin had been the father and placed the baby under the care of a convent or monastery. Neither were true but the real debate is whether Alexandra had been physically pregnant and miscarried, or did she suffer from a psychological phenomenon that fooled her body in to believing she was pregnant, when she was in fact not.

If Alexandra had a full term pregnancy then conception must have occurred at the end of October/beginning of November 1901. During that time she was receiving medication from Philippe. However, pregnancy symptoms were not recorded that far back as letters from that period only mention warnings about Philippe and do not signal any awareness of a possible pregnancy. So it is unlikely that it was a full term pregnancy as is suggested in a letter from Nicholas' sister Xenia dated 19 August 1902, in which she says *"nine months"* suggestive of a phantom occurrence.

"We have all felt so terribly disappointed since yesterday. Can you imagine anything so awful, it seems poor Alix isn't pregnant after all for nine months she had nothing, then suddenly it came, but completely normally, without pain." — XENIA ALEXANDROVNA

Alexandra had been through four successful pregnancies so it is a wonder why she would feel such a compulsive need to consult Philippe over the advice of her own doctors; royal accoucheur (male midwife) Professor Ott and royal surgeon Girsh. When Ott was finally permitted to examine Alexandra on 17 August 1902 he confirmed that everything internally was fine and that she was not pregnant and never had been. According to Grand Duke Konstantin Konstantinovich (Nicholas' cousin,) Alexandra cried a lot when she was told that it had been a false pregnancy. Both of Nicholas' sisters Olga and Xenia mention a discharge in their letters. Olga wrote that some blood was released which is suggestive of a miscarriage and on 20 August 1902 Xenia wrote the following:

"This morning Alix had a minor miscarriage if it could be called a miscarriage at all! – that is to say a tiny ovule came out! Yesterday evening she had pains, and at night too, by morning it was all over when this event happened! Now at least it will be possible to make an announcement and tomorrow a bulletin will be published in the papers with information about what happened. At last a natural way out of this unfortunate situation has been found."
— XENIA ALEXANDROVNA

The following bulletin appeared in newspapers from Alexandra's doctors, as an explanation for the previous misleading press release:

CHAPTER IV

"A few months ago, the state of Her Imperial Majesty the Empress Alexandra Feodorovna underwent changes, pointing to a pregnancy. At the present time, thanks to the departure from the normal course, the interrupted pregnancy has resulted in a miscarriage, which occurred without any danger, the temperature and pulse remaining normal. Peterhof 20 August 1902." — MSSRS OTT and GIRSH

The popular belief is that Alexandra was not pregnant and therefore the diagnosis being pseudocyesis meaning that all the symptoms were in her head. Xenia clearly described a discharge, or rather precisely the release of a tiny ovule. Wikipedia describes it as a 'molar pregnancy.' Dr Ott informed Alexandra after he examined her that such phantom pregnancies did happen, caused by anaemia. But he had examined her prior to the appearance of the ovule and may well have had a different diagnosis otherwise, if he had seen the ovule and shifted his diagnosis of phantom pregnancy to a miscarriage.

In a molar pregnancy the symptoms are severe nausea and vomiting which Alexandra did have. It presents with bleeding at around four to five months and means that she would have been pregnant as a sperm is required. It is the egg that is defective and leads to a disease whereby grape sized nodules form on the inside. If indeed Alexandra had a molar pregnancy then it would rule out pseudocyesis and phantom pregnancy because she actually conceived and therefore the symptoms she had of pregnancy were real.

Pseudocyesis is a condition where a woman who is not pregnant shows physical signs of pregnancy like amenorrhea (a lack of menstruation). That Alexandra was a victim of somatic disorders is apparent as she is known to have suffered from back pain since her youth and also headaches and fatigue was a common theme with her. But pseudocyesis is a psychological disorder and this we can attribute to the incredible stress that she was constantly under to produce an heir, whether for real or much of it perceived.

Since the late 17th Century it was known that the symptoms of pseudocyesis have their origin in the mind and common symptoms are chronic stress and depression. Today it's known that two thirds of women that have false pregnancies have a desperate desire for a child. Henry VIII's daughter Mary Queen of Scots, during her unhappy marriage to Philip of Spain believed herself to be pregnant several times, having the symptoms, which were attributed to her intense desire to have a child and heir. Yet she remained forever childless with no physical evidence of a pregnancy.

Within a few years of Alexandra's so-called phantom pregnancy it had been observed through psychological behavioural studies that a woman's perception of herself can dry the milk supply and the study was suggestive therefore, that the opposite could also be true in that someone believing they were pregnant could miraculously produce milk. This explains somewhat how Alexandra experienced the symptoms of pregnancy if it was a phantom.

The mind and body are connected by the pituitary gland, the part that controls hormones. Biochemical changes in the brain from strong emotions such as stress, produce increased hormone release that can produce physical changes consistent with pregnancy. The reader should consider whether Alexandra's famed phantom pregnancy was caused by pseudocyesis or did she have molar disorder and was technically pregnant.

When the phantom / molar pregnancy was finally over, her confessor Bishop Theophane, whom the Imperial couple were very fond of, advised them to reconsider their devotion to the occultist ways of Philippe and asked whether their disappointment at not yet producing an heir was a warning from God for indulging themselves in such trickery.

Considering the embarrassing situation Philippe had very publicly brought upon them in convincing Alexandra that she had been pregnant, and the considerable consternation that it had caused within the extended family, Philippe then had the temerity to blame Alexandra for having consulted with her own physicians which he said showed a lack of divine faith in him and God and which was why the pregnancy had ended without a child. Needless to say, Philippe was banished for his insubordination and sent back to France where he lived until his death in 1905.

Empress of Russia

ALEXANDRA FEODOROVNA

(1903)

Painting by Friedrich August von Kaulbach, 1903, future court painter of King George V. This was Nicholas II's favourite portrayal of his wife. She looks at her best, and considering at this time she had four children, a miscarriage, phantom or molar pregnancy, and is pregnant with the heir to the Russian throne, her beloved son Alexei.

CHAPTER IV

The Drugs Legacy

In the world of mysticism at the turn of the century the connection between drugs and hypnotics was studied widely, particularly in Russia. Given Philippe's intense interest in hypnotics he would have familiarised himself with the works of Russian medical doctors such as Dr N.O. Buhnow and Dr V. Bekherev who were at the front of scientific pioneering. He would have known about Alexandra's fears, that she believed she had a heart condition and often complained of it. There was a possibility that she had Graves Disease (hyperthyroidism) a condition resulting in high levels of the thyroid hormone which can lead to atrial fibrillation.

She had genuine physical ailments like back pain, sciatica and headaches, so bad sometimes that she could not walk. She had facial neuralgia, cyanosis (blue lips), acute earache, and swollen legs and feet. She suffered conditions like insomnia, fatigue, excessive stress and worry, panic attacks, and a chronic depression that was written across her face. How much of her life was spent resting on a couch or on the veranda, sitting in a wheelchair or in bed reading and writing while propped up on pillows. In short, she was more than likely suffering the mental illness of hypochondria.

The view generally given of her is that she was lazy and a recluse, but it goes further than that; she was narrow-minded and stubborn, described by Witte as *"hysterical and unbalanced"*. One of her German aunts told Queen Victoria, *"Alix is very imperious and will always insist on having her own way; she will never yield one iota of power she will imagine she wields."* This was a time when lethargic disorders like MS were not known about. No wonder she welcomed the crude mysticism presented to her by Grand Duke Nikolai Nikolaevich, which in due course she infected the entire court with. But a closer look at her life reveals the incredible work load she undertook, attending functions, charities, opening hospitals; the patron of many causes. Some accounts tell how she could hardly walk at the end of a day, familiar to every hard-working individual. By the end of 1908, 33 charitable societies were under her patronage, some are listed below.

- The communities of Sisters of Mercy, shelters
- The Peterhof Society for Helping the Poor
- The Imperial Womens' Patriotic Society
- The Society for Helping the Poor with Clothes in St. Petersburg
- The Alexandra Womens' Shelter
- The Guardianship of Labour Assistance
- Her Majesty's Nursing School in Tsarskoe Selo
- The Charity House for Mutilated Soldiers

One thing that may explain the negative labels appended to Alexandra and to some extent her health issues is prolonged drug use. Philippe was looking in the right direction in prescribing Adonis Vernalis and Barbital for her, the two drugs she continued taking up to her untimely death. Both are concoctions with hypnotic characteristics. Adonis Vernalis to regulate her pulse and Barbital to help with insomnia and anxiety, both having a sedative effect contributing to her lethargy. By comparison her legitimate physician Dr Botkin treated her anxiety with gentle medications and spas.

In 1879 Dr N.O. Buhnow introduced alcoholic extracts of Adonis Vernalis making a herbal tincture that acts as a cardiac stimulant similar to digitalis, it is the glycocides in the plant that are the sedative. Dr Vladimir Bekherev in 1898 mixed the Adonis Vernalis extracts with sodium bromide (a known irritant of the respiratory tract,) to treat heart diseases and various other conditions such as dystonia and epilepsy. It's evident that Philippe was offering this as a treatment for a possibly non-existing heart condition.

Both drugs, the Adonis Vernalis extract mixed with sodium bromide and the barbital, are based on Adonis Vernalis, a poison in large doses; in animals it causes vomiting and diarrhoea. The effect of two sedatives would explain Alexandra's worsening anxiety, lethargy and depression and one can only wonder whether it was contributing in preventing an otherwise healthy pregnancy or did it cause a molar pregnancy. Barbital which was introduced as a sleeping aid in 1903 and marketed as Veronal from 1904, was the first barbiturate (i.e. depressant) requiring higher doses over time for the sedative and hypnotic properties to remain effective. Codeine can be used instead of sodium bromide which is yet another sedative and an opiate that is addictive.

Dr Bekherev was interested in mental suggestion which he said was different to hypnosis. Barbital is a drug that leaves you very susceptible to suggestion, like believing you're pregnant maybe. When you consider Philippe's intervention in Alexandra's psyche and his experimentation with drugs whilst operating as a quack doctor, then it becomes plausible how all these parts may have led to a phantom pregnancy. By 1914 Alexandra was still using barbital and confessed to a friend, *"I'm literally saturated with it."* That drug use left Alexandra with a vulnerable susceptibility cannot be refuted. On this canvas, when Rasputin came to the Russian court, Alexandra was ready to be painted on with hypnotic suggestions.

Some discussion has explored whether Nicholas had cocaine and Alexandra was on opium. The discredited Prince Felix Yussoupoff in his memoirs suggested that Nicholas took drugs that made him calm, supplied by chemist Pyotr Badmayev, one of several Tibetan brothers that were licensed to practice medicine in St Petersburg. Badmayev had converted from Buddhism to Russian Orthodoxy and is best known for translating the Tibetan book of traditional medicine 'Gyushi'. In those times cocaine was used to relieve dental distress and Nicholas had notoriously bad teeth and a

CHAPTER IV

halitosis that Alexandra was constantly on to him to attend to. Opium was used as a sedative for various things; in Leo Tolstoy's Anna Karenina, she spirals in to opium addiction after her doctor prescribes it as a sleeping aid. Arsenic too was commonly prescribed for depression and anxiety although there is only evidence of daughter Olga Nikolaevna that used it, having been prescribed arsenic injections in 1915 by nurse Valentina Chebotaryova when she became anaemic.

Drug use did contribute somewhat to the mental and physical states of Nicholas and Alexandra if only because of the prevalence of mind altering substances at the turn of the twentieth century. They were young and hanging out with the Montenegrins and must have experimented with all sorts of concoctions; Philippe and Badmayev being their drug dealers.

Today we view cocaine and opium as highly addictive drugs, cocaine more of an upper and opium a downer. They were once regarded as helpful every-day pharmaceuticals. The Bayer company coined the name 'heroine' in 1898, the year before they introduced aspirin (*page 162*), and were the makers of 'heroine cough syrup.' Appreciating that cocaine and opium back then were as acceptable as the milder modern psychotropic drugs of nicotine and caffeine, helps in understanding the Imperial couple's idiosyncrasies; their reclusiveness, paranoia at times, mood swings and depression.

Tibetan physician Pyotr Badmayev

CHAPTER V
Industrialisation & War

IN 1902 Nicholas appointed the reactionary Vyacheslav Plehve as his Minister of the Interior. Plehve's attempts to suppress reformers led to a speech in 1903 when he warned them:

"Western Russia some fifty per cent of the revolutionaries are Jews, and in Russia generally – some forty per cent. I shall not conceal from you that the revolutionary movement in Russia worries us but you should know that if you do not deter your youth from the revolutionary movement, we shall make your position untenable to such an extent that you will have to leave Russia, to the very last man!"
— VYACHESLAV PLEHVE

Having displayed great opulence in February 1903 with an overly lavish grand ball, a number of anarchistic organisations began to appear in spite of Plehve's warnings. The Chernoznamentzy group formed from peasants, factory workers, Jews and students, calling for death to the bourgeois. The opposition to autocracy that Nicholas had inherited from his forebears was always present and worsened since his father Alexander III had severely persecuted the non-Russians that made up half of the population in Russia. In Finland the Russian governor was also dealing with rebellion and was given more powers by decree allowing him to imprison anyone for virtually anything. The order was short and broadly scoped, and gave the Governor the following powers:-

- ❖ To forbid any kind of public or private gatherings.
- ❖ To dissolve private associations and their branches.
- ❖ To forbid persons regarded by him as detrimental to political order and public tranquillity from residing in Finland.

CHAPTER V

In August 1903, the revolutionary Vladimir Lenin's actions had the effect of splitting the Russian Socialist Democratic Labour Party in to three factions, Mensheviks, Bolsheviks and Socialist Revolutionaries. It allowed over the ensuing years for a socialist agenda to sanction a rebellion that in 1905 started the First Revolution and culminated in the 1917 civil war.

The Financial Crisis

The Russian financial crisis of 1899-1902 was self-inflicted by the large-scale investments made by banks in loans to heavy industrial companies as working capital in the 1890s. These loans had high interest rates but could not be readily liquidated when urgently required. Between 1899 and 1904 a worker's wealth increased by nearly 10% but almost 40% of that was wiped away by inflation.

The response by government was to work with banks to prop up the large industries where necessary, to protect their initial investments. This limited the credit available for smaller companies. Between 1900 and 1904 large industrial companies prospered whilst smaller companies went in to decline. Metal works were the largest employer accounting for 60% of factory workers; the Putilov Works employed 30,000 workers making it the world's largest factory.

In 1900 the huge mining industry increased output by 5.3%. Yet over the same period the price of coal fell by 35.3% (oil by 57.3%, cast iron by 33.7%). In response to rising inflation and decreasing prices the larger companies downsized their labour and maximised their efficiency.

How could large industry increase output and profit when prices fell so much and while they were reducing labour by an average of 3% per year? It's not surprising that between 1897-99 coal mines became over six times more dangerous for workers and the first unions appeared in 1903 following the worsening conditions. Strikes took place in 65 of the 78 Russian provinces, starting out localised in the south and becoming general strikes towards the end of 1903 and during 1904.

Employers refused their demands initially but as regional strikes became general strikes with increasing demands, employers were compelled to negotiate and workers received a wage rise and better conditions. Unlike in the past when protesting was met with a wall of soldiers, these strikes did a lot of good. However, the hard liners gave it a political character by using slogans like *down with autocracy* and *long live the democratic republic*.

People do not usually protest against oppressive regimes in fear for their lives, that's what activists do. Having much success in collective bargaining the hard-liners were afforded some momentum which they carried to the Red Square and to the Tsar himself in the form of a letter addressed directly to him from the people and delivered by the people's representative Gapon in February 1905, and which led to the First Revolution 1905. There were around 2.3 million industrial workers in Russia and the majority did not seek to bring down the tsar or bring in socialism. In their minds the tsar was not associated with the government and its policies and their every-day lives. And they were right, as it was the government that was to blame, namely Sergey Witte the Minister of Finance (1892-1903).

Count Sergey Yulyevich Witte

Witte had been a politician under the previous two emperors and commanded much authority. His role as Finance Minister was during the time of the financial crisis. He was on a mission to increase the speed of Russian industrial development identified following the Crimean War but which was slow moving due to a skills shortage. This problem he overcame by importing foreign engineers. He relied on foreign investors for much of the industrial growth, having put Russia on the gold standard in 1897 to attract investments. Witte's policy for industrialisation worked and by 1900 Russia was producing three times as much iron as for 1890 and more than twice as much coal. But for the reasons outlined so far, the investments and commitments to repay foreign investors tied up the economy and having been successful in modernising Russia's industrial base, Witte had unwittingly created a financial crisis.

CHAPTER V

The Siberian Railway 1891–1916

Keeping Manchuria and Vladivostok supplied and reinforced was completely reliant on the Siberian Railway. The huge project of creating the longest railway line in the world (4,960 miles) from Moscow to Vladivostok, began in March 1891 by Alexander III. Nicholas II served as chairman of the Siberian Railroad Committee and laid the first stone of the Ussuri Railway near Vladivostok in May 1891, officially inaugurating the commencement of works which he supervised until its completion in May 1916. It was unarguably the greatest achievement of his reign.

A railway line already existed from St Petersburg to Moscow built in 1851. The government did not invest in Siberian infrastructure due to the small number of enterprises there but it would become important eventually to transport cheap grain from the interior to the west and to transport troops and supplies to the east. Roads through Siberia were rough where they existed and frozen rivers became roads for some months of the year. Steam ferries were used but limited. Having surveyed extensively for ten years it was concluded that a railway was viable between Moscow and the far east.

At the start of construction the country was thrown in to famine (1891-1892). 85% of the population lived in the countryside working in agriculture, 77% of the population were peasants. The famine drove many to seek employment elsewhere so it's a tragedy that instead of using localised labour much of the railway was built using thousands of prisoners. Over 3,500 civil engineering structures were built; 100 million cubic metres of earth was moved; more than one million tons of tracks laid; over 60 miles of bridges, tunnels and retaining walls built; 16 rivers and 87 towns crossed.

The term 'Trans–Siberian Railway' was a name given to this grand feat of engineering by the West. It is today the world's greatest railway journey and the backbone of transportation in Russia. The journey from Moscow to Vladivostok takes about a week and it's the shortest means of travelling between Europe and Asia by land. Although the project lasted until 1916, completing around 44,000 miles of railway, the main functionality of the Siberian Railway had been completed on 21 July 1904, not long after the war with Japan started on 8 February 1904. Moscow station opened in 1902 although certain sections were running before that, Moscow started running passengers from 1903. In 1904 the railway provided access to Manchuria.

Sergey Witte was well acquainted with the project, having been concerned with Russia's industrialisation and mobilisation. He had started out his career in the railway industry selling tickets before moving in to management and finally occupying the highest position of Transport Minister. It was Witte that convinced Alexander III to appoint Nicholas II as the chairman of the Siberian Railway Committee. Having a royal patron was essential for the project to be able to cut through the red tape and keep the construction on schedule. Witte went on to become the Finance Minister in 1892 which ensured that finances were always in place for the project and, as outlined earlier, that was done with unrestricted loans which ultimately helped to contribute to the financial crisis.

The problem with the railway was that it was a single track service; only one train could run in any direction. When two trains were travelling towards each other one was required to move in to a siding to let the other one pass. This caused huge problems during the war with Japan, with troops and munitions heading to the front and wounded troops trying to make it back to the hospitals in Moscow. Between 1911 and 1914 a second track was constructed that resolved this poorly anticipated problem.

By far the larger issue was at Lake Baikal, to take the railway around it in either direction was a huge undertaking in itself, and this is why the prisoners on that section were essential otherwise the territories in the east were unsustainable and a war could not be maintained. In 1902 there were around 9,000 workers on the Baikal railway which rose to 13,500 in 1904 when construction was accelerated. In all, the project employed around 100,000 workers achieving around 466 miles (750 km) of line a year. The track flowing around the southern part of Lake Baikal required thirty-three tunnels and over a hundred bridges costing about 11 million rubles (of the estimated 350 million for the whole project). The materials, excepting local stone, came by barges in the summer and horse drawn carts in the winter.

CHAPTER V

Above: Horses pulling railway cars across an ice covered Lake Baikal; the world's largest freshwater lake by volume, containing 22–23% of the world's fresh surface water. Before the ferries came the crossing was done by horse power alone.
Below: The English built ice-breaker steam ship SS Baikal ferrying trains on the Siberian Railway across Lake Baikal c1903-1904. When the line first opened railway cars and passengers would use an ice-breaker ferry to cross the lake. (4,200 tons, length: 290 feet, speed: 12 knots)

Two ferries operated across Lake Baikal until a track was completed in 1905 to circumnavigate this largest lake in the world by volume and the deepest. Known as the Pearl of Siberia it holds 20% of the world's surface freshwater. The ferry could take across 27 railway cars and 300 passengers and crew. Having completed the hardest part of construction in taking the railway around Lake Baikal, the priority turned to connecting it through Manchuria to Port Arthur, a vital link required to transport troops and munitions for the war against Japan. After the war the track in to Manchuria was abandoned and the Siberian Railway was connected from there directly to Vladivostok following the Amur River and bringing the entire railway within Russia.

The idea had been to start construction from both ends at Moscow and Vladivostok and meet in the middle at Chelabinsk, the second largest city in the Ural Federal District after Ekaterinburg. The construction was divided in to seven sections with three phases planned that would be completed in ten years. First off, The South Ussuri railway pushed out from Vladivostok to Grafskaya around 250 miles and the West railway pushed out from Chelabinsk about 870 miles to the River Ob, and the Central railway pushed out from Ob to Irkutsk about 1,150 miles.

The second stage took the Zabaikalsky railway to the east side of Lake Baikal and the Ussuri railway continued another 223 miles to Khabarovsk (named after the Russian explorer Yerofei Khabarov), a town founded in 1858 as a military outpost for defence of the Russian-Chinese border.

The third stage involved the circumnavigation of Lake Baikal. By 1901 much of the Siberian Railway had been built with the hardest final 1,240 miles left to finish between Sretensk and Khabarovsk. It was at this point that Nicolas II decided to divert the railway through Manchuria.

The Circum-Baikal Railway was completed in 1905 which ended the need for trains to use ferries to cross Lake Baikal. It took nearly four weeks to make the journey at 20mph from start to finish. The rush of construction because of the Russo-Japanese War involved using cheap materials so the railway often broke down. During the civil war in 1917 the White Army was to use the railway extensively and also blew up parts of it. It wasn't until 1920 that proper long term repairs could be made. The Siberian Railway has lasted until the present day with 30% of Russia's imports and exports using it to transport around 300,000 containers each year.

War with Japan 1904–1905

The Russo-Japanese War lasted for eighteen months starting on 8 February 1904 when Japan broke off diplomatic relations and attacked the great fortress of Port Arthur in the Yellow Sea, the Gibraltar of the far east

CHAPTER V

which symbolised the extent of Russia's domination. In the words of the Russian Minister of Internal Affairs, "[To] *Hold back the revolution, we need a small victorious war.*" In 1904 the army and navy were no more ready for war than they had been ten years earlier when Nicholas II became the Tsar, despite his penchant for the military and that way of life.

> *"As far back as 1901 our Headquarter Staff had estimated that in the event of war our Pacific Ocean Fleet would be weaker than Japan's"*
> — GENERAL ALEXEY KUROPATKIN, War Minister

Overtime was compulsory when manufacturers had military orders to fulfil. Striking fell drastically because the government sent any rebellious workers to the front. The war with Japan is one of the six or seven major contributing factors that Russian historians say led to the First Revolution 1905. The front was in Manchuria (north-eastern China today) but despite thousands of casualties on the ground it was primarily a naval war happening around the Korean peninsula with the Commander-in-Chief of the Fleet being Nicholas' uncle, Grand Duke Alexei Alexandrovich.

In 1904 three quarters of Russian land was in Asia. Most of the Empire, namely Siberia, is frozen during winter including the Baltic Sea. The Russian fleet was only operational at the shipping base at Vladivostok and from the warmer waters of Port Arthur, being land on the Liaodong Peninsula that had been leased from China in 1897 for 25 years. Manchuria and Korea are natural buffer zones between China, Russia and Japan, yet Japan and Russia were prepared to go to war for control of it. Japan had not long finished a war with China in 1895 in which Russia had given military support to China, so Japan knew that China and Russia would jointly oppose any Japanese aggression in Korea.

Therefore, Japan offered Russia complete control in Manchuria in exchange for control over Korea. Russia refused and consequently Japan surprise attacked Port Arthur in the night. The Japanese crippled three of the largest Russian naval vessels with torpedoes; *Tsesarevich*, *Retvizan*, and *Pallada*, and prevented the Russian navy from coming out to engage them at sea. The port was repetitively under bombardment while ships attempted to break free without any success. On 10 August 1904 Nicholas ordered six battleships, four cruisers, and fourteen destroyers to make a break for the open sea and engage the blockading Japanese fleet of four battleships, ten cruisers, and eighteen destroyers. It would be the first major naval battle fought between steel battleships, known as the Battle of the Yellow Sea. Casualties were Russian 444 – Japanese 226.

The Russians succeeded but became scattered and were so badly battered that they limped back to port. With no fleet in the Sea of Japan, Russia called for the Baltic Fleet and began delay tactics so that reinforcements and supplies could be transported to Manchuria via the Siberian Railway while the fleet was given time to make way to engage Japan. The Battle of Mukden was about to be fought in Manchuria, the last major land battle and the largest there had ever been in history, in terms of the amount of munitions used. The Japanese surrounded the Russians and they managed to break free and retreat to Russia and severed the Trans-Siberian Railway connection. The campaign had cost 8,705 Russian and 15,892 Japanese casualties.

Japan was receiving intelligence from Britain about the Russian Baltic Fleet under sail in co-operation under the Anglo-Japanese alliance of 1902 and were waiting when the Baltic Fleet arrived in the Sea of Japan. 24 of the 27 ships of the Russian task force were destroyed causing 5,000 casualties with Japan only losing 3 ships and 116 casualties. Nicholas had sent the army unprepared in to Manchuria and the aging Pacific and Baltic fleets to face a far more modern adversary and it had been disastrous. As in the Crimean War (1853-1856) which was the first to publish daily media coverage, so had the Russo-Japanese War gathered the world's press to witness Russia's humiliating defeats. In the spring of 1905 after the Battle of Tsushima Strait, the Russian navy was completely wiped out and the war was lost.

The American President facilitated peace talks at the Portsmouth Naval shipyard in Kittery, Maine, in New Hampshire between Russian and Japanese diplomats during 6-30 August 1905. It was known as the 1905 Treaty of Portsmouth and was signed on 5 September 1905 by Sergey Witte and Roman Rosen for Russia with Komura Jutaro and Takahira Kogoro for Japan. The treaty marked peace between the two nations but Russia had to pull out of Manchuria and recognise Japan's claim on Korea. Militarily it was a disaster and caused a public outrage that was irreparable. Having lost Port Arthur there was no longer any influence in the East and Russian ambitions stopped at Vladivostok.

Japan suffered as much politically because they had to acknowledge China's claim on Manchuria and control of the Liaodong Peninsula, which contained Port Arthur, extended only to taking over the lease. Japan could have negotiated so much more and the public outrage led to the Hibiya riots in Japan and the collapse of Prime Minister Katsura Taro's government in January 1906. Cessation of hostilities meant Russia did not need to deal with an existential threat from Japan and were able to regroup militarily. In the meantime the 1906 Nobel Peace Prize was awarded to Theodore Roosevelt for negotiating the peace between the two countries. However, Roosevelt had not been totally impartial because the US and Japan had the secret Taft-Katsura Agreement, signed before the peace talks, which recognised Japan's claim on Korea in exchange for Japan's recognition of the US claim on the Philippines, the existence of this treaty was not revealed until 1924.

The West saw Japan as under developed even though they boasted the sixth largest army in the world and a navy that had some modern British ships. Japan had borrowed 38% of the total cost for the war from Britain, Canada and the US yet Nicholas II could not comprehend how such a small country had defeated the Russian Empire and as Cossacks retreated from Manchuria they slayed whole villages for no reason, leaving 5 million Jews and 23 million Muslims in Russia to face their return. It was a gross underestimation marking the first time in modern history that an Asian nation had defeated a European one and the beginning of Japan's rise as a world power.

Above: Flagship of the Russian fleet Petropavlovsk hits a mine returning to Port Arthur and sinks with 599 souls on 13 April 1904.
Below: The Russian front at Mukden in Manchuria.

CHAPTER VI
Arrival of an Heir

WHEN Master Philippe visited Nicholas and Alexandra in Paris back in 1896 he made three prophecies; that an heir would be born in 1904 and that a revolution and a great military defeat would follow. Before he left Russia in 1903 he made two more; that it would be Seraphim of Sarov that would grant them a son and that another healer would come to them speaking about God. All of Philippe's predictions came true.

When Nicholas sponsored the canonisation of Seraphim on 1 August 1903 he also attended the festivities with Alexandra, his mother and other family members and even paid for the cypress coffin holding the relics. Nicholas and Alexandra bathed in the sacred River Sarova where once Seraphim himself had bathed. They prayed that he would bless them with a son. Before Nicholas' intervention Seraphim had been a relatively unknown figure in the Russian Orthodox Church having died just seventy years earlier but he became one of the most renowned saints in the Church for his healing powers and prophecies.

At age nineteen Seraphim joined the Sarov monastery located in the province of Tambov, near the town of Arzamas. He moved in to the woods living as a hermit for twenty-five years; for three of those years eating only grass. After a short spell back at the monastery he returned to spend 1,000 successive nights in continuous prayer, for which the Church deemed to be a miraculous feat of achievement. And surely it was if true; likewise was the news that Alexandra became pregnant two months later. Their prayers to the elder Seraphim of Sarov had paid off. As her due date neared, a newspaper printed what was on the collective minds of everyone – would God grant her a son and provide the country with an heir?

> *"A few days will decide whether the Tsarina is to be the most popular woman in Russia, or regarded by the great bulk of the people as a castaway, under the special wrath of God."* — from a newspaper clip

CHAPTER VI

A rare photo of a pregnant and smiling Alexandra with Nicholas II, 1904

On 25 August 1904 (G) Alexandra gave birth to an eleven pound boy at the Peterhof Palace. The labour lasted less than an hour but the umbilical cord when cut took several hours for the bleeding to finally stop and which unfortunately would transpire to be a serious health condition for the child.

Imagine the relief and exhilaration that Alexandra must have felt. The birth affirmed that Nicholas and Alexandra were blessed by God and that they had been right to put their faith in Philippe and Seraphim. Nicholas asked Militza to pass on their gratitude to Philippe which he received shortly before he died. Nicholas' sister Olga was more rewarding to Seraphim, *"I am sure it was Seraphim who brought it about,"* she wrote.

ARRIVAL OF AN HEIR

The procession of the shrine of the relics of Seraphim of Sarov, carried by members of the royal family with Nicholas II leading, 1 August 1903

"Today was a great and unforgettable day for us, when divine grace was bestowed upon us during which we were clearly visited by the grace of God. At 1.30pm Alix delivered a son, we've praised the Lord and named him Alexei. There are no words to thank God enough for sending us this comfort in a time of sore trials." — NICHOLAS II

Announcing the birth of an heir in St Petersburg the enormous cannons of the Peter and Paul fortress fired while the Cathedral of Our Lady of Kazan started church bells ringing across the city. This is how the people heard the news that a boy had been born at the Peterhof Palace. From the moment he was born the Tsarevich inherited the title of 'Hetman of all the Cossacks'. With Russia at war with Japan, all military personnel were named honorary godfathers. Alexandra's maternity dress was consigned to the wardrobe for ever and the baby was shown off to the public at every opportunity. At three years old he would be on parade in his miniature military uniforms; wearing a Cossack uniform in the winter, complete with fur hat, boots and dagger, and a naval uniform in the summer. When asked what he wanted to be when he grew up, he answered, 'a warrior tsar to lead armies like his ancestors'.

Alexei Nikolaevich Romanov
on the day of his christening
6 September 1904 (G)

Alexandra Feodorovna's
maternity dress
(1903-1904)

From the workshop of
A. Brizak, St. Petersburg.
Made from wool, silk and lace.

The Royal Disease

News of a tsarevich spread rapidly and celebrations took place in the villages. The christening twelve days later was celebrated like a pageant in the streets. For the first time, at the christening, the young Olga and Tatiana had been present at an official ceremony. A few weeks after the birth the boy was found to be bleeding continuously from his navel. It was about six weeks in that his parents began to notice bruises on his arms and legs and as the weeks rolled on, they noticed that he suffered terribly from the faintest knocks. The awful realisation descended upon them that Alexei was a victim of the royal disease.

CHAPTER VI

The exaggerated bruising and swelling and tummy bleeding were due to haemophilia, a blood clotting condition passed through the royal family and originating with Queen Victoria. One third of haemophilic cases occur by spontaneous mutation, and this had been the case with Queen Victoria who passed it unwittingly to the European royal houses through marriages. Alexandra being one of the most famous royal carriers of the rarer type Haemophilia B. The female carries the defective gene and she is largely immune to it but haemophilia presents in the male offspring depending on their chromosome make up.

The Imperial Family at Peterhof Palace after the christening of Alexei

This heredity disease meant that the damaged cell (i.e. the spontaneous mutation,) had occurred in Queen Victoria or someone in her distant past had it and it resurfaced generations later. She passed the trait on to three of her nine children. *"This disease is not in our family,"* she protested when her son Leopold presented with symptoms soon after he was born in 1853. Alexandra's son, her two nephews, brother, and uncle were haemophiliacs and her daughter Anastasia, a sister, mother, grandmother and several other female family members were haemophilic carriers.

Alexei was diagnosed with the milder form of haemophilia B, which is also known as Christmas Disease, named after Stephen Christmas the first person to be diagnosed with the disorder in 1952. Today, Alexei's condition would be perfectly treatable and he would have a normal life. There are several classifications of the disease; severe, moderate, or mild. Had Alexei had the severe type of haemophilia he would not have lived much past seven years old and most likely would have suffered from arthropathy, a disease of the joints resulting from frequent bleeding in to the joints, an extremely painful condition that can prevent walking and cause permanent disability.

At the time, what is called the Edwardian period in the UK, there was no treatment for the mild type other than the alleviating of pain. In the previous generation doctors were still bloodletting haemophiliacs and the disease was regarded as an early death sentence with a life expectancy of between seven and sixteen years. 50% of affected boys would die before the age of seven and 11% lived for twenty years with an average life expectancy of thirteen years. Today, the FDA and European Commission approved Behring's haemophilia B gene therapy is the most expensive drug in the world at US$3.5 million a dose.

Treatment for haemophilia made no meaningful advancement until the 1930s when thinned snake venoms were found to be coagulants. Indeed, the first ACE inhibitor (medications that help relax the veins and arteries to lower blood pressure) used to treat high blood pressure was developed from snake venom. From that starting point the research took off and treatments improved but it was about thickening the blood and reducing blood pressure as the disease impairs the ability to clot and stop bleeding resulting in longer bleeding and easier bruising all the while being at serious risk from internal haemorrhaging which is almost impossible to stop. Today, coagulants are made synthetically without animal origins that might risk the transmission of other diseases but the aim is still to replace the missing blood clotting factor concentrates by injection.

Haemophilia is a disease carried by the female and affected in the male, as discussed (*see image on next page*). The associated genes are on the X chromosome which is one of the two sex chromosomes. A female carrier's son has a 50% chance of having the disorder and a daughter has a 50% chance of being a carrier. The name itself means 'haemorrhage' (i.e. an escape of blood from a ruptured blood vessel). The term *haemorrhaphilia* was first used in 1828 and later shortened to haemophilia.

Alexandra must have understood that with Alexei not expected to survive through his teens that they were back at the drawing board required to produce another son; usually the objective for succession is to produce an heir and a spare. Having waited for so long the prospect of going through it all again must have been mentally depleting on top of the tremendous guilt that Alexandra had for passing the disease and all of that pain to Alexei.

CHAPTER VI

The most recent study at time of publication of this book was in the online European journal 'haemophilia' (Volume 29, Issue 2 - published: 31 January 2023). The study was concerned with the emotional experience of mothers of children with haemophilia and found that 40% indicated a guilt for passing the X chromosome associated with the condition and for having put their child through painful infusions. This is difficult enough to deal with let alone atop of Alexandra's undiagnosed manic depression, more commonly referred to as bipolar disorder today.

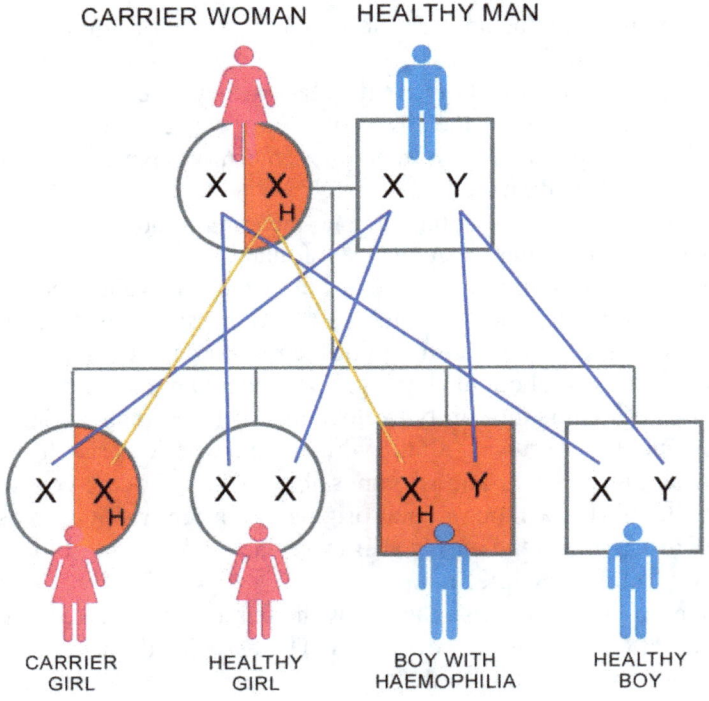

Alexandra's mother Alice also passed the disease to Alexandra's sister Irene and younger brother Frederick. Irene married cousin Prince Henry of Prussia and it passed to their two sons. Tests on Anastasia Nikolaevna made after the discovery of her remains in 2007 confirmed that she was a carrier. In Russia they called it the curse of the Coburg's but Xenia Alexandrovna described it more appropriately as *"that terrible illness of the English family"*. As things stood, Nicholas' brother Mikhail was next in line to the throne to revert to heir apparent on Alexei's passing. So it's a mystery why the Imperial couple didn't set about producing more children from here on.

In spite of the disease Alexei appeared well developed and went through teething well and grew up quite normally. But he did have bad episodes and Alexandra prayed for divine providence to intervene and hoped that the length between episodes would get longer until the affliction left him. Once, two whole years passed without an episode but alas it inevitably returned.

The Palace staff were not informed about Alexei's condition and did not understand why a sudden illness would visit him or why he was sometimes in a wheelchair or being carried by a military aide. Alexandra made the publication of bulletins concerning her son's ill health forbidden on pain of imprisonment. There were whispers about it but even Maria Feodorovna was not told until Alexei was around two years old that he had the royal disease and it was as late as 1912 after a particularly severe episode at Spala that Xenia learned from her sister Olga that Alexandra finally admitted that Alexei had haemophilia.

> "Alexei was the centre of this united family, the focus of all its hopes and affections. His sisters worshipped him. He was his parents' pride and joy. When he was well, the palace was transformed. Everyone and everything in it seemed bathed in sunshine." — PIERRE GILLIARD

The Austrian neurologist and founder of psychoanalysis, Sigmund Freud, once remarked that a family tends to organise itself around its most damaged member. For the Romanovs that had been Alexandra for a long time but now it became Alexei. The Imperial Family had unprecedented access to the medical and psychological pioneers of the day, working in fields of science being advanced in Russia as much as anywhere else in the world.

The Russian psychoanalytic scene was well established in 1904 when Alexei was born. For example the Russian translation of Sigmund Freud's *The Interpretation of Dreams* appeared nine years before the English edition was published. In fact, the Russian Institute was unique in receiving state support for its activities, including publication of translations of works such as Freud's. It is somewhat surprising that they instead placed their faith in God and mysticism.

The Imperial Family had a contingent of medical professionals at their disposal which included doctors, several nurses under an English head nurse and Alexei was afforded a full time nurse. Tatiana, wrote extensively in her memoirs about the respect the entire family bestowed upon the court physicians. When they travelled their medical care went with them whether to another palace or aboard the Imperial Yacht where facilities were second to none. There is no doubt they used the standard medical practices of the day and normally this would have been fine, but Alexei had haemophilia and doctors then, had limited medical knowledge about it.

CHAPTER VI

CZAR'S HEIR HAS BLEEDING DISEASE

Long a Characteristic of European Royal Families and Still Persists.

ALFONSO'S SON IS A VICTIM

Hohenzollerns Also Afflicted. as Well as Some Relatives of Queen Mary of England.

Special Cable to The New York Times

LONDON, Nov, 9. – The medical publication Hospital in commenting on the recent pronouncement of the Czar's physicians that the Czarevich has haemophilia says that this malady was frequently observed by scientists among European royal families in the early and middle ages. It goes on:

"In popular language, the victims of this constitutional disease have a tendency to bleed excessively and have been said to have 'only one skin instead of three.' The truth is, of course, that haemophiliacs have just as many skins as any one else, to wit, one; but their blood lacks to a greater or lesser degree that power of coagulation or clotting which in normal persons leads to the natural arrest of hemorrhages after any except very serious injuries to the large blood vessels.

"At the present time it would seem that haemophilia was more prevalent than ever among Princes. The late Duke of Albany suffered from it and eventually died of it. The second son of the King and Queen of Spain is said to be afflicted with it and to be incurably deaf in consequence of hemorrhages in the inner ear. Rumors also credit the Hohenzollerns with not being exempt from it, and it is said that some of Queen Mary's relations are haemophiliacs to a slight degree.

"The disease hardly ever occurs in females, but is handed down almost exclusively through the female line."

CHAPTER VII
The First Revolution 1905

THE dire news coming back from the Manchurian front since March 1904 and Port Arthur since April 1904 made people realise that the war with Japan was hopeless. At the start of 1905 it was still raging in the far reaches of the 14.3 million square miles of the Russian Empire and its effects were kindling for an uprising. Pogroms were an initial fight back against the revolutionary sentiment whereby the monarchist Black Hundred blamed Jewish dissents and Muslims and organised attacks on their communities.

It was harder in the cities to identify the leaders but quite successful up in the Caucasus mountains where Cossack troops were identifying uprisings. From 1905 Nicholas became markedly agitated and there was a hardening in his character against the people per se. They were supposed to be his subjects but instead of understanding their plight he was stuck in his conviction that they were beneath contempt and battle lines were being drawn for what may lay ahead.

Although the First Revolution 1905 was eventually put down, it was the start of a wave of pogroms by the regime led by the grand dukes in over a hundred towns that were raided without mercy. This slaughter was ignored by Nicholas who remained convinced that the pogroms and subsequent quelling of public strikes and protests was the only way to show that he was tough and to maintain his tsardom. His inherent hatred of Jews cannot be readily dismissed as he believed entirely that they were responsible for all hostile activities and had been programmed to eliminate any threat to the power of the Romanovs. In this regard the pogroms did not seek and destroy the revolutionary element but targeted peasant men, women and children.

On 15 January 1905 the Zubatov Assembly of Russian Factory and Mill Workers in St Petersburg, called a strike at the Putilov Works factory over the dismissal of some workers. It was headed by Russian Orthodox priest Georgy Gapon. He drafted a petition containing seventeen demands and handed it in at the Winter Palace.

CHAPTER VII

Bloody Sunday

A petition was a traditional method used in Russia, there was even a Petition's Officer in Moscow to receive it, or it could be handed directly to palace aides and even presented to the Tsar himself. Gapon had spent the year 1899 in Crimea to clear his head and on returning found himself attending to the concerns of impoverished families of unemployed factory workers. His petition demanded improved living conditions, minor reforms, an end to the disastrous war with Japan, and the implementation of reforms that had been previously agreed for improved working conditions, universal suffrage, et al, but that had not been implemented thus far. The social and economic demands were so basic that the three major political bodies did not approve the march because it lacked sufficient political content worthy of a demonstration; they wanted revolution not resolution.

Menshevism: The model of western democracies and working towards liberalism and a democratic party

Bolshevism: Authoritarian model controlled by one leader without freedoms or opposition factions

Socialist-Revolutionaries: Agrarian socialists and working towards a democratic socialist Russian republic

A resident of Zhmerynka, Ukraine, submits a petition to Nicholas II, 1904

Gapon was, by the time of the petition, well known to the Okhrana secret police for his association with hard liners calling for the downfall of the Tsar and for working with the Assembly of Russian Factory and Mill

Workers, a group that he headed since 1903. Everything had led Gapon to this point and he delivered his petition with a notification that he intended to lead a march to the Winter Palace on the forthcoming Sunday. A week later, on 22 January 1905, 140,000 protestors, mainly factory workers, marched across St Petersburg, many descending on the Winter Palace with the hope of an audience with the Tsar to receive his response to their petition.

It really was just a protest march against the government and not the monarchy. Ordinary people blamed the government for their problems believing that if the Tsar was made aware of their discontent he would intervene and help them; they could not know that he cared little for their plight. The government and the Tsar saw only social unrest in these demonstrations. One account is that Nicholas wanted to appear to the crowd hoping to appease them believing that they would disperse on seeing him but that he was advised not to. Another account has it the other way around, that Nicholas was advised to appease the crown but he believed that when the crowd realised he wasn't there they would go home. The latter is the likeliest version because on the preceding evening a special train took the Imperial Family back to Tsarskoe Selo.

Bloody Sunday – Russian Revolution 22 January 1905.
Imperial guards wait outside the Winter Palace, St Petersburg.

On the day of the march crowds formed at various locations across St Petersburg, waving religious icons and chanting *God save the Tsar*. The guards were typically confused, some crowds were ignored while others met with barriers to stop people gathering. Other groups were dispersed and

CHAPTER VII

others saw the guards joining in and sadly some crowds were fired upon. In Palace Square outside of the Winter Palace 3,000 protestors arrived expectant to see the Tsar and were met with a very violent response that earned the ensuing calamity the nickname 'Bloody Sunday'.

Artist impression of Bloody Sunday in Palace Square, 1905

Gapon was not at the march on Palace Square but led a column near the Narva Gate at Stachek Square, about three and a half miles west of the Winter Palace. His group was fired upon resulting in forty deaths. Most of the other groups were unaware of any shootings or deaths and so the main group continued towards Palace Square. On arriving they were met by two lines of Cossacks with orders not to let anyone on to the square.

As the protestors entered Palace Square a bugle sounded the order to fire. Other groups that had met with a military response were cut down by sword-wielding Cossacks on horses, that chopped and stabbed anyone in their way, not sparing women nor children. The number of deaths varies widely depending on accounts, the government stated that under 100 protestors had died, the hard-liner Leon Trotsky said that hundreds had been killed and the more radical anti-establishment groups put the figure at around 4,000 that had been murdered. Academic literature that discusses *Bloody Sunday* usually places the number of deaths at between 150 and 200.

The discontent that had been building up for a long time turned in to a rebellion brought about by a careless and brutal regime which in turn is

THE FIRST REVOLUTION 1905

another of the key factors for the cause of the First Revolution 1905. Ironically it was started by Gapon's organisation, the Assembly of Russian Factory and Mill Workers, a trade union established by Interior Minister Plehve to quell economic discontent among the workers, before he was assassinated in 1904 by the Socialist Revolutionaries, the party that had carried out over 2,000 assassinations by 1905.

To make matters worse, a newly evolved brutalising Nicholas was not discerning between a radical and rowdy revolutionary mob and a crowd of petitioning peaceful workers. Blatant terrorism was rampant in the streets, ministers were being assassinated daily and activists were being sentenced to death in their thousands. Against this backdrop the political parties that had wanted nothing to do with peaceful demonstrations, as soon as innocent workers were massacred, gave the marches a political purpose. They used Bloody Sunday to intensify the revolutionary element against the regime to further their cause. Not even the uprising that was quickly unfolding from a peaceful march could shake Nicholas' belief that anything could be quelled with enough force and brutality.

When Alexander II had freed the peasants from serfdom in 1861 he had in effect bought the landowners' lands and sold them to the peasantry in the form of loans. It was highly feasible because people didn't pay taxes with money back then so the idea was that they could work the land and afford so-called Redemption Payments. In reality only the wealthier peasantry got some land with the majority remaining landless and working in worsening poverty for the new peasant elite, known as the kulaks.

When famines came, kulaks couldn't make the repayments and the peasants that worked for them starved to death. The years 1903-1904 are known as 'the years of the Red Cockrel' when peasants seized much land in an attempt to beat starvation. This is why the peasants and the workers, being largely one and the same, were in no mood to fight Cossacks in Red Square on Bloody Sunday. But Nicholas had violently confronted them in his ignorance of what was happening in Russia and in so doing he accelerated the course of history from which there could be no redemption.

"Nicholas II inherited an empire and a revolution but not a single quality that would have made him capable of handling either."
— LEON TROTSKY

In a letter of 27 January 1905 from Alexandra to her cousin Princess Louise of Battenberg, she wrote the following:

"All over the country, of course, it is spreading. The Petition had only two questions concerning the workmen and all the rest was atrocious: separation of the Church from the Government, etc., etc. Had a small

CHAPTER VII

deputation brought, calmly, a real petition for the workmens' good, all would have been otherwise. Many of the workmen were in despair when they heard later what the petition contained, and begged work again under the protection of the troops."
— ALEXANDRA FEODOROVNA

The rebellion was like a champagne cork popping from decades of fermented discontent. People no longer believed the Tsar was ruling in their interest or was even capable of ruling at all. At an emergency meeting with ministers at Tsarskoe Selo Nicholas was asked to consider political concessions to appease the people and lay the foundation for the reforms he had originally promised but not kept. He told them that they were talking as if a revolution might break out at any moment, at which he was told: *"your majesty the revolution has already started."* On the following day he published a rescript (i.e. an official announcement,) promising a consultative assembly allowing religious tolerance and freedom of speech. The ministers had finally persuaded him to act and he responded by announcing his intention to establish an elected duma (assembly) to advise the government.

But the revolt would not go away with over 110,000 workers on strike in St Petersburg by 8 January 1905. Disorders increased and became more aggressive. On 17 February 1905, Nicholas' uncle Grand Duke Sergei Alexandrovich was assassinated at the Moscow Kremlin with a bomb. It was the worst terrorist act to hit the royal family since Sergei's father (Nicholas II's grandfather) Alexander II was assassinated with explosives on 13 March 1881 (J). Both assassinations being similar with a bomb having been thrown in to their horse drawn carriages.

In Alexander II's case the ringleader was herself a descendant of Peter the Great, Sophia L. Perovskaya, a twenty-seven years old well-to-do teacher whose father had once been Governor-General of St Petersburg. She belonged to a terrorist group called the People's Will and was soon arrested and publicly hanged with her four conspirators. On 15 April 1881 (J) she became the first female terrorist to be executed in Russia and after the October Revolution 1917 she became a heroine of the people for her efforts to bring down the monarchy. In 1991, when the Soviet Union collapsed, monuments and street names bearing her name were removed or renamed.

In the next few months since Sergei Alexandrovich's assassination, 90% of factories were on strike, peasants were rising up all across the country, army units were refusing to obey orders and the crew of the battleship Potemkin mutinied with a major military uprising of the Black Sea Fleet ensuing in November. The Imperial Court moved briefly to Alexander Palace awaiting the preparations to be relocated to the Peterhof Palace. The Imperial Family remained at Alexander Palace and Nicholas was asked by his ministers not to undertake any journeys by land in the years

THE FIRST REVOLUTION 1905

between 1905-1909. This was agreeable to the reclusive Imperial Family especially as Nicholas disliked St Petersburg for not being traditional enough and Alexandra did not trust the high society in St Petersburg or even Moscow saying of it, *"Moscow is a rotten town, and not one atom Russian."* Seclusion was fine with them and offered the opportunity to regroup and wait for things to blow over.

The document ending the war with Japan was signed on 5 September 1905. A month later on 30 October 1905 (G) Nicholas signed the October Manifesto (officially: The Manifesto on the Improvement of the State Order,) which addressed Gapon's January petition calling for the election of a state Duma. It also demanded that no law should be passed without having gone through the Duma. Nicholas' uncle Grand Duke Nikolai Nikolaevich was more critical about the way events were being handled:

> *"The government (if there is one) continues to remain in complete inactivity, a stupid spectator to the tide which little by little is engulfing the country."* — GRAND DUKE NIKOLAI NIKOLAEVICH

Dmitry Merejkovsky was a Russian writer and poet that was nine times nominated for the Nobel Prize for literature. He was taken by the annihilation of the Russian Fleet by Japan and blamed it on *"... the anti-Christian nature of the Russian monarchy."* He saw The First Revolution 1905 as a blank canvas to reform the Church, meaning the severing of ties between the state and religion.

> *"In the house of the Romanovs, as in that of the Atrides, a mysterious curse descends from generation to generation. Murder and adultery, blood and mud, the fifth act of a tragedy played in a brothel. Peter I kills his son; Alexander I kills his father; Catherine II kills her husband. The block, the rope, and poison – these are the true emblems of the Russian autocracy."*
> — DMITRY MEREJKOVSKY, words on the 1905 Revolution

Thus started the First Revolution 1905 from the many problems of the interior and fuelled by the thoughtless actions on Bloody Sunday for which the liberal press blamed Nicholas without reservation. In June 1905 the riots of the battleship Potemkin had been quashed. The riots of the Black Sea Fleet in Odessa were similarly quashed. The bloody pogrom on Odessa saw the Black Hundred on the streets and 800 Jews murdered while the police looked on and did nothing. On 30 October (J) the October Manifesto was finally published but the rioting continued and by mid November 25,000 more Jews had been killed that month with a total of 690 pogroms recorded for that year alone. The First Revolution 1905 would last for two and a half years until 15 June 1907 when the Second State Duma was dissolved.

CHAPTER VII

The State Dumas

Also known as the Imperial Duma, it was the lower house of the state legislature, while the upper house was known as the State Council. The duma was initiated as a result of the First Revolution 1905 and there were four distinct dumas in all operating from 27 April 1906 to the February Revolution 1917. The Duma shared with the Tsar and Government the powers to make laws and some saw it as a step on the road to a constitutional monarchy. Legislative elections were held throughout the Russian Empire from 26 March 1906 to 20 April 1906 for the 478 seats of the assembly. Duma sessions were held at the Tauride Palace in St Petersburg.

Imperial State Duma Tauride Palace built between 1783-1789 in the Palladian style by Russian architect Ivan Starov, and the former home of the military leader Prince Grigory Potemkin

The idea of a house of representatives came from the boyar dumas that existed during medieval times and the City Dumas that operated during the 19th Century. It describes the ruling elite who were effectively in control of the peasantry but it did not mean they were in direct consultation with the tsar. They gained seats on the councils but their power was local, the ruler's will was exacted through his Imperial Guard who were essentially the de facto police.

During the reign of Peter the Great there was a great influx of foreign officials and high ranking military officers regularly meeting with the tsar. These meetings derived the term 'duma' signifying advice or counsel. Somehow this was woven in to exchanges between the tsar and council members and surfaced as 'blizhnyaya (privy) duma' in documents and later as the term 'boyar duma' in the writings of Russian historian Nikolai Mikhailovich Karamzin (b. 1766-1826) to describe the groups of boyars, okolnichy (court) officials, military nobles and counsellors that ran the local councils. This assembly of the governing elite is why many accounts give the word duma to mean 'assembly', essentially a correct association notwithstanding the complexity involved.

Nicholas II would have studied Karamzin who put aside his military career in the Preobrazhensky Guards (1781-1783) to write Russian history becoming historiographer to Alexander I in 1803. He began the History of the Russian State (Magnum Opus) in twelve volumes over the remainder of his lifetime. In addition he presented his work on autocracy to the Emperor in 1811 and moved to St Petersburg in 1816 to form closer ties with the Emperor with whom he would regularly discuss the historical issues of his main literary work.

Karamzin uncovered many sources of Russian history that would have provided a remarkable historical insight had it not been that much of it perished in the Moscow fire of 1812. He was critical of Alexander I's policies as evidenced in his memoirs but supported autocracy and serfdom. Karamzin offers a genuine perspective. As the so-called founder of modern Russian literature Alexander Sergeyevich Pushkin (b. 1799-1837) put it, referring to Karamzin's History of the Russian State, that it was, "*The heroic deed of an honest man.*"

In 1803 Karamzin said that "*people should write as they speak and speak as they write.*" He made the obligatory tours of the age (1789-1797) spending time in Berlin, Leipzig, Geneva, Paris, and London, returning to Russia to kick off his writing career by publishing his travel journal 'Letters of a Russian Traveller' in the Moscow Journal. On his travels he met with such luminaries as German philosopher Immanuel Kant, he tutored the future historian Petr Viazemsky and Karamzin's influence can be seen in 19th Century Russian literature such as in Fyodor Dostoevsky's first novel, Poor Folk. The first eight volumes of Karamzin's historical opus was published in 1818 and although it received mixed reviews was still a bestseller. Three more volumes followed between 1821 to 1824 and the final volume was published posthumously, a year after his death, in 1827.

The Tauride Palace was the home of one of Russia's grandest noblemen and its design served as a model for innumerable manors across the Empire. It was ideally suited to the workings of a parliament and after the February Revolution 1917 housed the Russian Provisional Government and Petrograd Soviet in opposite wings of the palace. This was where the Bolsheviks named themselves the Russian Communist Party before relocating the government offices to the Mariinsky Palace that March (today the Mariinsky Palace in Kiev is the official residence of the President of Ukraine).

CHAPTER VII

The First Duma was made up of experienced politicians and statesmen like Prince Georgy Yevgenyevich Lvov, a social reformer who in 1905 became a Kadet (Constitutional Democratic Party) and was subsequently elected to the first Duma when it convened in May 1906. He was nominated for a ministerial post that year and became the first head of the Provisional Government established during the February Revolution 1917. He resigned his post on 15 March (G) leaving Alexander Kerensky to succeed him as Prime Minister. When the Bolsheviks overthrew the Provisional Government during the October Revolution 1917, Lvov was arrested but escaped and made it to Paris.

The arrival of deputies of the First State Duma for the opening session - 1906

Alexandra Feodorovna was not at all happy about the reforms of 1905 that her husband had succumbed to, it was another example of his weakness, as she perceived it to be. Her fanatical belief in absolute autocracy was far stronger than his and she made it her mission to restore the powers to protect the legacy for her son. Many regarded the October Manifesto as a great opportunity for Russia, Alexandra made sure Nicholas felt threatened by it. She wasn't alone, the general elections to the State Duma that took place in March 1906 were boycotted by the Bolsheviks and some socialist groups.

The original manifesto was issued on 6 August 1905 for the Establishment and Organisational Rules of the first parliament chamber, i.e. the State Duma. The State Council was established as the second chamber. This gave the Duma limited power but on 30 October 1905 (G) the Tsar signed a new

Manifesto whereby new laws required approval from the State Duma before they could be enacted. However, Nicholas mitigated this in April 1906, one month before the Duma's first session, by issuing an instrument depriving them of effectively having anything to do with the law making process. In his characteristic way, Nicholas had again agreed to do one thing and then did another.

Nicholas delivered a speech on the opening day of the First State Duma. His curtailing of their powers was not thought of as a terribly harsh measure because their primary focus was for agrarian concerns. This was somewhat disingenuous because the State Duma's main tasks were categorically agreed to be their involvement in making laws and having the means to control the activities of the Government. When delegates of the First State Duma attended the first session on 9 May 1906 (G) their first order of business was concerned with land and peasantry matters as anticipated but liberal and socialist opposition groups dominated the Duma seats and demanded extensive reforms far removed from agrarian reforms.

What Nicholas wanted was for the State Duma to be the Government's bureaucratic arm, a Russian typing pool for filing the run of the mill decisions. By limiting their powers he thought he had achieved this and removed them from the more serious workings of the Government so that they might not have any legal leverage. He had not understood that a revolution had brought him to this point and that many delegates represented a revolutionary force that turned the Duma in to a political side show of anti-autocratic sentiment which grew increasingly louder. While the decent members wanted to debate better working conditions the hard-liners asked for the release of political prisoners and attacked the government.

Instead of having tamed the State Duma it became a thorn in the side of the tsarist regime and when members demanded the resignation of Prime Minister Ivan Goremykin it pushed Nicholas to issuing a 'ukase' (an Imperial decree with the force of law) which dismissed the Duma after just 72 days. He told them that instead of making laws they had been investigating the government and thereby questioning the authority of the regime. The creation of a Duma had not appeased the people as their conditions had remained the same but it did give an official platform to dissidents who abused its purpose. The dispersal of the First Duma was perceived by the revolutionary parties as a signal to take offensive action. Industrial workers remained steadfast and strikes were dealt with brutally; between October 1905 and April 1906, roughly 15,000 peasants and workers were killed by the tsarist regime, 20,000 received injuries and 45,000 were sent to exile in Siberia.

Many of the representatives from the first Duma regrouped in Vyborg, an autonomous part of the Russian Empire that would later become Finland. Around 200, mostly Trudoviks (social democratic party) and Kadets

CHAPTER VII

(constitutional democratic party) focused their anger on the Government and collaborated on a document promoting defiance such as non-payment of taxes and draft dodging, known as the Vyborg Manifesto. On the day preceding the first Duma session, on 8 May 1906 (G), Pyotr Stolypin had been appointed as Minister of the Interior, the most important post in government at that time. He rounded up around one hundred of the Vyborg attendees and imprisoned them for several months.

Deputies of the first Duma arrived at Tauride Palace on 21 July 1906 (G) for their next meeting and found the doors were locked and a manifesto hanging from a column outside signed by the tsar officially announcing the closure of the Duma. It was seen as a hostile act and as justification for a renewed rebellion.

As harsh as it sounds, Stolypin was dealing with insurgents actively engaged in terrorism but he only had the effect of upscaling their activities. Up to the end of October 1906, no less than 3,611 government officials of all ranks had been killed or wounded. Stolypin's home on Aptekarsky Island was bombed and his family injured when three assassins entered his house on 25 August 1906 and bombed a reception he was holding. The First Revolution 1905 had been a remarkable achievement given the establishment of 450 years of autocratic rule. It transformed autocracy to a semi-constitutional monarchy and in retrospect was a general rehearsal for the Russian Revolution 1917, largely due to autocratic inflexibility which the rest of the world was beginning to learn about.

THE FIRST REVOLUTION 1905

"Eastertide in Russia will probably see another massacre of these people (Jews, and neither age or sex is spared). Nicholas will not raise a hand. The 'vicegerent of the Almighty' as he blasphemously styles himself, will tacitly permit this slaughter of his children. Count Witte seems to be powerless. The grand dukes are now in the saddle again, and only wait the propitious moment to give word to the Black Hundred to begin the dreadful slaughter. Such is the Russia of today."
— THE HERALD DEMOCRAT, US, 1 April 1906

"I most urgently advised Tsar Nicholas, repeatedly, to introduce liberal reforms within his country, to summon the so-called Great Duma, which existed and functioned even as far back as the reign of Ivan the Terrible. In doing so it was not my intention to interfere in Russian internal affairs; what I wanted was to eliminate, in the interests of Germany, the ferment going on in Russia, which had often enough been deflected before to foreign conflicts, as I have already described.

"I wished to help toward eliminating at least this one phase of the internal situation in Russia, which threatened to cause war, and I was all the more willing to make the effort since I might thereby serve both the Tsar and Russia.

"The Tsar paid no heed to my advice, but created a new Duma instead, which was quite inadequate for coping with the situation. Had he summoned the old Duma he might have dealt and talked personally with all the representatives of his huge realm and won their confidence." — KEISER WILHELM II, memoirs, page 314

This extract above from Wilhelm II's memoirs refers to the First Duma that was dissolved by Nicholas. There were in this group many experienced politicians that had he taken time to listen to them instead of imprisoning them, they may have put him on the path to an amicable constitutional monarchy. But instead, succeeding Dumas consisted of less experienced or astute members which meant increasing intolerance by the Government and active terrorism from the activists. This is what Wilhelm II could see, that Nicholas II could not.

A Second Duma convened on 3 March 1907. Stolypin tried to restrict the entry of known dissidents but still the proceedings became a platform for socialists and once again Nicholas closed it down after three months, on 16 June 1907, this time it had lasted for 102 days and this time fifty-five delegates were accused of being part of a plot against the monarchy. Perhaps the government had sought a closer unity with the regime as terrorist activity went way out of control. The government at the time was sat in the middle between the anti-autocracy socialists and the Black Hundred, the rich, pro-

CHAPTER VII

autocracy and antisemitic movement in Russia during 1905-1916, headquartered in St Petersburg, that were secretly led by the grand dukes (i.e. Nicholas's uncles).

On the world stage Russia was seen as harsh with a tyrant who positioned himself on an equal footing with God. Yet the world's most powerful autocrat was being described by observers as *remarkably passive* and unable to take direct action when his regime was threatened with revolution. The allegation of harshness came from his ability to turn a blind eye to the slaughter of his subjects and the weakness from his inability to prevent it from happening.

The Third Duma met on 14 November 1907 and ran for a full term of five years. It was dominated by landowners and businessmen, was conservative and generally supported the government's agrarian and military reforms. Stolypin established a special court to deal with terrorists which in the first six months passed 1,042 death sentences and a further 3,000 revolutionaries were hanged by 1909. Stolypin having obviously fallen out with the terrorists in a big way, was assassinated in September 1911.

Deputies of the Fourth State Duma pose for a photograph during a break in their session

The Fourth Duma convened on 15 November 1912 and was also predominantly conservative. During World War I Nicholas dissolved the Duma in 1914 but after he took direct control of the army in 1915 and it wasn't going well, the Duma was recalled and as the war progressed it became increasingly dissatisfied with the Government's incompetence and negligence, especially in supplying the army. By the spring of 1915 the Duma had become a focal point of opposition to the Imperial regime.

The instabilities of the Duma had more or less been ironed out when the Third Duma ran its full course undisturbed, but this isn't to say that irreparable damage had not been done; things simply changed from friction between the tsar and parliament to friction between parliament and the revolutionary element of the extremist parties. This rupture was evident during World War I when both sides could not jointly manage the infrastructure to run the army because they had opposing opinions on involvement in the war, and which ultimately contributed to the lead up to the February Revolution 1917. The Duma and Soviet shared equal levels of power at this time whereby nothing much could get legally done by one side without involvement from the other.

This was why the Provisional Committee of the Duma was established which formed the Provisional Government and subsequently accepted the abdication of Nicholas II. During its tenure the Provisional Government struggled to maintain this equilibrium and the Fifth Duma only held five sessions before it was dissolved when the Russian Revolution 1917 overthrew the Provisional Government and the Soviets took full control.

"The revolution had its brief spell of optimism."
— TAMARA KARSAVINA, prima ballerina, from Theatre Street

CHAPTER VIII
Rasputin

THE story of Rasputin has been told so often that there should be no need to expound upon it. Once again the reader is asked to stray from the path of the life of Nicholas II to examine the roots of Rasputin, a mini biography within this biography. Rasputin was a larger-than-life character who had a huge impact in the lives of each member of the Imperial Family. He experienced the court for the briefest time and has been as misrepresented as Nicholas. Their similarities end there but an examination of Nicholas' character would not be adequately expressed without looking at how Rasputin became entwined in his life and the fate of the Romanovs.

Some explanation of the so-called 'mad monk' is in order and deserving if only to correct some misrepresentations of him that have cast a shadow over Nicholas II and these falsities should be put to rest; Rasputin was neither evil, mad, nor a monk. He was however, dirty, uncouth and a rapist. Hopefully the reader will appreciate the level of detail that has been afforded him to demonstrate the complex relationship Rasputin had with the Imperial Family. As a married couple might attribute the longevity of their bond to a marriage counsellor, similarly Rasputin strengthened the devotion between Nicholas and Alexandra with his remarkable spirit permeating their lives.

The mystery around Rasputin starts with the date of his birth which was not known until the author Joseph T. Fuhrmann secured access to the Russian State Archives during research for one of his books and he confirmed the correct year to be 1869. He was the first researcher to visit the state archives after they opened in 1991 and examined records from the official investigation of Rasputin in 1907. He noted that the police had recorded the same personal information from the official birth registration documents which listed a Gregori, son of Efim, that was born on 9 January 1869 (J), a fact that was not able to be known during the Soviet Union era.

There was some confusion over Rasputin's birth date because his daughter Maria wrote three books about her father published 1929, 1934 and

CHAPTER VIII

1977, believing him to be born in 1873, when a great comet passed by to mark the divine event. The book *From Autocracy to Bolshevism* by Baron P. Graevenitz (1920) also gives Rasputin's birth date as 1873 on page 50, and it's probably where Maria found it. When the Soviet archives opened it was like a gold mine to historians like Fuhrmann. Since 1991 it has therefore been established that Maria got her father's birth date wrong and that there had not been a comet in 1873 and neither did one appear in the true birth year of 1869.

Grigori Efimovich Novykh was born to a peasant family in Pokrovskoe, a village on the borders of western Siberia between Tyumen and Tobolsk. Receiving little or no schooling some villagers said he possessed prophetic powers, some said that he could be extremely cruel. From the first off it seems he was compromising every woman that he came across, indeed the evidence for this is compelling. Yet Theodora Krarup in her memoirs, who knew him in St Petersburg much later in his life, strongly refuted that he was a womaniser and described him as a kind person without ambition. She was perhaps or maybe not one of his conquests but she certainly knew him well, having painted sixteen live portraits of him in just a few years.

Pokrovskoe, Tyumen Oblast, western Siberia

In 1886 Rasputin set out on a pilgrimage to the Znamensky monastery near Tobolsk and there he met Praskovaya, the woman that he married on 2 February 1887. They had four children that died and three that survived; Dmitri (b. 1895), Matryona – aka Maria (b. 1898), Varvara – aka Barbara (b. 1900). Only Maria would survive the Bolsheviks in 1917, the rest suffered terribly at the hands of the murderous Bolsheviks.

In the spring of 1897 Rasputin left his wife and child and headed for the St Nicholas monastery at Verkhoturye. A religious peasant without holy orders was known as a stranniki; neither monk nor priest, moving from place to place seeking food and shelter. In 1897 there were one million wandering holy men of which Rasputin became one and stated that on this pilgrimage, he found God. In 1890 he was ready for another major pilgrimage this time to Greece where he believed God had called him to visit Mount Athos despite his family trying to convince him otherwise.

The name 'Rasputin' is said to derive from the Russian word *rasputnik* which means debauchee, licentious or woman-chaser although there are some that associate it with the Russian word *Rasputie* meaning a crossroads, which is a fitting descriptor as Rasputin was born *where the rivers meet*. There are indeed two major rivers that join near Pokrovskoe, the Tavda and Tobol, a recognisable natural landmark that describes adequately the geographical location of the settlement at Pokrovskoe. Rasputin had the family name of Novykh and some way along his many pilgrimages, as they got further and further from Pokrovskoe, he started announcing himself as Rasputin of Tobolsk and in due course he changed his family name legally to Rasputin-Novykh.

On his return to Pokrovskoe from pilgrimage he claimed that from Greece he'd embarked on a pilgrimage to Jerusalem which according to Fuhrmann's book *Rasputin the untold story,* the explanation for his leaving Greece so soon in that same year 1902, was that he had not been welcomed there. He travelled to Kazan, still in 1902, in the south of Russia (approximately 870 miles southwest of Pokrovskoe and 500 miles east of Moscow). The Bishop of Kazan at the Seven Lakes Monastery was impressed with Rasputin at the start, the Church were desperately in need of people like him to sow optimism and renewed faith among the people. He earned a good reputation as a holy man but there were plenty of insinuations about his sexual exploits with female admirers. He became interested in the Khlysty that operated in that region and generally along the south-western side of Siberia. The Khlysty regarded Rasputin's behaviour as a religion; flagellation, orgies, some even strangulated each other using asphyxia to bring about spiritual exhilaration.

The Khlysty gave a validity to Rasputin's fantasies and perversions. He sat between the orthodoxy of the mainstream Church and the unorthodoxy of a fringe cult and although he aligned with the Orthodox Church for most

CHAPTER VIII

of his life, he also retained much of the Khlysty mentality along with the practice of flagellation and his addiction for sexual fulfilment. He had an unusually high sex drive which he accepted as a hindrance to his spiritual progression.

Returning from Jerusalem he was resolute to practice sexual restraint; he stopped drinking and became a vegetarian overnight. Inevitably on occasions he would relapse to his sexual exuberances usually after bouts of drinking. He had women wash his genitals to test his fettle against carnal temptation. But the salvation of repentance could only be attained through sin meaning that his resolve to resist the ecstasy of physical debauchery was directly proportional to the level of alcohol that entered his body.

One account suggests that Rasputin believed his destiny was to influence people on a grand scale therefore the Khlysty offered only a limited platform whereas aligning with the Orthodox Church offered a far greater audience, this being the reason he aligned with the Orthodox Church, presumably to access the wider female community as well as the cloistered nuns. Bishop Andrei just wanted him out of Kazan and suggested he go to St Petersburg and meet Sergei Stragorodsky, the rector of the St Petersburg Theological Seminary.

He arrived at Stragorodsky's Academy by train during Lent 1903 with a letter of introduction from Bishop Andrei. The monk Sergei Mikhailovich Trufanoff (soon to be ordained as Iliodor) in his biography spread a rumour that the chief of the Korean mission, Bishop Chrisanthes Schetkivsky had brought Rasputin to the capital, which was not the case. Initially Rasputin stayed at the Alexander Nevsky Monastery where he was introduced to many notables. There, he was invited to give a speech and amazed them all with his psychological perspicacity. Meanwhile Trufanoff was patiently waiting for the opportunity to meet him. The priest Theophane who had already met Rasputin in Tobolsk was also humbled by the larger-than-life stranniki and waited excitedly to meet him again.

Meanwhile Rasputin met the priest Hermogenes who had recently (1903) become the Bishop of Saratov. He was also introduced to the highly respected archpriest Father John of Kronstadt who was singularly impressed with Rasputin and would give him many letters of introduction to well known aristocratic circles in and around St Petersburg.

Trufanoff and Theophane did not encounter Rasputin for some months. On 29 November 1903 (G) Trufanoff was ordained a hieromonk (both a priest and monk in the Russian Orthodox Church) and took the name Iliodor. In the future Iliodor would become the head of the Russian Orthodox Church during 1925–1943. Iliodor's initial impression was that Rasputin looked dirty and smelled awful and then he hated himself for having such unkindly thoughts about this holy man whose reputation had preceded him and whose enigmatic presence was enthralling them all.

Rasputin had not lived in a thriving metropolis before. Unlike Moscow with its narrow lanes and dead end streets, St Petersburg had been designed to be big and the city was easy to get lost in but also very easy to get around. People met at markets and public baths and every precinct, every street, had a salon for the plying of a more focused social discourse to cover every interest. Rasputin wasted no time and frequented many salons, establishing a reputation for his healing abilities and prophetic powers.

His doctrine was one of rebirth through the experience of sin. In order to be truly forgiven through holy communion one must first be immersed in sin. As well as the Khlysty doctrine he continued with self-flagellation of which he was well accustomed, having been thrashed in his youth and even publicly whipped by order of the Ispravnik (the official in charge of law enforcement in a certain region). One time when he was publicly whipped was after a man stepped out of his house to catch Rasputin stealing his fence, he was caught loading it on to a cart.

Soon Rasputin had a following of mainly female admirers that became his spiritual slaves. He would instruct them on holy life and take them to church to pray with him. As more introductions came his way from John of Kronstadt and Bishop Theophane he moved through the richer salons and eventually was mingling with high society. The first notable of his well-to-do clientele was Madame Lochtina, the wife of a counsellor of state and whose son Rasputin cured of a serious illness that her doctors could not treat.

In spite of Rasputin's shortcomings his followers took good care of him, he was after all a bona fide stranniki. A wandering holy peasant would offer prayer, prophesy, healing and spiritual therapy, and in exchange people would feed, wash and clothe as needed. The aristocratic women of St Petersburg brought him shoes and garments to the extent that he had several wardrobes by the autumn of 1903. Having found fame he was often seen dressed in his soon to become signature silk shirts and high boots.

Left to attend to himself, Rasputin's dishevelled and malodorous appearance was like a shape memory alloy that would inevitably return to its original state. He took no interest in personal grooming or hygiene and had a certain naivety about how to present himself. On the inside there is plenty of evidence to show a caring individual that always held peace and love at the centre of his being, but equally on the outside, he was a beast, a defiler of peasant women and lover to women of nobility.

In recent years his life has been re-assessed, not least in this book, with some historians believing that he was actually a very humble and decent person. He was a devout Christian and loved his family and even through his rising fame and later connection to the Imperial Court, always remained humble and poor. Sometimes he has been regarded as a fool that by chance appeared on the stage mistakenly from a trap door, like Chauncey the gardener in the film Being There (1979) played by Peter Sellers.

CHAPTER VIII

GRIGORI EFIMOVICH NOVYKH

Yet, some accounts credit Rasputin with great ingenuity stating what an effective manipulator and political wrangler he was. The open question thus far about Nicholas II is whether he was a good or a bad man. In the same vein the reader is asked to consider whether Rasputin was a skilled exploiter for his own personal gain or was he unintelligent, illiterate and ignorant of the world around him as others have suggested. That Rasputin was illiterate has been established. The Russian Imperial Census of 1897 was the first and only one performed in the Russian Empire and confirmed that the residents at Rasputin's house were illiterate and in addition when Rasputin's journal was discovered his writing was described as infantile.

Lack of schooling in itself does not equate with being unintelligent and Rasputin appreciated that to move up the ecclesiastical ladder a basic level of literacy was required. A future book that he wrote for the Imperial couple on returning from another pilgrimage to Jerusalem was said to have been dictated and if that was true then it would be no different than using a ghost writer today. Rasputin's lacking in literary skills could explain why he didn't pursue ordination but certainly the diversity of opinion about the man will ensure that his infamy as a manipulator and predator of women will live on.

Arrival at the Imperial Court

> "*The appearance in court of Grigori Rasputin, and the influence he exercised there, mark the beginning of the decay of Russian society and the loss of prestige for the throne and for the person of the Tsar himself.*" — MIKHAIL VLADIMIROVICH RODZIANKO, President of the State Duma

For a long time the influence of the Church and the doctors of the court had fallen behind the influence of the many mystics that had been allowed to occupy the court. Russia's obsession with occultism was never greater. Bishop Theophane had been very critical of Master Philippe towards the end of 1902 following the phantom pregnancy. After meeting Rasputin around Easter 1903 Theophane was sure of his healing powers. With Philippe gone and Papus and Badmayev also having fallen out of favour and left the court, Theophane saw an opening for Rasputin. Word spread fast and Rasputin's reputation was preceding him through the many connections he established during this time. Madame Lochtina, mentioned earlier, is credited by Iliodor for bringing Rasputin to the Russian court although this is up for debate and likely happened through Theophane who introduced him to the Montenegrins.

In his book, *The Mad Monk of Russia – life, memoirs, and confessions of Sergei Michailovich Trufanoff (1905)*, Iliodor states that Rasputin used Madame Lochtina to engage Nicholas and Alexandra on religious matters and mysticism. Iliodor's account is not a trusted source, notorious for his

CHAPTER VIII

exaggerations, himself admitting that his book '*was the truth with a little added on*'. However, Rasputin's secretary Aron Simanovich also described how Madame Lochtina helped to position Rasputin so that he could have influence over the Imperial Family.

> "*She* [Madame Lochtina] *was a proud, clever, highly educated woman of unusually stubborn disposition who, before her acquaintance with the saint* [Rasputin], *had been considered virtually the first lady in society for her beauty and her exquisite gowns. She devoted herself to Rasputin partly, at least, in order to acquire with him power over the czar and the czarina, and inasmuch as only 'prophets' and 'prophetesses' could exert this influence, she soon began to play the part of one of these.*"— ILIODOR

In the future Iliodor came in to the possession of Madame Lochtina's extensive collection of diaries which revealed that she became so obsessed with Rasputin that she left everything behind to join the Verkhouturye convent, located in the Urals on the Tavda River north of Tyumen. Rasputin looked after her mansion in St Petersburg and held salons there. The more likely scenario is that Rasputin had found a highly susceptible Lochtina whom he hypnotised, seduced and then made use of her residence for his own purpose. Iliodor makes no bones about her feebleness in his book.

> "*She left her husband, her two sons, and her daughter Lada, and began to wear queer dresses, decorating herself from head to foot with all kinds of ribbons, crosses, and icons. She wore a hat of camel's hair with the inscription, 'In me lies all power. Hallelujah!' In this attire she would come to the palace, where she spent all her time drinking tea with the Imperial Family, and interpreting the wise sayings and prophecies of Father Gregory.*" — ILIODOR

Maybe it was a combination of forces working in tandem that brought Rasputin to the court. The case for Lochtina is made but Iliodor's account remains conflicting because Rasputin according to other accounts did not visit the palace for tea, his meetings with the Imperial couple, especially in the early years, took place at the house of Alexandra's lady in waiting Anna Taneyeva. Perhaps they were dilly-dallying around the palace, but when Theophane introduced Rasputin to the Montenegrin sisters, Rasputin knew then, that they would be his connection to the Imperial Family and for whatever reason, he left things there and headed back to Pokrovskoe.

In many accounts it's Anna Taneyeva (later Vyrubova) that is given credit for bringing Rasputin to the Russian court. She appeared at the palace in 1905 as Alexandra's confidant but in her biography of Alexandra she denied any involvement in Rasputin's arrival at the court.

Page 153: *"I am aware that the public generally believes that it was I who introduced Rasputin into the Russian Court, but truth compels me to declare that he was well known to the Sovereigns and to most of the Court long before I ever saw him. It was about a month before my marriage in 1907 that the Empress asked Grand Duchess Peter* [Militza] *to make me acquainted with Rasputin."*
— MS ANNA VYRUBOVA, Memoirs of the Russian Court

Rasputin returned to St Petersburg at the start of 1905. Iliodor in his book states that Theophane and Rasputin had by Easter, made several visits to the Tsar, but Iliodor was mistaken because on Rasputin's return to St Petersburg, as if to pick up from where things had left off, Theophane took Rasputin to visit Militza and her husband Peter Nikolaevich for Easter that year. Learning that Philippe had died on 2 August 1905, Alexandra once more turned to Militza and was advised about a healer that was circulating the city who was every bit as devout an Orthodox Christian as Nicholas and Alexandra were and Alexandra asked to meet him at once. Coincidentally it would seem at first, Rasputin asked Theophane to arrange an introduction and he proceeded to advise the Imperial couple to receive Rasputin which Nicholas recorded in his diary for 1 November 2005 (J), the first meeting taking place at Peterhof Palace.

Of other accounts of how Rasputin managed to infiltrate the court, one falsehood should be put to rest; the story told by William John Warner (1866-1936), an Irish occultist (mainly a palmist) who also went by the name of Count Louis Hamon and wrote under the pseudonym Cheiro (pronounced Ki-ro). He told of a Madame Gutjen Sund, a Swedish medium with a large following in St Petersburg for many years. In the story he places her at Reval in 1908 in the company of Nicholas II and Edward VII, before her mysterious death occurs. She has no presence outside of the two books that mention her; *Confessions: memoirs of a modern seer (1932)* and *Mysteries and Romances of the World's Greatest Occultists (1935),* both written by Cheiro, and Sund is most likely a figment of his imagination.

The first book states that Cheiro met Rasputin when Rasputin arrived in St Petersburg in 1903 and that Cheiro met Gutjen Sund a year later, by which time Sund and Rasputin had already met. Cheiro credits Sund for having introduced Rasputin to the Tsar but credits himself for having steered Rasputin and Sund to meet each other. Sund's character is portrayed as in a novel: *"Many rumours have been afloat in Europe as to the identity of the woman often spoken of as Madame X, who was for some years famous as a medium in St Petersburg."* Cheiro masks her details by placing her in a world of subterfuge: *"Her real name was Madame Gutjen Sund, a Swedish woman who married a German officer, who afterwards was a prominent assistant under Herr Stanmers, the chief of the great Spy Bureau in the Wilhelmstrasse, Berlin."*

CHAPTER VIII

Cheiro's other book recaps on what was already said in the first book and includes the story of a séance held by Sund at the house of the Foreign Minister Alexander Isvolsky, of which there is no mention in *The Memoirs of Alexander Isvolsky - Formerly Russian Minister of Foreign Affairs and Ambassador to France* in which only Philippe and Rasputin are mentioned.

> Page 27: *"Philippe's stay at the Court of Russia was of short duration and had no particularly serious consequences. The butcher's boy of Lyons appears to have had only pecuniary gains in view, and never sought to put his influence to the uses of a Court cabal or a political intrigue. His death left a place free for a much more formidable person, Grigori Rasputin, who contributed materially to the downfall of the Romanov dynasty and the dismemberment of the Russian Empire."* — ALEXANDER ISVOLSKY, memoirs

Cheiro places Sund at the court between 1903 and 1908 but there is no mention of her in the memoirs of those that were around the court, including Sophie Buxhoeveden's biography of Alexandra, which is exceptionally comprehensive. How convenient for Cheiro that when he published his book Isvolsky had been dead for nearly thirteen years. The likeliest scenario is that Cheiro fabricated the whole story about his connection to Sund to pad out his books and she likely never existed at all.

THE SUND STORY:

Cheiro attended a séance by Madame Sund hosted at the home of the Foreign Minister Alexander Isvolsky overlooking the Winter Palace. She invoked her regular guest *William de Morgan*, the spirit of a previous Governor of Bermuda, who predicted that Japan would win the Russo-Japanese War, that a disastrous war would follow, that the Tsarevich would never see the throne and that the Romanov dynasty would fall. Remarkably true predictions. Sund had met Rasputin a couple of days earlier and introduced him at the Russian court.

Having learned of the influence Sund's predictions had on the Imperial couple, Rasputin used his hypnotic power to encourage her to tell them that she had been wrong about the Tsarevich and that she had met someone who could perform miracles and save the boy from his illness. It followed that Alexandra ordered Sund to bring Rasputin to her.

Sund had a large following in St Petersburg and at the Russian court and held regular séances with the Imperial couple. When King Edward VII met Nicholas II at Reval in 1908, Madame Sund was brought in after the dinner for a performance, Cheiro was having dinner with the Tsar later that evening at Peterhof Palace and the Tsar recounted the story to Cheiro which he happily published as a first hand account.

Meeting the Imperial Family

For his first encounter with the Tsar Rasputin took along a hand-painted wooden icon of the Orthodox Saint Simeon of Verkhoturye, the patron saint of the Ural region, spiritual centre of Siberia, and whose feast day was fast approaching on 31 December 1905. Nicholas and Alexandra took a great interest in the saint after that. The monastery at Verkhoturye was built ten years after the village was founded and was the first monastery in the Asian territory. With Nicholas' patronage the cathedral on the grounds was upgraded between 1905-1913 demonstrating the influence Rasputin came to have on the Imperial couple from the very start.

On meeting Rasputin, Nicholas recorded in his diary: "*We have got to know a man of God – Grigory, from Tobolsk province.*" This marked almost the completion of predictions made by Master Philippe: a son had been born, a revolution had followed, and they had just met a man that was talking to them about God. Philippe's final prediction of there being a war like no other to follow the revolution, was yet to come in 1914. Following his introductory meeting at Peterhof Palace Rasputin headed back to Pokrovskoe and did not return to St Petersburg for seven months to attend a second meeting with the Imperial couple at Peterhof on 18 July 1906.

Why had Rasputin returned to Pokrovskoe instead of capitalising on his royal introduction in the capital? It was as though he was taking stock of his success and needed to think it through before taking things to the next level, or did he fear staying in the capital would present carnal temptations that he knew he would be powerless to resist. Either way it shows a degree of restraint and a determination to advance through the court instead of the Church. A third meeting followed in October 1906 at which he met the Imperial children for the first time, at Alexander Palace. During this time Rasputin's popularity in St Petersburg was mounting despite restricting his time there. His presence to attend the best salons was in high demand and his Khlysty spirit found the drinking and dancing enthralling not least the new introductions that might advance him in some way, especially the aristocratic female clientele who accepted him and believed in the strength of his prayers.

High ranking royal women were accustomed to having several ladies in waiting; Alexandra had over 200 during her time. One was Anna Taneyeva who joined her in 1905 with a monthly salary of 270 rubles and whose parents had worked at the court of the preceding two emperors. She kept a reasonable house in Tsarskoe Selo, was described as plump, featureless, and unintelligent, but it was her loyalty and quirkiness that endeared her to Alexandra. In one interpretation of Taneyeva, Alexandra introduced her to Rasputin who recognised her feebleness and moulded her to do his bidding. In another interpretation, Rasputin instilled her at the palace as part of his plan to infiltrate the royal family.

CHAPTER VIII

Of course, the negative interpretations of Taneyeva's role at the court may be totally false but if the possibility of an accomplice at the palace is to be considered, as is discussed further on, then there was no better candidate than Taneyeva, in possession of a pliable mind and who was always seemingly in the right places at the right time. What a horrendous betrayal by her if it were true as the Imperial couple enjoyed social visits to her house; Alexandra brought with her little cakes and Nicholas would provide a bottle of sherry. In the privacy of this small house they became entwined in each other's lives.

Taneyeva's simplistic and limited experience of life perhaps offset the Imperial couple's extensiveness. Her calmness put them at ease to discuss the popular trends of the day and topics like mysticism that they were all developing a keener interest in. In an interview given by Taneyeva in later years from her home in Finland, she confirmed that meetings between Alexandra and Rasputin had usually taken place at her house. She was in daily attendance with Alexandra and no one understood her relationship with the Tsar better than Taneyeva.

The house of Anna Taneyeva, Tsarskoe Selo c1905

Almost two years later towards the end of March 1907 Alexandra asked Militza to introduce Taneyeva to Rasputin. In her book, *Memories of the Russian Court*, Taneyeva said how she was struck by his piercing eyes. The daughter of the British ambassador, Merial Buchanan, would describe in her book *Recollections of Imperial Russia*, that, *"he had a face that probed deeply, that seemed lit with fires not human and had a voice that could be charming but with a distorted mind."*

Taneyeva became one of Rasputin's ardent followers and a religious bond was formed between Rasputin and the palace through her. Her relationship with him has not been given due consideration because she always maintained there had been no relationship and was reluctant in her memoirs to discuss the matter. One imagines the huge forces at work that prevented Rasputin from descending upon a young unmarried woman living alone with a direct royal connection; she was an obvious successor to Madame Lochtina and a facilitator for his ambitions.

One account from Mikhail Vladimirovich Rodzianko, the State Councillor, tells that Nicholas appointed Rasputin as the Emperor's lamp-keeper so that he could be slightly compensated for his efforts in attending the palace as he was never paid any fees for his visits. It was his job to keep the lamps burning in front of religious icons and thus he could come and go as he pleased. This is rejected by lady in waiting Sophie Buxhoeveden, *"Rasputin never had any official position in the Palace. He was never 'lampadary,' a non-existent post, nor did he ever get any pecuniary assistance from either the Emperor or Empress."*

Meetings between Rasputin and the Imperial couple took place at the house of Taneyeva. Anyone granted an informal meeting with either of the Imperial couple did it through Taneyeva. Rasputin didn't start calling at the palace informally until the end of 1907 after he was once called there by Alexandra in her desperation over Alexei's health. Rasputin and Theophane made an Easter visit to Alexander Palace on 6 April 1907 and were greeted in the palace dining room by Alexander holding Alexei in her arms. Theophane explains that they were discussing Russia when suddenly Rasputin jumped up and knocked his fist on the table staring straight at the Tsar who was startled by it. Alexandra stood up, Alexei started crying and Theophane became apprehensive. Rasputin asked *"Where do you feel a throbbing, here or there?"* pointing to the Tsar's head then heart. Nicholas pointed to the heart saying, *"Here."* Rasputin said, *"Good, when you are about to do something for Russia, consult your heart, and not your brain. The heart is more certain than the brain,"* at which Alexandra reached out and kissed Rasputin's hand and said, *"Thank you, teacher."*

During the time of the meetings with Rasputin, Alexandra helped in arranging the marriage between Taneyeva and the war veteran Alexander Vyrubov which took place on 30 April 1907. Rasputin warned Taneyeva that the marriage would not last and sure enough the couple divorced after eighteen months. One account is that Vyrubov was so horribly wounded that the marriage was never consummated while another asserts that Vyrubov was so outraged on learning that his wife was the go-between for Alexandra and Rasputin that he divorced her over it. In any case the likeliest scenario was that the now Mrs Vyrubova had become so integral to palace life that she simply had no interest in a husband and divorced him.

CHAPTER VIII

Rasputin's next visits to the palace were on 19 June 1907 and on 12 August 1907. He was also invited by Prime Minister Stolypin to pray for his daughter who was left with broken legs following the failed assassination attempt when his house was bombed in 1906. Stolypin would later turn against Rasputin as he wormed his way in to palace concerns convincing Alexandra that he was the holy man sent by God that Master Philippe had foretold would visit her. Once, Alexandra sent Nicholas a lock of Rasputin's hair which he carried on his person, she also gave him one of Rasputin's combs to help him make decisions in a meeting of the Council of Ministers. In August 1915 she wrote to him as he departed for Moghilev, "*You have Gregory's St Nicolas to guard & guide you...*" Nicholas was an obsessive believer in superstition and carried the relics of saints around with him.

There is no doubting that Rasputin utilised his abnormal sex drive to exploit women for his gain. There are few that knew him that were not taken with his hypnotic influence or did not have some sexual complaint about his behaviour. One woman of note that knew him well was the Danish artist Theordora Krarup (1862-1941) who arrived in St Petersburg in 1895 as a portrait painter for the court. Among her clients was Rasputin who would often visit her studio on Nevsky Prospekt to sit for the sixteen portraits she made of him, of which a handful survive today. In her memoirs she records the first time she met Rasputin. Whether she is talking hypothetically or literally referring to the sexual act of falling on ones knees is left to the discretion of the reader.

"My impression of him was not so that I felt like immediately throwing myself on my knees as I later saw so many women do . . . but I cannot deny that from his person flowed a great, one can safely say domineering, power." — THEODORA KRARUP

At the end of Ms Vyrubova's memoirs she mentions that Iliodor sent his wife to meet Alexandra at Ms Vyrubova's house where she produced a manuscript and asked for sixty thousand rubles. It was Iliodor's book about Rasputin, the original title being *The Holy Devil*. Alexandra was not amused with the indelicate writing and had the police department investigate the matter and they confirmed that Orthodox bishops had been responsible for Rasputin's arrival at court but were unable to establish any truth in Iliodor's claims about Rasputin's relationship with Alexandra.

"In terminating this inquiry I believe it necessary to repeat that Bishops Theofane and Hermogenes contributed importantly to the introduction of Rasputin at Court. It was because of their recommendations that the Empress, in the beginning, received Rasputin cordially and confidently."
— ANNA VYRUBOVA, Memoirs of the Russian Court, page 399

Iliodor would have to wait some years for it to be safe to publish his interpretation of what was happening between Alexandra and Rasputin, undoubtedly adding many elaborations intended to promote the book.

Rasputin Investigated

During 1907/08 Rasputin's past finally caught up with him and an investigation by the Church was conducted on his alleged connections to the society known as the Khlysty (cited as meaning 'whips' or loosely based on the word Christ). They were an underground spiritual sect that split from the Orthodox Church in the 1600s and were in to self-flagellation and wild trance-like dancing. Khlysty believed that they could get closer to God whilst in a state of ecstasy obtained during 'Radenie', a ritual of rejoicing.

He was also accused of being a Khlysty member by a local priest from his home town Pokrovskoe. The police report dated 15 May 1908 found no evidence and the charge was withdrawn. Today, historians are of the opinion that Rasputin was not of the Khlysty and although the Church could not progress it, there is usually some truth behind such accusations. The Khlysty were principally in the regions of Kazan, Saratov, Renburg and Tobolsk, the same areas that Rasputin had been circulating. In another report, in Kazan one evening Rasputin came out of a drinking establishment driving before him a naked prostitute whom he was thrashing with his belt, which caused a great consternation in the town.

> *"After a certain time, however, Rasputin's head was turned by this unexpected rise to fame; he thought his position was sufficiently secure, forgot the caution he had displayed when he first came to St Petersburg, and returned to his scandalous mode of life. Yet he did so with a skill which for a long time kept his private life quite secret. It was only gradually that the reports of his excesses spread and were credited."* — PIERRE GILLIARD, Thirteen years at the Russian court

Pierre Gilliard, Dr Botkin and others received total respect from the Imperial Family but there was a sense that where Alexei was concerned, their caring for him was paled by Rasputin who would ultimately be credited for every improvement, whether he was actually present at the time or not. Not even Alexandra and Nicholas gave themselves any credit for their tremendous efforts to find a cure and to alleviate their son's pains.

> *"When, after nights of watching, they had the joy of seeing their young patient out of danger, the improvement was attributed, not to their care and efforts, but to the miraculous intervention of Rasputin!"*
> — PIERRE GILLIARD

CHAPTER VIII

Nicholas and Alexandra wanted to verify their impression of Rasputin and asked several people to make his acquaintance. Alexandra dispatched both Ms Vyrubova and Theophane to Rasputin's village Pokrovskoe to do some digging. Stolypin separately asked his men to gather information from the Tobolsk regional office. Ms Vyrubova and Theophane returned with favourable reports. Stolypin's report however was damning, concluding that, *"the man is truly of a deplorable morality."* But the Imperial couple had already made up their mind having trusted Rasputin from the start and believing in his prayers to cure Alexei from haemophilia. The Montenegrins also believed they had finally found a divine healer that lived up to his reputation and together with Ms Vyrubova it meant that the three women closest to Alexandra were avid promoters and devotees of Rasputin.

In the summer of 1907 Alexandra sent for Rasputin late at night when Alexei was having a severe episode of internal bleeding. He remained at the foot of Alexei's bed praying for a few hours until the bleeding stopped. The next morning Alexi's auntie Olga Alexandrovna reported that the boy was doing well – it was truly miraculous. After that, Rasputin was called whenever it became necessary to attend to Alexei's bleeding. Alexandra would call him on the telephone believing that Alexei only had to hear his voice to begin recovery.

Herein lies the suggestion of an accomplice helping Rasputin, as whenever Alexei had an episode Rasputin was always close by and able to stop the pain and bleeding, as if having benefitted from ardent planning. According to Baroness Sophie Buxhoeveden (who would become a lady-in-waiting for Alexandra in 1913,) the fact that Rasputin and Ms Vyrubova had both turned up at the court in 1905 was no coincidence, or *"fortunate timing,"* she called it, and she was convinced that he had an accomplice within the palace walls. Ms Vyrubova certainly shared some ambition.

If that was true then it had to be a palace servant and appreciating the relationship between Rasputin and the former Anna Taneyeva, the identity of the accomplice becomes obvious as Rasputin had use of her house and Taneyeva was the servant closest to the Imperial Family. It also explains her reluctance to mention it in her writings as presumably she realised after they were all dead, that she had been duped and her silence became the unwitting attestation that it was her failing loyalty that had betrayed the Imperial Family.

Sophie Buxhoeveden was not alone in her assertions that when he was not called for, Rasputin would anyway appear at the opportune moment to intervene in Alexei's recovery. Others at the court gossiped that Alexei was being administered irritant drugs that were discontinued at the appropriate time when Rasputin was due to appear. Rasputin had simply to hang about for a few hours after his arrival for the miracle recovery to play out. Rasputin was known at one time to be on close terms with Badmayev who is believed to have supplied the drug that was administered to Alexei's food by the accomplice prior to Rasputin's appearance. Aside from the wicked deed of poisoning a child there was a drug that likely contributed to Alexei's bleeding, aspirin, which some accounts give as an explanation of how Rasputin was able to control the bleeding.

The account of Russian historian and renowned writer Robert K. Massie suggested that Rasputin's advice not to let the doctors disturb Alexei had in fact aided recovery by preventing the administering of aspirin. Rasputin would send the doctors out of the room on his visits and advise Alexandra not to let them near Alexei. Therefore while Rasputin was around and perhaps for some time afterwards, Alexei received no aspirin which allowed his blood to return to its regular viscosity which in turn helped to slow down or stop any bleeding.

However, the evidence is lacking that Alexei took any aspirin at all. The assumption that he did is made because Alexei's doctors were faced with a patient in incredible pain and they knew about the successful clinical trials of aspirin for pain relief. Alexei developed stomach problems in later years when aspirin, by 1917, had become the drug of choice for all GPs and which was discovered to target bleeding of the stomach, strengthening the case that aspirin was the root cause of much of Alexei's internal bleeding.

This is all well and good except that Alexei actually did have haemophilia which is the known cause of his bleeding. Haemophilia is a serious disease with or without aspirin and the assertion is that aspirin probably just made it worse. It was the wonder drug of the day that alleviated blood disorders and cancers because diseases move to areas of inflammation which aspirin targets. The German company Bayer had been extensively marketing it since 1899 as an anti-inflammatory agent; its blood thinning properties were not discovered until 1971, by Sir John Robert Vane who received a Nobel Prize for his explanation of how aspirin works, so the drug was actually working against Alexei preventing blood clotting. In summary, aspirin is an antiaggregant and nonsteroidal anti-inflammatory drug with blood-thinning properties which can actually raise blood pressure in people with hypertension. All haemophiliac boys are hyperactive and aspirin is not therefore a medicine for them. In addition the medical fraternity didn't learn that aspirin is not suitable for children until 1963, because of a link to the metabolic disorder Reye's Syndrome.

By the end of the 19th Century, St Petersburg was at the centre of practical medicine where many methods of clinical practice were being first introduced and aspirin was only part of the story. In 1912 Alexei was to suffer his most debilitating episode and Rasputin was able to stop the bleeding. Even allowing for the possibility that Alexei was being administered an increasing dosage of aspirin to combat his pain, which was exacerbating his internal bleeding, Massie said that it was, "*one of the most*

CHAPTER VIII

mysterious episodes of the whole Rasputin legend," and that the cause of Alexei's recovery remained unclear. In simpler terms, there was more to Alexei's miraculous recoveries than blood control alone, which Massie hinted at but seemed to have overlooked.

Aspirin had been around for a long time, since the ancient Greeks and Assyrians. Ancient Egyptians used willow bark and leaves to alleviate pain and fever. The Greek physician Galen recorded its anti-inflammatory effects. In 1763 Reverend Edward Stone described the use of powder from the willow to treat malaria fever. In 1826 Henri Leroux isolated 'salicin' from willow bark and in 1838 Raffaele Piria in Paris made salicylic acid from salicin.

In 1853 Charles Frederic Gerhardt created a version of salicylic acid called acetylsalicylic acid but it was unstable until in 1897 a German chemist Felix Hoffman (of Bayer) arrived by his own path to create acetylsalicylic acid which he named aspirin. Acetylsalicylic being more tolerable to the stomach than salicylic acid, in order to make it safe for consumption.

The Scottish doctor Thomas Maclagan used Salicin to treat rheumatism, which was reported in The Lancet in 1876. Aspirin mostly introduced the widespread use of a drug for pain relief. The latter half of the 20th Century revealed aspirin's anti-inflammatory and analgesic properties and how it works at a molecular level. The by-product of turning salicylic acid in to acetylsalicylic acid gives it the ability in low doses to prevent cardiovascular events, first reported by an American General Practitioner Doctor Lawrence Craven whose observations were verified by clinical trial decades later.

Today doctors only advise daily aspirin as primary treatment for helping to prevent heart and circulatory problems in those most vulnerable. Even in healthy people aspirin is no longer advised and only prescribed within certain age groups if deemed appropriate in those with hereditary concerns because taking aspirin daily can cause ulcers and internal bleeding.

"As soon as the tsarevich became ill, Vyrubova would remind the Tsarina that Rasputin alone could restore him to health. Rasputin would appear and the illness would immediately vanish, the powders having been discontinued. Then Rasputin would be in high favour again and would be allowed everything he desired." — ILIODOR

Iliodor in his books also named accomplices that wanted to remain in favour with Alexandra; Ms Vyrubova and Pyotr Badmayev (the Tibetan pharmacist). He stated clearly that Alexei was being administered powders to make him ill without endangering his life. In the previous quote, 'powders' are a reference to the concoction provided to Rasputin by Badmayev and administered to Alexei by Ms Vyrubova. She waited for the opportunity to administer the drug and Rasputin would turn up to alleviate the suffering with prayer and waiting long enough for the effects to wear off. Iliodor also tells that Rasputin once told him that the Tsarina had been neglecting him of late and that all it would take was 'the little yellow powder' to restore her faith in him.

In the foreword of his book Iliodor wrote that everything he had written was witnessed by him personally or sourced from evidence held in his possession. Although Iliodor offers a valuable insight he was a controversial and discredited figure, defrocked and exiled, who made money from his renditions and even starred in a silent movie *The Fall of the Romanovs* (1918) in which he played himself. Iliodor if nothing else, confirms that the mystics at court were unscrupulous and in some part contributing to the ill health of the tsarevich. Badmayev appears to be the drug dealer in all this but he also turned against Rasputin when he realised what the powders were intended for.

He was not interested in power and was busily compiling his famed pharmacopceia. Badmayev's work brought together chemicals from legit pharmacies to create dangerous anaesthetics, narcotics, emmenagogues and aphrodisiacs. He would prepare medications and remedies giving them such marketable names as *Essence de lotus noir* and *Elixir du Thibet*. Before Rasputin appeared in St Petersburg he was called to the palace several times to attend to Alexei when his doctors couldn't stop the bleeding, and this was where and how he met Rasputin. Badmayev didn't approve of Rasputin, choosing to side with Iliodor when Rasputin was later investigated. His grandson Boris Gusev, in his book *Peter Badmayev: The Emperor's Godson, Healer, and Diplomat*, stated that it was because of his desire to expose Rasputin that Badmayev was eventually banned from the court.

Page 143: *"Badmayev does not hesitate to treat the most difficult and obscure cases in the whole realm of medicine. Yet he has a preference for nervous diseases, mental affections and the baffling disorders of feminine physiology."* — MAURICE PALÉOLOGUE, French Ambassador

The obstacle for Badmayev was that he didn't have any medical training in Europe or from the Russian Imperial Medical and Surgical Academy and often came under attack for it. He was called a fraud and a swindler and accused of discrediting oriental medicine per se, whereas the doctors of the

CHAPTER VIII

Ministry of the Imperial Court were well established professors in medicine with their entourage of expert consultants. At the turn of the century court medicine had a well-established structure, whereby the Imperial Family and other Russian nobles and elites could expect to receive the highest medical care available anywhere in the world at that time.

They refused to admit Badmayev to the Imperial Family while he did not have sufficient qualifications to participate in their treatment, despite his popularity in St Petersburg as a practicing Tibetan physician. This does not mean Badmayev was a charlatan, his family had served in ministerial posts for two emperors and he was a godson of the late Emperor Alexander III. Pyotr Badmayev became the official gateway between Russian scientific medicine and the Asian alternative system known as Tibetan medicine (also called Lamaist or Buddhist medicine,) of which little was known about in the West at that time.

Badmayev researched and collected many herbs and plants during his work in the Asian department of the Russian Ministry of Foreign Affairs which covered a vast landmass across two thirds of Russia having borders with Mongolia and China and including the regions of Buriatia and Kalmykia, where the majority of the population were Buddhist, favouring traditional Tibetan medicine. He came from a Buddhist family and was an ethnic Buryat from Buryatia in the trans-Baikal region bordering Mongolia.

His brother, Doctor Sul-Tim-Badma, had been invited by the Governor of Siberia in the 1850s and moved to St Petersburg where he formed ties with the emperors Alexander II and Alexander III and even changed his own name to Alexander Badmayev to be more Russian sounding, as well as converting to the Orthodox Church. Pyotr Badmayev followed his brother to St Petersburg and their younger brother joined them soon after. Pyotr Badmayev established a clinic on Poklonnaya Hill around 1862 which was the first of its kind in Europe with Count Sergey Witte being one of his many high ranking political clients.

It would be unfair to slight Pyotr Badmayev for preparing his own medicines because that was how things were done back then. Tibetan, Chinese and Indian doctors would prepare their remedies from minerals, plants, herbs, fruits, and animals and turn them in to powders and ointments. Today most alternative medicine practitioners tend to prescribe pre-prepared and controlled medicines. For preparing his own medicines and for not having scientific medical endorsements, he was accused of quackery by his contemporaries. Badmayev made several publications on Tibetan medicine during 1898-1903, one of his achievements was to finish his brother Alexander's work to translate the work of tantras, Gyushi, in to Russian books. The work received acclaim from the respected academic professor Sergei M. Vasilyev who said that Tibetan medicine had achieved an amazing development that was in some respects ahead of medicine in the West.

After the publication of Gyushi, Dr Isaak Solomonovich Kreindel of St Petersburg, wrote to the editor of the newspaper Novosti, in 1902, reporting five cases of alleged incorrect treatments by Badmayev and calling in to question Badmayev's knowledge of Tibetan medicine, because *"he did not live among his own people and abandoned them when he was a boy."* They repeatedly argued in periodicals until Badmayev finally sued Kreindel for libel. The first doctors of Tibetan medicine in Buryatia were Buddhist monks who arrived from Mongolia in 1712, Badmayev's roots could not therefore be challenged. However he lost his case on a technicality because he had once signed a death certificate when not officially qualified to do so. Not having a medical doctorate had caught up with Badmayev in the end.

Then there is the accounts of a second cousin to Ms Vyrubova, Yulia Smolskaia. In 1907 she married Carl Akimovich von Dehn, one of the naval officers from the Imperial Yacht Standart, and was known thereafter as Lili Dehn. After Dehn's marriage Alexandra took to her and made her a lady-in-waiting. Through Ms Vyrubova, Lili Dehn called on Rasputin to pray over her son when he was dangerously ill and soon after her son gained a full recovery. Lili Dehn was insistent that coincidence alone had been responsible for Rasputin's so-called healing power, a view shared by several members of the extended Imperial Family. Lili Dehn was highly suspicious of Rasputin, and was of the opinion that he was only attending the palace because Alexandra could not admit that she had been wrong about him. How much of this she discussed with Alexandra is unclear but they did become best friends and no doubt in later years it was discussed perhaps in an 'I told you so' manner.

The reason Rasputin and Ms Vyrubova could be active in conspiring against Alexei during this particular time was because Alexandra's personal physician Dr Girsh had died so there was a period when Alexei could be accessed directly until a replacement doctor was appointed in 1908. This opportunity afforded Rasputin closer ties to the palace and the relationship between Rasputin and Ms Vyrubova was a strangeness noted by the new Doctor Eugene Botkin who resisted their influence and obviously witnessed the manipulation at court as he mentioned in a letter to his brother:

"You would need to have a mind as perverted as theirs and a disordered soul to defeat all of their unbelievable plots. I have decided I am old enough to dare to be myself. I will do the things which I believe to be right and am ready to stand up and defend my actions because they are really my own, and have not been forced upon me."
— DOCTOR EUGENE BOTKIN, court physician, letter autumn 1909

Ms Vyrubova was sent to inform Dr Botkin of the Military Medical Academy in St Petersburg, that he had been appointed as physician to the

Imperial Family. Those that did not subscribe to the yellow powder plot theory, such as tutor Charles Sydney Gibbes, were of the belief that Rasputin was using hypnotism and this was the view that Dr Botkin came to share along with many others in and around the court.

Dr Eugene Botkin, court physician 1908 – 1918

As the court physician Botkin participated in the welfare of Alexei and his haemophilia. He would see the girls twice a day at 9.00 am and 5.00 pm to make sure that all was well with them. Mostly his duties were taken to dealing with Alexandra's many psycho-somatic ailments. He became a loyal and well respected member of the court and was well liked by the children. He typically always looked the same with a blue suit and pocket watch, and used a rather strong scent from Paris. As a pass-time the girls would move from room to room trying to track him down by following his scent. He was on friendly terms with Ms Vyrubova at first until he refused to befriend and accept Rasputin which placed a barrier between them.

Medical advances in haemophilia wouldn't come for many years and Alexandra found no assurances from her doctors or the Orthodox Church. She knew that medical science could do little for her son beyond bedrest and the wrapping of wounds in the hope of stopping any bleeding. She had to keep a constant watch over her son and was herself in a state of permanent worry. Only Rasputin could stop Alexei's bleeding at will, it seemed. In Alexandra's talks with Ms Vyrubova she came to realise that he was the only answer to her prayers and she was strengthened in her belief that he had been sent to her by God to cure her son and to alleviate her own pains and suffering.

"Rasputin took the empire by stopping the bleeding of the Tsarevich. It was perhaps an imposture but it is also possible that by hypnotism or a similar method, he was able to produce a contraction of the small arteries. Their contraction can be provoked in the body of a hypnotised subject." — J. B. S. HALDANE, British Scientist

Dr Botkin's journal monitoring Alexandra's health from 1913 to 1917

CHAPTER VIII

Rasputin's salon at his home. The telephone can be seen on the wall.
The old man on the edge of the table is Rasputin's father

Rasputin portrait by Theodora Krarup, 1915

CHAPTER IX
Seclusion at Tsarskoe Selo

MARGARETTA Eagar, the children's nanny that abruptly returned to Ireland in 1904 (*page 71*), had decided to leave the Imperial Court because of tensions over the Russo-Japanese War. Her memoirs had Alexandra's approval, *Six Years at the Russian Court*, published while the Imperial Family were still living which means it's likely that any sensitive revelations were omitted. Up until the Imperial Family settled in at Tsarskoe Selo in 1905 her book is a viewport in to their everyday lives at the Winter Palace. In leaving Russia when she did, she missed the First Revolution 1905, Rasputin and quite possibly her own execution.

A New Norm at Alexander Palace

Margaretta's book may have been respectfully written but still offers an honest insight to Imperial life before mysticism arrived at the palace. For example, on the question of why Alexandra was so accepting of mysticism, Margaretta reveals that she was in fact not convinced by it. Her scepticism over Father John of Kronstadt given in the extract below proves this and adds weight to the theory that Philippe, Papus, and Rasputin all had a peculiar occult power to influence people and kept Alexandra believing that they were the answer to all of her health concerns.

> "*I once suggested to the Empress that he* [Father John of Kronstadt] *was probably simply a natural hypnotist, who had practiced his powers; however, she was not pleased with the suggestion. Both she and the Emperor look upon these occult sciences with grave suspicion. The Empress says if there is anything in them at all, it is the work of the devil, and is the witchcraft spoken of in the Bible.*"
> — MARGARETTA EAGAR, Six years at the Russian court, page 39

CHAPTER IX

Nicholas II's reign saw the fullest development in Russia of the Orthodox Church. He was seen to revive it amid the Lutheran, Jewish and Muslim Churches that were suffocating the Russian culture. Mostly this was being done with a heavy hand with pogroms that unashamedly massacred whole communities and with russification. Under his rule the number of Orthodox churches increased by more than 10,000, Nicholas having laid many cornerstones personally. The number of monasteries increased by 250, and many ancient churches and several cathedrals were renovated.

The religious beliefs of Nicholas and Alexandra were reflected in their family life and the children had a very pure Orthodox upbringing with prayer at the centre of their lives. Outside of Alexander Palace the children knew very little of the world and now that they were also shielded from the revolution that was happening outside of the palace, their world was further limited to the grounds within its wrought iron gates.

"In short, the whole charm, difficult though it was to define, of these four sisters was their extreme simplicity, candour, freshness, and instinctive kindness of heart." — PIERRE GILLIARD

Alexandra Feodorovna (note her camera) with her children, Tsarskoe Selo c1906

Secluded at Alexander Palace, Alexandra fell gradually back in to depression and sickness, whether real or perceived. Perhaps her health was failing in sympathy with her son whom she knew was destined to die young. For Alexandra and Alexei sickness would be a constant affair for the rest of their lives. The girls were healthy but had a loneliness visited upon them by their mother who as a result of her depression made herself lonely too. Their confinement could arguably be said to have been cruel and was compounded by their mother's abandonment as she withdrew for longer periods as her condition appeared to get gradually worse by degrees.

The girls were treated unpompously whereas Alexei was allowed to behave as he pleased receiving special treatment because he was the heir apparent and with his debilitating illness. In his younger years he was a little mischievous. One time at a dinner he went under the table and removed a shoe from one of the ladies in waiting, showing it to his father like a trophy. Nicholas ordered him to return it immediately. Suddenly its owner gave out a scream, Alexei had inserted a strawberry in to the toe of the shoe. There are varying descriptions of his behaviour and one view is that he was a spoilt child, arrogant and constantly reminding others of his importance and who loved to exert his authority over the guards and his sisters.

At six years old (1911) he walked by his father's study and saw the soon to be appointed Russian ambassador Alexander Isvolsky,(*mentioned earlier as having invited Madame Sund to his house for a séance*). He was waiting patiently for the Tsar when Alexei sternly crossed him, *"When the heir to the Russian throne enters a room, people must get up!"* As this trait developed his father turned a blind eye, instead of correcting it. Alexei entirely ignores his duties and even what his mother tells him. No one is allowed to rebuke him or even contradict him and if anyone displeases him, he threatens punishment. He beats his sisters and acts like a tyrant over his servants. The words 'beats' and 'tyrant' are surely exaggerations.

How much of this was true is anyone's guess but if there was some truth it's a mite surprising that the girls didn't develop a mental disorder on top of their already restrictive seclusion and perhaps it was because they had each other that the rest of the family could tolerate Alexei, and if it were true, you might expect to find more references to it. Similarly it's said that he was not allowed to ride a bicycle or a horse, or play with his cousins, in order to avoid a potential injury. Yet, from the remarkable collection of photographs that are preserved, Alexei is seen on ponies, donkeys, bicycles, boats, sleds and even climbing trees without much ado. What can be said with certainty is that he lived with his condition without grumbling and was open to all the treatments his mother offered and to the various doctors and mystics that came along. He enjoyed games and most of all loved sailing with his father and making photographs with the family. He does not on the whole appear to have been a spoilt child and perhaps it is the same with all children that they will continue to push the boundaries if left unpunished.

In 1908 Alexandra's heart was troubling her more than usual and she was often not able to attend meals. For most of the day she might lay on a couch or sit in the garden with a nurse. She would lock herself away and send messages, sometimes very critical ones to Nicholas and later apologise for them stating that it was important for her to have aired what she had said.

CHAPTER IX

The girls also started communicating like this where a code system was used numbered one to three to describe Alexandra's condition or pain level. She might inform them that her heart was at number two which might imply that she didn't want to receive visitors that day and the children would reply with something like, *"I'm sorry to hear that your heart is at number two, I miss you so much and long to see you."* Because of this estrangement the girls grew closer to their father with whom there is no doubting their exceptional closeness to him.

What started out a very close-knit family was turning into something else, sometimes seemingly uncaring or even harsh, nevertheless they made a comfortable home of Alexander Palace. The girls have sometimes been portrayed blandly or as boring even and of little interest but they were hugely creative and energetic, each having unique qualities and skills. They created photograph albums, read to each other. Olga and Tatiana did embroidery and drawing, Alexei rode on his pony or played with his dog and his donkey called Vanka.

Alexei on his pony, 1910

Nicholas set out his day and followed it religiously, so many hours for official duties, so much time for prayer, so much for exercise, and the rest for reading to improve his knowledge. Mr Stcheglov was the Tsar's librarian whose job included the presentation of ten or twenty of the latest books just out and worth reading. He would display them each month in Nicholas' study for him to scrutinise. Nicholas would arrange the books in a particular order according to his interests and each evening select one to read to Alexandra, usually it was a Russian novel that he preferred.

> *"These readings aloud were at all times the favourite leisure occupation of the Imperial couple, who looked forward to the quiet homely intimacy of their evenings."* — ALEXANDER MOSSOLOV, (Head of the Chancellery of the Imperial Ministry)

Alexei with his Spaniel dog, Joy

There were some 18,000 books in the many library rooms with another 6,000 distributed around the private rooms of Alexander Palace. Alexandra brought several hundred with her when she arrived in Russia, mostly books that had belonged to her mother Alice and written in German or French. She kept many of her wide-ranging books in the famous Mauve Room with its Becker upright piano that she sometimes would play on. She liked the bestselling Marie Corelli (the pseudonym of English novelist Mary Mackay) of whom Queen Victoria once said would one day number amongst the greatest writers in the world. She mostly wrote about Christianity and mysticism, which might suggest that mysticism also held an interest at the German and English courts, as it did in the courts of Paris and St Petersburg.

Alexandra's early reading matter according to letters she sent to her elder sister Victoria, were François Guizot's *Reformation de la Litterature*; *The life of Oliver Cromwell*; and *Geschichte der Hohenstaufen* in nine volumes by German historian Friedrich von Raumer. In 1903 when she was heavily in to mysticism she was reading works written by the German and

Dutch theosophists of the 15th and 16th centuries. Nicholas the novelist, liked Chekhov and Arthur Conan Doyle and one of his favourites was Dmitri Merezhovski, who also worked for him as a Privy Councillor. He tried to read daily, before lunch and in the evenings. He was so busy on 14 May 1916 that he noted in his diary, *"Returned to the train at 6 o'clock. Didn't have time to read before lunch."* He was remarkably gifted and could read in Russian, English, French, German and even Danish. For such a well read individual, much of what he consumed was fiction.

Alexandra Feodorovna in the Mauve Room surrounded by her books

After the October Revolution 1917 the Bolsheviks stormed the palaces and stately homes. The Bolsheviks needed funds and removed everything of value, including much of the personal collections of the Imperial Family. Around 2,800 books from the Imperial palaces were acquired by the Library of Congress (LOC) in America, including the personal library of Nicholas II and 21 books from the library of the children. According to the LOC many were presentation copies to the Tsar that were never actually read by him whereas some had clearly been read. There were so many books that they were being sold by the weight and it wasn't until 1991 that the full extent of these sales to the West was fully appreciated.

Some families escaped Russia with their most valuable treasures that were then acquired by collectors. In 1921 Lenin's government established the Antikvariat to control the continuing sale of these confiscated state treasures to the West, which was the source of many items that passed in to the hands of mostly American collectors and who in turn bequeathed much to the museums.

The Maple Room – Alexander Palace. Fabergé egg cabinet in corner

Alexandra kept her Fabergé eggs on display in the Maple Room. Of the 50 Imperial eggs made, 8 went missing following the revolution of 1917 and many more were damaged or the 'surprise' inside was lost. Other families purchased Fabergé eggs too, for example the collection of Alexander and Barbara Kelch who commissioned seven eggs in 1898.

Fabergé was appointed Supplier to the Imperial Court in 1885, the same year Alexander III commissioned the first egg which was originally intended for a wedding anniversary present. He placed an order for an egg to be delivered to his wife every Easter after that. The Fabergé workshop worked to great secrecy and it was a very complex process to design and craft, which took a dedicated team the whole of the year. Each egg cost an average of 10,000 rubles, which in today's terms would be around £76,000.

Of course eggs were just one item made by Fabergé, arguably of equal prestige are the jewellery, animal sculptures, exquisite boxes and picture frames of all descriptions, enamelled flowers, glassware and various objet d'art ranging from cigarette holders to mother-of-peal fans, crystal bells and parasol handles. What really established Fabergé was the patronage of the Danish sisters Maria Feodorovna and Queen Alexandra. Being fashion icons they inadvertently created the greatest publicity which gave Fabergé commissions from most of the royal houses of Europe. Especially between Russia, England and Denmark, the customary gift within and between families for birthdays, anniversaries, Easter and Christmas, were uniquely crafted Fabergé items. Alexandra Feodorovna and Maria Feodorovna received their precious eggs from the Emperor on Easter Sunday.

Queen Alexandra and Edward VII were also avid collectors, ordering many for gifts. At one auction they bought no less than fourteen eggs as gifts and many of them remain in the royal collection today. Indeed they were so fanatical about their collection that their children Victoria and George (future George V) also developed a passion for Fabergé. It was an exciting time for collectors during the first half of the 20th Century in no small part due to the Antikvariat, who between 1930-1933 sold fourteen Fabergé eggs. In Britain, The Royal Collection retains several Fabergé eggs, including one of the Kelch eggs acquired in 1933.

Also, in the Royal Collection is one of Alexandra's first teeth from when she was a child, crafted in to a lily-of-the-valley brooch for Queen Victoria whom she adored. Brooches became Alexandra's favourite gift item and her personal jewellery told the story of her life from the lily white tooth to the 2,000 diamonds on the coronet that crowned her as Empress. Her collection started with a bracelet from Queen Victoria that contained a picture of her father Ludwig IV. She learned to associate jewellery with memories and everything she wore had a sentimental connection. In 1889 Alexandra illuminated a ball in St Petersburg wearing white diamonds and at the Romanov Tricentenary ball in 1913 she wore pearls and emeralds. She was always fashionably elegant without being ostentatious. Alexander III gave her a sautoir of pears on a fine gold chain set with jewels (one account says they cost 250,000 rubles,) and she said of it in her thank you letter to the Emperor, "*It gave me quite a shock when I opened up the case and saw those beautiful stones.*"

According to the book *A Lifelong Passion* Nicholas gave her a bracelet before they were married and she wrote him back, "*… you naughty monkey, how could you dare to give me such a magnificent thing."* How many jewels would Alexandra receive from the Emperor after the marriage; so many indeed, that they would one day be sown in to undergarments to avoid detection by the Bolsheviks. One can only imagine the hurt she must have felt towards her end when she was forced to leave her *Faberg*é collection behind, and was stripped by the Bolsheviks, quite literally, in the search for her jewellery.

A World of Cameras

Have you noticed how old photographs or paintings of royalty depict toddlers of both sexes wearing a dress? It's only since the advent of cameras that people have noticed this but it was a European practice for thousands of years. It was common practice with the poor also but they could ill afford to have their image captured for posterity. It was mainly to do with toilet training as the fastenings on breeches and the wearing of hose and tights could be rather complicated back then. King James II of Great Britain is depicted in a dress in a Van Dyke portrait and his son James Francis Edward as seen on the next page. See also *page 210* for an image of Marie Antoinette and Louis XVII. It's less common to find Nicholas II wearing a dress but there are a multitude of Alexei thanks to the photographic collections.

Throughout the Romanov photograph albums there are seen many people with a portable camera. The family members each had their own and it was an instrument they kept close by like a soldier with his rifle. What started as a hobby with Nicholas turned in to a family and court obsession. The photograph albums created by the Imperial Family and others around them made it possible for the first time, to see what life was really like for an Imperial Family. If not for these, we would know only about the brutal regimes depicted in history books. Anyone that sees these photographs cannot fail to be enamoured by the loving family they depict. Their fascination is in how relatively humble the Romanov Imperial Family members each were aside from their wealth and status and they can easily be imagined as the nice neighbours in your street. These photographs have become highly collectable items.

'*Poignant 1913 signed photograph of Tsar Nicholas II's teenage duchess daughters who went on to be brutally executed in the Russian Revolution is set to go up for auction for £45,000.*' — MAILONLINE, 4 February 2022

CHAPTER IX

Right: The Tsarevich Nicholas wearing a dress, with his mother Maria Feodorovna

Below: A 1690s Van Dyke portrait of Queen Mary (of Modena), the wife of King James II of England, Scotland and Ireland, with her first surviving son, James Francis Edward
– *by Benedetto Gennari the younger*

The world's first full length documentary movie was taken at the coronation in Moscow 1896 (sometimes wrongly attributed to Nanook of the North (1922)), but the camera had been invented a little earlier and the portable camera was invented by American George Eastman in 1888. The Kodak #1 camera was a box (i.e. a dark room.) with glass plates for 100 exposures. It came out in February 1900 and sold over 150,000 units in the first year. Although it was originally priced at US$25, Eastman wanted to widen its popularity believing the profit was in film sales and developing. The price fell to $1 each (5 shillings in the UK), the equivalent of $33 today.

The sturdy box was designed by Frank Brownell in 1889 (hence the 'Brownie' name given to future models). He was a Canadian cabinetmaker who went on to design many other early Kodak cameras for George Eastman until 1906. A wood block supported a jute board wrapped in a strong leather covering. It was light and easy to use. To take a photograph it was necessary to look along the V shape at the top of the camera, a string would set the shutter and at the right moment a button was pressed on the side to trip the shutter. The key on the side was used to wind the film to the next frame. After 100 exposures the whole camera was sent to Kodak for developing, at a cost of $10. A new roll cost just 15 cents.

When the Brownie camera arrived in Russia the Imperial Family were trained how to use it by Kodak staff and the family built their very own dark room at Tsarskoe Selo. They were some of the first to own portable cameras and the Russian court were pioneers of photography therefore photographs from this period are highly valued. Photography and cinematography were the new technologies for the 20th Century which St Petersburg embraced with shops throughout the city.

Kodak was well established with many outlets where members of the Imperial Court placed their orders. Some of the main retailers were Levitsky, Pasetti, Hahn and Boissonnas & Eggler. These brands carried a special approval to be able to distribute images taken of the Imperial Family. Portrait photographs of Imperial Family members were delivered to the palace to be signed and dated individually by them and sent to whomever they wished. It served as the greatest publicity for Kodak. The real explosion in photographic popularity came in 1900 with the portable Brownie #1.

Left: Eastman Kodak No1 Box Brownie camera. *Right*: No.2 Bulls-Eye, Model D Camera – The camera on the right (H132 x W150 x D116 mm) belonged to Pierre Gilliard, the Imperial children's French language tutor. He passed it to his godson, whose son Jacques Moser donated it to the Tsarskoe Selo State Museum and Heritage Site in 2014. These were the models that set off the portable camera boom.

In 1902, Eastman introduced a roll of negative film and the Brownie No.2 appeared for $2. It was produced until 1935 and remained the standard method of taking photographs until Kodak invented the digital camera in

CHAPTER IX

1975. Many old photographs including of the battlefields of World War I, were taken with a Brownie or a Bulls-Eye. Digital cameras started the long decline of roll film and have been outselling film cameras since 2003.

Nicholas was an insatiable photographer; Alexandra and the rest were also hooked. They ordered some equipment and professional photography services directly from England which became a significant part of their leisure expenditure. All the bills for their photography hobby were paid from their own pocket. The portable camera put the latest technology in to the hands of amateurs who were able to capture impromptu moments on a massive scale. Wherever the family were in the world one of them always had a Brownie camera to capture the moment. They loved taking photographs of each other and Nicholas was happy to pose on his own or in group shots. They rarely took photographs of scenery without people or of official gatherings. The court employed professional photographers to capture ceremonies, S. Levitsky and C. Bergamasco and one expert whose sole duty was to develop and print the photographs and mount them in frames and albums.

According to Nicholas' diaries, the family spent many evenings together working on their photo albums and enjoyed arranging the images and even colouring some. They took care to file each with the correct date and location and ultimately created something that was truly a remarkable record for posterity. Ms Vyrubova often worked with Alexandra on their personal albums, with Nicholas leaning over them, as fastidious about neatness as a Fabergé workmaster. Ms Vyrubova wrote in her memoirs, *"He could not endure the sight of the least drop of glue on the table."*

The many dozens of albums they created were kept close to them at Alexander Palace. One account asserts that Nicholas kept his albums in his personal study, another account says that they were kept in the combined billiard and sitting room. If no writings were to exist of Nicholas II there would still be a comprehensive photographic biography of him. The others kept their albums in their rooms.

In the future when the family were moved to Tobolsk under house arrest they took what albums they could carry and unfortunately this is one reason why many were lost. Fortunately many did survive, some are in the hands of private collectors and hopefully some are out there yet to be discovered and undoubtedly many will remain lost for ever. The newly discovered albums that were on display for the Blood and Revolution exhibition in London 2019 and those held by the Zlatoust City Museum in Siberia as well as those at the Library of Congress in America, and at several other collections, were discovered completely by chance. This is a strange phenomenon that such important photographic evidence in world history should be uncovered in this random way and demonstrates the lack of regard the Bolsheviks and Communist Russia had for their own history.

One such Romanov archive in private hands is a collection of telegrams, photographs, drawings and letters totalling more than 200 items dating from 1860 to 1928 that found their way out of Russia with the fleeing family members following the Bolshevik coup. This find gave a valuable insight in to the growing foreboding of the family leading up to the 1917 revolution. In a letter from Grand Duke Nikolai Mikhailovich (an uncle of Nicholas II's) he knew his end was near and his diary tells it as it was, *"We continue to descend down a slope and it is not difficult to imagine what awaits us."* The Bolsheviks eventually killed him on 28 January 1919.

The collection was sold by an anonymous owner in July 2017 for 70,000 euros to the state-owned Sberbank Russian bank who put it on display in Tsarskoe Selo for a 2018 centenary exhibition. It's thanks to organisations like Sberbank that works of exceptional public interest are brought to the public in temporary exhibitions, otherwise they would be lost behind the walls of private collectors indefinitely. These historical documents are of huge interest to researchers and historians and there is always excitement over what could still be awaiting discovery.

BEINECKE COLLECTION AT YALE

In 1925 a large collection of documents of Nicholas II and his family ranging from 1894 to 1935, were transferred to the Beinecke Rare Book and Manuscript Library at Yale University to form the new Romanov Archive. The majority of the collection was added in 1951 with six albums of photographs and letters ranging from 1907 to 1915 that had originally belonged to Ms Vyrubova; the images were taken by her and others close to the royal family.

Ms Vyrubova escaped Russia in 1920 after being imprisoned in St Petersburg for a time and took seven large albums and some letters with her. The first album she bequeathed to Prince Ludwig of Hesse and is stored in Darmstadt today. In 1937 a Yale University student called Robert Brewster visited her, having become fascinated with the Romanov story, to enquire about the remaining six albums and talked her in to selling them to him.

He later gifted his collection to the Beinecke library. There are many placeholders with traces of glue for missing photographs. These items were pulled by Ms Vyrubova and sent to Bryan Ludbrook over a six year period in gratitude for the periodicals he sent her such as *The Sphere An Illustrated Newspaper For The Home*. The 139 missing photographs are known as the Ludbrook collection.

Ms Vyrubova died in Finland four days before her 80th birthday on 20 July 1964. In 1966 the Pulitzer Prize author Robert K. Massie when he learned of the Beinecke Romanov Archive said that it was the most complete set of intimate photographs of the Imperial Family to survive the holocaust of the revolution and when he saw it was reminded of the moment Howard Carter first peered into Tutankhamun's tomb and was asked what he could see and he replied, *"Wonderful things!"*

THE LUDBROOK COLLECTION

On 27 November 2008, 139 photographs of the Imperial Family contained in two albums bound in textured leather were sold by Swedish collector Bryan Ludbrook at the Stockholm auction house of Bukowskis to an unknown buyer for 16,500 euros. The photographs had been sent to him by Ms Vyrubova by way of thanking him for sending her various reading matter, as discussed (*page 181*).

Several of the yellowing album pages hold postcards and sketches. The Swedish auctioneer had online records dating back to the time just after this sale and so no further information could be found. At the time of researching for this book, Bukowskis were acquired by Bonhams and this author was unable to get any information about the sale from either auctioneer.

Ms Vyrubova browsing one of her albums at her residence in Vyborg, Finland, 1937. One of seven grand photograph albums that she gifted and sold. She wears a cassock having taken the vows of a Russian Orthodox nun in 1923.

From the Library of Congress collection: *Top*: May 1917 Tsarskoe Selo. Tatiana and a guard carry lumps of sod on a stretcher. She is helping to plant a kitchen garden. *Bottom*: Between August 1917 & May 1918 Tobolsk. The four girls stand on left, Alexei in centre and Nicholas on far right.

CHAPTER IX

LIBRARY OF CONGRESS

The two photographs on the previous page were discovered in 2007 by a college student visiting the Library of Congress, while he/she was looking through uncatalogued files. They were stamped with a copyright notice dated 1921 by Underwood and Underwood, a photograph seller. The LOC already had seven Romanov photographs in its collection of which some were taken by Pierre Gilliard on his No.2 Bulls-Eye camera. This is known because his writing appears on the notations.

THE BENCKENDORFF COLLECTION

Alexander Konstantinovich Benckendorff (1849-1917) was the last tsarist ambassador to the court of St James in London having been sent there by Nicholas II in 1902. He died in office, one of the first from the influenza epidemic that swept across Europe in 1917. His brother Pavel Benckendorff was a Marshal of the Imperial Court and wrote regularly to him in London, keeping him abreast of state affairs back home; their letters cover the period from 1892 to 1916. Alexander also kept in regular contact with his wife Countess Sophia (Shuvalova) who mainly stayed in Russia, there being around 600 letters between them dating from 1903 to 1914. These combined letters form part of the Benckendorff collection.

Alexander and Sophia were amateur photographers and a substantial number of their photographs, many taken in Russia, ranging from 1890 to 1905 form part of the collection as well. Not long after Alexander's death his wife Sophia was visited by their son in 1918 at her country house in Suffolk, England. While there he discovered a hoard of letters and photographs in the attic and sent them to the Central Archives of Historical Research in Moscow. Queen Alexandra acquired some of these photographs that remain in the Royal Collection. The main archive for the Benckendorff collection is at the Columbia University Rare Book and Manuscript Library.

ZLATOUST CITY HISTORY MUSEUM, SIBERIA

A collection of over 200 Romanov family photographs taken between 1914 and 1916 were found in the vault of a remote museum in the Urals (about 195 miles south of Ekaterinburg,) The Siberian Times reported on 8 May 2013. It's known that one of the guards who escorted the Romanovs from Tobolsk to Ekaterinburg, a guard called Dmitry Chudinov, was from Zlatoust and known to have appropriated some possessions and it's reckoned that he stole the album but how it ended up with the museum is unknown. In one photograph fifteen year old Anastasia and her father are sharing a cigarette. A year earlier she wrote to her father: *"I am sitting here with your old cigarette that you once gave me, and it is very tasty."*

Anastasia and father Nicholas II with cigarette, there was no stigma attached to smoking back then, 1916, Zlatoust City Museum

FERDINAND THORMEYER COLLECTION

Ferdinand Thormeyer (1858-1944) was a Swiss French language and literature tutor who travelled to Russia when he was eighteen to tutor military cadets until he was assigned to the children of Alexander III from 1886 to 1899. He returned to Switzerland around 1900 and worked for the Red Cross. For the rest of his life he kept in touch with all the Imperial children, George, Nicholas, Olga and Xenia. Strangely Olga continued writing to him even after his death.

His artifacts from Russia were carefully packed in suitcases by his relatives and stored in the loft until one day in 2010 they were opened by Thormeyer's descendants who discovered around 2,000 items. 1,000 letters, 400 telegrams, 150 photographs, 200 postcards, 12 Imperial menus and other objects, including a silver and rose gold cigar case with an engraving inside the lid: '*Nicholas and George to M. Thormeyer in the memory of three good years*'.

The items went on exhibition in Geneva at the Hôtel des Ventes where they were auctioned. A year later the Thormeyer family found another remarkable hoard in the same loft of around 300 new photographs, some were signed and dated by Nicholas II and his siblings. These new items were auctioned in 2011 for £1.3 million. A scrap of paper went for £64,464 which contained a scribble that Nicholas II had done. Both auctions were won by private collectors.

Nicholas II, c1881, from the Thormeyer collection

GENERAL COUNT ALEXANDER GRABBE

An extraordinary collection of some 200 never before published photographs of the Imperial Family seen through the eyes of General Count Alexander Grabbe with notes from his journal. This is a book compiled by his son Paul Grabbe.

The private world of the last Tsar : in the photographs and notes of General Count Alexander Grabbe

THE SBERBANK COLLECTION

A collection of more than 200 telegrams, photographs and drawings dating from 1860 to 1928 that left Russia in 1917/18. They were purchased by Sberbank at auction in 2017 and exhibited at Catherine Palace from 24th May 2018 to 30 December 2018.

SCIENCE AND MEDIA MUSEUM, BRADFORD, UK

A crate of twenty-two albums was discovered in 2018 by the National Science and Media Museum in Bradford and these were the centre piece of the Blood and Revolution exhibition at the Science Museum in 2019. The images were captured by Herbert Galloway Stuart, an English tutor to the nephews of Nicholas II, between 1908 and 1916.

Then again in July 2018 the Collections Services team were renovating the Print Archive and stumbled on a series of photographs taken during the coronation in 1896 by British photographer George William Totten using a Kodak Bulls-Eye No. 2 portable camera.

VICTOR ALEXANDROV

Wooden boxes were taken out of Russia following the Russian Revolution 1917 by White Army investigator Nikolai Sokolov. One box contained photographic plates which were lost for decades, resurfacing at a Paris auction and recovered by the Russian writer Victor Alexandrov who included many of them in his book *The End of the Romanovs* (1966). Many had been taken by Nicholas II (see *page 467*).

Olga Nikolaevna looking at an album on a sunny day, c1917.

CHAPTER X
The Imperial Yacht Standart

THE word Standart refers to the banner of the Imperial Family that was flown on vessels that welcomed the Emperor aboard. Standart was the third vessel of the Russian Imperial Navy to bear that name. The first ship was built for Peter the Great in 1703, the second for Alexander II in 1857 and the third in 1895 was the grandest and most magnificent successor to an historic line of Imperial yachts and the last Imperial yacht. Standart (III) was ordered by Alexander III on 19 June 1893 because the royal fleet did not have sufficient capacity to accommodate the needs of the royal family. It was to be bigger and grander than the current flagship Polar Star and was built in preparation for his son Nicholas' reign, his legacy anticipating an expanding Russia as a growing world power.

Several previous royal yachts were built in Great Britain, having a tradition of shipbuilding second to none, namely in Scotland. The Queen of England and the Empress of Russia being Danish sisters, ensured that the contract for Standart (III) was awarded to Burmeister & Wain, Danish shipbuilders with a worldwide reputation. It was the largest shipbuilding project undertaken by Denmark and the port and docks had to be modified to accommodate the construction and later re-modified for the launch and its release to sea.

Polar Star was a sister cruiser yacht, slightly smaller and less powerful than Standart but looking almost identical which remained in the royal fleet as the primary yacht used by Maria Feodorovna for visits to Denmark and England, as well as being utilised by other members of the royal family. There were already several yachts aside from the Polar Star available to Alexander III but building Standart was a matter of national pride and a sign on the waves of Russia's ability to extend its influence across the seas. Its design set a benchmark for royal yachts at the turn of the twentieth century with engines that were the largest the ship builder had ever made.

A team of officers from the Imperial Navy were assigned as resident supervisors in Copenhagen to oversee the construction work. Alexander III

CHAPTER X

and Nicholas visited the site at least once to catch up with the build. Alexander III would not see it completed, he wasn't really meant to, and by way of coincidental planning, the ship was ready for Nicholas II almost as soon as he was crowned. It surpassed all expectations in every respect.

1. **Alexandria**, 1851, built in England, 55 metres, 228 tons
2. **Standart** (II), 1857, built in France, 70 metres, 895 tons
3. **Derzhava**, launched 1872, built in Russia, 95 metres, 3,115 tons, 16.72 knots, design based on HMY Victoria and Albert
4. **Tsarevna**, 1874, built in England, 57 metres, 840 tons, 13.5 knots
5. **Livadia**, 1880, built in Glasgow Scotland, 79 metres, 4,442 tons
6. **Polar Star**, launched 1890, built in Russia, 96 metres, 3,949 tons, 17.5 knots
7. **Standart** (III), 1895, built in Copenhagen Denmark, 128 metres, 5,557 tons, 21.18 knots

Standart at ship builders. Burmeister & Wain, 1894/5

On 1 October 1893, Alexander III and his son arrived in Copenhagen on the Polar Star to watch the keel being laid and for Alexander III to place the first rivet. They were astounded at what they saw and immediately upgraded its construction to a yacht cruiser which left the shipbuilder with a problem that nearly bankrupted the company. The whole design had to be reworked which took six months. In addition, the contract had not stipulated the extravagant furnishings that were being added ad hoc with no expense being spared and the shipbuilder could not afford to bankroll the mounting expenses. This financial dilemma continued until Alexander III died and Nicholas II personally arranged for the settlement of all outstanding costs incurred by Burmeister & Wain; in total £232,000.

The first phase was completed in the winter of 1893 and the ship was ready to launch but it needed to wait several months for the ice in the bay to thaw. For his financial expediency in settling the costs, Burmeister & Wain were asked by Nicholas to make haste with the launch and set a provisional launch date for 21 March 1895 (G), his father's birthday. The ship builder was obliged to meet the request but it was a tremendous struggle because of the unusually severe weather that year. In Hinnerup (a small town in East Jutland,) on 13 February 1895, −27.3°C was the lowest temperature ever recorded in Denmark's history.

At the Burmeister and Wain Shipyard there was a blistering storm raging on the day of the launch, preventing Nicholas, Alexandra and Maria Feodorovna from attending the ceremony. The only observers were the Danish royal family who watched from a shelter at the quayside. After the launch, the next phase took eighteen months of final fitting out and sea trials by which time the ship was again besieged by forty centimetres of thick ice and locked in. Once more the Danes worked relentlessly around the clock to release the ship from the harbour. Two hundred men were used to cut a channel through the ice in order to meet the Tsar's completion schedule with sea trials being conducted in the summer of 1896.

The contract specified that Standart should sustain a speed of 20 knots over 12 consecutive hours. It achieved 21.5 knots on average with 21.75 knots being its best performance over a distance of 27.5 nautical miles. Final operational speed could reach 21.18 knots in almost all sea conditions. It was a double hulled steel panelled twin screw vessel powered by two Triple Expansion Steam Engines. Each propeller had a diameter of 4.87 metres with three blades made of delta metal and studs of phosphor bronze (an alloy of phosphorus and tin); materials that were lightweight and resistant to corrosion for smooth operation and reliability. Fuel compartments with a capacity for 850 tons of coal were next to two boiler rooms housing twenty-four boilers lined back-to-back, separated by a waterproof bulkhead. Two bilge pumps in the engine room delivered water to toilets and various outlets including fire pumps. A water desalination unit fed the boilers at a rate of 60 tons of fresh water in 24 hours, and in the bottom of the ship a separate reservoir of 154 tons of fresh water supplied bathrooms and kitchens.

CHAPTER X

It had three decks, with three masts made from steel and pine and two funnels, essentially it was a schooner with a clipper stern. The steering wheel was directly above the rudder and controlled by Brown Brothers and Co (Edinburgh) patented hydraulic steering gears, which could be operated manually by four men if required in an emergency. After the redesign the public rooms were nearly twice as large as the Polar Star with the main deck boasting a huge dining saloon lined with mahogany panelling with seating for up to seventy-two guests around one long table and fixed chandeliers hanging overhead. Below deck dining areas and family suites were in birch wood, corridors in ash and Imperial suites on the mid deck fitted in the most prized solid cherry and walnut. There were thirty rooms in all.

A private chapel was arranged in a semi-circle around one of the masts and whenever Standart sailed a chaplain was appointed by the Holy Synod to conduct a daily service. There was even a stable for a cow so the Imperial children could have fresh milk. Standart's strength was in its well designed structure; there was no unnecessary gilding or decoration and it perhaps had a trim more in line with the simplistic Dutch and British tastes, the reasoning being that if it wasn't functional, then it wasn't necessary. The exact numbers of personnel making up the full complement slightly differs from one account to the next. In the main, Standart housed a compliment of 275 crew of the Imperial Navy as well as a brass band and orchestra, stewards, butlers, cooks and a platoon of marines, together forming a crew of around 375-400 people.

The sister ships Polar Star and Standart provided the Russian Emperor and his family a combined tonnage of 9,506 which was 5,000 tons over and above what his ruling cousins had at sea for their royal excursions. Germany had the sleek but outdated paddle-wheel steamship *Hollenzollen* (II – 1892-1823) at 4,280 tons for the Keiser's use. Britain had the *Victoria & Albert* (1855) and the *Osborne* with a combined 4,326 tons. Both Wilhelm II and the Prince of Wales (future George V) were known to have been unsatisfied with their yachts and in this Nicholas II ruled supreme, as intended.

Wilhelm II was rather envious of the Russian yachts having boarded Standart on two official occasions. His yacht Hohenzollern (the second to hold that name,) was a converted destroyer lacking the style and elegance of the Russian yachts and neither matching their sleek seafaring capabilities. George, Prince of Wales, saw Standart during its maiden voyage in 1896 and requested the drawings so that the Admiralty could design a new *HMY Victoria & Albert* (III) that was duly built in 1899 and launched in 1901.

Due to the shallow waters around Peterhof, the larger yachts would remain anchored at Kronstadt and smaller vessels took family members and guests between Peterhof and Kronstadt Island. The yachts formed an important part of Russia's overseas diplomacy at the turn of the century acting as palaces on the waves and conveying all the splendour befitting the greatest Imperial leader on the planet. The Russian Imperial yachts were always accompanied by several navy cruisers and were a sight to behold. Nicholas would use Standart in an official capacity and for taking family holidays in the Gulf of Finland as technically anywhere the Tsar wanted to go was official to some degree. He was onboard Standart when the news reached him of the assassination in Sarajevo of Archduke Franz Ferdinand that led to the start of World War I. So many memories were to be made on Standart and many photographs documenting their adventures at sea.

Upon Standart's completion in August 1896 it was the largest royal yacht that had ever been built. It had cost four million rubles in comparison with Nicholas' personal wealth at that time of two million rubles with an additional 350,000 francs in foreign banks and a yearly Imperial stipend of 200,000 rubles. 1896 was a relatively prosperous time across Europe with World Fair expositions and exhibitions held in Russia, Austria-Hungary, Germany, Sweden and even Wales. People travelled to the exhibitions to be impressed with the technological and industrial advancements, with Standart providing the Tsar unrivalled luxury travel.

World Fairs ran between the start of May and the end of October and were a regular attraction since the first one held at Crystal Palace in 1851. Before the advent of television nothing else reached so many individuals for the arts and technology. The fin de siècle winner in Europe was Paris with almost 110 million visitors to its five Parisian Expositions Universelles held at eleven year intervals. But in 1896, the Millennium Exhibition in Austria-Hungary was the most popular, focusing on entertainment with lovely gardens, circus acts and beer drinking, in all nearly 250 pavilions. In Germany, the Berliner Gewerbeausstellung trade exhibition in Berlin, had star attraction French Dr Alexandre Lion's baby incubators that proved a great attraction. Six prematurely born babies that would not have been alive but for the temperature-controlled incubators they were occupying, were drip fed drops of milk for nourishment. In France there were some notable exhibitions for photography and cinematography and the Colonial Exposition at Rouen in Normandy, but the focus in France was on preparations for the Russian state visit that year.

In Russia Nicholas and Alexandra attended the All-Russia Industrial Exhibition on 10 June 1896 (G), it was a week after the Khodynka tragedy, which opened slightly later than traditional May because of the coronation celebrations. In construction, the world's first steel tensile framing and hyperboloid structures were on show and it was ironic that a thunderstorm destroyed the complex on the opening day, which included the world's first radio receiver for measuring thunderstorms. Following the opening of the All-Russia Industrial Exhibition in June 1896 (G), Nicholas and Alexandra returned to St Petersburg to make preparations for the coronation tour of European state and family visits. Along the way they would be boarding

Standart for its maiden voyage. Nicholas couldn't wait to collect it but first they had a lot of appointments to attend in Germany and Denmark.

The Royal Visits

The Imperial Family left Russia on the Imperial train for Ukraine, crossing the border and arriving in Vienna on 27 August 1896 (G) for a short stay with Emperor Franz Josef of Austria-Hungary. The second day was reserved for hunting at Lainzer Park on the outskirts of Vienna, which the Austrians knew the Tsar had a passion for. A week later they headed north to Breslau (Wroclaw in Polish); a small city of under 400,000 inhabitants. Breslau is 185 miles south of Warsaw and was annexed by Prussia in 1871 and incorporated in to the German Empire. They arrived on 5 September 1896 (G) to visit Wilhelm II and his wife the Empress Augusta at their Viennese styled Stadtschloss (royal palace). It was the first of several state dinners in German-held Poland and Germany.

The Russian and German Imperial couples had a two and a half hour train ride to the small border town of Görlitz between Poland and Germany, some said it was the most beautiful city in Germany and labelled it the Paris of the eighteenth century. Then they headed 235 miles northwest to Berlin. Great festivities marked the three day state visit along the route from Breslau to Görlitz and then to Berlin, with people celebrating in the streets and military parades at each stop. There is no record of them visiting the Berliner Gewerbeausstellung exhibition that was running until 15 October 1896.

Circa 8 September 1896 they left Berlin. German princes and court officials were waiting on the platform for the Imperial families to arrive at the train station. Nicholas and Alexandra bade farewell to those gathered and with warm embraces the two empresses were visibly moved at their parting. Nicholas thanked Wilhelm II and boarded the train. A band played the Russian anthem as the train pulled away to begin the four hour journey to Kiel, the capital of Schleswig-Holstein; a rather dull seaport town and natural harbour for Germany's Baltic Fleet. The families would meet again on Nicholas's return trip through Darmstadt and then again in the summer of 1897 when Keiser Wilhelm II and his wife visited Russia.

On 17 September 1896 the newspapers reported that the conferences between the Russian and German statesmen in the respective suites of the Russian Tsar and German Emperor resulted in the complete agreement on all political questions existing between the two powers. According to the book *Letters From The Keiser To The Czar* (1920), author Isaac Don Levine stated that it was believed at the time of the Breslau meeting that both Emperors had reached complete accord concerning the Eastern Question having agreed each to maintain the status quo in Turkey.

As a result, it was surmised by Britain that Turkey may suffer as a consequence, meaning the strategically vital Bosporus Strait, naturally cutting Constantinople in two and linking the Black Sea and the Marmara Sea, was under threat of invasion. That region held the contentious political issues of the day and unfortuitously for Nicholas he was due at Balmoral Castle on 23 September 1896, where he would no doubt be subtly quizzed over the matter by Queen Victoria and the British foreign office. But that was a way off just yet and the next leg of the grand tour was a visit to Kiel and then on to Denmark where Standart was waiting to be collected.

From Vienna the Imperial Family arrived at Breslau then visited Gorlitz and Berlin. Then they visited Kiel and sailed on to Denmark.

The Imperial Family arrived in Kiel as guests of Wilhelm II's younger brother Prince Henry of Prussia. His wife Princess Irene was Alexandra's older sister. They were all essentially cousins, being grandchildren of Queen Victoria. Alexandra was recently pregnant whereas Irene was heavily pregnant with her second child. They must have discussed the possibility that either of them might produce a haemophilic child. Irene's first child Waldemar was seven years old and a haemophiliac; he would live to 1945 which was quite an achievement.

Unknown at the time, Irene who wanted a daughter was carrying a son, Sigimund, who was born in November 1896, unaffected by the disease and Alexandra who wanted a boy was carrying her second daughter, Tatiana, who was born in June 1987. Alexandra didn't know that she too was a haemophilia carrier. Irene was to have a third son Heinrich in January 1900 who was also haemophilic and died in February 1904 and Alexandra's son Alexei was born that same year in August 1904 also with the disease. Of the ten male descendants of Queen Victoria that had haemophilia, the immediate families of Irene and Alexandra accounted for four of them.

Prince Henry was a successful naval officer and expert seaman who would in due course become commander of the High Seas Fleet (1906-1909) reaching the rank of Grand Admiral. His marriage to Irene in 1888 had displeased Queen Victoria, yet they seemed to have been born for each other. They were a very pleasant and calming couple nicknamed 'the very amiables' by their closest friends. Alexandra visited Kiel on the previous two years staying at Prince Henry and Irene's residences at Kiel Castle and Hammelmark, and this time she brought her family and would have no doubt preferred to stay in Kiel with her sister so close to giving birth if not for looking to the prospect of seeing Queen Victoria again.

The details of the journey from Kiel to Copenhagen are a bit sketchy but the likeliest course of events was that they left Kiel on Polar Star and arrived at Copenhagen on 10 September 1896. They were to spend eleven days with Nicholas' grandparents the king and queen of Denmark. Finally the day had come for Nicholas to take possession of Standart. Although the Captain was in charge, officially each Imperial yacht was the responsibility of an individual Admiral. The captain for her maiden voyage was Ivan Ivanovich Tchagine who became a personal friend of the Imperial Family. Captain Tchagine took Standart out of port and headed for Britain.

The date for leaving Copenhagen is also a bit sketchy. The accepted date is on the morning of 21 September 1896, arriving at St Abb's Head on the morning of 22 September 1896; that's a twenty-four hour trip. It's not an important distinction to make but it should be noted that it takes five or more hours from Copenhagen to Kiel, eight hours to traverse the Kiel Canal and eighteen hours to cross the North Sea. Even at twenty knots it would probably take a day and a half to get from Brunsbüttel to St Abb's Head on the shoulder of the British northeast coast. It's more likely that Standart sailed a day earlier on the 20th and took two days to reach its destination.

On the morning of that momentous day on 20 September 1896 (G) when Standart left Copenhagen on its maiden voyage, Nicholas was with his wife and daughter Olga and Polar Star was accompanying them alongside. That afternoon they arrived back at Kiel. It was originally the Keiser Wilhelm Canal when it opened on 21 June 1895 but was widened and renamed. The canal cut through the 61-mile width of Schleswig-Holstein, from Kiel-Holtinau on the Baltic Sea to Brunsbüttel on the North Sea, saving 250 nautical miles of navigation around the Jutland peninsula. Standart and Polar Star sailed out of the canal and in to the North Sea. After some distance Standart turned northwest for St Abb's Head, a sleepy fishing village in the Scottish Borders and Polar Star continued westward through the English Channel for Portsmouth on the southern tip of England.

On the morning of 22 September 1896 Standart arrived at St Abb's Head where the Imperial Family transferred and travelled with the Prince of Wales on his ship to the port of Leith in Edinburgh, the traditional place for royal visits to Scotland. Standart headed back to the English Channel. Edinburgh city requested for the tsar to inspect the guard and enjoy a tour of the city but Nicholas chose not to and asked for the welcome ceremony to be conducted at Leith so that he might continue the journey to Balmoral without delay. The Channel Fleet greeted the Russian escort ships and at Leith a grand welcome was given, despite the inclement weather which didn't deter a great turnout, as reported by the Scotsman newspaper, "*It was one of those days which does Scotland no favours – dreich and misty, with driving rain.*"

Having been welcomed by the Lord Provost of Edinburgh and the Provost of Leith and other regional dignitaries, the Imperial Family were accompanied by the Prince of Wales in open carriages to the Leith Railway Station. The Scottish people having been deprived of a city procession still lined the streets in the awful weather. Unfortunately, a slight oversight by the planners not anticipating rain meant that everyone in the carriages were soaked by the time they arrived at the waiting train.

It was a day travelling along the eastern coast to Ballater, stopping several times to change trains or fill the tanks with water for steam, via Dundee, Arbroath, Montrose and Aberdeen. Along the journey they crossed the new Forth Road Bridge, a modern feat of engineering built in 1890 and holding the status of the world's longest bridge. They arrived at Ballater in the evening and were met by the Duke of York and a guard of honour of the Black Watch. From the station they transferred to carriages for the last hour of the trip, along the Braemar Road to Balmoral.

They arrived at the castle almost frozen, on 23 September 1896. Queen Victoria greeted them at the entrance and for the first time met her ten month old great-granddaughter Olga. Alexandra's pregnancy was not discussed during the visit 'apparently' because it wasn't officially announced yet, but undoubtedly she thought to inform the queen privately of it. Nonetheless,

CHAPTER X

seeing Olga must have been the greatest present for Queen Victoria from her favourite granddaughter, especially on such an historic date because it marked to the day, the very moment that she surpassed George III as Britain's longest reigning monarch. Queen Victoria it's said did not wish to make a fuss of it and requested it be combined with her diamond jubilee taking place in nine months' time. How proper that Queen Victoria should value seeing her granddaughter and great-granddaughter over the relatively meaningless celebration to mark the longevity of her reign.

Of course, there were still the pressing issues of the day to discuss and Nicholas expected to be quizzed although perhaps he wasn't as prepared in diplomacy to deal with the British government who seized the opportunity to gauge his views on the 'Eastern Question'. For this purpose the statesman and Foreign Secretary Robert Cecil, Marquess of Salisbury, was at Balmoral. The British government were anxious to determine the Tsar's position on what they regarded as the pressing matters of India and Turkey. Lord Salisbury was able to gain assurances regarding India that Russia held no intentions in that direction.

The Queen was duty bound to discuss the issue of the political and economic instability in the Ottoman Empire. Her peremptory discourse on the 'Eastern Question' prompted Nicholas to assure her and the British Prime Minister that the alliance of 1894 between Russia and France was not aimed against Britain which was what had been meant by 'pressing matters'. Nicholas gave the same assurances to Queen Victoria that he had given to Wilhelm II in a perfect example of how Nicholas would say one thing and then do as he pleased, which made him unpredictable and unreliable on the world political stage. Witte described it in his memoirs thus:

"He is incapable of playing fair and he always seeks underhand means and underground ways. He has a veritable passion for secret notes and methods." — SERGEY WITTE, memoirs page 183

It's worth mentioning how the situation with Turkey played out so that Witte's statement above can be appreciated. Following Nicholas' assurances that Russia had no ambitions in Turkey there came a massacre of Armenians in Constantinople. Somewhere between 70,000 and 300,000 Armenians were slaughtered, known as the Hamidian massacres named after the Sultan who tried to preserve Imperialism and prevent the Ottoman empire from collapse. It followed the Russian success of the Russo-Turko War (1877-1878) and took place between the years of Nicholas' ascension and his coronation (1894-1896) and is probably to be considered as the first phase of the Armenian genocide that followed during World War I.

It was a time preceding the Franco-Russo Alliance (1894) and France was attempting to take advantage of Russia's financial debt to France by manipulating Russia in to imposing control over the Ottoman Public Debt largely owed to Russia as reparations for the Russo-Turko War. The Russian ambassador to Turkey A. I. Nelidov was adept at using Russian leverage to control Ottoman finances and met Nicholas to discuss whether Russia was planning to use force with Turkey as was being rumoured. On 3 December 1896 the ambassador suggested that they create insurgent incidents to force a military response and thereby take the Upper Bosporus, which was what the Eastern Question was really all about in military terms.

The War Minister supported the idea but Count Witte advised against the use of force saying that it would create yet another European incident equalling the Crimean War in magnitude. Nicholas sided with the plan and preparations were made for landing troops in Turkey launching from Sevastopol and Odessa. Witte refused to sign the minutes on 9 December 1896 unless his objection was noted, to which Nicholas dictated a note to be inserted at the head of the minutes:

> *"In the opinion of Secretary of State Witte the occupation of Upper Bosporus without a preliminary agreement with the Great Powers is,* at *the present moment and under the present circumstances, very risky and likely to lead to disastrous consequences."*
> — NICHOLAS II

Somehow uncharacteristically of Nicholas, he allowed himself to be coerced by ministers that sided with Witte who demanded that he cancel the covert offensive plan before their ambassador arrived in Constantinople. Witte notes that from then on Nicholas held a grudge against him. The first thing that Queen Victoria and Keiser Wilhelm II would have known about it, if the plan had been enacted, was when Russian troops had invaded the Upper Bosporus. In the meantime the Russian ambassador to Turkey did return to his post to enact the plan and monitor the effects of the insurgency. At the right moment he was to send a telegram to his financial agent in London for a purchase of grain. This was the signal to invade and would be passed on to the Director of the Imperial Bank and from there to the War Minister and Minister of the Navy. To this end a secretary was placed on listening duty at the Imperial bank waiting day and night for the telegram that never came.

Perhaps this was another example of something Nicholas promised to do and then did the opposite, this time it was perhaps in part due to the pressure from Queen Victoria, rather than from the French or German governments of which he cared little about. Wilhelm II's whimsical letter to Nicholas of 12 November 1896 demonstrates his belief that their policies in Turkey were aligned and how Nicholas had given him that impression over their discussions on Turkey during his recent visit to Germany.

CHAPTER X

"... in the hopes that you will kindly trust me as you did till now and that nothing has or can change between us two since we arranged our line of action at Breslau. Vladimir [Nicholas' uncle] *has come from Paris with the best of impression that all is quiet there, which I can corroborate from the reports of my ambassador who is on the best of terms with the Government and is quite full of admiration for the capabilities and sang froid of Hanotaux. The latter I hear is rather nervous about Turky* [sic]*, but as I have heard nothing alarming from there I suppose there is no real cause, he, I hear, is strongly opposed to any conference about Turky* [sic] *and in that is perfectly right."* — WILHELM II, letter to Nicholas II, 1896

The British also knew that Nicholas loved hunting and presented him with plenty of it, being the start of the Scottish gaming season. Perhaps he was not overly flattered because he knew the tour would end with a stay in Spala, Poland, his hunting ground and he surely would have preferred to be with his family at the castle. He wrote to his mother informing her that his hosts had laid on hunting *"all day every day"* which was a gross exaggeration but shows how overwhelming it was for him. The weather remained awful until the last days of their stay when the rain stopped and finally Nicholas could take a break from hunting to go for long walks with Alexandra and even having a picnic on the moor. They also managed to take in a visit to the Duke and Duchess of Fife.

Polar Star leaves Portsmouth to join the British escort at the Isle of Wight

On 3 October 1896 they left Balmoral. Alexandra noted, "*It has been such a very short stay and I leave dear, kind Grandmama with a heavy heart.*" Carriages took them to Ballater where they boarded an overnight train from top to tail through Scotland and England to arrive in Portsmouth on 4 October 1896, where Polar Star was waiting. Standart had been making way from St Abb's Head and was scheduled to rendezvous at their destination at the port of Cherbourg. Nicholas made a diary entry for 5 October 1986 (G) describing being on the deck of Polar Star at 7.00 am leaving Portsmouth at low speed to the Isle of wight where the British squadron was waiting to escort them across the English Channel. The flotilla was assembling and almost ready when the wind grew stronger until the waves nudged them out to sea and they were prematurely sent towards Normandy.

The two locations are geographically on opposite sides of the English Channel. At 11.00 am the flotilla met French ships that took over the escort and the British ships turned smartly and headed back. Nicholas slept through much of it while Alexandra and Olga were very seasick, confirming just how rough the crossing was. At 2.00 pm they entered the inner harbour at Cherbourg. Polar Star weighed anchor with Standart arriving on schedule and positioned itself on Polar Star's port side. It was a superb way to arrive for a state visit. Standart was the largest yacht in the world and having recently entered Russian naval service it held a fascination with the crowds. The largest yacht since 2013 has been the Azzam at 180 metres, compared to Standart's 128 metres. Some years later RMS Titanic would make a similar impression on 12 April 1912, arriving at Cherbourg from Southampton on the second leg of her maiden voyage, also being at that time the largest vessel of its class.

Nicholas and Alexandra went ashore to be met by President Félix Faure. They planned stays at Cherbourg, Paris, Versailles, and Châlons. At 7.00 pm Nicholas was invited to a small dinner at the port's arsenal which he attended without Alexandra, who was still recovering. Cherbourg was left disappointed like the people of Edinburgh because Nicholas again chose to decline an invitation to tour their city. At 8.30 pm they boarded the Imperial train heading to the outskirts of Paris and arriving at Versailles-Chantiers station on the following morning at 8.50 am. President Faure had arrived on his Presidential train slightly earlier at 8.30 am. Nicholas and Alexandra transferred to the Presidential train; little Olga remained on the Imperial train.

After a short journey they arrived in Paris at 10.00 am then went in to the city centre where the crowd had gathered in extraordinary numbers; more than two million had come from all over France to see them and was quite possibly the largest turnout for a single event in the history of the French capital. It must have been exhilarating for Alexandra to hear the crowds cheering, "*long live the Empress!*" The newspapers would report that she had 'conquered Paris.'

CHAPTER X

Nicholas II and Alexandra disembark Polar Star at Cherbourg and are greeted by President Félix Faure on 5 October 1896. (Cover of Le Petit Journal, Supplement Illustre, 11 October 1896). The Russian yachts would make their way back to Russia leaving the Imperial Family to continue their visits and return to Russia by train.

The street decoration was so impressive that Nicholas, overcome with emotion, said, "*I can only compare it with my entry in to Moscow.*" French and Russian flags were tied to every mast completely lining the Champs-Elysées and the Jardin des Tuileries. Garlands were hung from make-do hooks, balconies were draped and an incredible profusion of illumination emitted from lamps on the girandoles that were woven between street posts and building protrusions.

A few months earlier for the coronation in Moscow, cinematographers Camille Cerf and Francis Doublier had made cinematographic history for the Lumière brothers. In Paris they were expected to likewise capture every minute of the Emperor's historic visit. People were still flocking there a week after the event to view the Lumière film; screening at the Café de la Paix (The peace café) every day from 2.00 pm to 6.30 pm. Less than a year had passed since the Lumière's first commercial screening of the factory workers at the Grand Café, Paris on 28 December 1895.

"The animated scenes relating to the Tsar's trip to France obtain considerable success every day. The public flocks to the Lumière Cinematograph to admire the remarkable scenes full of life which give such a perfect idea of the superb celebrations that Paris offered to the Russian sovereigns." — Le Journal de Guignol, Lyon, 18 October 1896

The *Lyon Republican* newspaper lauded the merits of cinematography and the importance of the new visual medium for recording historically important events for posterity and cited the Tsar's visit as evidence of the absolute necessity of it for the good of the public record.

"Cinématographe Lumière has just given us striking proof of its precious usefulness and of the services that can be expected from its invaluable assistance. The magnificent festivals, unique in the history of peoples, which marked the visit of the tsar and the tsarina to France, the Cinématographe Lumière recorded, with all their life, the most remarkable scenes, thanks to the assistance of skilful operators sent to Cherbourg and Paris by the Maison Lumière. Everything of which even the illustrated newspapers only manage to give a very imperfect idea, such as the enthusiasm of the people at the passage of the Russian sovereigns, the appearance of the crowd at the time of the parade of the cortege, the magnificent decorations of the streets and boulevards, etc., the Cinématographe Lumière gives us an idea of it as exact as if we were transported to one of the best placed points in Paris to admire this unforgettable spectacle. This is a truly extraordinary historical document that will forever immortalise these wonderful celebrations. It's the way we write history at the end of our century. How much should we regret that our ancestors did not know the Lumière Cinematograph!"
— Lyon Republican newspaper, 11 October 1896

The Imperial Family stayed in Paris for two days attending functions and visiting locations to great crowds. On the first day in Paris they visited the Russian Embassy and the Russian Church, attended a splendid dinner at the Elysée and a gala performance at the opera later that evening.

CHAPTER X

Nicholas II and President Félix Faure apply cement and tap the granite foundation stone for the Pont Alexandre III. (Cover of Le Petit Journal, Supplement Illustre, 18 October 1896). The inscription later added on the inauguration reads '*On April 14th 1900, Émile Loubet, President of the French Republic, opened the Exposition Universelle and inaugurated the Pont Alexandre III*'.

1900 was a busy year for Paris with the Olympic games opened by then President Émile Loubet. The Petit Palais and the Grand Palais were also constructed for the Exposition Universelle. During the Exhibition and the Olympics, an estimated fifty million people visited the Pont Alexandre III. It was listed as an historic monument in 1975.

Day two in Paris was given to sightseeing at the Cathedral of Notre-Dame, the Palais de Justice, the Sainte Chapelle and the Pantheon. In the crypt of the Church of Saint-Louis-des-Invalides, they visited the tomb of Napoleon Bonaparte situated under its Hardouin-Mansart dome. Napoleon's remains were transferred from St Helena and have stayed in Paris since 10 June 1840. Nicholas stood in front of the sarcophagus in his smart linen and wool tunic adorned with gold-tasselled epaulets and metal threads and brass buttons, his hands crossed his chest and he bowed his head, showing respect to the French Emperor whose Grande Armée had once crossed the Neman River and invaded Russia.

The most significant event in France was a visit to the new bridge across the River Seine spanning the 7th and 8th arrondissements (*previous page*). On one side was the Esplanade des Invalides and on the other lay the Petit Palais and Grand Palais being built for the Exposition and summer Olympic Games of 1900. While Nicholas had still been in Portsmouth, on 4 October 1896, President Faure decreed the bridge to be named Pont Alexandre III, in honour of the peaceful relationship that existed between France and Russia since Alexander III had signed the Franco-Russo alliance in 1893 with Sadi Carnot, the President of the French Republic at that time, and whose tomb at the Pantheon Nicholas visited and placed flowers upon. The alliance was a response to Germany's Triple Alliance which ended France's diplomatic isolation and had the effect of undermining the perceived power of the German Empire.

A granite block was positioned and a golden trowel and hammer were provided for Nicholas and Faure to spread cement on the stone and tap it home; the foundation stone was thus laid. French newspapers reported that the joint act symbolised the future harmony of the alliance. The compliment was repaid the following year with a French state visit to Russia when President Faure laid the foundation stone for an even more impressive bridge, the French built Trinity Bridge over the River Neva in St Petersburg. At that event (1897) Faure officially proclaimed the Franco-Russo Alliance. Although it was superseded by the future Triple Entente, it remained in existence in its principle form until 1917 when the Bolsheviks changed the nature of their relationship with France, ringing true the words of Keiser Wilhelm II who once said that democratic and autocratic alliances cannot last for long.

On 8 October 1896 they visited the Louvre; today it's the most visited museum in the world. Nicholas had requested it to be scheduled on the same day as a trip to Versailles whilst Alexandra scheduled some Paris shopping. In the first days since their arrival in France it became evident that they had scheduled too many excursions and they ended up being rushed through the Louvre so that they did not get to view a single gallery and Alexandra did not get to visit the fashionable delights of the Avenue des Champs-Élysées.

CHAPTER X

Alexandra was most disappointed, having looked forward to shopping in Paris, which she fervently discussed with her mother-in-law. Her French was fluent but surprisingly until now she had never set foot in France. She was unsatiated and came to realise their visit was politically less concerned about them and more to do with the relationship between the two countries. Behind this seemingly innocent royal visit the landscape of Europe was being redefined for 'le nouveau siècle'. Perhaps their disappointment with not having the time for their personal sightseeing was somewhat tempered by the crowds and the reception they had received and in spite of the hidden agenda, it was they, that occupied every inch in the newspapers.

After Paris Nicholas became more settled and was appreciative of the moment and managing his schedule better. As they were whisked away to the next pressing engagement at Versailles, located around twelve miles west of Paris, they managed to squeeze in a couple of detours. First they called on Sèvres and visited the triumphal arches; one for Peter the Great 1717 and the other for Nicholas II 1896. Then they went to a principle European porcelain factory, Manufacture Royale de Sèvres. Finally they arrived at the Château de Versailles at noon where they had lunch and stepped out on to the balcony with President Faure and his wife, and where 45,000 people in the gardens below had gathered to see them.

The Imperial couple with President Félix Faure riding through Paris, 1896

Just before the evening meal, they were shown to the rooms of Louis XV where they freshened up, rested and dressed for supper. According to the usually trusted account of Sophie Buxhoeveden, they were given the rooms of Marie Antoinette, a personal heroine of Alexandra's whose image she would keep on permanent display in her boudoir after this trip.

The official publication (*Relation officielle des fêtes organisées par la ville de Paris pour la visite de LL. MM. II L'Empereur et L'Impératrice de Russie les 6, 7 et 8 Octobre 1896*) published by Paris Imprimerie Nationale, in 1897, gave a detailed and definitive account of the Russian state visit, including the rooms that were provided for use to the Imperial couple at Versailles. In this instance, the Imperial couple had not used the suites of Marie Antoinette as told in the many accounts, indeed they were not shown those rooms at all and even if they had been, they contained no furnishings at that time. There was no bed there until renovations began in around 1960.

> "To the Empress the most interesting day was at Versailles, where she was thrilled by the palace, its artistic beauties and historical associations. The rooms placed at her disposal were those of Queen Marie-Antoinette, to the suppressed horror of her suite who, superstitiously, found the association ominous." — SOPHIE BUXHOEVEDEN

The 'association' stated by Sophie Buxhoeveden was a reference to the striking similarities between the two women. A young Marie Antoinette had arrived in France from a foreign court (Vienna) ill-prepared for the Grand Court. Similarly, Alexandra had arrived from the English court and was unprepared for the Russian court. Their husbands ascended the throne when they were at a very young age; Marie Antoinette at 18 to Louis XVI and Alexandra at 22 to Nicholas II. Sadly, the happy comparisons end there and the two women came to be aligned more by their tragic circumstances. Marie Antoinette not producing an heir for over eleven years and for Alexandra it was to be eight years. Marie Antoinette became increasingly unpopular and derived a false reputation for harbouring sympathy for the enemy of her adopted country; likewise Alexandra was unpopular and during World War I was accused of sympathising with Germany. Marie Antoinette saw a revolution topple the monarchy, was placed under house arrest, and was executed at thirty-seven years old; Alexandra would also see revolution, house arrest and execution at the unrespectable age of forty-six.

The wrongful connection of Marie Antoinette to the Imperial couple's visit at Versailles falls to Buxhoeveden who published a biography about Alexandra in 1929 in which she mentioned Marie Antoinette, on page 75. Buxhoeveden was not at Versailles in 1896 and her account was therefore derived from a secondary source but still it has been quoted multiple times in publications, not least by the renowned Robert K Massie.

CHAPTER X

For example, the attribution appears in a biography of Marie Antoinette by Lady Antonia Fraser *Marie Antoinette: the journey* on page 538. Also, in a biography of Alexandra by Greg King, *The Last Empress,* page 115, Alexandra is said to have spent the night underneath the damask canopy of the doomed queen's bed, when it's known the Imperial couple did not spend the night at Versailles. These are small and perhaps insignificant details but demonstrate the problem with Romanov history when trying to establish the facts from an age when it was fashionable to embellish memoirs. Even the respected accounts given by the aforementioned authors are easily challenged in the Paris Imprimerie Nationale, the primary record that provides the conclusive evidence. In this case, the association with Marie Antoinette is better suited to the memoirs of Buxhoeveden who may have decided the myth to be more appealing for her readers.

The evening performance in the Salon d'Hercule (or the Hercules Drawing Room on Level 1 at the Château de Versailles), ended at 11.00 pm. By 11.30 pm the Imperial Family were at Versailles station boarding the rather dated Imperial train of Napoleon III and heading for their next engagement at Camp de Châlons. Nicholas and Alexandra had thoroughly enjoyed their time at Versailles and Nicholas noted the resemblance to Peterhof Palace that had been modelled on the Palace of Versailles. Nicholas believed Peterhof just pipped it because Versailles had no sea. Today the Peterhof Palace gets 5.8 million visitors each year, far out-pipped by the Palace of Versailles with its 15 million yearly visitors.

On the following morning, 9 October 1896, the Imperial couple attended military manoeuvres at Camp de Châlons where 90,000 personnel presented for inspection by their President and the Russian Emperor. It was witnessed by an estimated 500,000 spectators and held on a large open field not dissimilar to Khodynka Field; with a similar sized crowd this event was a lesson by the French in event management. The Moscow Gazette reported that the speeches given at Châlons had been a solid guarantee of peace of greater value than a written treaty.

Their reception in France gave them an intimate experience, Nicholas had arrived half-hearted and learned to relax and was now reticent about leaving. Despite Alexandra's ongoing lethargy, she had accompanied her husband to all the events, except the Cherbourg armoury dinner. Politically it was a huge success in placing both nations at the centre of Europe and at such a vibrant time in world history, e.g. the approaching new century, Olympic Games and World Fair. Russia had arrived on the world stage as never before and even Fabergé were the masters of the intricate decorative arts in Paris. In the words of the French adage it was a time for, '*out with the old and in with the new*'. As the train left for Hesse to visit Alexandra's family on the next stop, Nicholas wired President Faure that the recollection of his visit to Paris would remain deeply engraved in his memory.

President Loubet and Nicholas II inspect the naval guard at Kronstadt, May 1902

Crossing the border in to Germany Nicholas was writing a letter to his mother just before he retired at bedtime:

> *"We arrived at the frontier at eleven in the evening. There for the last time, we heard the strains of our national anthem. After this began German helmets and it was unpleasant to look out of the window. At every station in France one heard 'Hurrah' and saw kind and jolly faces, but here everything was black and dark and boring."*

The Imperial train arrived in Darmstadt on 11 October 1896. Alexandra was back with her family in the heart of her ancestral home at Stadtschloss (The Residential Palace). How much she remembered being there with her mother up until the age of six is hard to say. In 1893 her brother Ernest (the last grand duke of Hesse,) built a tea house adjoining the property that suited their pseudo English culture which Alexandra would have found amusing. The House of Hesse directly descended from the House of Brabant and would come to an end towards the end of World War I. On 19 October 1896 the Imperial Family travelled to the Biebrich Palace in the small town of Wiesbaden, about twenty-eight miles northwest of Darmstadt, where Wilhelm II travelled out to greet them. Wilhelm II was in actuality a passionate supporter of Nicholas and the Russian cause which had continued to a point during World War I when Wilhelm II decided he had been betrayed too many times by Nicholas. On 21 October 1896 the Imperial train left Wiesbaden and went to Spala marking the end of their grand tour.

There were many state visits at the turn of the century, perhaps none as grand as Nicholas and Alexandra in France though, and if stability relied on them alone then maybe there would not have been a world war in 1914. 1901 was another busy year for state visits, like coronation year, but this time their French host was President Émile Loubet, the successor to President Félix Faure and who during 7-10 May 1902, visited Russia, arriving at Kronstadt and staying in Tsarskoe Selo for the duration of his visit.

CHAPTER X

Loubet was presented with a silver-gilt, translucent and painted filigree enamel traditional bread and salt dish. Alexandra was likewise presented with a traditional gobelin (i.e. tapestry). It was a representation of a portrait of Marie Antoinette with her children (*see below*). The empty cradle is in remembrance of the queen's youngest child, Sophie-Béatrice, who died shortly before the painting was completed. Note the absence of jewellery, just a simple pearl earring and bracelet signify the importance of her children over material wealth. It had been completed in the wake of the so-called 'Affair of the Diamond Necklace' scandal in 1785 which had nothing to do with Marie Antoinette but for which she suffered ridicule when the trial caused a sensation in Paris by her implication.

Marie Antoinette with her children, 1787
Oil painting (275cm by 216.5cm) by Élisabeth Vigée Le Brun

The painting was commissioned by Louis XVI who wanted to portray Marie Antoinette in a sympathetic way being that she was at that time very much disliked by the people. It was painted by French artist Élisabeth Vigée

Le Brun and today the original is housed at the Palace of Versailles and considered to be a French masterpiece and national treasure. Three gobelins were made of it, each in 1814, 1822 and 1897. One was presented to Empress Elizabeth of Austria in 1868, the second is held at the Élysée Palace and the third was presented to Alexandra Feodorovna in 1902.

On 8 May 1902 Loubet visited the tomb of Alexander III and the next day was taken on a tour of St Petersburg. On the morning of the 10th he had breakfast with Nicholas aboard the French cruiser *Montcalm* just before his departure. It had been another memorable state visit for both allies. Paris continued its diplomatic missions receiving Edward VII in May 1903 and Loubet visiting London in July 1903. The next major French visit came from Spain; King Alfonso XIII visited Paris between 31 May 1905 to 4 June 1905. Interestingly, King Alfonso and Loubet survived an assassination attempt meant for the king. After attending the opera, a bomb was thrown at their carriage on Loubet's side as they passed the Hotel de Louvre on Rue de Rivoli. Arrests were made but the assailant, thought to have been 'Arnould', was never found and the Spanish anarchist Alexander 'Farras' thought to be responsible for the plot was never caught. The terrorist threat had existed for several decades around politically sensitive state visits.

Left: The Chinese theatre gala   *Right*: Loubet playing with the children in the nursery at Alexander Palace. In 1906 Loubet became the first President of the Third Republic to end a full term of office.

CHAPTER X

The Alliances

The war between France and Prussia started because Prussia wanted to ally with Spain, thereby sandwiching France on two fronts. France had been left feeling vulnerable since the Franco-Prussian War of 1870-1871, and following the formation of the German Empire in 1871, when Prussia had defeated France and annexed the provinces of Alsace and Lorraine.

From 1891 France was progressing foreign policy with Russia. Alexander III had not been enthusiastic about France and neither side dared utter the word 'alliance' until the formalities were upon them, having taken a lot of political zeal and French loans to establish the Franco-Russo alliance. It was no small feat considering the wide expanse between a republic and an autocracy and their opposite ideologies, returning once more to Keiser Wilhelm II's statement that democratic an autocratic alliances cannot last.

The coronation state visit to France in 1896, although traditional for newly crowned monarchs to visit foreign courts, was foremost a political demonstration by France of the shared mutual interests between the two nations, particularly on their views about Germany. France did not have the European royal connections that its neighbours England, Germany and Russia did, as a result of marriages, which was thought to be a disadvantage for France. But its physical location has always given France a strategic importance encompassing an empire of just under four million square miles by 1914. It 'lended' its language to the international language of diplomacy (langue diplomatique) ever since the Treaty of Rasstatt (1714) that marked the end of the War of Succession in Spain. Thereafter French was used for treaties and across the European courts and was the language of the nobility that in Russia was used by Catherine II for all her correspondence.

France's insecurity in the face of a growing and ever more aggressive German power continued well in to the new century. In 1904 she allied with Britain in the Franco-Anglo treaty better known as the Entente Cordiale. When Kaiser Wilhelm II arrived in French Tangiers on 31 March 1905 to declare his support for the sultan of Morocco, he once more provoked France, in what was called the Tangiers Crisis, which meant that Britain automatically backed France because of their alliance.

France led the initiative in Europe for a decade but its treaties with Britain and Russia became better arranged under one joint venture forming a stronger deterrent in the form of the Triple Entente Alliance. Had it been down to the monarchs, things may have turned out very different. Wilhelm II and Nicholas II sought an alliance against the British and Japanese. They viewed France as a member ally that was only needed if it became necessary to help them against the British. Had this scenario played out then Russia and Germany would have been allies in World War I.

However, it was the governments of the Triple Entente that set about in opposition to the obvious signs that Germany was preparing for war. Since the Tsar's coronation visit to France in 1896, Germany was under no illusion that Russia had aligned its foreign policy with Germany's arch enemy. To guard against an attack on two fronts from France and Britain, Germany had secretly negotiated the Russo-German Reinsurance Treaty in 1887 but had allowed it to lapse in 1890 after Wilhelm II removed Chancellor Otto von Bismarck from office. Russia asked for a renewal of the treaty but Germany refused, and to reiterate once more, Wilhelm II believed that democratic France and autocratic Russia could never reconcile against Germany.

The Triple Entente between Britain, France and Russia was designed to counter Germany's growing power on the continent. It was a merger of three existing alliances; Franco-Russo 1894, Anglo-Franco 1904 and Anglo-Russo 1907; these pacts became the Triple Entente from 31 August 1907. Additional agreements with Portugal and Japan effectively restrained the perceived menace of German expansionism.

"Thus England, France, and Russia had, though for different reasons, an aim in common to overthrow Germany. England wished to do so for commercial-political reasons, France on account of her policy of revenge, Russia because she was a satellite of France and also for reasons of internal politics and because she wished to reach the southern sea. These three great nations, therefore, were bound to act together. The union of these ambitions in a common course of action, duly planned, is what we call the 'policy of encirclement'."
— KEISER WILHELM II, memoirs, page 308

Between 1907 and 1914, France, Britain and Russia exchanged five major visits in addition to the two separate state visits made between Russia and France. Standart was the conveyor of the Triple Entente meetings for Russia but it had to sail past Germany which required utmost diplomacy as the alliance in effect was an overt measure against Germany, of which Wilhelm II regarded as a hostile encirclement. He called Russia a satellite of France, meaning in financial terms, as Russia's foreign debt was predominantly owed to France accrued from financing the Russo-Japanese War. This meant France was better placed to influence Russia than Germany was. The fact that Wilhelm II and Nicholas II were distant cousins only went so far in foreign policy. The Austrian newspaper *Neue Freie Presse* considered:

"... the visit to Reval as an almost irresponsible proceeding in view of the consequences involved, and heaps reproaches on Russia for turning away from her true German friend to welcome England who has always been her bitter enemy." — NEUE FREIE, Austrian newspaper

CHAPTER X

The Triple Entente naval visits took place over two waves, first from 1907 to 1909 and then from 1912 to 1914. The pact was a defensive measure but served to provoke Germany and led to a world war. Not every nation was happy that the dominant powers were squaring up to each other, for example, Italy stubbornly resisted any involvement until 23 May 1915 when it had no option but to declare war on Austria-Hungary and entered World War I on the side of the Triple Entente.

For Russia and Britain the meeting at Reval in 1908 served a diplomatic purpose in the aftermath of the 1907 Anglo-Russo alliance. It settled colonial disputes and was a formal way to sort out the old alliances between them over Persia, Tibet and Afghanistan. Although the British Foreign Secretary Sir Edward Grey (first viscount of Falloden) announced in the UK House of Commons that the Reval visit was not being used to discuss future alliances between France or Russia it was essentially marking the beginning of the Triple Entente meetings which facilitated those discussions.

Imperial Yacht Standart in the Bay of Reval, 9 June 1908.
The Union Jack flies at the bow. A launch takes Nicholas II to Polar Star.

Reval had once been under Russian control and represented for them the resounding success at the naval Battle of Reval on 13 May 1790. During the Russo-Swedish War (1788-1790) Sweden sent an armada of more than

26 ships to obliterate the Russian fleet of 14 ships anchored in the Harbour of Reval. The wind hampered the Swedish effort as they entered the harbour and they were easily fired upon and dispersed by three tactical defensive lines firing cannon and iron grapeshot. One account gives casualties of Swedish 51, Russian 8. A revised account states Swedish 130, Russian 8 - either way, the low casualties are telling of Russia's most successful naval battle.

Reval (now Tallinn, Estonia) 9 June 1908 – Edward VII (successor of Queen Victoria,) comes aboard Standart, welcomed by nephew Nicholas II and sister-in-law Maria Feodorovna. This was a British monarch's first visit to Russia.

Reval now in German hands (until 1918) was the first visit of a British monarch to Russian waters. Edward VII crossed the North Sea onboard *HMS Victoria and Albert* and entered the Kiel Canal. On entering the canal at Brunsbüttel the British flotilla were greeted by an escort of German cavalry along the banks. The Royal Yacht *Alexandra* damaged a propeller blade on the canal wall but made it through. It was Wilhelm II's idea to greet the British ships as they entered the canal and escort them for a while.

On the day, they were disorganised, not having rehearsed it and when the British yachts came in to view the cavalry started moving along the bank,

CHAPTER X

but the yachts were moving much faster and overtook the escort and were soon heading away at speed. The cavalry tried desperately to catch up, all the while making a mess of it. It's said that the crew on the decks watching the palava couldn't contain their laughter. The flotilla passed from the Kiel Canal in to the Baltic Sea and arrived at the Bay of Reval on the morning of 9 June 1908. The senior Russian yachts were waiting side by side. The Imperial Family arrived by Imperial train and transferred to *Standart*. Nicholas' mother and siblings boarded *Polar Star*.

Reval, June 1908 – (LTR)

Ladies –   Princess Victoria (Older sister of Empress Alexandra), Empress Alexandra, Grand Duchess Olga Alexandrovna (younger sister of Nicholas II).
Children – Marie, Alexei, Olga, Anastasia, Tatiana.

As well as for state matters these get togethers offered the opportunity to catch up with family members and other royals at no personal expense to them. Security around such ports as Reval could not be guaranteed and so in 1908 all parties remained on their respective yachts, inviting each other to dinners and dances, yacht hopping to kept themselves entertained.

It was a brilliant sunny day, gun salutes were exchanged and the yachts were awash with small craft all around them and people cheering from the bays. Queen Alexandra and First Sea Lord Admiral Sir John Fisher were watching from the deck of *Victoria and Albert*. Nicholas transferred to *Polar Star* and welcomed his uncle Edward VII aboard for lunch as a guest of the Dowager Empress Maria Feodorovna. In the evening a grander banquet was held aboard *Standart* and the members of the royal parties stayed on deck until after midnight listening to the music. The next day, Wednesday, lunch was aboard *Standart* and dinner was on *Alexandra*, then after dinner they met aboard *Victoria and Albert* for a relaxing evening.

An awkward moment arose at the first dinner party aboard the *Victoria and Albert* and was another example of Alexandra Feodorovna's resistance to Russian etiquette. The Dowager Empress, having precedence in such matters in accordance with Imperial etiquette, was in a slight quandary over Alexandra Feodorovna's defiant gestures looking like she might walk off if her mother-in-law entered the dining room first. Edward VII averted the potential storm by stepping in at the moment dinner was announced taking them both on each of his arms and bringing them to the table together thereby avoiding a scene.

"It is with feelings of deepest satisfaction and pleasure that I welcome your Majesty and her Majesty the Queen to Russian waters. I trust that this meeting, while strengthening the many strong ties which unite our *houses, will have the happy result of drawing our countries closer together and of promoting and maintaining the peace of the world."* — Opening lines of the Tsar's speech addressed to Edward VIII

It was fortunate that Reval 1908 brought together the royal families of Britain, Germany and Russia, with a notable absence; France was not an Imperial power with relatives to contribute. Alexei fell on the deck and hit his forehead and the swelling was so extreme that he could hardly open his eyes and suffered blindness for three months. If Cheiro is to be believed of his story about the existence of Madame Sund being present at this event, then Sund performed an after-dinner séance for the royal guests which also places her conveniently with Alexei at a time when he was unwell and with the addition of Rasputin having been summoned there – all rather unlikely. Overall, the visit to Reval was a resounding success and a return outing to England was arranged to visit Cowes on the following year, i.e. 1909.

When the children were quite young they were each assigned a member of the crew known as a sailor nanny or diadka to watch over them and ensure they didn't fall overboard and to accompany them when they wanted to swim or go ashore. Diadka's were rewarded by the Imperial couple at the end of a voyage with something nice like an expensive watch.

CHAPTER X

The children with their diadkas (sailor nannies)

From 1905 *Standart* was assigned to the marine guards and whether on *Polar Star* or *Standart* when the Imperial Family were at sea they lived on the yacht at anchor, with launches taking them to and from shore as required. In the summer they would take a trip to a small island off the coast of Finland which the children nicknamed the Bay of Standart. On that uninhabited piece of land they could relax together, undisturbed. What irony for a family that ruled over one sixth of the planet's surface, that it became their only real place of refuge, as an extension of the isolation they enjoyed at sea.

In late summer 1909 the family sailed to England as guests of King Edward VII for the Isle of Wight regatta, arriving on Monday, 2 August. *Standart* moored at Cowes next to *HMY Victoria & Albert III*. The Imperial couple remained onboard and Edward VII and Queen Alexandra took a launch out to greet them. Living onboard was the protocol even in England due to the high level of security that was being provided. Although it was almost ten years before the Irish Republican Army formed in 1919, the seeds of terrorist activism were being formed in 1909 when Na Fianna Éireann was established, the organisation that would provide the officers skilled in weapons handling to the Irish Volunteers in 1913 and thereafter to the IRA.

In 1909 the perceived threat came from Germany (*Chapter XVIII*). Indeed, the Daily Mail advised its readers to refuse to be served by a German waiter and should they claim to be Swiss, to ask to see a passport. Prime Minister Herbert Asquith was convinced that German spies were plotting in the UK and the Secret Service Bureau was established in the previous month, July 1909, which was basically the new Home Office, and which first began field operations in October 1909. It's fair to say there was a high state of alarmism present at the Cowes Regatta as a new era of terrorism against the British was unfurling.

Security fears were largely unfounded in relation to any German spy networks operating in the UK during Germany's preparations for war. But a network of spies was discovered working for German Naval Intelligence that posed a significant threat due to the naval arms race and was therefore a high risk at the regatta where so many Allied yachts were gathered. In the following years (1910-1911) British intelligence services really took off when Home Secretary Winston Churchill extended every resource to them. Churchill to British Intelligence was like J. Edgar Hoover to the CIA.

The increased security didn't keep Europe's nobility away from Cowes. Far from it. Edward VII's sister Princess Helena was present (now Princess Christian of Schleswig-Holstein). She was the most active of the British royal family; one of the founding members of the British Red Cross and a few years earlier had translated and published the letters of her sister Alice, the mother of Alexandra Feodorovna. Also present at Cowes was Empress Eugénie de Montijo, the Spanish widow of Napoleon III. There were no less than four empresses at Cowes in 1909, if Eugénie de Montijo is to be counted among them: Empress of India Queen Alexandra, Dowager Empress Maria Feodorovna, Empress of Russia Alexandra Feodorovna, and Dame Eugénie de Montijo the former Empress of France.

Dame Eugénie de Montijo came to have an important influence on her husband regarding foreign policy. During the war in Spain her father had fought on the side of Napoleon I and she had moved to Paris after Louis-Napoléon became president of the Second Republic in December 1848. They were married on 30 January 1853 after he became Emperor and after the Franco-Prussian War (1870-1871) when the Emperor Napoleon III was overthrown on 4 September 1870, and Eugénie de Montijo joined her family in exile in Britain, relinquishing her title in 1873 to be known as a grand dame.

At Cowes Nicholas was made an honorary member of the Royal Yacht Club and he greeted the Lord Mayor of London aboard *Standart* while that day Alexandra Feodorovna visited the Royal Yacht *Victoria & Albert III* to inspect the British Fleet. In the evening Nicholas and Alexandra paid a visit to Empress Eugénie on her yacht *Thistle*. Nicholas and Alexandra had a full week of yacht hopping and yacht racing to enjoy which they watched from the British yachts *Alexandra* and *Victoria & Albert III*.

CHAPTER X

Nicholas II and Edward VII each hosted marvellous formal dinners on their respective yachts. *Standart* was particularly suited for banqueting with its long cabin at deck level offering functional space as required, it could accommodate a banquet with plenty of room for waiters to move around the edges. The high windows allowed for the flooding of natural light with rigid chandeliers illuminating the evenings.

A formal dinner on Standart, August 1909. Nicholas II on left in military dress and Alexandra sits opposite wearing an elegant hat with a large feather

The mainland was rife with picnics, luncheons and teas. How near Alexandra was to the famed residence of Osborne House near Cowes where she grew up with her siblings after the death of their mother. The Romanov children did get to visit Osborne House for a tour including the room where Queen Victoria had died and they played on the beach gathering sea shells. After lunch Olga and Tatiana went in to the village and purchased some postcards but had to ask how to make the purchase, such was their sheltered life that they didn't understand cash transactions. It was an experience they thoroughly enjoyed and the girls documented how they had wished they could have stayed on the Isle of Wight much longer.

A more intimate family gathering took place near Osborne House at a farmhouse called Barton Manor. On that memorable get together the strong ties between the two families are plain to see in the photograph on the next page. The girls took great pride at demonstrating their English language fluidity and they had tea at the manor and posed for photographs taken by Arthur William Debenham. Debenham was a portrait photographer and miniature painter with studios at Ryde and Sandown on the Isle of Wight, who was chosen to take the royal portraits for the regatta.

Barton Manor 4 August 1909. Nicholas II and Edward VII family portrait

Barton Manor Photograph Identification — L to R:

Standing: Prince Edward of York (future Edward VIII), Queen Alexandra of Denmark (consort to Edward VII), Princess Mary Countess of Harewood (daughter of George Prince of Wales), Princess Victoria (daughter of Edward VII, future Princess of Wales), Grand Duchess Olga (daughter of Nicholas II), Grand Duchess Tatiana (daughter of Nicholas II).

Seated:- Mary Princess of Wales (consort to George Prince of Wales and future Queen Mary of Teck), Nicholas II of Russia, Edward VII of Great Britain, Tsarina Alexandra (consort to Nicholas II), George Prince of Wales (future George V), Grand Duchess Marie (daughter of Nicholas II).

On ground:- Tsarevich Alexei (son and heir to Nicholas II), Grand Duchess Anastasia (daughter of Nicholas II).

CHAPTER X

Barton Manor on the green expanse of East Cowes had been purchased as a guesthouse by Queen Victoria in 1845 and modernised by Edward VII who developed the gardens. The land was listed in the Domesday Book in 1086 and from 1282 to 1430 functioned as an Augustinian monastery, then reverted to the Christian Church that donated it to Winchester College.

In the Barton Manor photograph Edward VII and Nicholas II sit at the centre as heads of the British and Russian empires with consorts bookending them. Queen Alexandra stands on Nicholas' right and Tsarina Alexandra sits on Edward VII's left side. The obvious similarity can be seen between first cousins Nicholas II and George, Prince of Wales. In this portrait, Edward VII only had around six months to live, ending the short-lived Edwardian period (1901-1910). He died on 6 May 1910 at Buckingham Palace at which time Queen Alexandra became a Dowager like her sister Maria Feodorovna. The young Prince George of Wales (far right) ushered in the Georgian period as George V. Edward VII's other son Edward (far left) would succeed George V briefly as Edward VIII before abdicating in favour of his nephew George VI (i.e. George V's son and the father of Elizabeth II).

The photographer's name may sound familiar being that his antecedents of Debenhams fame in Oxford Street, were enthusiastic about photography and one of the first to use the bromide print method that came in to use around 1880. It used paper containing silver bromide that was sufficiently sensitive to light to be used for enlargements. It was the most popular format for black and white photography in the twentieth century. While Arthur William Debenham was developing the regatta portraits, the American retailer Harry Gordon Selfridge opened the first British custom-built department and the world's largest store, on Oxford Street in 1909. Debenhams had been in the West End since 1778 selling expensive fabrics and apparel for women, and in 1919 bought outright the Marshall & Snelgrove department store complex on Oxford Street, in an attempt to directly compete side-by-side with Selfridges; the rest as they say is history.

Standart left the Isle of Wight on 6 August 1909. On the return trip from England the next official state visit was to Italy at Racconigi on 24 October 1909. The state visit was really disguising the conclusion of their secret agreement known as the Racconigi Bargain, in which Russia and Italy would include each other in meetings regarding territorial matters in Eastern Europe. Queen Elena (of Montenegro) consort to King Victor Emmanuel III gifted Nicholas II a donkey which went by train to Odessa then boarded *Standart* to cross the Black Sea to Sevastopol and whence it was transported to Livadia Palace. Nicholas wrote to his mother about it:

"As a goodbye present, the queen gave my children a donkey with a cart from Calabria and insisted I take it onto the train with me. This

was done and the donkey arrived to Yalta on board the Standart. It kicked a lot while in Odessa when it was being taken aboard. But when the donkey got onto the deck, it felt at ease and relaxed. Now the children often take rides and are very pleased." — NICHOLAS II

Standart in the Kiel Canal, Germany, 1909, on a visit to Prince Henry of Prussia (the husband of Alexandra Feodorovna's sister Irene)

Royal Romances

The Imperial couple were aboard *Standart* for extensive periods, of which they wholeheartedly loved every minute. They are full of praises for the crew and in particular the medical staff who made them feel like the most pampered royals alive. Notwithstanding their position they were down to earth and allowed people in to their inner family circle. Nicholas and Alexandra would talk for ages on the decks to simple sailors or cooks. And the girls played and even innocently flirted with some of the young sailors.

In this setting it is unfortunate that rumours were over-zealously circulated that the girls could be somewhat indiscreet and had inappropriate liaisons with the sailors. It should be considered whether young sailors would be at will to develop unseemly affections with the grand duchesses, given the severe punishment that would face the sailor. Would the navy not have employed the strictest behavioural conduct and warned crew about holding such delusions.

CHAPTER X

Nicholas II tasting a recipe and conversing with a ship's cook. He once commented that being on *Standart* meant he could eat proper food. He took great enjoyment from simply prepared meat dishes, particularly chicken. He loved porridge in the mornings and soup in the evenings. There was not much in the way of desserts prepared for him as he did not like sweet things. For an apéritif he was partial to Benedictine liqueur and for a digestif he liked cognac.

THE NIKOLASHKA

The sailors were well aware of a chaser invented by Nicholas during his formative days in the military. The recipe is rather lost but seems to involve a slice of lemon dried and powdered, ground coffee, sugar and a shot of cognac.

There are just several credible instances when the girls developed a crush. Tatiana favoured Lieutenant Nikolai Rodionov from Tula, he was the Assistant Commander of the Imperial Guard. Olga had a crush on *Standart* officer Pavel Voronov and later during World War I she would fall for an injured cavalry officer Dmitry Malama. Marie became obsessed with an officer, Nikolai Demenkov, while on a visit to her father and Alexei at the Stavka in Moghilev. Prince Carol of Romania formally proposed to Marie in 1916 while visiting Russia but was declined because she didn't like him.

Anastasia was the youngest, not flirty but mischievous. Nicholas once jokingly told the Countess Ekaterina Kleinmichel, *"Anastasia is our family clown!"* Countess Kleinmichel was a Maid of Honour to Alexander II's wife Maria Alexandrovna and the auntie of Countess Olga Kleinmichel. The Kleinmichel's were one of the most affluent aristocratic families in Russia. The abundant joyfulness of the girls has sometimes been misinterpreted as flirtatious. Consider that up to the end of the first wave of the Triple Entente visits when *Standart* returned to Sevastopol, the eldest daughter Olga was just 14 years old, not exactly on the scene looking for romance. It isn't until the second wave of Triple Entente visits that Olga by her own admission fell in love in 1913, when she was eighteen. Assuredly most young ladies would relish the company of young sailors and no more than that should be read in to the matter.

Olga Nikolaevna had known an officer on *Standart* for some years, Pavel Voronov, with whom in 1913 she became emotionally compromised. She was open about her feelings to her father who brushed it off as a crush. She kept a detailed diary and recorded one time when *Standart* pulled in to Livadia and the family had to disembark, how mortally painful it was to leave the yacht, in particular Pavel Voronov. It's unlikely that Voronov reciprocated Olga's emotional advances; she had just come in to adulthood turning 18 in November and he approached 27 in December. But Voronov was already betrothed to a different Olga, Countess Olga Konstantinovna Kleinmichel, whom he met in 1911 at a dance given by Princess Leonilla Ivanovna Bariatinsky of Sayn-Wittgenstein from another of the most influential families of the Russian nobility.

Voronov had served on the ship *Admiral Makarov* moored at the port in Messina when on 28 December 1908 an earthquake hit Sicily for 30 to 42 seconds and the crew rushed to help. Thousands of lives were lost. Pavel's bravery came to the attention of the Tsar who promoted him to a Lieutenant on *Standart*. Quick on the scene had also been Queen Elena of Italy (the Montenegrin sister) who endeared herself by arranging a hospital ship for the wounded and a fundraiser for the victims.

The Messina earthquake occurred along the Straits of Messina between the island of Sicily and mainland Italy. A total of 293 aftershocks were reported between 28 December 1908 and 31 March 1909 which triggered a local tsunami. Both the cities of Messina and Reggio di Calabria were completely destroyed and covered by rubble up to five metres high. It remains even today, the deadliest natural disaster to have occurred in Europe with anywhere between 60,000 to 120,000 deaths.

Olga Kleinmichel and Paval Voronov went to many more dances together and in 1914 were married at the Feodorovsky Cathedral in the presence of the Emperor and Empress. Due to Voronov's parents being deceased, the Empress stood as his pseudo mother and the Grand Duke Alexander as his

CHAPTER X

pseudo father, as is explained in the book Upheaval by Olga Kleinmichel. The rumour mill speculated that the wedding was a way of dealing with the Grand Duchess Olga Nikolaevna's unshakable infatuation for Voronov. Voronov and Olga Kleinmichel would have one daughter and they named her – Tatiana. Olga Kleinmichel said the following in her book *Upheaval*:

> *"I was presented to the Emperor and to two of the young Grand Duchesses, Olga and Tatiana. The latter, to my idea, was the prettier of the two, but both had the simplicity of manner that is the greatest charm in every person and especially in anyone who holds such a position as theirs. they were not blasé in the least, and their faces shone with pleasure and excitement."*
> — COUNTESS OLGA KLEINMICHEL

<u>THE END FOR STANDART</u>

At the outbreak of World War I the Imperial yachts were placed in dry docks. Standart was kept in Helsinfors and converted for naval service in 1917, renamed to 'Marta' on 18 March and later to 'Marti'. One account says the names were references to the February Revolution (March in the newer Gregorian calendar) and another says they were variations of the name of a leader of the French Communist Party. It was far from the end for these magnificent vessels but their prestigious days and noble history were over.

From 1906 *Standart*'s second in command had been Nikolai Pavlovich Sablin. He continued to serve but only took over as ship's Captain for a short while in 1914. His father was Vice Admiral Pavel Sablin and his brother Nikolai was also a naval officer. His command was interrupted by World War I and after the revolution he was expelled from the Russian Navy. Captain Tchagine's service came to an end on 11 October 1912 (J) under unfortunate circumstances when he became involved with a considerably younger woman whose family pursued him to do the honourable thing. He was so embarrassed by it and wanting to avoid a scandal for the Emperor, that he committed suicide.

Standart served as a minelayer and was damaged during the siege of Leningrad. After the war it served as a training ship and was again renamed, this time to Oka in 1957. The ship was finally retired from service in 1963 and scrapped at Tallinn, Estonia. Such an ignoble end given by a Soviet Union far removed from its own history. Before construction of the Imperial yachts a model was made in the scale of 1:96 by the modelmakers of Burmeister & Wain. *Standart*'s model is housed at the Burmeister & Wain Museum in Copenhagen. Another impressive model is the intricate gold worked Fabergé surprise in the Standart Fabergé Egg (1909).

THE STANDART FABERGÉ EGG

Alexandra received the Fabergé Standart Egg for Easter 1909. It containing a miniature three inch long (8cm) replica model crafted by Fabergé's most skilful craftsman Henrik Wigström in pure gold and platinum. It rests on a sea of rock crystal cocooned in a transparent shell with a double headed eagle on each end in reference to the figure on Standart's bow. It rests on its stand held up by the tails of two dolphins. It is housed at the Armoury Museum of the State Museum of the Moscow Kremlin.

CHAPTER X

Nicholas and Alexandra on the Standart.
A rare photograph of them smiling together.

Marie and Anastasia reading above deck on the Standart,
a favourite pass-time. Can you spot the camera?

THE IMPERIAL YACHT STANDART

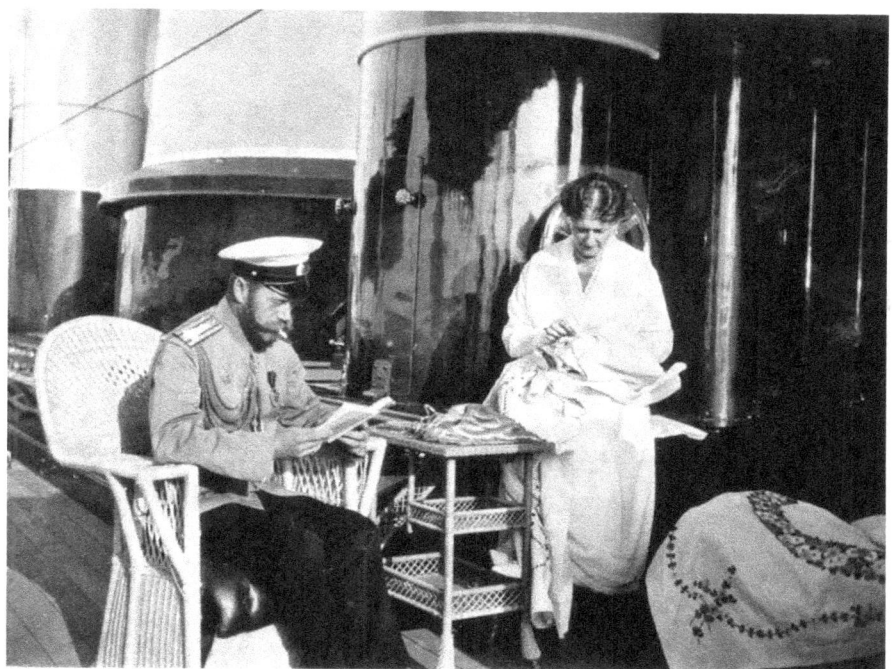
Nichola II reading and Alexandra sewing on the deck of Standart

Alexei on the deck of Standart with his toy yacht c1908

CHAPTER X

The crew of Standart in the ship's mess having dinner

Nicholas II with sister Olga Alexandrovna and his daughters on an excursion to 'Standart Island' on the Finnish Archipelago, 1911

CHAPTER XI
Mad Monks & Hypnotism

NOT long after Dr Botkin's letter to his brother, in November 1909, Iliodor was having some problems with the authorities and Rasputin gave him shelter at his home in Pokrovskoe. On the journey Rasputin began telling the most monstrous stories of which Iliodor says he corroborated personally. "... *the whole story of which in all its details he described to me in the most shameless way.*" They stopped along the way to rest at Tyumen for the night. There Rasputin came upon a nun that he had once met on a pilgrimage and a trunk-maker Dmitri Dmitrievitch who had a good looking wife. Iliodor was left to his own devices and later learned that Rasputin had been alone with the trunk-maker's wife for several hours and had stayed out all night thereafter, presumably with the nun.

Iliodor stayed with Rasputin for Christmas and one evening, Rasputin full of drink boasted of kissing the Tsarina and of his sexual exploits and influence over the Imperial Family. Iliodor didn't believe him so Rasputin produced a stack of letters from a trunk that he had received from Alexandra and her daughters. They were affectionately written but he chose to boast of sexual connotations. At this, Iliodor's temper flared and he removed himself immediately back to Tsaritsyn in an outrage, vowing to do something about Rasputin's indiscretion and disrespect for the monarchy. In the final quarter of 1911 hectographed copies of these intimate letters started appearing in the newspapers and the story goes that Iliodor had stolen a few in the night to prove that Alexandra and Rasputin were lovers, although he always denied ever being in possession of such letters.

They were apparently love letters between Alexandra and Rasputin but of course in reality they were nothing of the sort and innocently toned in harmony with the fondness Alexandra used in all her letters. There were altogether seven, including a few written by the children expressing their adoration. The publishers were never found but the original letters were retrieved and given to Nicholas who confirmed their authenticity. The famed letter of 7 February 1909 from Alexandra is usually quoted because in it she mentions that she loves him. In another account Iliodor handed the letters to Nicholas and then met Alexandra at Ms Vyrubova's house and threatened to publish them if she continued to befriend Rasputin. The most likely scenario is that Iliodor stole a sampling of the letters and sold them to the highest bidder for personal gain and to stitch up Rasputin with whom he had fallen out.

Rasputin's behaviour was seemingly connected to his frequent intoxication. A BBC radio interview with Louisa Andrews who had known Rasputin when she worked for an aristocratic family was asked, *"What was Rasputin like?"* and she replied succinctly, *"If he wasn't drunk, he was alright."* Alcohol was his drug of choice and the root cause of his troubles.

Between the First Revolution 1905 and 1911 it was a time of great divide among the State, the people and the Church. Pyotr Stolypin was a statesman during which time he was a supporter of the autocratic system attempting to find compromises between all sides. One of the fundamental debates was around the institutional racism that existed and rather worryingly much of it originating from the Orthodox Church. Stolypin stressed that the Church needed to be tolerant of rival denominations but instead it was siding more and more with the right wing Black Hundred (the pro-anarchistic and antisemite group,) with many clerics constantly attacking the government and the Duma.

Iliodor was one such monk that went a little overboard even for the Holy Synod. In 1906 he chose his side and published material criticising the Jews and the Church and called for a reinstatement of the death penalty to address those who would oppose the state. The Tsar and Rasputin did not think too much about it at the time but the Church did and called for his dismissal. By 1909 Rasputin had the special favour of the Imperial couple and was highly influential in Church matters whereas Iliodor was embroiled in this stand against the Church. Rasputin arranged for Iliodor to meet with Alexandra at Ms Vyrubova's house in Tsarskoe Selo to talk things over. She was not impressed and confronted him saying that his actions were a threat to the Tsar's authority at which Iliodor agreed to back off. Nicholas was impressed at how well the matter had been handled and asked Rasputin if he would talk to Bishop Hermogenes of Saratov who was also behaving roguish.

1909 was to be another extremely busy year for the Imperial couple and as they set out on their state visits, Rasputin went to Saratov in September 1909 to deal with Hermogenes. The two men got on well at first and Rasputin had the impression that everything had been sorted out and that Hermogenes too had been satiated and so he returned the 380 miles south to Tsaritsyn to check up on Iliodor whom he found still to be contented. That was until Iliodor caught him kissing some women and became angered. Although Iliodor had stopped openly protesting against the authorities the

Church used the tsar's absence to press for the removal of Iliodor to a much quieter region, deep in Siberia. But with Rasputin to protect him that didn't get far.

Understanding the vulnerabilities of Iliodor and Hermogenes, in having fallen out of favour with the Tsar and the Church, Rasputin set about trying to help them in order to gain their loyalty. He told Iliodor that he would arrange with the Church for him to stay in Tsaritsyn and gave Hermogenes a similar assurance. But no sooner was Nicholas back at Alexander Palace in December 1909, while Iliodor was staying in Pokrovskoe with Rasputin, than complaints about Rasputin were on his desk and this time there were too many to ignore.

During 1909, having taken no heed of the investigation in to his conduct of 1907, Rasputin had set off on another path of debauchery in his private life. M. V Rodzianko during the third Duma wrote in his book *The Reign of Rasputin* on page 8, "*I had in my possession scores of letters from mothers whose daughters had been seduced by Rasputin.*" Alexandra was apparently not remotely interested as godly saints can do no wrong but an ecclesiastical court was interested and summoned Rasputin to explain his behaviour towards the women that had brought forward serious complaints of rape.

LTR: Rasputin, Bishop Hermogenes, Bishop Iliodor, Tsaritsyn 1909

CHAPTER XI

This time Rasputin was at a disadvantage, during his extended time away from the court he could not now easily call on the Imperial couple to rescue him and in any case, he could not defend the allegations and neither would palace aides involve themselves in any such connivance. Theophane, the Imperial couple's beloved priest, banished Rasputin for one year to a monastery outside of St Petersburg. It seemed as though this time the Holy Synod had secured the tsar's support but Rasputin wrote to the Tsar rather arrogantly explaining that his spiritual followers could not be separated from him for that long and Nicholas recalled him to the capital.

His vulgarities had become evident to all but Nicholas and Alexandra. Having seduced a mother and her daughter simultaneously at the baths, the news of Rasputin's sexual depravity spread throughout St Petersburg. Like painters of the early seventeenth century who became aggressive and unpredictable from heavy metal poisoning, Rasputin's behaviour was likewise unexplainable, the only elucidation being his frequent intoxication. He does not portray a bad man and his biography could equally describe a good man, but when he was drunk even rape was not beyond him, an act that can only ever be regarded as a heinous crime and ergo he was a beast.

Rasputin was sufficiently astute to behave himself accordingly around the Imperial couple and never to cross the line. Others were not so taken in by his ways and attempted to bring him to task, usually without any success. His enemies were growing and he was being watched constantly by those wanting to catch him in the act of something or other. The police were observing his frequenting of bathhouses to meet aristocratic women and prostitutes which was in itself strange as he purposefully resisted bathing or fresh clothes in his religious beliefs and avoided touching his own flesh to stave temptations; his twisted logic was its own curiosity and quite bizarre.

Following the assassination attempt on Pyotr Stolypin on 26 August 1906, Nicholas had convinced Stolypin to utilise Rasputin's healing services after his daughter had been disabled by the bomb. Stolypin took over as Prime Minister after Goremykin's resignation on 21 July 1906 (J) and continued as Minister of the Interior making him the most powerful politician in Russian history. Having taken Nicholas' advice, Rasputin turned up and attempted to hypnotise him, which Stolypin reported to the Tsar and thereafter put a watch on him.

Of the women that had approached Theophane, he first heard from Khioniya Berlatskaya in 1909 accusing Rasputin of raping her. Theophane felt some guilt as he'd presented Rasputin to the Montenegrin sisters in 1903 after they had returned from Compiègne. He also helped introduce Rasputin to various salons in St Petersburg, not least the Imperial couple themselves. Berlatskaya was one of Rasputin's earliest followers and was shaken enough to have gone to Theophane for redress. Then there was the woman from Kazan (where Rasputin had driven the prostitute through the street.) who described in a letter to Theophane some of Rasputin's perversions and brought the vilest charges against him. There were others that came forward and an embittered Theophane resolved to turn against Rasputin, which, at that time was not a fruitful or wise thing to contemplate.

> [RASPUTIN] *"... was quite considerate of his wife. They lived in sincere friendship and never quarrelled. When Praskovaya* [Rasputin's wife] *was showing a couple around Pokrovskoe one day, they came upon her husband 'exorcising a demon' – that is having sex with a female devotee. The visitors were appalled, but Praskovaya was not surprised or even displeased."*
> — ARON SIMANOVICH, Rasputin's financial secretary

With Rasputin back in the capital creating his own mischief, Iliodor was likewise continuing to attract influence in Tsaritsyn. Having told Iliodor that he would help him, Rasputin then persuaded Nicholas to investigate him, suggesting that the young Captain Alexander Mandryka be sent to Tsaritsyn to evict Iliodor for good. Why Rasputin did this is unknown and appears to be out of revenge for Iliodor having chastised him in December 1909 in Pokrovskoe. By Rasputin's arrangement, Captain Mandryka was to be met at the nearby Balashevskaya Convent where Rasputin had a hold on the Mother Superior. On Mandryka's arrival she was delayed in town and he was able to talk with the nuns unsupervised and was shocked when they revealed Rasputin's frequent visits, bathing with the younger sisters and seducing them, even engaging in orgies. They would wash his genitals whilst he boasted of his sexual exploits with the Tsarina. The nuns told him this had been happening for some time. Having found all he needed Mandryka rushed back to Alexander Palace and presented his written report to Nicholas and Alexandra on 10 February 1910. This time the Imperial couple were angered and took note but did nothing about it.

Rasputin learned about Mandryka's fateful visit, presumably from the Mother Superior and stayed away from the palace, waiting for them to make the next move and fearing that he had finally pushed the boat out too far. Meanwhile at the palace, in the early spring of 1910, the governess of the girls since 1907, Sophie Tyutcheva, discussed with Nicholas' sister Xenia Alexandrovna that Rasputin was visiting the children's rooms at bedtimes when they were in their night gowns which she found unsettling with Olga not yet fifteen and Tatiana just thirteen years old. Xenia discussed it with her sister Olga Alexandrovna who then brought it up with Alexandra.

In another account in March 1910 Alexandra learned that Rasputin had taken advantage of Olga and Tatiana. That source was perhaps being a tad exuberant exemplifying yet another instance of elaborating historical events by introducing conflict to sell books and there is no mention of anyone being

CHAPTER XI

taken advantage of in the actual recorded conversations at that time, only of there being a concern about Rasputin and perhaps some conjecture was also involved. What exactly was said between them may never be known outside of the letter between Xenia and Olga, but the sisters disapproval is known as demonstrated in the extract below:

> "...*the attitude of the Tsarina and the Grand Duchesses to that sinister Grigory, whom they consider to be almost a saint. He's always there, going to the nursery, he sits there talking to them and caressing them. They are careful to hide him from Sofia Ivanovna* [TYUYCHEVA] *and the children don't dare talk to her about him. It's all quite unbelievable and beyond understanding.*"
> — XENIA letter to her sister OLGA, c1907

Reacting to the letter, Olga visited Nicholas at Alexander Palace and he took her to the children's nursery to see them. They were comfortably in their nightgowns with Rasputin sitting among them. That was the first time Olga had met Rasputin and noted the children appeared to be completely at ease with him. Nicholas spoke with Rasputin after that and the practice of him visiting the girl's bedroom stopped. However, Tyutcheva's accusations were not believed and her approach to Xenia was not appreciated by Alexandra. Her position became tenuous and she was forced to resign in 1912 and her connection to the court was severed. Her memoirs written in 1945 offer another valuable insight including the Imperial couple's visits to England and Kiel; *A Few Years Before the Catastrophe: The memoirs of Sofia Ivanovna Tyutcheva*. And yet again, like so many memoirs of the period the reader remains the final arbiter in determining the extent of the truth, as in this case some suspicions are cast by Buxhoeveden.

> "*Mlle. Tyutcheva did not stay many years, however, she and the Empress disagreed on the subject of Rasputin. Mlle. Tyutcheva was deeply distressed at leaving, as she had got to love her charges. She was the unconscious originator of many false legends about the Court. What she said carelessly was twisted and turned into marvellous stories, which did the Empress a great deal of harm.*"
> — SOPHIE BUXHOEVEDEN

Indeed, in determining the likelihood of Tyutcheva's account the case is strengthened with other concurrences or corroborations. Also in 1910, Maria Vishnyakova, nursemaid first to the girls and then to Alexei from 1905, told Alexandra that she had been raped by Rasputin at the palace. She was another of Rasputin's devotees and had gone to Pokrovskoe with Ms Vyrubova where Rasputin had tried to lay with her. Predictably, Alexandra didn't believe her and apparently insisted that everything Rasputin did was holy. Vishnyakova was monitored, some might say set up, even Olga Alexandrovna reported that Vishnyakova had been caught in the bed of a Cossack of the Imperial Guard. Discredited, she was sent to a sanatorium in the Caucasus where she met Bishop Anthony of Tobolsk (a member of the Holy Synod 1912-1916). She told him what had happened to her and he travelled to see Nicholas who promptly told him to mind his own business. Vishnyakova was quietly retired in 1913 and left St Petersburg for good.

Gossip was rife in 1910 when the Moscow Gazette launched the first of many press campaigns against Rasputin. One report displeased him, saying that he was only fit to scrub the palace toilets and that was the only thing the Imperial couple should use him for. On 30 April 1910 the Moscow News called for the Holy Synod to investigate Rasputin with the editor Lev Tikhomirov citing Theophane as his direct source for the concerns that Rasputin was receiving money for favours from women that asked him to advance their husband's careers.

He would get the Tsar to approve this and that and sometimes took sexual favours for payment and blackmailed others. This was to continue right up to the outbreak of world War I when the going rate to keep from being sent to the front was the equivalent of around £200. This money stream is probably accurate as Rasputin was fastidious in his recording of monetary transactions. The extract below from a blackmail letter from Rasputin was published by William Le Queux demonstrating his shameless effrontery, but keep in mind that this author was known for his exaggerations and untruths, so how reliable can it be.

> *"Friend,—It is now many days since His Majesty appointed you Privy Councillor of the Empire, but I have received no word from you or from your bank as we arranged. If I receive nothing by next Thursday, the facts concerning your son's implication in the Platanoff affair (the blowing up of a Russian battleship in the Baltic by German agents) will be passed on to the Admiralty. If double the sum we arranged passes to my bank before the date I have named, I shall remain silent. If not, I shall take immediate action.— G"*
> — WILLIAM LE QUEUX, Rasputin the rascal monk

The newspapers exposing Rasputin's sexual antics during 1910 had done no real damage, as his licentious behaviour and the skulduggery at Tsaritsyn was already known to the Imperial couple. His enemies always devising ways to denounce him, paid a Finnish ballerina to invite him to her house where she got him drunk; so drunk that he was stripped and positioned among prostitutes and a series of compromising photographs were taken. In due course there came a knock on the door and Rasputin was handed an envelope containing the photographs with a warning to leave St Petersburg or they would be given to the Tsar. Having nowhere to turn Rasputin handed the envelope to the tsar himself declaring that he'd been set up in a move to dislodge him from the Tsar's favour. Nicholas suggested that he go on a long pilgrimage to the Holy Land and even paid for the trip.

Meanwhile in Tsaritsyn (later renamed Stalingrad and then since 1961 to Volgograd) Iliodor had increased his following and his sermons turned to criticism of the government and individual ministers. The Holy Synod had made several attempts to deal with him but were obstructed by his high ranking allies in the Tsar and Rasputin but by 1911 his constant attacks on Prime Minister Stolypin formed a part of the terrorism that would eventually lead to Stolypin's assassination in September 1911. This placed the Tsar in a predicament and with the state and Church being unified against Iliodor, Iliodor once more turned to Rasputin, but Rasputin had been sent on pilgrimage for his own wrongdoings leaving Iliodor to fend for himself.

Iliodor had taken things too far this time. His followers barricaded themselves inside the Tsaritsyn monastery in protest against the authorities and refused to stop the protest which in truth was only about Iliodor trying to prevent the Church from removing him to Siberia. While people gathered at the monastery to support Iliodor, he continued to denounce Stolypin and the Church, indeed he called for the Prime Minister to be flogged, while protestors armed themselves with weapons. How fortunate that Nicholas backed down and allowed Iliodor to stay in Tsaritsyn fearing that another bloody massacre might ensue like Bloody Sunday, and thereby he obstructed the Holy Synod yet again from taking action against Iliodor.

Rasputin returns from Pilgrimage (1911)

In March 1911, Rasputin and a group of Russian pilgrims journeyed to the Holy Land. First they went west to the Holy Dormition monastery of Pochayevsk Lavra in Ukraine and from there to the Sophia Cathedral in Constantinople where they crossed in to the Mediterranean and sailed by the islands of Rhodes and Cyprus to land at the port of Jaffa. They travelled directly to Nazareth finally arriving in Jerusalem. It was a rather nicer form of exile that Rasputin had been used to with Nicholas having funded the trip and on his return Rasputin had a journal book made of his experiences as a gift for Nicholas and Alexandra.

Alexandra's uncle King Edward VII died in May 1910 and having not long since returned from England the Imperial couple sent a contingent to Westminster Abbey for the coronation for George V and Mary of Teck in June 1911 and not least because Alexandra's health would not permit her to travel. Therefore the Imperial Family were at home in Alexandra Palace when Rasputin returned from the Holy Land. First he stopped at Tsaritsyn to catch up with Iliodor and where Hermogenes happened to be staying. He planned to nurture their support by picking up where they had left off before he had been banished on pilgrimage. He found himself sharing a room at the Balashevskaya Convent with Hermogenes when in the middle of the night Rasputin slipped out and Hermogenes followed him and caught him seducing the wife of a priest who was away on business. Hermogenes resolved at that moment to side with Iliodor in doing something about this sexual pest once and for all.

Nicholas may have financed the pilgrimage but it had been Stolypin in early 1911 that strengthened it by banning Rasputin from the capital because of the overwhelming evidence of his scandals. Nicholas detested Stolypin for having cleverly steered this outcome thereby also preventing Rasputin's return. It was not until Stolypin's assassination in September 1911 that Rasputin dared to venture back to St Petersburg. The reader will recall (Chapter VIII – Rasputin,) that Bishop Theophane received Rasputin at St. Petersburg in 1903 and introduced him to the Church elders such as Father John of Kronstadt, a controversial figure heavily in to hypnotism who was singularly impressed and provided letters of introduction to the high society salons. Through Theophane and Madame Lochtina, Rasputin had met the Montenegrin sisters and whether through them or his own devices came upon their mutual acquaintance Anna Taneyeva in 1905. This time Rasputin needed only to visit her for a new opportunity to reconnect with the Imperial Family. If anything, he was adept at getting back on his feet, being that he habitually fell out of favour.

Rasputin was therefore back in St Petersburg nearing the end of 1911 and the opportunity also arose for Iliodor and Hermogenes to do something about him. Of course the conversation was still about the letters which were circulating in the newspapers, which precluded any contact with the palace. Nicholas and Alexandra tolerated Rasputin, such were the high hopes for their son's healing but they were not blind to his appearance and behaviour and Rasputin would have been repugnant to them in spite of the evidence portraying their respect and adoration for him. Rumours of an affair between Rasputin and Alexandra and the insinuations made from the published letters had crossed a line.

Rasputin accused Iliodor of having stolen the letters at Pokrovskoe and passing them to his enemies or there is another account that Iliodor passed the letters to Hermogenes for him to decide what to do with them. Another account is that Rasputin himself showed the letters to people and wilfully released them to the newspapers to incriminate Iliodor. Finally, the supposition is that Rasputin leaked the letters to raise funds for his return to St Petersburg as he could not expect any hospitality from the Church. An investigation was held by the head of the police department, A. T. Vasiliev,

CHAPTER XI

in which he stated there was nothing compromising in the correspondence and confirmed that no additional letters were being held by Rasputin. Alexandra was extremely offended by it all and sent a telegram to Pokrovskoe reprimanding Rasputin and refused to see him when he did appear at the palace to discuss the matter. Vasiliev was to examine the evidence again in 1913 and confirmed his initial findings.

In the 1920s Lili Dehn wrote a biography called *The Real Tsaritza* to refute the hearsay about the supposed relationship between Alexandra and Rasputin. Then there's the letter from political activist and writer Maxim Gorky to his friend Alexander Amfiteatrov that suggested Alexei was Rasputin's son. That was an impossibility seeing that Rasputin was nowhere near the court before Alexei was born. The French Ambassador Maurice Paléologue spent ten months in Russia and one thing that truly amazed him was the freedom with which the Imperial Family were openly discussed without fear of retribution.

LTR: Ms Vyrubova (lady in waiting), Rasputin, Tamara Antonovna Rodzianka lady in waiting whose first husband (1901-1910) was Colonel Pavel Rodzianko

The gossip was taking its toll on Alexandra's health. She would never come to terms with how her family could interest the whole country, especially about Alexei when he was ill, *"It is my personal business ... I wish people would not meddle in my affairs,"* she would say. Rasputin had done a lot of damage to Alexandra's reputation and the people blamed her for everything that was wrong in the country; including a useless heir to the throne. In November 1911, the newly built Livadia Palace had just been completed and Olga Nikolaevna celebrated her sixteenth birthday there. At the party Olga Voronova (the woman that married the man Olga Nikolaevna fell in love with) recorded Alexandra's condition in her diary:

"The Empress appeared only after dinner. She suffered frequently from her heart, receptions were a strain on her, and the eternal anxiety about her son made her long to avoid appearing in public. Her face usually wore an expression of weariness and sadness which 'society' took for coldness and haughtiness on her part and sulked. This caused much of her unpopularity, which natural timidity increased, and misunderstanding led to a feeling of bitterness on each side." — COUNTESS OLGA VORONOVA

Hermogenes and Iliodor set a trap for Rasputin in December 1911. Iliodor was in St Petersburg attempting to resolve the issue of the Church wanting to remove him from Tsaritsyn when Rasputin telephoned him to arrange to meet up. Iliodor suggested Vasilievsky Island, at the residence of Hermogenes. In this plot to lure Rasputin, Iliodor would disavow any complicity in his future book. On 16 December 1911 Iliodor and Rasputin arrived at the residence of Hermogenes and on entering the reception room Hermogenes was standing there in his vestments holding a large cross. With him were Colonel Ivan Rodionov and Dmitry Kolyaba. Hermogenes accused Rasputin of raping women, being a drunkard, undermining the Imperial Family and of involvement with the Khlysty.

In his memoirs Iliodor describes the moment when Hermogenes grilled Rasputin over the rape of a nun, *"Oh, you ungodly man, why did you torture so that poor, innocent girl, the nun Xenia?"* To which Rasputin replied *"I did not torture her, I relieved her."* Rasputin would often convince women that by giving themselves to him they were passing on their sins and being freed from their carnal desires. It was a measure of how great the man truly was that he was prepared to do that for any woman requiring sexual relief.

The assailants dragged Rasputin to the nearby chapel and forced him to agree to stay away from the Imperial Court. The story goes that they grabbed his penis threatening to cut it off if he forced himself on to another woman again. Hermogenes instructed him to confess his sins and then to leave Russia and not return for a period of not less than three years.

CHAPTER XI

Rasputin was furious and the minute he was freed headed straight for Ms Vyrubova's house and arranged for an audience the following morning with Nicholas and Alexandra and told them everything that had happened. The Procurator of the Holy Synod deprived Hermogenes of his See and sent him to a distant monastery in Khirovitsy, Lithuania. The man that had once been described by Duma President Rodzianko as, *"having no more than average intelligence,"* had succeeded in removing the most powerful bishop in the Russian Orthodox Church.

Meanwhile, Bishop Theophane had gathered more sexual complaints against Rasputin including the statements from Sophie Tyutcheva, Maria Vishniakova, Miss Timofeyev, Khioniya Berlatzkaya, the nun Xenia Goncharova, Helen (a coachman's wife), A. Vostrikova (a priest's wife) and her sister Madame Bourkova and her daughter Madame Vargoun, Madame Golovkova, A. M. Lebedeva (a shopkeeper), Madame Lochtina's daughter Lada, et al.

Bishop Theophane 1912

The Montenegrin sisters now joined with Theophane's concern and visited Alexandra to advise her about Theophane's evidence. Not only did Alexandra reject everything but she instructed the sisters not to mention Rasputin to her again. Ms Vyrubova, advancing her own and Rasputin's agenda advised Alexandra that the Montenegrin sisters and Theophane were no longer of any consequence at the court. Rather bizarrely Alexandra then cut the Montenegrins out of her family circle entirely and Theophane despite his written testimonies and the fact that he was their confessor, was exiled to Crimea.

The court, government ministers, Duma representatives, and Church leaders, could all see the influence Rasputin had attained. It was in part due to Nicholas' feebleness around his wife who only became more emblazoned with the notion that she knew better how to handle things as time went on. She had made enemies of the ministers among them Stolypin and Witte, the two most prominent ministerial servants whom she felt Nicholas wasn't firm enough with.

In a conversation between the French Ambassador Paléologue and Madame Blavatsky, at which he marvelled at the frankness with which Blavatsky spoke of her emperor, she said to him, *"He is mortally afraid of Witte, he'll never have the courage to deal with him. ... He's always been the same since the beginning of his reign; he has neither courage or will. No, he hasn't an ounce of will. How could he expect to have, seeing that he hasn't the slightest personality."*

Count Witte was fully aware of Alexandra's negative attitude towards him personally, or as he put it, *"I am aware of having been the object of Alexandra's particular enmity."* This, Witte attributed to an incident that had happened at Livadia in the autumn of 1900 when Nicholas was laid up with typhoid fever. He was attended to by court doctor Girsh, a man without any formal medical qualifications that Nicholas had inherited from his father.

Court physicians needed to be always present, usually living at the palace and travelling with the monarch. A medical career could be ruined over a sudden illness when a doctor was not on hand. Maria Feodorovna suffered from nausea during her pregnancies and Girsh had advised her to eat raw ham in bed each morning, such was his way. He was insistent that Nicholas did not have typhoid fever, yet the family wanted a second opinion and a physician was sent for from St Petersburg.

> *"Girsh is adamant, that it isn't typhoid, we asked him. Girsh asked Nicky to call someone else, to put everyone's mind at rest - it was decided to call for Tikhonov."* — XENIA ALEXANDROVNA, diary 27 October 1900

Those that happened to be there when Nicholas fell ill, Witte included, discussed what would happen in the eventuality of the Emperor dying. The first suggestion was to make Alexandra regent in consideration that she could be carrying an heir, as it was thought that she may currently be with child. Indeed, she was already three months pregnant in December 1900, when Nicholas was at the most dangerous point of the disease, having conceived in September with Anastasia who was due to be born in June 1901. Witte was against the suggestion and convinced the others, chiefly the Ministers for the court, interior, exterior, and Grand Duke Mikhail Nikolaevich, to stick to the Pauline law which extended the succession to the next male in line, that is, Nicholas' brother Mikhail Alexandrovich. All those present agreed. The success of Witte's intervention was interpreted by Alexandra as an underhand move against her future son and Witte believed this to be the source of the animosity she held against him.

"Girsh is adamant, that it isn't typhoid, we asked him. Girsh asked Nicky to call someone else, to put everyone's mind at rest - it was decided to call for Tikhonov." — XENIA ALEXANDROVNA, diary 27 October 1900

Eventually the scandalous tales about Rasputin compelled Prime Minister Vladimir Kokovtzev (previously the Finance Minister and the successor of Stolypin since his assassination,) to report Rasputin's sordid actions to Nicholas and to advise that Rasputin's connection with the Imperial Court was damaging the monarchy. Nicholas saw no alternative but to remove Rasputin once more from the court and sent him back to Pokrovskoe where he was told to remain indefinitely.

Proof of Haemophilia

For the first quarter of 1912 Rasputin remained back in Pokrovskoe in exile until the Imperial Family's yearly trip to Livadia when Ms Vyrubova stowed him on the Imperial train assuming that he would be forgiven in the Easter spirit, a traditional time for forgiveness. When she eventually told Nicholas he stopped the train at the next station and threw Rasputin and his luggage off the train. Undeterred Rasputin continued the journey by other means but was turned away at Livadia Palace and he returned to Pokrovskoe to sink in to the bottle and contemplate his strategy.

When Alexei was born Ms Vyrubova had described the baby as *"beautiful, healthy, normal,"* but her observations were not correct and the child was anything but healthy. It was a ridiculous situation for the crown, the heir apparent could not outlive his father short of an assassination and there had been no spare heir produced. Alexandra's denial that there was a problem with Alexei only strengthened as he grew and suffered fewer life-threatening haemophilic attacks.

Nicholas II recovering from typhoid fever at Livadia Palace, December 1900. Known as 'the illness that did not discriminate' his uncle Edward VII contracted it while staying in Scarborough and it was the disease believed to have killed Edward's father, Prince Albert. Nicholas' father and grandmother had it, sister Xenia had it in the winter of 1888 and daughter Olga Nikolaevna would contract it in the spring of 1901.

Alexandra attended to Nicholas tirelessly and it was another example of how her own ails would vanish when she had something else more serious to worry about, like the threat that her husband could be dying from typhoid fever. Xenia Alexandrovna noted in her diary for 27 October 1900 (J) *"Poor Alix has forgotten about her own sickness and is moving around more."* In general, Nicholas exercised well and was rarely ill. In later years under house arrest he ordered a horizontal bar to be placed in his bathroom so he could keep in shape and later set it up in the exercise yard at Tobolsk.

CHAPTER XI

"Alexei was told constantly that his existence was precious but the truth was finally dawning that there was little hope that he would reach manhood, and this knowledge impelled heartfelt sympathy towards his parents, who, after having longed for so many years for the birth of this heir, now had to resign themselves to the probability that his days were numbered." — PIERRE GILLIARD, memoirs

Letters between Nicholas and Alexandra have been translated and published and offer a first hand account of the extent of Rasputin's influence over them. But it is their diaries that interestingly do not make the slightest mention of a blood disorder problem for Alexei. What references there are about his condition suggest that the problem was related to blood vessels and not actually to do with the blood itself. This is why for a long time some accounts suggested that he didn't have haemophilia but a lesser disorder of the blood vessels.

"The Tsarevich certainly suffered from the hereditary trouble of thin blood vessels which first became apparent after a fall at Spala, but he was otherwise a normally healthy boy." — LILI DEHN

"The child had a rare disease. The blood vessels were affected, so that the patient bled at the slightest touch." — ANNA VYRUBOVA,
(from an interview after the abdication of Nicholas II)

Perhaps doctors and family members referred to Alexei's condition in terms of bleeding caused by abnormal blood vessels, through ignorance or in pandering to Alexandra's hope that the underlying cause was curable. They were all fully aware that Alexei had the royal disease. In years to come, with the development of biological technology, Alexei's remains were analysed for mitochondrial DNA, which revealed a causal substitution in the splice acceptor site of exon 4 in the F9 gene. This mutation is responsible for haemophilia B thereby proving that Alexei did indeed suffer from haemophilia. Things revolved around the denial that Alexei had the disease and it left outsiders and even close family members without any confirmation of Alexei's true condition and were compelled to refer to the ailment as a constriction of the blood vessels.

The name of the disease comes from the German word hämophile, originating from the Greek 'haima' meaning blood. Philia means 'to love', so haemophilia means literally 'a love of blood' and it was named in 1828 at the University of Zuric. Unfortunately, no one was permitted to use that term in Russia on pain of imprisonment. In 1803 American doctor John Conrad Otto reported that haemophilia was hereditary and mainly affected males and was transmitted by healthy women. Prince Leopold was the first of the British royal family to present with haemophilia and he died in 1873, at thirty years old. He was the reason that Queen Victoria had known that her granddaughter Alexandra was a potential carrier. Queen Victoria finally did admit that her family had the disease called haemophilia and towards the end of her life would have also realised that she alone was responsible for passing the disease around the royal houses of Europe.

> *"Our poor family seems persecuted by this awful disease, the worst I know."* — QUEEN VICTORIA, 1900

Spala 1912 – Rasputin Returns Again

The word Spala loosely means 'sleeping' so this is the 'sleeping lodge' or resting place. Another account attributes the name to a previous owner, a saw-miller Marcin Spala, which if he did exist is the obvious explanation. The region is dominated by plains, hills and forest, that are ideal for hunting. Alexander III built the complex in 1885 that encompassed a wooden palace, military barracks, guest houses, and even a casino, all within a landscaped park. Each year the last trip before Christmas was a stay in Spala.

Byelovvyezh hunting lodge, Spala, Poland

Alexei was climbing out of a boat when he stumbled and knocked the inside of his leg on the oar lock which caused bruising and swelling. Dr Botkin examined it and sent him to bed for some days until the swelling went down. But the pain didn't leave him and on further examination a haemorrhage was found in the left thigh and torn vessels in the leg.

CHAPTER XI

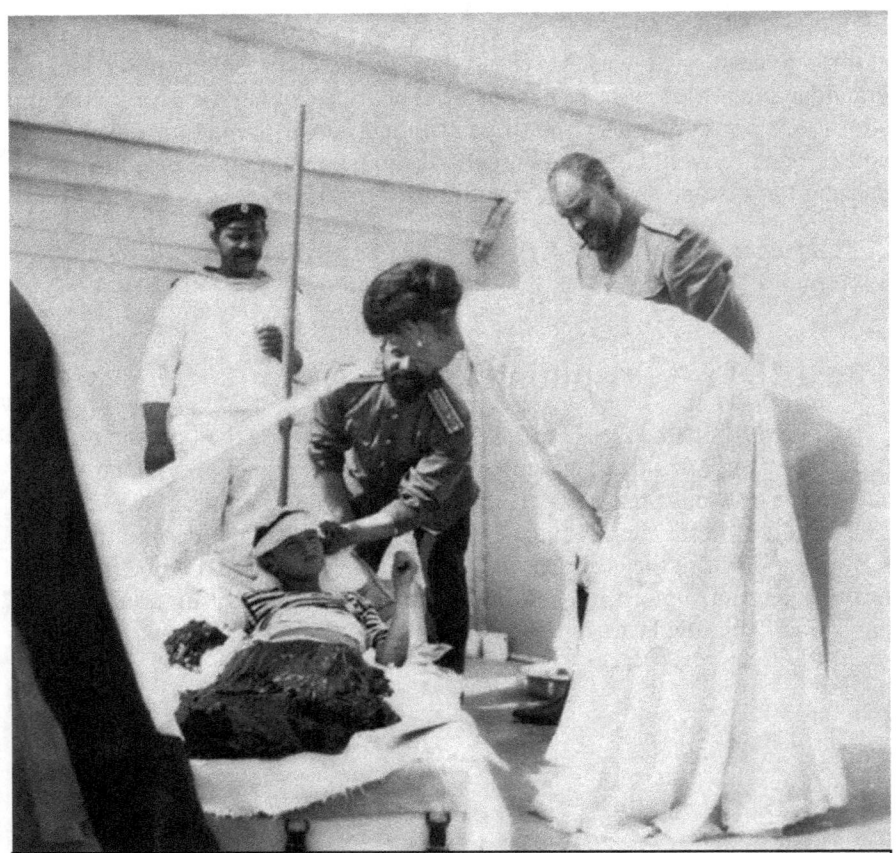

Alexandra checks on Alexei resting on his orthopaedic bed, taking a mud bath to treat his legs following the accident at Spala in 1912 which made them rigid. The mud was specially imported for its curative properties. This image of Alexei is on the following year after the boating accident at Livadia Palace 1913.

Alexei's agony was intense, he would become delirious screaming with agony as his legs stopped working and the haemorrhage moved to his abdomen (or kidney in one account). Dr Botkin summoned the best doctors but they were no wiser to it. The situation seemed dire and it began to look like nothing could prevent a slow death. Alexandra was at his bedside not able to sleep at night, for days on end. The bleeding could not be controlled and became so bad that she arranged for the first draft of his death announcement to be prepared and he received the sacrament of Anointing of the Sick (i.e. the Last Rites).

Alexandra had become overly worried about the slightest thing ever since Alexei's head injury at Reval but this time it was evidently more serious and having insisted for eight years that Alexei's haemophilia be kept secret, now for the first time the illness was publicly announced in anticipation of his death. She asked Ms Vyrubova to send a telegram to Rasputin asking for his prayers who replied immediately from Pokrovskoe, 2,000 miles away:

"God has seen your tears and heard your prayers. Do not grieve. The little one will not die. Do not allow the doctors to bother him too much."
— RASPUTIN, telegram to Alexandra, 1912

Alexei also complained of an earache that was preventing him from sleeping and over the telephone Rasputin told him that he didn't have earache and to go to bed and ignore the pain. Rasputin received a call fifteen minutes later to inform that Alexei had fallen asleep. The next day the fever which had been worsening for eight days suddenly abated and the bleeding inexplicably ceased and Alexei recovered. He was to remain crippled for most of the next year but he survived and Alexandra was left with no doubt that Rasputin was her heaven sent saviour. Alexandra had returned Rasputin to St Petersburg officially and his place by their side was secured as the story of Rasputin's deed spread throughout Russia. All hopes for the heir apparent were now pinned to one man alone who convinced Alexandra that not only Alexei but also the monarchy and Russia depended on his guidance. His control was complete and from this time on, Rasputin develops a cockiness, favouring Alexandra over Nicholas.

"The Tsarina is a painfully wise ruler, I can do everything with her, I will reach everything, and he (the Tsar) is a man of God. Well, what kind of Emperor is he? He would only play with the children, and with flowers, and deal with the garden, and not rule the kingdom."
— RASPUTIN

The Imperial Family were returning to Tsarskoe Selo on the Imperial train but they still had a final engagement that year before making their preparations for the Christmas season. It was for the centenary anniversary of the French invasion and retreat of 1812, when Napoleon invaded Russia and was repelled. In Moscow the Tsar inaugurated a monument to his farther Alexander III and in Smolensk the Tsar commemorated a famous battle there. At the famous battlefield of Borodino (about 66 miles west of Moscow) another monument was erected dedicated to the memory of the 70,000 Russian defenders that fell on the deadliest day of the entire Napoleonic Wars. For Alexandra, 1912 had turned out to be every bit as stressful as the preceding years.

CHAPTER XI

Alexandra suffered intense mental pressure over Alexei who had had his most serious episode in October at Spala. Time at Spala and Livadia had taken their toll and she slipped slowly back in to her woes and started to be seen in a wheelchair more and more until she was rarely seen out of it getting about unaided. By the end of the year both Alexandra and Alexei were getting around in wheelchairs and from November 1912 to March 1913 between Spala and Livadia Palace there would be 27 visits by Dr Federov, 15 by Dr Vreden and 124 by neurologist Dr Dmitriev to monitor Alexei.

Alexandra and Alexei in wheelchairs, Spala, November 1912

Rasputin's associates claimed that up until 1912 he scarcely touched alcohol and that there was a great change in him when the drinking started and his sexual appetite became excessive. Most accounts disagree as it's known that his life was full of drinking and womanising. Discussed earlier was that most of Rasputin's misdeeds happened when he was drinking; in one story of him he drank twelve bottles of Madeira in as many hours. It's simply untrue that he started drinking in 1912 but perhaps he did increase it while he was in exile. Maybe his home town saw him fall in to a prolonged drunken stupor after the Tsar banished him and Hermogenes had given him a severe beating, who during the attack is said to have beaten Rasputin about the head with his staff. During this time Rasputin also denounced the Church as Iliodor had done and became very embittered. It was typical of the way the man became reborn from the ashes of debauchery and he nonetheless returned to St Petersburg a changed man looking to regain his status. Within a year the Imperial couple had welcomed him back, such was their folly.

Alexei's miraculous recovery in Spala meant that Rasputin would be kept nearby, Nicholas was unwilling to separate him from Alexei again, in spite of his continued presence being an embarrassment to the Imperial couple. In 1913 Nicholas' diary suggests they were seeing Rasputin at least once or twice a month. Maria Feodorovna's impression of Alexandra had mellowed in the years since the coronation but this re-introduction of Rasputin at the palace reversed that and she was horrified at the extent that Alexandra had allowed the standing of her house to deteriorate.

"My unhappy daughter-in-law is incapable of realising that she is bringing about her own downfall and that of the dynasty. She deeply believes in the holiness of that dubious individual [RASPUTIN].*"*
— MARIA FEODOROVNA, 1913

"The children never mentioned Rasputin's name, and in my presence even avoided the slightest allusion to his existence. I realised that in so doing they were acting on their mother's instructions."
— PIERRE GILLIARD, Thirteen Years at the Russian Court

самодержавие / autocracy. In a St Petersburg magazine 1916, suggesting that Rasputin had a hold on the Empress.

CHAPTER XI

By December 1916 Alexandra's sister Elizabeth tried to warn her about Rasputin, as she had also attempted to do in a letter about Master Philippe in 1902 (*page 100*). This time Elizabeth went to Alexander Palace just days before Rasputin's murder. Was she trying to warn Alexandra to stay away from Rasputin because she knew what was about to happen? One account, from Nikolai Sokolov's book of 1925 suggests that Elizabeth had wished for a sinister outcome for Rasputin, but to her chagrin she was turned away again by Alexandra.

"In December 1916, Grand Duchess Elizabeth Feodorovna strove to avert the impending catastrophe. She came to Tsarskoe thinking of persuading the Empress to eliminate Rasputin. After the first conversation she, by order of the Empress, was given a train, and she was forced leave against her will." — NIKOLAI SOKOLOV

The Science of Hypnotism

During the time that Rasputin had been in exile he admitted that he had been losing his powers. As a boy in Pokrovskoe he was known for healing animals because he possessed a natural ability to calm them. On his return to St Petersburg he gave the outward appearance of a changed man but soon started to frequent the public baths, on some days he might meet with one or even two prostitutes there. But it was not entirely a sexual deviance because in Russian folklore the baths are places that conjure up the spirits. Rasputin would often not have sex with his bathing partners but was testing his resolve and only when he could no longer resist did he relent to the flesh.

He had no friends left in the Church and instead of seeking salvation he turned his hand to seeking out the devil and at the baths there were evil spirits to be confronted. At least that's what is reckoned was going through his head. Back in 1910 when his moral compass was being attracted by the nuns of Siberia his wife sent their daughters Maria and Varvara to stay with him at his small flat in 64 Gorochovaja Street, St Petersburg, in the hope that they might keep him grounded.

The girls were nervous when they were introduced to the Romanov girls at the palace but they hit if off straight away and the Romanovs were curious about how they lived, the names of their cows, and so forth and gifted them each a beautiful porcelain doll. Nicholas and Alexandra would tell their mother in 1917 that they considered Maria and Varvara as their own, as described in Maria's third book about her father which was published posthumously in the same year she died. (M*ore about Varvara in Chapter XIII – Rasputin is done for*). Maria was the only one to escape Russia and made it to London by 1934 and then went on to settle in America.

The books written by Matryona Grigorievna Rasputina

- ❖ 1929, *The Real Rasputin* (A strong defence of her father)
- ❖ 1932, *My Father*
- ❖ 1977, *Rasputin: The Man Behind The Myth* (biography)

When Rasputin believed his powers had left him it was probably that he failed to appreciate that he needed to start all over again from the beginning, because his method of persuading people to do his bidding relied on a lot of preparation relating to the power of suggestion which has to be implanted in to someone. Today it might be described as grooming and in this respect Rasputin had invested years of his time. His excessive drinking perhaps left him with no patience as he came to believe that his gift for persuasion was a divine power. Therefore when the fires within him calmed and the phoenix rose once more, Rasputin began with Ms Vyrubova to welcome himself back to the capital, his devotee and accomplice that always accepted his explanations for unsavoury rumours no matter how grotesque and whose house was just opposite the palace. That he was still deranged, a drunkard and a sexual pest in 1913 is certain but he returned with a level-headedness, determined to restore his former power.

On 16 July 1913 Nicholas recorded that Alexei's arm was hurting from waving it about too much when he had been playing and the pain was so great that it would not allow the poor boy to fall asleep. Rasputin arrived the next morning to see Alexei but this time he couldn't just walk in and had to wait by the gate for the sentry to clear him. Vladimir Voeikov took over palace security in 1913 and was surprised that no effort was being made to conceal these visits considering the leaked letters and the general view that Rasputin was unsavoury and disruptive. No sooner had Rasputin left the palace than the pain also left Alexei who fell straight to sleep. Was this instant recovery the same as it had been for the miraculous incident at Spala 1912, was it down to the yellow powder, did Ms Vyrubova administer a drug before Rasputin attended and was this now their modus operandi?

It's quite conceivable that Ms Vyrubova could have been coerced by Rasputin using hypnotism. Despite her devoutness to Rasputin, she was in all other respects a loyal lady in waiting and loved the Imperial Family, never having said a word against them. But she had a malleable disposition and a simple mind. The art of hypnotism and the key factors of the hypnotic process are to put the subject at ease and then to implant a suggestion. Can there be any other explanation for how Alexei fell ill and got well again other than with the use of drugs and hypnosis. Hypnotic intervention for illness and pain relief is one of the oldest adjunctive treatments in medicine and Rasputin is believed to have been an expert at it.

CHAPTER XI

Rasputin said that during the time when the Tsar had sent him away on the pilgrimage to the Holy Land, that he met many priests that passed on the old secrets to him. Hypnotism was more of a thing then than it is today, everyone messed with it. It was approved in 1955 by the British Medical Association and it's well known that psychological intervention with hypnosis shows positive results for disease management and is effective with chronic pain. Positron Emission Tomography (CAT) and Electroencephalograms (ECG) have shown that the parts of the brain that deal with pain can be affected through hypnosis and the general consensus today is that it can help decrease pain from haemophilia.

There have been many studies to link pain to stress. Hypnosis reduces pain because pain itself is caused by multiple factors, like stress. With haemophilia sufferers one of the bleeding risk factors is anxiety (Hoirisch-Clapauch, 2018). Pavel Kurlov was a former Interior Minister and head of the security guard at Tsarskoe Selo responsible for the Imperial Family's security. After he fled to Berlin in 1918 he said the following in his book:

"Rasputin has undoubtedly the ability to calm people down and beneficially influenced the underage heir during his illness."
— PAVEL KURLOV, The end of tsarist Russia

At Spala Rasputin had stopped Alexei's bleeding over the telephone; words play the major role in hypnosis and it offers the only explanation for how blood can be controlled in a haemophiliac. Dr Botkin and others were certain that he was using hypnosis on Alexei. Rasputin believed wholly in his ability to control people with his suggestive force and there's no doubting he was an expert practitioner and that many had succumbed to and many stronger-willed personalities had equally resisted. Duma President Mikhail Rodzianko in his book *The Reign of Rasputin* described what Prime Minister Stolypin told him about the time he was interrogating Rasputin at the beginning of 1911 and resisted an attempt to be hypnotised:

"He ran his pale eyes over me, mumbled mysterious and inarticulate words from the scriptures, made strange movements with his hands, and I began to feel an indescribable loathing for this vermin sitting opposite me. Still I did realise that the man possessed great hypnotic power, which was beginning to produce a fairly strong moral impression on me, though certainly one of repulsion. I pulled myself together and addressing him roughly, told him that on the strength of the evidence in my possession I could annihilate him by prosecuting him as a sectarian. I then ordered him to leave St Petersburg immediately ... and never show his face here again."
— PYOTR STOLYPIN, Minister of the Interior and future Prime Minister

In the following passage from his book, Duma President Mikhail Rodzianko describes the time he encountered Rasputin in the Cathedral of Our Lady of Kazan at the time of the tricentenary celebration where Rasputin had attempted to hypnotise him (*page 80*).

> *"Rasputin faced me, and seemed to run me over with his eyes; first my face, then in the region of the heart, then again he stared me in the eyes. This lasted for several moments. Personally I had never yielded to hypnotic suggestion, of which I had had frequent experience. Yet here I felt myself confronted by an unknown power of tremendous force. I suddenly became possessed of an almost animal fury, the blood rushed to my heart, and I realised I was working myself into a state of absolute frenzy. I, too, stared straight into Rasputin's eyes, and, speaking literally, felt my own starting out of my head."*
> — MIKHAIL RODZIANKO

Mikhail Rodzianko also described the suggestive hypnotic power of Rasputin and further ascribed the whole of Rasputin's relationship with the Imperial couple to this force.

> *"It goes therefore, without saying that the neurotic and mystically inclined Empress, whose tortured soul suffered continual agonies of fear for the fate of her son, the Heir to the Throne, and for that of her exalted husband, fell under the influence of Rasputin's hypnotism to an extraordinary degree. ... I can confidently assert that by this force of suggestion he gained absolute control over the will of the young Empress."* — MIKHAIL RODZIANKO, The reign of Rasputin (1927)

Rasputin had once asked Iliodor to persuade Hermogenes to see him. Hermogenes responded with, *"Let him come in but I shall not face him. I shall speak to him with my back turned toward him. I shall not let the curse come near me."* The curse Hermogenes referred to was Franz Mesmer's animal magnetism. Hermogenes was guarding himself against being hypnotised or mesmerised by Rasputin whom he evidently knew was skilled in its use. Iliodor describes when he ushered Rasputin in to the room that day in his book. Such was the power of Rasputin.

> *"Hermogenes stood with his back toward him with his face almost squeezed into the corner where the icons hung, he stood chewing a wafer and drinking holy water."*
> — ILIODOR, The mad monk of Russia, 1918

A respected expert was the Austrian/German physician Franz Mesmer who established a theory of internal magnetic forces that aligned with the Earth's magnetism and which he called animal magnetism and is better known as mesmerism. It differs from hypnotism; whereas hypnotism relies on words to enter a state readily open to suggestions, mesmerism uses energy to induce a trance-like state. Hypnotism can be used for behavioural conditions, to stop smoking for instance (i.e. maladaptive behaviour), and mesmerism can be used for physical conditions, with arthritis for example (psycho somatic conditions). Hypnotism would be ideal to aid Alexandra's mental stress whereas mesmerism would aid Alexei's haemophilia. Most recently hypnotherapist Judith Prager explained how suggestion can be used to stop blood flow altogether. She is a physician that has trained medical professionals and first responders in the use of Verbal First Aid.

D. Tocantins M.D. (1901- 1963), Director of the Cardeza Foundation for Haematologic Research and internationally recognised for his work on haemophilia, gave a medical statement confirming hypnotism/mesmerism had the ability to stop bleeding. He accepted the use of hypnosis for haemophilic patients finding that it caused vascular constriction. Alexei's doctors had been right to talk about a vascular condition therefore, if perhaps they weren't fully conversant with haemophilia at the time.

Franz Anton Mesmer
(1734-1815)

Mesmerism / hypnotism, was not like on a stage when fingers are clicked and immediately the behaviour is affected. Better described as self-hypnosis, it is the skill of implanting things with suggestion that gets results over time and cannot be rushed. This was the technique learned by Rasputin.

Not everyone is susceptible to hypnotism and results are unpredictable, as evidenced by the many reports of Rasputin's failed attempts to hypnotise them. It's not a scientific observation but the many women Rasputin preyed on were weak-willed and easily fell under his spell while stronger characters like Teffi and Tamara Rodzianko, recognised what he was up to and dismissed him. He particularly enjoyed influencing the well bred, literate and glitterati; those who possessed a superior intellect and by 1914 most of the ministers believed that Alexandra was under Rasputin's full control.

CHAPTER XII
War In Europe

IN 1913 Nicholas II approved the great army programme in response to increasing tensions in western Europe which added nearly 500,000 men and 11,800 officers to the Russian armed forces. He increased it again in March 1914 to a total of 1,700,000 active duty military personnel (1,400,00 soldiers), the largest army in the world made up of 115 infantry and 38 cavalry divisions – it was the largest display of Russian force ever and Russia also had the largest air force in the world. Yet, for generations its policy of russification had largely failed and for a country having more Muslims than the Ottoman Empire and more Jews than other nations in the world combined, it would now have to deal simultaneously with the cultural issues mounting at home whilst the army was waging war in Europe.

The military leaders had stayed loyal to the Tsar since the First Revolution 1905 and the Duma and government supported him too. Just five Bolsheviks had voted against the government's strategy for war and they were exiled to Siberia and had their property confiscated. The people had enjoyed the tricentenary celebrations of 1913 but now in July 1914 anti-government sentiment against the war peaked with a general strike in St Petersburg known as The July Crisis of 1914. Former Prime Minister Sergey Witte and the current Minister of the Interior Pyotr Durnovo and even Rasputin, attempted to persuade Nicholas against war with Germany. Even his distant cousin Keiser Wilhelm II tried to appease him but without having exerted any influence on him at all.

Witte believed Russia would lose a war despite its large industrial power base even though, due to his efforts alone, the production of iron and steel had risen by 50% since 1905 and Russia had become the fourth largest producer of steel, coal and iron in the world by 1914. Witte blamed the politicians for not ensuring the country was in a state of readiness for war. The problem was with logistics; Russia lagged well behind the efficiency of Germany. The French Ambassador Maurice Paléologue sent the following

CHAPTER XII

communiqué to his government in 1914, *"I am obliged to report, at the present moment, the Russian Empire is run by lunatics."*

After the assassination of the heir to the Austrian throne Archduke Franz Ferdinand in Serbia on 28 June 1914, Austria blamed Serbia and Russia promised to support their Balkan ally against aggression from Austria-Hungary and Germany. Austria then declared war on Serbia on 28 July 1914 and bombarded the capital Belgrade. Russia mobilised forces on 30 July 1914 to assist Serbia. Then it all got rather messy: Germany declared war on Russia and France; Britain declared war on Austria-Hungary and Germany; Austria-Hungary declared war on Russia; France declared war on Austria-Hungary; and Japan declared war on Germany. There were all told twenty-three declarations of war in 1914 alone and more followed in 1915 and later in 1917.

<u>World War I – 1914 declarations of war</u>
❖ = ('declares war on')

July 28	Austria-Hungary ❖ Serbia
August 1	Germany ❖ Russia
August 3	Germany ❖ France & Belgium
August 4	Britain ❖ Germany
August 5	Montenegro ❖ Austria-Hungary
August 6	Austria-Hungary ❖ Russia
August 6	Serbia ❖ Germany
August 8	Montenegro ❖ Germany
August 12	Britain ❖ Austria-Hungary
August 12	France ❖ Austria-Hungary
August 23	Japan ❖ Germany & Austria-Hungary
August 25	Austria-Hungary ❖ Japan
August 28	Austria-Hungary ❖ Belgium
November 1	Russia ❖ Turkey
November 5	Britain & France ❖ Turkey
November 11	Turkey ❖ Russia & Britain & Japan
December 2	Serbia ❖ Turkey
December 3	Montenegro ❖ Turkey
December 5	Japan ❖ Turkey

The immediate effect of Germany's declaration of war unified the Russian cause behind the Tsar and strengthened support for the monarchy. Almost overnight any discontent from the 1913 general strikes were doused with the immediate sense of urgency to attack Germany. In July 1914 Grand

Duke Nikolai Nikolaevich (Nicholas' great uncle and husband to Anastasia of Montenegro,) was appointed the Supreme Commander of the Russian Army. General Nikolai Yanushkevich (1868-1918) became his Chief of Staff and General Yuri Nikiforovich Danilov (1866-1937) became the quartermaster general. Danilov would publish the only biography of Grand Duke Nikolai in Paris in 1930. The Stavka was located at a strategic railway junction in Baranovichi, Belarus with military personnel residing on the railway carriages and not being quartered in the town itself.

At this early time in World War I, Grand Duke Nikolai Nikolaevich was popular with the army. Had the Russian public known the fullness of his blame over Khodynka perhaps he would not have been as respected but war blanketed his sins and Nicholas not having learned it, now appointed his poor strategist uncle to lead the war in the West. The strategic planning fell naturally to General Danilov during 1914-1915, leaving the less than ideal Supreme Commander with the job of handling the army's political front and the management of the occupied territories.

On 2 August 1914, Russia invaded the largest German province of eastern Prussia (now Poland). At the outbreak of war countries expected short territorial disputes but it turned in to a prolonged war of attrition. There had not been war in Europe since the Napoleonic Wars when the French Emperor stormed across Germany and Russia with the aim to stop them from helping Britain which he planned to defeat next.

The biggest test at the start was the Battle of Galicia also known as the Battle of Lemberg (18-19 August 1914 to 11 September 1914). It brought a huge victory against the dual monarchy of the Austro-Hungarian empire. Each side threw about one million men in to the battle. It consisted of three Russian armies from the Russian southwest front which was also their border. Both sides took a week to position their armies along the border. When fighting started Russia found itself outflanked and outnumbered in places. One corps (the 17th) retreated and another (the 25th) was almost encircled. The Russians managed to regroup and fierce fighting ensued.

Russia's 3rd Army met the Austro-Hungarian 3rd Army at the River Gold Lipa and won the battle. The Austro-Hungarian Army retreated almost unhindered while the Russian 3rd Army advanced and broke through the front at Przemyst causing more Austro-Hungarian forces to retreat. Other Russian units had similar successes at Lviv and Galich forcing yet more Austro-Hungarian retreats. But they were organised retreats, and once regrouped they made a stand and began a series of counter attacks with limited success. Fearing encirclement the Austro-Hungarian army halted and began a full scale retreat on 12 September 1914 across the River San. With the Russians on their tail, they were pushed 120 miles while Russia retook Przemyst and secured Galicia in a series of engagements. From this springboard Russians also took Lemberg.

CHAPTER XII

The Austro-Hungarian Army lost a third of its forces on their eastern front totalling 360,000 to 400,000 casualties (100,000 at Galicia alone) and lost 120,000 prisoners of war. Russia lost 230,000 to 300,000 casualties. The effect of such a devastating loss was that it had diverted a considerable military force away from its ally Serbia and thereby Prussia could no longer depend on its eastern front being protected by Austro-Hungarian forces. The battle for Galicia was one of the most significant battles of World War I.

Napoleon had studied previous attempts to invade Russia that had failed due to inadequate support services for the advancing troops and he learned that logistics played a crucial part in a military campaign. Russia's interest in defending Serbia in 1914 was because they were allies, but wholly because big countries regard little countries as buffer states where it is preferable to engage in military conflicts without incursions in to their own borders. Russia knew that Serbia was the best place strategically from which to launch and support an invasion in to Russia and therefore it was the most important western territory that needed to be defended. And so Russia intervened to help Serbia as a necessary step in ensuring Germany did not establish a border with Russia.

However, the supreme Commander, Grand Duke Nikolai Nikolaevich, was not as astute or militarily proficient as Napoleon and the success at Galicia masked the small role he played in its accomplishment in terms of military leadership. In the first month of the war, at the Battle of Tannenberg (26-30 August 1914) 30,000 Russian troops had died fighting Germany, 120,000 were wounded and 92,000 taken prisoner. At this point Russia was well and truly in the thick of it with their victory at Galicia masking the greater battlefield tragedies that followed. Much worse came in September 1914 at the first battle of the Masurian Lakes when Russia lost two entire armies, over 250,000 troops, making the bloody sacrifice at Borodino in 1812 against Napoleon's troops look pale by comparison.

General Samsonov, responsible for the blunders at the Masurian Lakes was unable to face the Tsar to account for the huge losses and instead walked in to the woods and shot himself. By December 1914, twenty-three countries had dug in to trenches for 1,500 days in unbearable weather (snowing or raining 42% of the entire time). To account for losses the Russian army rapidly increased to 6,553,000 personnel but they had only 4,652,000 rifles. Like Napoleon, this time it was Grand Duke Nikolai Nikolaevich that had not appreciated the importance of logistical planning.

Warfare analysis has shown that the side which can manufacture the most equipment and armaments always wins irrespective of the quality of their men or their leadership. But the supply of armaments is dependent entirely on the supporting logistics infrastructure. Had Nikolai Nikolaevich been the least bit competent in supplying the troops, then his military inadequacies may have remained inconsequential but as it happened, due to the poor communication and his lack of organisational skills, Russian troops were ordered in to battle without adequate arms, ammunition or food of which the only outcome can be excessive deaths and loss of territory. Russia had the greater number of troops, had they possessed the same level of German expediency then they may well have overran Europe by force.

As for medical treatment on the battlefield, that was close to zero with medical staff spread across a 600 mile front with one surgeon for every 10,000 men. In the Napoleonic Wars injured soldiers were left on the battlefield, waiting for help that came only after the fighting had stopped. Many soldiers died from simple wounds and an army could suffer defeat because of it. Sickness had killed more troops than the enemy in most wars until World War I. In terms of medical attention this war saw advancements in medical care overall, but on the Russian front it was still as dire as ever. Antibiotics were still twenty years away but in 1858 the discovery by Louis Pasteur that garlic had antibacterial properties saw its use as a battlefield antiseptic in both World Wars of the twentieth century, and was nicknamed 'Russian penicillin'.

Nicholas II arriving at the western front Stavka, September 1915

The battle of Tannenberg had the effect of emboldening Germany because they had repelled an aggressor. They began the headstrong push to drive Russia out of Prussia. The only notable response from Russia was to

CHAPTER XII

rename St Petersburg to Petrograd because it was thought too German sounding. 'Petro' in honour of Peter the Great and 'grad' being a suffix meaning 'city of', similar to the suffix 'stan' that is used for middle eastern countries to indicate 'country of'; e.g. Pakistan, Uzbekistan, etc. Petrograd was later renamed to Leningrad in 1924. After the fall of the Soviet Union in 1991 Leningrad returned once more to being called St Petersburg.

The government's inability to organise logistics led to shell shortages which allowed Germany to break through the front line at Gorlice-Tarnow in May 1915. It started the strategic withdrawal from Russia's western front and by July 1915 the entire Russian army was retreating, known as the Great Retreat (13 July 1915 – 19 September 1915). It gave up hard won territory like Galicia and Russian held Poland, territories that Grand Duke Nikolai Nikolaevich was supposed to have been fortifying while his staff were doing his job at the front.

In St Petersburg, Rasputin had been warning Nicholas for a long time that the Russian army would suffer defeat after defeat until the Tsar took over direct control of the military. What had been happening on the battlefield for two months was exactly how Rasputin had foretold it, defeat after defeat. With the same encouragement in his other ear from Alexandra, Nicholas removed Grand Duke Nikolai Nikolaevich on 21 August 1915 from overall command of the armies fighting Germany and Austria-Hungary. It was a move long overdue but worryingly not done because of the Grand Duke's incompetence, but because Nicholas had been persuaded to remove him under pressure.

The Stavka was ordered to move to Moghilev and on 23 August 1915 (G) (or 21 August in another source or 22 August according to Sophie Buxhoeveden,) Nicholas set out to take over control at the western front. He arrived at the front in the face of a strongly advancing German army on 5 September 1915 to assume supreme command. Military representatives from the Entente countries were there at Stavka from Britain, France, Serbia, Belgium, Montenegro, and later Italy and Romania.

"It's a heavy cross Nicky takes upon himself, but with God's help it will bring better luck. ... He will guide the whole thing here as the other place [Moghilev] *is still further off and then he will constantly go and see the troops and know what's going on at last."*
— ALEXANDRA FEOFOROVNA, letter to her sister Elizabeth Feodorovna

General Mikhail Vassilievich Alekseev (1857-1918) was appointed Chief of Staff and General Mikhail Savvich Pustovoitenko (1865-1918) as the Quartermaster General. Nicholas planned to guide operations directly from the Stavka because as Alexandra suggested in the letter to her sister Ella, Nicholas was not being reliably informed about the situation at the front. The irony of an emperor that had to go to the front in order to get reliable information is demonstrative of the ineffective communications.

Nicholas was not afraid to take the lead in military matters, but it was his timing that was significant. When Maria Feodorovna heard that he was going to the front she cried, but it had no effect on Nicholas who proceeded with his mission to change the course of the war. When Rasputin suggested that he accompany Nicholas to the front to bless the troops, Nikolai Nikolaevich promised to hang him if he dared to show up. Instead, the Tsar is usually seen in photographs blessing troops on the battlefield.

By taking the reins when he did, Nicholas became inextricably linked to the Great Retreat and all of the military failures thereafter. When Napoleon's Grande Armée crossed the Niemen in to Russia in 1812, the Russians retreated just as fast as the French could advance. Now Russians were retreating just as fast as the Germans were advancing.

Nicholas II blessing troops at the western front, September 1915

The Generals at the Stavka may have felt relief at the removal of Nikolai Nikolaevich and their morale fortified by the presence of the Tsar, like in medieval times when the sight of the king on the battlefield leading a charge helped to win the battle. But Nicholas was also regarded by others as scarcely competent to command a regiment let alone to lead an army of seven million. Effectively, tactical military decisions were made by General

Alekseev, but in practice Alekseev was overwhelmed in working tirelessly to improve logistics and expediate the hasty retreat of the army. Alekseev was in need of a superior that was tactically proficient and a masterful logistician at his side but instead he appears to have been left struggling with all roles.

However noble Nicholas' intentions to turn the war in Russia's favour, it could never be anything but a hopeless retreat. He believed that he was a good judge of character but in the twenty years of being tsar he'd failed to understand the root cause of his own inadequacy that was not able to match the right people for a given task, Nikolai Nikolaevich was evidence enough of this. He could choose anyone from the largest military pool ever assembled, but instead left the major military and political appointments to providence waiting for candidates to materialise instead of actively seeking them out. British writer Sir John Squire, editor of the London Mercury during the war years, was convinced of Nicholas' sincerity but not of his political, diplomatic or military nous.

> *"He has a strong sense of duty, a generous nature, a great capacity for affection, a desire to serve his people, no malice, no liking for cruelty and slaughter: adversity sweetened his character, and at the worst moments he never complained. But he was not intelligent, he was not educated, he did not know what was going on in Russia, and he was a poor judge of men."* — SIR JOHN SQUIRE, writer

Similarly, the famed writer Mohammed Essad-Bey portrayed an image of a ridiculously inept but gallant knight with noble intentions, in the foreword of his book *Nicholas II Prisoner of the Purple* by describing Nicholas II as the 'Don Quixote of autocracy'. Sophie Buxhoeveden used a different metaphor to convey the magnitude of what Nicholas was trying to achieve.

> *"It was the Emperor's fate to face such a task so titanic that it would have demanded a reincarnation of Napoleon and Peter the Great, thrown in to one, to carry it through successfully."*
> — SOPHIE BUXHOEVEDEN

The War From the Palace

Nicholas remained at the front for two years directing the war from the Stavka. For all his bravery in the field he would miss the drama unfolding in Petrograd for when he left to take personal command, Alexandra became regent and Rasputin consequently gained political leverage in addition to his social and religious clout. The pinnacle of power in Russia resided in the absolute autocracy of the emperor, now that power was in the untested hands of two individuals who the country suspected were in collusion with Germany. The ministers referred to Alexandra as '*that German woman*'.

Duma President Rodzianko was the first to put a spanner in the works between the Tsar, the Duma and the Government. He strongly advocated that Nicholas refrain from directly leading the army from the Stavka and made it plain that he regarded his so-called 'special advisor' Rasputin, as a German spy. But the extent of Alexandra's influence over her husband was such that she was already directing the affairs of state, with Rasputin looking over her shoulder. Nicholas responded in his typical non-confrontational fashion by removing Rodzianko from military concerns, having discussed the matter with General Mikhail Vassilivitch Alekseev, his new Commander in Chief.

> "*Dear Mikhail Vladimirovitch,*
>
> "*You have addressed, through the intermediary of our attaché in France, a telegram to General Joffre and M. Albert Thomas concerning the supply of aeroplanes for the Russian army, and have determined, according to your own lights, both the type and quantity of the machines, without any relation to the general programme worked out by common agreement between ourselves and the French and British Governments.*
>
> "*Copies of the correspondence conducted by you, though after the despatch of your telegram, were forwarded by you to the Grand Duke Alexander Mikhailovitch. On this correspondence being submitted to his Majesty the Emperor, his Majesty commanded me to notify you of his wish that you should abstain from direct interference in war matters which do not concern either the President of the Imperial Duma or a member of the Special Council.*
>
> "*A business possessing several masters, each deeming himself to be independent of the others, equally competent and invested with full powers, is liable to come to ruin in a very short time.*
>
> "*I beg to assure you of my absolute respect and loyalty.*"
>
> — MIKHAIL ALEKSEEV, letter to Duma President Mikhail Rodzianko

With Nicholas away, all focus was on Alexandra and for a time she did well but Rasputin was at the height of his power, hated by the Russian people and at odds with the government and Church alike. Alexandra would do everything he asked, sending messages to the field telling Nicholas why this minister or that one had to be replaced with the number of these replacements being something she would be questioned about in future. She arbitrarily dismissed capable ministers replacing them with nonentities favoured by

CHAPTER XII

Rasputin. These decisions were being constantly made, sometimes weekly and it gravely tainted the Tsar's reputation and destabilised the country. No one could keep abreast of the church leaders, officials and ministers currently in office.

The government alone, between September 1915 and February 1917 went through four Prime Ministers, three War Ministers and five Interior Ministers. Alexander Mossolov said in his memoirs that in December 1916, while he was in Petrograd, Alexandra offered him the post of Deputy Minister of the Interior which he declined. She told him, *"Everybody is criticising, nobody is ready to give any help."* He further elaborated that he might have considered the position, *"... if I had had the least hope that it was not already too late to combat her mysticism and all that it involved."*

Similarly, when Rodzianko was offered the post of Prime Minister he would only agree to accept it on the condition that Alexandra would reside at Livadia until the end of the war. Alexandra responded by removing his rank at court and thereafter referred to him as a 'scoundrel'. The ministers on the whole went to great lengths to secure an audience with Alexandra, which gave her an insight in to the connivances they were all plotting against each other and a summary of which she would try to communicate to her husband at the front. She was always having to verify what was being told to her by the ministers, with some difficulty because she possessed the same lack of judgement as her husband and was not aptly skilled to determine the mood of the ministers or to distinguish sincerity from duplicity.

With Nicholas at the Stavka he stopped receiving reliable information from Petrograd. Alexandra talked only about ministerial appointments which is a measure of how busy she became. Nicholas' decision to elevate Alexandra was an extension of his lack of foresight considering that she was regarded as a political incompetent by most. Rasputin continued with his favours for money as his influence grew, having Alexandra get the authentication he needed from the Tsar. Ministers rarely ventured away from Petrograd and unsurprisingly Nicholas little by little dropped out of the loop, learning things only from the contents of Alexandra's communiqués. Some ministers questioned whether the Tsar knew anything at all about what was happening in the capital and if he knew anything of what Alexandra was up to at home or of the antics of Rasputin.

> *"The Tsar saw only what the Empress allowed him to gather from her personal letters; and these letters were, of course, neither objective nor even informative."* — ALEXANDER MOSSOLOV, memoirs

Alexandra was not the type to go in to the heart of government and be among them, she ruled at arm's length from Tsarskoe Selo and received information from her valet Alexei Volkov, who watered down anything that might displease her. Volkov received reports on the telephone from the Minister of Interior Alexander Protopopov (the last Imperial Minister of Interior), who got his information from various and mainly unverified sources. It was like the game of Chinese whispers. Nicholas and Alexandra might have done better to regularly talk to each other on the telephone and one wonders why they didn't.

> *"On one occasion I recall, Nicholas referred to Her Majesty as 'a person in whom I have absolute faith.' The fate of many millions of human beings is actually in the hands of that woman. Surely the poor Emperor, and all of us who are his devoted servants, and, above all, Russia, would have been much happier had Princess Alix married a German Duke or Count."* — SERGEY WITTE

Lady in waiting Sophie Buxhoeveden may have also held an opinion that Alexandra was not up to her new leadership role saying that, *"she was no born politician,"* and was, *"highly strung* [and] *struggled through a maze of difficulties and opposition, The full extent of which she did not realise."* 'Opposition' that came from all directions and for which Volkov is partly to blame. She learned that the ladies of the court were criticising her for turning some of the lesser graded palaces in to hospitals after the tsar had left for the front, such as the Neskoutchnoe Palace in Moscow. It seemed that even her good deeds went under scrutiny and she would always be stuck between a rock and a hard place when making the slightest recommendations.

The rumours that circulated about Alexandra and Rasputin working for the Germans became ridiculous; Rasputin was selling food supplies on the black market and Alexandra had a radio transmitter under her bed to communicate with Berlin. In 1917 the Provisional Government would appoint a commission to investigate any documentary evidence on suspicions of treason, which even included a full search of Alexander Palace looking for the transmitter. No evidence was found of course. Indeed, Alexandra's letters during this time confirm how completely devoted she was to Russia and the task at hand, even though her competency may have been in question.

The French Ambassador said, *"Her education, her intellectual formation and her morals were entirely English."* But she was of German birth and such an eventuality should have been anticipated before she was left at the helm. Some politicians believed that Nicholas just didn't have any awareness of these things and despite his intelligence was better suited to ceremonial and philanthropic duties. Rodzianko, despite being an ardent opponent of the Tsarina Alexandra, rejected the accusations levelled against her that she was sending and receiving letters to Germany or making any other treasonous communications.

CHAPTER XII

One such letter came with the Mademoiselle Marie Alexandrovna Vassilitchikov who arrived in Petrograd in late autumn 1915 from Austria to visit Sergei Alexandrovich and his wife Elizabeth (Alexandra's sister). At this time there existed tensions with Austria so anything coming in to Russia from there was treated with suspicion. Lenin wrote to Maxim Gorky, "*A war with Austria would be a splendid little thing for the revolution.*" Russia needed any excuse to escalate with Hungary.

Alexandra and Marie were acquaintances since their youth but Alexandra sent the letter back unopened. She suspected, for whatever reason, that Mlle Vassilitchikov was attempting to lay the foundation for a bridge between Germany and Russia to discuss a separate peace and Mlle Vassilitchikov was sent in to exile under virtual house arrest for the remainder of the war. There is no evidence that Alexandra conspired against Russia, indeed her two closest confidants and only friends Ms Vyrubova and Lily Dehn were completely of Russian origin and other prominent ladies in waiting, such as Sophie Buxhoeveden documented how ridiculous the notion was that Alexandra was anything but loyal to Russia.

Mossolov's opinion about Rasputin's effect on the government was that, "*Rasputin's influence over affairs of state became virtually paramount.*" Consider the story of Tamara Rodzianko from his memoirs *At the Court of the Last Tsar: Being the Memoirs of A. A. Mossolov* (1935). He describes Tamara as the daughter of a fellow officer Novosiltzev who married M. Rodzianko. Confusing though it is to distinguish, this is not the same Tamara Rodzianko (*page 240*) that was married to Pavel Rodzianko nor is it a reference to the Duma President Mikhail Rodzianko.

Exactly who M. Rodzianko was and Tamara's connection to the court is difficult to ascertain with any certainty. In fact, the real name was probably disguised by Mossolov to avoid legal action after publication. Putting aside Mossolov's motive for masking the identity, the story gives a level of understanding in to the administrative relationship that existed between Alexandra and Rasputin while Nicholas was away at the front.

The story goes that Tamara married M. Rodzianko and they moved to Italy. They had children and something went wrong because the husband had his wife confined in a lunatic asylum. She escaped and returned to the Russian capital to try and reclaim her children. Alexandra had shown some animosity towards Tamara some months earlier, possibly believing in the reason given for her being clinically sanctioned. But now Alexandra wanted to assist her with regaining her children and approached Mossolov for help. He asked Tamara how she had secured the attention of the Tsarina and was told that it had been down to Rasputin. Straight away, with Rasputin having an involvement, one suspects a sexual connotation around a vulnerable woman.

Tamara told Mossolov that she was intending to visit Rasputin the next day to thank him personally. When she arrived at Rasputin's house the ladies of his salon were present and on seeing her they quickly left the house, leaving her alone with Rasputin. *"They made no secret of their intention of leaving me alone with that man. Then Rasputin literally threw himself upon me. I boxed his ears and ran away."* Two days later Tamara discovered that Alexandra had withdrawn the letter to assist her with her children. How it turned out for this poor woman is left in the crevices of history and one day she might be identified and her story told in its fulness.

Sergey Witte, who had been Russia's first Prime Minister (appointed 6 November 1905) said of Nicholas II, *"He married a completely abnormal woman and took her in to his arms, which was not difficult given his weak-willidness."* This weakness, or 'willidness' as Witte put it, was always the mole in the camp. In November 1916 there were 1.7 million military dead and 5 million wounded. The public attributed this bloodshed to Alexandra and her assassination, according to the daughter of the British ambassador, was openly spoken of in aristocratic circles as the only way of saving Russia.

> *"She might have been a good enough consort for a petty German prince, and she might have been harmless even as the Empress of Russia, were it not for the lamentable fact that His Majesty has no will power at all."* — SERGEY WITTE

On the battlefield of Europe World War I raged on. Events within Russia were destined to become a geopolitical conflict that became an extension of the war in Europe for several years after it ended. Wilhelm II blamed Nicholas' stupidity for having marched against Germany in the first place and not recognising the Keiser's open hand. In his memoirs Wilhelm II stated that he tried to mend the relationship between the two countries because of a promise he once made to his grandfather on his deathbed and pointed out that had Queen Victoria been alive, she would never have allowed them to enact such a terrifying and devastating world war. Keiser Wilhelm II essentially washed his hands of Nicholas II and of Russia.

> *"The words of the old General at Brest have remained unforgettably engraved upon my memory; they induced me to bring about my many meetings with Alexander III and Nicholas II, at which my grandfather's wish, impressed upon me on his deathbed, that I watch over our relations with Russia, has always been my guiding motive."*
> — WILHELM II, memoirs page 18

> *"Tsar Nicholas was weak and vacillating; whoever had last been with him was right; and naturally, it was impossible for me always to be that individual."* — WILHELM II, memoirs page 313

* * *

Ambulances arriving at the Tsarskoe Selo infirmary

Nurses at the Palace

As soon as war broke out Maria Feodorovna became the head of the Red Cross and Alexandra and her eldest daughters trained to be nurses of the Sisters of Mercy. Women played an important role in humanitarian work during World War I (e.g. Marie Curie) and many private committees were directed by high-society women, including the Red Cross. Italian Queen Elena (of Montenegro) studied medicine and became the first Inspector of the Voluntary Nurses for the Italian Red Cross from 1911 until 1921. She turned the Quirinal Palace in Rome in to a hospital between 1915 to 1919 and worked as a nurse during World War I. Queen Marie of Romania fled to Moldova, and there she worked with her three daughters as nurses in military hospitals.

Alexander Palace was seconded as a military hospital during the war. The Tsarskoe Selo infirmary was the idea of Vera Gedroitz who became its director and who ran it with military discipline. She was highly decorated for her medical practices during the Russo-Japanese War and served as a physician to the Imperial Court until the start of World War I when she became the first female military surgeon in Russia. At the Tsarskoe Selo infirmary Gedroitz turned one of the wings in to a state-of-the-art facility encompassing beds for 200 soldiers and 30 officers, a well-arranged operating theatre, an X-ray room and laboratory.

Alexandra asked Gedroitz for herself and daughters Olga and Tatiana to be instructed in the art of nursing the wounded. They trained for three months alongside other students without receiving any preferential treatment. Ms Vyrubova also joined but was more suited to a clerical role. The first two months was for intensive training, mornings were given to bandaging and changing dressings with two hours in the afternoon for studying. After they passed their exams they started the nursing day at 9.00 am, usually working to around 9.00 pm.

The wounded received first aid at mobile operating theatres at the front and were then moved by car or carriage to the hospital train and then taken to the various hospitals, usually still covered in mud and blood from the battlefield. At Tsarskoe Selo the hospital train pulled in at the tsar's private station. The wounded were transferred to a waiting team of medical staff that toiled day and night to care for them, they were bathed and allotted a freshly made bed. Their shift officially ended at 2.00 pm but sometimes they would still be labouring until 2.00 am with just a few hours of sleep until their next shift.

The Romanov nurses reported to Gedroitz and other surgeons just like the other nurses and threw themselves completely in to nursing the sick and the dying. There are many photographs of them assisting with surgery and comforting the sick. Gedroitz placed the highest importance on cleanliness and sanitation which greatly improved battlefield surgery. The Romanov nurses weren't afraid of mopping floors and changing bedding and were very active, giving most of their allowances to charities for the afflicted.

Alexandra was described by the journalist Waclaw Czerneewski, "*She works quietly and laboriously.*" She was again presented with a situation when the injuries of others were more pressing than her own ailments. The American newspaper Richmond Times-Dispatch reported in August 1915 '*The Empress forgot all about her ailments and spleen, the war has cured all of them.*' Marie and Anastasia were deemed too young to become nurses and helped where they could. They are seen in photographs looking in on patients and doing other supportive work.

Alexandra was metaphorically born for this work and was not spared any toil in the slightest. She would directly assist a surgeon and carry away amputated limbs, indeed all of the Romanov nurses disposed of amputated limbs and looked after fetid dressings. Tatiana was also said to be gifted in the calling and was described by doctors as cool headed. She would often assist Gedroitz during operations although at just seventeen years old it was decided not to expose her to the more gruesome cases. Still, after a few months she became physically drained and distraught and needed time off for rest. In autumn 1915 Olga became anaemic and weary and also needed time off. She was cared for by her mother and senior nurse Valentina Chebotaryova who prescribed arsenic injections and rest. She returned to work in January 1916, but was not permitted in the operating theatre again.

> "*This morning we were present (I, as usual, help to feed the instruments, Olga threaded the needles) at our first major amputation (the arm was taken away from the very shoulder). Then we all engaged in bandaging ... I had to bandage the unfortunate with terrible wounds ... I washed everything, cleaned it, anointed it with iodine, covered it with Vaseline, tied it up - it all turned out quite well - it's more pleasant for me to do such things myself under the guidance of a doctor.*"
> — ALEXANDRA FEODOROVNA, In letter to Nicholas II, 22 November 1914

CHAPTER XII

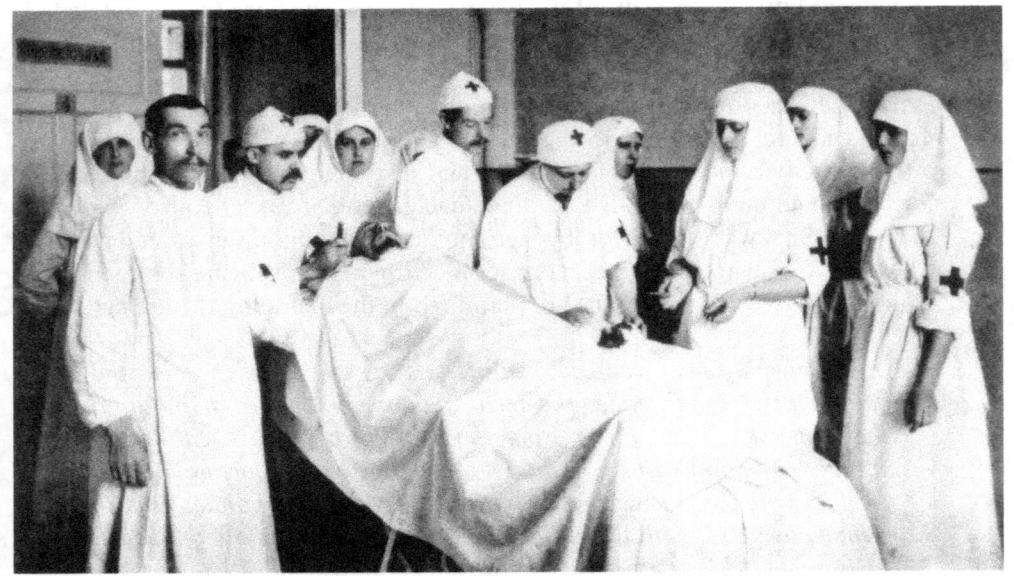

Marie and Anastasia visiting soldiers at the Tsarskoe Selo infirmary

Alexandra providing instruments to surgeon Vera Gedroitz. Behind Alexandra, LTR are Tatiana and Olga. Ms Vyrubova stands behind the patient's head.

"All the doctors who saw the Grand Duchess Tatiana at her work said that she was born to be a nurse, that she gently and fearlessly touches the most serious wounds, that all of her dressings are done by a confident and skilful hand. Meanwhile, just the sight of some of these injuries could deprive another person of sleep and rest."
— VALENTINA CHEBOTARYOVA

Valentina Chebotaryova had been a nurse in the Russo-Japanese War and had asked to work at Tsarskoe Selo where she started as a senior nurse. She kept a journal noting everyday things that she published in newspapers and magazines. She came to love the Imperial nurses. After the October revolution, six months after the royal family met with their end, she attributed their fate to Alexandra's liaison with Rasputin and believed that Alexandra's promiscuity or her fallibility around Rasputin had led to their demise. Chebotaryova died of typhus in April 1919. Alexandra's friend Lili Dehn, who must have heard many contemporary opinions, recorded in her memoirs, *"It is hardly possible to come up with some kind of crime in which she* [ALEXANDRA] *would not be accused."*

"I feel terribly sorry for her [ALEXANDRA] *and yet it is all so painful that I cannot find the warm feelings of old, after all she is the awful cause of all the misfortunes of our land, she ruined her entire family, the unfortunate sick of soul, sick with mysticism and arrogant pride."*
— VALENTINA CHEBOTARYOVA, 10 August 1917

In 1914 The International Committee of the Red Cross (ICRC) had already been operating for over 50 years since 1863. The Russian branch formed in 1867 (which in 1918 would rename itself to the Soviet Red Cross and was recognised by the ICRC in 1921). The organisation monitored compliance with several international war agreements, namely the 1906 Geneva Convention and the Hague Conventions of 1899 and 1907. Its job was to be in the field where direct action was needed and in the diplomatic circles where complaints and violations could be reported to the countries concerned and the international community.

World War I saw an outstanding number of medical precedents; the use of chemical agents for example that caused unimaginable devastation and of which the Red Cross campaigned vigorously against. At no time previously had the treatment of soldiers or civilians in a time of war been so comprehensively considered. With the shifting front lines came the displacement of ordinary people; between 1914 to 1917 this amounted to 5,000,000 on Russia's western front fleeing their homes and heading to Petrograd for shelter.

The displaced were regarded as refugees by the government and as such proper records were not kept about them. Tatiana was just seventeen years

CHAPTER XII

and three months old in September 1914 and established a committee to help the government carry out a census of refugees to provide financial aid to return them home or re-settle them with employment. It was financed partly by the state and with public donations that came from as far afield as Britain and the US. Her committee ultimately secured a law on meeting the needs of refugees that remained in place for decades.

Meanwhile, just a few miles within reach of Tsarskoe Selo, the renamed capital city of Petrograd was in turmoil. A series of auctions took place to fund hospitals, one art auction alone made 6,000 rubles. Many infirmaries were created within existing institutions such as museums and even the Winter Palace opened on 10 October 1915 with 241 staff. But it was still not enough to deal with the numbers arriving from the front, night and day. Almost 15 million Russian soldiers went to war with an estimated 1.8 million casualties and 2.8 million returning home wounded.

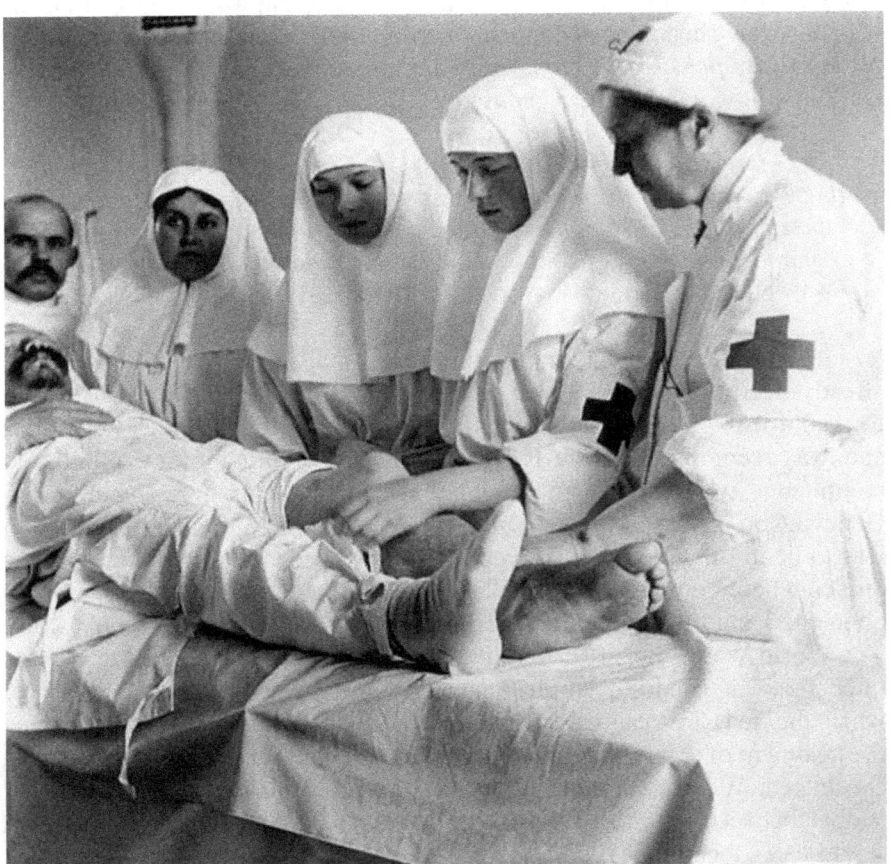

The dressing room at Alexander Palace infirmary, 1914. LTR nurses: Ms Vyrubova, Tatiana Nikolaevna, Olga Nikolaevna, Vera Gedroitz

As the wounded continued to pile in so too did refugees and inhabitants from the countryside whose menfolk had gone to the front and were themselves now seeking employment as servants, cooks etc. in the cities. Children committing crimes became a major problem; it would have been prudent to send them to the countryside to alleviate the shortage of labour. Even prisoners of war were sent to Petrograd, 1.4 million Germans by the end of the war. So many were on the streets that legislation was introduced to forbid them from interacting with Russian civilians. But it was food shortages that had the severest effect and nutrition was a critical problem. Many of the agrarian production problems and issues of the peasants that the Dumas had tried so desperately to address before they were shut down, had never seriously featured in Russia's strategic planning. The importance for organised logistics, proper handling of public disorders and peasant food riots, and the impact of war on economics had been largely ignored.

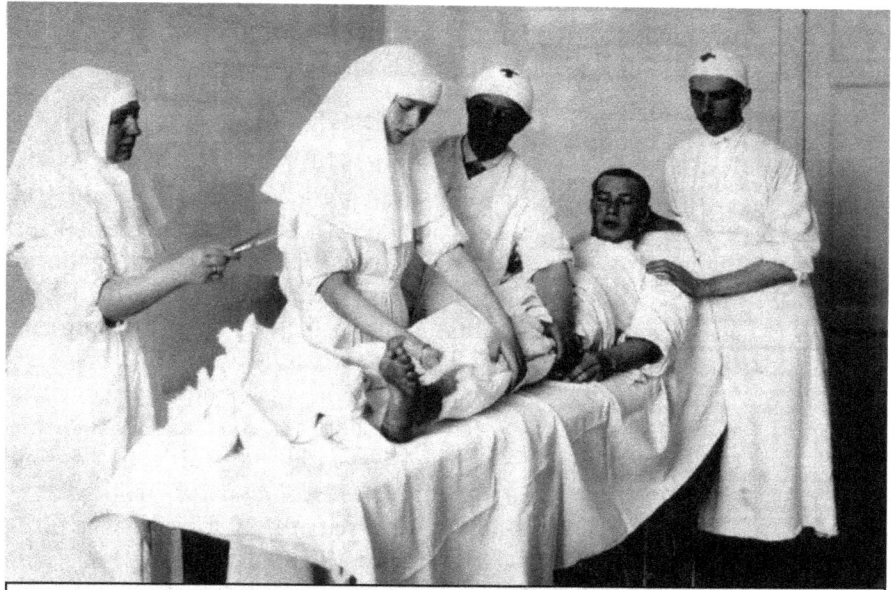

Tatiana dressing the wound of Dmitry Malama, an officer of the Imperial cavalry. A romance developed between them after he was appointed an equerry at the Imperial Court. The other nurse is possibly Valentina Chebotaryova.

Between 84% and 88% of the fifteen million conscripts for the war were peasants, having previously held a role in the production of foodstuff, and their removal from the countryside caused a food supply issue. These

CHAPTER XII

conscripted soldiers required army rations of sufficient nutrition to be able to fight, whereas previously the larger percentage of them had been self-sufficient or malnourished. Generally the output of crops reduced, therefore the food supply to cities reduced but the food supply to the army increased.

Ironic that people coming to the cities to find work were being passed by the many people from the cities migrating to the producing areas, where they assumed held the grain for them to survive. By 1917 the problem of food and nutrition superseded everything in wartime Russia and starvation had become a reality for everyone and is one of the major factors that historians attribute to the underlying cause of the Russian Revolution 1917.

The fortunate thing for injured soldiers were two-fold, firstly they were entitled to full rations and second that hospitals were under the auspices of the various national Red Cross groups, for example Russian Red Cross, British Red Cross and the American Red Cross, all having a strong presence in wartime Russia with ample supplies. Alexandra looked at the distribution of around eighty-five hospitals and restructured them to receive mass casualties. She founded and supported two schools for training nurses which noticeably increased the efficiency of the hospital system in Russia.

Alexandra's nurse uniform

There were 109 Red Cross schools of nursing in 1914. 25,000 Sisters of Mercy received training between 1914 and 1916. In comparison to the many achievements of women in World War I, Alexandra is easily overlooked but her contribution in Russia during the conflict was admirable and showed what she was truly capable of.

Alexandra was honoured with The Red Cross Portraits egg. It was one of the treasures taken by the Bolsheviks during the Russian Revolution 1917 and sold by the Antikvariat in 1930 for a pittance $250 to Armand Hammer, an American oil magnate with close ties to the Soviet Union. He sold it in 1933 to Mrs Lillian Thomas Pratt, a collector of more than 400 Russian Imperial jewels. She owned five Imperial Fabergé eggs: Red Cross Portrait egg, Peter the Great egg, the Tsarevich egg, the Pelican egg and the Rock Crystal egg. Mrs Pratt's collection was donated to the Virginia Museum of Fine Arts upon her death in July 1947 (*page 278*).

TYPHUS & TYPHOID FEVER

Typhus and Typhoid Fever are separate diseases, both are infections but caused by different types of bacteria that are spread in different ways. Both commonly occur in areas where overcrowding and poor hygiene are prevalent and can be difficult to diagnose because the symptoms are similar.

The similar binomial names are because both have the epithet 'typhi', which came about because they were once thought to be the same disease. Yet they have little in common at the molecular level and treatment and prevention can be very different, but good hygiene and basic sanitation is essential in the prevention of both diseases.

Typhus: Rickettsia typhi
- *flea-borne infection*
Spread by lice, ticks, mites, rats, cats, i.e. arachnid, insect or animal.
Prevent with repellents and insecticides

Typhoid Fever: Salmonella typhi
- *food borne infection*
Spread by person to person, contaminated food and drink.
Prevent by avoiding contaminated food and water sources

TYPHUS IN WORLD WAR I

Living conditions at home and in the trenches caused the typhus epidemics during World War I, characterised by malnutrition, squalor, and the lack of hygiene. It first appeared in November 1914 among refugees and prisoners and spread rapidly to the troops. Half of the 60,000 Austrian prisoners taken by Russia died from typhus and it was also one of the main causes of death for British troops.

There was uncertainty about what caused typhus and how to prevent it so that by the winter of 1918 it appeared in epidemic form. It was kept from ravaging the armies only because medical science was learning how to defeat it at a rapid pace.

For the twenty years previous to war, Russia had an average of 82,000 cases per year. In the final two years of the war 2.5 million deaths were recorded on the Russian front alone. Lenin said in 1919, *"Either socialism will defeat the louse, or the louse will defeat socialism."*

CHAPTER XII

FABERGÉ RED CROSS PORTRAITS EGG

Made by Henrik Wigström in 1915 for Maria Feodorovna in recognition of her role as Head of the Red Cross in Russia during World War I. It has the lowest purchase price of 3,875 rubles, reflecting the austerity in wartime with a simple design of two red enamel crosses over five bands of white guilloché enamel. The centre band has a Slavic gilded inscription, *'Greater love hath no man than this, that a man lay down his life for his friends.'* When opened there's a depiction of Christ's resurrection with the patron saints of Grand Duchesses Olga and Tatiana on either side. The surprise inside is a folding screen of portraits painted by Zuev within opalescent white enamel with gold edging. The five portraits are: Alexandra Feodorovna, Olga Nikolaevna, Tatiana Nikolaevna, Olga Alexandrovna, and Maria Pavlovna the Younger (daughter of Paul Alexandrovich brother to Alexander III and first cousin to Nicholas II).

The collection of the Virginia Fine Arts Museum, Richmond, Virginia, US

Russian Jewish Soldiers on the western front

Occupying the social issues at the start of World War I the German Keiser was giving some thought to the many Muslims that could if called to Jihad be mobilised in Europe being that Turkey was already allied with the Ottoman Empire. Russia was more concerned with the Jews in the western extremes with half a million living along the western front. Conscription came in to force for the war and for most poorer Jewish soldiers this meant compulsory military service. Richer Jews had more avenues to avoid conscription and it was this small element that the Russian authorities focused on by labelling all Jews cowards and continuing the persecution that stemmed from their inherent hatred for the Jews. However, in World War I, Russian Jews proved that their blood was equally worthy to be spilled for Mother Russia.

In 1891 some 20,000 Jewish reserve soldiers and their families had been banished from Moscow. They were accused of being unpatriotic, unfit for combat and draft-dodgers. Those that were in military service were forbidden any religious identity, they had to eat the same food as everyone else and Russian officers that showed any sympathy were disciplined by the War Ministry. Things went from bad to worse following the First Revolution 1905 and by 1908 Jewish soldiers were being called cowards and traitors in the Duma by the far-right groups.

Of course, the revolutionaries behind the manufacture of the revolution were mostly Jews who saw the revolution as a mission to take control and put an end to their oppression. The far-right elements in the Duma attributed all of Russia's social and economic problems to the Jewish socialist cause and argued to ban Jews from the armed forces entirely. They were backed by the Black Hundred who had among their supporters almost every high ranking Russian officer in the army. Jews were forbidden to take NCO or commissioned ranks.

Despite this, in 1907 Jewish soldiers made up 5 percent of the entire military (compared to making up 4 percent of the population of the Russian Empire). In Poland and Ukraine some Russian regiments were made up of up to 20 percent Jewish soldiers with around 90 percent of them serving in combat positions (75 percent infantry, 20 percent artillery, 5 percent cavalry). By the outbreak of World War I, 400,000 Jewish men had been conscripted predominantly for the western front which was also their homelands; altogether around four million Jews were occupying that zone.

The pogroms did not stop while Jewish soldiers were at the front. In spring 1915 for example, at Cortland (a country before it became part of western Latvia in 1918) and parts of Lithuania, 200,000 Jews were expelled from their homes by the retreating Russian army who pillaged and raped Jewish settlements. In May 1915 all 40,000 Jews living in Kovno (Kaunas)

CHAPTER XII

were forcibly removed from the city. It was a nonsensical exercise because the expelled Jews just moved towards the Russian interior and had to be resettled somehow anyway. The Germans during their advance also expelled many Jewish communities in their wake.

Germany offered reward to Jews that helped them and Russian General Staff believed Lithuania and Latvia in particular was littered with spies. For this reason they expelled many Jews and held some to ransom so that other Jews would think twice about collaborating with the Germans. It was up to the socialist element in the Duma to speak up for the plight of the Jewish soldiers and in 1918 Duma Deputy Naftali Friedman with Prime Minister Alexander Kerensky travelled to Lithuania to examine the basis for the accusations that Jews in Kuzhi had helped the Germans. Their investigation concluded that the claim was totally unfounded.

> *"At the beginning of the war, the newspapers reported about large numbers of Jewish volunteers. These were volunteers that, judging by their education, were entitled to officer ranks. They knew that they would be denied such ranks, and volunteered anyway."*
> — NAFTALI FRIEDMAN, Deputy of the Fourth Duma

Deputy Naftali Markovich Friedman (Third & Fourth Dumas) was a Jewish Lithuanian Kadet. He gave a speech on 19 July 1916 and backed it up in the Duma by reading aloud a letter from an unnamed Jewish soldier who had gone to America but then returned to Russia to join the Russian Army to fight. Part of that letter is given below:

> *"I became a soldier, and lost my left arm almost to the shoulder. I was brought into the governmental district of Courland. Scarcely had I reached Riga when I met at the station my mother and my relatives, who had just arrived there, and who on that same day were compelled to leave their hearth and home at the order of the military authorities. Tell the gentlemen who sit on the benches of the Right that I do not mourn my lost arm, but I do mourn deeply the self-respect that was not denied to me in alien lands but is now lost to me."*

Immediately following the February Revolution 1917, the Provisional Government removed all anti-Jewish regulations in the military making it possible for courses to be available for Jewish officers. Religious services were introduced and Rabbis were able to serve but it only lasted until February 1918 when religious services were discontinued in the Red Army. The military Rabbis from Poland and Lithuania took up the cause for the Jewish soldiers; one said, *"Jewish soldiers have never been traitors to their motherland; they have proved it with their loyalty and self-abnegation."*

Over 3,000 Jewish soldiers received the Decoration of the Military Order of St George (a disproportionately high number) but featuring a double-headed eagle instead of St George, which was given to non-Christian soldiers receiving the award. 100,000 Jewish soldiers were killed in world War I with many more murdered at home by the tsarist regime and the Red Army of the Jewish led Bolsheviks. It's estimated that somewhere between half a million and one million Jewish civilians were forced from their homes between 1914 and 1917, roughly a quarter of the Jewish inhabitants.

Indifference to the Keiser

The world's most powerful autocrat was described by observers as *remarkably passive* and unable to take direct action when his regime was threatened with revolution. If Nicholas was timid then was he completely to blame when his wife, an empress, was also sworn to share his tribulations. At their coronation they had taken salt and bread and shared in the responsibility of ruling. Some accounts attribute all of the blame for a disastrous war solely to Alexandra which is overstretching it; an emperor is the supreme being and therefore solely accountable for the way the empire is managed; a leader with the power to shut down parliament cannot be otherwise. Whatever was the true relationship between emperor and empress, it had formulated long ago after they retreated to their palaces and buried their heads in the sand.

Was the Triple Entente more important to Nicholas than preventing a world war and could he alone have prevented World War I? Most certainly there is evidence to suggest this. Even if hindsight be impossible to garner in advance, the emperor has many advisors for him to base pre-emptive judgements. Even Wilhelm II who is regarded as a rather eccentric bungler, in comparison to Nicholas at this time appears to hold a better grasp of what was happening in and out of Russia. He attempted to discuss matters that could have helped Nicholas II such as the urgent need for reforms and a military alliance with Germany to dominate the central European plateau.

Wilhelm II believed that an alliance would address Germany's encirclement worries. Germany's eastern flank and Russia's western flank would be secured with the territory in between falling under their influence. The major opposing powers in Europe would be clearly split between the east and west. Wilhelm II tried to make Nicholas see this but failed, in all probability because Wilhelm II had ended the secret Reinsurance Treaty that existed between them since 1887. A level of stubbornness, revenge, petulance or simply just uninterest from Nicholas should not be ruled out. Wilhelm II learned not to trust Nicholas; he thought him a double-dealer whose word could not be trusted. At the onset of the Russo-Japanese War he personally had given Nicholas the assurance for securing the Russian western flank.

CHAPTER XII

"When the Tsar resolved upon war against Japan, I told him that I would assure him security in the rear and cause him no annoyances. Germany kept this promise." — KEISER WILHELM II, memoirs

In a passage from Wilhelm II's memoirs (*page 141*) he refers to the first Duma which was disbanded. The members met in Finland and wrote the Vyborg Manifesto to encourage peaceful demonstrations of discontent. These were experienced politicians that could have helped Nicholas to transition to a constitutional monarchy but instead the next Duma members were less astute. Nicholas had placed a distance between himself and the ebbing tide of revolution. The passage given below from Wilhelm II's memoirs, demonstrates how uninterested Nicholas was with home matters at the outbreak of World War I. Wilhelm II is referring to the Marshal of the Court, either Vasily Dolgorukov or more likely Grand Marshal of the Court Count Pavel Benckendorff, in the given text.

"This shows plainly how little we had expected, much less prepared for war in July 1914. When, in the spring of 1914, Tsar Nicholas II was questioned by his Court Marshal as to his spring and summer plans, he replied: 'Je resterai chez moi cette année parceque nous aurons la guerre' (I shall stay at home this year because we shall have war). This fact, it is said, was reported to Imperial Chancellor von Bethmann; I heard nothing about it then and learned about it for the first time in November, 1918.

"This was the same Tsar who gave me, on two separate occasions at Björkö and Baltisch-Port entirely without being pressed by me and in a way that surprised me, his word of honour as a sovereign, to which he added weight by a clasp of the hand and an embrace, that he would never draw his sword against the German Emperor — least of all as an ally of England — in case a war should break out in Europe, owing to his gratitude to the German Emperor for his attitude in the Russo-Japanese War, in which England alone had involved Russia, adding that he hated England, since she had done him and Russia a great wrong by inciting Japan against them."

— KEISER WILHELM II, memoirs

When Germany and Austria were messing with each other Nicholas amassed troops along Russia's western borders without understanding what was happening in the region. This troop movement was wrongly interpreted by Wilhelm II and Germany declared war on 1 August 1914. Wilhelm II maintained that he tried to prevent the confrontation but things were made worse with Nicholas having taken no interest to respond when war was imminent and while he was being beseeched to prevent a state of war.

> "On your appeal to my friendship and your call for assistance began to mediate between your and the Austro-Hungarian Government. While this action was proceeding your troops were mobilised against Austro-Hungary, my ally. thereby, as I have already pointed out to you, my mediation has been made almost illusory.
>
> "I have nevertheless continued my action. I now receive authentic news of serious preparations for war on my Eastern frontier. Responsibility for the safety of my empire forces preventive measures of defence upon me. In my endeavours to maintain the peace of the world I have gone to the utmost limit possible. The responsibility for the disaster which is now threatening the whole civilized world will not be laid at my door.
>
> "In this moment it still lies in your power to avert it. Nobody is threatening the honour or power of Russia who can well afford to await the result of my mediation. My friendship for you and your empire, transmitted to me by my grandfather on his deathbed has always been sacred to me and I have honestly often backed up Russia when she was in serious trouble especially in her last war [Russo-Japanese].
>
> "The peace of Europe may still be maintained by you, if Russia will agree to stop the military measures which threaten Germany and Austro-Hungary."
> — KEISER WILHELM II, letter to Tsar, 31 July 1914

Wilhelm II sent a further telegram (*next page*) to Nicholas on 1 August 1914 having received no responses to his previous communiqués. It reached Nicholas seven hours after Germany declared war so leaving the door open for negotiation right up until the last minute, even after hostilities had started Wilhelm II was still asking for a response to avoid hostilities.

> "When the Emperor came, it was with the news that Germany had declared war. At first the Empress could not grasp it. War ! her nightmare ! She knew the completeness of German organisation; she knew that Russia was not prepared for war at that moment; and that England had not yet joined Russia and France. She was in despair, but, then and always, she had the conviction that Russia would win in the end."
> — SOPHIE BUXHOEVEDEN, The Life and Tragedy of Alexandra Feodorovna (1929) page 185

* * *

CHAPTER XII

TELEGRAM: Wilhelm II to Nicholas II (transcript below)

TRANSCRIPT OF TELEGRAM : *Thanks for your telegram. I yesterday pointed out to your government the way by which alone war may be avoided. Although I requested an answer for noon today no telegram from my ambassador conveying an answer from your government has reached me as yet. I therefore have been obliged to mobilize my army. Immediate affirmative clear and unmistakable answer from your government is the only way to avoid endless misery. Until have received this answer alas I am unable to discuss the subject of your telegram. As a matter of fact, I must request you to immediately order your troops on no account to commit the slightest act of trespassing over our front lines.*

CHAPTER XIII
Rasputin is done for

IN 1915 the gossip surrounding Alexandra and Rasputin being German spies had had a limited impact. So, when Duma member and former political prisoner Pavel Milyukov made a speech at Tauride Palace where the State Duma was sitting on 14 November 1916, he really let the cat out of the bag by referring to them as Rasputin and Rasputuiza. He followed a speech given by Alexander Kerensky who accused ministers of being guided by Rasputin. Kerensky was forced to leave the chamber for it but Milyukov took more care in his delivery in highlighting government failures and hinting at a government sympathetic to Germany.

Since 1912, Alexandra had kept Rasputin within close proximity, because of her son Alexei, despite the gossiping that they were in an affair. In 1914 she came out of her hypochondriac insensibility to become a nurse and now in 1915 she took control in running the government. It seemed that the more she tried to do for Russia the more it turned against her.

WAS RASPUTIN A DRUNKARD?

Louise Andrews interviewed by the BBC for a documentary on Rasputin.

BBC : *"What sort of control did he* [RASPUTIN] *have over the Empress?"*

Louise : *"Well you see, he had a control over her on account of the son because he's supposed to have had these medicines that cured the boy when he had these very bad attacks, or else I suppose he would hypnotise him, the child would get well again for a little while and then a month or so later he'd have another terrible attack, the Empress would call for him* [RASPUTIN] *immediately, she wouldn't have a doctor."*

CHAPTER XIII

Rasputin at the Helm

Milyukov's speech at the Duma was so successful that the military formulated a plan to imprison Alexandra for treason but the investigation could find no evidence. The Duma just couldn't accept that in the war against Germany they were being led by the *Niemka*, 'the German woman'. Rasputin, they believed was spying for personal profit, to access black markets but at the height of his power it also came with increased threats including several failed assassination attempts on him.

First on 12 July 1914 (G) a 33 year old woman called Chionya Guseva stalked him in his village Pokrovskoe and stabbed him in the stomach, almost fatally but for the local doctor that saved his life. She had read about Rasputin in the newspapers and believed him to be the antichrist. She was found to be not responsible for her actions by way of insanity. Rasputin and the police believed that Iliodor had played some role in the assassination attempt. Then in February 1916 the Minister of the Interior Alexei Khvostov, firmly believing the German spy conspiracy, along with Iliodor plotted to kill Rasputin. It failed and he was imprisoned and Iliodor exiled.

Alexandra was slightly less culpable for her actions as it was understood that Rasputin controlled her and through her he also controlled the Tsar. The danger was that people also believed she was being controlled by Germany. Rasputin's obvious hand at court was in the many replacements of officials and Church leaders; he would suggest a replacement and Alexandra would get Nicholas to endorse it. This way Rasputin became a focal point for anarchistic propaganda, but even the posters and magazine cartoons of him puppeteering the Emperor and Empress appeared not in the slightest to offend the Imperial couple.

Alexandra removed the ministers that criticised Rasputin. Two notable ones were; Scheratov (Minister of the Interior) replaced by Protopopov, a convicted armed robber that had spent ten years in prison; and Goremykin (the man Nicholas had replaced Witte with,) who was replaced by Sturmer, who promptly set about embezzling the treasury. President of the Duma Mikhail Rodzianko recounts in his book *The Reign of Rasputin* what he had once told the Tsar:

> "... *The constant changes of Ministers at first created confusion among the officials, which finally gave place to complete indifference. Think, your Majesty, of Polivanoff, Sazonoff, Count Ignatieff, Scherbatoff, Naumoff – all of them honest and loyal servants of yourself and of Russia, who were dismissed for no cause or any fault whatever. Think of such venerable statesmen as Golubeff and Kulomsin."*
> — MIKHAIL RODZIANKO, memoirs

"She exercises a deplorable influence on all appointments, even those in the army. She and the Emperor are surrounded by shady, incompetent & evil persons. Alexandra Feodorovna is fiercely and universally hated, and all circles are clamouring for her removal. While she remains in power, we shall continue on the road to ruin."
— GD MIKHAIL ALEXANDROVICH, speaking to MIKHAIL RODZIANKO

Some accounts are unconvinced that Rasputin had any real influence on the government. He had always clashed with the Duma who saw his hold on the palace as a threat but their complaints had resulted in legislation that only reduced their own authority. Following the dissolvement of the Duma in September 1915, Rasputin took charge of just about everything in Petrograd; holding meetings on state matters and forwarding discussions to the relevant minister for their attention. He entrenched himself in the war by examining military plans so that he could pray for successful outcomes which was the reason he was suspected of spying. The contradiction of whether Rasputin was important in governmental affairs comes from the memoirs of those who were not in the sphere of government or immersed in the gossip and knew not with any certainty what was really happening in government or at the court. For example, Count Pavel Benckendorff in his memoirs believed there may have been some influence in religious matters but that there was none in politics; which was just his opinion.

"During the last years of his reign there was often talk of the influence, political and other, that Gregori Rasputin had exercised over their Majesties. Neither the Emperor nor the Empress ever mentioned him to me. I am convinced that the political influence of Rasputin was nil. The appointment of ministers, which, during the latter years, proved so fatal, can be explained otherwise, and if certain persons thought it necessary to approach that person for their private ends, they may have derived personal advantage, but he never had any influence on the course of political events."
— COUNT PAVEL BENCKENDORFF

By February 1916 when the Duma resumed briefly, the war was still going badly with no end in sight; fuel was in very short supply, Poland was lost to Germany and the people were hungry. Having vaguely considered arresting Alexandra the government focussed on Rasputin. Two days after Kerensky and Milyukov had openly criticised Alexandra and Rasputin at the Duma, politician Vladimir Purishkevich returned to Petrograd having requested a meeting with the Tsar at Stavka. He had left on 3 November to discuss the problem of Rasputin's uncontrolled power and assumed authority but had it actually been to seek permission for Rasputin's assassination?

CHAPTER XIII

Purishkevich was a hard line supporter of the Tsar but despaired at how the government was being misused. Three days after Purishkevich returned from the Stavka on 19 November 1916, he gave another speech at the Duma about the continuous government reshuffles saying that the Tsar's ministers had been turned into marionettes whose threads were firmly in the hands of Alexandra and Rasputin, whom he called: *"the evil genius of Russia and the Tsarina who has remained a German on the Russian throne."* Presumably Nicholas had refused to sanction Rasputin's murder. While it can never be known how Purishkevich was received by Nicholas it was highly likely that he was waved away, considering the speech he subsequently gave at the Duma immediately on his return. It would seem Purishkevich had exhausted all options including approaching the Tsar to back the removal of Rasputin and had been left with no alternative but to personally take responsibility for the plot against Rasputin, to proceed immediately.

Coincidentally, at this time Rasputin gets nervy and even afraid from rumours circulating in Petrograd that he would soon be done away with. His assistant Aron Simanovich, also the court jeweller of dubious character, in his memoirs, described how Rasputin was fearing for his life. What was most fearful for someone with so many enemies was having no idea who was conspiring against him or where the real threat lay waiting and therefore Rasputin was constantly looking over his shoulder and fearful of being imminently murdered.

Rasputin decided to act and he put a buffer between himself and any plot against him. He wrote a letter to Alexandra dated 7 December 1916 (J) in which he was really addressing the Tsar with a fearful prediction, stating that he didn't expect to live past 1 January 1917 and added a warning to his would-be assassins. This famed letter appears singularly in Simanovich's book published in 1928. He states the letter fell in to his possession shortly after Rasputin's death at the end of December 1916. If it existed at all, it was remarkably accurate as just 23 days later Rasputin was murdered and 19 months later so were the Imperial Family. It was all rather convenient for Simanovich's book in yet another example of memoir elaboration.

But, there was another source that corroborated Rasputin's predictions, from famed Russian author Nadezhda Lokhvitskaya, better known by her pen name Teffi. She wrote about Russian society and eventually she too, had to escape the Bolsheviks via Crimea and Constantinople. She met Rasputin on two occasions during World War I. The first time was at a function where he tried to seduce her. *"Drink,"* he told her, and she declined, *"Drink, I'm telling you, God will forgive you."* Teffi stated that he was drinking a great deal and that she could see straight through him and saw him for what he was. She believed he played at being a holy peasant in order to accomplish things, after all without this what was Rasputin but a peasant. The second time, Teffi described that he stood in the centre of the room *"thin *and black – a gnarled tree, withered and scorched."* Before she left him, he made a prophesy that he would be killed and that his death would signal the end for Russia, which evidently came to pass.

RASPUTIN'S PROPHETIC LETTER

"I wish to make known to the Russian people, to Papa [Nicholas II], to the Russian Mother [Alexandra], and to the children, to the land of Russia, what they must understand. If I am killed by common assassins, and especially by my brothers the Russian peasants, you, Tsar of Russia, have nothing to fear for your children, they will reign for hundreds of years.

"But if I am murdered by boyars, nobles, and if they shed my blood, their hands will remain soiled with my blood, for twenty-five years they will leave Russia. Brothers will kill brothers, and they will kill each other and hate each other, and for twenty-five years there will be no peace in the country. The Tsar of the land of Russia, if you hear the sound of the bell which will tell you that Grigory has been killed, you must know this:

"If it was your relations who have wrought my death then no one of your family will remain alive for more than two years. And if they do, they will beg for death as they will see the defeat of Russia, see the Antichrist coming, plague, poverty, destroyed churches, and desecrated sanctuaries where everyone is dead.

"The Russian Tsar, you will be killed by the Russian people and the people will be cursed and will serve as the devil's weapon killing each other everywhere. Three times for 25 years they will destroy the Russian people and the orthodox faith and the Russian land will die. I shall be killed. I am no longer among the living. Pray, pray, be strong, and think of your blessed family."

— GRIGORY RASPUTIN, letter to the Tsarina, 17 December 1916 (J)

Sir John Hanbury-Williams offers an insight in his memoirs about Rasputin, a man he never met, and his connection to Germany and Ms Vyrubova as a suspected accomplice. He was an officer stationed at the Stavka and was very well known to Nicholas and Alexandra. Following the death of his young son, Alexandra had comforted him. Despite his focus on the military and British intelligence, it demonstrates how deep relationships existed between the Russian court and foreign dignitaries operating in Russia and between the Stavka and the foreign military staff.

CHAPTER XIII

> "*How much he* [RASPUTIN] *was a paid agent of the enemy it is difficult to say, but there is no doubt that he received money from some sources which did good work for Germany at the time, and bad for Russia.*
>
> "*There seems but little doubt that his principal agent at Court was, wilfully or not, the celebrated Madame Vyrubova, who was very rarely away from the Empress.*
>
> "*The known influence he exercised over the Empress, and thus upon the Emperor, made him the court of appeal for all those intriguers and place-seekers who had their own axes to grind, and knew full well that here was a means of assuring their success. No doubt, wherever the money came from, whether from German sources or others, it became well spent by those who, for their nefarious purposes, brought about, by 'slow drops of poison,' as it were, the ruin of Russia.*"
>
> — MAJOR-GENERAL SIR JOHN HANBURY-WILLIAMS, memoirs, 1-3 January 1971 (G)

The Murder of Rasputin

It would not be a valid telling of Rasputin's end without a woman being involved. That woman was the beautiful Irina Yussoupoff. One account says that Rasputin had once attempted to compromise her while another maintains that they had never met. Irina's husband Prince Felix Yussoupoff made a plan to lure Rasputin to their home at Moika Palace (aka Yussoupoff Palace) using Irina, also the very beautiful niece of Nicholas II, as bait that his insatiable curiosity could not refuse. So that Yussoupoff's parents were not alarmed the meeting was arranged for midnight. Rasputin turned up for a party expecting to seduce Irina, so the story goes.

That evening Rasputin told Ms Vyrubova about the invite and she in turn mentioned it to Alexandra who became suspicious because she knew that Irina was in Crimea. This was just a few hours before the appointment. Had Alexandra or Ms Vyrubova sent word to Rasputin then he may well have suspected that he was walking in to a trap. On 30 December 1916 (G), the conspirators met at Moika Palace to prepare the ruse by soundproofing the cellar. There were five men waiting for Rasputin to arrive that evening:

- ❖ Prince Felix Yussoupoff (aristocrat)
- ❖ Grand Duke Dmitry Pavlovich (Nicholas II's cousin)
- ❖ Vladimir Purishkevich (Duma member)
- ❖ Lieutenant Sergei Mikhailovich Sukhotin (Preobrazhensky Regiment)
- ❖ Colonel Stanislaus de Lazovert (Military doctor)

Rasputin arrived expecting a light social event and was lured in to the cellar where he was murdered. The question beckons why he wasn't suspicious on his arrival when he wasn't taken directly to meet the other guests. In some video reconstructions Rasputin is shown to be almost prophetic at this point knowing he was there for the purpose to be murdered but his arrogance would not have entertained that eventuality as he believed that no one could harm him because of his divinity and that he was untouchable. Why didn't the conspirators just drag him to the basement and kill him on his arrival, instead of playing out the ensuing charade. These questions arise because most of what took place comes from Felix Yussoupoff's unreliable accounts. Nonetheless, he was a participant and gives a valuable insight even though the facts may have been distorted and exaggerated to create the material for his book.

The cellar in the Yussoupoff Palace where Rasputin was murdered

The popular story goes that Rasputin was given cakes and wine laced with cyanide, the poison had no effect so he was shot several times and still he did not die, so he was taken outside and shot in the head. Two men had fired, Yussoupoff and Purishkevich, each claiming to have killed Rasputin. There were three bullet entry holes found on the body, one in the chest that travelled through his liver and stomach, a second in the kidneys and a third went bang smack in the middle of the forehead.

CHAPTER XIII

Rasputin's body was taken in Purishkevich's car to the Great Petrovsky Bridge and dropped in to the nearby icy Malaya Nevka River. Still he breathed so they went down to the river and drowned him in an ice hole. The body did not drift away as intended but resurfaced and the frozen corpse was spotted a couple of days later, its legs and wrists tied by the same rope, mouth half open, teeth clenched, and with arms reaching out as if trying to claw out. Water was found in the lungs indicating death by drowning but as that could appear in the lungs anyway it was not a conclusive cause of death.

"This devil who was dying of poison, who had a bullet in his heart, must have been raised from the dead by the powers of evil. There was something appalling and monstrous in his diabolical refusal to die."
— FELIX YUSSOUPOFF

Rasputin's murderers all got away with it because it was such a popular murder with the people. When news circulated of his slaying the city was jubilant and the murderers were hailed as heroes. The Yussoupoffs and Pavlovich were placed under house arrest in the Sergei Palace, the home of Sergei Alexandrovich and Princess Elizabeth. From January 1916 that palace was functioning primarily as a British Red Cross hospital to treat Russian soldiers. Then they were banished from Russia which inadvertently saved them from the Bolsheviks and they ended up in Paris.

Purishkevich escaped Russia and died from Typhus in 1920, Sukhotin married Sophia, the granddaughter of the famous Russian author Leo Tolstoy and died in 1926. Pavlovich died from a sudden attack of uremia in 1942. Felix Yussoupoff died in 1967 and Irina three years later. And Dr Lazovert also escaped and died in France much later in 1976.

In 1932 Metro-Goldwyn-Mayer made the film *Rasputin the Mad Monk* originally called 'Rasputin and the Empress'. The part of Prince Yussoupoff was played by Prince Paul Chegodieff and Irina was played by Princess Natasha, both fictional characters. Felix Yussoupoff seized the opportunity to cash in and sued MGM in 1934. But he was a self-proclaimed murderer so it was Irina that brought the law suit, for libel.

The Yussoupoff's claimed the film had not accurately portrayed Rasputin's murder and was defamatory. They argued that the character representing Irina was seduced by Rasputin and that it was obvious the characters were recognisable as the Yussoupoffs. In the film Rasputin hypnotises and rapes Princess Natasha but in real life Irina and Rasputin had never met - they alleged. Felix Yussoupoff took the stand and coldly described his part in slaying Rasputin, even testifying that Rasputin had told him he was working for Germany. Irina was awarded £25,000 in one of the largest court awards of the time. The offending scenes were cut and the film was removed from circulation for some years with MGM losing their appeal.

THE KNOXVILLE INDEPENDENT

NOBLES SLEW MONK?

6 January 1917

Petrograd Papers Hint Murder of Czar's Confessor.

Reported That Young Aristocrats Killed Gregory Rasputin and Threw His Body in River.

London, Jan. 4.—The newspapers, in their Petrograd dispatches feature stories of the reported death of Gregory Rasputin, the Russian monk who, it has been reported, exercised great influence over Emperor Nicholas.

The reports of the death of Rasputin evidently are making a stir in Russia, not only on account of his personality but owing to allegations that two persons of exalted rank and a well-known former member of the duma were concerned in his taking off.

The general assumption in the stories is that Rasputin was murdered, and some of the accounts say so unqualifiedly. According to one story, two young aristocrats drove in an automobile the night of Friday-Saturday to a house on Korokhovaya street, where a man, assumed to have been Rasputin, entered the car, which then went to Yussupoff palace, which is owned by the young Prince Yussupoff, heir to Gen. Prince Yussupoff, aid to Emperor Nicholas.

Afterward the police heard shots and cries coming from the palace garden. Hastening there to make inquiries, they saw blood on the snow in the garden and were shown the carcass of a dog, which, they were told, had been shot because it was mad.

Meantime, according to another version, the body of a murdered man, wrapped in a fur coat, was placed in an automobile. The aristocrats took seats in the car and drove to Petroasky Island, in the Neva. Investigation Saturday and Sunday led to the discovery of a freshly made hole in the ice, traces of blood, and many footprints near by. Divers descended into the river and found the body of Rasputin.

The names of the persons suspected as being concerned in the alleged murder are not printed, but it is stated that young Prince Yussupoff, after the events of the week-end, quit Petrograd for his Crimean estates, but that he subsequently returned to the capital. Young Yussupoff is related to the imperial family by marriage.

One of the researchers at MGM, Mercedes de Acosta, had pointed out the potential libel case when she was asked to write the sexual scene, *"such a sequence would be absolutely unauthentic and probably libellous,"* she warned, and was dismissed for stating this. Yet the film company had restrained from using another sexual scene between Rasputin and Alexandra, depicting Rasputin who once pulled out his penis to show what he *"gives to the old girl"* and which carried no risk of libel with it at all.

CHAPTER XIII

MGM had used a short message on the film, '*A few of the characters are still alive, the rest met their death by violence.*' Seeing that all characters except for the Yussoupoffs had been murdered the judge advised that it would have been better for the film company to have stated that the film was not intended as an accurate portrayal of real characters. That's what MGM eventually did and all films since have carried the now familiar disclaimer, '*Any similarity to actual persons, living or dead, or actual events, is purely coincidental*'.

The many accounts given by Yussoupoff slightly differed from each other, with no two being identical versions. Despite his account being regarded as heavily fictionalised, it has become accepted over time and particularly because it's one of the few eye-witness accounts available, and because he was the main conspirator, head of the richest family in tsarist Russia and the husband of Nicholas II's only niece. His autobiography *Lost Splendor* was the source material used for the television drama by HBO in 1996, making Yussoupoff's version the de facto account on the murder of Rasputin based entirely on his testament without any supporting evidence.

Rasputin's body recovered from the Malaya Nevka River near the Great Petrovsky Bridge on 19 December 1916. Police found the body floating in a hole in the ice, arms frozen in a raised position.

Having left Russia in 1919 the Yussoupoff's sold two Rembrandt paintings (now in the National Gallery of Art in Washington,) as well as Princess Irina's jewellery. In 1924 they started a *House De Couture* perfume shop in Paris and London called Maison Irfé, the name coming from the first two letters from their names. But they closed in 1931 owing to the world-

RASPUTIN IS DONE FOR

wide depression leaving the Yussoupoffs in financial ruin. Yussoupoff described as being penniless, continued to sue MGM for transgressions around the world, and anyone that made a film or book explicitly referencing either of them. Notably, another large payment came in 1965 from MGM which secured the Yussoupoffs in total an estimated £600,000 that keep them in the lifestyle they were accustomed to for some time to come.

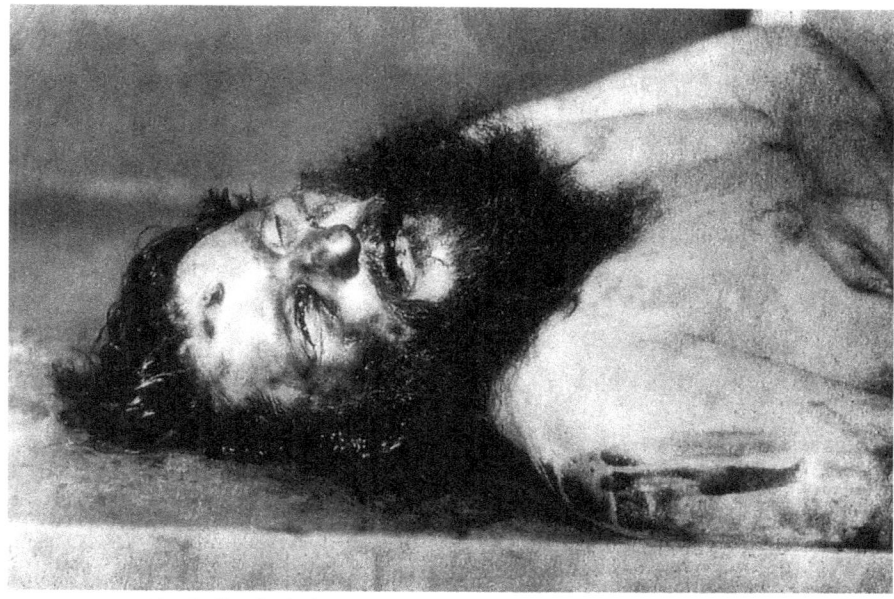

The bullet hole in Rasputin's forehead can be clearly seen

Yussoupoff resorted to writing his memoirs to ease their finances further which made a modest income for many decades. His first book *Rasputin* was an account of the murder. The next book was an autobiography with the English title *Lost Splendor* and French title *En Exile*. Yussoupoff made several statements nearer the time before his books published, all of which were discredited professionally. First there was the initial statement he gave to the police in St Petersburg; then the account given from exile in Crimea in 1917; the account in his first book; and the final accounts given at the libel cases of 1934 and 1965 under oath.

- ❖ *Rasputin: His malignant influence and his assassination*
  Published: 1929 Russian; 1934 Paris; 1955 English

- ❖ *En Exile* (Avant L'Exil) – Published: Paris 1952

- ❖ *Lost Splendor: The Amazing Memoirs of the Man Who Killed Rasputin.* Published: 1954 New York, London

CHAPTER XIII

Even Purishkevich's statement contradicted Yussoupoff in many details. They agreed on one point only, that the first attempt to poison Rasputin had failed. Some cakes were left on plates half eaten to avert any suspicion, others had their cream filling injected with potassium cyanide and Rasputin had eaten several. The post mortem performed by Professor Dmitry Kossorotov found no evidence and stated that, *"the examination revealed no trace of poison."* In 1993 a Russian forensic expert Dr Vladimir Zharov, re-examined the Rasputin evidence, and disputed the cause of death by drowning stating that the water found in the lungs was a common finding in autopsies and also suggested that cyanide had been injected before baking the cakes which could have killed off its potent effect, so enabling Rasputin to consume the cakes without being poisoned.

The simplest explanation would be that Rasputin had declined the cakes. Rasputin's daughter Maria said that her father avoided anything with sugar. It could be that when Yussoupoff's finances needed a boost he had embellished his book with fanciful untruths, a common trait discussed so far. Felix showed no remorse in his books or in court and portrayed his victim as inhuman and a beast to be slain. Perhaps he had little empathy with the character because he had made most of it up. How many murderers profit from boasting about a cold blooded murder, openly detailing the motive and opportunity and how the deed was accomplished, with such enthusiasm.

Another expert that was asked to take a look at the autopsy report was Professor Derrick Pounder, Head of Forensic Medicine at Dundee University and a government pathologist. If Rasputin was indeed poisoned by cyanide but did not die as a result then the only logical conclusion is that he did not ingest sufficient cyanide. He quoted the founder of modern toxicology, Paracelsus, that the poison is in the dose.

"Poison is in everything, and no thing is without poison. The dosage makes it either a poison or a remedy."
— PARACELSUS VON HOHENHEIM

Yet Yussoupoff claimed that Rasputin had ingested enough cyanide to kill a horse. Dr Stanislaus de Lazovert was responsible for providing the cyanide, as well as for the disposal of the body, so was it he that had been remiss with the dosage. Professor Pounder also discounted the theory that sugar could have neutralised the cyanide because of the way cyanide is absorbed by the body without having time to react chemically with any sugars. This being a reason why sugar is not used for an antidote.

To the court's surprise British Member of Parliament Oliver Locker-Lampson (Conservative MP for Birmingham Handsworth and former naval officer,) was called in the MGM libel case. He had served as the British Ministry of Information's representative in Russia and was seemingly in court to add weight to Yussoupoff and claimed, astonishingly enough, to have been personally asked to participate in the assassination of Rasputin by Purishkevich. It was an insinuation intended to link British intelligence with the murder. But he wasn't the only British agent to make that claim. One account says that Yussoupoff involved another British agent Oswald Rayner in Rasputin's murder and not only did he participate, but allegedly fired the third and fatal bullet to the forehead.

Rasputin's body once recovered was required to be buried within forty days according to Russian tradition. Alexandra wished for an Imperial funeral – not something that Nicholas would approve or the country would accept. What happened with the body depends on the source. Ms Vyrubova was in the process of building a small chapel not far from Alexander Palace, off the property of the Imperial Family. It was decided to bury Rasputin there under the bell tower.

The burial service took place three days after death on 2 January 1917 (G) in the bell tower of the chapel. It was attended by the Imperial Family (Alexei was ill and did not attend,) including Ms Vyrubova, Rasputin's general secretary Akilina N. Laptinskaya and around eight others whose identity is mysteriously withheld from Ms Vyrubova's memoirs. None of Rasputin's relatives were invited. Just a month earlier Ms Vyrubova had gathered Rasputin and Iliodor there, to bless the foundations. That winter the palace was in mourning, no Christmas presents were exchanged and Alexandra, it was reported, would cry for hours on end.

When the people and soldiers at the palace found out about Rasputin's grave they went there to desecrate it. For a time Alexandra and Ms Vyrubova visited the grave daily to mourn and presumably keep it in fresh flowers. It was found with the most awful graffiti and with litter over the grave and the smell of urine. A letter dated 7 January 1917 (G) confirms this, from Anna Rodzianko to Princess Zinaida Yussoupoff, the mother of Felix Yussoupoff.

"She [ALEXANDRA] *visits the grave daily, and always finds it couverte d'ordures* [covered with rubbish].
— ANNA NIKOLAIEVNA (Golytsin) RODZIANKO to ZINAIDA NIKOLAIEVNA YUSSOUPOFF

Relating to the quote given above, Anna Rodzianko was the wife of the Chairman of the State Duma and short-lived Prime Minister Mikhail Rodzianko. She was formerly Anna Golytsin. The Golytsins were one of the largest Russian noble houses. Zinaida Yussoupoff (Felix's mother) also of a noble family, was twenty-one years younger than her husband and when he died aged forty-six, she became heiress of Russia's largest private fortune.

The soldiers smashed axes in to the coffin, spitting and urinating over it. The body was removed and taken to the Tsarskoe Selo town hall and put on display where the bullet hole in the forehead could be clearly seen. After a time, the Provisional Government secretly buried the body at Konyushennaya Square in Petrograd. Prime Minister Kerensky had it removed to outside of the city but on their way the truck broke down and the body was buried in nearby woods or another account says the remains were burnt to ashes and yet another that the remains were taken to the Petrograd Polytechnic Institute under mysterious circumstances. Joseph Fuhrmann in his book *Untold Story*, confirms some of this, stating on page 238 that Rasputin's body *"spent ten weeks buried in the foundation of Anna Vyrubova's small church."* He continues that on 17 March 1917 drunken soldiers scrawled on the nearby church *'Here lies Grishka Rasputin, shame of the House of Romanov and the Orthodox Church,'* and also left obscene drawings.

In 2005 Rasputin supporters erected a memorial Russian wooden cross at the site of the original grave on the edge of the estate (now an open-air museum). Seven years later in September 2012 vandals attacked the wooden cross during a spate of crimes on religious symbols, showing that almost a hundred years on, Rasputin was still relevant to some people.

Were British Intelligence behind Rasputin's assassination as first suggested by modern day author Oleg Shishkin. He writes that Yussoupoff was just a patsy, in his books *Kill Rasputin* (2000) and *Rasputin. A History of Crime* (2004). Shishkin suggests that several foreign intelligence agencies particularly the British and German were actively seeking a coup d'état in Russia. Nothing new here, but it may strengthen the notion of a foreign government being responsible. Another account points out that the British and Germans had become so established in Russia that they were essentially a de facto government. Rasputin was decidedly against a war with Germany and tried to convince the Tsar to pull out of World War I and because of his influence may well have succeeded. If that were to happen, the allies could not defeat Germany without Russia and therefore the only recourse was to assassinate Rasputin. (See *British Intelligence in Russia, page 401*).

In the aftermath of Rasputin's murder many of his associates were arrested. The state made an inventory of his possessions and assessed the estate to be worth somewhere around a year and a half the salary for a bishop. All of his family were persecuted, in due course the Bolsheviks took their possessions and exiled them to Salekhard in Siberia; except for daughter Varvara who for some time continued working as a stenographer for the justice department in Pokrovskoe.

With a little help from one of Rasputin's previous secretaries Aron Simanovich, Varvara attempted to leave for Germany in 1923 but was searched at the station and a manuscript was found on her detailing the events that had taken place in Ekaterinburg regarding the royal family's disappearance. She was arrested and sent to a Siberian prison where she disappeared and it's thought she was poisoned in 1924 or 1925. Every family member was forced to work in the freezing camps of the Arctic Circle and by 1933 all of them, except for Maria, had died from dysentery or been worked to death.

Maria was the only family member that survived the Bolsheviks. She fled to Vladivostok with her husband and then to France where she became a performer, even working in London in a circus act for a time. She attempted to sue Felix Yussoupoff for her father's murder but the French court would not deal with affairs that were out of their jurisdiction. She settled in America and died in 1977. In February 1980, Boris Yeltsin in charge of Siberia before he became President of Russia, had Rasputin's house in Pokrovskoe torn down to curb the increasing numbers of pilgrims that were visiting there to pay homage. And so ended the tale of Rasputin.

Rasputin's daughters Varvara and Maria

CHAPTER XIV
Revolution & Abdication

WHEN Nicholas II stepped on to the balcony of the Winter Palace in 1914 to announce Russia was at war with Germany, the many thousands in the square below fell to their knees. By autumn 1915 the gossip was about Alexandra and Rasputin being German spies which had had a limited impact but it would catch up with them both as World War I progressed. The disastrous Duma sessions of autumn 1916 had voiced such strong opposition to them that Nicholas cancelled the next due session for February 1917 and quite possibly also suspected that some Duma representatives had been involved in Rasputin's murder in December 1916. The mood during this time is described in the following quotes by Duma and military members.

> *"The idea of the Emperor's compulsory abdication had been persistently circulated in Petrograd since the end of 1916. ... At the beginning of January [1917] General Krymov arrived from the front and asked to be given an opportunity of unofficially acquainting the members of the Duma with the disastrous conditions at the front and the spirit of the army."* — MIKHAIL RODZIANKO, Chairman of Duma

> *"The spirit of the army is such that the news of a coup d'etat would be welcomed with joy. A revolution is imminent, and we at the front feel it to be so. If you decide on such an extreme step, we will support you. Clearly there is no other way. You, as well as numbers of others, have tried everything, but the Emperor attaches more weight to his wife's nefarious influence than to all honest words of warning. There is no time to lose."* — LIEUTENANT GENERAL KRYMOV

On 16 February 1917, the British general Sir Henry Wilson was in Petrograd for the allied conference and recorded in his diary, *"The Emperor*

Nicholas II on the balcony at the Winter Palace 1914

and Empress are riding for a fall. Everyone – officers, merchants, ladies – talk openly of the absolute necessity of doing away with them."

The February Revolution 1917

The first warnings that the monarchy was unrecoverable came from Mikhail Rodzianko, the highly competent statesman that was viewed in low esteem by the Imperial couple. Of his many achievements he is better known as the man that relentlessly tried to warn the Imperial couple of the impending revolution. Alexandra's ignorance of politics was double folly with her refusal to take counsel from notable and experienced politicians such as Rodzianko. Indeed, her disrespect extended to referring to him as 'that fat Rodzianko.'

Alexandra's thinking had never wavered in that she was deserving of all the benefits of her noble inheritance. Her grandmother and father-in-law were models of how to keep a grip on power and rule an empire and since the moment she had decided to become tsarina had been convinced with the notion of an unsinkable autocracy. After her son was eventually born in 1904 her resolve hardened as she sought only to protect and strengthen what would one day be rightfully his to inherit. She had exerted her influence on Nicholas from the very start, and no action towards her aim had a firmer effect than the tsar's first speech that she undoubtedly had co-authored.

In the third month of his reign Nicholas gave a momentous speech on 17 January 1895 in the great concert hall of the Winter Palace that stunned those that heard it. He announced that he would continue his father's autocratic legacy. The country had high hopes after thirteen and a half years of tyrannical rule under Alexander III and people wanted reforms to take the country feet first in to the 20th Century. The millennium was a symbolic marker for technology and science and other countries had been preparing with grand exhibitions ever since the construction of the Eiffel Tower for the World Fair of 1889. Now, with five years to go the new tsar appeared to be taking backward steps with a speech that was for all intents and purposes a decree that the status quo would remain and possibly be more stringent.

The effect of that speech signalled the tsar's laziness to re-evaluate and consider progressive possibilities. He had absolved himself of the onus to change anything, legally, morally or otherwise. His assertion to be tough only kept him in the cocoon of his father's legacy which was incompatible in the modern world. Future prosperity lay with industrialisation and in construction but to position oneself on the world stage required reforms. Nicholas instead gripped autocracy and shackled the country to a bygone age of medieval feudalism, religious superstition and brutality. Everyone in Europe wanted to move on from the Victorian age in to the modern era, just as the medieval had transitioned from the age of exploration to the age of discovery. One might assume that such speeches are prepared years in advance for an ascending monarch, but deplorably not so, it would seem.

"Let everyone know that I, devoting all my strength to the good of the people, will protect the beginning of the autocracy as firmly and unswervingly as my unforgettable late parent protected it."
— NICHOLAS II, speech 17 January 1895

Days after the speech, Konstantin Petrovich Pobedonostsev, statesman and adviser to three tsars, was in conversation with one of his admirers, Princess Catherine Radziwill, whose mother belonged to the Vorontsov-Dashkov family (*page 36*). Catherine wrote around two dozen books on the royal courts of Europe using the pseudonym Paul Vassili for her book *Behind the Veil at the Russian Court* (1913). She spent two years in Roeland Street Prison (1901-1903) in Cape Town for attempting to defraud Cecil John Rhodes (the British mining magnate and South Africa politician) of £6,000 to pay off her mounting debts.

Conversation between Pobedonostsev and Radziwill:

Pobedonostsev: *"Do people actually think that I authored that speech."*

Princess Radziwill: *"Of course."*

CHAPTER XIV

Pobedonostsev: *"I always thought I was credited with more intelligence and sound common sense."*

Princess Radziwill: *"But who else could have suggested such an unfortunate idea to the Emperor?"*

Pobedonostsev: *"You don't know then? Who else but the young Empress."*

Princess Radziwill: *"But what does she know about Russia?"*

Pobedonostsev: *"Nothing ... but she presumes to know everything. She is more autocratic than Peter the Great and more cruel than Ivan the Terrible. Her limited mentality makes her believe she is gifted with great intelligence."*

Of course it wasn't just Alexandra that Nicholas listened to and his mother would have maintained the ideals of autocracy, after all being an Empress had not done her any disfavours. She knew that to maintain tsardom it was necessary to encourage in Nicholas a tougher demeanour. She would reprimand him, *"Nicholas, be Tsar!"* But the hard line that Nicholas had taken in his speech had much more to do with Alexandra who told him to *"be more autocratic than Peter the Great and sterner than Ivan the Terrible."* By 1905 Maria Feodorovna had been pushed out and retreated to Gatchina leaving Alexandra as sole advisor, confidant and even as minister during the First Revolution 1905.

> *"If you could only be strict, my dear! It is so necessary; they must hear your voice and see the discontent in your eyes. But they are too accustomed to your sweet, indulgent goodness. Your voice must make them understand that you are protesting and reprimanding forcefully. Never ask, order!"* — ALEXANDRA FEODOROVNA, June 1905, Letter

Another revolution was approaching when all the various political and social problems would manifest as the February Revolution 1917. Alexandra found Duma President Rodzianko particularly irritating when he pleaded for her to remove herself and her children out of harm's way and always refused for fear that it might be seen that she was running away. She was steadfast and could not accept that a decaying dynasty was coming to an end. Rodzianko became more persistent from January 1917 for the Imperial Family to make plans for their own safety. The statements by Nicholas and Alexandra, that they would never leave Russia, did nothing to align the public with them and only served to show how out of touch they were and eventually even Rodzianko gave up the lost cause. At his final audience with the Tsar, he pleaded for him to reconsider his family's safety.

"Save yourself your Majesty. We are on the eve of tremendous events, whose outcome cannot be foreseen. What your government and you yourself are doing is irritating the people to such an extent that anything is possible." — MIKHAIL RODZIANKO

For his genuine concerns Rodzianko was dismissed. He bowed to his tsar and left him with these prophetic words:

"I leave your Majesty in the firm conviction that this is my last audience with you. Hardly three weeks will pass and the revolution will have swept you away. You will be Tsar no longer, You shall harvest what you sowed." — MIKHAIL RODZIANKO

Nicholas announced that he would also be cancelling the Duma session for April. It was a bad move and on 8 March (G) the February Revolution 1917 started (23rd February Julian calendar) with riots in Petrograd. The Duma refused to comply with the Tsar's wishes and formulated a Provisional Government that encouraged Nicholas II to abdicate. There were differences of opinion among the Duma leaders and the representatives of the working men (Soviets). The leaders feared that in the physical absence of a government there should be a regency under the Grand Duke Mikhail Alexandrovich. The workers wanted to leave the form of a new government and monarchy undecided until after the holding of a constitutional assembly.

Grand Duke Alexander Alexandrovich (Nicholas' uncle and dearest family friend of the Imperial couple,) wanted to impress upon them both that the revolution was at a point where autocracy was being swept away, and that the government instead of saving the tsardom had turned to sacrificing the tsar to satiate the people. Alexandra predictably advised Nicholas not to share his divine right to rule with the government or the people.

Troops fire on Bolshevik demonstrators in Petrograd on 4 July 1917 (G)

CHAPTER XIV

Alexandra was completely missing the point and Nicholas had not yet acknowledged that his absolute power had ended on 30 October 1905, after the first Revolution 1905 began. Like Rodzianko, Alexander Alexandrovich faced immeasurable stubbornness and stood up, raised his voice at the two of them and in frustration stormed out of the palace.

> *"I kept my silence for thirty months, but now I see that you two are resolved to go down to destruction. Still, you have not the right to take the rest of us with you. I refuse to continue this conversation!"*
> — GRAND DUKE ALEXANDER ALEXANDROVICH, memoirs

Alexandra's pontificating discourse was determining how things would unfold for them. The admirable Rodzianko still did not fully give up on the Imperial Family. He sent countless telegrams for several weeks after his dismissal without ever receiving a reply. The final telegram was on 13 March 1917 (G), after the revolution broke out in Petrograd. Nicholas read it and instructed his trusty Minister of the Court Count Adolf Frederiks not to respond, thus trivialising the February Revolution 1917 as he once did the First Revolution 1905, without any awareness of its severity. *"That fat Rodzianko has wired me all kinds of nonsense again. I do not believe I shall bother to answer."* he told a nonplussed Frederiks.

Telegram: *"Steps must be taken immediately as situation is more threatening than ever. Tomorrow will be too late. The last hour has struck which will decide fate of country and dynasty."*
— MIKHAIL RODZIANKO, his last cable warning the Tsar of revolution

Nicholas ignored Rodzianko's warnings and wasted no time leaving the Stavka on 13 March 1917 on the 400 mile journey to Petrograd naively believing that he could quell the discontent. That same day Maria Feodorovna in her diary wrote of Alexandra Feodorovna, *"For this we can thank her stupidity and hunger to rule in Nicky's absence."* Along the journey Nicholas received a telegram from Alexandra asking him to return immediately to Tsarskoe Selo because the children were ill and their situation was dire.

The Imperial train headed east and after a couple of sleepless nights Nicholas arrived at the administrative centre of Malaya Vishera at 3.00 am where the train had been diverted because the way ahead was occupied by revolutionaries. The safest route was to head for the town of Pskov, 160 miles from Petrograd, where General Nikolai Vladimirovich Ruzsky was barracked. General Ruzsky had learned on 10 March 1917 that the Tsar was preparing to return to Tsarskoe Selo, so he was surprised to receive a telegram in the middle of the night informing him that the Imperial train would be arriving at Pskov at 8.00 pm on 14 March 1917.

Nicholas learned from Ruzsky that Petrograd was completely overrun and there was talk of his abdication. His siblings Mikhail and Xenia were in Petrograd that day and in great danger. Nicholas proposed sending Ruzsky with a few divisions from the war front to march on Petrograd, but a futile last stand was not on the cards from his beloved military. The last thing Ruzsky wanted to do was march on the government and lead a civil war.

"From the Tsar's first words I was convinced that he was in the hands of fate. Nicholas usually said little, and on this occasion he was even more curt and economical of words. Events had not only agitated him, but also made him angry." — GENERAL NIKOLAI RUZSKY

"As I was walking along the Millionaïa this afternoon, I saw the Grand Duke Nicholas Michaïlovitch. ... I know him well enough to have no doubt that he is sincere when he says that the collapse of autocracy will now mean the salvation and greatness of Russia; but I do not know whether he will keep his illusions for long and hope he will not lose them. ... In any case he has honestly done his best to open the Emperor's eyes to the approaching catastrophe, he actually had the courage some time back to send him the following letter, which was shown to me this morning: — MAURICE PALÉOLOGUE, 21 March 1917

"You have often mentioned your determination to continue the war to victory! But do you really think victory is possible in the present state of affairs?

"Do you know the situation within the Empire? Are you told the truth? Has anyone pointed out where the root of the evil lies?

"You have frequently told me that men were always deceiving you and that the only thing you believed in was the views of your wife. I tell you that the words she utters are the result of clever intrigues and not in accordance with the truth. If you are impotent to rid her of those not in accordance with the truth. If you are impotent to rid her of those influences, the least you can do is to be always on your guard against the schemers who use her as their tool. Clear these dark forces out, and you will immediately recover the confidence of your people which you have already half lost.

"I have hesitated long before telling you the truth, but I have made up my mind to do so, with encouragement from your mother and two sisters. You are about to witness fresh disturbances, nay, an attempt on your life.

"I speak as I do in the interests of your own safety and that of your throne and country."

— NIKOLAI MIKHAOLOVICH, letter to Nicholas II

CHAPTER XIV

Final Words on Weak Willidness

"The failure to move with the times brought Russia to the disaster of 1917.
— BARON P. GRAEVENITZ, Autocracy to Bolshevism

Naturally there was a softer side to Nicholas behind his public image and in fact the typical view of him is that he was too gentle and unsuited to head a tough regime in tough times. But succession is what it is and the next ruler in line is not always suitable or even sufficiently prepared to rule, as strange as that may seem. Nicholas II attracts much attention because of his apparent weakness that lost an empire and cost a dynasty. However, he can be judged equally loving or brutal and an interesting and complex character emerges under scrutiny. But the common view has come to be that on all sides of his personality he was pliant and easily coerced and manipulated.

One example was when he received a letter in an illiterate scrawl from a peasant widow called Vorobjova and Nicholas understood that she was pleading for her son to return from military service because he was needed to work on their land. He commanded, *"Send her son home otherwise the entire farm may be ruined."* Even though his order went against the law. Perhaps more decisions like this one would have left a better legacy and made him more compassionate while at the same time powerful.

Nicholas possessed all the attributes of a loving and caring son, brother, husband and father. He was reserved and enjoyed the simpler things in life. He loved animals, long walks and to smoke cigarettes in peaceful surroundings. He found pleasure in chopping wood, rowing a boat, arranging photo albums, growing vegetables and had a compulsion for heavy reading. It might be fair to call him a family man and it's easy to see how his easy-going character could be misread for weakness and attributed as the basis for his poor leadership. It was a view held by some of the closest people around him from his wife to his Prime Minister Count Witte. This perceived weakness which went hand in hand with his timidness was a reflection of his inner nature and the young man that had eventually crawled out from under his father's shadow.

The time when monarchs went in to battle with their troops was long gone and they became better suited as emblems for their cause. Russian tsars and tsarinas were honorary commanders of military regiments with their individual patron saints. Ceremonial uniforms and feast days were the large part of that cultural tradition and if that was all that was required from a tsar then Nicholas was well suited for it. Alexandra had her uncle Edward VII to look to in this regard, who was known as Edward the peacemaker and was one of the best examples of how a monarch should behave at the head of a Church and constitutional monarchy. He was the epitome of a ruler that trained well at court and was adept at representing his country abroad.

Still, Nicholas was not afraid to show up at the front unlike his cousins Wilhelm II and George V that had stayed well away from the battlefield. George V had the benefit of his father's counsel while he was heir apparent but Wilhelm II on the other hand looked to the military and was commissioned as a second lieutenant at the age of ten in the 1st Foot Guards, without having any field experience; he too was regarded as a poor leader. How ironic that both cousins George V and Wilhelm II thought Nicholas to be the weak one when he in fact was the stronger military leader.

Nicholas took tremendous interest in the smallest details, for example he would test a soldier's uniform before giving it his approval and literally donned it with a pouch, rifle, ammunition, one day's ration of bread and salt, and some water. He then marched a half marathon (13 miles) completing the march without sores or pains and then approving the new kit for general issue. Commitment to the military meant a slight detachment from political and social concerns. He preferred to deal with non-military matters from his study and didn't retire until all official papers were cleared from his desk. Here he made the subtle changes that trickled down to the minions and for which his expediency reaped benefits that fed down to the rank and file for rubber stamping, and all the while he looked to strengthen his legal powers.

He once said, *"I shall never, under any circumstances, agree to a representative form of government because I consider it harmful to the people whom God has entrusted to my care."* Two hundred years earlier, Peter the Great also believed that God had enthroned him and sanctioning his acts but he had carried a great humility with the role and once shared a meal with a servant from the same bowl. Nicholas took almost until the end of his life to learn such humility, when under house arrest he too would share the same food bowl with his servants.

The fundamental question is whether he was suited for the role of tsar with its overwhelming responsibilities or was it all way over his head? Afraid of the Government, Duma, military, and Church he was not, so timidness cannot in all fairness be levelled at him in these arenas. Yet conversely, in some accounts he is portrayed as a brutal ruler on a scale that was worse than his father. How could a ruler with such admirable family attributes and a clam grip on the political front also be labelled a tyrant? Had he lost apathy and empathy as he became detached from his ministers and the people? How did he really view his role; was it a calling or a sense of duty or did he regard his existence as a lifestyle of privilege, imperial traditions, military pageantry, state visits, sailing on fabulous yachts, dancing at balls and sumptuous feasting? Was it a nine to five occupation that attended to paperwork in the morning, met with ministers in the afternoon and enjoyed evenings with family in privacy.

Nicholas' first speech had been a warning not to harbour delusions, *"senseless dreams"* he called them. People would get more of the same.

CHAPTER XIV

Leon Trotsky was fifteen years old when he heard that speech and resolved to fight against those impositions. When Nicholas became tsar in 1894 Russia was still thought of as a medieval country. But just a year later, working hours were limited and night work was forbidden for women and minors under seventeen years old at a time when the majority of countries had almost no labour legislation at all. William Howard Taft the 27th President of America (1909 – 1913) said in 1908 following a visit to Russia, *"The Russian Emperor enacted labour legislation which not a single democratic state could boast of."* The campaign for womens' suffrage and equality in Russia gained momentum during the First Revolution 1905 and by July 1917, women over twenty had the right to vote and hold public office. After 1905 Russia entered a period of such agricultural and industrial growth that had World War I not happened, Russia had the potential for becoming the leading industrial nation of the world.

Despite the tsarist regime's criticism abroad, in 1901 Nicholas was nominated for the Nobel Peace Prize. On 12 August 1898 the Russian government had proposed that future difficulties between nations should be settled by peaceful means through international arbitration. With the aim of strengthening the Franco-Russo alliance Nicholas had initiated the Hague Convention of 1899, designed to end the arms race. It became part of the laws of war and he, along with Russian diplomat Friedrich Martens who contributed, were nominated because of it.

In the early years of Nicholas' reign his interest lay in strengthening his predecessors' territorial legacy and his ambitions of expansionism extended to hostilities with Mongolia, Manchuria and China and a war with Japan. None of it could have happened without Witte's successful industrialisation policy and guidance and without Witte the country may well have regressed to serfdom. Nicholas was able to ride 'Witte's wave' until his removal from office. And herein was Nicholas' greatest flaw, his ineffective management of ministers meant that in many cases a post depended solely on whether the tsar liked him, and later on, on whether Alexandra liked him.

In comparison with the level of attention Nicholas gave to the military down to uniform design, ministers felt that even in face-to-face discussions they were not being heard. His distance from political issues meant that his impulsive decision making was often the rule. If a minister was headstrong, Nicholas would listen to him and avoid confrontation and agree in principle until the minister left feeling satiated. A while later they would receive word that they were to be reprimanded or if they had upset the emperor or empress by their tone, would be told they had been dismissed from their post and in rarer cases exiled. This made him unpredictable and his 'two faces' was the foremost complaint levelled against him by his ministers in their memoirs.

In Count Witte, Nicholas had arguably squandered his most valuable ministerial asset. He was the single most minister that Nicholas was weary of because of his remarkable political and diplomatic skills. He'd served under Alexander II and Alexander III of whom he told his wife Maria Feodorovna that he considered Witte to be his ablest minister. When Witte married a Jew he knew that his political career would be over but Alexander III admired his moral courage and continued business as usual, overlooking that Jewish predicament and never mentioning it. Nicholas in comparison used his Jewish prejudice to remove Witte from office. In 1903 when there was a particularly raised hatred for the Jews and police were actively organising antisemitic riots and pogroms, Witte spoke out. One example was with the Kishinev pogrom, an Easter massacre of about fifty Jews when soldiers smashed their homes and raped the women. Witte openly highlighted the antisemitic cultism that was ingrained in the government, the police and the monarchy. Nicholas intervened in defence of the police and Witte was pressured in to resigning.

> *"His Majesty, it must be noted, hardly tolerates people whom he considers superior to himself either intellectually or morally. He is at ease only when dealing with men who are either actually his inferiors or whom he considers as such or finally, those who knowing His Majesty's weakness, find it expedient to feign inferiority."*
> — SERGEY WITTE, memoirs page 406

The many inconsistencies in attempting to unravel such a complex personality can be generalised. During the first two years of his reign Nicholas attempted to assert himself with guidance from his experienced mother. For the first half of the next twenty years of his reign he leans on Alexandra for inspiration. After Rasputin's appearance Alexandra's counsel takes on a different form where Rasputin is allowed to interfere which caused scandal in the monarchy, political instability and a rift in the Church; major factors contributing to the eventual fall of the dynasty.

> One source: *"He [NICHOLAS] was an affectionate creature, weighed down by a sense of responsibility to which he was utterly unable to rise; dependent for his inspiration upon an irresponsible wife who was in her turn the victim of an unscrupulous adventurer [RASPUTIN]".*

Nicholas' uninterest in political matters gave Alexandra a space to fill, she was the Empress after all, and even Rasputin could see that Nicholas showed little interest in ruling. As the world went to war Alexandra found herself at the helm of enormous power with only Rasputin at her side that she trusted. Finally, fate had placed her where she could bridge her husband's lacking and protect the autocracy for her son. Unfortunately the presence of Rasputin ostracised the ministers and the clergy.

CHAPTER XIV

Nicholas' father had been the wiser to retain Count Witte and Nicholas quite demonstrably did not value good counsel. The partnership with Witte had built the Siberian Railway and transformed the economy. Witte was not whiter than white and believed Russia's abundant grain production could serve as currency to pay for imports but as Russia was competing with America, Australia and Argentina, who produced grain more cheaply, he exploited the peasants with a ruthless hand which Nicholas happily approved of. In this arena the two men had no scruples about the manner in which they achieved their objectives.

Alexandra gained power in equal proportion to Nicholas losing it, signalling that he all but gave it away. It's unsurprising that this should be attributed as a weakness but had she been looking to overthrow her husband as previous consorts had done previous to the Pauline laws, then she may well have succeeded but she was just holding the fort. In any case, she possessed even less political nous than her husband and with the inclusion of Rasputin and the fact that she was of German origin meant that her ill fate was already written in the stars. Had Nicholas married the wrong woman and should he have listened to his father and married Elena of Montenegro, a far more interesting and stronger woman. A great Russian empress she would have made and what an Emperor he might have become.

"I have no patience with Ministers who prevent him [NICHOLAS] *doing his duty. The situation requires firmness. The Emperor, unfortunately, is weak; but I am not, and I intend to be firm."*
— ALEXANDRA FEODOROVNA, said to SIR GEORGE BUCHANAN, British ambassador in Russia

Alexandra's German roots were always going to be the bone of contention for a country that was at war with Germany. Her loyalty to Russia is not in question and, in her defence, Lili Dehn who was well informed about Germany's role in the Russian Revolution 1917, in her book exonerates Nicholas, Alexandra and Rasputin of being directly responsible.

"It is both unjust and untrue to ascribe the Revolution as directly consequent upon the Emperor's weakness, or the pro-Germanism and hysteric sensuality of the Empress. I have endeavoured to show that Rasputin was probably one of the unconscious tools of the Revolution against Imperialism: there is no doubt that German intrigues brought Lenin back from Switzerland to overthrow the milder rule of Kerensky, who was not ready to offer the country an efficient substitute for Tsardom, but the Empress was entirely innocent of pro-Germanism."
— LILI DEHN, (Alexandra's friend) quote taken from the last page of her book The Real Tsaritza

In April 1917 Lenin moved from Switzerland through Germany to Sweden and thence to Russia where the Bolsheviks fanned anti-war sentiment against the war. Had Nicholas dealt with this incursion and stopped Lenin's party from organising in Russia then civil war may not have happened in August 1918 during which time the Bolsheviks granted Germany economic rights on Russian territory in exchange for military assistance in helping to defeat the White Army that dominated Ukraine, Crimea and large parts of south Russia.

That Nicholas allowed Rasputin directly to influence matters of state is another common belief and falsity. With regards to Rasputin's role in government and Church, he had none outside of the commissions he was tasked on behalf of the tsar or tsarina. Many contemporary politicians have said that Rasputin had no influence at all but it has been demonstrated thus far that he did have an effect on the government, the Church, Alexandra, the Tsar and ultimately on the people and therefore the country as well.

"I must insist that Rasputin had not a particle of influence over him [NICHOLAS II], *It was Nicky who eventually put a stop to Rasputin's visits to the palace and sent the man back to Siberia."*
— OLGA ALEXANDROVNA

Ms Anna Vyrubova
(Courtesy, The Last Days of the Romanovs)

The argument is made that if Nicholas had been forceful and prevented Alexandra from bringing Rasputin in to their home then the Imperial Family would not have met their fatal end. Aside from ministers and other officials,

CHAPTER XIV

some of those closest to the Imperial Family wrote that neither Alexandra nor Rasputin influenced the tsar to a degree that was relevant. Ms Vyrubova who probably knew the tsar and tsarina better than anyone outside of the Imperial Family, in her book attests to a stronger Nicholas.

> *"The Emperor understood all this well and very frequently acted against her advice, guided by his own experience. Sometimes his decisions coincided with the Empress' wishes. But to claim indiscriminately that the Emperor acted in state matters only according to the Empress' wishes is a great mistake. This means ignoring the facts as well as the character and principles of the Emperor. Emperor Nicholas was far from being as simple-minded and weak-willed as many thought."* — ANNA VYRUBOVA

> *"... after his marriage, his mother's influence rapidly waned and Nicholas fell permanently under the spell of his wife ...* [Alexandra was] *possessed of a sufficiently strong character to master him completely and infect him with her own morbidity."*
> — COUNT SERGEY WITTE

Nicholas' relationship with the military differs somewhat in that he had a real interest in it. There is ample evidence of the heartless acts of violence and murders perpetrated by the regime with his knowledge and approval. The Black Hundred didn't have official approval but carried out plenty of assassinations on those who were considered a threat to the monarchy including ministers. One of its founders was Vladimir Purishkevich, who was among those named responsible for the killing of Rasputin in 1916. Notable members from the Church were John of Kronstadt, the hieromonk Iliodor and Bishops Hermogenes and Sergius (Stragorodsky - future Patriarch of Moscow). Nicholas was highly supportive of this group, made up of various unions and factions across Russia. There is no objection from Nicholas that voiced any disapproval of the terrifying deeds of the Black Hundred, on the contrary, he wore the badge of its largest union, the Union of Russian People (URP) of which the Black Hundred served as its paramilitary wing.

He was so embroiled with the need to rid the country of non-pure Russians that it's hard to see how he could have avoided any involvement in the regime's ethnic cleansing ethos. By accepting the URP badge, perhaps inadvertently, he had become a high ranking member of the Black Hundred and the Church also being members added legitimacy and essentially provided a ring of protection around the monarchy. Uprisings in the countryside were met by military force and the worst of the pogroms were perpetrated by the Black Hundred, such was the method for implementing institutional racism.

Nicholas II was nominated for the first ever Nobel Peace Prize in 1901, notwithstanding the killings being perpetrated by his regime. It demonstrated that the world was prepared to turn a blind eye on population culling. The award was won by Frédéric Passy for his work on international peace conferences, almost for the same reason that Nicholas had been nominated and perhaps it was this juxtaposition of a tyrant receiving a peace prize that had ruled him out. His expansionist aims in the East were comparable to his need to control the interior where sporadic rebellions in the cities and uprisings in the countryside needed to be put down and it seemed appropriate to blame such matters on the Jews and Muslims; being that racism was virtually passed by heredity through the Romanov dynasty.

His prejudice extended to Britain which he believed was controlled by Jews, he would say, "*An Englishman is a zhid* [Jew]." He also loathed the Japanese who he referred to as monkeys, even in official documents. The Black Hundred organisation were a staunchly monarchist movement and in many ways led the interior offensive which Nicholas supported and thereby he was the de facto figurehead of the far-right movement against the minority groups of his own subjects. The margins of Nicholas' state papers, where he would often leave comments, help to reveal the tyrant in him that some biographers have tended to ignore. His words alone portray an unsympathetic and much darker side at odds with the gentle words with which he filled his personal diaries and the gentle behaviour and meekness for which he is usually attributed. At no time did he believe it could be possible to overthrow the entire tsarist system as would happen in 1917.

In August 1905 when Cossacks were operating in the Caucasus it was reported that they had suppressed an uprising without bloodshed. In his marginal comments Nicholas wrote "*That is no good! In such cases one must always shoot.*" On 6 August 1905 General Trepoff reported that his Cossacks had 'unfortunately' used nogaikas (thick whips) on a group of doctors that were siding with the peasants of Saratov in disorders. Nicholas underlined the word 'unfortunately' and noted "*Very well done!*" On 5 November 1905 he was informed that 162 anarchists were stirring up strikes in Vladivostok, and he wrote "*They should all be hanged.*"

Nicholas approved the use of excessive and cruel force to deal with uprisings, public disorders, protestors, rioters, dissidents and terrorists. Whilst he got along with the military and even his uncles and the Black Hundred, he was not likewise supportive of the government. Loyal officials like Count Witte and Stolypin that were risking their lives at the rock face were alone in dealing with the *Socialist Revolutionary Battle Organisation* that had undertaken a terrorist campaign involving many assassinations and attempted murders of government officials. That terrorist movement spread widely and the government had no effective policy to deal with it which ultimately had resulted in Stolypin's assassination in 1911.

CHAPTER XIV

TSAR NICHOLAS DIARIES

Keeping a diary was something Nicholas picked up from Alexandra during the period of their engagement. It seems that she abandoned her journal to kick start his, as there are no entries in her journal after 11 May 1894. She insisted on access to his private diary and made her own entries in it. Shortly before the death of his father she wrote *"I have been able to pray with you in church for your darling father. What a comfort! You near me, all seems easier. I know you will always help me."* (cite. Sophie Buxhoeveden page 39).

From the start of Russia's switch from the Julian to Gregorian calendars, Nicholas and Alexandra recorded both date formats in their diaries. Nicholas kept a simple diary with remarkable regularity, throwing light on his character, his interests, and noting official visits. Indeed, a diary meant to log official affairs became a focal point of his family life. It revealed the deep sorrow after his abdication because of the absence of an entry for several days. He said to Ms Vyrubova, *"It has shaken me badly, as you see. For the first few days I was so little myself that I could not even write my diary."*

Nicholas amassed many volumes of diaries, fifty-one have survived. They are kept at the Novo-Romanov Archive in the State Archive of the Russian Federation in Moscow. They were partially translated to French (Les Journal Intime de Nicolas II), then in to German in 1923 and in 1925 they received a first translation in to English. His early diaries can be quite difficult to come across.

It was the same across the dominion territories which were difficult to control because of the empire's vastness so Nicholas empowered governors with the legality to perform atrocities in his name. In his manifesto of 1899 for example, he abolished the Finnish constitution and placed the function of the government of Finland under the Russian Imperial Council. It was done because the governor of Finland reported that the Finnish people had become increasingly difficult to control (*page 109*). With a flurry of his pen, Nicholas transferred the capstone of power from Finland to St Petersburg and the governor of Finland was given carte blanche.

The head of the police promised him, there would be no revolution in Russia for a hundred years if Nicholas sanctioned 50,000 executions, which he did not do, thankfully. In 1908 he was similarly presented with an industrialisation plan that would require far more money than was available and cost between ten and fifteen million premature deaths but again he refused, resisting the temptation to become the biggest genocidal perpetrator in world history. His decisions offer a unique perspective, as he could have had many more people killed by his regime. However, the number of people murdered by the Bolsheviks following the Russian Revolution 1917 were comparable and ironically had Nicholas decided to massacre 50,000 people then the deaths of many millions might well have been saved.

The loss of both the war against Japan and the Great Retreat from the Germans is largely attributed to Nicholas not having involved himself enough in the Russo-Japanese War and having involved himself too much in World War I. For both, industrialisation had been readied thanks to Witte's rapid growth plans but the inefficient management of supplying the front had been the primary cause for the military defeats. The result of ineffective logistics during World War I meant that Russia lost territories inhabited by more than one-quarter of its citizens that provided more than one-third of its grain harvest (namely Ukraine). How much of it was directly attributable to Nicholas is debatable but what was the point of millions being sent to fight and the government not adequately managing their provisions. Although logistics is a partnership between the war department and the Ministry of the Interior it may be inferred that Nicholas should have intervened as tsar, and disarray ensued as a consequence of not having this relationship developed with the ministers over a two decade reign.

The Soviet demographer Boris Urlanis estimated that 1.8 million Russian soldiers were killed in world War I, that's 30% of the total deaths of the Entente powers. Otherwise the figure of Russian deaths is usually given as 1.451,000 deaths (1.7 million according to UK and US estimates). 4.9 million were wounded, a third of a million were taken prisoner and there were 1.5 million civilian deaths above the pre-war level. Russia suffered the highest number of military, civilian and total fatalities in World War I. How much of this was due to the divisions within the Russian structure?

CHAPTER XIV

"I was surrounded with members of the suite who were thoroughly honourable men and ready, as I was, to worship the Tsar and to die for the dynasty. Each one of us felt that we had never succeeded in inspiring in the Sovereign the confidence without which the difficulties of our task inevitably became more than mortal man can overcome." — ALEXANDER MOSSOLOV, Head of Chancellery of the Imperial Court Ministry

It is inconceivable that Nicholas alone could have orchestrated such a chaotic set of circumstances that produced failure upon failure which lead to the February and October revolutions of 1917. The failings of others certainly played their part with Alexandra and Rasputin contributing to that instability. While those closest to the tsar have refuted that Alexandra and Rasputin had any influence over Nicholas, such as Olga Alexandrovna, Anna Vyrubova and Lili Dehn for example, to accept their testimony is to reject any influence on events from Alexandra and Rasputin during the two years that Nicholas was at the front. He had been persuaded to go and was remiss in leaving behind the government to be dismantled by them.

From 1914 to 1917, the price of flour increased fivefold because grain was not being brought to the cities which caused the hunger that led to both revolution and civil war, this was the real internal issue aside from a thriving black market that was selling flour with as much chalk as wheat in it. Yet conversely the construction of the Siberian Railway had been the greatest facilitator for movement of goods in Europe, not least for grain supplies to the cities. If Nicholas had not seen that project through to its completion the calamity that would have faced Russia is truly unimaginable.

The debate is whether Nicholas was weak and it cannot be assumed that the atrocities perpetrated in his name were because he was too weak to prevent them or that he was manipulated in backing the paramilitaries. Any mention of weakness seems moot considering he presided over the deaths of millions; who ever heard of a gentle tyrant, by definition he had to be unsympathetic. There was an acceptance of the suffering of others and even those closest to him did not agree that he was weak nor influenced in any way. Yet the memoirs of his ministers are the primary source and they use the words, weakness, failing intellect and limited intelligence, interchangeably to describe him.

What then do we make of his mental state. When Nicholas was ten years old he was conversant in Russian, French, English and German and studied history ardently. He could read a great work of non-fiction in several days. Someone capable of that mastery could not have been without intelligence. His intelligence and intellect have been universally questioned, which are two separate things. Perhaps his intellect was lacking but hardly the same can be said for his intelligence which was above average and certainly he was not the dunce that his father had thought of him.

"Some time after I left the post of Prime Minister, His Majesty received me very amiably and asked me to return all letters and telegrams with his autographed commentaries which were in my possession. I did so, and I now regret it. These documents would shed a remarkable light on the character of this truly unhappy sovereign, with all his intellectual and moral weaknesses."
— COUNT SERGEY WITTE

Chairman of the Council of Ministers (effectively Prime Minister,) Count Witte, credited Nicholas with the average education of a Colonel of the Guards and deficient of intellect. Chairman of the second Duma F. A. Golovin (February-June 1907) knew Nicholas for the shortest time and described him as weak willed, a description shared by so many others in the Duma (parliament) and the Council of Ministers (government).

"Devotion to his home, and trust in a deep, superstitious religion – these were the prevailing consolations of a weak and wavering intellect." — THE DAILY TELEGRAPH, 1 March 1919

Abdication of a Dynasty

The Grand Duke Pavel Alexandrovich (Nicholas' uncle,) sent a message to the army generals asking for their views on replacing the Tsar. Their responses surprised Nicholas and must have deeply affected him as evidenced by General Ruzsky's earlier quote that the normally calm tsar was angered (*page 315*). To learn the unfavourable consensus from his beloved military which he assumed he could always count on was simply shattering. His mother remained convinced that if Nicholas had stayed in Moghilev then he would have had vital days to regroup and even to muster support and turn the troops towards Petrograd, but he was always going to respond first to Alexandra's call to come home.

At 2.00 am on the morning of 15 March 1917, Nicholas sent for Ruzsky and told him *"I have decided to submit and to give the people a responsible Ministry."* At 3.00 am Ruzsky began repeatedly calling Duma President Rodzianko's office until the telephone was finally picked up later that morning, presumably when Rodzianko and his staff turned up for work. The conversation lasted for two hours during which Ruzsky informed that the Tsar wanted Rodzianko to process the abdication, in fact it was one of the pointless stipulations, Nicholas believing his abdication was negotiable.

Rodzianko had no intention of going out to Pskov and abandoning the disarray that was unfolding in parliament and the government. He apprised Ruzsky of the serious nature of things in Petrograd and stated his opinion that the only way forward was for the Tsar to abdicate the throne. Rodzianko must have felt some vindication having warned the Imperial couple of this eventuality so many times only to be scorned and dismissed.

Ruzsky communicated the Tsar's wishes to Moghilev where Chief of Staff General Alekseev sent telegrams out to the generals on the various fronts and the senior admirals of the fleets. He asked for their response regarding the Tsar's abdication, on the question they had previously been asked by the Grand Duke Pavel Alexandrovich (Nicholas' uncle). All but one of the nine high ranking military staff sent their response in the affirmative for the Tsar to abdicate.

The die-hard monarchist Admiral Alexander Kolchak was the only military commander that did not consent to abdication. In fact, Kolchak did believe that reforms were desperately needed but in order of priority the emerging civil war was the current and pressing issue. It required a robust leadership structure to succeed, in order for the military to obey the orders of a stable government, and not such talk of abdication. Many military leaders that sympathised with White Army objectives during the civil war (1918 - 1920) sooner or later went over to the Red Army. Kolchak in contrast established an anti-communist government in Omsk and became recognised as the Commander in Chief of the White forces until January 1920 when the Czech-Slovak regiment handed him over to the Socialist Revolutionaries and soon after that, in February 1920, he was shot at Irkutsk, Siberia. If Nicholas had stayed in Moghilev he might have found in Kolchak the loyalty that would have marched on Petrograd.

Senior staff that voted on the question of Nichols II's abdication:

- Chief Of Staff General Mikhail Alekseev – Yes
- Commander of northern armies General Nikolai Ruzsky – Yes
- Commander of the Baltic Fleet Admiral Adrian Nepenin – Yes
- Black Sea Fleet Vice Admiral Alexander Kolchak – No
- Grand Duke Nikolai Nikolaevich (Nicholas' great uncle) – Yes
- Commander of 7th Army General Vladimir Cheremisov – Yes
- General Alexei Evert – Yes (removed from service March 1917)
- General of the Cavalry Sakharov – Yes
- * Commander of the 8th Army General Alexei Brusilov – Yes

* The Iron General as he was nicknamed, was appointed Commander in Chief of the Russian Army from May 1917 to July 1917.

The memoirs of Russian military officers are concerned chiefly on the formative days of the revolution of 1917 offering an understanding of the mood during this time and indeed during World War I. For example, General Brusilov stated that in the spring of 1917, in other words at the moment of Nicholas' abdication, "that *the pre-war army formations had already been destroyed.*" This simple statement from Brusilov underpins the necessity for which the admirals and generals believed the Tsar had to resign. There were twelve million personnel at the front who were poorly equipped and no better disciplined, and transport logistics were a nightmare. For example, up until World War I the whole industrial base in St Petersburg, including the Putilov Works, relied on coal shipped in from Cardiff, England. This source being stopped at the outbreak of war meant that coal had to be sourced from the Donets Basin requiring in turn a new railway. By January 1917 blast furnaces were stopping production because they could not receive coal and with no coal there was no iron to forge for the railway and a stalemate ensued which as a consequence saw the reduction of armaments production and the lack of artillery shells and ammunition supplied to the front.

From the memoirs of military officers a clear picture of what happened in the carriage where Nicholas signed his abdication can be derived. In this case two accounts can be referenced; one by Ruzsky and another by Vasily Vitalyevich Shulgin a representative of the Duma during the abdication. Ruzsky's account was published a few days after the abdication in *Russkaya Mysl* (Russian Thought), a magazine established in 1880 that would be shut down by the Bolsheviks in 1918.

At 10.00 am on the morning of the day of the abdication, Ruzsky entered the Tsar's coach to begin the official process. He had with him General Yuri Danilov, the Chief of Staff for the northern front, and a commissary officer General Savich. Nicholas wanted updates from the front and Petrograd but Ruzsky having no direct instruction from the Executive Committee gave no response. This time it was Ruzsky that said very little. He knew the situation in Petrograd was hopeless even with 20,000 anti-revolutionary troops that were mustered at Gatchina waiting for orders. Ruzsky had all that was needed in his pocket. He pulled out the telegrams from the generals and laid them out on a table in front of Nicholas, each one asking him personally to abdicate in favour of his son. The one from Nicholas' second cousin Nikolai Nikolaevich must have driven home the message. Not a single general was prepared to march on Petrograd for him.

Nicholas turned to Count Adolf Frederiks and dictated a letter to the President of the Duma, Rodzianko. Finally, Nicholas was humbled at the eleventh hour to recognise the power of the Duma. He asked that Rodzianko arrange for his renunciation of the throne in favour of his son Alexei. At 3.00 pm on 15 March 1917 Ruzsky received the instrument of abdication from Nicholas II. But two Duma representatives were already eagerly heading towards Pskov from Warsaw. Ruzsky on returning to his office found a telegram waiting, informing him that Duma dignitaries Alexander

CHAPTER XIV

Guchkov and Vasily Shulgin would be arriving that evening and therefore he did not act on the document in his possession and decided to wait for the Duma contingent. Nicholas was glad to learn of the Duma envoys believing they would affect a positive change in the situation and offer an agreeable and well considered solution. Frederiks was with Nicholas the whole time, not leaving his side for a moment. He would later tell a Soviet investigator that the Tsar never asked him for any advice on his abdication, *"... and if he had asked me, I never would have advised him to do so."*

At 10.00 pm the dignitaries arrived and were led to the Tsar's carriage. Guchkov and Shulgin exchanged pleasantries with Nicholas and Frederiks. Both sides sat opposite each other amid the green velvet walls and soft furnishings of the Imperial carriage cum-drawing room. Ruzsky and Danilov joined them and sat quietly to one side. Guchkov was aware of the significance of this moment in history and was very nervous, not once looking the Tsar in the eyes. He updated the Tsar on the situation in Petrograd and informed him that his personal guard at Tsarskoe Selo had gone over to the Red Army. Then he went in to a lengthy but unnecessary speech aimed at smoothing the process and putting the Tsar at ease. When he had finished, Nicholas asked simply *"What is to be done now?"* at which Guchkov explained that he was there to persuade him to abdicate the throne. His nervousness in the carriage with Nicholas came as a surprise to his colleague, as Guchkov had volunteered for the Boer War and fought in numerous duels. The Duma representatives completed their task and found Nicholas to be rather blasé about the whole thing and certainly he had not required any persuasion to abdicate.

Nicholas had submitted mentally to the abdication the moment he learned of the situation at Tsarskoe Selo; the utility power was down with water pipes that had burst and no running water or electricity and the children had for a time sat in the cold and dark. Now and again just outside of the peaceful palace grounds the family heard intermittent gun shots. When Alexandra had asked the guard if they would be loyal many had fled leaving Alexander Palace unprotected and open for marauders. Alexandra, the children and their servants were left unguarded while everyone outside the gates held Alexandra responsible for the troubles in Petrograd. Something terrible could happened at any time. It must have been the bitterest pill to swallow for Nicholas, his only option having been to abdicate with no support from the military. He had lost the monarchy and his dynasty.

> Nicholas replied to Guchkov, *"Very well. I have already signed the act of abdication in favour of my son but now I have come to the conclusion that my son's health is not strong enough and I do not wish to part from him. Therefore, I have decided to make over the throne to Mikhail Alexandrovich."*

"I considered all this, decided to abdicate. But I do not deny it in favour of my son, since I must leave Russia, since I am leaving the supreme power. I [do not] consider it possible to leave my son, whom I love very much. That is why I decided to pass the throne to my brother, Grand Duke Mikhail Alexandrovich." — NICHOLAS II

Nicholas wrongly assumed that he was entering in to negotiations about his impending house arrest and believed he would be setting out conditions for his family's relocation in exile at Livadia Palace. In a final display of ignorance he reappointed Grand Duke Nikolai Nikolaevich, whom he had previously relieved of command at the front, as Commander in Chief of the army. But when he deleted his son from the proclamation to abdicate, he set the normal course of events in the opposite direction. The generals would have supported the promotion of Tsarevich Alexei, however with Alexei out of the frame there could be no military support for the monarchy or the family.

Nicholas naively signed the document in haste which is evidenced by his shaky scrawl on the document. It was made with the wrongful belief that his family would be protected under these broad terms, *"... to take under the protection of the government all members of the imperial house, since in such difficult times, all kinds of surprises are always possible."* French ambassador Maurice Paléologue (1914-1917) is considered to have written one of the most revealing and significant memoirs of this time in Russia and he recorded that Nicholas had listened to no one for advice leading up to his abdication. His naivety was astonishing and in taking only cursory advice from Frederiks, he assumed that he was dealing with a stable government that would meet the terms of his perceived agreement.

He totally underestimating the momentum of the revolution because he neither understood it nor appreciated the resolve of the people. The February Revolution 1917 was a culmination of a long series of political and social developments that was demanding a constitutional monarchy. Nicholas' naivety and lack of foresight led him to believe the country was preparing to form a republic. The single act of forfeiting Alexei from the succession meant that Nicholas II had unwittingly changed the focus of the revolution from a demand to modernise in to a call for the removal of the monarchy.

Nicholas entered the Adjoining carriage with Frederiks to compose the letter of his abdication. It took just ten minutes and they returned with a typed sheet containing Nicholas' signature and Frederiks' countersignature. Two copies were made, one each for Ruzsky and Guchkov; this was agreed because of the stormy situation in Petrograd where the document might easily fall astray. Effectively the regency was now with Nicholas' brother Mikhail Alexandrovich and Alexei had no recourse in accordance with the laws of succession because abdication removed any claim from descendants. Alexei would later question the validity of his father's action to withdraw his claim to the throne, which of course was legal as the decision had been made by a sitting tsar.

The Duma representatives were surprised by how easy things went. Guchkov commented to Ruzsky that he had not noticed anything stirring in Nicholas, surmising that he had met a man who lacked all emotion and had conducted the abdication as though he were handing over a platoon of soldiers. Shulgin wrote in his memoirs, *"In my soul there was rather pity toward this person who in that moment was redeeming his mistakes. Noble thoughts illuminated his resignation of power."* Having accepted the Tsar's abdication on the Imperial train Guchkov came away believing that he was dealing with an abnormal individual with a lowered intellect and believing the Tsar was completely unaware of the significance of the event.

Guchkov and Shulgin handed Ruzsky a chit for their copy of the abdication document and headed back to a broiling Petrograd. Half an hour later the Imperial train also left Pskov heading back to Moghilev overnight and arriving at the Stavka at 2.00 pm (6.00 pm according to Ruzsky) on 16 March 1917. From the moment he had abdicated Nicholas was not permitted to communicate with Alexandra. He wrote in his diary, *"I had a long and sound sleep. Woke up beyond Dvinsk. Sunshine and frost ... I read much of Julius Caesar."* He made no further entries until 19 March 1917 (G) such was his misery during this time. If ever there was a time to sit on a train for hours in despair, staring out of the window contemplating the how and why of what went so wrong, this was it. Yet Nicholas slept and found solace in reading, his mind undistracted by the significance of his abdication. Julius Caesar can only be read with a clear head.

The wiry old frame of Commander in Chief General Alekseev was waiting to receive Nicholas on the platform at Moghilev station. He looked at his former Tsar respectfully over his gold spectacles and informed him just a few minutes later at 2.30 pm that his brother Mikhail Alexandrovich had also renounced the throne having received no support from the Duma as was his prerequisite for accepting the title. Nicholas and Alekseev crossed platforms where Maria Feodorovna's train had also arrived that afternoon through a snowstorm (one account says she arrived on the next day). Maria Feodorovna called this day the greatest humiliation of her life.

No sooner had Gutchkov and Shulgin returned to Petrograd than rumours were spreading again about Nicholas and Alexandra working with Germany to restore the monarchy and that in collusion with them were tsarist ministers like Gutchkov, Lvov and Milyukov. The Petrograd Soviet on 20 March 1917 (G) subsequently demanded that the government immediately place them all under arrest and that evening four Duma members left Petrograd for Moghilev to carry out those instructions. Guchkov, a former Chairman of the Duma (1910-1911), had already been arrested on the evening of 15 March 1917. He had the abdication document in his possession but didn't hand it over fearing that it might be destroyed in the hurricane of confusion that was consuming Petrograd. His copy of the letter of abdication remained unaccounted for until it was discovered in the archives of the Academy of Sciences in Leningrad in 1929. Both Guchkov and Shulgin, the Duma contingent that had gone to Pskov, were supporters of the White movement and were routed out by the Bolsheviks; Guchkov emigrated to Germany and Shulgin managed to get to Yugoslavia in 1920. This was the level of distrust the Soviet had for the Duma.

The abdication marked the victory for the February Revolution 1917. By 21 March 1917 (G) military dignitaries, government representatives and the Duma task force were in Moghilev. The Act of Renunciation speech was written by the Vice Director of the Chancellery of the Ministry of Foreign Affairs Nicolas A. de Basily who was serving at Moghilev as the Chief of the Diplomatic division. Whether Nicholas read out his speech before or after he was arrested is up for debate as are the many translated versions of its contents. In the presence of the assembled parties the former emperor Nicholas Alexandrovich Romanov was formally told that he was under arrest and would be held indefinitely by the Provisional Government. That evening at an event in Petrograd, Nikolai Mikhailovich (first cousin to Alexander III) showed ambassador Paléologue a copy of a letter he had sent to Nicholas (*page 307*).

Nicholas was put on the Imperial train and taken to Tsarskoe Selo. It rolled in to the station at 11.30 am on 22 March 1917 (G). Nicholas alighted from the train but before he made it to a waiting car a shot rang out; the train driver had shot himself in his sorrow over the abdication of the Tsar after that saddening final train journey. At Alexander Palace, Nicholas found Alexei, Olga and Marie with measles and Tatiana and Anastasia with painful ear abscesses. Marie was literally at death's door with a temperature of 40°C (104°F) and having double pneumonia with Alexandra attending to her personally. Kerensky visited later that day to determine that the arrangements were adequate and to introduce Colonel Korovichenko who was soon to replace the existing Commandant de Kotzebue who had become too friendly with the prisoners, it had been judged.

Kerensky informed the Tsar that he had ordered the arrests of Ms Vyrubova and Lili Dehn and members of the royal family and their close aides. The Imperial Family were officially placed under house arrest on 25 March 1917 (G). Ms Vyrubova was detained for several months and Lili Dehn for a few days only. Nicholas from this point turns his attention to moving to England. He noted in his diary on 23 March 1917:

"*Cleared up my books and things, and began to set aside everything I want to take with me, If I have to go to England.*"
— NICHOLAS II

CHAPTER XIV

THE TSAR'S RENUNCIATION SPEECH AT MOGHILEV

"We, Nicholas II, by the grace of God, Emperor of Russia, Tsar of Poland and grand duke of Finland, and so forth, make known to all our faithful subjects:

"In the day of the great struggle against a foreign foe who has been striving for three years to enslave our country, God has wished to send to Russia a new and painful trial. Interior troubles threaten to have a fatal repercussion of the final outcome of the war.

"The destinies of Russia and the honour of our heroic army, the happiness of the people and all the future of our dear fatherland require that the war be prosecuted at all cost to a victorious end. The cruel enemy is making his last effort and the moment is near when our valiant army, in concert with those of our glorious allies, will finally chastise the foe.

"In these decisive days in the life of Russia we have thought that we owed to our people the close union and organisation of all its forces for the realisation of a rapid victory; for which reason, in agreement with the Imperial Duma, we have recognised that it is for the good of the country that we should abdicate the Crown of the Russian State and lay down the Supreme Power.

"Not wishing to separate ourselves from our beloved son, we bequeath our heritage to our brother, the Grand Duke Mikhail Alexandrovich, with our blessing for the future of the Throne of the Russian State. We bequeath it to our brother to govern in full union with the national representatives sitting in the Legislative Institutions and to take his inviolable oath to them in the name of our well-beloved country.

"We call upon all faithful sons of our native land to fulfil their sacred and patriotic duty of obeying the Tsar at the painful moment of national trial and to aid them, together with the representatives of the nation, to conduct the Russian State in the way of prosperity and glory."

— NICHOLAS II, 15 March 1917, 15.00 (G)

REVOLUTION & ABDICATION

REVOLT SUCCEEDS QUICKLY

New Cabinet Selected Exclusively from Present and Past Duma Members.

FREE PRESS, FREE SPEECH

BULLETIN.
London, March 16.—The abdication of Emperor Nicholas and the appointment of Grand Duke Michael as regent has not yet been carried into effect, though it has been decided on by the executive power, Andrew Bonar Law, chancellor of the exchequer, announced today in the House of Commons.

(By Associated Press.)

London Thinks Czar Will Leave Russia

London, March 17. It is believed here that the Czar and his family will leave Russia immediately.

The phrase in the manifesto "not wishing to separate ourself from our beloved son" is interpreted to mean that he has been ordered to go at once. It is possible for him to come here or even to go to Denmark, but his plans are not known only to a very few.

There is a possibility that following his departure Russia will establish a limited form of republic. Much depends on the attitude of the Grand Duke Nicholas. Many expect him to be the "man on horseback" who, it has long been predicted, would dominate the Russian revolution when it came.

Things continued to escalate in Petrograd with workers organising in to soviets and revolutionaries criticising the Provisional Government for their continuation with the war. It was time for officers to pick a side in a sea of shifting loyalties that depended on which side was winning at any time. For example, Lieutenant General Krymov was ordered to bring his troops to Petrograd on 25 August 1917 to guard against a Bolshevik uprising, it was a last ditch effort but like Nicholas at Pskov thinking he could rally the troops, Kerensky had also left things way too late. Two days later, Kerensky having appointed himself Commander in Chief of the army, ordered Krymov to turn back. However, the Cossack divisions switched sides and continued marching on the city under Bolshevik leadership. On 30 August 1917 Krymov tried to explain to Kerensky that his troops had aligned themselves with the Soviets but Kerensky scheduled a military trial. On the following day Krymov sat in a quiet room and shot himself (aged 45).

CHAPTER XIV

In America the abdication was reported as a victory of the democratic revolutionaries over the authoritarian state (*image below*) but were also reporting the Bolsheviks as the enemy of democracy. In London the Russian Revolution 1917 was hailed as the advent of a free press and free speech. In due course American troops would arrive at Vladivostok and join the campaign with the British, to support Kolchak's White movement.

In his study at Alexander Palace, Nicholas showed the telegrams from the generals and admirals to Pavel Konstantinovich Benckendorff (Grand Marshal of the Imperial Court). Nicholas stood facing his former chargés d'affaires no more than a Russian citizen, seeking an explanation for such blatant disloyalty and such affrontery from the people who now referred to him as citizen Romanov.

"He showed me the telegrams of the Generals commanding the different fronts, who all, with one accord, had told him that the only means of saving the monarchy was to abdicate in favour of the Tsarevich." — COUNT PAVEL BENCKENDORFF

"The Emperor as Supreme Commander of the army had, in the presence of the enemy, been betrayed by his Generals and had been forced to give way to pressure because the last support of the monarchy, the army, was going over to the revolutionaries. History has never known the like of this." — COUNT PAVEL BENCKENDORFF

Perhaps Nicholas should have abdicated much sooner if he really had not wanted to rule. Perhaps he shouldn't have taken over the military in both the Russo-Japanese War and World War I. Perhaps he shouldn't have let Rasputin anywhere near the court and perhaps the Duma should have been treated respectfully and afforded some credence. Perhaps he shouldn't have let his wife run the affairs of state. So many maybes that 'perhaps' the debate on whether Nicholas II was ill equipped intellectually to deal with his responsibilities has been answered.

"The crowned heads of this country are so far from their people, and the Empress through shyness and a nervous nature is but rarely seen, though she has worked splendidly for the sick and wounded and has a really kind and sympathetic nature, which unfortunately no one experiences except those who are very near her, or who happen to have seen a good deal of her, as I have done. ... At present she stands alone. It is a sad business, and when one looks at those pretty daughters one wonders what will happen to them all."
— MAJOR-GENERAL SIR JOHN HANBURY-WILLIAMS, Military Secretary to Secretary of State for War, Head of British military mission with the Stavka in Russia, 4 January 1917 (G)

Previous tsars valued ministerial advice and the counsel of experienced nobles and statesmen alike, but alas Nicholas II did not as evidenced by Frederiks up until the final hours. According to those around Alexandra when she heard the news that her husband had abdicated, she didn't believe that he had actually done it and remained reasonably calm. She had been unable to go out to Moghilev because she was nursing her children and telecommunications were no longer possible. But had she gone out to Moghilev, she would not have permitted him to sign away the future of their son and it's hard to imagine how Nicholas could have made that momentous decision in renouncing the throne for himself and his son, without consulting with his wife the Empress.

"When she found out about the renunciation, she controlled herself, keeping calm." — PIERRE GILLIARD, French tutor

"She treated the events and the very abdication of the Sovereign calmly, showing courage and endurance." — ALEXEI VOLKOV, Alexandra's valet

The tragedy was that Nicholas realised his folly when it was all too late for him and his family. Vasily Yakovlev transported Nicholas from Tobolsk to Ekaterinburg in April 1918, and knowing him for the briefest time, described the tsar as a pleasant enough person but of *"extraordinarily limited intellect."*

CHAPTER XIV

"The combination of an Emperor so devoted to his Empress that her word was law, and of an Empress led unconsciously by the worst possible advisers, brought about their ruin and that, for the time being, of their country." — SIR JOHN HANBURY-WILLIAMS, memoirs

"Though it could hardly be said that the Tsar governed Russia in a working sense, he ruled as an autocrat and was in turn ruled by his strong-willed if weak-witted wife. Beautiful, hysterical, and morbidly suspicious, she hated everyone but her immediate family and a series of fanatic or lunatic charlatans who offered comfort to her desperate soul." — BARBARA W. TUCHMAN, The Guns of August (1962)

Pavel Mikhailovich Bykov, Chairman of the Ekaterinburg Soviet and renowned author of Nicholas and Alexandra's letters in 1929 also wrote the first accounts of the fall of the Imperial Romanov dynasty in his books, *The Last Days of Tsar Nicholas* and *The Last Days of Tsardom*. A more thorough investigation of Nicholas the man and the fall of the Romanov dynasty cannot be had, and he described Nicholas II quite succinctly as *"weak-willed and intellectually limited."*

"I can in no way forgive myself for having given up power. I never expected that power would fall to the Bolsheviks. I thought that I was giving up power to the representatives of the people." — NICHOLAS II

The remarkable thing about the abdication was that it happened so fast. The Duma delegates that met with Nicholas on the Imperial train at Pskov were seeking a transference of power to the tsarevich not a full abdication. Just a day or two earlier the Duma was demanding only the dismissal of tsarist government ministers. Nicholas knowing little about what was happening was manoeuvred in to a corner by his uncles and the military leaders and the cost to him was his abdication and the forfeiture of his son's claim to the throne, which ultimately led to the end of the monarchy.

Nicholas revealed the bitter sentiment in his diary, *"At one o'clock in the morning left Pskov with a heavy feeling, due to all I have lived through. Am surrounded by treachery, cowardice, and deceit."* The moment he realised that all was lost was when at Pskov he was unable to persuade the army to march on Petrograd to quash the revolution. He had not accounted for the reality that his military forces were absent from the cities because they were on the western front and there was no physical way to put down the agitators in Petrograd.

The Duma might have accepted Alexei in some capacity but when Nicholas learned that his son would be separated from the family he could not accept it and passed the succession to his brother Mikhail. It may seem bizarre considering Alexei could have reversed things upon receipt of legal powers but the boy had a serious illness and was not expected to live much more than a few years. Returning to Alexandra without the throne was one thing but returning without their son was not something she would forgive.

Nicholas detested the Duma but had been humbled to ask Chairman of the State Duma Mikhail Rodzianko to accept the abdication document personally. Rodzianko refused to go out to him because pressing matters in Petrograd demanded his urgent attention. Nicholas therefore signed his abdication document on the Imperial train late in the evening on 15 March 1917 and handed it to General Mikhail Alekseev, the current Commander of the Russian armies in Europe. Nicholas backdated it to 3.00 pm to give the impression that it had not been signed under duress from the Duma. General Alekseev then handed it to General Ruzsky who presented it officially to the Duma representatives. The following is roughly translated from Nicholas II's diary entry for the day of his abdication.

> *"General Ruzsky came this morning to advise me of a telephone conversation which he had with Rodzianko. The situation in Petrograd is such that the Duma is unable to do anything because they are in opposition to the socialist parties in the form of workmens' committees. My abdication is necessary. Ruzsky has transmitted our conversation to General Headquarters, and Alekseev has passed it to all the Commanders-in-Chiefs. At 12.30 came answers from all, the sense of which is that to save Russia and keep the Army at the front quiet, I must take this step. I have consented. General Headquarters have sent a draft of a manifesto. In the evening arrived from Petrograd Guchkov and Shulgin, with whom I had a long talk, and handed them the signed manifesto as agreed."*
> — NICHOLAS II, Diary, 15 March 1917

The Duma told Mikhail Alexandrovich that should he accept the throne his safety could not be ensured and Mikhail subsequently renounced his claim. Both the abdication of Nicholas and the renunciation of Mikhail were officially announced on 17 March 1917. Whilst the royal family moved in to house arrest and the government and Duma were preoccupied with World War I, insurgents were arriving and organising in Russia. In April 1917 Lenin left Germany and travelled through Switzerland and Finland, arriving in Petrograd to end his exile; the anti-war league had come to Russia.

The Provisional Government which had formed on 15 March 1917 reasserted its commitment to continue the war against Germany in a telegram to the Allied Powers. That telegram from Foreign Minister Pavel Milyukov was leaked creating further unrest but also giving greater support to the Bolsheviks after Lenin expressed his condemnation of it. Milyukov was forced to resign. Kerensky was blamed for having allowed the statement to be made but remained undeterred and in the following month the Kerensky Offensive began (aka June offensive (J), July Offensive (G), or Summer Offensive). The telegram became known as 'the Milyukov note' and would in due course lead to the downfall of the Provisional Government in November 1917.

In May 1917, General Alekseev resigned; the man that had planned the successful offensive on Galicia in 1914. This time, it was the Provisional Government that began the Kerensky Offensive on Galicia, which collapsed within three days revealing the poor state that the military was in. The newly appointed Commander in Chief General Lavr Kornilov and his officers believed this was mostly due to poor discipline and called for the death penalty at the front to deal with the increasing numbers of soldiers that were refusing to fight.

Kornilov was a Kalmyk Cossack born in East Kazakhstan from a Mongolic-Turkik ethnic group, He was involved in the Battle of Mukden (1905) and in the Battle of Galicia (1914). His father was strongly linked with the political activist (and historian,) Grigori Potanin who advocated the idea of an independent Siberian state and had spent years in hard labour for supporting separatism for Siberia. This became the driving force behind the White movement and its furtherance to military activities through Admiral Alexander Kolchak who established the Provisional Siberian Government.

Six months of wranglings had been taking place in the Provisional Government with demonstrations on the streets and strikes in the factories. The Bolsheviks voted for a military uprising to overthrow the government. It started on 7 November 1917 (G) (25th October Julian calendar) and became known as the October Revolution 1917 (aka Bolshevik Revolution). The Bolshevik army was raised for revolution but wasn't officially founded as the Russian Soviet Federative Socialist Republic army until 28 January 1918 and would become the Red Army of the Soviet Union in 1922.

The Winter Palace was stormed and almost immediately people realised that the new political faction led by Leon Trotsky and Vladimir Lenin was not friendly and things were going to get a lot worse before they got any better. Lenin issued a decree on the press legitimising the suppression of publications and by July 1918 all opposition to the new regime had been closed down. The Russian Revolution 1917 mildly described, had succeeded because of a lack of leadership, a discontented peasantry, an isolated government and a disorganised military.

CHAPTER XV
House Arrest

BY 1917 there were 65 family members of the House of Romanov in Russia. On the day before the abdication (i.e. 14 March 1917), Colonel Eugene Kobylinsky made preparations for 350 of his men to replace the Imperial Guard at Alexander Palace. On the afternoon of the day that Nicholas II had been arrested, on 21 March 1917 (G), General L. Kornilov, Commander of the troops of the Petrograd military district, and Colonel Kobylinsky, arrived at the palace to place Alexandra Feodorovna under house arrest; the official date being recorded as 25 March 1917. Colonel Kobylinsky remained in command of the new guard and placed it at the disposal of the Commandant, Captain de Kotzebue.

> *"Towards 3 o'clock the company of the combined regiment was formed before the front entrance and received the colours of the regiment which had always been guarded at the Emperor's. This was a melancholy ceremony; everybody was in tears. After so many years of good and loyal service the combined regiment, composed of the flower of the Guard and of the army, was obliged to give place to a revolutionary horde, horrible even to look at. For the last time the colours passed the threshold of the palace; God knows what became of it."* — COUNT PAVEL BENKENFORFF, memoirs

Home to Prison

When Nicholas arrived at Alexander Palace on 22 March 1917 the palace gates were locked. As his car approached the sentries did not immediately open them and waited for the officer on duty to give the order. Then came a shout from afar, *"Open the gates to the former Tsar."* General Kornilov gathered everyone in the palace and announced that whomever

CHAPTER XV

wanted to stay with the royal family could remain on the same terms as those being officially under house arrest.

When General Alekseev had received the Tsar at Moghilev a week earlier, he also received a telegram from the Provisional Government informing that a decision had been made to release the Tsar and his family with orders for them to be transported immediately to the port of Mermansk. This was a tactical move to get them as far from the cities as possible. Mermansk is the furthest northern terminal sitting over 2° north of the Arctic Circle, it has railway access to Europe being just 67 miles from the border with Norway and 113 miles from the Finnish border. It lies at the end of a deep bay and offered the possibility of an extraction from the Barents Sea.

For the Provisional Government it was Pavel Nikolayevich Milyukov the Minister of Foreign Affairs, that was negotiating with British ambassador Sir George Buchanan to extract the royal family. He had close relations with the British as the most senior politician and was trying to keep Russia in the war. As far back as 6 March 1917 Milyukov had been told the Tsar and his family could go to England but that Prime Minister Lloyd George preferred they exiled to a neutral country. Ironically it was Milyukov who had requested the British release Leon Trotsky from an internment camp in Nova Scotia, after which on his release, Trotsky made his way to Russia and became one of the Bolshevik Party leaders that overthrew the Provisional Government, albeit he was soon after exiled to France in April 1921.

On 21 March 2017 the Executive Committee of the Petrograd Soviet, made up of Mensheviks and Socialist Revolutionaries, discovered the government's plan to extradite the royal family. They had assembled to vote and all hands went up in agreement to bring the royal family under Soviet control because the government could not be trusted not to facilitate an escape. On the following morning Soviet guards were posted at all the major railway stations intended to prevent the royal family from attempting to leave Tsarskoe Selo.

According to Kerensky, there were plenty of officials wanting to imprison the royal family at the Peter and Paul fortress or at Kronstadt Island, and many of them from all parties called for their execution. The various groups petitioning for the release of the royal family were arguing among each other and missing opportunities for a rescue. By placing the royal family under house arrest in Tsarskoe Selo, Kerensky believed that he was also placing a guard around them to protect their lives until more suitable arrangements could be found.

Trusted advisor Marshal of the Court Prince Vasily Alexandrovich Dolgorukov was at Tsarskoe Selo with Alexandra to greet Nicholas when he arrived from Moghilev. He informed Nicholas that it was rumoured that Germany was demanding their immediate release at which Nicholas replied, *"I assume their intention is to humiliate me. If it were to save me I would consider it an insult.*" Alexandra possessed a forced smile that always made people hurry their words so that she could continue talking, this time she simply added, "*I would rather die in Russia than be saved by outsiders.*"

That the Romanovs should have planned for an escape abroad goes without saying but they stubbornly refused to leave Russia and their folly would be their undoing. Nicholas refused invitations from Germany, Italy, England and Spain, and doggedly dug in his heels waiting for the political mood to turn in his favour so that he could negotiate the terms for his exile. It was a dangerous chess game he played and somewhat disingenuous if it wasn't that he didn't fully appreciate the gravity of his situation. The royal family members were panicked and made their arrangements. How was it that the natural tendency for parents to protect their children didn't kick in and at the very least the children should have been preemptively evacuated.

Had Mikhail Alexandrovich accepted the throne then it would have been unlikely the former Imperial Family would have gone under house arrest at all. Nicholas maybe regarded his cousin George V, and even to a lesser extent Wilhelm II as exit strategies if things became untenable but how much more dire could the situation have become for them. For a man that had to be told in 1905 that, unbeknown to him, the First Revolution 1905 had already started, and who gave up power so easily on a train ride from Moghilev to Pskov (250 miles,) perhaps the assessments by his contemporaries that Nicholas possessed an extraordinary limited intellect is indeed the best explanation for his actions.

Prime Minister Kerensky's next of several visits to Alexander Palace, was on 3 April 1917. He brought with him Colonel Korovichenko (a lawyer by profession) and put him in charge of the palace, replacing Kotzebue as the Commandant. Kotzebue's mild manner suited his interim position as Commandant but he was closely watched and found to have developed a friendship with Ms Vyrubova with whom he would often sit and chat in the courtyard. He was seen handing letters to her for the royal family without first opening and reading them. As a result he was denounced. Kerensky held several interviews with Nicholas and Alexandra, but in particular he tried to get to the bottom of the accusations that Alexandra was spying for Germany and the reasons for her numerous ministerial appointments. He found no evidence of wrong doing by Alexandra.

"*I inquired about the health of the members of the family, informed them that their relatives abroad were solicitous of their welfare and the King and Queen of England had notified the Provisional Government of their concern for the Imperial family.*" — ALEXANDER KERENSKY

Back in August 1909, at their last meeting, when Nicholas had been a guest of George V on the Isle of Wight for the regatta, their relationship had

CHAPTER XV

strengthened but Nicholas had not been receiving any correspondence from England since he was placed under house arrest and he could not pursue talks for exile. The reason was because letters were being addressed to the 'Emperor of Russia', a subtlety that was overlooked as if the Russian diplomatic service didn't know exactly who the letters were intended for.

Had George V received a reply from Nicholas then a way out of Russia could have been negotiated, even at that late point just before the Bolsheviks took over the government, it may have been possible. Of the fifty-three Romanovs still in Russia when Nicholas II abdicated, thirty-five managed to escape and the rest were not so fortunate. As early as 19 March 1917 (G) George V had written to Nicholas; in the quote below George V is referring to the February Revolution 1917.

"Events of last week have deeply distressed me. My thoughts are constantly with you, and shall always remain your true and devoted friend as you know I have been in the past."
— KING GEORGE V to NICHOLAS II, communiqué, 19 March 1917

Nicholas II - 1913　　　　　**George V - 1925**

In April 1917 as the White Army was scattering, the Kerensky government was pressed for a solution for the royal family. They favoured the British and once more approached them on the issue of asylum. Buchanan received word on 23 April 1917 that the previous offer extended to the Tsar and his family had been withdrawn due to internal political concerns and Kerensky was left without an alternative other than Germany.

> "... King George V had invited them to come to England, but this had met with the opposition of the British government in the person of Lloyd George. The King of Spain had also offered them hospitality, but the Emperor had refused, saying that no matter what happened neither he nor his family would ever leave Russia."
> — FELIX YUSSOUPOFF, Lost Splendor, page 283

During Prince Felix Yussoupoff's lifetime it was not known that it was in fact George V and not Prime Minister David Lloyd George, who became Prime Minister in December 1916, that had blocked the royal family's invitation to exile in England. George V took advice from his secretary Arthur Bigge, the first Baron of Stamfordham, over concerns that Nicholas' presence in England and the connotation with 'revolution' might provoke an uprising like the previous year's Easter Rising in Ireland. Lloyd George was believed to have made the decision until Cabinet papers from his tenure were released in 1986 revealing that it was indeed George V that rescinded the invitation. According to the royal author Lady Colin Campbell, it was Queen Mary's doing because she disliked Alexandra and persuaded her husband not to help the Romanovs, fearing the same fervent desire for an uprising against the British monarch could take hold with the Romanov family in the country.

The American writer Eugene Gore Vidal wrote that George V, Queen Mary and their son Edward were having breakfast at Buckingham Palace one morning when an aide handed the king a note. Having read it he passed it to his wife who turned to her husband and said, *"No."* The king then told the aide *"No."* Later Edward asked his mother what the note was about and she told him that his father's government was ready to send a battleship to rescue the former Imperial Family, but she didn't think it would be good for them to have their Russian relatives in Britain.

Another story from an Anglican chaplain Reverend G.V. Vaughan-James, of Warminster, England, told of when he was on a British ship sent to a port on the Black Sea to rescue the Tsar and his family and bring them to England. The crew were very excited by the mission. When they arrived at the port, a telephone message came from London ordering the ship to return to England without the former Imperial Family. No reason was given and the crew were most upset and turned back.

> *"I nearly hate the Allies. When will they help – or won't they. All words and no actions. No tanks yet here – nothing that can help us."*
> — OLGA ALEXANDROVNA

Nicholas' sister Olga was a nurse at a field hospital in Kiev during 1916. She often communicated with her mother and sister Xenia. In 2017 a collection

CHAPTER XV

of 52 letters between Olga and Xenia were sold at auction by Olga's grandson providing an insight in to the fears of the royal family at this time. Olga mentions her hate when she thought the British were not doing enough to protect them.

Many years earlier Alexandra Feodorovna had felt some affinity with Marie Louise (Napoleon I's second bride), and now during her final period at Alexander Palace she shared a homogeneous set of circumstances with Marie-Antoinette, whose portrait surrounded by her children was hung in Alexandra's bedroom. She had faced the French Revolution and been under house arrest in the Tuileries Palace (October 1789). She had taken a decisive role in urging her husband, the King of France Louis XVI, not to concede to demands for reforms. She promoted in him a determination to show strength against his opposition. Alexandra knew how it ended for them; they were duly dispatched and beheaded on the guillotine.

As soon as the royal family went under house arrest they became inmates and the whole attitude towards them changed and got gradually worse as they moved from month to month and from place to place. Their home at Alexander Palace became their prison. At least they were allowed to exercise twice daily between 11.00 am to 12.00 pm and 2.30 pm to 5.00 pm which was very important for them to do so. Nicholas made several observations about the changes in their circumstances.

"An unprecedented event happened; we were placed under house arrest, without the slightest possibility of communication with Mama or others. ... The faces of the guards have not been as free and easy as before. They usually talk with us and give us their impressions of the revolution." — NICHOLAS II, 7 April 1917

"I learned why yesterday's guards were so mean. They were completely from the staff of the Soldier's Soviet and had replaced the guards from the 4th Infantry Reserve Battalion."
— NICHOLAS II, Saturday 8 April 1917

"The soldiers of the new Guard were horrible to look at; untidy, noisy, quarrelling with everybody; the officers, who were afraid of them, had the greatest difficulty in preventing them from roaming about the Palace and entering every room."
— COUNT PAVEL BENCKENDORFF

Kerensky believed the public didn't care for the Romanov's lifestyle in captivity, still living in their palace with staff to wait on them. The guards complained a lot about their freedoms, begrudging every luxury they saw the family enjoy. Wine was rationed at meal times but the soldiers wanted to stop this and raided the cellar for themselves. In the end Commandant

Korovichenko had to lock it up and issue the wine at meal times himself.

From the very start of house arrest the family experienced disrespect and abuse from the Bolshevik soldiers. One example was Nicholas riding a bicycle and as he passed by, a sentry thrust out his rifle into the wheel spokes and laughed when he fell off. Inside they had to contend with the offensive guards and outside with the jaunts from angry members of the public that came to the gates daily to stare at them in the grounds.

> *"The guards usually chose a place close to the fence of the park, and the inhabitants of Tsarskoe Selo gathered on the other side of the fence to stare and make remarks. Often crude and rude, the Tsar continued his work as if he heard nothing. They spoke to him as if he were a caged animal unable to hear or do anything about it."*
> — MARIE NIKOLAEVNA

Finally on 9 June 1917 Nicholas appears to comprehend the magnitude of the predicament he had placed his family in, his strategy for exile in Crimea had not transpired and the realisation hit him that they were in fact, real prisoners. Nonetheless, he got wind that preparations were being made to relocate them, possibly and hopefully to Crimea. At this point Nicholas cares only for his immediate family and mother. A trial in Moscow, he believed, would afford a global platform from which to recover the hopeless situation. It didn't matter where they would be taken, so long as it was away from Alexander Palace, their home that had become their prison.

> *"It has been exactly three months since I came from Moghilev and we have been prisoners. It is difficult to be without news from dear Mama, but as to the others I am indifferent."*
> — NICHOLAS II, Friday 9 June 1917

Exile in Siberia

> *"The Imperial Family were no doubt buoyed up by the hope of their removal to some place at a distance from the turbulent seat of trouble at Petrograd, possibly out of the country altogether, or to the spot to which the Emperor himself told me he wished to go – Crimea. It was not until mid-August, however, that they were warned to start for a destiny unknown to them, but which turned out to be Tobolsk."*
> — SIR JOHN HANBURY-WILLIAMS, memoirs, page 220

After three months of house arrest at Alexander Palace Nicholas learned that they were being moved from the cook who had been asked to prepare food for a five day journey. A month later they set out for Tobolsk. It was a

CHAPTER XV

small town of 20,000 inhabitants, one of the oldest towns in western Siberia and was selected for its remoteness, being more than two hundred miles from the nearest railroad, far too remote for a rescue attempt. The family at this time were still unaware that negotiations with England had ended some months back.

A group of thirty-five people left Tsarskoe Selo on 31 July 1917 (G) by train on a thirty-six hour, 1,700 mile trip. Despite the early hour a large crowd had gathered at the palace that booed them, whistled and jeered as they left their home for the last time. Their hearts must have sunk when the train headed eastwards in the opposite direction to Crimea, and again when they continued past Moscow. On 15 August 1917 they reached the Urals and Tyumen on the Tura River, the first settlement to have been established in Siberia during Russia's eastward expansion.

At the quayside they transferred to three waiting steamships; the family boarded the *Russia* (or Kouss according to Sophie Buxhoeveden,) the servants went on the *Kurmiletz* and a tug steamer the *Tyumen* carried their baggage. The steamships set out on the Tura at 6.00 am, the *Russia* first with the other two vessels following. On Sunday 6 August 1917 (J) they entered the wider Tobol River and sailed by Rasputin's village of Pokrovskoe. Nicholas was reminded of the prophesy Rasputin had made that willingly or unwillingly they would one day pass by his home. Had not he also warned that "*If any harm comes to me the Russian Empire will crumble.*" Alexandra fondly mentioned that they were on that part of the river where Rasputin caught the fish that he brought to them at Tsarskoe Selo. They had hoped to go to Moscow for Nicholas to face trial but instead were being exiled to Siberia. The realisation grew as their ships steamed deeper in to the expanse that they had been abandoned by England and betrayed by the Provisional Government. On the following day Nicholas described it:

> "*We got over the Ural Mountains and felt the cold air. The train passed Ekaterinburg in the small hours of morning. It dragged on and on incredibly slowly, so that we arrived in Tyumen only at 11:30 pm. The train pulled in almost to the quay and the only thing we had to do was to board a ship. We departed from Tyumen by the river at 6 am.*"
> — NICHOLAS II, 7 August 1917 (J)

> "*After yesterday's thunderstorms until dinner, today's weather was cold and rainy with a strong wind. All day we unpacked photographs of the Journey of 1890-1891.* [His trip around the world} *I brought them on purpose so that in my spare time I could put them in order.*"
> — NICHOLAS II, 14 August 1917 (J)

The family took their prized photographs with them to Tobolsk as the quote above from Nicholas' diary confirms. It's not known if they all made it but there were enough to fill one large trunk. How many made it on the next journey from Tobolsk to Ekaterinburg also is not known but many that did survive ended up at the Zlatoust City Museum collection in Siberia.

They arrived in Tobolsk on 19 August 1917 (G) and were taken to the Governor's Mansion on the recently named Freedom Street (formerly Mira Street). The town turned out to welcome them and did not share the hatred that was prevalent in Petrograd. The building had once been a governor's residence and was later used for barracks. No preparations had been made and the building was officially declared uninhabitable. The situation was truly dire; it was freezing with no heating; the temperature never went above 10 degrees Celsius in winter months and at night fell anywhere between -20 to -50 degrees Celsius.

Alexandra recorded temperatures daily in her journal using the Celsius scale, even the entry she made on the eve of her last evening alive on 16 July 1918 had ended with a temperature reading, *"10 ½ to bed – 15 degrees of heat."* She also monitored the body temperatures of the family members daily, (a normal temperature is 37 degrees Celsius, equivalent to 98.6 degrees Fahrenheit). Presumably it was her nursing training that she might use the information as an early indicator that someone might be falling ill and considering the conditions they all remained generally in good health.

TOBOLSK   I JANUARY   †

−4°   MONDAY

7.15.	Got up. At 8 went to Church.
	Olga in bed 37.3°. Tatiana too 38°. German measles (rubella) Tatiana has a strong rash all over, headache & eyes bloodshopt. Aleksei alright again. Sat with the girls, sowing. I lunched with them in their bedroom at 12. Beautiful, sunny weather, sat on the balcony for 35 m: & then with the girls til tea-time
4.30.	Kolia Derevenko also took tea.
6.00.	rested til 8, reading & writing.
2.00.	Olga 37.4° Tatiana 38.5°
6.00.	" 37.5° " 38.7°
8.00.	Dined with Olga & Tatiana
9.00.	Olga 37.7° Tatiana 38.5°
	Played bezique with Nicholas, then he read to us & I knitted.

Page from Alexandra's journal. She recorded religious feast days, the weather, body temperatures, bed times and trivialities.

CHAPTER XV

List of people that journeyed from Tsarskoe Selo to Tobolsk.

1) General Adjutant Ilya Leonidovich Tatishchev
2) Marshal Prince Vasiliy Alexandrovich Dolgorukov
3) Doctor Eugene Botkin, physician to the royal family
4) Tutor to Alexei - Peter Andreevich Zhilyar from Switzerland
5) Lady in waiting Countess Anastasia Vasilievna Hendrikova
6) Governess of A.V. Hendrikova - Victorina Vladimirovna Nikolaeva
7) Maid of A. V. Hendrikova - Paulina Kasperovna Mezhants
8) Lady in waiting Anna Stephanovna Demidova
9) German language tutor - Ekaterina Adolfovna Schneider
10) Maid of Y. A. Schneider - Ekaterina Zhivaya
11) Maid of Y. A. Schneider - Maria Gusmavovna Tumelberg
12) Helper of Y. A. Schneider - Elizaveta Nikolaevna Ersberg
13) Lady in waiting Sophie Karlovna Buxhoeveden
14) Governess to the children - Alexandra Alexandrovna Tegleva,
15) English language tutor - Charles Sydney Gibbes from Great Britain
16) Footman to tsarevich - Klementy Grigorievich Nagorny
17) Doctor Vladimir Nikolaevich Derevenko
18) Valet of the Tsar - Terenty Ivanovich Chemodurov
19) Assistant of T. I. Chemodurov Stepan Makarov
20) Valet of the Empress - Alexei Andreevich Volkov
21) Cook Ivan Mikhailovich Kharitonov
22) Cook Ivan Vereshchagin
23) Cook Kokichev
24) Cook in training Leonid Sednev
25) Kitchen Servant Sergey Mikhailov
26) Kitchen Servant Franz Pyurkoesky
27) Kitchen Servant Terekhov
28) Waiter Frantz Zhuravsky
29) Head of the cellar Rozhkov
30) Footman Alexei Egorovich Trupp
31) Children's servant Ivan Dmitrievich Sednev
32) Hairdresser Alex Nikolaevich Dmitriev
33) Attendant Smirnov
34) Footman to grand duchesses - Mikhail Karpov
35) Footman Dormedontov
36) Footman Ermolai Gusev
37) Clerk/janitor Alexander Kirpichnikov
38) Cloakroom attendant Stuipel
39) Footman Kiselev
40) Waiter to I. L. Tatishchev and V. A. Dolgorukov - Tyutin
41) Footman to P. Gilliard - Sergei Ivanovich Ivanov

* Possibly) Cameraman Ma Riya Gustavovna, Footman G. Solodouhin

Buxhoeveden's story is rather interesting in that she not only volunteered to be with the royal family during their house arrest at Tobolsk but travelled there under her own steam to join them, having secured a travel permit in Petrograd on the last day before the Provisional Government fell to the Bolsheviks. Her train was jam-packed with people evacuating the capital. She had travelled on the carriage roof for part of the journey, clinging to the ventilator with both hands; as she recalled it, "... *I had never been so much frightened in my life.*". On arriving at Tobolsk she visited Commandant Colonel Kobylinsky and henceforth her captivity started. Once there, she befriended the former General Adjutant Tatishchev who said to her:

> "*I can only hope that some loyal people in Petrograd may know the danger the Emperor is in and that some International Red Cross Society may take steps to rescue the family.*" — ILYA TATISHCHEV

It's uncertain what Buxhoeveden might have expected on her voluntary internment at the Governor's House. Certainly she could not have believed she was placing herself in line for execution and therefore must have had a more than reasonable assumption that she would survive the ordeal. The central main part of the mansion was open plan, rather like a dance floor or concourse hall. Cubicles were put up that did not touch the floor or reach as high as the ceiling, resembling a lavatory style separation. These were make-do rooms and Buxhoeveden was assigned one to occupy. Alexandra furnished it with some of her own things but they would see each other only intermittently as Buxhoeveden was mainly confined with Tatishchev, Hendrikova and the cubicles of other prisoners, kept apart from the family.

Commandant Kobylinsky thought the atmosphere at Tobolsk less strained than the hustle and bustle of Alexander Palace. He had been responsible for arranging transportation to Tobolsk and the living arrangements there. Some decoration was brought from Alexander Palace separately, carpets and some pictures because otherwise there were no comforts at the Governor's Mansion. Initially, the servants were permitted to go for brief walks around the town. The court dentist Dr Kastritzky travelled from Crimea to keep dental appointments, Alexei was allowed weekly visits from his best friend Kolya Derevenko, and it was approved for the ballroom to be converted in to a chapel, which pleased them greatly. Even the hardened Kobylinsky was eventually disarmed by the royal family's friendliness.

For a time they were allowed to attend Sunday service at the Church of Intercession of the Virgin, but on Christmas Day 1917, Father Aleksei Vasiliev gave up a prayer for the long life of the *Imperial Family* and for that crime he was banished to a distant monastery in Siberia and services

CHAPTER XV

after that were restricted to the chapel. The new priest Vladimir Khlynov was more discrete about his sympathies following that episode.

> "*I have never seen, and I shall probably never again see, such a happy and united family. The time will come when the Russian people will realise what terrible tortures this family was subjected to, from the first days of the Revolution when the newspapers published scandalous stories about their private life.*" — EUGENE KOBYLINKSY

The royal family were expected to pay for their own upkeep, energy, food et cetera. Once, when their finances were low, unbeknown to them the staff came together and secured 20,000 rubles so that things could continue as they were for a while longer. Nicholas complained about the toilets not flushing and the lack of clean water, being fundamental necessities, which were duly sorted out by Kobylinsky.

Walking on the grounds was permitted between 10.00 am to 12.00 pm and from 2.00 pm to 4.00 pm daily. Although four hours a day seems plenty for exercise, to Nicholas that was a constriction as he was a great walker. Wherever he would go he made sure to take minimum fifteen minute walks every few hours. When his staff accompanied him they fell behind or turned back, not able to sustain the pace. Confined to a small courtyard at Tobolsk he paced up and down continuously, doing intermittent push-ups and chin-ups on his trapeze which he set up in the courtyard. The aides were not allowed to engage with the family in the courtyard where they too exercised.

Even with the space constriction, the guards would chastise them, "*you can't go there*" or "*come back that's far enough.*" Nicholas noted on 4 September 1917 (G), "*What a marvellous day. One gets frustrated at not being able to take walks along the riverbank or in the woods in weather like this.*" Three days later he wrote, "*Walks in the garden are becoming incredibly tedious, here the sense of sitting locked up is much stronger than at Tsarskoe Selo.*"

As they settled in, they busied themselves with whatever they could to fill the days which passed one after the other much the same. The family would often huddle together outside on the balcony in the cold to take in the fresh air. It was not uncommon for their fingers to freeze so that activities like writing became impossible for hours after. When the children had measles they cut their hair very short and their appearance on the balcony was a revelation for the locals of the quiet town who came daily to see them; they thought the haircuts must have been fashionable in Petrograd.

In the yard Tatishchev and Dolgorukov took turns to saw logs with Nicholas who would never stop and could continue sawing for hours. To alleviate boredom the family created a little farm with some turkeys and pigs. They loved to grow things together and look after animals. George V once remarked to Wilhelm II that Nicholas was best at ease when he was tending the land, upon which Wilhelm II replied that Nicholas was only good for growing turnips. Alexandra was not so active, she regressed to her lethargy and was rarely seen downstairs before dinner at 1.00 pm, she slipped in to her bible and the spiritual books that she'd taken with her.

The Governor's Mansion, Tobolsk, Siberia

They thought of Tobolsk as a midway point before they would be moved to their final destination, presuming that to be Crimea. If they had left Tsarskoe Selo to be expediated they would have been shot already; their personal safety was therefore being assured and they just needed to wait it out and hope that the White Army could retake Petrograd or rescue them from captivity first. But as power began to slip from the Provisional Government to the regional Soviet authorities in Omsk, the effects were felt at the Governor's Mansion. The first instruction from the Bolshevik Soviet in Omsk was to move the royal family to a prison which was mercifully ignored by the Socialist Revolutionaries Soviet in Tobolsk.

One account says that Kerensky had created the circumstances for the royal family to escape by having placed them under house arrest in Siberia under a guard that was less loyal to the revolution, in anticipation of a rescue attempt. The family got on so well with the guards that if they had tried to escape many of the guards would not have tried to stop them including the head of the guard Kobylinsky. The only thing that stopped them escaping was themselves. They were either too proud to run, or wouldn't leave without the aides. Most likely they were mindful of Lieutenant Colonel A. Matveev's orders to his men to shoot them all if anyone tried to escape.

CHAPTER XV

Tobolsk, Nicholas II and Pierre Gilliard sawing logs. Just look at the pile behind them! The Tsar could saw logs all day long without breaking in to a sweat.

Tobolsk, Nicholas II and Alexei looking after turkeys on their animal farm

With pressure mounting from the new regime, Kerensky appointed Commissars Pankratov and Nikoisky to take over at the Governor's Mansion. Kobylinsky remained but subordinate to the new commissars. Pankratov had been a prisoner in the tsar's infamous Schlusselburg Fortress on Orekhovy Island near Petrograd for 14 years; (Bykov says 27 years and Sunday Times dated 25 February 2017, says 20 years,). He could be counted on not to allow an escape. The commissars were Socialist Revolutionaries and arrived in Tobolsk on 14 September 1917 (G), on the same day that Kerensky in Petrograd proclaimed Russia to be a republic. Nicholas it seems, had been right.

"The heart bleeds at the thought of what you have gone through, what you have lived and what you are still living! At every step undeserved horrors and humiliations. But fear not, the Lord sees all. As long as you are healthy and well. Sometimes it seems like a terrible nightmare, and that I will wake up and it will all be gone! Poor Russia! What will happen to her?"
— XENIA ALEXANDROVNA to NICHOLAS II, letter November 1917

Alexandra found the irony mildly amusing that the prisoners had become the jailors. Nicholas found it less amusing because from that day the new republic stopped saluting the ex-tsar. The presence of Kobylinsky was a godsend to them, because he was friendly and the guards obeyed him because he had the military authority from General Kornilov.

Two months later the Provisional Government fell to the Bolsheviks. Kerensky would describe the event thus, *"Without Rasputin, there could have been no Lenin. Certainly, without Lenin, there would have been no Communist Russia."* Immediately following the Bolshevik coup d'état Lenin withdrew Russia from World War I and a bloody civil war ensued between the Bolsheviks (Red Army) and the conservative White Guard (White Army). The Bolshevik War Commissar Filipp Goloshchekin announced the following in relation to the prisoners at Tobolsk:

"All those under arrest will be held as hostages, and the slightest attempt at counter-revolutionary action in the town will result in the summary execution of the hostages." — FILIPP GOLOSHHEKIN

On 27 February 1918 Commandant Kobylinsky received a telegram instructing him that from 1 March the family were to be put on soldiers' rations and each member was only allowed a maximum of 600 rubles per month from their personal estate. It meant they had to be more frugal and it became necessary to release ten of their staff. The Russian Bolshevik Party became the Russian Communist Party and the Tobolsk Soviet now run by Bolsheviks, set up a Commission to strengthen the regime at the Governor's

CHAPTER XV

Mansion. They blamed Commissar Pankratov for the lackadaisical element of the guard and demanded he run the place like a prison, sending out a hundred Bolshevik guards to keep things in order. Pierre Gilliard noted in his diary, *"These are the first Bolshevik soldiers in the Tobolsk garrison. Our last hope of escape is gone."*

This meant strictly curtailing their freedoms until they were experiencing the harshest conditions of prison life. The aides were moved out to a house opposite the mansion, in so doing the family's connections to sympathisers on the outside became severed. Nicholas and Alexandra had each been smuggling information out to would-be rescuers. One such was Hermogenes the newly appointed Bishop of Tobolsk. He'd been persecuted by the tsar and stripped of his clerical standing after beating up Rasputin so the Soviet authorities believed that he was no friend of the Romanovs. But in fact Hermogenes tried to help them many times. When Father Aleksei Vasiliev was exiled, Hermogenes had protested and stuck up for him which meant pitting himself against the Bolsheviks. But no matter how many times he tried to assist the royal family in their plots to escape, they ignored him because Alexandra didn't trust him nor even liked him for what he had done to her saint Rasputin.

It was a lovely sunny day on 1 March 1918 when Nicholas started the book Anna Karenina. On 12 March Lenin published his argument to move the capital to Moscow and the first items started to disappear from the dining table at Tobolsk; butter and coffee at first, being considered luxuries. Dentist Kastritzky was still allowed to visit and it was through him that information was still being smuggled out. On one occasion returning from Tobolsk, he delivered a message from Nicholas to Irina Yussoupoff, *"When you see Princess Yussoupoff, tell her that I now see how right she was. If I had listened to her, many tragic events might have been averted."* He finishing the book on 13 March as foodstuff started arriving from local people that had heard they were on soldiers' rations. They brought in butter, coffee, pastries and prepared meals.

As the final signs of autocracy were dismantled so the guards manifested increasing levels of cruel disregard for the royal family. They would sit on Alexandra's bed with her in it and stand in and around the room when Alexandra and the girls were getting dressed. Several guards could not stoop to that level of indignity and asked for transfers to the front. Eventually only the crudest guards remained that spat and swore around their captives, made lewd remarks and did disgusting things.

Letter writing continued to be the favourite pass-time. Alexandra did not understand why some people were not replying to her letters, not considering their fear that by association they might place themselves in danger. In March 1918 Alexandra wrote to her friend Lili Dehn asking if she had received her previous correspondence of October 1917. They had not seen each other since the previous March when the house arrests had started at Tsarskoe Selo. Letters to Lili Dehn were smuggled out, but Dehn had her own problems in trying to secure the safety of her son whilst under house arrest herself. Dehn moved south ahead of the Red Army to Odessa and with the help of the French boarded a ship for Constantinople.

> *"My Dearest, I am for such a very, very long time without news of you, and I feel sad. Have you received my post card of the 28th October? Everybody is well, my heart is not up to much, fit at times, but on the whole it is better. I live very quietly and seldom go out as it is too difficult to breathe in frozen air."*
> — ALEXANDRA to LILI DEHN, letter, 15 March 1918 (G)

Tobolsk, the last know photograph of Anastasia

Journey to Ekaterinburg

The seats of the Tobolsk Soviet were firmly in Bolshevik hands when the Red Army arrived in Tobolsk from Omsk on 7 April 1918. Once again talks started about moving the prisoners to a prison somewhere in the Urals, under Goloshchekin's jurisdiction. Goloshchekin, the War Commissar, went to Moscow to inform headquarters that monarchists in Tobolsk were increasing their activity. The Central Executive Committee decided to move the prisoners to Ekaterinburg as a precaution. Goloshchekin was placed in

CHAPTER XV

charge and he in turn put all his detachments at the disposal of the extremist Bolshevik revolutionary Vasily Yakovlev, whom Moscow had already appointed in March 1918 to escort the ex-tsar to Moscow to face trial.

Yakovlev sent a detachment to Tyumen a day ahead to survey the route and the mood of the people. When the main troop caught up at Tyumen, Yakovlev had learned that people were supportive of the tsar and would help him escape if presented with the opportunity and therefore he arrived at the Governor's Mansion with 150 horsemen on 22 April 1918 and a letter for the Commander of the Guard Kobylinsky to cooperate on pain of death.

Yakovlev immediately set about planning for the trip to Ekaterinburg. Alexei was seriously ill, so he decided to leave him behind with three of his sisters to care for him, the rest he would take with him; Nicholas, Alexandra, Marie, Dr Botkin, and most of the servants. The lakes they needed to cross were still frozen so a lot of the journey would be done by carriage. In the spring when the rivers opened up the others could follow with their baggage, transported by steamship. As far as the family knew, they heard they were being taken to the Ural Mountains. Pierre Gilliard, the French language tutor, stated that Yakovlev had told him they were being taken to Moscow for Nicholas to face trial. The first group left Tobolsk at 5.00 am on 25 April 1918 travelling all day and resting several times along the 186 mile journey on the first stage to Tyumen.

On one of the rest breaks while they were stretching out, a villager saw Marie alight the carriage to arrange her mother's cushions furiously rubbing her hands together and it was a long while before she could move the cushions because her fingers were so numb from the cold. The journey took them over several rivers at which they had to get out and help to lay planks where the ice was unsafe.

Rasputin's home in Pokrovskoe

On the first day, they crossed the River Irtysh, the carriages sank half way up the wheels, and at one place Nicholas carried Alexandra in his arms across a river, wading knee-deep in the ice-cold water. They stopped on the first evening at the village of Bochalino on the River Tobol and set out again at 8.00 am. Later that evening they held up at Pokrovskoe and tied the horses almost directly opposite Rasputin's house. This time Rasputin's words must have really resonated, that they would one day pass by his home, and literally there they were standing outside his house in Pokrovskoe, the very place they had exiled him to several times. On the third evening when they arrived at Tyumen there was a train waiting to continue on phase two of their journey. From Tyumen Yakovlev sent a telegram to the authorities confirming that they would be taking the train for Moscow in the morning. In the meantime, they rested for the night at a peasant's house.

Yakovlev feared an ambush on the train along the way to Ekaterinburg so he set out at 5.00 am on 28th April 1917 heading in the opposite direction. Instead of heading west to Moscow he headed east towards Omsk from where he planned to take a train on a direct route to Moscow, making the detour to avoid an ambush, but on nearing Omsk the authorities stopped the train fearing Yakovlev might be helping the prisoners to escape. Some confusion existed since Yakovlev had sent his telegram to Moscow. The authorities had responded several times but received no acknowledgement by 10.00 am because Yakovlev's train had already left by then. The Soviet were taking no chances and declared Yakovlev a traitor and had the train intercepted at Liublinskaya just outside of Omsk.

Yakovlev had to go in to Omsk to explain why he was taking a route heading away from Moscow. He explained that his orders were to protect the royal family by all means available to him and as his own life depended on their security he was being exceptionally cautious in taking steps to disguise their destination and he convinced the Soviet but was not permitted to continue further eastward and was turned back to Tyumen. Instead of setting out for Moscow, they left Omsk heading directly for Ekaterinburg. The trip to Moscow had been cancelled because it was feared the White Army by now had been updated on their movements and were certain to make a rescue attempt along the long route to Moscow, of which the White Army controlled much of the areas the train would pass through.

At Ekaterinburg station they were met by the Ural Soviet who took control of the prisoners and arrested Yakovlev's guard. The Soviet authorities had not been entirely convinced of Yakovlev's sincerity. He was sent to Moscow for questioning and eventually the guard were released one by one over several days to not attract any suspicion from the residents of Ekaterinburg. Yakovlev was angered by his treatment and before he left obtained a receipt dated 30 April 1918 (G) in case he might need the proof that the prisoners had been handed over officially. This was pretty much it

CHAPTER XV

for Yakovlev who became embittered with the authorities and turned against the Bolsheviks and the last thing heard about him was that he joined the White Army and was killed fighting.

> "I, the President of the Regional Uralian Council of Deputies, Beloborodov, have taken over from the member of the All-Russian Tsik comrade Yakovlev the interned: former Tsar Nicholas Romanov, the former Tsaritsa Alexandra Feodorovna, the former Grand Duchess Marie Nikolaevna, and the persons accompanying them. All these persons are under arrest and under guard." — THE PRESIDENT OF THE URALIAN REGIONAL SOVDEP (Signed) BELOBORODOV

Print of Nicholas II, Alexandra, Marie and aides arriving at Ekaterinburg, 30 April 1918

Goloshchekin took over overall soviet responsibility at Ekaterinburg. Several cars were waiting for the prisoners at the station, Goloshchekin took the royal family in his personal car. It would have been a strangeness for anyone that caught a glimpse of them going by, to see the ex-tsar in the front seat and the ex-tsarina and ex-grand duchess sitting in the back. The convoy proceeded without a guard escort and arrived at a smaller premises than the Governor's Mansion in Tobolsk and the former house of a local engineer named Nikolai Ipatiev; Ipatiev House, 49 Voznesensky Prospekt.

On their arrival the living arrangements were sorted and the following aides were isolated and taken to a prison for interrogation: Dolgorukov, Tatishchev, Hendrikova, Schneider, and Volkov. A few days later Nagorny, Chemodurov and Ivan Sednev joined them in prison. The only prisoners allowed at Ipatiev house in addition to the royal family were Doctor Botkin, cook Haritonov, valet Trupp, kitchen boy Leonid Sednev, and lady-in-waiting Demidova. The remaining aides were released and told to leave the Ural Soviet district; except for Dr Vladimir Derevenko and his son Koyla. Dr Derevenko was permitted to remain in the city and practice medicine and was called several times to attend to Alexei following his later arrival at Ipatiev House, when Koyla was also permitted to visit now and then and they were left to continue their activities unhindered.

The Commandant at Ipatiev House was Alexander Avdeev, a factory worker and a drunkard. The guards were a rabble, not regular soldiers but made up of workers from the local factories, predominantly the Zlokazov Brother's factory and Sysertskoe Works. In the secluded parts of Russia that didn't have a permanent garrison, or were spread thinly, men were seconded in to the civil guard as and when required.

Nicholas and Alexandra were not kept updated about their children still in Tobolsk or about Alexei's health condition. Alexandra did received a telegram from Olga informing that Alexei's health had improved but no more details than that were given and there was little communication between the family with letters. For a while the prisoners were allowed to do their favourite things; reading books, writing diaries and taking photographs although strangely there are no surviving photographs since their arrival in Ekaterinburg.

The following extracts passed between Olga and Marie during the time they were separated. The reference to the windows is because it was a particularly hot summer that year and during the intense heat of June 1918, Avdeev permitted only the windows in Nicholas' bedroom to be unsealed.

> Letter from Tobolsk, 28 April 1918 (G) *"Today was warmer than yesterday and the windows are wide open. We took the evening tea in the dining room. Yesterday, we ate the poor turkey. Mama, you would have said 'one should not,' dear little soul."* — OLGA NIKOLAEVNA

> Letter from Ekaterinburg, 2 May 1918 (G) *"This morning we heard the church bells. That was the only pleasant and agreeable event. We were happy to learn that the pigs sold so well. What is he going to do with the piglets? Mama, speaking about the turkey, said you should not have."* — MARIE NIKOLAEVNA

If they were not as yet fully aware of their rapidly waned chances for survival then Anna Demidova was the first to sense the imminent danger.

CHAPTER XV

Soon after arriving at Ipatiev House she sent a letter to Alexandra Tegleva at Tobolsk instructing her to conceal the family jewels in to the undergarments of the girls. The reader will recall Tegleva was Anastasia's nurse and Pierre Gilliard's wife. She set about immediately sewing diamonds and pearls in to bodices, hats, fur linings, and buttons with the help of chambermaid Elizaveta Ersberg. Fortunately, Ersberg and Tegleva on their arrival in Ekaterinburg were among those separated and sent to Tyumen, then released.

Colonel Kobylinsky was eventually replaced on 17 May 1918 with the bullying Commissar Rodionov who would take over the responsibility for moving the remaining prisoners from Tobolsk to Ekaterinburg. As soon as spring caught up, the children and twenty-seven servants left the Governor's House on 20 May 1918 and boarded the steamship *Russia*.

Charles Sydney Gibbes wrote of the journey from Tobolsk to Ekaterinburg escorted by the Soviet police. His account does not mention any sexual attention the girls received from the guards on that journey as was inferred by others like Colonel Pavel Rodzianko, serving with the British Expeditionary Force in Siberia, who believed that Olga, Tatiana and Anastasia were sexually abused. Gibbes and Rodzianko were to return to Ipatiev House (with Pierre Gilliard) to assist White Army investigators in 1919 so it's interesting that these three who were equally close to the royal family have given opposing views. In Recent publications the contentious version has been preferred; the authors of the book *The Fate of the Romanovs* suggest that Olga was sexually abused or even raped, based on the interpretation of a photograph and the following excerpts also imply sexual abuse as if incontrovertibly proven.

"Alexei Romanov (13) suffered an attack of bleeding as a result of the haemophilia that beset the family at this time and only joined his parents three weeks later, along with his sisters Olga, Tatiana and Anastasia, who were sexually assaulted by their guards in transit."
— BELFAST TIMES, 21 July 2018

"The teenage Alexei suffered an attack of bleeding and had to be left behind; he came to Ekaterinburg three weeks later with three of his sisters. The girls, meanwhile, were sexually molested on the train."
— TOWN & COUNTRY, 12 October 2018, quoting Simon Montefiore

Another insight from Sophie Buxhoeveden about the second journey from Tyumen to Ekaterinburg describes how the servants were placed in a cattle carriage and the conditions were filthy, it was bitter cold and they were not provided any food for the whole journey. The guards were edgy and watched over them like hawks. She portrays that there was not much privacy afforded and it would have been almost impossible for anything to happen without the others in the carriage knowing about it. There is no mention in her account of the girls and guards in any sexual context. On that journey, General Adjutant Tatishchev predicted that the royal family would be separated from the household servants and lady in waiting Hendrikova predicted that all their days were numbered. What they did know for sure was that Marshal Dolgorukov had been separated from the royal family at Ekaterinburg and sent to a prison. Their overriding fear was that they did not know what was waiting for them at their destination.

They arrived in Ekaterinburg at night and were kept on the train until the morning. When word got out that the Romanov children were in Ekaterinburg people flocked to see them and threw flowers at their feet but the guards brushed the people aside. The children were immediately taken to Ipatiev House. Those considered of particular interest were taken straight to prison; the rest including the tutors and lady-in-waiting Sophie Buxhoeveden, were kept on the train carriages for a further ten days, then released and were eventually swept up by the advancing White Army.

At Ipatiev House the arriving children were ordered to carry their personal luggage, Alexei's sailor nanny Klementy Nagorny attempted to assist him but was pushed away by the guards and Alexei was made to carry his own belongings. The family had been apart for nearly three weeks so imagine the elation when they were reunited on 23 May 1918 (G). It was very unfortunate that the original plan to take them to Moscow was changed because they were to spend just 56 days together and would not leave Ipatiev House alive.

Alexei and Olga on the ferry to Ekaterinburg, May 1918.
This is the last known photograph of the Romanov family

CHAPTER XVI
The End of Days

THERE had been no effective leadership for Russia since August 1915 when Nicholas took personal control of the army and Alexandra had been handed control of the government. How ironic that they, representing the only organisation structure with any legal and historical legitimacy, were blamed for all of the ensuing problems which ultimately led to the most significant year in Russian history and one of the explosive events of the twentieth century. The two decisive revolutions in 1917 resulted from several factors loosely attributed to political corruption and mismanagement of economic resources which were not compatible with World War I. But in the main, it was really down to the tsar who had become detached from the plight of his people who by the start of 1917 were yet again facing starvation.

The most abled workers were fighting in the war and the government was leading the country in to economic collapse. By February the factory workers were striking on the streets of Petrograd numbering in the thousands. 100,000 women were also marching to celebrate International Womens' Day and over the ensuing two days these groups merged in to a larger protest calling for the end of the monarchy. Nicholas made the fateful decision to fire on the crowd but this time, unlike Bloody Sunday, the soldiers refused to carry out his orders and unit by unit they joined with the protestors. It was left for the police to confront the crowd and serious disorder ensued, known as the uprising of 1917, the peoples' revolution, or better still as the February Revolution 1917, which had started as a civil demonstration but quickly became political when the crowd were fired at.

There had been no effective deterrent from the Duma because Nicholas had closed it down. When the Duma resurfaced following the rioting they processed the tsar's abdication and formed the Provisional Government which became lively with conservatives, socialists and the Petrograd Soviet, each vying for overall control of the country. The Petrograd Soviet was always going to win a show of hands because it represented the workers and soldiers. In the military, those with monarchist allegiances such as Admiral Kolchak, the only commander that had not voted for Nicholas II to abdicate, were dismissed following the February Revolution 1917. Kolchak was a veteran of the Russo-Japanese War and became the youngest vice-admiral in the Imperial Russian Navy, commanding the Black Sea Fleet. He had reported a lack of discipline in the navy to the Provisional Government, as General Kornolov had also done (*page 332*), and likewise had recommended capital punishment.

Nicholas II's abdication in March 1917 had helped to steer the outcome, with the Kerensky Offensive following briefly during July 1917 that tried to shift focus back to the war in Europe and the liberation of the oppressed from Austria-Hungary. Russia had a contractual agreement and could not just pull out of the war and the Allies would not release Russia from its obligation because a peace between Russia and Germany would turn the German divisions of General Erich Friedrich Ludendorff, the military tactician who played a central part in winning the battle of Tannenberg, to engage the Allies and almost certainly claim victory in Europe.

The mainly conservative Provisional Government was at odds with the socialist Petrograd Soviet over the priorities for running the country, particularly participation in the war which the socialists wanted to stop with immediate effect. Furthermore, the Provisional Government was concerning itself with ambitions to secure the Bosporus from the Ottoman Empire, whilst the socialists had no interest in external matters like Constantinople or any form of territorial expansion. Preoccupation with the war meant that formulating a policy for dealing with internal issues was kept on hold until the war ended and elections could then be arranged but they became so disorganised among themselves that they mismanaged the logistics for food and arms resulting in more civilian uprisings and military defeats.

Without elections there was no validity to the Provisional Government and it gave the socialists reason to organise against them. Between February and October many anti-Bolshevik factions were developing in Petrograd and the Bolshevik Lenin cleverly changed his tact. He promoted no confidence in the Provisional Government and led a campaign using the slogan 'All power to the Soviets'. This way Lenin aligned the largely non-political groups made up of representatives of factory workers and soldiers with the political group of Bolsheviks.

Had the Provisional Government dealt with the existential threat from socialism and arranged for elections while the workers were in disarray on the streets and the soldiers were fighting a hopeless war, then they may well have succeeded in appeasing them and survived. In allowing Lenin to adopt the Soviets it gave a political arm to the people and the government was short lived after that; their tenure which started with the people's revolution would soon come to an end with the Bolshevik revolution.

With the increasing distrust Kerensky viewed Admiral Kolchak as a threat whilst he was in Petrograd forming ties with anti-Bolshevik leaders and sent him away. He went to England, Canada and America to discuss the situation around Constantinople with his naval counterparts and did not return to Russia until December 1917 when it was under Bolshevik rule. General Kornilov was another that fell on the wrong side of Kerensky even though he had fought with distinction during the Kerensky Offensive. Both Kolchak and Kornilov, to an extent, came to be regarded as British puppets.

Kornilov had been captured by Austria-Hungary in April 1915 and escaped in July 1916 returning to Russia to continue in military service. His loyalty to Siberia and his hatred for the Bolsheviks was never in doubt and he was put in charge of the Petrograd Military District. After Nicholas II's abdication, Kornilov replaced the guards at Alexander Palace and placed the Romanov females under house arrest there. However, Kerensky's military failures had severe political consequences and although both Kolchak and Kornilov had not been granted the drastic disciplinary measures they had called for to bring the army in to line (namely corporal punishment), Kolchak began to organise for the establishment of an autonomous Provisional Siberian Government in Omsk and Kornilov turned his attention to ridding Petrograd of the Bolsheviks that he believed had taken control of Kerensky's government.

Kornilov put his troops on alert in the capital knowing the Provisional Government was no match for the powerful Petrograd Soviet now allied with the Bolsheviks. As he continued to bring troops in to Petrograd, the effect was to put Kornilov and Kerensky on opposite poles and Kornilov was dismissed from service. Kerensky's misinterpretation that Kornilov was attempting to dislodge the government prompted him to call on the Petrograd soviet for military assistance which ultimately left no confidence that Kerensky could take forward the ground that had been won in the February Revolution 1917. Although the matter lasted only four days, the coup attempt is known as the 'Kornilov Affair' and had inadvertently strengthened public support for the Bolsheviks. Kornilov and his officers were captured and incarcerated at the Bykhov Fortress.

Opinions are divided on whether Kornilov's actions were intended to help the Provisional Government or stage a coup d'état. Four years before his death in 1970, Kerensky gave a Soviet interview in which he gave his belief that Winston Churchill, who was notoriously opposed to the Bolsheviks, had been at the centre of the attempted coup d'état. British military historian Sir John Keegan reinforced Kerensky's view and believed Kornilov had been manipulated by the British whose expertise in these matters was exemplary. This was happening during September 1917 when British agent Oliver Locker-Lampson was supporting Kornilov; British policy being to assist any cause by any means, that opposed the Bolsheviks.

CHAPTER XVI

Civil War

Having led the failed Kerensky Offensive and locked up his Petrograd generals following the Kornilov Affair, Kerensky had made judgemental errors similar to Nicholas II by alienating the military. Now, when he needed them the most, the troops were in far off trenches with their officers locked up and he faced the ensuing hostilities and the October Revolution 1917 without them; and it had turned out to be disastrous. The Soviet Red Army was controlling Ekaterinburg and Moscow with the Bolsheviks having control of Petrograd essentially through the Petrograd Soviet which had assumed complete dominance over the Provisional Government.

However, it wasn't the end for Kornilov, who was rather adept at escaping and he broke out of captivity in November 1917 to raise an army and continue to fight the Bolsheviks. Indeed, by some accounts Kornilov's opposition helped to define Bolshevism. Kolchak had found a very different country on his return to Russia and offered to serve in the British military, prepared to serve as a private. He was accepted and deployed in Harbin to take control of the Russian troops guarding the Chinese Eastern Railway in Manchuria. The British wanted control of the Siberian Railway and to defeat the Bolsheviks so that Russia could rejoin the war against Germany.

German military incursions could not be effectively met until after the American Expeditionary Force entered the war and established in numbers along the western front to preoccupy German forces. With Russia effectively out of the war since the October Revolution 1917, the Bolsheviks solicited the German troops already in Russia to fight the anti-revolutionary groups that were mainly in the southern regions which effectively met the British led effort. General Mikhail Vasilyevich Alekseev brought the anti-revolutionary groups together by creating the first White army. The reader will recall that he was the former Chief of the Stavka and had handed over the tsar's abdication document to General Ruzsky (*page 331*).

Opposition to the Bolsheviks took the form of the 'White movement'; because it was supposedly the colour of the tsarist government according to one account. The Russian flag was decreed tricolour white, blue and red in coronation year 1896; if red symbolised the Bolsheviks and blue symbolised clarity of which there was an absence in the government, white remained symbolising perfection and purity, but the more likely view is that 'white' was associated with anti-revolutionaries since the French Revolution 1789, when the white flag had been adopted by the Bourbon dynasty.

Alekseev recruited disgruntled officers to form volunteer armies with leaders who were experienced generals like Alexey Kaledin in Saratov, Anton Deniken in Novocherkassk (northern Caucasus), Nikolai Yudenich in Lithuania (northwestern Russia), Pyotr Wrangel in southern Russia, and many more including Lavr Kornilov in Siberia and Alexander Kolchak in

Omsk (southwestern Siberia). These competing generals began offensives as early as November 1917. Bolshevik authority was established throughout most of Siberia but British backed Kolchak seized control of the Siberian Railway and moved westwards to Omsk and established a Siberian government. Kornilov took his army south to the cultural capital of the Cossacks at Novocherkassk on the Don River, where Alekseev had the support of the Don Cossacks and the non-Cossack population on the fringes of the southern Russian lands that surrounded the second most important river in Russia after the Volga. Generals Kornilov and Alekseev set up headquarters there with a combined force of 4,000 men.

The armistice between Russia and the Central Powers was signed on 15 December 1917 which left the Bolsheviks in a rut with German forces evacuating Russia en masse. On 28 January 1918 a decree was issued forming the Workers' and Peasants' Red Army, henceforth beginning a fully fledged civil war that was to last for some years until Joseph Stalin was appointed General Secretary of the Communist Party in April 1922 and the subsequent creation of the Soviet Union in December 1922. At this point the difference between the opposing armies was that the Soviets since the Provisional Government was toppled had been restructuring the Red Army, whereas the White Army, despite its experienced generals, was a loose alliance of poorly trained and not well organised volunteer armies. By February 1918 the Whites were consuming vast territories, controlling much across the Urals and the south of the country and the majority length of the Siberian Railway and were even surrounding the Bolshevik units. But they were far outnumbered by the Red Army which started to advance on what they called the White Guard.

The Red Army was able to mount well structured counter offensives and pushed from the north so that Kornilov was forced to slowly retreat across the frozen steppes in what became known as the Ice March after a number of officers froze to death crossing an icy river. In Siberia, the White Army was still some distance from Ekaterinburg but advancing slowly, allowing the Bolsheviks time to decide what to do with the royal family and the other prisoners being held in the Urals. Even the grand dukes had joined the White Army to hasten the relief of Ekaterinburg so that they could reach the royal family. But they would remain at a disadvantage until the Czech-Slovak regiments and other anti-Bolshevik factions joined with the White movement. On reaching Kuban at the end of March 1918, the White Army ranks swelled by 1,000 men led by Colonel Viktor Pokrovsky (a World War I pilot who was awarded the St George Cross for bravery).

The next major battle was at Ekaterinodar in April 1918 where an artillery shell made a direct hit on the headquarters and Kornilov was killed outright. He was buried in Ekaterinodar but later when the Red Army retook the region they dug up Kornilov's corpse and burnt it. When news reached

CHAPTER XVI

Moscow of the victory Lenin said, "... *the civil war has ended!*" The city was renamed to Krasnodar in 1920 by the Bolsheviks but history was to preserve General Kornilov at Krasnodar when in 2013 the Don Cossacks (aka Kuban Cossacks,) erected a monument to him. The Ice March ended in June 1918 when Kornilov's men, or rather Alekseev's army, had returned to the Cossack capital of Novocherkassk, now led by lieutenant-General Pokrovsky, Commander-in-Chief of the Kuban army.

The escalation had started with British and Japanese troops entering Vladivostok on 5 April 1918 and as troops poured in to the Russian interior ambitions grew and in July 1918 Japan landed over 70,000 troops at Vladivostok intent on securing the entire eastern Siberian coast for themselves. That same month the Soviets introduced mass conscription to swell the Red Army to one million men within a year, to three million by 1920 and by the end of the civil war the number had reached five million. It attracted attention from further afield and on 10 August 1918, 10,000 American troops and 4,000 Canadian troops landed at Vladivostok to assist the White movement in Siberia, essentially in guarding the Siberian Railway from Vladivostok to Lake Baikal. Other countries landed troops in Siberia, notably 15,600 French troops, 30,000 Greek troops, 2,500 Italian troops and significant numbers from Estonia, Serbia and Romania. The British all told eventually had 60,000 troops in Russia; the main access points being at Vladivostok in the east and Arkhangelsk in the northwest.

Also in the autumn of 1918, Kolchak promoted himself to an Admiral and when General Alekseev died of heart failure on 8 October 1918, Kolchak became the Commander in Chief of the White Army in Siberia with between 70,000 to 100,000 personnel at his disposal and a further 7,000 British troops made up of volunteers and demobbed soldiers that Winston Churchill had arranged to remain in Siberia to provide assistance and training. The White movement had renewed and unequivocal goals; to expunge German troops from Russia and the Bolsheviks from Petrograd. To this end, the brutality of the White Army had no bounds.

Within three months it turned from a liberating force with the full backing of external nations such as Britain and America, in to a murderous group of death squads equalling the Bolsheviks in their inhumanity. The individual military leaders had little in common with each other and became far removed from the perfect and pure ideals of their white flag. General Pokrovsky, for instance, was sadistic holding a penchant for executing prisoners. Deputy Supreme Ruler to Kolchak, Polish born Lieutenant General Anton Ivanovich Denikin, implemented the White Terror that lasted throughout the civil war carrying out up to 100,000 executions and mirroring the Red Terror campaign that also started in September 1918 which was responsible for quite possibly twice as many executions. White Army insignia which appeared on the uniforms and flags was a skull & crossbones, the symbol for death, which was well suited to Lenin's Bolsheviks and Kolchak's equally bloodthirsty officers who went on murderous sprees killing many thousands of innocent people.

Although Kolchak was described as being immature and petulant with a simple demeanour, as well as kind, he could be a complicated person with a short fuse and possessed a fearful temper. In some regards he had more in common with Nicholas II in that he was under the influence of whomever spoke to him last and was therefore malleable and easily influenced by the British. Many thousands were being recruited in to the White Army on pain of death and opposition to Kolchak meant being strung up on a telegraph pole along the Siberian Railway.

Thousands of dissenters were held in concentration camps which became so crowded that groups were forced to dig their own mass grave before being mowed down by machine gun. Rape and pillage were the order of the day throughout White Army controlled areas. It wasn't that Kolchak couldn't control them but rather that he was no humanitarian, once stating that the civil war had to be won even if three quarters of the Russian population had to be sacrificed to achieve a victory. It was almost a blueprint for the Nazis that would rise in Germany in the following generation.

Admiral Kolchak inspecting White Army ranks

The first step for the end of World War I came on 29 September 1918 when Bulgaria became the first of the Central Powers to pull out of the war. By 3 November the only remaining ally of Germany was Austria-Hungary and on 9 November, the German government met with Marshal Ferdinand

CHAPTER XVI

Foch in France at Compiègne to receive the armistice terms which included the surrender of all military instruments and the Allied occupation of Germany. The German government collapsed on the following day and a Provisional Government was installed. The Keiser abdicated and because his safety could not be assured, he exiled to Holland. Just two days later at 5.10 am on 11 November 1918, still at Compiègne, the German contingent signed the Armistice which became effective at 11.00 am.

Of course, during this time the royal family had been under house arrest during which they always believed they would be rescued by monarchists. It really was a case of the inmates running the asylum with the royal family imprisoned and the governance of the largest country in the world in disarray. They were long since departed by the time of the Armistice, yet there were still several years of fighting before the civil war ended. Pierre Gilliard and Charles Sydney Gibbes amid the madness believed there was no way home for them, yet they survived. While countries accepted the atrocities being done for the greater good, American Major General William S. Graves made his disgust very clear and was not afraid to distribute his daily reports highlighting the terrors perpetrated by the White Army.

"At Krasnoyarsk I learned something of General Rozanov with whom I was to try to work in Vladivostok. He was the man who, on March 27, 1919, issued [the following] *instructions to his troops:"*

> - *"In occupying the villages which have been occupied before by bandits* [partisans] *to insist upon getting the leaders of the movement, and where you cannot get the leaders, but have sufficient evidence as to the presence of such leaders, then shoot one out of every ten of the people."*

> - *"The villages where the population meet our troops with arms, should be burned down and all the full grown male population should be shot; property, homes, carts, etc. should be taken for the use of the Army."*

"We learned that Rozanov kept hostages and, for every supporter of his cause that met death, he would kill ten of the people kept as hostages."
— MAJOR GENERAL WILLIAM S. GRAVES, America's Siberian Adventure, 1931

For his efforts to expose the barbarism of the White Army, Graves received only criticism from France, Britain, Japan and the other nations but at least President Woodrow Wilson agreed with his communiqués. In contrast to Graves' opinion, Winston Churchill described Kolchak as honest and intelligent and Sir Samuel Hoare (*page 403*) called him a gentleman. In London, Paris and even the newspapers in Washington, Kolchak was praised for his patriotism and for having created a stable government in Siberia. Much of this praise was for want of an opposing figurehead to Lenin, Kolchak was all they had to symbolise the good versus evil. Since the summer of 1918 the Bolshevik leaders were being categorically denounced in the world press as paid agents of Germany. The New York Times called them, "our most malignant enemy," notwithstanding America was not at war with Russia.

However, Raymond Robins of the American Red Cross and British diplomat Robert Lockhart, each working for their respective intelligence services, established that many of the military leaders of the factions of the White Army were funded by German Intelligence to create incidents as a pretext for a prolonged German military intervention in Siberia. Most countries had initially offered the White Army every assistance with troops and supplies but fell short of officially recognising Kolchak's Siberian government; only the British had done so which was undoubtedly singularly down to Winston Churchill.

Was it really the case that Germany was funding their enemy to kill their own soldiers so that they could remain in Russia to defeat their Soviet ally? In any case, Kolchak slowly lost the support of the local militias because he could not develop relationships with those he considered inferior. He had no diplomatic skills at all and saw himself purely as a military leader and therefore lost valuable resources, like Finland which could have played a very significant role in the outcome of the civil war.

In April 1919 a major Red Army counter-attack began, capturing Ufa in Bashkortostan (233 miles southwest of Ekaterinburg as the crow flies) in June 1919, which punched a hole straight through the centre of the White Army lines. The White Army retreated to Tobolsk and by October 1919 they were falling back to the Siberian central government in Omsk and were forced to evacuate it on 14 November 1919 retreating to the Irkutsk redoubt. The new administration at Irkutsk was overthrown in December 1919 by Socialist Revolutionaries and a trap was set for Kolchak who believed he was being taken to the British contingent in Irkutsk but was instead handed over to the Red Army and tried and sentenced to death by firing squad by the Bolsheviks in January 1920. He was subsequently executed on 6 February 1920 (some accounts give 7 February 1920) and his body dumped in the frozen Angara River, never to have been recovered.

The White Army continued its retreat eastwards until it was kicked out of Russia entirely with officers arriving in British controlled Harbin daily. The Northern Russian Expedition had failed long ago with French and British troops withdrawn from Murmansk on 12 October 1919 and by November 1920 the White Army had largely been pushed out of Crimea and any foreign support had retreated to Arkhangelsk. The Siberian Expedition had withdrawn all foreign troops by April 1920, although Japanese troops remained until October 1922. The Russian Civil War had cost anywhere between 7 and 15 million lives (depending on sources) mostly civilians.

CHAPTER XVI

House of Special Purpose

Nicholas was fifty years old on 19 May 1918 which went unnoticed. The royal family had reduced staff at Tobolsk and at Ekaterinburg the numbers were further reduced with some going to prison and others being released. Anna Demidova, Alexandra's lady in waiting who arrived at Ipatiev House with the royal family on the first trip, told Charles Sydney Gibbes before they were separated, *"I am so frightened of the Bolsheviks, Mr Gibbes. I don't know what they will do to us."* The first Commandant Alexander Avdeev was a man that could not be reasoned with when he was drunk, in fact he and the guards were always drinking. His two assistants, Alexander Moshkin and Pavel Medvedev allowed all sorts of behaviour from the guards who were a very rough bunch.

The two-storey house in Ekaterinburg was built towards the end of the 1880s in the Russian style. It stood on the junction with Vosnesensky Prospekt and Vosnesensky Pereulok (lane) facing a large square with a church at one end and a prison on the other side of the lane. In 1908, mining engineer Nikolai Ipatiev (sometimes described as a mill worker) purchased the property and converted the first floor (Level 1) in to his workplace. In April 1918 he was ordered to vacate the premises and it was designated by the Ural Soviet as a 'House of Special Purpose'.

It was much smaller than the Governor's House at Tobolsk. Wooden fencing was built around the property exterior with a second paling that was erected after the children arrived creating a moat area around the perimeter. Both panes of the secondary-glazed windows were painted black so that no daylight entered the bedrooms at all and only the top part of the windows could be seen from the street. The prisoners occupied level one with the Commandant occupying an ante room on the same floor and the guards were barracked on the ground and basement levels.

There were 300 guards in the area with regular perimeter patrols and on the inside at least three guards were stationed on level one at all times with the orderly officer making patrols twice an hour during the night. The family had three rooms at first and three more assigned when the children arrived a few weeks later. Many doors were removed so the guards could have a line of vision, including toilet doors; there was no privacy and with only one toilet downstairs for the guards the prisoners used the single upstairs toilet. They were not permitted to move outside of their rooms and doors that still remained in place had to be left open at all times so private communication between the prisoners could be overheard, and they were instructed to speak only Russian so they could be understood by the guards. Sentries were on the landings, in the rooms, near toilets, and at every convenient point throughout the house. It was a secure prison and daily life was pretty mundane as Nicholas described in his diary, until the children arrived.

THE END OF DAYS

"The weather remained overcast and rainy. The lighting in the rooms was poor, and the boredom in the rooms was incredible."
– NICHOLAS II, Saturday 18 May 1918 (G)

Ipatiev House, Ekaterinburg

Ipatiev House surrounded by 20 foot high pilings, (postcard 1920)

CHAPTER XVI

Several groups were raising funds to rescue the royal family but there was no co-ordinated escape committee. Count Benckendorff raised a large amount to finance a rescue attempt and Bishop Hermogenes was still doing his best to rally support for them. Both Nicholas and Alexandra were in secret communication with one or more of these monarchist groups finding ingenious ways to pass secret messages. One note was discovered stuffed in to the cork of a bottle of milk, another inserted in to a slice of bread. Despite these being discovered by the guards the family always harboured the hope for a rescue one day. Nicholas received newspapers for a while and knew how hostile the workers of Ekaterinburg were towards him but the local people were generally sympathetic to the royal family. However, while the Red Army were in Ekaterinburg, suspicion and duplicity prevailed and people were afraid to voice their opinions for fear of being imprisoned or shot for no other reason than being in the wrong place at the wrong time.

As each day passed things got worse for the prisoners. They were stripped of their possessions and their money was confiscated so that they were unable to get any personal supplies in. They lived through their indignations without fuss or complaining about the awful conditions, their food rations or their treatment. The house was cold and very damp and there were no beds for the children when they first arrived so they slept on the floor making a mattress of whatever clothing could be gathered. Marie gave her bed to Alexei until camp beds were eventually brought in for them all.

In comparison with how things had deteriorated in Tobolsk, the food situation had improved. At Tobolsk they had three daily meals comprising a skimpy breakfast, cabbage for lunch (12.00 pm – 1.00 pm) and baked potatoes for supper. Here they had tea and black bread in the mornings (a simple dense rye sourdough bread, sometimes called Borodino bread) but often there was no tea because the guards would use up the hot water and certainly there was never any sugar. According to notes left by the valet Terenty Chemodurov, they had meat soup and a roast of usually cutlets for lunch (2.00 pm).

But it was short lived and lunch came at irregular hours brought in from an eatery whenever the guards could be bothered to fetch it and dinner consisted of left-overs from lunch. The food became so bad that Alexandra could hardly keep it down and Nicholas once went several days without eating. According to Majordomo Parfen Dominin, *"Food was very scarce. Generally only herring, potatoes and bread were given, at the rate of half a pound daily to each person."*

Before meals the guards would pick at the food and even from their plates while they were eating their meals. There was no cutlery allowed and the prisoners used wooden spoons to eat out of shared bowls. Nicholas insisted on taking meals with their fellow prisoners, all being of equal social status under these extraordinary circumstances.

The girls' room at Ipatiev House. British tutor Charles Sydney Gibbes visited the house with White Army investigator Nikolai Sokolov and retrieved several items, taking them back with him to England. One such item was the Murano glass chandelier seen here, made from Venetian glass and hand crafted by highly skilled master artisans.

This exquisite example of Murano craftsmanship was displayed at the Blood & Revolution exhibition at the Science Museum, London, from 21 September 2018 to 24 March 2019 (*see next page*).

The Murano glass chandelier from the girls' room at Ipatiev House

"The guards sang revolutionary songs devised to hurt and shock the feelings of the prisoners, containing foul words such as no man should dare to utter in the presence of innocent girls, but the revolutionary warriors delighted in wounding the modesty of the grand duchesses in this and in other still more repulsive ways, by filthy scribbling and drawings on the walls and by crowding round the lavatory, there was only one for the prisoners and the warders. They went reeling about the house, smoking cigarettes, unkempt, dishevelled, shameless, inspiring terror and loathing. They did not scruple to help themselves liberally to the clothes and other property of the prisoners whenever anything came within their reach."
— NIKOLAI SOKOLOV, The Last Days Of The Romanovs

Alexandra rarely got out of bed before lunch and spent her time in a chair reading or sewing. Alexei's friend Koyla Derevenko lived at the Popov house close by and became the only constant they looked forward to. Nicholas read like crazy and sawed wood like a maniac after exercise time was reduced to twenty minutes a day. The girls took photographs although none exist from Ipatiev House. Anastasia wrote to her friend Ekaterina Zborovskaya, "*It is not too bad, but we spend most of the time searching for balls in the ditch. We sit on the window sills and entertain ourselves watching the public passing by.*"

Alexander Avdeev's room at Ipatiev House

"I was a little boy, just twelve years old. I did not know of the evil in people's souls. ... In the middle of the summer of 1918, I was afraid and worried for Alexei." — KOYLA DEREVENKO, memoirs

Dr Botkin acted as the go-between between the prisoners and Avdeev but usually his complaints and even minor requests were ignored. Guards would later testify at a White Army inquest that Avdeev took great pleasure in denying their requests; Anastasia once asked for her shoes from a box among her possessions and was abruptly told that the ones she was wearing would last for the remainder of her life. The majority of their possessions were kept in a room downstairs or in the loft, or in an outhouse by the courtyard, depending on which source is the correct one. It's likely their things were spread around with the bulk of their belongings being kept in a room downstairs. They were not permitted access to their things and the guards rummaged and stole many items. The guards could appear anywhere in the rooms at any moment, day and night, taking the prisoners by surprise.

In April 1918 news was circulating about the death of Bishop Hermogenes which travelled extremely slow throughout the Russian interior. If it wasn't in a newspaper it might take several weeks for word to travel between Tobolsk and Ekaterinburg and even the Tsar's abdication took four to five months before the whole country learned about it by which

CHAPTER XVI

time the revolution was over and there was a sitting dictator, the son of a Jewish father, who after his marriage to a Christian (Ulianov) had changed his surname from Zederbaum to Lenin.

Hermogenes had come to the attention of the authorities when he held a religious parade through Tobolsk without a permit, notwithstanding that he was the then sitting Bishop of Tobolsk. He was moved to Ekaterinburg for processing but due to protests for his release he was sent back to Tobolsk. The story goes that on the return journey, at the section between Tyumen and Tobolsk, the guards decided to kill him. First he was tied to the paddles of the steamship and when he did not drown a weight was tied to his body and dropped in to the River Tobol. It would seem a very drastic perpetration by soldiers with simple orders to deliver a bishop to Tobolsk. Apparently they were angered about recent military defeats and the deaths of their comrades and this they took out on the bishop whom they suspected of being in collusion with the Whites. It's more likely that the decision to kill Hermogenes had already been made in Ekaterinburg and orders were given for the crime to be enacted after they crossed the Ekaterinburg boundary. It was no doubt due to his sympathies for the royal family, for which his loyalty had never been appreciated by them.

In May 1918 things started hotting up in Ekaterinburg and the Regional Extraordinary Committee were routing out the counter-revolutionary element in Ekaterinburg. On 20 May 1918 other Romanov members and captured counter-revolutionaries in Ekaterinburg were rounded up and taken 85 miles northeast to a camp near Perm. It was a place of detention used by the Ural Soviet at the Nizhnyaya Selimskaya mining site about 11 miles from Alapayevsk on the Irbit Nizhniy-Tagil Railway. What to do with the prisoners now was a matter of disagreement between the Ural Soviet and the Central Kremlin Soviet.

Towards the end of May 1918 a priest was allowed to give a weekly service at Ipatiev House. He reported that Alexei was so thin that he looked almost transparent. This moved the nuns from a local convent to bring eggs and milk for him every day but these nutritional goods didn't always find their way past the guards. By June 1918 Nicholas and Alexandra were also poorly; Nicholas was laid up for several days with kidney trouble and Alexandra was remaining in her bed for most of the day, for days on end.

Many things were happening simultaneously in June 1918 including a disruptive break in the communications network between Moscow and the Urals, possibly being the work of White Army insurgents. Because of this, important decisions were taken without the approval of the Central Committee in Moscow. The Ural Soviet was far more radical than the Bolsheviks in Moscow and wanted to execute all of the prisoners but still they didn't want to face the consequences of going against the Central Committee. Nevertheless the decision was made on 12 July 1918 (G) to execute all of the prisoners at Ipatiev House. The book *The Last Days of the Romanovs* said, *"It is absurd on the face of it to hint that the Ural Regional Soviet was overriding the decisions of Moscow."* It was not that the Ural Soviet was overriding Moscow but rather that they were cut off due to a physical break in the telecommunications infrastructure.

The break of communications was of course a weak argument as the Ural Soviet could have probably found some other way to communicate with Moscow, but it did mask the decision taken to begin the cull of the Romanovs. That same day (i.e. 12 June 1918) an unofficial group of soviet activists and workers headed by Grigori Nikulin (Yurovsky's assistant) turned up at the King's Hotel in Perm where Mikhail Alexandrovich (Nicholas' brother) was staying. Mikhail Alexandrovich was at the hotel with his secretary Nicholas Johnson and they refused to leave. Mikhail had not long turned down the throne and was living at Gatchina Palace since March 1917. In June 1918 his wife Countess Brassova met with Lenin seeking permission to leave the country with her husband which was denied and at a subsequent meeting of the Petrograd Soviet the workers called for his death sentence and a team was promptly dispatched to take care of it. Nikulin was a ruthless Bolshevik killer who on 13 June 1918 returned to the hotel and presented forged documents from the Regional Extraordinary Commission asking Mikhail Alexandrovich and his secretary to leave with him, again they refused but this time were forcefully restrained. The victims were driven out of town and shot and then news of their faux escape was released. Countess Brassova who did not hear from her husband again, made for the border and escaped Russia unharmed.

Marje Spiridonova (Socialist Revolutionary of the Central Committee,) went to Ekaterinburg in another attempt to return the royal family to Moscow for Nicholas to face trial. She came to realise how impossible that task was and decided to conduct the trial in Ekaterinburg instead. Leon Trotsky was to be the Public Prosecutor against the ex-tsar for his crimes against the people. So Goloshchekin was ordered to arrange the public trial for July 1918 but he sent word that there was not enough time for a hearing before they were overrun by the White Army which left the Ural Soviet with a difficult decision to make while allegedly being cut off from Moscow.

Meanwhile at Ipatiev House, despite Avdeev and his men exemplifying the foulest most despicable behaviour, still some of the guards had been humbled by the suffering and humility of the royal family. Even the drunkard Avdeev who enjoyed tormenting them so much, had received no complaints and did not remain unaffected by the gentleness of the royal family, and for this weakness he too was replaced on 10 July 1918 by Yakov Yurovsky. On 4 July 1918 Yurovsky was appointed a member of the Presidium of the Regional Extraordinary Commission and subsequently was also made Commandant at Ipatiev House. His second in command was Grigori Nikulin,

CHAPTER XVI

the Bolshevik killer that had disposed of Mikhail Alexandrovich and his secretary (i.e. valet). On the day Yurovsky took over at Ipatiev House he dispatched Nikulin to kill Court Marshal Vasily Dolgorukov and General Adjutant Tatishchev, both being held at the nearby prison.

Back at Tobolsk, Court Marshal Vasily Dolgorukov had been discovered smuggling pencil written notes to the British Consulate besieging them to help the Romanov family. Now that they were imprisoned at Ekaterinburg, Cheka agents accused him of having plotted a rescue and on 10 July 1918 they took him and General Adjutant Tatishchev to the Ivanovskoe Cemetery just outside of the city where they were shot in the head by Nikulin and their bodies thrown in to a pit, never to be recovered.

On 10 July 1918 Alexandra recorded in her diary that for a couple of days the guards did not bring them their meals at all and they lived on macaroni stores that the cook had brought with him from Tobolsk. The prisoners were suspecting that some development was afoot but nothing so sinister as the murders of their friends Dolgorukov and Tatishchev. They were more believing that they were just days away from being rescued when in fact the purging of Romanovs had only just begun.

> *"We spent an anxious night, and kept up our spirits, fully dressed. All this was because a few days ago we received two letters, one after the other, in which we were told to get ready to be rescued by some devoted people, but days passed and nothing happened and the waiting and the uncertainty were very painful."*
> — NICHOLAS II, 10 July 1918 (G)

Yakov Yurovsky

Now in charge at Ipatiev House was a former watchmaker by trade, the Marxist Yakov Yurovsky, member of the Cheka secret police formed in December 1917 with powers to arrest and execute without trial. The day after the murders of Dolgorukov and Tatishchev, Alexandra was ecstatic at some eggs brought in by the nuns for Alexei. Yurovsky confronted the nuns to confirm that Commandant Avdeev had previously given them permission to deliver these supplies and thereafter he approved only milk deliveries. Nicholas' diary referred to the constant tightening of restrictions by Yurovsky, *"We like this man less and less,"* and in another entry, *"This specimen we like least of all."*

Yurovsky was a Jew (like almost everyone in the revolution) from Tomsk who had converted to Lutheranism. He hated the tsarist regime that had repressed the Jews and Alexandra in particular for having turned away from Lutheranism, in his view. He once worked as a photographic dealer in Ekaterinburg and now so many photographs belonging to the royal family were in a chest on the ground floor under his control that would one day become treasures of photographic history; but alas only one album would survive, now owned by the Zlatoust City Museum, Siberia.

The Moscow Soviet had established that there was not enough time to expediate a trial for the ex-tsar and the pressing problem was of inadequate numbers of Red Army troops in the Urals and Ekaterinburg to repel the advancing Czech-Slovak regiments of the White Army that were attacking from the south and flanking Ekaterinburg on both sides. It was the major city controlled by the Red Army that if lost would be a humiliating defeat. Bolshevik War Commissar Goloshchekin was also a member of the Central Executive Committee of the Ural Regional Council and by 12 July 1918 he was asking for a final solution from Moscow on what to do with the prisoners at Ipatiev House and those at the internment camp in Alapayevsk.

Goloshchekin and Yurovsky were summoned to Moscow by Yakov Mikhailovich Sverdlov, the Chairman of the Central Executive Committee, who asked them how long the White Army could be held from entering Ekaterinburg. He was told the city could hold for just three more days as the White Army were already approaching the city gates. The time finally came when the order was given to dispose of the royal family and their aides at Ipatiev House and various family members being held at Alapayevsk. Goloshchekin and Yurovsky returned at once to Ekaterinburg to set about planning the murders posthaste.

An assumption has to be made that Sverdlov made his decision pending the approval from Lenin. There is some confusion on who exactly gave the order for the murders; Sverdlov or Lenin. It does not have anything to do with telecommunications problems because Goloshchekin was given his order to proceed with the preparation for the murders in person. It does have to do with not having a link back to Lenin, that's how plausible deniability works. According to one account Sverdlov gave orders to execute only the tsar and two of the guards later stated that their orders had been to relocate the remaining prisoners to a secret and more secure facility. Another account states that Goloshchekin acted on his own accord making the decision to kill all the prisoners because he was cut off from Moscow and being pushed for a decision. The chain of command was very simple: Lenin – Sverdlov – Goloshchekin – Yurovsky. An investigation in 2011 concluded that no document exists to prove that Lenin or Sverdlov ordered the murders.

At Ipatiev House Yurovsky faced growing attention when it was least wanted. A diversity of people were gathering outside daily, hoping to get a glimpse of the inmates at the windows or glean information from the guards. Foreign dignitaries, snooping priests, reporters clamouring for information, they all came to the city. Approaches to the guards were brushed away and on one occasion a boy tried to climb the paling and was caught, sent to prison and later shot. The residents were less afraid to discuss the comings and goings of Ipatiev House but still they would wait a while longer for the White Army liberators before they could walk the streets unchallenged wearing their Imperial uniforms. Sophie Buxhoeveden described the scene outside in her book *Left Behind* (1928), *"The streets were full of sailors and soldiers ,,, A great many cars rushed hither and thither, full of Commissars."*

Only the false news of Mikhail Alexandrovich's escape was released by the authorities and when this reached the Alapayevsk camp they tightened their own security fearing another daring and humiliating escape. Various stories were circulating in the absence of real news, purely speculative with some doubting the Tsar was still alive and eventually the general consensus was that he and Alexei had been executed and the focus of the world media shifted to the wellbeing of the remaining prisoners.

According to historian David Bullock, the Bolsheviks believed at this time that the White Army were planning a daring rescue ahead of their main attack on Ekaterinburg and that a snatch raid on Ipatiev House was imminent therefore security was tightened. According to Sophie Buxhoeveden additional machine gun nests were installed to bolster the fortifications. She had been fortunate to be released and left Russia in February 1919 for Brussels and wrote *Left Behind* which is a first hand account of the mood of the people during this remarkable time in world history.

Execution of a Dynasty

Goloshchekin and Yurovsky, were brutal men, it was Goloshchekin who first suggested to Lenin that the prisoners be moved from Tobolsk to Ekaterinburg. Yurovsky received the order from Goloshchekin to execute the Ipatiev House prisoners on 13 July 1918. At church services on 14 July

1918, the new priest Vladimir Khlynov reported that the royal family looked sad and dejected and for the first time the girls did not sing. He was the last person to see them alive.

That same evening Yurovsky drove out to an abandoned mine in the Koptyaki Forest, about ten miles northwest from Ekaterinburg, to prepare a cache of petrol, sulphuric acid and firewood at a pre-determined burial ground. For the place of execution he selected a cellar room in the basement at Ipatiev House. It had a single window which was nailed shut that at eye level met the sloping ground outside. Finally he prepared ten assassins personally picked by him and brought to Ipatiev House. When this was done he informed Goloshchekin that the preparations were completed and the deed could go ahead whenever the confirmation order came. Goloshchekin arrived at Ipatiev House on 16 July 2018 to tell Yurovsky that a truck would arrive at midnight to collect the bodies and that it should back on to the basement entrance and keep the engine running to mask the gunshot sounds. He remained at Ipatiev House awaiting Sverdlov's call to proceed.

Confirmation to proceed with the murders came at 12.30 pm. Only then did Yurovsky tell his assistants that the killings were to take place that evening and told them to prepare rolls of canvas to wrap the corpses with. On the previous morning when the nuns had delivered milk, Yurovsky had asked them to bring 50 eggs for the following day which they did. They were not intended for the prisoners and were probably sustenance for the guards for the task that lay ahead and indeed the future investigation found egg shells around the burial ground at the Four Brothers mine. At 4.00 pm Yurovsky became nervous and returned to Ganina Yama in the Koptyaki Forest with Goloshchekin to double-check the cache was still there undisturbed and to run through the dress rehearsal with Goloshchekin.

The prisoners were blissfully unaware as they waited to be rescued that the Bolsheviks had already killed Nicholas' brother Mikhail Alexandrovich on 13 June 1918 and that the operation to dispose of the royal family members in Ekaterinburg and Alapayevsk was already underway. Nicholas' cousin Sergei and his wife Elizabeth Feodorovna (Alexandra's sister) would be executed on the following day, on 17 July 1918.

On the morning of 16 July 1918 the royal family got up at 9.00 am for morning prayers as usual, they had breakfast and the day went like any other. Alexandra made her last diary entry, the next day's date was written on the next blank page but she would be dead by then and it remains eerily blank for eternity. She noted that the trainee cook Leonid Sednev, whom she called Lenka, had been taken to Popov House across the lane. The Bolsheviks decided to spare the boy's life but his father Ivan was already murdered. At 8.00 pm Yurovsky revealed the mission to his executioners to kill the royal family and their aides. Three of the detail refused to participate and walked off. To compensate for the gaps in the firing squad, Yurovsky stepped in and

CHAPTER XVI

with his assistant Pyotr Ermakov (who was also charged with disposing of the bodies,) they each had two prisoners to execute; so in total this meant there were nine executioners to execute the eleven prisoners and their dogs.

Ekaterinburg 3/16 July [Diary, last entry of Alexandra Feodorovna]

Irina's 23rd birthday. [Nicholas' niece and wife to Felix Yussoupoff]

Grey morning, later lovely sunshine. Baby has a slight cold. All went out ½ hour in the morning. Olga and I arranged our medicines.* Tatiana read ... They went out. Tatiana stayed with me and we read: ... Every morning the kommandant comes to our rooms. At last after a week brought eggs again for Baby.**

8. Supper.
Suddenly Lenka Sednev*** was fetched to go and see his uncle and flew off - wonder whether it's true and we shall see the boy back again! Played bezique with Nicky. 10:30 to bed. 15 degrees.

* Medicines: code for valuables sewn in to clothing. / ** Baby: Alexei.
*** Kitchen boy and son of the Imperial children's personal carer Ivan Sednev.

The identification of the organisers of the executions was included in the investigatory work of Nikolai Sokolov who ascertained them to be:

      Y. Yurovsky (Cheka organiser)
      P. Ermakov (Cheka detachment)
      G. Nikulin (Bolshevik assassin and assistant to Yurovsky)
      P. Medvedev (head of the guard)

The eminent Professor of history Ivan Egorovich Plotnikov, established the identity of the remaining executioners as:

      M. Medvedev (aka Kudrin)
      S. Vaganov
      A. Kabanov
      V. Netrebin
      Y. Tselms

On the late evening of 16 July 1918, Nicholas, Alexandra and Alexei were asleep in one room and the four girls and their maid were asleep in the adjoining room, Dr Botkin slept in the dining-sitting room. Over the past few nights the guards repeatedly walked through the rooms making the girls scream in fright. Presumably this is the source of the account that one or more of the prisoners was raped just prior to their execution. Later in the night, as they were being led along the basement corridors to the cellar, they were reportedly seen smiling and appeared to be jovial, therefore rape is likely a myth albeit there is some measure of truth behind myths it is said. From Buxhoeveden's book 'Left Behind', *"They were at the absolute mercy of their gaolers, who spared them no humiliation they could devise."*

Summer nights in the Urals are short so there was only around seven hours of darkness. At 10.00 pm Yurovsky initiated the operation. Eight assassins went to a basement and waited in a room adjoining the designated killing room. At 11.00 pm Yurovsky came to the room and assigned a prisoner to each executioner with the instruction to shoot at the heart to avoid excessive bleeding. He handed out the weapons selecting for himself a Mauser and Colt to kill Nicholas and Alexei. Ermakov picked up three Nagan revolvers, a Mauser semi-automatic pistol and a bayonet, for killing Alexandra and Dr Botkin.

The massacre was planned for 11.30 pm but the truck didn't arrive so they had to wait leaving the executioners with nothing other than to continue drinking. The truck arrived at 1.30 am and got in to its position. The next phase was to lure the victims to the killing room. Yurovsky went upstairs to wake Dr Botkin and instructed him to raise the others and tell them to get dressed because the White Army was approaching and they were leaving Ipatiev House as a matter of urgency. They should make haste and wait downstairs for further instructions when they would be moved for the time being to the basement until it was safe to leave the house.

The prisoners took between 40 and 60 minutes (depending on accounts,) to wash, dress and gather some belongings, while Yurovsky waited in his office mere metres away. No one was alarmed and the prisoners believed they would be taken to Moscow and were relieved to be finally leaving Ipatiev House. Ermakov was on the upper corridor with Yurovsky, and paced along the corridor listening out, *"I heard them walking around in the bedrooms, putting on their clothes and talking,"* he said. According to the book *The Fate of the Romanovs* Nicholas told the family, *"Well, we're going to get out of this place."*

Alexei was unable to walk so Nicholas carried him and they were the first to go downstairs followed by Alexandra hobbling on her walking cane, then the daughters wearing white blouses and dark skirts and then Dr Botkin, Alois Trupp (the valet), Ivan Kharitonov (the cook), and Anna Demidova (lady-in-waiting). When they had gathered downstairs, Yurovsky led them out to the courtyard and back inside through an adjoining door. A short way in, and Yurovsky opened a set of double doors gesturing for them to go down the staircase to the semi-basement. They followed Yurovsky along a corridor, through a suite of rooms where guards were barracked and to the southern end of the building so that they were almost below the rooms they had been occupying on the upper level.

Inside the courtyard at Ipatiev house

The double doors inside the courtyard. The prisoners were led out of the left door and back in through the right door

The cellar doors were held open and the prisoners were motioned in to a vaulted cellar measuring 18 feet by 16 feet. They put down their cases and waited for guidance. Alexandra asked for a chair and two were brought in by Nikulin; she sat on one and Nicholas placed Alexei on the other. Nicholas was standing almost in the centre of the room between the chairs with the servants standing behind Alexei and the girls standing behind their mother. They were informed that the White Army was expected to overrun the house that night and they were to wait for a truck that was being readied for them.

One account states that Yurovsky played to his professional interest in photography and told them he wanted to take a photograph. According to

Alexander Strekotin, a guard manning the downstairs machine gun post, he claimed to have seen and heard Yurovsky directing them, "*Stand on the left ... and you on the right ... a little more over.*" Yurovsky was spreading them out for a very different type of shoot in an exercise that would have haunted any photographer for the rest of their life; except that Yurovsky was not normal, he was a Bolshevik killer. When they were in position he told them to wait while he went to retrieve his camera. He left the room and closed the cellar doors behind him.

Doors leading to staircase   Staircase leading to basement

Yurovsky headed upstairs to the waiting truck and told a guard to keep the engine revving. Goloshchekin was unnerved and pacing up and down along the moat walkway between the inner and outer palings. The barking of the dogs in the cellar was making the guard dogs outside bark and this concerned him. Everything had come down to this moment, the essence of the revolution was in doing away with the monarchy, and here they were. In the cellar eleven prisoners were already lined up and ready to be executed. A composed Yurovsky returned to the basement and entered the cellar room with his armed detachment of assassins to find the prisoners positioned exactly as he had left them. It was at that moment the prisoners would have missed a few heart beats when they saw that Yurovsky didn't have a camera but a gun and they realised that something was terribly wrong.

CHAPTER XVI

Reconstruction of the positions of the family and servants. Of the many sketches depicting a reconstruction of this scene there are none that show the three family dogs, some accounts mention Alexei's dog called Joy, Anastasia's dog Jemmy and Tatiana's French bulldog Ortipo being present.

Yuroksky stood facing the prisoners with Ermakov at his side. Spread out behind them were two more associates and the five Latvian killers that Yurovsky had personally selected. Although accounts give the time as 2.15 am, there was two hours daylight saving time in Russia up to 1918 and therefore the true time was likely fifteen minutes past midnight which also fits the timings of the truck and which was now revving so loudly from the courtyard that the window in the cellar was rattling wildly giving Yurovsky a sense of urgency to get the job over and done with. He stepped forward and addressed the prisoners, *"your relations have tried to save you. They have failed."* Yurovsky told them that a hearing had taken place that had found them guilty of crimes against the people. He referred to the document he was holding and read it aloud. *"Nikolai Alexandrovich, in view of the fact that your relatives are continuing their attack on Soviet Russia, the Ural Executive Committee has decided to execute you."*

When Yurovsky mentioned 'relatives' he was referring to the British troops in Russia helping to supply the White Army that was fighting against the Bolsheviks. Although the British government's policy was not to commit troops to the civil war, Winston Churchill was openly very anti-Bolshevik making British involvement an inevitability. Since troops had landed in Murmansk on 6 March 1918 the British had been supplying the White Army.

Nicholas shouted out, *"Oh my God No!"* Doctor Botkin said rhetorically, *"So we're not going to be taken anywhere."* A shocked Nicholas addressed Yurovsky, *"I can't understand you ... read it again please."* Yurovsky read it a second time after which Nicholas muttered in disbelief, *"What!"* and a second time, *"What?"*

"This!" Yurovsky answered, or according to the account given by one of the guards called Letemis, Yurovsky's words were, *"You're life is finished."* Without further ado Yurovsky pointed his pistol at Nicholas and shot him in the chest (or in the head according to one account,) from which Nicholas died instantly and dropped to the floor. Contrary to firing at their assigned targets, the inebriated assassins all fired in to Nicholas, Medvedev alone fired five rounds at him. Both Yurovsky and Medvedev would later claim to have fired the bullet that killed the ex-tsar but in a statement given by one of the executioners he stated, *"Mikhail Medvedev shot Nicholas II dead with the first bullet. ... I also shot into the prisoners."*

There being such a volley of bullets directed at Nicholas, the bullets that missed him hit the men standing behind. Dr Botkin received two shots to the abdomen and one to his kneecap and fell to the floor. Trupp received two bullets and then a fatal one to the head. Kharitonov was hit by several bullets at once and fell dead. Once the frenzy had started it didn't stop. The shooters at the rear were firing over the shoulders of Yurovsky and Ermakov.

CHAPTER XVI

Propellant gases filled the air with smoke and the smell of gunpowder. In their drunken state the assassins fired indiscriminately into the smoke which got so thick that they stooped to fire under it. One of the assassins would later describe it as *"complete chaos."* The room suddenly became quiet as the Latvian assassins left the room momentarily to allow the smoke to clear.

Goloshchekin was still pacing about outside, he sent the guard Alexei Kabanov down to tell the detail to use their bayonets as shots could be heard above the revving engine and barking guard dogs. He also instructed them to shoot the dogs first to stop the frantic barking. The concentrated firing at Nicholas left much of the room untouched and as the smoke began to clear the women were huddled and frozen with fear, screaming for help. Ermakov turned to Alexandra and pointed his Mauser, she turned away and did the sign of the cross but before she could finish a bullet entered the left side of her skull. For all that firepower just Nicholas, Alexandra, Trupp and Kharistonov were dead. Even Doctor Botkin who was severely injured was trying to get to his feet. The Latvians came back in to the room to finish the job. The screams and moans of injured victims on the edge of death could be heard but not so easily seen through the lingering smoke as the executioners worked their way across the small room with probing bayonets.

Yurovsky stood over the 53 year old Dr Botkin, as he looked up at him Yurovsky placed his Mauser to his head and shot him. Alexei, was sitting in the chair terrified and covered in his father's blood. Nikulin stood in front of him and fired five bullets from his Browning pistol until the boy slipped from the chair and lay on the floor next to his father. Still alive and writhing with agony he made a movement to touch his father's coat but his hand was kicked away and he was kicked in the head and then finished off with an eight-inch bayonet. Blood ran from the bodies in streams.

Next the attention turned to Olga and Tatiana. Yurovsky and Ermakov moved towards them through the clearing smoke. Seeing them approach, both girls wrapped their heads around each other, crouched down and covered their heads with their arms, both screaming and crying in terror. Yurovsky shot Tatiana in the head, blowing her brains out over her sister. As Olga tried to get up, Ermakov kicked her sending her reeling backwards and shot and killed her. Ermakov next heard screams from Marie and thrust his bayonet in to her several times but she did not die so he shot her in the head. Then Anastasia, who had fainted, came to and rolled about screaming and drawing attention to herself. She fought desperately with one attacker until Ermakov plunged his bayonet in to her but she continued to fight on so he shot her in the head.

Demidova was the last to be slain. She was screaming hysterically and running back and forth along the back wall, (in one account she had fainted when the ex-tsar was shot and came to and said *"God has saved me."*) She was set upon with multiple bayonets and attempted to protect herself with a cushion containing hidden gems that she was holding but it was to no avail and she fell having received more than thirty stab wounds. Along the back wall also lay Anastasia's spaniel dog Jemmy with its head pierced by a bayonet.

Quite possibly the pistol that killed Nicholas II

Pyotr Ermakov c1917/18 – *"I shot him point blank and he fell instantly."*

Later, upstairs in the house a guard would comment on how quiet it was without the prisoners and his testament is confirmation that the dog Joy did survive. How did it escape from the basement and make it upstairs? One account says that after the massacre, *"one of the guards then took pity and cared for the spaniel."* When the White Army arrived at Ipatiev House they found a half-famished, blind and traumatised dog which Colonel Pavel Rodzianko rescued and took care of for the rest of its life. One source says that he gave over the dog in to the care of Edward VII on his return to England. At one time when Buxhoeveden visited Rodzianko, she described Joy's excitement at seeing her, perhaps by association it believed that Alexei might be with her.

CHAPTER XVI

These two photographs are from the evidence in the Sokolov investigation for the White Army, carried out in 1919 and eventually headed by Nikolai Sokolov. **Above**: The cellar room at Ipatiev House — The damage is not from the gunfire. White Army investigators recovered more than thirty bullets that were embedded in the wall and floor. Most were fired from a revolver but also some from a Colt and a Mauser pistol. **Below**: Some of the bullets of various calibres recovered from the cellar room.

"The door from the hallway to the room where the royal family lived was closed, but the room was empty. Not a single sound was heard from there. Previously, when the royal family lived there, one could hear the life in their rooms: voices, footsteps. Now there was no life. Only the dog stood in the hallway near the door in to the room where the royal family lived and waited to be let in these rooms. I remember thinking at the time: you're waiting in vain."
— Guard from Ipatiev House

What should have been an orderly execution taking one minute or so, had been a bloody and chaotic massacre lasting nearly ten minutes. The bludgeoned bodies lay heaped on the floor with pieces of face and brain on top and blood running heavily from the mass of flesh. In 1922 Yurovsky would write, *"after checking again to see that all were dead, I ordered the men to start moving them."* Yurovsky and his team were only part way completed, albeit the dastardly deed was done and the Rubicon had been crossed but they were also half way in to the allotted time of darkness with daylight fast approaching in three hours. A tarpaulin that had been used to cover the prisoners' belongings in the courtyard room was laid on the floor of the truck and the bodies were carried out on canvas sheets and loaded on to the truck. Ipatiev House had been finally cleared of prisoners.

A cleaning crew was assigned that scrubbed the cellar to remove evidence that might one day cost them their own lives if found and used as evidence against them. They proved surprisingly inept at the task leaving much for the White Army investigators to find. The furniture was gathered in the courtyard by the guards and set alight. The possessions were also burned and presumably it included the trunk of photographs excepting the one album taken by the guard Dmitry Chudinov that turned up in 2013 in the archives of the Zlatoust City Museum.

The man that gave the order to murder the royal family, Yakov Mikhailovich Sverdlov, was honoured for his contribution to the Bolshevik Revolution 1917 and Ekaterinburg would be renamed to Sverdlovsk in his honour for sixty-seven years during 1924 to 1991. He died in mysterious circumstances in 1919 aged 33 years old.

In July 1918, World War I was not yet over and Germany was in Crimea and the south of Russia fighting factions of the White Army at the request of the Bolsheviks. France and America had troops in Russia, but the British support for the White Movement was reason enough for the Bolsheviks to have broken off any remaining negotiations affecting the release of the royal family and it had resulted in their tragic deaths.

PART II

CHAPTER XVII
The Aftermath

IN the wake of the murders confusion existed even within the Soviet, the Cheka and the Bolsheviks and even after the civil war the climate of secrecy would continue as the hallmark for the new Soviet Union. What was really happening during 1918 was rather complicated and many theories arose about the fate of the royal family. From the partial release of information in 1991 and the many memoirs that were written shortly after the events, much can be pieced together and looked at afresh and of course, there is always the White Army investigations that can be referenced.

Eleven corpses were on the truck that left Ipatiev House at 3.00 am (allowing for daylight saving time, 1.00 am in actuality) heading northwest of Ekaterinburg on a nineteen mile journey to the derelict iron mine shafts at Ganina Yama near the town of Koptyaki. The road was boggy and the truck struggled. Yurovsky, Ermakov and Vaganov rode in the truck for about half a mile where twenty-five of Ermakov's men were waiting with horses and carts and the bodies were transferred from the truck and then they continued on the journey to dispose of the evidence.

One account is that Ermakov's waiting men were drunk and were angered when dead bodies turned up as they were expecting to rape the women and be involved with the executions. It didn't stop some of them from molesting the female corpses but Yurovsky threatened to shoot them if they didn't stop, not out of decency but to keep to schedule as daybreak was nearing. That story came from the official White Army's 295 page investigation by Nikolai Sokolov published in 1925, in which he wrote:

> *"One of the witnesses cited in the preliminary inquiry had described overhearing a conversation between several Bolshevists about the bodies. ... They spoke cynically of feeling the corpses while they were still warm. Levatnykh boasted that he had felt the Tsaritsa and that he could now die in peace."* — NIKOLAI SOKOLOV

CHAPTER XVII

As Ermakov was the Commissar for the district he had arranged for a cordon around the Koptyaki woods. At Ganina Yama, so named after the pond at its centre, Yurovsky kept five men and sent the rest back to Ekaterinburg. The bodies were laid out on the ground and stripped naked. The clothes were burned and this was when precious stones were discovered sewn in to bodices and cloth buttons. It suddenly became clear to Yurovsky why it had been so difficult to finish off two of the girls and lady in waiting Demidova with bayonets.

"Only in the forest did I finally discover the reason why it had been so hard to kill the daughters and Alexandra Feodorovna ... the daughters had on bodices almost entirely of diamonds."
— YAKOV YUROVSKY

One source even suggested that two of the daughters were still alive as they were being carried out to the truck and even that one of them was groaning after being placed on the truck and that it was only then that they were killed. That scenario would appear a mite exaggerated but there is always a slight possibility that it could have happened that way. Considering the importance of these executions to the Bolsheviks it also seems unlikely for such an unorderly drunken rabble of men to be entrusted with such an important task. What is known for sure is contained in the accounts given by some of the guards for the preliminary White Army investigations and in those additional statements gathered by Nikolai Sokolov later for his book in 1925.

The bodies were left out at the mine, several miles from Lake Isetsk, until the next day and then mutilated and thrown in to the Four Brothers pit, named after the four pine trees that once stood there. Sulphuric acid from the pre-stored cache was poured over the dismembered parts to dissolve the bones and then everything else belonging to them was thrown in to the pit as well. But it was only three metres deep and they soon realised that wasn't deep enough. Grenades were tossed in to try and widen or deepen it but that did not have the effect hoped for except that it made the site a lot messier and Yurovsky's aim to leave no sign of their presence became hopeless.

"In my attempt to collapse the mine shaft with the help of hand grenades, evidently the bodies were damaged and a few parts torn off." — YAKOV YUROVSKY

Yurovsky returned to Ipatiev House to update Goloshchekin who consulted Moscow about the problem with the mess at the pit. It was decided to move the corpses to a deeper copper mine some miles further on. The next day at 4.00 am Yurovsky and Goloshchekin returned to Ganina Yama with some men and hastily removed the body parts and the mess there. Along the way to the copper mine the truck became stuck in the mud near the Gorno-Uralsk railway. Yurovsky's men were losing patience and daylight was fast approaching so Yurovsky decided to bury the bodies in the road where the truck was stuck. A shallow grave was made just 6 x 8 feet and 2 feet deep and when the body parts wouldn't fit, the remaining sulphuric acid was used and the body parts crammed in tightly using rifle butts. But still the grave was too shallow and two corpses were left out. The equivalent of nine corpses were in the grave and railway sleepers were placed over it and the truck driven back and forth over the top to embed them in to the soil, so that it might look like a road repair to fortify the way for the passage of carts.

Pyotr Ermakov standing on the shallow grave near the Starya Koptyakovskaya Road, 1920. On 10 June 2014 the Sverdlovsk regional government listed this place with the National Cultural Heritage so that it would be looked after and protected for future years. The investigation by Nikolai Sokolov searched this place but did not think to look under the railway sleepers that were embedded in the road covering the grave.

The corpses of Alexei and Marie were buried in a pit some 230 feet further along and off from the road. The story goes that Yurovsky thought that if eleven bodies were discovered together they would be instantly connected to the eleven executions at Ipatiev House; so he had made two graves to

CHAPTER XVII

confuse potential discoverers. This explanation seems unlikely and it was probably the case that an inebriated and incompetent crew dug a shallow grave because they hit frozen ground and they did not have enough sulphuric acid remaining to reduce the mass. Consequently they were left with no option but to search for softer ground and dig a second grave.

In the early morning of 19 July 1918 the disposal of the bodies had been completed. Back at Ipatiev House the guards were still scrubbing the cellar floor and removing blood from the walls. The valuables recovered from the bodies and from the house were taken to Soviet headquarters by Goloshchekin and the rest of the belongings that were not burned were looted by the guards. Several of the possessions would turn up elsewhere such as a cross of Alexandra's that was sold and turned up years later in someone else's possessions and also the photograph album that found its way to Zlatoust. Nicholas' 'bloomers' were also stolen by the guard Leonid Vasilev Lubushev and were recovered on 7 August 1918 from his private flat by the Ekaterinburg Criminal Investigation Department.

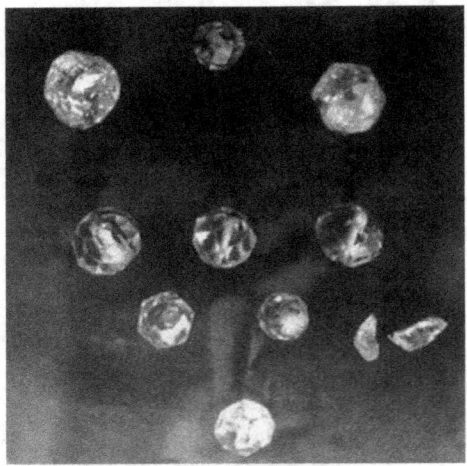

Jewels found at Ganina Yama

Those jewels that Yurovsky did not find when he first stripped and searched the Romanov family at Ipatiev House were later discovered when he stripped their corpses at Ganina Yama. There were so many hidden jewels that they had formed a protective jacket against the bullets and bayonets. Many of the jewels were passed up the Soviet chain but Yurovsky secretly handed the majority of them to Pyotr Voykov, the procurer who had supplied the sulphuric acid and who has thus far not been mentioned but who played an important role in Yurovsky's plans. The cleaning detail, in their utter incompetence left a lot of evidence at Ganina Yama, including several jewels that the White Army investigators unearthed.

THE AFTERMATH

The Chairman of the Ural Council Alexander Beloborodov (Jan 1918-Jan1919) sent a coded telegram to Lenin's secretary, Nikolai Gorbunov. It was deciphered by the White Army investigation (1919-1922); 'the evacuation' refers to the Bolsheviks leaving Ekaterinburg in haste before the arrival of the White Army. Could this be considered a link to Lenin?

TELEGRAM *"Inform Sverdlovsk the whole family have shared the same fate as the head. Officially the family will die at the evacuation."*

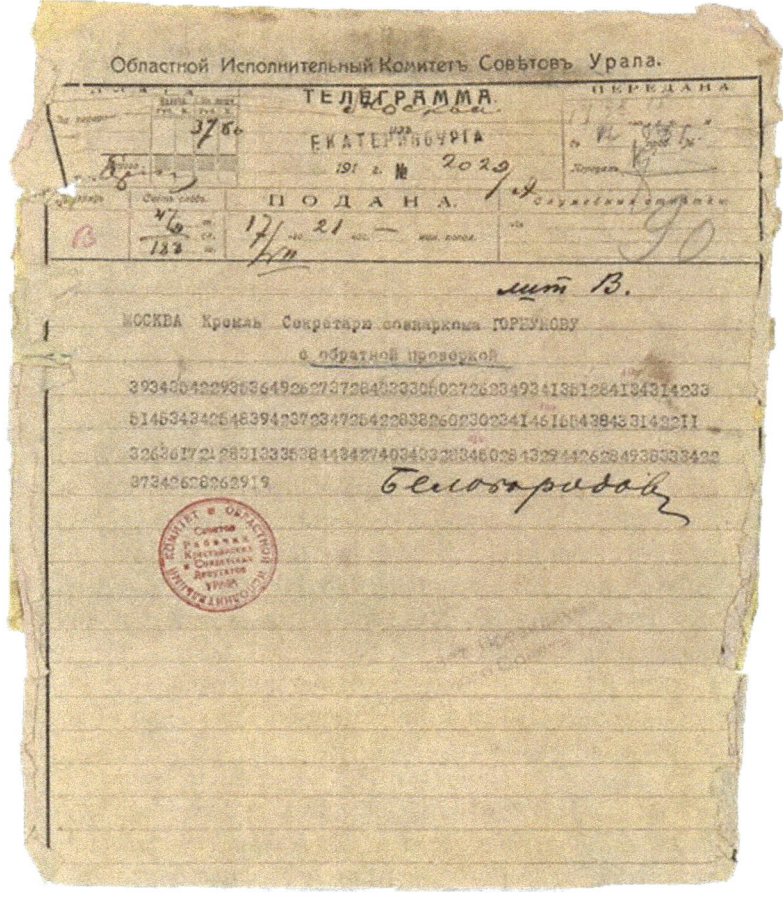

The coded telegram from Ekaterinburg to Moscow confirming the prisoners had been executed. It was obtained by the State Archives during the exchange of archival materials with the ruling prince of Liechtenstein, Hans-Adam II.

CHAPTER XVII

On 18 July 1918, twenty-four hours after the Ipatiev House murders seven more Romanovs were executed by the Bolsheviks ahead of the advancing White Army. The massacre took place at the mines near Alapayevsk. One account says they were thrown down a shaft but didn't die so grenades were thrown in but still they didn't die, so logs were thrown in and set alight in a bonfire. This story has been accepted as an untruth and the victims were already dead when they were thrown in to the pit. On the following day a decree was issued by the Council of People's Commissaries confiscating all Romanov property and proclaiming it to belong to the Soviet Republic, which officially started the Romanov flee from Russia.

News of the Alapayevsk executions were published in Ekaterinburg on 22 July 1918. In spite of the White Army investigation report that refuted the story that the victims had been buried alive at Alapayevsk, most accounts since have persisted with it. Even a description of Elizabeth Feodorovna on the Royal Collection Trust website (RCIN 401319) states the following, *"She was arrested by the Bolsheviks in 1918 and later that year she was thrown alive down a mineshaft with several other prisoners."*

The forensic medical examination and autopsy report concluded that the victims at Alapayevsk were already dead when they were tossed in to the pit. The cause of death was a blow to the back of the head with a blunt object such as the back of an axe. Grand Duke Sergei Mikhailovich Romanov (second cousin removed to Nicholas II) survived the blow and tried to get away but was shot in the attempt. As they were being executed the bodies either fell in to the pit or were pushed in when they died. Several grenades were tossed in but only one exploded. The pit was then sealed and the corpses remained there for three months awaiting discovery by the White Army. They took Ekaterinburg on 23 July 1918, arriving at the internment camp at Alapayevsk on 28 September 1918, but it was not until 8 October 1918 that the pit was excavated. Because the corpses were in relatively good condition considering the length of time they had been in the ground, the initial view was that they had not died from an injury but were thrown in to the pit alive and had perished from starvation, hence the myth that the victims were buried alive was created.

> *"It is not true that they threw their victims down the shaft before life was extinct. The autopsy has dispelled that legend. The murderers even exploded hand grenades down the shaft, probably to make assurance doubly sure."* — NIKOLAI SOKOLOV

Twenty-eight bodies were discovered at the Alapayevsk internment camp. They were buried in a mausoleum at a church in Alapayevsk. The locals were instrumental in the summary executions and knew what was happening at the internment camp. They had pressed the guards to take severe action,

THE AFTERMATH

calling for their deaths and had shown no humanity towards the captives at any time. The White Army in turn showed no mercy to the workers and peasants of Alapayevsk for helping to expediate the deaths and reprisals made the residents pay dearly for their treachery. Later when the Red Army were returning, the coffins of the royal family members and some aides were recovered by the White Army and taken ever eastwards as the battle lines shifted during the civil war. By 1920 they had arrived in Peking, current day Beijing, near the Andingmen city gate where they were buried in the cemetery of the Russian Orthodox Mission (ROM).

The victims of Alapayevsk were (18 July 1918):

- ❖ Grand Duchess Elisabeth Feodorovna
- ❖ Grand Duke Sergei Mikhailovich of Russia
- ❖ Grand Duke Sergei's secretary Varvara Yakovleva
- ❖ Prince Ioann Konstantinovich of Russia
- ❖ Prince Konstantin Konstantinovich of Russia
- ❖ Prince Igor Konstantinovich of Russia
- ❖ Prince Vladimir Pavlovich Paley

In 1957 the ROM in China was demolished and in 1986 a parking lot was constructed over the adjoining cemetery. The Romanov descendants have been trying to recover these remains ever since without much success. The remains of Elizabeth Feodorovna were exhumed from the ROM in January 1921 along with a fellow nun and transported to Jerusalem where they were reburied in the Church of Mary Magdalene in Gethsemane and where they remain undisturbed to this day. Elizabeth Feodorovna became a nun after her husband Grand Duke Sergei Alexandrovich was assassinated by a bomb in February 1905. She founded a convent and became its abbess, working with the poor in Moscow until her arrest by the Bolshevik Abramov, the Alapayevsk Cheka leader whom Lenin had personally ordered to arrest Elizabeth Feodorovna and detain her at Perm. Thereafter she was moved to the Alapayevsk internment camp and processed for execution.

Also involved in the arrest of Elizabeth Feodorovna was Alexander Beloborodov, the Ural Regional Soviet representative mentioned earlier (*page 352 & 393*), that gave Yakovlev the receipt for the transfer of custody of the royal family at Ekaterinburg station and who also sent the telegram to Moscow confirming the executions at Ipatiev House had taken place.

The Bolshevik purge on the royal family and their supporters had started several months earlier in April with the murder of Bishop Hermogenes who

CHAPTER XVII

was suspected of helping the royal family. As discussed (*page 372*), Hermogenes was killed on the orders of the Bolshevik Pavel Khokhryakovk, the official in charge of the detail assigned to transport Hermogenes back to Tobolsk. The bishop's body was discovered in the river Tobol on 3 July 1918 and buried nearby and was later moved for reburial at the Saint Sophia Cathedral (built in 1686) in his bishopric town of Tobolsk. Also, on 13 June 1918, Nicholas' brother Mikhail Alexandrovich was murdered in a forest in Perm.

In January 1919 the Bolsheviks murdered the following Romanovs:

- ❖ Grand Duke Dmitry Konstantinovich
- ❖ Grand Duke Nikolai Mikhailovich
- ❖ Grand Duke Pavel Alexandrovich
- ❖ Grand Duke George Mikhailovich, who had been held in the prison of the Peter and Paul Fortress in Petrograd

There are very few stories of people that managed to escape from Bolshevik captivity, the most notable being Alexei Andreevich Volkov (*page 267*), a valet to Alexandra Feodorovna, whom the media reported had been shot alongside lady in waiting Anastasia Hendrikova and German language tutor Ekaterina Schneider who were being held captive in Perm. Volkov's story is worthy of inclusion so the reader may rejoice that for Volkov there was a light at the end of the tunnel, in stark contrast to the sad way in which this book is drawing to its inevitable end with listing the many Romanov victims of the Bolshevik purge.

Volkov had once worked for the Grand Duke Paul Alexandrovich of Russia, the youngest child of Alexander II, brother to Alexander III and uncle to Nicholas II. From 1910 he was in constant service with Alexandra Feodorovna, often pushing her around in her wheelchair. He had been with her under house arrest at Tsarskoe Selo and Tobolsk. His family had followed him to Tobolsk and was staying at a nearby convent. He was one of those arrested that had been separated at Ekaterinburg and eventually found himself in a prison cell at Perm.

Near midnight on 3 September 1918 (G) a guard entered his cell and asked *"Which one is Volkov? - Get dressed, Come with me."* Volkov, Hendrikova and Schneider were told that they were being moved to another prison and were escorted by three young soldiers. They travelled by foot and along the way they joined another group making them in total eleven prisoners and 25 soldiers. The prisoners were closely flanked by soldiers and as it got colder and darker, just outside of town some peasants and carts crossed their path and the cohort of prisoners came to a halt. For a brief minute earlier Volkov had passed a pedestrian and asked him how far it was to the prison and was told that they had already passed it.

It suddenly dawned on Volkov that they were being taken to a place of execution. He looked for a place to run and hide under cover of darkness but it was too late, they were ordered to start walking again. Three shots rang out behind them, Volkov dared not look back, perhaps it was the pedestrian he met earlier that had just paid with his life for their encounter. Volkov's intuition was warranted; approaching the dawn they turned off the track heading in to a forest along a path lined on both sides with hedges. They were ordered to stop. He stood there frozen and holding on to Ekaterina Schneider's belongings. This was the moment it also dawned on the others that they were about to be executed and he could feel their fear.

This time Volkov wasn't going to lose the opportunity that might cost him his life. Without a moment to reason or weigh the risk, he threw himself over a hedge and bolted away for his life. A shot was fired and he felt the bullet race past his ear, a second came and coincidentally at that instant he tripped and fell and the guards presumed that he had been hit. He could not risk waiting for them to come to check if he was dead so he got up and started running and a third shot fired out and whizzed past him. The forest was still thin with trees so he didn't look back and kept running until he reached a lake where he could stop and appraise the distance he had put between himself and the guards and where he rested for an hour, flat on his back, more exhausted than he could ever remember being.

The countryside he traversed was a series of fields and clumps of thick forest. By evening he had been on the run and without food for twenty-four hours and rested again. At dawn he continued, weaving in and out of field and forest, chewing on wheat stalks for sustenance. He could not ask for help at the houses he passed or from the peasants he saw because he dared not trust anyone. He was resting under a tree when a man approached him holding an axe. Volkov placated him and the man offered to take him in to town and show him where to get some free bread. He took the hat from a scarecrow to hide his face and tried to tidy his dishevelled appearance.

He was surprised by the kindness of the villagers who offered him food. Some smiled because they knew who he was. The peasants were not friends of the Red Army although there were sporadic Bolsheviks scattered about here and there. Some women gave him bread and cucumbers and he was able to spend nights sleeping in haystacks as he continued to move through the countryside. He hoped that he was moving in the direction towards the White Army lines but he couldn't be sure. He came upon a church where the deacon and his wife were most hospitable and the deacon made him a map highlighting the proper route and the houses of Bolshevik sympathisers to avoid. He also provided ten rubles and his wife packed a bag with some bread and butter for his journey ahead.

CHAPTER XVII

For a short while he was back dipping in and out of field and forest. One night sleeping in a thicket, he heard loud breathing next to his ear, he snapped his head around and was staring at a wolf; frightened, he shouted at it loudly until it ran away. Finally, after several weeks he came to a railway station controlled by the Czechs and purchased a ticket to Ekaterinburg. He headed straight for the prison at Ekaterinburg where he had been an inmate for a time, not being one of those prisoners permitted at Ipatiev House. He was recognised by the prison officials who were shocked to see him as they had performed his funeral service on the previous day. After a dinner he went to the barber and then to the baths with the local officials, where he put on new clothes. Before leaving town he visited Dr Derevenko who was still practicing there. Dr Derevenko helped the White Army investigators after they arrived in Ekaterinburg but he was fated to die at the hands of the Red Army years later and was executed in 1936 during Stalin's Great Purge.

Volkov left the city and that evening he was in Tyumen. He called upon Sophie Buxhoeveden who was shocked and excited to see him and gifted him fur boots and a winter coat. This was where the royal household survivors had gathered, Gilliard, Buxhoeveden, Tegleva and Ersberg, existing rather *"mediocrely"* Volkov recorded in his memoirs. He stayed with them briefly until he regained strength enough to continue to Tobolsk to reunite with his family at the convent there. They too had believed that he had perished at Perm with Hendrikova and Schneider. The Volkov family were moved to Omsk by the authorities and that's where the White Army investigator Nikolai Sokolov caught up with him to take his deposition. The family emigrated after much diplomatic wrangling to Denmark where they were well received for Volkov's loyalty to the former Imperial Family.

In his memoirs, Volkov described his last encounter with Nicholas II and Alexandra Feodorovna as they were leaving Tobolsk for Ekaterinburg.

"The Emperor said goodbye to me, we hugged and he said 'Soon, I hope.' The Empress gave me her hand, which I kissed, and said to me 'Keep a good watch on Alexei.' Then they left. The sadness like a death hung over the house. Before, there had been a certain liveliness. After the Imperial couple left, silence and desolation descended on us."
— ALEXEI VOLKOV, valet of Alexandra Feodorovna

On 19 July 1918 Bolshevik War Commissar Filipp Goloshchekin of the Ural Soviet announced at the Opera House on Glavny Prospekt (today home to the Ural Opera and Ural Ballet on Lenin Avenue,) that 'Nicholas the Bloody' had been shot and his family taken to a secure location. A multitude of false press releases and speculation followed around the world. Over the next 84 days fourteen more Romanovs and thirteen of their entourage, were murdered by the Bolsheviks.

The Countess Anastasia Hendrikova, the devoted lady-in-waiting to Alexandra who had followed her in to exile before being separated at Tobolsk was asked if she had willingly followed the family. She replied that she had. When asked if she would return and continue to serve them if she were set free, she said: "*Yes! Up to the last day of my life!*" On 4 September 1918 (G) she was taken to the woods with others, and shot.

> "*According to Mr Gilliard's account of the last days of the Imperial Family, those fine qualities of the Empress which showed themselves in her care and devotion to the sick and wounded during the war became still more evident in the days of distress, misery and ignominy which crowned the end.*
>
> "*Even her critics and her enemies, and she had many, will accord her a mead of praise for the courage and devotion which, even in what must have been the worst intense purgatory to her, she showed unselfishly for her husband and children.*
>
> "*And so in death they were not divided.*"
>
> — SIR JOHN HANBURY-WILLIAMS, memoirs page 220

Dr Derevenko had stopped making visits to Ipatiev House at the start of July 1918 when Yurovsky took over as Commandant. He returned after the White Army had taken Ekaterinburg on 23 July 1918 with his son Koyla who recalled the experience in his memoirs:

> "*There was a terrible scene. The house was in complete chaos; diaries, letters, albums, and other things were strewn all around in the house. 'But where is Alexei?' I asked my father, but he stayed silent. I was confused. 'Papa, where is my Alexei?' I asked. 'They killed him,' he said, and I started to cry. 'But how?' I replied. 'They killed the Tsar, the Tsarina, and the Grand Duchesses too. They are all dead.' said my father. 'But I don't understand. Where are their bodies?' - 'We don't know, maybe we will never find them.'.*"
>
> — KOYLA DEREVENKO

The pet dogs belonging to the children shared the same fate at Ipatiev House except that Alexei's spaniel Joy survived and was taken to England to live a happy life. The frozen body of Anastasia's spaniel Jemmy was found a year later at the bottom of the mine at Ganina Yama, with its right paw broken and a fatal head injury. According to Ms Vyrubova's memoirs (pages 53-54) Jemmy was a gift from her to Tatiana but the dog took a liking to Anastasia so she kept it; in her letters Anastasia referred to it as 'my Jim'.

The children's English tutor Charles Sydney Gibbes identified Jemmy when he was assisting the White Army investigation in 1919. Tatiana's

CHAPTER XVII

French bulldog Ortipo was given to her by Dmitry Malama, the cavalry officer she had grown fond of while nursing him at the Alexander Palace infirmary. Alexandra once told Nicholas that he would have made a nice son-in-law, if only royal princes were as nice, she would say. There is no evidence of what happened to Ortipo, it's said she was not in the cellar but was killed outside by the guards, perhaps when they had heard enough of her constant yapping and silenced her.

Tatiana and Anastasia with Ortipo at Alexander Palace, 1917

CHAPTER XVIII
Plots & scheming

British Intelligence in Russia

Sir Mansfield Cumming, a British naval Captain, was the first chief of the secret intelligence service (SIS), the forerunner of MI6, from 1909 to when he died in 1923. He shaped the newly formed foreign intelligence service and was the originator of the legends about spy agencies; using blades hidden in canes, invisible ink, disguises and poison tipped jewellery; he even wore a monocle and had a wooden leg, all the things that would make a John le Carré spy novel.

He was the first intelligence head to use a single letter to refer to the Chief of the Service and it's how M appeared in the James Bond books and films. In reality he was C, not because his name was Cumming but rather because the War Office was handling an Austrian agent known as B to monitor activity in German ports so Cumming became C and the single letter title has been bestowed on every Chief ever since. D was one of three agents being handled in Germany to provide an early warning on the likelihood of war in Europe.

Europe was a cauldron of political strategy and skulduggery, increasing threats from European rivalries and shifting allegiances and alliances forming various pacts and treaties, each surpassing the other in their scope. Germany was seen as the belligerent nation with the strongest economic and military power in Europe. It wanted to build its naval fleet to rival the British and push out in to the North and Baltic Seas.

Germany's expansionist aims were the reason the formation of the Triple Entente in 1907 was necessary. Whitehall was convinced that Germany was targeting Britain and had flooded it with German agents. Before World War I Germany encouraged migration to study and forge business partnerships and England was a popular destination for aspiring Germans. However, British officials became insanely paranoid about a network of German espionage being formed by the settlers. But there were

CHAPTER XVIII

no spy rings of that nature in Britain at that time. A study by the War Office revealed that France and Germany had effective intelligence services in place whereas Britain was relying on the age old system of informants since Elizabeth I of England and there was no real knowledge about the state of foreign affairs outside of political and diplomatic means.

Cumming therefore had three objectives; to organise home intelligence so that it could be known who was spying in Britain and what their intentions might be; to set up a secret headquarters and outline a method of tradecraft, recruitment and training; and to establish a global network of agents to gather military information in the national interest as well as economic and industrial information for Britain to prosper commercially. During World War I therefore, MI6 was still in its infancy but establishing itself fast.

Cumming started out with his informant B, an Austrian agent reporting on German port activities and ship building. The network was expanded from there so that by 1915 there were around 1,000 people in the field. Cumming learned that it was better to recruit a few well vetted agents than to increase the eyes in the field. Loyalties were, he discovered, a complicated issue. For example, B was providing the highest quality information out of Germany but would not inform on Austria where four German battleships were being built at Pola.

Greed also became a factor in the handling of non-British agents. Whenever a meet was necessary the agent would choose the most expensive restaurants and hotels, so becoming the format for novels in portraying the tuxedoed spy. Perhaps Ian Fleming's notion of a Martini swilling Bond had something to do with one agent that Cumming wanted to send to Germany in August 1910 who made it a condition that he receive an allowance for Champagne. In any case, handling the handlers also required discretion and a bogus shipping company was established as a front, creating yet another de facto for the spy thriller, the imports and exports cover.

In 1912 Cumming witnessed the double agent at play. In his meetings with his French counterpart they realised that some agents were working for both sides, so by 1913 France and Britain were exchanging intelligence. One triple agent was found to be also working for the Russians. Cumming met him at the London Savoy Café in April 1913 and learned that he had allowed himself to be recruited by the Russians in order to widen the availability of information to sell. He also gave Cumming the vital detail that Russia was intent on war with Austria under any pretext and that war in Europe was imminent. Cumming resolved to getting agents in St Petersburg posthaste.

The minutes of the Secret Service Bureau committee meetings from 1912 to 1913 supported Cumming's work and he was well placed when war broke out in April 1914, one year after his meeting with the triple agent, and when a high demand for operational intelligence was being requested by the War Office. Inroads were made in Africa, South America, the far east, and a trade and commerce network was being started in Russia, separate to the existing military structure already there. Because of the secrecy around the true nature of the endeavour, there were a lot of wranglings with the British military and diplomatic staff who became incensed when decisions from London ruled in favour of the intelligence mission.

On the military side, General Sir John Hanbury-Williams was sent out by the Secretary of State for War Lord Kitchener. He was the head of the British mission at the Russian General Headquarters, the Stavka in Moghilev, Poland, and reported directly to Kitchener. Cumming had planned to visit Petrograd in person but although his plan was approved the Admiralty forbade him from going so instead he sent Captain Archibald Campbell as his representative in August 1914. He was accompanied by Lieutenant Stephen Alley, born and bred in Russia. They arrived in Petrograd in late September 1914.

Their mission was to contact the relevant officers of the Russian General Staff dealing with intelligence and obtain information about Germany but had no direct involvement with espionage. The Russian military staff regarded them as a hindrance and Campbell was revealed as not having any diplomatic skills. Therefore in May 1915 he was replaced by an Indian Army officer, Major Cudbert Thornhill who was more apt in dealing with Russian military staff and was on the whole successful in maintaining an intelligence service that many British military staff still regarded needless.

By the end of 1915 Cumming had got around to preparing for a firmer footing in Russia and recruited Sir Samuel Hoare (a Conservative MP since 1910), appointing him the rank of Lieutenant-Colonel. Meanwhile in Russia in 1916, Thornhill was transferred to the embassy as assistant military attaché. Cumming's deputy Frank Stagg assigned Lieutenant-Colonel Samuel Hoare to the British intelligence mission with the Russian general staff as the head of the British Secret Intelligence Service in Petrograd. Alongside him were Oswald Rayner, John Scale, and Stephen Ally. Cumming now had a proper intelligence mission in Russia.

For a while after Hoare took over in July 1916 things went well. Then intelligence started picking up gossip and rumours of the war soon coming to an end for Russia. John Scale in his notes recorded, "*German intrigue was becoming more intense daily. Enemy agents were busy whispering of peace and hinting how to get it by creating disorder, rioting, etc.*" Soon Rasputin came in to their field of view, he was already considered a Germanophile and a threatening anti-war force, and Cumming was concerned by the influence he exerted on Russia's foreign policy.

Michael Smith, the author of *Six: The Real James Bonds 1909–1939* originally published in 2011, argued that MI6 were ordered to arrange the assassination of Rasputin. Richard Cullen, a former Scotland Yard commander and author of *Rasputin: The Role of Britain's Secret Service in his Torture and*

Murder (2010), went further by claiming to have uncovered evidence in 2004 when he examined newly released files linking MI6 to the murder. He stated that Hoare suggested to Cumming that he believed Rasputin was sabotaging the Russian war effort and that if he was murdered, *"the country would be freed from the sinister influence that was striking down its natural leaders and endangering the success of its armies in the field."* Cullen also stated that the plot was conceived through the personal relationship that existed between Felix Yussoupoff and Rayner and that prominent agents Oswald Rayner, John Scale and Stephen Alley made contact with Yussoupoff and Purishkevich and were involved in the plot; Raynor actually being in attendance and having fired the fatal shot to the forehead. The Tsar accused MI6 of involvement and British ambassador George Buchanan put it to Samuel Hoare who angrily retorted that the allegation was "*incredible to the point of childishness*".

The Yussoupoff/MGM court case made public the possible involvement of British Intelligence in the murder of Rasputin. A good case can be made to support British involvement as has been explained thus far. The main instigator Felix Yussoupoff, son of the richest man in Russia after the tsar, studied at Oxford (1909-1912) where he met people that would later be recruited as British intelligence agents working in Russia. Yussoupoff and the British had different motives for wanting to murder Rasputin; Yussoupoff saw him as a threat to the Romanov dynasty and to Russia and the British wanted to prevent his influence on the Imperial couple to make a separate peace with Germany. If that were to happen, it would free up 400,000 German troops on Germany's eastern front to go to their western front and face the British, a contemplation that Britain would have done anything to prevent.

While it's unavoidably true that Yussoupoff had a firm connection with British agents – Oliver Locker-Lampson, the MP that appeared at Yussoupoff's court action and Oswald Raynor, his best friend that translated the book *Rasputin* for him and who was deployed in Russia by MI6 – there is no reason why Yussoupoff didn't have as many connections in Russian intelligence, albeit the Soviet were not at all accommodating to the nobility. The point is, that if Yussoupoff was trying to enlist help to murder Rasputin, he could have approached the British, as he said he had done, because he certainly knew the people of MI6 in Russia well.

The theory that British agents were involved with Yussoupoff in the murder was largely discredited for lack of any evidence until author Cullen claimed to have found some. Even so, British involvement was never seriously considered on account the assassination was conducted with such downright ineptitude. The police chief Serda described it as the work of incompetent killers whose methods were clumsier than he'd ever seen in his career and it was hardly the work of the British. Yet it might be argued that such an overly chaotic scene was exactly how the British would want to leave things in order to avert suspicion. Three shots fired within 200 mm of the body, one to the liver, a second to the kidney and yet it took a third bullet to the head to kill Rasputin!

The craze for Cullen's theory will have to wait for other authors to catch up and examine the new findings because as it stands the supporting evidence for British involvement rests on the third bullet to the head. Cullen examined the forehead wound in detail and identified the gun as a .455 calibre Webley revolver manufactured by Webley and Scott in Enfield, England. The Webley was a common weapon for British troops in World War I, whereas Russians used Nagant revolvers. This was an interesting discovery assuming it to be true. But how would it prove that the gunman was a British agent. That gun could easily have been used to incriminate the British. Furthermore, Historian Douglas Smith while researching for his book *Rasputin* at the Russian State Archives in Moscow, found a receipt for a Webley-Scott revolver, filed for a Lieutenant Colonel Polyakov, thus proving that Russian police had previously used Webley revolvers.

Talks of Rescues and Executions

In October 1917 Leon Trotsky called for the Soviet Congress (a minority of the people,) to represent the revolution and no longer acknowledge the Provisional Government. Civil war broke out and by November thousands of troops were returning home with German troops left behind Russian lines on the outskirts of Petrograd. It caused confusion and uncertainty that was reflected in the shifting of power across middle Russia between the opposing sides in the civil war. There was renewed hope for the Tsar and his family and aides, that they might be rescued. Unfortunately, the hatred carried by the Bolsheviks ensured that never happened.

The Treaty of Brest-Litovsk signed on 3 March 1918 effectively ended Russia's participation in World War I with the Bolsheviks accepting the independence of Estonia, Latvia, Finland and Ukraine. The Bolsheviks then committed to a Romanov purge by killing Mikhail Alexandrovich in a Siberian wood on 13 June 1918. It turned in to a killing spree when within a month, they had extended the purge to the Romanov Household and Vasily Dolgorukov and Ilya Tatishchev were shot at the Ivanovskoe Cemetery on 10 July 1918. Finally, the ultimate sacrifice was a massacre of the entire ex Imperial Family on 17 July 1918. Reports of these killings appeared in the media except that there was nothing about the inmates of Ipatiev House which stirred speculation and rumours of their execution or escape or rescue.

Goloshchekin was the de facto communist press bureau spokesperson and had one day to clear up the mess at Ipatiev House before making the official announcement on 19 July 1918 that the ex-tsar had been executed and the remaining prisoners moved to an undisclosed location. Goloshchekin, was one of a few that really knew what was going on. No news was good news some thought. The British knew just a few hours after the murders on 17 July 1918 because Thomas Preston of the British Consul sent the following telegram to London, *"Emperor of Russia shot in the night of 16 July by order of the Ekaterinburg local Soviet ..."* A communiqué that Goloshchekin intercepted and changed the wording from '*Emperor*' to '*Ex-Emperor*' correcting a mere technicality and proving the British knew.

The British secret service was quite ahead of the game in Russia, having established itself effectively. The British interest was with Russia pulling out of World War I. British diplomat Sir Robert Bruce Lockhart was sent to Russia in January 1918 as the Consul-General in Moscow to establish a direct line of communication with the Provisional Government concerning both the war and the predicament of the royal family. In truth Lockhart went to handle the activities of British spies placed by Mansfield Cumming and Lockhart's real purpose was in bringing together spies and diplomats to sabotage the Bolshevik regime, albeit there was genuine concern for the welfare of the royal family, being they were relatives of King George V.

"In 1918, behind-the-scenes helpers such as ... Sidney Reilly, the erstwhile Russian double agent who was operating on Britain's behalf, were involved in the formulation and execution of various attempts to snatch both Russia and the Romanov family from the Bolsheviks."
— SHAY McNEAL, Historical author (The Secret Plot to Save the Tsar)

Lockhart was hand-picked by Prime Minister David Lloyd George for the special British diplomatic mission to Russia because for five years he had held the post of British Consul-General in Moscow and not least because he spoke fluent Russian. He had returned to London just six weeks before the Bolshevik Revolution (i.e. the October Revolution 1917). He arrived in Petrograd, in January 1918 while Foreign Minister Leon Trotsky was at Brest-Litovsk heading the Soviet peace delegation. Trotsky was the principal agitator and did not want to sign the peace agreement. He was there to delay the negotiations while Lenin attempted to convince Russia's allies to get involved in the civil war. Trotsky ignored any civility by turning down invitations to dinners and all social events and generally was distant and behaved oddly.

It was a great misjudgement by Trotsky and the Germans did not delay. They gave Russia twelve days to decide whether to sign the peace treaty, two days to open negotiations with Germany, and three days to conclude them; after which a war footing would resume. Lenin had to threaten to resign unless the Central Committee members voted to sign the treaty; The voting was 116 to 85 in favour, with Trotsky abstaining.

Lockhart soon confirmed that the Bolsheviks were pulling Russia out of the war, "*The Bolsheviks are the more extreme party. They are at heart anti-war. In Moscow at any rate the Mensheviks represent today the majority and are more favourable to the war.*" Lenin didn't sign the agreement; it was accepted but Russia refused to discuss the terms. Lenin had been unable to convince Britain and the Americans to support his struggle against Germany but they were helping indirectly by supporting the White Army that were fighting German forces in Russia. When it was clear that Lockhart's efforts had failed to scupper a peace deal and after Germany had invaded, he turned instead to backing the intervention of allied military forces in Russia, in whatever form.

Ten days after the Treaty of Brest-Litovsk came in to effect German forces began a major offensive along the entire Russian western front. They washed through Poland and Ukraine, reached Petrograd and headed towards Moscow. It was to all intents and purposes an invasion and would have been successful under a crumbling Red Army had not the end of World War I come sooner.

Not long after Lockhart's arrival in Russia he began a relationship with Maria Zakrveskia, who gained notoriety as the 'Red Mata Hari'. She later would have affairs with Maxim Gorky and H. G. Wells. Lockhart probably believed that he had recruited her and some accounts say that she was later working for the Soviet Union secret police (OGPU). Lockhart once described her, "*She was, perhaps, the soviet Union's most effective agent-of-influence ever to appear on London's political and intellectual stage.*"

In this context the Okhrana were the special police that operated for the tsarist regime and the Cheka were the special police that operated for the Bolsheviks. Within a year of the formation of the Soviet Union on 15 November 1922, the Cheka became the OGPU. In 1934 it became the NKVD; in 1943 it was the NKGB; in 1946 the MGB; and in 1954 the KGB.

The Cheka were quick to learn the West's technique of infiltration and Zakrveskia had possibly been recruited much sooner than 1923 by the Cheka, because they were becoming so effective in 1918 that they foiled the efforts of British Intelligence to organise a coup d'état and disrupted the effectiveness of Germany's considerable spy network within Russia.

Lockhart was severely compromised from the start due to his weakness with women. How unfortunate that he was in direct contact with the King of England who on 18 March 1918 approved a daring plot to snatch the royal family from Tobolsk and take them to Constantinople from where they would be taken to America. Thirty British soldiers from the 20th Hussars Regiment left for Russia to link up with White Army Cossacks for a reconnaissance mission and quite possibly the Cheka got to hear about it from Zakrveskia. Was it a coincidence that one week later, on 25 April 1918, the ex-tsar was moved from Tobolsk to a more remote and secure location?

CHAPTER XVIII

Sidney Reilly (proper name Sigmund Rosenblum), the renowned Russian born secret agent who became known as the 'ace of spies', was sent to help Lockhart organise anti Bolshevik factions and counter the work of German agents against the White Army. If there was any possibility of bringing Russia back in to the war Reilly was the one man that could do it. Between 1914 to 1917 he worked as a munitions dealer in the USA for British Intelligence, by some accounts, to help bring the USA in to World War I. That happened of course, but how much credit, if any, should be given to Reilly is a matter for debate. Both men developed delusions of grandeur; Lockhart in wanting to impress London after his failure to achieve anything meaningful in Russia and Reilly in attempting to single-handedly arrange a coup d'état which was foiled by the Cheka.

In London, Cumming had promoted Reilly to Lieutenant and after a short while posted him to Germany to spy on munitions factories, being Reilly's area of expertise. The situation in Russia evidently required Reilly's brand of expedience and he was sent to liaise with Lockhart, arriving in Murmansk on 5 April 1918, the very day that Lenin announced to the All-Russian Congress of Soviets in Moscow, that Soviet Russia had reached its direst period. Lenin was referring to the clandestine activities by foreign powers attempting to pull Russia back in to the war and whose ulterior aim was most likely the removal of the Soviet government.

Lockhart had no time for field agents whom he considered mere information gatherers but he made an exception for Reilly, "*extremely able and by far the cleverest of our agents in Russia.*" Reilly was introduced to Alexander Nikolaevich Grammatikov, a lawyer with ties to the Socialist Revolutionaries and tsarist Okhrana police, and who had also helped to steal drawings of German warships from a naval shipyard in St Petersburg where he worked, which he passed to British Intelligence. Reilly had spied for British Intelligence in Russia during 1911 to 1914 as a naval contracts broker and therefore shared an affinity in naval matters with Grammatikov.

Through a former associate in the Okhrana called Vladimir Orlov who was now working for the Cheka, Grammatikov was able to provide Reilly with the paperwork to pass as a Cheka agent and thereby move about freely. Lockhart staying mainly in Petrograd was the controller and financier and Reilly was mostly the man on the ground in Moscow. In June 1918 Reilly became the Greek businessman Mr Constantine, operating from a flat owned by Grammatikov's niece. At this time, Czech regiments were fighting for the White Army and were in control of Omsk, Samara, and Cheliabinsk, and they were closing in on Perm and Ekaterinburg.

Seemingly June 1918 was an opportune time for a rescue. Foreign secret agents were circling Ekaterinburg and Moscow like sharks with submerged fins. The German spy network was operating freely in the Urals unhindered by the Cheka, but even they didn't really know what was happening, neither did the Bolsheviks in Moscow nor the government in Petrograd. Outside of Lenin in Moscow and Sverdlov in the Urals, the matter was in the hands of Goloshchekin, who had execution orders to carry out.

Within the country the Germans were the most determined nation to help the royal family, not least because Wilhelm II regarded Nicholas II as a brother even if the feeling wasn't mutual. Although Germany were extremely powerful in Russia militarily, politically they struggled to find co-operation being that they were not wanted in the country. In April 1918, Count Wilhelm von Mirbach was appointed as German ambassador to Moscow and because he had taken part in the Brest-Litovsk negotiations he was by default at odds with the Socialist Revolutionaries (mainly the peasants) and the White Army which had not wanted the war with Germany to end. Germany installed a puppet governance in Crimea and supported the anti-revolutionary White Finns.

Across the board German authority was not accepted anywhere and the level of disruption and guerrilla warfare surprised even the German conquerors. Mirbach made representations daily for the royal family to be treated well and tried to find a solution to the problem faced by the Provisional Government of what to do with them, but whatever he tried, the Soviet authorities were evasive and he was unable to make any meaningful progress for their release.

The Keiser's adjutant in Ukraine, General Werner von Alvensleben, sent out spies for wide area reconnaissance. Two agents went behind enemy lines to Moscow; two were despatched to Kotel'nich on the River Vyatka, a main transport junction along the route of the White Army controlled Siberian Railway and a third team went behind lines to Ekaterinburg. Their joint aim was to get the information necessary to plan a rescue mission on Ipatiev House.

The agents in Moscow reported on a rumour of the ex-tsar's execution but no evidence could be obtained and it was similarly disappointing in Kotel'nich where they found nothing substantive. The best place for intelligence seemed to be in Ekaterinburg where the ex-tsar had been held from 30 April 1918. Therefore, a German contingent arrived under cover of a Red Cross mission to help prisoners of war, which was surprisingly welcomed by the unsuspecting Bolsheviks, who at this time were highly suspicious of foreign services.

"A German mission arrived in Ekaterinburg at the end of June to inquire in to the situation of the prisoners of the Ipatiev House."
— ROBERT WILTON, correspondent The London Times

"Did this delegation know of the danger to the Emperor and his family, or were they deluded into believing in the Bolsheviks' feelings of

CHAPTER XVIII

humanity? Certainly had they themselves offered to do anything for them the Emperor and Empress would not have accepted their help, but I always wondered how it was that through this Red Cross delegation the news of the desperate plight of the Russian Sovereigns did not filter through abroad. I personally could not approach the Germans, for I considered that we were still at war with them, the Emperor never having recognised the peace treaty concluded with them by the Bolsheviks." — SOPHIE BUXHOEVEDEN, Left Behind

Mirbach wasn't completely ostracised, he had connections like Georgi Chicherin at the Kremlin who provided reasonably accurate information. The question posed is why General Alvensleben went to such extremes to gather information when Mirbach had diplomatic means. Could it be that the Keiser had grown impatient at Mirbach's stalemate or simply that Alvensleben offered a better alternative untainted by the political impasse that was obstructing Mirbach.

Alvensleben was, rather like Lockhart, out to impress his superiors and had a reputation for being a bit of a maverick. The hopeless situation in Russia meant that the most feasible option was a German assault on Ipatiev House, not an operation advisable for an ambassador to be directly involved in but a mission totally suited for a maverick.

The Bolsheviks had chosen Ekaterinburg for its remoteness and Goloshchekin chose Ipatiev House for its convenience; easily guarded with the Iset River at its rear. In the first seven of the eight months that the Provisional Government was in power, the prisoners had moved from Tsarskoe Selo to Tobolsk and then to Ekaterinburg, not much else had been achieved by way of a final solution in discussions with foreign powers.

In mitigation, some historians believe the complexity of events that were occurring during this time in Russia have never been matched but the fate of the royal family and members of the royal household was simple enough; their incarceration was symbolic for the White movement and if they were rescued it would send the strongest message of victory. It represented hope that Nicholas II would be at liberty to lead the counter revolution to a victorious conclusion and restore the monarchy.

The rescue groups in the vicinity were the Bolshevik's primary concern. There were many, but they were sectarian, each having been formed and being funded separately. This was the problem for the rescue planners; there was no joint co-ordination of their endeavours when their collective weight might have been more effective. Security at Ipatiev House was strengthened with extra guards and the prisoners were forbidden to go near windows where they might send out a signal, even though they were painted and boarded up, except for the ones in Nicholas' bedroom. On one occasion Anastasia did look out of a window and was fired at by a perimeter guard.

Sophie Buxhoeveden passed by one day and saw the girls pop in to view at the window and wave to her, then they immediately retracted themselves out of view. They had been waiting patiently for her to come along so that they might let her know they were alright. As soon as they spotted her they sprang at the window and waved, Buxhoeveden had seen them for a fleeting moment. She walked by many more times after that hoping for another occurrence but never saw them again, which makes her one of the last people to have seen the royal family alive.

The media in Europe during World War I, and particularly the British press were used solely for propaganda purposes. Their primary attention lay in recruitment which relied on misinformation to maintain interest in the war. They slowly turned to the reporting of German atrocities and the internal struggles of Russia where the imprisoned royal family had not been seen for some time. Not enough time had elapsed since the October Revolution 1917 for the Soviet propaganda machine to change from how it worked in tsarist Russia and publishers still received the official news from the Petrograd Telegraphic Agency (PTA) which for war news was supplied to them, unofficially, by the Ministry of Foreign Affairs and for internal news by the Ministry of the Interior.

Up until World War I censorship fell to the military districts and they adhered to a list of things that could not appear in the press, for example anything about Rasputin was forbidden. Much of the news before and after the war was either about the government or the so-called 'internal enemy', that is to say, non-Russians, but specifically implying Germans and Jews. Since 1916 newspaper circulation increased threefold. The February Revolution 1917 was supposed to have abolished censorship after a resolution was passed allowing the freedom of the press. Journalists who were heavily restricted under Nicholas II, were now free from state control.

In reality, the Russian media was being restricted even more, particularly from July 1917 when powers were given to the Ministry of the Interior to close publications at will which resulted in most Bolshevik publications being closed down, including Pravda, the official Communist newspaper. It was not until the formation of the Provisional Government that the press was afforded any real freedom, which they exercised with a passion. Foreign journalists of course, just wanted to report what they saw and this is what the authorities could not control.

Since the October Revolution 1917, things were controlled by the Bolsheviks and with the boot now on the other foot, they closed down 216 opposition publications by March 1918. This time, freedom of the press meant publishing anything related or favourable to the Bolshevik cause. The names of people suspected of German espionage had previously been censored, but now they could be legally named and shamed. A list of just under 200 names was published in *Obshchee delo* (Common Cause) of

CHAPTER XVIII

agents that had infiltrated Russia from Germany, including Lenin. It also meant the discussion around Alexandra and Rasputin resurfaced and their faux connection to Germany was used as anti-monarchist propaganda. This was the anti-German climate that Mirbach faced that had prevented him making any headway for the release of the royal family.

On 3 July 1918 the Bolshevik Yakov Yurovsky was promoted and arrived at Ipatiev House on the following day to take over as the new Commandant with a mission to dispose of the prisoners. Two days later at 3.00 pm on 6 July 1918 two Cheka volunteers, Yakov Blyumkin and Nikolai Andreyev, entered the German Embassy on Denezhny Lane in Moscow under orders from the Central Committee of the Socialist Revolutionaries party with the intention to assassinate Ambassador Mirbach in order to spark tensions with Germany and hopefully reignite the war. It was a pointless act considering the existing civil war in which both sides were already engaged in fighting.

Blyumkin told the counsellor of the Embassy Riezier that his visit was about the Ambassador's nephew Count Robert Mirbach in connection with him being suspected of spying for Germany; of which the evidence would have been readily obtainable to the Cheka agents. Blyumkin presented Riezier with a false letter of introduction:

'The All-Russia Extraordinary Commission for Combating Counter-Revolution empowers its member Yakov Blyumkin and the representative of the Revolutionary Tribunal Nikolai Andreyev to enter into direct negotiations with the German Ambassador to Russia, Count M. Mirbach, regarding a matter of direct concern to the Ambassador.'

Mirbach came out to meet them with his interpreter. After some petty discussion Blyumkin fired shots in to the ambassador, the counsellor and the interpreter at point blank range. But Mirbach wasn't killed so Andreyev thew a bomb at him but that didn't go off. Blyumkin quickly picked up the bomb and tossed it again at Mirbach; this time it exploded and killed him. The embassy guard opened fire at them and injured Blyumkin and with great difficulty the Cheka assassins got out alive and drove away. According to the book *The Assassination of Count Mirbach* by Alfred Erich Senn and Harold J. Goldberg they state, "*Despite the significance of the assassination, historians have tended to treat it but briefly. The identity of the assassins is clear ... yet there seems to be considerable confusion as to the purpose and even the nature of the deed.*"

The book rightly highlights the pointless murder but does not offer the possible explanation that Mirbach was assassinated to send a message to the Keiser to abort his ambitions for a rescue attempt on Ipatiev House. Mirbach had offered Moscow a way to offload the prisoners. In their ignorance the

Cheka had not known that it was Alvensleben and not Mirbach that had been entrusted with the task of arranging a rescue. What had Blyumkin and Mirbach discussed in those final minutes. Had Mirbach been given an ultimatum to call off the raid on Ipatiev House and when he claimed ignorance Blyumkin had acted. Otherwise why not just shoot Mirbach when he appeared and make for a clean get away. The Cheka had therefore assassinated the wrong man and the generally accepted reason for the assassination now remains that it was done to incite war. Blyumkin instead of paying for his crime became the personal bodyguard of Leon Trotsky.

The Bolsheviks acted quickly after Mirbach's assassination and kicked out the Socialist Revolutionaries from their seats, thus having one less faction of opposition to worry about. Lockhart, Grammatikov and Riley had not played any part in the assassination. Lockhart had failed diplomatically and it was not helpful to him that he was rather loose with his tongue for a diplomat and had a weakness as a womaniser. Trying to recover his situation, his efforts turned to backing a plot to assassinate Lenin. The operation would become known as the Lockhart Plot and this is thought to have been a joint mission between the German and British intelligence services.

In Moscow, the Italian, French, British, Danish, German and Spanish diplomatic services were ceaselessly enquiring for information about the royal family and receiving little news. The German and Spanish governments pressed for negotiations for the exile of the royal household prisoners to their respective countries and were largely ignored. Germany with substantial troops and an extensive spy network in place ironically had no political leverage. Nicholas II lost any possibility for freedom in not asking Germany for help. It's known he would not have accepted any offer from Germany but it was most certainly on the table which goes to show how naïve Nicholas II really was and perhaps even a little foolish.

During Kerensky's interviews with Nicholas II at Tsarskoe Selo, he had learned how stubborn Nicholas II could be and that he did not appreciate the magnitude of the situation that they were all in. Nevertheless, Germany did have a rescue operation in play. On the day that Mirbach was murdered, Alexander Mossolov met with Alvensleben and asked that he deliver a letter directly to the Keiser asking for his urgent intervention, as Mirbach was a personal friend of the Keiser, which could offer some explanation why the Keiser was taking pressure off Mirbach and using Alvensleben.

The reader may recall that Mossolov had turned down the post of Deputy Minister of Interior offered by Alexandra Feodorovna (*page 266*). Since the royal family were put under house arrest, the mantle passed to the Head of the Imperial Court Chancellery, Alexander Mossolov. He suggested the Keiser write to Nicholas II to personally guarantee a safe passage. Crimea was basically a protectorate of Germany albeit officially they didn't offer civil administration until November 1918. If Alvensleben could get the

CHAPTER XVIII

royal household to there, then they would have safe passage to Germany through Crimea and most of Ukraine. Evidence exists of Nicholas II and Alexandra's view about their objection to German involvement (*page 335*).

In any case, the Keiser had ordered for the rescue mission to begin. Immediately following the meeting with Mossolov, Alvensleben brought together Prince Alexander Dolgoruky (Maria Feodorovna's secretary, and the Chairman of the North-Western Region in Ukraine), and Colonel Fedor Nikolaevich Bezak. He told them that the Keiser had ordered the rescue of the ex-tsar and that arrangements would be made to facilitate this. Dolgoruky and Bezak became integral to the plot and invaluable for its chances of success. Alvensleben gave them each a travel permit pertaining to a Red Army officer and dispatched them to German occupied territory to verify the current status of the royal family in Ekaterinburg.

Alvensleben believed that when the ex-tsar was rescued the Bolsheviks would, in order to counter any anti-revolutionary fervour, release the news that he had been executed. He told Dolgoruky and Bezak to watch out for this false news between 16 - 20th July 1918 and not to divulge the plot to anyone and that in the company of others they should pretend to believe the news that the ex-tsar was dead if they heard it until the ex-tsar was safely in Crimea. Even Maria Feodorovna, who hated Prussia, was exerting her influence at this time to help break up the alliance between Germany and Austria-Hungary. Plots and scheming were rife.

The only real possibility of a diplomatic release lay with the British who were already in negotiations and had the best intelligence. The British Consul in Ekaterinburg had sent a message to London as early as 18 May 1918 (G) informing on the relocation of the royal family and their aides from Tobolsk, five days before the children arrived at Ipatiev House. Goloshchekin was receiving daily visits from Thomas Preston, the British Vice-Consul at Ekaterinburg, who was in turn being pressured by tutors Pierre Gilliard and Charles Sydney Gibbes to expediate an exile.

There were plenty of teams in Ekaterinburg planning a rescue, some of which the ex-tsar knew about and some that were discovered by the jailors. On one occasion a false letter was smuggled in by the Bolsheviks so that the ex-tsar might incriminate himself in the plot to escape and could then receive summary execution, but nothing came of it because no evidence was had.

According to Prince Michael of Kent, a rescue was ordered by George V. The story goes that Air Commodore Peregrine Fellows, an Australian officer in the Royal Navy, was to fly an aeroplane in to Ekaterinburg and fly the ex-tsar straight out but the mission was cancelled. Fellows is known to have been shot down on a bombing mission over the Ostend Canal in the spring of 1918 which he survived and became a prisoner of war. He appeared to have been indisposed unless it was planned long before he went to Belgium. In 1933 Fellows was the first pilot to fly over Mount Everest.

The German rescue effort is shrouded in mystery because there is nothing to be found that adequately explains what happened next. The announcement of the death of the ex-tsar came as a shock to Germany. They assumed that having control of large parts of western Russia meant they exerted some influence, at least as much that an execution of the ex-tsar could not happen without their prior knowledge or even their consent. Why did the press take so long to report it. On 21 July 1918, two days following the announcement of the execution, the Norwegian newspaper *Aftenposten* reported that the Tsar was killed. In London it was on 22 July 1918; The Times reported that Nicholas had been served a military execution.

Dolgoruky and others under Alvensleben's influence like Generals Bezak and Skoropadski, believed that the rescue of the ex-tsar had succeeded because of what Alvensleben had told them to expect, which was playing out in the newspapers as foretold. This is where the facts meet the theory. There was no raid on Ipatiev House but the story goes that the royal family were spared and relocated to live out their lives in secret. This is perhaps too unbelievably far-fetched to accept but it has persisted because the details went missing from the public record and nothing fuels a conspiracy more than a cover up.

In August 1918 the bodies of the ex-tsar and ex-tsarevich were yet to be seen and the remaining prisoners yet to be confirmed alive. The Germans demanded confirmation on the wellbeing of the remaining prisoners which they believed had been taken to Perm. In the end the Soviet authorities admitted that they had lost track of the royal household prisoners after the White Army had arrived in Ekaterinburg and it became increasingly evident that the prisoners had all perished with the tsar.

The missing documents or cover up depending on how you look at it, has to do with the communications between British High Commissioner (also renowned botanist and marine biologist) Sir Charles Eliot and King George V. The reason it's known about is from Dolgoruky's memoirs in which he describes the contents of Eliot's original report sent to London, before it was cleaned up and presented to the King. Eliot reported that the Tsar had not been executed but placed in German custody and that a train had left Ekaterinburg on 17 July 1918 with all the blinds down, and with the royal family on it. This revelation is a bombshell and one would ask why Dolgoruky would record it in his memoirs if it was not the truth. If true, then they would have been able to travel almost the entire length of the Siberian Railway from Penza to Vladivostok as it was under Czech control.

On the fourth day after the occupation of Ekaterinburg by the White Army, on 27 July 1918 (G), charred remains were discovered at Ganina Yama by White Army investigators. Charles Sydney Gibbes, the English language tutor who returned to Ekaterinburg to assist the investigators, gave a detailed account to the British High Commissioner in Siberia, Sir Charles Eliot, stating that General Dieterichs, Commander in Chief of the Siberian Army, had given Mr Miles Lampson, British High Commissioner for Siberia at Peking, a despatch box once belonging to Tsarina Alexandra, containing the ashes that had been found at Ganina Yama. Eliot sent his report to the Foreign Office which was presented to the King.

Decades later, on 22 July 1999, the respective Foreign Ministers of Russia and the United Kingdom, Igor Ivanov and Robin Cook, signed a collaboration agreement and exchanged secret files. Among these, Ivanov received the reports by Charles Sydney Gibbes and Sir Charles Eliot. A note was appended to the top of Eliot's report stating that a summary had been given to George V but leaving out the gruesome details. A letter from the King dated 4 July 1919 was also included, confirming that he had been informed of the murders in a dispatch from a Colonel Robertson and preferred for the gruesome details not to be published. There is no mention of Dolgoruky's claim in the papers exchanged in 1999 which do not contain details of an incredible rescue attempt or escape.

The Lockhart Plot (to defeat Bolshevism and kill Lenin)

Not much has been investigated about the alleged joint venture between Germany and Britain of the plot to kill Lenin. The British believed the notion of Bolshevism, which had taken over the peasantry and the workers, revolved entirely around the philosophies of two men. To bring down the Bolsheviks required simply the removal of Lenin and Trotsky, which would potentially save thousands of lives.

On 30 August 1918. Lenin was shot at point blank with a Browning pistol as he was leaving the Mikhelson arms factory in Moscow and was severely injured. Three bullets were fired (notched and poisoned) and he fell to the ground. One bullet passed through his neck and part of his lung. The second lodged in to his shoulder without exiting. One account says the third bullet went through his coat and another by author Semion Lyandres says it hit a woman standing nearby, perhaps both accounts had been true.

The Socialist Revolutionary Fanya Kaplan shot Lenin. One story says she tried to kill him because she regarded him as a traitor to the revolution for signing the Treaty of Brest-Litovsk. This was why she had gone to the Socialist Revolutionaries to offer herself as an assassin, because they were the opposition party to the Bolsheviks. A suggestion is made that there were several shooters and that not necessarily was Kaplan acting alone. Another account says that she did it because she lost her job in January 1918 when the Soviets dismantled the non-communist governmental organisations.

Can it be believed that the Socialist Revolutionaries would entrust an unhinged stranger, as she had spent time in mental correctional institutions, for such an important hit. Or did she take such a drastic action to take out the leader of the nation, knowing that she would surely be put to death if she survived it, because she lost her job? With assassinations, the first question is always to ask who had the power to withdraw the security, in this case, it may also be asked how a blind woman got hold of a gun and put herself in close proximity to Lenin.

It was easy to place the blame on the Socialist Revolutionaries not just because they opposed Lenin but earlier on that same day 22 year old Leonid Kannegisser had assassinated the Chief of the Petrograd Cheka, Moisei Uritsky. While he did it because Uritsky had signed the execution orders for his friend, Kannegisser was a member of the Popular Socialist Party which had been founded in 1906 by members of the Socialist Revolutionaries Party. It could be construed that Kannegisser was acting as the terrorist wing of the Socialist Revolutionaries and therefore the two attacks had been part of a terror spat on the two most senior Bolsheviks in Petrograd and Moscow.

The details around Lenin's failed assassination attempt rely on the 18 witnesses questioned that day from the Cheka investigation report. One account states that the plot remained a secret and there has been no indisputable proof that it had ever existed and also that Kaplan acted largely on her own accord as a lone gunperson. That theory is easily dismantled in the memoirs of the Socialist Revolutionary Boris Savinkov. In his book *Memoirs of a Terrorist*, he disclosed that he passed to Kaplan the gun that had been given to him for the assassination by none other than Sidney Reilly, thereby linking British Intelligence to the Lockhart Plot. Savinkov's account cannot be dismissed as he was a former Assistant Minister of War in the Provisional Government from July to August 1917 and did not need to make up material about himself as so many do in their memoirs. He had been involved in the assassinations of Grand Duke Sergei Alexandrovich of Russia (Elizabeth Feodorovna's husband.) and also that of the Minister of Interior Vyacheslav Plehve and was already destined for the history pages.

Lockhart mentions Reilly's role to overthrow the Bolsheviks, in his book *Memoirs of a British Agent* (1932). There's no doubt Lockhart and Reilly were connected to the assassination attempt on Lenin. That's a strong tie to British involvement whereas a link to German involvement is less conclusive and as for the assassination of Uritsky, was it a coincidence that after the shooting and during his escape Kannegisser ran to the British Embassy. The Lockhart Plot therefore, is aptly named.

Kaplan was a patsy. When she was in custody she told the Cheka, *"Today I shot Lenin. I did it on my own,"* and she would not incriminate anyone. Her mental state should have been enough to place her in a mental institution, but instead the order to execute her came from Sverdlov, just six weeks after he had ordered the executions at Ipatiev House. Albeit according to the diaries of Leon Trotsky it was Lenin that decided to kill the Imperial

CHAPTER XVIII

Family. Kaplan was shot on 3 September 1918 in the back of the head and her body was thrown in to a barrel and set alight. She was 28 years old.

It's widely accepted that Kaplan could not have acted alone due to her limited mental capacity or fired off shots with such precision, two out of three bullets, because she became blind in 1909 and following an operation was at best partially sighted by 1918. Lenin's speech started at 8.00 pm so by the time he emerged it was dark and Kaplan had never had any experience with guns. Despite the accounts saying that she was seen firing the gun, the eighteen witness testimonies taken that evening do not attest to that. No one saw her fire the gun and no one saw Lenin get shot.

A bullet recovered from Lenin, probably the one from his shoulder, was found not to have been fired from a Browning pistol. The Savinkov memoirs prove that Kaplan was in possession of a Browning pistol which some will insist she was seen carrying, but the facts are that no one saw her do anything, yet Lenin had been shot with a different calibre gun than the one she was carrying and the patsy Kaplan was executed four days later. Her remains were never recovered and there's even doubt over her true identity.

Irrespective of Kaplan's role, within days of the failed assassination attempt the Bolsheviks began the campaign of 'Red Terror' which lasted for the next four years. Thousands of political opponents were murdered by the Cheka. Lockhart's political upheaval, plotting and loose talk around his lover Zakrveskia was indirectly responsible for all the subsequent deaths. Lockhart and Zakrveskia were arrested for their suspected involvement in Lenin's shooting but released soon after; Lockhart on diplomatic grounds and Zakrveskia, one account says, because she was recruited by OGPU although there is no evidence of this, but more likely because she was already working for British and German intelligence services.

Boris Savinkov and Sidney Reilly were executed by Soviet agents in 1925. Maria Zakrveskia, on her arrest spent time at the famous Lubyanka prison in Moscow. Lockhart, on his release from incarceration at the Kremlin, used his diplomatic clout to release Zakrveskia from Lubyanka. She continued her affiliations with multiple men, even Joseph Stalin was an admirer and she was described in an MI5 report as *"A very dangerous woman"*. She died in London in November 1974. Lockhart was deported in exchange for a Soviet attaché (i.e. a spy) called Maxim Litvinov.

Lockhart worked in finance and then journalism. During World War II he was utilised in charge of all the propaganda directed at the enemy, as the Director-General of the Political Warfare Executive. He died on 27 February 1970.

Reilly managed to get out of Russia after the Lockhart affair before a trial could be arranged. Both Lockhart and Reilly were sentenced to death in their absence and Reilly, uncharacteristically for him, had been foolish to allow himself to be lured back to Russia and was there shot in 1925.

CHAPTER XIX
The Great Escape

THE rescue task force to Russia that George V had approved on 18 March 1918 arrived in Russia after Nicholas II and his family were already dead. However, one account asserts that they did manage to rescue some family members which is the basis for the notion of survivors. White Army investigator Nikolai Sokolov, in his book published in 1925, stated that the massacre at Ipatiev House happened on the night of 17 July 1918, instead of the night of 16 July 1918 in the official version of events, a simple discrepancy demonstrating how common mistakes are made. In this case as previously discussed there were two hours of summer time so 11.30 pm 16 July, becomes 1.30 am on 17 July and hence the date discrepancy is explained. Although this book has clarified these rather insignificant finer details, one thing is known for sure, that the Bolsheviks lied about everything and were the source of much confusion to hide the truth that they had murdered the royal family; as Sokolov put it, *"They lied, I give them their due, skilfully. But they sometimes overestimated themselves and their caution."*

The cover up was brought about by a handful of powerful men; Sverdlov, Goloshchekin and Beloborodov. The Provisional Government, whom the Bolsheviks considered insignificant, tried to find solutions for the royal family and for their protection placed them under house arrest and later moved them to safety. They failed to extract them from Russia because the foreign governments had not responded when they were needed, despite having lobbied the Russian authorities constantly. The only meaningful possibility was through the more advanced negotiations with the British. However, during the term of Prime Minister Georgy Lvov between 15 March 1917 and his resignation on 20 July 1917, the Minister of Foreign Affairs Pavel Milyukov since stated that he felt obliged to keep ongoing discussions with the British Ambassador Sir George Buchanan, he knew that these ties once severed would mean certain death for the royal family and it confirms that the hold-up was from the British side.

CHAPTER XIX

Both Lvov and Milyukov were Kadets (Constitutional Democratic Party). Lvov, a former deputy of the First State Duma 1906, was married briefly to Countess Julia Alexeievna Bobrinskaya, the great-great-granddaughter of Count Grigori Grigoryevich Orlov and Catherine the Great (*page 57*). Milyukov, elected to the Third and Fourth Dumas, was also at one time a political prisoner and no friend of the tsarist regime. A philosopher of history at heart, he is one source that attested to the influence that Rasputin had on the government in 1914. It was Milyukov that gave the 'Rasputin and Rasputuiza' speech (*page 285*) in November 1916, a month before Rasputin's murder. Indeed, following that speech he was accommodated at the British Embassy for several months under the security of Sir George Buchanan and that's when the negotiations over the release of the royal family had started (*page 334*). Ironically at this time Alexandra Feodorovna was petitioning her husband to send Lvov and Milyukov to Siberia and ultimately the discussions fell apart not long before the Provisional Government itself did, albeit easy to forget that war in Europe was their preoccupation.

Milyukov had turned from being an anti-monarchist to a republican and was now supporting a monarchy albeit under the Tsarevich Alexei. Through his close ties with Buchanan he pressed for action to facilitate the exile of the royal family and was finally informed that a British cruiser was on its way. Nikolai Sokolov would write that he believed George V was personally involved in this decision but the cruiser never arrived; despite the efforts of Lvov and Milyukov the British had reneged. During the abdication process Nicholas II called on the Duma, not the Soviet, to handle his renunciation and sent a letter to Prime Minister Lvov entrusting him with his fate and the safety of his family, which is why Lvov tried so hard to get the royal family far away from the Bolsheviks. Because Lvov had no assurance to give that could guarantee their safety, in most part because he had been let down by the British, Nicholas II had boarded the Imperial train and at Psov signed his abdication papers therewith believing he had also secured a safety deal.

The Kerensky government took over the enterprise with Kerensky himself stating, "*The Provisional Government has tried to find out from the English government the possibility of the departure of the royal family to England.*" Kerensky was a skilled orator and negotiator but whom Lenin described as an 'idiot' and it follows that he had no support from the Bolsheviks. He started out like Milyukov in ardent opposition to the tsarist regime but came to view the royal family in a new light after he assumed responsibility for their welfare and met them at Alexander Palace. His government ultimately fell because he supported a war that the soldiers at the front were tired of fighting but his efforts to exile the royal family failed because he too hit a brick wall with the British. He kept trying until he received an official response from the British government who did not consider it any longer desirable to offer hospitality to the former tsar and his family.

Kerensky came to appreciate that it was already too late to save the royal family despite having moved them to the less hostile safety of exile in the remoteness of Siberia. Dutch negotiations were concerned with assisting the safe passage of Maria Feodorovna. German envoys concerned with Alexandra Feodorovna were ignored with those envoys that had no direct connection with the prisoners such as Spain also being ignored. America had not been sufficiently involved in Russia to be a part of any discussions. The French had similarly been ignored since July 1917. Russian diplomat Petr S. Botkin, a former envoy to Britain, America and Portugal, was pressed by French Minister of Foreign Affairs M. Pichon to intervene but a year later on 2 July 1918, Botkin sent Pichon a letter, *"With great regret, I must state that all my efforts were in vain, all my steps remained without results, and as answers to my letters, I have only receipts of couriers, honoured believing that my letters have reached their destination."*

The publication of *The File on the Tsar* (1976) by Summers & Mangold, addressed successfully the theory that the Romanov females lived months after the date of the alleged murders. This attributes some success to the envoys as the Bolsheviks realised how useful the prisoners could be to trade perhaps for prominent revolutionaries imprisoned in Germany. Indeed it has been suggested that Lenin held the Romanov females for the single purpose of trading them with the Keiser for an alliance with Germany. The White Army investigation (*discussed in detail in Chapter XX*) was at one point headed by Judge Ivan Sergeev who investigated for several months and said, *"I do not believe that all the people, the Tzar, his family and those with them were shot there* [i.e. at Ipatiev House].*"* When Sergeev was replaced by Judge Nikolai Sokolov the official line suddenly assumed that they were all shot there – why were these opinions polarised?

The Bolsheviks had announced that the ex-tsar had been shot and the other prisoners taken to another location. One theory is that the murders in the cellar were staged by the White movement and news needed to be released quickly to portray the Bolsheviks as heartless killers to the world press. Evidence of murders and the identities of victims were liberally left about and when viewed in a sequential list the official version of events might appear to have been planned.

July 1918

- 16th - Murders are planned.
- 17th – Murders are carried out.
- 18th – Sverdlov reports execution of ex-tsar to the TsIK presidium.
- 19th – First reports appear in the Moscow press.
- 20th – Goloshchekin announces death of ex-tsar to Duma President.

- 21st – Posters go up in the cities announcing the death of the ex-tsar.
- 22nd – Foreign press publishes news of the death of the ex-tsar.

The Band of Royal Women

Due to the lack of bodies rumours emerged that Marie, Anastasia and even Alexei had survived. The work of Summers & Mangold for instance, said that the Romanov females all survived and the tsar and tsarevich had been executed. There is no record of George V's reaction on learning of Nicholas II's death outside of the diary entry made by Queen Mary of Teck for 24 July 1918 when she noted that the news of the murders of the royal family had been confirmed. By confirmation, she meant the official announcement made by the Bolsheviks.

Princess Victoria of Hesse and by Rhine (Alexandra's sister) became extremely concerned from the moment the royal family had arrived in Ekaterinburg because of the worsening circumstances since the increase of Bolshevik control in Siberia. She formed an alliance with the king and queen of Spain and this pressure group kept the issue of the Russian royal family's imprisonment at the fore with her cousin George V. Princess Victoria sensed him distance himself but she would not be put off. She sent a telegram asking him flat out to intervene internationally, unaware that he had already closed the door to them and in effect sealed their fate.

Wilhelm II whom Lenin was attempting to pacify, for the most part remained loyal to Nicholas II but believed that he was responsible for his own downfall. Not enough credit has been attributed to Wilhelm II for his efforts to avert war and the fall of the Romanov dynasty and despite his bungling ways he was spot on about many things. He felt a responsibility to steer Nicholas on the right path. Neither has Wilhelm II's first wife Augusta Victoria of Schleswig-Holstein (m. 1881-1921), daughter of Queen Victoria's daughter Helena, been credited for steering Wilhelm II's continued support of Nicholas and Alexandra.

It was royal women such as Wilhelm II's wife that held much influence during the war years albeit the Empress Augusta was towards the end of it quite ill and died in 1920. The royal women were busily trying to enlist the heads of states to intervene in securing the safety of members of the royal household. Together they pushed the authorities further than diplomatic ties were able to. Similarly to Wilhelm II's view about Nicholas II, the royal women believed that it was more by Alexandra Feodorovna's hand that the prisoners were in their predicament. In a letter from Queen Ena of Spain to Queen Marie of Romania, she says, "... *and to think that Alix is a great deal to blame for having brought ruin to her whole family.*" Queen Ena (i.e.

Victoria Eugenie Julia Ena of Battenberg – daughter of Beatrice), was geographically limited on the fringe of western Europe but together with two other granddaughters of Queen Victoria, her first cousin Victoria of Hesse and Queen Marie of Romania, they formed a formidable diplomatic alliance. Also on their team was Queen Elena of Italy (Montenegrin sister).

Of the group, it was Queen Marie's connection to Russia that gave them a foothold, albeit a weak one as a direct descendant of Catherine the Great counted for nothing much at that time but it was more to do with her strength of character and her riveting personality. She was a remarkable woman in her own right having made tremendous achievements worthy of mention here. The last queen of Romania was a first cousin to Wilhelm II and Alexandra Feodorovna. Her father was Prince Alfred the second son and fourth child of Queen Victoria. Her mother was Maria Alexandrovna of Russia, a daughter of Emperor Alexander II by his first wife. She was born in England in 1875 as Princess of Edinburgh and moved to Romania when she was seventeen years old. When she married Prince Ferdinand of Romania in 1893 (the year before Nicholas and Alexandra were married,) she became the first English princess to marry a Roman Catholic in almost three centuries.

"Queen *Marie of Romania was one of the most fascinating crowned heads of Europe and one of the most extraordinary and independent women of our century."* — MAUREEN DIANA CLEAVE, British journalist

In her teens she was one of the most talked about royals and a trend setter on par with Queen Alexandra of the UK and was also considered to be among the most desirable women in the world alongside her cousin Alix of Hesse and by Rhine of which the cousins shared some physical similarities (*next page*). She had many suitors but dismissed them all; not least George V when he was still a young Prince of Wales who proposed to her and was promptly rejected. This might have been a reason why Queen Alexandra of the UK had not joined with this band of royal women petitioning for the release of the Russian royals.

Romania entered World War I in 1916 by which time Queen Marie was already a renowned equestrian. In 1909 she became one of the first women to obtained a driving license in Germany and was the first woman to be appointed a member of the French Academy of Fine Arts recognising her endeavours in promoting the Art Nouveau movement with her own designs. She also wrote poetry and was a successful journalist. Romania capitulated to Germany in March 1918 and despite its criticism for doing so, by the summer of 1918 Queen Marie was described by the New York Times as, '*one of the vivid and unforgettable personalities of the war*'.

For almost all of World War I Queen Marie gained notoriety with her heroism as a Red Cross nurse, working at the front on sixteen-hour shifts for

CHAPTER XIX

months on end. It was whilst managing a network of field hospitals for the Red Cross that she finely tuned her negotiating skills in securing food and medicines and even vehicles from abroad. Germany entered Bucharest and occupied half of the country. However, by the time the war had ended, Romania had doubled its territory to become the fifth biggest country in Europe, in no small part due to Queen Marie.

Alix 6yo (Alexandra Feodorovna)   Marie 13yo (Princess of Edinburgh)

Another great woman was Queen Ena, wife of King Alfonso XIII of Spain and the daughter of Prince Henry of Battenburg, the Battenberg's being essentially a branch of the House of Hesse-Darmstadt. She was the youngest child of Queen Victoria making her a first cousin to Alexandra Feodorovna. The securing and distribution of medicines, food and vehicles was something Queen Ena and her husband did on a large scale to help the war effort, in relation to the wounded and prisoners of war. They brought a lot of pressure to bear on the Russian government concerning the welfare of the royal family and Queen Ena and King Alfonso were probably the most ardent negotiators for their release. To paraphrase, 'foremost activists for the release of the royal family were King Alfonso and Queen Ena of Spain'.

King Alfonso was certainly the most skilled in negotiations and was also a great humanitarian particularly known for his hospitality of the Jews in Spain. During World War I, he sent telegrams to all the European countries involved in the war demanding the exchange of prisoners and the safe passage for American food provisions to alleviate their plight. He was one of the first to learn of the execution of Nicholas II, from his Palacio de la Magdalena in Santander, because he was so well informed due to his humanitarian efforts.

Despite the efforts made, by 6 August 1918 both King Alfonso and George V, had accepted that Nicholas II and his son had perished and they harboured grave doubts over the safety of the others. In a last ditch attempt the Spanish Ministry of Foreign Affairs brought together the European cabinets in a joint effort to pressurise for the release of the Russian royal family and in principle secured an agreement to transfer the prisoners to Spain. The Keiser personally intervened on 13 August 1918 and by 25 August 1918 it was believed that an agreement had been reached to receive the royal family in Denmark.

But neither side could make any progress with the Bolsheviks after that. King Alfonso wrote to Victoria of Hesse and by Rhine, "*I have started negotiations to save the Empress and girls, as Tsarevich think is dead.*" Victoria in final desperation showed George V the message and asked again for him to personally intervene but was advised by his staff to speak to the Danish government who were at a more advanced stage in the negotiations. King Alfonso and Princess Victoria were working on one flank it seemed, with Danish and German governments working on the other. Yet where Britain should have provided the frontal assault there was none coming and through this division Moscow was allowed to dictate the narrative.

The Spanish continued trying but made little headway and were still in negotiations up until 27 August 1918. King Alfonso must have constantly been told by his staff, "*No one seems to know anything, your Majesty.*" On 10 September 1918 the new German ambassador in Russia was informed that the ex-tsarina and her girls were being removed from any danger to a more secure facility at Perm. This was nearly two months after they had already been murdered, according to the official line.

Yet, German agents continued reporting that the royal family were alive and were being regularly moved between locations so that it was difficult to have sightings confirmed and therefore intel reports were based on assumptions as there had not been a single sighting of a royal family member. As reports faded it was believed that they had been moved north to the monastery fortress at Verkhoturye. By 18 September 1918 George V believed that all of the prisoners were dead and informed Princess Victoria in a letter.

On that same day Leon Trotsky implemented '*special order No. 30*' a zero tolerance move to deal with deserters, defectors and sympathisers of the White movement, particularly in the army. It was a measure against a new political situation which saw huge numbers of officers trying to flee the Red Army. The Bolsheviks had moved on with the civil war while the other nations still held on to the disillusionment that they could influence the events in Russia.

CHAPTER XIX

"*Cases of treacherous flight by members of the commanding apparatus in to the enemy's camp, though less frequent, are still occurring. These monstrous crimes must be stopped, without shrinking from any measures. The turncoats are betraying the Russian workers and peasants to the Anglo-French and Japanese-American robbers and hangmen.*

"*Let the turncoats realise that they are at the same time betraying their own families: their fathers, mothers, sisters, brothers, wives and children.*

"*I order the headquarters of all the armies of the Republic, and also the district commissars, to supply by telegram to Revolutionary War Council member Aralov, lists of all the members of the commanding apparatus who have gone over to the enemy camp, with all needful data about their family situation. I entrust Comrade Aralov with the responsibility for taking, in cooperation with the appropriate institutions, the measures necessary for arresting the families of deserters and traitors.*" — ORDER NUMBER 30

How unfortunate that the two most fervent petitioners for the release of the royal family, Germany and Spain, could not get along as jointly they may have persuaded Britain to get more involved. Their distrust of one another was a long running thing. In 1905 during a state visit by King Alfonso to Berlin, both leaders agreed to give their speeches in French for a banquet. Wilhelm II stood and promptly gave his in German knowing full well that King Alfonso would not understand a word of it. Having sat quietly without asking for any assistance, when it came to Alfonso's speech, he calmly stood and promptly gave his speech in Spanish and the guests at the banquet had no idea what their Spanish guest had said.

1918 was not the best of times for Wilhelm II who caught the Spanish Flu and was forced to abdicate on 9 November 1918 as a condition to ending the hostilities of World War I. Having originally blamed Nicholas II for the demise of the royal family, in exile after the war he blamed the British and in turn was labelled by George V as, "*the greatest criminal in history.*"

Leaving Mother Russia

Olga Alexandrovna worked as a nurse in Ukraine between 1915 to 1917 under the protection of the White Army but as the Red Army advanced her hospital was moved east to Kiev. As the advancing troops were soon to retake Kiev, a pregnant Olga with her husband and son took a train directly to the Imperial estate at Dulber Palace near Yalta. By February 1918 several other Romanovs had gathered there. The palace was soon placed under house arrest by the advancing Red Army and the prisoners soon after that were moved to the nearby palace at Ay-Todor, the home of Xenia Alexandrovna, about twelve miles from Yalta; except that is, for Olga who refused to leave. Other prisoners were held at the Villa Harax near Sevastopol and were later moved to Ay-Todor in March 1919 just after the British landed in force at Murmansk. Maria Feodorovna was also in Crimea and for the longest time stubbornly refused to leave Russia and her son and grandchildren behind, waiting for the British to reach her. Queen Marie of Romania tried desperately to rescue her using her connections in Malta but Maria Feodorovna had declined. Queen Marie did manage to help other Romanovs and continued to lobby Russian authorities for the release of the royal family held in Ekaterinburg.

British troops had landed in Murmansk on 6 March 1918, just days after the Brest-Litovsk Treaty. It was the first official British involvement in the civil war and as the treaty put Russia effectively out of World War I, the British turned to securing their supplies that had been sent to Russia since Murmansk had been created in 1915 (its official date of founding being 4 October 1916). The Allied Powers needed to prevent the supplies from falling in to German hands as they advanced and by January 1919 there were 40,000 British troops in the Caucasus, 1,800 in Siberia and 950 in Trans-Caspia (the region east of the Caspian Sea). The Japanese had done a similar thing in Vladivostok on 9 April 1918 and deposited over 70,000 troops in the region.

The issue was that Murmansk was supplying the White Army so it's hardly surprising the Bolsheviks decided to execute the Romanovs by way of severing ties with Britain and Germany. If the royal family were viewed as leverage then that had changed when Britain started supplying the White Army and probably caused the breakdown in negotiations to save the royal family. It also elaborates on Yurovsky's notice that he read to the Tsar before the execution, when he said, "... *your relatives are continuing their attack on Soviet Russia ...*", the 'attack' being the supplying of military aid to the other side in the civil war.

> *"I think the day will come when it will be recognised without doubt, not only on one side of the House, but throughout the civilised world, that the strangling of Bolshevism at its birth would have been an untold blessing to the human race."* — WINSTON CHURCHILL, 1949

Prime Minister Lloyd George was against sending troops. The British government and Winston Churchill were ardent anti-Bolsheviks and backed an intervention in Russia and certainly were not bothered about providing military aid. Considering how the British felt about the Bolsheviks it's hard to see how any discussions could have been had between them and as early

CHAPTER XIX

as August 1918 it was known that no ties could be formed with a Bolshevik government. The quote from Winston Churchill on the previous page was said in the Houses of Parliament in 1949 but it would have been equally fitting had it been said in August 1918.

Fortunately Bolshevik inexpediency resulted with a delay in arranging the killings and meant that the royal family members in Crimea were able to get away because in late April 1918 Ukraine with Germany's assistance had regained most of Crimea and the Germans had no issue with people moving freely. The military revolt that followed in May 1918 of 70,000 Czech-Slovak soldiers along the length of the Siberian Railway siding with the White Army, only hastened the need to rid Ipatiev House of its occupants. The Lockhart Plot too must have contributed somewhat to Bolshevik thinking since they believed the assassination attempt on their leader was linked to Germany. But the war was over for Germany by November 1918 and their army was retreating home. With their help the Romanovs at Ay-Todor were able to get to Sevastopol where they were protected for a while as Allied naval vessels were securing Crimean ports.

Many people left Russia on outbound French ships leaving Maria Feodorovna and daughters Olga and Xenia and their families and entourage, still in Crimea. The Bolsheviks having lost their prisoners at Ay-Todor, placed a bounty on the heads of all members of the Romanov family in Russia. Unofficially, but in actuality, anyone related to the royal family could now be shot on the spot without trial. Maria Feodorovna again turned down the offer of safe passage to Denmark from Germany, preferring to wait for the British which was a gamble seeing the Black Sea ports were controlled by the French whose assistance she had already declined with there being no obvious British route out of Crimea.

Grand Duke Dmitri Pavlovich of Russia was Nicholas II's first cousin and interestingly, first cousin of Prince Philip Duke of Edinburgh (the consort of Queen Elizabeth II). The reader may recall that Pavlovich had been involved in the murder of Rasputin. He became the youngest man with a title to have survived the Bolsheviks. When he arrived in England towards the end of 1918 he was told to leave by the Foreign Office which he refused to do unless ordered to do so by the King. Pavlovich and George V then met at Buckingham Palace and George V told him bluntly, *"You are here only by accident,"* and instructed him to leave England. The British royals were changing their image to look less German and renamed themselves from Saxe-Coburg and Gotha to the House of Windsor. Because Russia had pulled out of the Allied Powers alliance and was no longer a military ally, it was felt that receiving the Russian cousins was bad for business lest it draw unwanted attention in the form of stirring talk about a revolution.

Pavlovich went to Biarritz where he had an affair with French fashion designer Gabrielle Bonheur Chanel, better known as Coco Chanel, who was to become considered one of the most influential people of the twentieth century in fashion. He settled in Paris and was quite active in the Russian community and supported the claim of his first cousin Grand Duke Kirill Vladimirovich who proclaimed himself the Emperor of Russia in 1924, to wit Maria Feodorovna, his auntie, stated colloquially that she did not believe the title was vacant. Kirill was publicly rebuked by Maria Feodorovna who never accepted that her son was dead because there was no proof of it, albeit she must have reached that conclusion at some point, being the highly intelligent and astute person that she was. Pavlovich would finally emigrate to America where he married an American socialite in 1926 and died there in 1942.

The Allied military action in Ukraine that started in December 1918 is known as the Southern Russia Intervention. By April 1919 it had largely failed and British ships in the region were then involved in helping with the transportation of troops and supplies to assist the White Army. During this time the trusty aide-de-camp to Nicholas II and Captain of the Standart, Captain Sablin, who was dismissed from service following the February Revolution 1917, joined the White movement in Ukraine, eventually leaving Crimea in 1921 for Constantinople. He later moved to Berlin, finally settling in Paris where he died on 21 August 1937 aged fifty-seven years old.

Also at this time Xenia Alexandrovna's husband Alexander, a naval officer, known as Sandro within the family, left Yalta with their son Andrei in December 1918 on HMS Forsythe. They got to Paris where his daughter Irena and her husband Felix Yussoupoff would arrive four months later. Sandro became an amateur archaeologist until he succumbed to cancer in 1933. He was buried in Roquebrune-Cap-Martin, a village near Monaco.

Those Romanovs that were still in Crimea were waiting for the British battleship HMS Marlborough that was sent by Queen Alexandra to rescue her sister. It landed at Sevastopol on 5 April 1919 then proceeded to Yalta the next day to collect Maria Feodorovna and her entourage. There were eighteen Romanovs, among them Xenia and her family including eldest child and only daughter Irena with her husband Felix Yussoupoff. The rest were aides making in total a party of seventy people.

The captain was taken aback and was probably expecting just Queen Alexandra's sister and her children and grandchildren, but Maria Feodorovna refused to leave a single person behind. Had they remained they would not have been able to get away and would likely have been recaptured by the Red Army and shot. Before they set off, an Imperial troopship passed by on the way to engage the Bolsheviks; a compliment of 170 fresh soldiers undoubtedly sailing to their death. They cheered when they saw the black figure of Maria Feodorovna on the deck of HMS Marlborough and sang the Russian anthem. Maria Feodorovna set sail from Russia, leaving Olga and her family behind at Dulber Palace.

CHAPTER XIX

The Dowager Maria Feodorovna and Grand Duke Nikolai Nikolaevich onboard HMS Marlborough. Yalta is in the background, 8 April 1919.

Xenia and her husband Alexander Mikhailovich (first cousins once removed) are the ancestors of most of the current Romanov descendants living today; Queen Elizabeth II was the grandniece of Nicholas II. Alexander Mikhailovich wrote the following amazing tale in his memoirs:

"Two of my relatives owe their lives to an astonishing coincidence. A Bolshevik commander who was ordered to shoot them was once a painter whose paintings one of them had once bought. So he couldn't kill them and helped them flee to the White Army." — ALEXANDER MIKHAILOVICH

When HMS Marlborough weighed anchor on 11 April 1919, Maria Feodorovna sent a telegram to her sister Queen Alexandra that she was heartbroken. The next morning the ship anchored off Haiki Island (about twelve miles from Constantinople,) as there was some uncertainty over where exactly the royal family should be taken to. The Montenegrin sisters Militza and Anastasia disembarked HMS Marlborough on 16 April 1919 and boarded a waiting HMS Lord Nelson destined for Genoa. The Black Peril had survived Russia and husband Nikolai Nikolaevich was with them.

On Good Friday 18 April 1919, Maria Feodorovna had tears in her eyes as HMS Marlborough sailed out of the Black Sea and headed for the British naval base at Malta. She knew that it was unlikely she would ever return. One account says HMS Marlborough went next to Constantinople but this was not the case, they sailed first to Malta and disembarked and then the ship turned back and went to Constantinople with other passengers. When Maria Feodorovna arrived in Malta on 20 April 1919 she and her entourage were put up at the Palace of San Antonio and the nearby hotels. Their expenses to the tune of £750 (another account says £500,) were advanced by the Governor Methuen from the Maltese Civil Funds.

HMS Lord Nelson, after it had landed the Montenegrins at Genoa, called next at Malta for a brief refit in late April 1919. Then it returned to England with Maria Feodorovna, daughter Xenia and her family and some others. They stayed briefly with Queen Alexandra, who was now also a dowager queen-empress since the death of Edward VII on 6 May 1910. After a short stay, still in 1919, Maria Feodorovna returned home to Denmark staying with her nephew King Christian X (k. 1912 - 1947) at the Amalienborg Palace. She was there only briefly then relocated permanently to her summer villa in Hvidore just north of Copenhagen. Hvidore was the residence she shared with sister Alexandra after their father Christian IX died of heart failure in 1906 aged 87. With no more family reunions at Fredensborg Palace, the spring and autumn residence of the Danish royal family, the sisters bought Hvidore House in 1907. They met there from September to November every year until the outbreak of World War I when travel became too dangerous.

Once settled at Hyidore, Maria Feodorovna called for her youngest daughter Olga who was still in Crimea and the only remaining Romanov left in Russia. Olga had unwisely judged that she could remain in Russia with her husband and children when everyone else had either escaped or been murdered. The only reason they were not arrested sooner was due to Olga's morganatic marriage meaning that for a time Olga 'Kulikovska' was not a person of interest to the Bolsheviks. A year after the German army left Russia they had no choice but to flee, keeping just ahead of the Red Army troop movements.

They sought refuge just a small way along the coast at the Danish Consul in Novorossiysk where Olga received news for the first time that her mother was safely in Denmark. Olga, her husband Nikolai and their two young sons Tikhon and Guri, were shipped to an island in the Dardanelles Strait near Constantinople - there were no longer any living Romanovs in Russia. From there the family were taken to Belgrade where they intended to settle but on her mother's insistence Olga continued the journey to Denmark, arriving on Good Friday 1920, exactly one year to the day since Maria Feodorovna and daughter Xenia had sailed out of the Black Sea and left Russia forever.

That same year in 1920, a woman was rescued from a Berlin canal, she had no identification and insisted that she was Grand Duchess Anastasia Nikolaevna. Xenia went out to meet her and was convinced that it wasn't her; the 'imposter' was markedly taller for starters. Because the bodies of the royal family had not been found, many imposters emerged. The girl from

CHAPTER XIX

the canal is the best known example who maintained until her death decades later that she was Anastasia Nikolaevna even after it was proved that she was not. She was in fact mentally deranged and probably genuinely believed that she was a Princess.

The Danish sisters looking over the balcony of their residence at Hvidore

In 1927 Grand Duke Ernest Ludwig of Hesse and by Rhine (Alexandra Feodorovna's brother) funded an investigation that uncovered that she was in fact a Polish factory machinist called Franziska Schanzkowska who had worked in an arms factory during World War I. During a shift, a grenade had fallen out of her hand and exploded causing a head injury and the death of a co-worker. She became severely depressed after that and was declared clinically insane.

Franziska moved to America and changed her name to Anna Anderson living for years on the financial support of those who believed her claim. A German court ruled that Anderson had failed to prove that she was Anastasia which then attracted even more media coverage over the years bringing her further notoriety. After she died in 1984 a sample of her tissue that had been stored at a hospital in Virginia, America, following an operation to her intestine in 1979, was used to extract mitochondrial DNA. It was compared to Romanov DNA and there was no match found which proved that she was unrelated. It did however, match the DNA provided by Karl Maucher, a grandson of Franziska's discovered sister Gertrude Ellerik and having no royal antecedents.

Another mentally challenged would-be Anastasia was Nadezhda Ivanova-Vasilyeva who died in a mental asylum in 1971. And then there was the strange story from Helen of Serbia (the daughter of Princess Zorka of Montenegro,) who was among the nobility women that were trying to help release the prisoners at Alapayevsk, when in April 1918 her husband Prince Ioann Konstntinovich was sent to the camp with his brother and his cousin. Helen petitioned for their release and in June 1918 she went to Ipatiev House demanding to speak with the ex-tsar, with the aim of secretly passing him some letters from family members. She was arrested and imprisoned at Perm. One day a Bolshevik guard brought a girl to her cell who was claiming to be Anastasia Nikolaevna. Helen did not recognise the girl. Two weeks later Helen was taken by train to Petrograd and secured in the Peter and Paul Fortress. Fortunately, Norwegian diplomats were able to locate her and she was allowed to leave Russia with her children, arriving in Sweden and eventually relocating to Paris. Whether she was convinced that she had met the real Anastasia is unknown.

Author Gabriel Louis Duval published a book in 2004, *A Princess in the Family* in which he claimed that his foster grandmother Alina was in fact Marie Nikolaevna. Marga Boodts claimed to be Olga stating that a guard took pity on her by hitting her on the head to make her unconscious, then substituting her body with a girl that he had caught stealing from the bodies of the Romanov females and then he took her to Vladivostok where she made passage to Germany via China. Boodts was convincing because she seemed to know so much about Olga's life. She claimed that Wilhelm II met her and believed her to be Olga and even supported her financially from his exile until he died on 4 June 1941. She also discredited Anna Anderson's claim to a degree by stating that she had witnessed Anastasia's murder. There were several men that claimed to be the Tsarevich Alexei Nikolaevich

CHAPTER XIX

and there was an intriguing claim from Suzanna Catharina de Graaff who believed herself to be a fifth daughter born in 1903, coinciding with the time that Alexandra had her phantom pregnancy and whose claim was supported by Anna Anderson.

Grand Duchess Olga Alexandrovna a volunteer nurse in the Russo-Japanese War (1904-1905) and World War I (1914-1918). She came under heavy Austrian fire working so close to the front lines and was awarded the Order of St George by General Mannerheim, the later President of Finland.

The end in exile

Queen Alexandra of England was the longest-serving Princess of Wales in British history. She died from a heart attack in November 1925, aged 80 (two months before her 81st birthday). She is buried at the St George's Chapel at Windsor Castle with her husband George V. After her death there was a very noticeable decline in the health of her sister Maria Feodorovna. For the last three years of Maria Feodorovna's life the one time queen of European fashion was filling the cracks in her face with porcelain, like an image of the face of Elizabeth I of England, so that she could neither smile nor frown. It was the only self-inflicted indignity in her life for which she may be forgiven. She died at 7.00 pm on 13 October 1928 at villa Hvidore aged 80 (one month before her 81st birthday). She outlived four of her six children. Her son-in-law, Grand Duke Alexander Mikhailovich (i.e. Sandro) said, *"She was ready to meet her Creator."*

Maria Feodorovna was buried alongside other members of the Danish royal family in the Christian IX Chapel at Roskilde Cathedral in Denmark. During her last years she had expressed the desire to her daughters to lie next to her husband, *"when circumstances permit it."* In 2005 her wish was brought to the attention of Queen Margrethe II of Denmark, who approached the Russian President Putin about moving the remains to St Petersburg.

Following lengthy negotiations between the Danish and Russian governments, in September 2006 her coffin was taken from Roskilde Cathedral by the Danish ship *Esbern Snare* to Peterhof where on 26 September 2006 her statue was unveiled. The coffin was taken to Saint Isaac's Cathedral (once the largest cathedral in Russia, and today a museum since 1931) for an elaborate ceremony beneath its gold-plated dome, officiated by the Patriarch Alexis II. After the service the coffin was taken to the Peter and Paul Fortress in St Petersburg, the resting place of the Russian Imperial rulers and their family. Two days later on 28 September 2006, the coffin was lowered in to the Imperial crypt, seventy-eight years after her death, and placed next to her husband and son. The ceremony was attended by the king and queen of Greece, the crown prince and crown princess of Denmark, and distant Romanov relatives the Prince and Princess Michael of Kent.

Daughter Xenia Alexandrovna got on exceptionally well with her cousin George V and was said to be his favourite cousin. She visited Windsor Castle from time to time to a point where Queen Alexandra could not hide her jealousy at the fondness of their relationship. Unlike her mother, Xenia decided to settle in England permanently and in 1925 the King gave over Frogmore Cottage for her use, a property of the Crown Estate that passes from monarch to monarch. It was built in 1801 as a country retreat on the grounds of the Frogmore House estate at Windsor for Queen Charlotte, the wife of King George III and mother to George IV of Great Britain and Ireland (who was also the King of Hanover).

Perhaps Queen Charlotte built it in tribute to the Acts of Union which became official on 1 January 1801 bringing together Great Britain and Ireland. The cottage was much smaller than the house, the house being the traditional residence of the Prince and Princess of Wales, yet it was still a mansion in its own right boasting thirty-six rooms, including ten bedrooms.

CHAPTER XIX

One newspaper clipping described it thus, "*The cottage is a very modest affair and has often been lent by the Ruling Sovereign to distant relatives who, like the Princess Xenia, are not too well-endowed with this world's goods.*" In recent times it served as the residence of Prince Harry and Meghan Markle before they moved abroad.

An interesting aside is that Queen Charlotte was the first resident to move in to the newly constructed Buckingham Palace in 1762 and she constructed the timber-framed Kew Cottage (1772-1781) on the grounds of Richmond Lodge by the River Thames (today the Lodge is better known as Kew Palace). She even kept kangaroos in the rear paddock of Kew Cottage, circa 1792. There she developed her green fingers and was quite famed for her interest in horticulture. There is a dailily named after her called the Queen Charlotte Hemerocallis (i.e. a flowering plant of late spring or early summer – family: Asphodelaceae; genus: Hemerocallis). She also brought the Christmas tree to Great Britain from her native German Duchy of Mecklenburg-Strelitz and put the first known decorated tree up in December 1800 at Windsor. Her granddaughter Queen Victoria popularised the festive decoration of the tree and from around the mid nineteenth century it was absorbed as a national British Christmas tradition.

Frogmore Cottage and Kew Cottage are Grade II listed buildings today. In the book *The Boy Who Would be Tsar*, written by Xenia's grandson Prince Andrew Romanoff, the stories and illustrations are about his youth spent at Frogmore Cottage. One story tells of the time at Easter when a huge chocolate egg was delivered from Harrods or Fortnum's. After they had demolished the egg a courier from Frogmore House rapped at the door to enquire if they had received a large egg erroneously delivered to the cottage. Of course they owned up and sent a message back that they had eaten it and it was delicious. It had been intended for the princesses Elizabeth and Margaret, then living at Frogmore House.

Xenia's husband, Alexander Mikhailovich, known as Sandro to the family, did not live at Frogmore Cottage with his wife and children but remained in France. It was probably thanks to him that Xenia was able to leave Petrograd and make it to Crimea. Sandro lived at Ay-Todor and would go to Petrograd from time to time to get news on the political climate, he could come and go unnoticed as he was not one of the better known royals. He had warned Xenia when it became urgent for her to leave Petrograd which she did on 28 March 1917 rushing for Ay-Todor. They never divorced despite his infidelity and they were happily married until Sandro had an affair. Xenia in turn had an affair with whom is suggested to have been the husband of Sandro's mistress. They chose to remain married but lived separate lives after that. In his capacity as advisor to the tsar, like Rodzianko before him, Sandro had tried many times to warn Nicholas II to leave the city, but he too had been ignored by the Tsar.

> *"In conclusion I want to say that, strange though it may be, the Government itself is the organ that is preparing the revolution. The nation does not want it, but the Government is doing everything to make as many malcontents as possible, and is succeeding perfectly. We are witnessing the unparalleled spectacle of revolution from above, and not from below."*
> — SANDRO, last paragraph of letter to Nicholas II, 17 February 1917

There are several accounts suggesting Xenia took on several lovers but the details are obscure. The book *A Lifelong Passion* by Andrei Maylunas & Sergei Mironenko, mentions an affair but offers no identity. In another rather more interesting account, Xenia developed a relationship with Prince Sergei Alexeevich Dolgoruky. The story goes that Dolgoruky had been married for just three years when his wife committed suicide after she found out about his affair with Xenia. Another account states that the relationship took off when they were both under house arrest at Ay Todor. The Dolgoruky's were a huge family that also go by Dolgorukii, Dolgoruki or Dolgorukov, and the only Dolgoruky in the area to link to Xenia is Alexander Dolgoruky who was an equerry to Maria Feodorovna and who would have been around the same age as Xenia and was also a captive at Ay Todor. Have the names been confused; were there two 'Dolgorukys' at Ay Todor or was it just a rumour.

Xenia was essentially broke but after her brother was declared officially dead in 1928 following the death of Maria Feodorovna, Xenia was able to claim a small property in England (approx £500) that had belonged to her brother. The sale of the villa Hyidore in 1930 and some of her mother's jewellery helped to alleviate her financial stresses. But the money didn't go far enough and she continued to rely mainly on a small pension from the King up until he died in 1936. Sandro had never been to England and when he died in 1933 his funeral was one of the only occasions when Xenia left England. Their eldest son Andrei Mikhailovich and his second wife Nadine McDougall, of the wealthy McDougalls flour family, moved to England permanently after the funeral, staying at Frogmore Cottage with Xenia.

The new King Edward VIII requested the return of Frogmore Cottage for his own purpose and in March 1937, reluctantly Xenia moved to Wilderness House on the Hampton Court Palace estate, Richmond-upon-Thames with her son and his wife. It was a reasonably similar sized property, built around 1700 for the royal gardener, and between 1764 to 1783 was the residence of the most famous gardener of all, Lancelot 'Capability' Brown. Xenia was finally at peace and like her sister Olga loved to paint in exile. Olga used her talent to generate income and Xenia painted many small sketches and watercolours for joy, many she included in letters. Xenia died on 20 April 1960, three weeks after her eighty-fifth birthday, she was buried with her husband at the Roquebrune Cemetery in France.

CHAPTER XIX

At the end of World War II Olga once more was in the wrong place at the wrong time when the Soviet army liberated the easternmost island of Bornholm on 9 May 1945. Joseph Stalin accused Olga of having conspired with Germany against Russia during World War II. Soviet troops had a reputation for snatching people from the West, so with Soviet troops at the Danish border, Olga left with her family in 1948, aged sixty-six, on a troopship bound for Canada for her second forced exile, to avoid that eventuality.

They survived on the jewels that Olga's maid had smuggled out of Russia. Eventually Olga was able to purchase a small farm in Ontario, stating that she chose it because the vastness of Canada reminded her of Russia. She also published her memoirs and made around 2,000 paintings. Indeed, she came to regard her life on that farm as the happiest times of her life. As Olga and her husband grew older and were unable to adequately manage a farm they moved in to a suburban home in Ontario where husband Nikolai died in 1958.

In June 1959 Queen Elizabeth II was on a royal visit to Canada and invited Olga to dinner on the Royal Yacht Britannia. Olga believed she was too old to buy a new frock to attend a formal occasion. *"Honestly, all this fuss just to see Lilibet and Philip,"* she said. But her neighbours persuaded her and so in deteriorating health she sat at the head table on HMS Britannia with the Queen of England, a position once held by her auntie Queen Alexandra.

In 1960 she moved to a yet smaller flat above a shop in Cooksville, Toronto and soon after developed pneumonia. Xenia's children Andrei and Irina came from Paris to be at their auntie's side, and there, the last surviving Russian Grand Duchess died on 24 November 1960, aged seventy-eight, six months after her sister the Grand Duchess Xenia.

CHAPTER XX
The Official Investigations

THERE are two conflicting investigations that were undertaken by the white Army after they took Ekaterinburg and Perm. There was little time to organise and pick up momentum before the Red Army retook control of these cities but a good deal was learned about the fate of the prisoners of Ipatiev House, the nearby prison and the military camp near Alapayevsk. At Ekaterinburg the investigation was headed by the judiciary, by a lawyer, Nikolai Sokolov, that confirmed the ex-tsar and his immediate family had been murdered at Ipatiev House and buried nearby at one of the mines of Ganina Yama. At Perm, the Czech-Slovak General Rudolf Gajda conducted a completely separate investigation which contradicted the Ekaterinburg findings and concluded that the tsar and tsarevich were executed in either Ekaterinburg or Perm along with the royal aides but the Romanov females were imprisoned for some months thereafter leaving the door open for speculation that there may have been survivors.

Both investigations had equal resources and were competently handled yet the Ekaterinburg report entered the official history of events whereas the Perm one was quashed and forgotten about. The Ekaterinburg report is known as the Sokolov Investigation and similarly the Perm report is known as the Gajda Investigation. Unfortunately they were both far from finished when the White Army were pushed out by the rapidly advancing Red Army. There were yet many decades before the bodies were discovered and the investigations had revolved around interviews from guards and other witnesses. Why one investigation should have triumphed over the other is difficult to know but the thing about the Gajda investigation is that it contained material that cannot continue to remain under the carpet and it has kept popping up time and again until finally a documentary programme funded by the BBC *The File On The Tsar* explored the Gajda alternative theories in depth.

CHAPTER XX

The investigations each have their merits and seen as a whole they offer a complete picture of the confusion that prevailed during that time. The fact that one inquiry was judicial and the other was military serves to strengthen the understanding and unravel the mystery. Within each there are facts and untruths. Are we to believe that Sokolov travelled the length of Russia with the organic remains of the ex-Imperial Russian Family in his suitcase; to do so is to accept the official version of events. Also, when bodies were finally discovered decades later, discussed in detail in the next chapter, the DNA profiling that confirmed the identities cannot be disputed. How much credence then, should be given to the alternative theories that suggest there were survivors.

The story of Sokolov's involvement and his journey with the evidence certainly is fascinating but raises suspicions not least because Sokolov died very young in mysterious circumstances before he published his book. With so much secrecy in the air there will always be uncertainty over the exact order of events but that is inconsequential because Sokolov's evidence turned up in 1950 and the bodies were discovered and analysed in due course. The BBC documentary led to a book by the researchers and deserves its rightful place for consideration. It mainly concentrated on the Gajda Investigation which helped to confirm many aspects it and ignited a renewed interest in the alternative theories.

The White Army arrived in Ekaterinburg on 23 July 1918 (G), just one week after the massacre at Ipatiev House. Three days later investigators inspected it thoroughly, knowing it to be the last known address of the Romanov family and their closest aides. The Senior person in control of the White Army was Admiral Alexander Kolchak who went about replacing the Ural governance with his own Siberian government. He appointed Colonel Sherekhovsky to chair an inquiry to determine what exactly had happened at Ipatiev House who in turn assigned investigator Aleksei Nametkin who started his report on 30 July 1918 but did not yield much of any worth.

A second report was headed by Judge Ivan Sergeev (*mentioned earlier on page 421*) who looked in more detail for several months and believed that the ex-Imperial Family had not been shot at Ipatiev House. Sergeev's findings were more in line with the Gajda report but the story is that both Nametkin and Sergeev had been bogged down with many uncertainties and Kolchak had had enough of delays and therefore brought in a new lead investigator in Judge Nikolai Sokolov.

He was a young lawyer with the perseverance to search for the truth, or perhaps the real reason was that he was susceptible to manipulation. With hindsight the first item to note is that up to then, any notion of survivors or the ex-Imperial Family not having been killed at Ipatiev House was not entertained by the White Army and it was in their best interest to project the worst possible scenario about the Bolsheviks to the world.

THE OFFICIAL INVESTIGATIONS

When the first investigators entered Ipatiev House the first thing they did was dig up the grounds and look for bodies. They searched all locations that were the subject of local gossip, like the mines of Ganina Yama where it was rumoured bodies had been burned. A large barge steam engine was used to handle the lengthy process of pumping the water from the twenty-nine pits and at the initial stage they found a small heap of charred remains and among the ashes the ruby ring that Nicholas had given Alexandra when she arrived in St Petersburg for her sister Elizabeth's wedding. According to her maid, Alexandra always wore it hanging from a chain on her chest.

On 30 January 1919 a new inquiry chairman was appointed by Kolchak, General Mikhail Konstantinovich Dieterichs. As expected of a General, he was a veteran of the Russo-Japanese War; as a Lieutenant he had fought in Manchuria at the Battle of Mukden and during World War I he served as Chief of Staff of the Third Army under the renowned General Brusilov. He helped to plan the Brusilov Offensive also known as the June Advance which induced Romania to join the war on the side of the Allied Powers. The June Advance started on 4 June 1916 and was the largest operation of World War I which in military history is regarded as one of the most vicious offensives and probably only matched in ambition by the D-Day landings that took place exactly twenty-eight years later to the day, on 4 June 1944.

For his successes Dieterichs was offered the post of Minister of War by the Provisional Government which he declined and instead was promoted to Chief of Staff of the Stavka. In the Civil War he joined the White movement and moved eastwards to evade the Bolsheviks. When Admiral Kolchak tasked him with taking over the Ipatiev House inquiry, the ruby found in the ashes had been enough to presume they had found the remains of the royal family. What the White Army discovered at Ipatiev House was the focal point of the investigation because it substantiated the presence of the royal prisoners and that they appeared to have been rushed to their execution in the middle of the night and taken to Ganina Yama for burial.

The guards at Ipatiev House were unruly and stole many items of the prisoner's personal belongings like pearls and diamonds which eventually turned up for sale and the investigators also managed to retrieve items from the guards when their houses were searched. It throws up many questions like if the guards were such thieves then why was jewellery found at the house on display. The items found appear conveniently placed to deceive the investigators. Alexei's prescribed medication was still in his room and Alexandra's diary and the icon of the Romanov patron saint, the Feodorovskaya Icon of the Mother of God, was found, items that would confirm the presence of Alexei and Alexandra.

Everything that supports the official version was found in the Sokolov Investigation. Sokolov himself found a small casket containing 374 letters exchanged between Nicholas and Alexandra between 1914 to 1917; the longest period they had ever been apart, while Nicholas was at the front. Sokolov reckoned that they would never have left such things behind if they had prepared to leave Ipatiev House and therefore he deducted that they must have been hurried. If so, they must have been told to travel light and pack only clothes. Indeed the other issue with the Sokolov Investigation is that all of the clothes recovered were at the Ganina Yama mine. Evidence found at Ganina Yama likewise throws up suspicions and it could be argued that those items too, seemed to be in a deliberate pattern, as opposed to being randomly distributed.

The Sokolov Investigation

On 6 February 1919, thirty-six year old Nikolai Alekseevich Sokolov was handed the forensic materials from Nametkin and Sergeev and was appointed the Investigating Magistrate for Cases of Special Importance by the Omsk District Court on 7 February 1919. In due course he would also receive everything relating to the Gajda investigation. He was a staunch monarchist who was once captured by the Red Army and escaped at Sarov. He brought the much needed impetus to the investigation. The new lead investigator, sometimes referred to as just 'the Judge' understood the historical significance of his role. He was pedantic, meticulous in recording every detail, exceptionally thorough and left no stone unturned; at one time he disguised himself as a peasant in Red Army territory so that he might discover clues.

The testimonies gathered from the guards revealed that everyone except those on sentry duty were involved in the clean up operation and their own accounts say that it was done thoroughly. However well that was, some trace evidence would inevitably remain but what was found superseded any expectation. Why were there jewels on display when it's know the guards were rummaging through the bedrooms and the belongings of the prisoners. Dr Botkin may well have determined that Alexei no longer needed his medication, which had also been left behind, or maybe it was overlooked in the rush but there is less explanation for the cellar which was meticulously scrubbed. The cleaning detail were extremely inattentive and are portrayed as totally incompetent; more than thirty bullets were recovered and enough blood was in the wall that it seeped through for months despite several attempts to paint it over.

Furthermore, if the prisoners were rushed, then why did the Romanov females have enough time to put on their corsets which took a considerable effort to lace up. The corset was standard clothing that Alexandra insisted on being worn by every female in the household but these were now double-quilted bodices containing jewellery; the double bra was stitched together and used to conceal jewels in the cavity. The corsets were evidently given priority which may be the reason for leaving the other items behind. The jewels were their insurance for whatever lay ahead and are the best indication that they knew they were leaving Ipatiev House for good although they would not have suspected anything sinister was about to happen to them.

Left: General Dieterichs on left side wearing the Chez-Slovak uniform with a French General. *Right*: Nikolai Sokolov c1919

"As a result of the investigation, and the examination of persons who fell into the hands of the White Guards and were in one way or another cognisant of the shooting of the ex-Imperial family, it was established beyond possibility of doubt that the whole Imperial family had been executed." — PAVEL BYKOV, The last days of Tsar Nicholas

Whether or not the scene of the crime had been conspicuously prepared, the inescapable remains that following the Bolshevik announcement of the execution of Nicholas II there was no evidence forthcoming of it or of the fate of the other prisoners. According to the Gajda Investigation the Romanov females were alive and Sokolov would no doubt have heard about the rumours. His visit to Ipatiev House established that murders had been committed but the identities were unknown. At Ganina Yama he concentrated on trying to establish the identities from the remains but with the absence of

CHAPTER XX

bodies identification was impossible and he focused on searching the surrounding areas.

The charred remains were human and assumed to be from Ipatiev House but the problem was that there were not enough ashes to account for eleven bodies, so Sokolov doubled his efforts and widened the search radius. One account has it that in February 1919 the ashes were sent to George V and some items of jewellery and clothing were sent to Xenia Alexandrovna. In another account, the remains travelled with Sokolov in his suitcase when he left Russia in 1920 and ended up in Belgium.

Almost immediately on leading the investigation, in February 1919 Sokolov found the location at Koptyaki Forest where Yurovsky's truck had got stuck in the mud. Nothing was discovered there as he neglected to look under the railway sleepers where the hidden grave was located and it would remain undetected for decades. Having not found anything Sokolov wrongly concluded that all the bodies had been disposed of at Ganina Yama.

The investigation determined that an attempt was made to destroy multiple corpses at Ganina Yama and ascertained the identities of victims from the statements taken from the guards at Ipatiev House and from the items discovered there and also recovered from Ganina Yama. At pit number 7 among the items found were Dr Botkin's upper dentures and spectacles and a severed female index finger found in the shaft of the mine on 7 August 1918. Also found was congealed fat, skin, dismembered bones and charred bone fragments, shoes, keys, spent bullets, pearls and diamonds (*page 392*) and the metal parts of six corset ribs. In similar fashion to Ipatiev House, the items found at the pit appeared not to be randomised but intended to help identify the victims.

The severed finger is sometimes confused with a finger from Elizabeth Feodorovna. What a coincidence that both sisters should each have a finger preserved in formaldehyde. In one account the finger from Ganina Yama had been severed to remove a ring. In Yurovsky's report of 19 July 1918 he stated that it was blown apart by the grenade thrown in to the pit. Sokolov photographed it which is the proof that it existed (investigation photo No. 120) and he assumed it belonged to Alexandra Feodorovna on account that she was known to have rather long and slender phalanges. The author George Telberg referred to the Sokolov report in his book *The Last Days of The Romanovs* (1920), "*The finger is described as belonging to a woman of middle age. It is long, slender and well-shaped, like the Empress's hand.*"

Was Alexandra Feodorovna's finger really among the remains Sokolov collected, the story goes that it was placed in a flask of formaldehyde and travelled with him in his famed box of relics when he left Russia and was witnessed by Anna Rozanov (*page 452*). Another account states that the finger turned up in the vault of a New York bank, that source coming from the preface of Victor Alexandrov's book *The End of The Romanovs* (1966) but he doesn't state it as a fact, only as an open question, *"Have we not good reason to think that Empress Alexandra Feodorovna's index finger – one of Sokolov's macabre finds in a mineshaft near Ekaterinburg – today reposes in a bottle of formol in the basement of a New York Bank?"*

But what is the 'good reason' that Alexandrov talks of? It all suggests the finger went with Sokolov and presumably when he reached Harbin or Paris it was placed in 'formol', an aqueous solution of formaldehyde, and was later deposited at the bank for safe storage. Having Alexandra Feodorovna's actual finger preserved was the definitive proof that she had been at Ganina Yama. As for Elizabeth Feodorovna's finger, that story is also a little sketchy (*page 484*).

Working at the Four Brothers pit in Ganina Yama, around nineteen miles from Ipatiev House, Nikolai Sokolov's investigation searches but finds no bodies, only ashes and many items that point to the identities of the victims. Photograph taken from the Sokolov report, spring 1919, photograph No 70.

CHAPTER XX

On 16 March 1919, Yakov Sverdlov died, probably due to the Spanish flu although tuberculosis is sometimes given as the cause of his death. The reader will recall that he was the man who gave the order for Yurovsky to murder the prisoners at Ekaterinburg and Perm. He was also known as the Red Tsar in recognition of the power he wielded. (a title that passed to Lenin then Stalin). According to German archives Sverdlov had been receiving masses of German money up until November 1917 used to fund the Russian Revolution 1917. It's also given to support the theory that as Germany were in control of Sverdlov, so they too played a part in the fate of the Romanovs.

The Bolsheviks in the early days were to a large extent under the control of Germany who wanted Russia back in the war but on their side. The way to achieve that was for Nicholas II to return to the throne under German influence. As soon as word reached the Germans that Nicholas would not capitulate, the authority was given for his execution. As discussed, German ambassador Mirbach was involved at some level and possibly had not agreed to the murders, thus being a possible explanation for why he came face to face with Cheka assassins. The theory for German involvement was also evident at Ipatiev House where German markings were found on the walls made by the guards, implicating that some were German agents.

Dieterichs was in overall charge of the White Army investigation until July 1919 and then he was reassigned by Admiral Kolchak to take charge of the Siberian Army but resigned in December 1919 after they had a falling out. Dieterichs continued to fight independently until the Bolsheviks pushed him all the way to Vladivostok and from there he made his way to Harbin, a British redoubt for White Army officers in Manchuria.

He is the source for the theory that the murders of the royal family were ritual killings and wrote a book when he left Russia about the sadistic ritualised retaliation by the Jews, by which he was referencing the Bolsheviks, an essentially Jewish led movement. He was well known for his hatred of the Jews and believed in the Jewish conspiracy as many did, a vehement racist at odds with all non-Russians, deeply anti-socialist and a freedom fighter loyal to the monarchy. These similarities he shared with Nicholas II and likewise in contrast to his obvious aversions was also a deeply religious man. If he wasn't such a sinister character because of his views, it might be argued that his heart was in the right place.

When Dieterichs left the investigation in Sokolov's capable hands he continued to offer support and followed its progress. He played an important part throughout and has somewhat been underrated for his efforts. His book *The Murder of the Royal Family and Members of the Romanov House in the Urals*, published in Vladivostok in 1922, complements the Sokolov report for a complete understanding of the official line of what was happening at that time and without his input the investigation could not have progressed as it did.

Towards the end of 1919 Sokolov visited Ipatiev House with Charles Stanley Gibbes, the Imperial children's English language tutor. In the cellar they found *"unmistakable evidence of its being human blood."* which was the conclusive proof Sokolov needed to establish that the cellar had been the place of execution, but as discussed, exactly who had been executed was only assumed. Any evidence that was not directly related to the murders at Ipatiev House was omitted from the Sokolov report such as the deposition given by Charles Sydney Gibbes. It's hard to fathom why a first hand account would not be considered because a lot of what is known about has been gleaned from the memoirs of such notaries as Hanbury-Williams, Gilliard, Gibbes, Rodzianko, et al.

"I saw in the room in which the murder took place obscene drawings with inscriptions, partly obliterated since, but clear enough to read. There were horrible pictures of Rasputin and the Empress and inscriptions boasting of outrage, and the shrieks that were heard at night tend to confirm this." — COLONEL PAVEL RODZIANKO

The level of disrespect and indignity suffered by the prisoners at Ipatiev House was evident when Colonel Pavel Rodzianko visited there and saw the obscene images of Rasputin with Alexandra on the walls. It's a good example of how a first hand account such as this conveys more than a record of the event but also emotions. The reader will recall (*page 354*) that it was Pavel Rodzianko who claimed the Romanov women were sexually abused on the journey from Tobolsk to Ekaterinburg and that he also rescued the dog Joy found at Ipatiev House.

The Sokolov Commission, as it became known, was objective and ultimately proved that executions had taken place at Ipatiev House and that corpses had been taken to Ganina Yama for attempted disposal. Sokolov wrongly assumed the remains represented all of the victims only because a grave had not been found and he ignored the fact that hardly any bones had been found and that the ashes did not account for eleven persons. The return of the Red Army put an end to the investigation and Sokolov fled to France on an exaggerated journey through China and Japan, taking with him as much as he could carry, believing the Bolsheviks would destroy everything related to the investigation if they caught up with him. He could only move through areas occupied by the White Army which proved extremely dangerous as he encountered the many sects that were not receptive of his great mission. Sokolov was in possession of evidence of the ex-tsar's death which was the last thing the White Army wanted to prove. He became ever paranoid that his cargo would be captured and his evidence might be lost for ever.

The Sokolov Commission dossier was made up of eight volumes and many photographs that Sokolov had taken of documents and items. Three copies were made. George Telberg, Kolchak's Justice Minister and former professor of law at the University of Saratov, retrieved one copy and various other files from Kolchak's office and took them to Europe where they ended up with the law library at the Library of Congress. A second copy was claimed by special correspondent of The Times (London), Robert Wilton, who was around Sokolov in Harbin and stayed at the Paris hotel in 1920 where several political figures were gathered in exile. Wilton confirmed that the 'Sokolov dossier' passed to him and, *"I should be free at my own discretion to make it public in whole or in part,"* referring to his right to publish it. The third copy went with Sokolov of which, along with the majority of the material he possessed is located at the Houghton Library at Harvard University which holds seven of the eight volumes of the Sokolov Commission dossier.

After the investigation was interrupted when the White Army was pushed out of Ekaterinburg, Sokolov was in danger and by 1920 he had fled Russia with his evidence and the documents from the investigation. What happened to it is a story of letters between ex Russian politicians, diplomats, Romanov family members, banks, and auction houses, leaving things rather complicated to unravel but essentially Sokolov continued his work from exile in Paris having little support. The documentation and much of the evidence existing today can be attributed to Sokolov. In Paris he had just a few years left to live (d. 23 November 1924) and managed to write the definitive account of the murders, published posthumously in 1925.

Sokolov's Cargo Leaves Russia

Sokolov kept negative photographic plates and important documents in two oblong wooden boxes. The contents were itemised by Grand Duke Andrei Vladimirovich, (cousin to Nicholas II and husband to ballerina Mathilde Kschessinska – page 5). The relics (i.e. ashes), which presumably included the preserved finger of Alexandra Feodorovna and other valuables, he placed in a Russian army suitcase which came to be known as the 'Sokolov Box'. Clothing and such, from Ganina Yama and Ipatiev House was packed in to a small chest. There were four main containers in all.

Sokolov left Ekaterinburg travelling eastwards through Omsk and Chita until he reached the coastal town of Vladivostok towards the end of 1919. He arrived seeking the assistance of General Sergey Nikolaevich Rozanov, a White Army Lieutenant General who had come over from the Red Army and was once more switching allegiances and becoming sympathetic to the brewing rebellion against Admiral Kolchak. He was the general that had torn down the wooden palings around Ipatiev House and one of the first to enter after the murders. In September 1918 he had recommended to the

Ministry of Justice of the Provisional Siberian Government that the lawyer Nikolai Sokolov be appointed the Criminal Investigator to lead the judicial investigation which Sokolov filled on 5 November 1918.

The Sokolov investigation wooden boxes

Now in Vladivostok with his cargo; two wooden boxes, a chest and the Sokolov Box, Sokolov was asking Rozanov for help to get out of Russia. In October 1919 Rozanov had informed Admiral Kolchak of the strengthened opposition to his government in the eastern regions and the planned uprising by General Gajda. When in mid-November 1919 General Gajda launched the attack (with Czechs and Socialist Revolutionaries), he was pushed back by Kolchak to Vladivostok where Rozanov was supposed to engage him but didn't. For disobeying orders Rozanov was declared an enemy of the people by the Political Centre in Omsk.

Vladivostok was too risky to keep Sokolov's cargo but Rozanov was not able to offer much assistance due to his predicament so Sokolov turned to good old General Dieterichs who in January 1920 asked the British High Commissioner in Peking, Miles Lampson (who had been to Siberia in July 1919), to remove the cargo from Russia and preferably push it along with Sokolov to Britain. Lampson received three of the four containers on the next day, 8 January 1920, as Sokolov would not part with the Sokolov Box. Lampson used the Americans to transport the cargo to Harbin in Manchuria.

The Kolchak rebellion had arrived in Vladivostok on 31 January 1920 by which time Rozanov had fled to the safety of Japan and Sokolov had safely arrived in Harbin with his pregnant wife and his two assistants Robert Wilton and Paul Bulygin. In early 1918 Bulygin was backed by Maria Feodorovna to organise an escape of the royal family and his endeavour had come to nothing. In January 1919 she asked him to investigate the fate of the royal family and that's when Bulygin met Sokolov and was made Sokolov's assistant by Kolchak. Wilton was an entirely different matter altogether, unofficially attaching himself to the investigation and in some ways was detrimental to it because he was not liked and unreliable, which was the description given of him by the newspaper he worked for.

Harbin was 300 miles from Vladivostok as the crow flies, a town founded by Nicholas II in 1898 to support the construction of the Chinese Eastern Railway extension of the Siberian Railway. Today it sits within China's northernmost province of Heilongjiang. It was a White movement redoubt for officers, politicians, ministers and anyone that wanted to flee the Bolsheviks or move between Asia and Europe. For example, in 1919 the last of the Shirinsky-Shikhmatov family left their home town Kasimov; situated on the left bank of the Oka River, 158 miles southeast of Moscow as the crow flies. They were descendants of the Tatars, the people that came from the Mongol Empire, Genghis Khan and the Tatar princes – a common ancestry for noble families of the Russian Empire. Many of them joined the White movement and had been pushed to Vladivostok and subsequently out of Russia and ended up in Harbin.

The Sokolov Box, it is kept at the Russian Orthodox
Church of Saint Job in Uccle, Brussels.

One notable of that family was Prince Alexei Alexandrovich Shirinsky-Shikhmatov (1862-1930). He worked in law under several capacities for the Holy Synod. While the royal family were under house arrest he tried to organise a rescue without success and left Russia on 1 September 1918 but was to play a significant role in helping Sokolov to move his wooden boxes.

Despite arriving in Harbin with his family and assistants, Sokolov wrote that after admiral Kolchak was executed on 7 February 1920, the situation in Harbin was dire for them, he had no funds and there was some confusion over the cargo which arrived on separate trains from the British and the Americans. The confusion was over what to do with it. Sokolov contacted Miles Lampson for an explanation and asked that he be permitted to take the remains of the royal family (i.e. the Sokolov Box) to Britain. Lampson was in Beijing at the time so his secretary was dispatched to Harbin, arriving on 23 February 1920 to discuss the matter further. A little later on 19 March 1920 Sokolov was told that the British government would not accept him or any of his cargo and certainly not the alleged remains of the royal family which he had presumed was his ticket to London.

Dieterichs was also in Harbin, and with Sokolov, together they found General Maurice Janin, the Commander of the French Mission in Siberia, in charge of the Czech-Slovak Legion of the White Army. He was heading for Paris and had a special train arranged going to Vladivostok. He agreed passage for Sokolov and his wife, his assistant Bulygin, and the cargo. According to Sokolov it was thanks to Janin that the investigation evidence got out of Russia with the extra help from two Russians that he names Kupets and Shchelokov of whom he says, understanding of his mission, gifted him a gold ingot to the value of 3,000 yen which Sokolov used to get established in Paris.

Sokolov was once more in control with the Sokolov Box with him and the other containers in the trusted care of General Janin. When the train reached Vladivostok they boarded the French refugee ship S.S. André le Bon (aka Lebon). Built in 1914 it had served as a troopship then as a hospital ship from 1916 and in 1919 had recently returned to its owners and was placed on the Marseilles to Yokohama service. It arrived at Vladivostok delivering troops for the Whites, for the battle that was raging there. Sokolov's entourage boarded the euro-asian passenger liner along with many others leaving the zone, like tutors Pierre Gilliard and Charles Sydney Gibbes, Rozonov's daughter Anna Sergeyevna Rozanov-Naryshkin and her husband Kiril Naryshkin.

The Naryshkins shared a cabin with Sokolov and his wife. The Sokolov Box was kept hidden under Anna Rozanov's berth. She confessed to her future grandson Captain Peter Sarandinaki that she had once opened it and seen a finger inside. Sokolov was paranoid that there were secret agents onboard specifically assigned to part him from his relics. One account says

CHAPTER XX

that he feared German agents mostly because he carried documents that proved the German involvement in the executions of the ex-tsar and ex-tsarevich. Sokolov continued to look over his shoulder even after he settled in Paris believing that British as well as German intelligence agents were constantly watching him.

The ship sailed 4,014 nautical miles to the port of Colombo, Sri Lanka. There the Sokolovs and Rozanov-Naryshkins transferred to another ship taking them a further 5,452 nautical miles to Porto di Venezia, Italy. General Rozanov had not gone with them but had returned from Vladivostok to Harbin where he and Dieterichs had outstanding matters to attend to relating to the eight coffins that had arrived from Alapayevsk; six Romanovs and two aides (*appendices page 498*). Alapayevsk was a comparatively large iron smelting town with the only notable point being composer Pyotr Ilyich Tchaikovsky had lived there for a short time as a child.

The Romanov prisoners had arrived at the Perm internment camp on 20 May 1918 and were murdered two months later by the occupying Bolsheviks. The corpses were found in a pit by the White Army on 28 August 1918 (G), a month after the town was liberated and the bodies reburied at a nearby church for little under a year before the Red Army were again at the gates of Alapayevsk in July 1919. The White Army retrieved eight of the coffins and transported them ever eastwards across the length of the Russian interior until they finally arrived at Harbin in March 1920. Rozanov and Dieterichs ensured the coffins reached Beijing in April 1920 to be interred at the Russian Spiritual Mission, in a small Orthodox cemetery just by the city wall.

The British ambassador in Beijing Miles Lampson and General Rozanov settled there for a time before Rozanov moved to Meudon, France to reunite with his family, where he died in 1937. The coffins of Elizabeth Feodorovna and her companion nun, the former lady in waiting Varvara Yakovleva, were recovered in the future and taken to Jerusalem where they were laid to rest in the Russian Orthodox Church of Mary Magdalene, on the Mount of Olives, a church that was constructed by the sons of Tsar Alexander II and consecrated in 1888 in the presence of Elizabeth Feodorovna and her husband Sergei Alexandrovich.

Meanwhile, Janin was still in Harbin waiting on a decision on what to do with the three containers from the Sokolov Commission. That decision lay with Nikolai Nikolaevich (uncle to Nicholas II), de facto Commander in Chief of the White movement since Kolchak's execution on 7 February 1920. On that day the files of the victims at Alapayevsk had passed to Sokolov. Things had not been as straight forward with the containers and General Janin was ordered to take the cargo to Nikolai Nikolaevich at his residence in Venice where he was living in exile. Janin did as he was ordered and delivered the cargo to Venice in to the care of Mikhail Nikolaevich de

Giers who up until 1917 was the Russian ambassador in Italy and someone that would know where to store the cargo; perhaps he had even considered taking it across the border to Switzerland for long term protection.

By the time Sokolov arrived in Venice, Nikolai Nikolaevich had moved to the French Riviera. Sokolov and Kiril Naryshkin (*page 451*) tried to track him down without success and ended up settling in Paris at the Hotel du Bon Lafontaine, without the cargo; at the same residence where Pierre Gilliard and his wife Alexandra Tegleva were staying and other notable émigrés. Eventually Sokolov received a response from Nikolai Nikolaevich that he would not receive the boxes because Maria Feodorovna refused to accept that her family were dead. One source says this meeting took place at the French Riviera – Robert K. Massie. Another source says they were unsuccessful at trying to meet with Nikolai Nikolaevich – Greg King & Penny Wilson, which was in fact the case.

Sokolov knew precisely what was in the missing containers because he itemised everything but he would never see them again. He tried desperately to locate them and doubtless had learned in Venice that they had gone under the protection of de Giers. In his memoirs he said that he was unable to 'recover' the cargo, suggesting that he knew where it was. No one was really talking to Sokolov so he started to write a book making a great effort to interview as many relevant people as he could locate. As far as the world knew, the Romanov remains had quietly sailed over the horizon.

The Gajda Investigation

The Sokolov dossier at Harvard University was examined in 1971 by BBC researchers Anthony Summers and Tom Mangold for a television documentary. They had been told by Sir Anthony Royle, a former Under Secretary of State at the British Foreign Office, that a dossier existed from Naval Intelligence containing the details of a rescue mission for the tsar. Summers & Mangold retrieved a package containing some unpublished and therefore previously unknown interviews conducted by Nikolai Sokolov which suggested the royal family were transferred to Perm on the night of 16/17 July 1918. It was the same date given for the official version of events for the murders of the prisoners at Ipatiev House, suggesting that they had been removed from Ipatiev House and others had been murdered in their place to fit with the official line that they had all perished. Why would the Bolsheviks save the Romanov females unless it had been already agreed and the Bolsheviks could benefit by it.

Sokolov did not investigate the contents of the naval file in his work. It can be assumed that he might not have been privy to the secret negotiations but he surely knew of the file. Writing his book in Paris, he was miles apart from Cheka agents and still didn't discuss it – why? The Bolsheviks were in

CHAPTER XX

negotiations with the Germans and the British whose secret intelligence agents were prominent in Paris, so it's not unreasonable to assume that they had good reason to keep Sokolov quiet. Several authors in Paris were investigating the rumours of a survival story and they were silenced; one had his house set on fire and another was killed. It appears that someone was suppressing information arising from the Gajda Investigation that purported the Romanov females were alive.

The book that came from the research by Summers & Mangold, *The File On The Tsar – The Fate of the Romanovs – Dramatic New Evidence* (1976) initially received great reviews but had some criticism in the New York Times. The official line that the ex-tsar was executed and that the rest of the prisoners were relocated, was also the view held by Summers & Mangold, except that the authorities said that they had lost track of the Romanov females in the ensuing confusion whereas Summers & Mangold believed they were secretly hidden for months and had been disposed of when the negotiations broke down and which this book suggests happened because Winston Churchill continued to support the White Army with supplies.

Summers & Mangold offered an explanation that the ex-tsar and ex-tsarevich were killed at the military camp in Perm and not at Ipatiev House. The book which was based largely on material from the Gajda Investigation generally believed that the royal family had been removed to Perm while the negotiations were taking place between the Bolsheviks and Germans. This was not German led to free the prisoners but Bolshevik led to gain leverage over German incursions. The theory goes that when negotiations had ceased the ex-tsar and ex-tsarevich were taken back to Ipatiev House and executed and their corpses then taken to the Four Brothers mine at Ganina Yama for disposal. The official version and the Summers & Mangold book are not that far apart but the book at least discusses alternatives based on the information from the Gajda Investigation that was available to the authorities at the time but which was mysteriously ignored by the Sokolov Commission.

The negotiations at Perm lasted until the end of 1918 when Germany surrendered in the war and the Red Army retook Perm after which the respective positions of influence between the Bolsheviks and the Germans drastically changed. At this point Germany may have made concessions that involved supporting the removal of the ex-tsar and ex-tsarevich in exchange for the Romanov females, details of which German Intelligence feared was in Sokolov's possession. If the Romanov females really were imprisoned at Perm then it stands to reason that they needed to be moved before the Perm camp was overrun. The story goes that they were taken south heading towards Kazan, as there were witnesses along that journey. The Gajda Investigation and Summers & Mangold lose track of the Romanov females on that journey and so the presumption is made that they must have met with their fateful end before reaching Kazan.

THE OFFICIAL INVESTIGATIONS

In an interview given by the commander of the special detachment at Tsarskoe Selo, Colonel Eugene Kobylinsky, to the Sokolov Commission, he revealed that the ex-tsar's valet Chemodurov, who spent the first three weeks at Ipatiev House before being transferred to prison, had believed the royal family were alive even after the announcement of their execution. This simple statement supported the other interviews of the Gajda Investigation but Chemodurov was not taken seriously because how could he have known anything for sure when he was incarcerated. Sokolov came across many conflicting statements like this that didn't make it in to his investigation or the pages of his later book, albeit he died before it was finished.

Another variation of the ex-tsar being executed separately to the Romanov females is known as the 'lone execution theory' and is mentioned by several sources including *Pravda* (truth) which reported that the ex-tsar was taken from Ekaterinburg in mid June 1918, a month prior to the official date of the murders. The story goes that the royal family were moved to the military camp at Perm during the discussions between the Bolsheviks and the Germans. Lenin's view almost certainly was that the ex-tsar and his heir had to die if the Romanov females were to live. Nicholas must have known that his and his son's death were prerequisites for the royal family's survival. At this time the negotiations were going well since the Keiser personally intervened following the assassination of Mirbach on 6 July 1918. The Bolsheviks feared a full German invasion and were receptive to negotiations knowing there to be little hope for the ex-tsar and turning their focus on negotiations for Alexandra because of her German background which naturally included her children.

Mirbach's interim replacement at the German mission in Moscow was Dr Rietzler who on 23 July 1918 visited Georgy Vasilyevich Chicherin, who since March 1918 was the first Commissar for Foreign Affairs in the new Soviet government. Chicherin had acted as Leon Trotsky's deputy during the negotiations that led to the Treaty of Brest-Litovsk. Now Dr Rietzler was before Chicherin warning him of the implications of any harm coming to the Romanov females. "*Chicherin listened to my ideas in silence,*" said Dr Rietzler. But Chicherin's pro-German policy was not enough to interfere with the plans of the Moscow Bolsheviks who saw no way out of murdering the entire royal family after negotiations had broken down. The evidence that Germany was negotiating to recover the Romanov females is confirmed by Sokolov, "*On 14 June 1921, I was received in Berlin by Dr Rietzler. He is familiar with and gave me the contents of four German official documents. September of the same year I received copies of them.*" One of these documents contained the proof that the Germans believed the Romanov females were alive and that they were negotiating for their release.

Lenin knew that to kill the royal family meant his regime would never be accepted by any foreign government, but the death of the emperor alone

CHAPTER XX

would be acceptable for the outcome of a revolution. Bolshevik discussions were apace, with Filipp Goloshchekin moving between Moscow and the Urals meeting Lenin, Sverdlov and Beloborodov, during which time the decision to execute the ex-tsar alone was made. Goloshchekin sided with the decision but Beloborodov was under mounting pressure from Bolshevik hardliners to kill all the prisoners at Ekaterinburg and Perm. Sverdlov would have the final decision nearer the time with the authority to change the plan as he saw fit. Historians agree that these were probably the busiest and most complicated few months in Russia's history; so the question arises - what was it that persuaded Sverdlov between 6 July and 16 July 1918 to go against Lenin's order to kill only the ex-tsar, and decide to murder all of the prisoners?

In those final days before the official murders of 16 July 1918, Yurovsky was pressing Goloshchekin for the confirmation to proceed. Goloshchekin was pressing Sverdlov who in turn was waiting on Beloborodov for an update on the negotiations with Germany. The killings took place two days after Goloshchekin returned to Ekaterinburg from Moscow and it would seem everyone was in agreement to kill only the ex-tsar and his son, so once more the question beckons why Sverdlov changed the orders. But of course, the Gajda report suggested that it had not been the royal family that was actually executed on that fateful night. Assuming the ex-tsar, the ex-tsarevich and the Romanov females were already imprisoned at Perm, on the official date of the murders, then Sverdlov's decision makes sense because he knew that it was not the Romanov females that were being executed at Ipatiev House.

The theory that the royal family were in Perm comes from Sokolov's naval file that Summers & Mangold had located at Harvard. The lone execution theory has it that having made the decision to kill only the tsar, he was taken from his cell by Red guards without prior warning and while they walked was told that he was being taken to his execution. His composure was said by the guards to be calm and he asked to speak with his family one last time which was denied him, suggesting they were nearby as Ekaterinburg is 200 miles to the southeast of Perm as the crow flies.

A slight variation of the lone execution theory is that the ex-tsar was instead taken from Perm directly to Ganina Yama for his execution. The Gajda report is made of many conflicting stories like this but each deserves consideration such as Chemodurov's statement mentioned earlier (*previous page*). There were also reports published in *Pravda* which explicitly recorded the royal family moving from Ekaterinburg to Perm and a report from Sir Charles Eliot (*page 415*) stating that the Romanov females left Ekaterinburg by train on 17 July 1918 and at least one witness claimed to have seen the royal family leaving Ipatiev House in the middle of the night. One could easily overlook the Gajda report but corroboration in this instance is provided by the official Communist newspaper itself and a British Lord which raises the question of why these reports were similar.

THE OFFICIAL INVESTIGATIONS

There is more evidence to support the story that the Romanov females were imprisoned at Perm for five months after the ex-tsar's execution until 24 December 1918 when the town fell to the White Army. At that time one account states they were killed and another that they were moved to Kazan. It's not clear whether the ex-tsarevich was shot with his father because one account states that he died some weeks earlier from an accident that possibly required medical treatment that was not provided. Nicholas II's Majordomo Parfen Dominin published his account of these final weeks and confirmed that, *"The former heir to the Imperial throne, Alexei Nikolaevich, was ill all the time. Once he was coughing and spitting blood."*

To accept the Gajda Investigation and the book from Summers & Mangold is to entertain the alternative and unofficial version of events. Once on that road, it's easy to read in to things that are purely speculative. For example, in siding with the theory that the Romanov females were killed in Perm because the White Army was approaching then it can be demonstrated how murderous the Red Army were before they were overrun; a French Intelligence agent who arrived with the liberating White Army reported that *"... all the children under the age of one are dead,"* strengthening the possibility that the Romanov females would similarly not have been spared. The observation that personal items were deliberately left for White Army investigators to be found is strengthened by one revelation that most of the jewellery items were recovered at the house and most of the clothes were found at the Four Brothers pit; an observation that in itself means nothing more than coincidence unless one wishes to be convinced of a conspiracy. A problem for an alternative theory is that the bodies were discovered many decades later and using DNA profiling were proved to belong to the royal family members, somewhat obfuscating theories of survivors.

The likeliest scenario assuming the Romanov females were in Perm is that they did eventually leave, evidenced by several accounts from witnesses that saw them outside of Perm. The testaments from the Gajda report imply that there were people murdered at Ipatiev House in place of the Romanov females. All of the anomalies discussed only make sense when accepting that the Ipatiev House scene was staged - the incompetent cleaning detail; the evidence found at the house (blood and bullets) and at the mine (jewels and clothing); items appearing to be laid out deliberately to identify victims; and, why so much effort had gone in to making things look like the prisoners were in a great rush with the approaching White Army on their heels. It also neatly explains why the Gajda Investigation was passed to Sokolov for it to be suppressed and why Sokolov didn't mention anything in his writings.

So it comes full circle to determine the legitimacy of the Gajda report and a slight backtracking is needed. General Gajda had accepted an offer to join Admiral Kolchak's forces and played a significant role in securing the Siberian Railway. He would also play a large part in the formation of

CHAPTER XX

Czechoslovakia at the end of World War I (28 October 1918). Essentially he was an Austrian fascist holding the nickname of the Czech Führer and was eventually driven out of the Army in 1926 having made enemies of Czech President T. G. Masaryk and Foreign Minister Edvard Beneš.

On 23 July 1918 Gajda's Czech-Slovak troops liberated Ekaterinburg and then Alapayevsk on 28 September 1918 and Perm on Christmas Eve 1918. He was therefore au fait with what had taken place at Ipatiev House and Sokolov's investigation report on the murders of the royal family. After taking Perm he set up his own investigation that was handled by the new Criminal Investigating Division (CID) being more of a military affair unlike Sokolov's judicial inquiry and separate to the Sokolov Commission. It was centred in Perm and became the alternative version of events to the official line of what had happened in Perm. CID agents soon established that the royal family had been moved to Perm and that the ex-tsar and ex-tsarevich had been returned to Ekaterinburg to be shot. The man with many enemies, General Gajda, had done history a favour in digging for the truth.

CID collected statements confirming that the Romanov females had been in Perm including a very credible witness statement from a local nurse called Natalya Mutnykh whose brother was a Cheka agent working directly for the Chairman of the Ural Soviet, Beloborodov. Her story and statements are a matter taken up in the book of Summers & Mangold in chapter 25. From the main points of her final statement she said that the ex-tsar and ex-tsarevich were executed just outside of Ekaterinburg; pointing to Ganina Yama. The Romanov females were being held by the Regional Soviet at the Excise Office on Obvinskaya Street until one of them tried to escape so they were moved to the more secure Berezin House on the same street, in the basement with no electricity nor furniture. Mutnykh once visited with her Cheka brother and described them as looking poorly.

Natalya Mutnykh found the room lit by a single candle and the Romanov females sleeping on pallets without sheets nor other bedding. A second escape was attempted which resulted in the death of one of the girls, not identified. One account says the escapee was Anastasia and that she got away and managed to get to Berlin; turning up eventually as the so-called Anna Anderson (*page 433*). The remaining Romanov females were again moved, according to Mutnykh, "*... to a convent under more strict arrest.*" That convent according to another account was somewhere in the Urals. CID located several witnesses that saw the Romanov females moving away from Perm but it's not known whether they were travelling north to the convent or south to Kazan. The reason for the uncertainty is that when the Bolsheviks left Ekaterinburg they went in the direction of Verkhoturye, 224 miles to the north, situated in the middle of the Ural Mountains on the left bank of the Tura River. If the prisoners went to the convent there, then do we believe they lived out their lives in religious service and was this location something to do with the convent founded by Alexandra's sister, Elizabeth Feodorovna, who were helping. It's easy to believe the deeply religious Alexandra Feodorovna would take holy orders but not so easy to accept that three young daughters could live out their lives under such secrecy in a convent.

The Soviet were always looking to finance their own cause. There is a theory that says the Romanov females were killed because so much Romanov treasure had been stolen that the legitimate owners had to be disposed of so that the items could never be identified. The treasure was contained in two railway carriages sitting at Perm since 7 February 1918 when Bolshevik forces began arresting local leaders and nobles. February 1918 was also coincidentally when the anti-Bolshevik Provisional Government of Siberia (PGS) was forced out of Ekaterinburg by Bolshevik forces and fled further eastwards to re-establish itself at Chita. Following major Red Army counter offensives in 1919 the PGS would flee again to Harbin and Vladivostok, the last strongholds. This somewhat lost track of the mass of gold and jewels that had accumulated in Perm of which the Gajda Investigation located much.

From Sokolov's book, "*We have already reported that her* [Alexandra] *stock of gold has been taken from here* [Ekaterinburg] *for two are on the wheels of Perm.*" This indicates treasure was taken from Ekaterinburg. However, the White Army counter offensive that first threatened Perm meant that this train had returned to Ekaterinburg but as the White Army approached Ekaterinburg in June 1918 again the train was sent back to Perm and later would be sent on to Moscow. Sokolov managed to compile an inventory of the contents of the carriages for his book and confirmed that the treasure was, "*sent from Ekaterinburg to Moscow.*"

He also recorded a statement from a guard called P. Lylov of the Ural Regional Soviet who said on 4 September 1918 that the majority of the treasure was collected during the flight of the Bolsheviks from Ekaterinburg and he incriminated Beloborodov who according to Sokolov, "*kidnapped,*" the treasures. It can be seen that as well as an organised collection of wealth by the Moscow Soviet, the Bolsheviks were prolific pilferers. White Army investigators found valuables at the homes of the Ipatiev House guards with Lylov himself possessing gold crosses taken from the corpses in the cellar among other items that were found at his house.

Gajda and Kolchak were destined to fall out and on 5 July 1919 Gajda was dismissed for leading the revolt against Kolchak. The Gajda Investigation came to an end and the CID dossier went over to the new commander in the Urals, General Dieterichs who stopped all further CID involvement and forwarded the entire Gajda dossier to his newly appointed investigator Nikolai Sokolov. Thereafter everything related to the victims was sent to Sokolov. Unfortunately he made little use of the CID material and effectively buried it. He was aware of its contents as he signed every document on receipt in to the Commission dossier. How curious he must have been to receive so

CHAPTER XX

much new material from a parallel investigation and he must have been totally overwhelmed by the sheer amount and imagine the scene when he realised much of it contradicted his own findings. In fairness, he didn't have any time or opportunity to look in to the new evidence and evaluate it.

One imagines that when Sokolov settled in Paris and started to work on his book, his time would have been filled with researching his own leads and not unravelling the entirety of the Gajda material. Even so, it is a shame that at the very least, the testament from Natalya Mutnykh wasn't explored and that it hasn't featured more prominently in the Romanov story, considering the validity of her source, Beloborodov, who was one of the three men that knew the unfiltered truth of what had happened to the prisoners. Such a substantiated testament is not found anywhere else but remains recorded in the Gajda report and in the book by Summers & Mangold for future scrutiny. Perhaps Sokolov just didn't write about matters that he had not personally investigated or maybe he had plans for a second book, before he died prematurely.

By and large the men directly responsible for the Russian Revolution 1917 lived out their lives in Moscow, except for Leon Trotsky who in 1938 opposed Stalin and was assassinated in August 1940 in Mexico City by Ramón Mercader, an agent of the Soviet NKVD. The organisers of the Romanov murders, except for Sverdlov who died in March 1919 at thirty-three years old, all lived for some years.

Yurovsky never expressed remorse and donated his guns to the Museum of the Revolution in Moscow, and was to see his wife and sons die before he too died in 1938 in physical and mental agony. Beloborodov was shot in 1938. Goloshchekin was shot on 28 October 1941 by a monarchist. Ermakov was shot in 1939 (Victor Alexandrov - *The End of the Romanovs* – page 244) or died of cancer in May 1952 (Wikipedia).

CHAPTER XXI
The Search For The Remains

HAD there been no remarkable world events during 1918 then the Romanov females may well have made it out of Russia but Germany had lost leverage since Lenin moved the Bolshevik government to Moscow on 12 March 1918 and renamed the Bolshevik party to the Russian Communist Party. German ambassador Mirbach was assassinated in July 1918 and Keiser Wilhelm II abdicated on 9 November 1918 with Germany surrendering to the Allied Powers two days later. The German negotiating team had faced impossible odds in their attempts to secure the release of the Romanov females and were finally pushed aside. The White Army were searching for bodies and the Civil War was raging.

The Last Tango In Paris

Meanwhile Russian escapees were arriving in France and the most liberal capital in Europe filled with talk of the Russian Revolution 1917 and the fate of the Russian royal family. For many of Russia's well to do Paris was already a second home and those not already established there, they would depend to some extent on the émigré community for support. Many turned to writing their memoirs and published their work in Paris, London, New York and Berlin, where the active publishing centres were based; Paris being by far the most popular destination. Mentioned earlier (*page 444*), Gustav Telberg was one of the first to publish the story of the fate of the Romanovs with, *The Last Days of the Romanovs* (1920). Sokolov also arrived in Paris not far behind him and completed the Sokolov Investigation.

Sokolov used the remaining four years of his life to bring his research together in the book *Judicial Inquiry into the assassination of the Russian Imperial Family*. It was a definitive work when the French edition was

CHAPTER XXI

published in 1924 posthumously, and then in Berlin in 1925. Like others working on their memoirs he was strapped for cash and needed to write to survive but he also had benefactors and received a respectable amount from Maria Feodorovna to continue his research and received a regular amount from Count Nikolai Vladimirovich Orlov. He arranged to meet with Maria Feodorovna in Denmark but at the last minute her daughter Olga Alexandrovna sent a telegram to Paris cancelling the meeting believing it would be too traumatic for such a poorly woman to learn the terrible truth. Although they never met, her support kept the search for the royal family alive for a time. Sokolov did offer a sliver of hope after he interviewed Alexander Dolgoruky, also living in exile in Paris, who was the source of the rumour that some of the royal family members had survived the massacre at Ipatiev House (*page 414*).

Sokolov met the forty-eight year old ex-general Alexander Dolgoruky on 5 February 1921 but the interview was omitted from Sokolov's book as he did not consider accounts that contradicted the official line albeit the type of material that sold books. Some might view the omission as a kindness to Maria Feodorovna so as not to give her a false hope in the same way that Nikolai Nikolaevich had not accepted the Sokolov Box. Perhaps the reason was that Dolgoruky's information was simply old hat following the discovery of a manuscript by Mikhail Pokrovsky, the author of Yurovsky's memoirs (i.e. the testimony of the chief executioner,) which put an end to rumours of any survivors.

Sokolov's other benefactor, the Orlov family, were long respected descendants of Count Grigori Grigoryevich Orlov (*page 57*). Orlov's reward back then had been the creation of the charter of the Orlov title in 1763. Vladimir Nikolaevich Orlov (1868–1927) was one of Nicholas II's closest advisors who along with Interior Minister Vladimir Dzhunkovsky (appointed in 1913,) had tried to discredit Alexandra and Rasputin in a newspaper and they were consequently banished to the Caucasus. Vladimir Orlov was in Paris from 1920 with other likeminded anti-Bolshevik émigrés like de Giers, that believed the revolution had been a necessary transition for a new Russia. His son Nikolai Vladimirovich Orlov was the husband of Princess Nadejda Petrovna, a daughter of Grand Duke Peter Nikolaevich and Princess Milica of Montenegro. They were among the nobility that left Crimea on HMS Marlborough in 1919. Now in Paris, Nikolai Orlov provided Sokolov with regular funding and accommodation on the Orlov estate just slightly southeast of Paris.

In the early 1920s German Intelligence was largely dismantled and no one had yet seen a royal survivor, they existed only in testaments collected by the Gajda Investigation. So with the investigation dossiers closed, why was Sokolov found dead in his garden in Salbris under mysterious circumstances on 23 November 1924, he was forty-one years old. Sokolov is buried at the

Salbris Cemetery and on his grave is written "*Your Truth is Truth forever.*" The Sokolov Commission had answered many issues such as how messages were communicated between the prisoners under house arrest and the outside world. Sokolov had discovered notes were smuggled out by the priests Fr Meledin and Fr Storozhev during the occasional Sunday Service that was still permitted at Ipatiev House, before the arrival of Yurovsky.

It was a dangerous activity and Yurovsky tried several times to catch the ex-tsar in the act of planning an escape and even encouraged an escape so that he could be caught and shot for attempting to evade justice for crimes against the people. One story goes that a note was found with information about the numbers and routines of the guards at Ipatiev House which included the location of a machine gun post. Yurovsky's trap went nowhere and he eventually would have realised that there was no longer the need for incrimination because the ex-tsar was as good as dead anyway.

Majordomo Parfen Alexievitch Dominin began service for Nicholas II in 1896 and accompanied him under house arrest. He kept a record of what took place in the final hours of the ex-tsar's life which explained in detail the moment Nicholas II believed that his execution was imminent. According to Carl William Ackerman, a foreign war correspondent for The New York Times working in Siberia, Dominin's account is the only authentic version of the events of those last hours. The quote below was written in Russian and most probably translated for Ackerman:

> "One day the former Tsar returned to the house from his walk in the garden. He was unusually excited and after fervent prayers before an icon of Holy Nicholas the Thaumaturgist he lay down on a little bed without undressing. This he never did before. '*Please allow me to undress you and make the bed,*' I said to the Tsar. '*Don't trouble yourself old man,*' the Tsar said, '*I feel in my heart I shall live only a short time.*' " — P. DOMININ, 15 July 1918

We venture back to the Gajda Investigation. On the late evening of 15 July 1918 the Commissary of the Guard came for Nicholas II and delivered him to the Ural District Soviet. He asked "*Tell me straight, are you taking me to be shot?*" and was told nothing would happen to him until a decision was made. The kangaroo court took place at midnight. The ex-tsar stood alone without representation, dressed in his standard basic military attire facing a council of the Soviet District of Workers, Cossacks and Red Army Deputies. He was accused of conspiring in a rescue attempt with leaders of the rescue committee Generals Dutov and Dogert. Dogert had passed the ex-tsar notes informing him to be ready for a rescue, and it was Dogert's notes that now incriminated the ex-tsar who stood accused of a counter-revolutionary plot to escape in order to reorganise to suppress the workers.

CHAPTER XXI

The soviet feared an escape because it would have the effect of rallying the people behind the White movement to return Nicholas II to the throne. Two and a half hours later he was back in his room at Ipatiev House and told Dominin *"They have informed me that I shall be shot within three hours."* In this theory the ex-tsar was only permitted to see his wife and son alone before his departure and they had both cried hysterically and were inconsolable up to the last moment he left them. Dominin did not know where the ex-tsar was taken but knew enough that in the early hours of 16 July 1918 he had been shot by a firing squad of around twenty guards.

This was the 'lone execution theory. The remaining members of the royal family were told they were being moved and to pack lightly, no more than between 30-40 pounds each. Dominin didn't know where they were taken either, only that they left immediately in a truck. This fascinating account was from the reporter Carl Ackerman who arrived in Ekaterinburg towards the end of 1918 when the press believed the ex-tsar was dead because there had been no news about him for some time. Then, a statement was released by Lieutenant Michael de Tchihatcheff that the ex-tsar and his family were alive. His statement appeared in an Associated Press dispatch from Warsaw on 24 December 1918 and contradicted the official line that the ex-tsar had already been shot.

Tchihatcheff was an interpreter to the British Russian Expeditionary Force. He would eventually move to the UK but was unfairly judged to be working for Russian Intelligence. Why did Tchihatcheff believe that the ex-tsar was alive five months after the official line had stated that he was dead? This would confirm that the former Imperial Family had been together at Perm for five months before the ex-tsar was shot alone. However, Ackerman reported in January 1919 that the ex-tsar had been shot which, rather suspiciously the New York Times retracted a month later.

"I have obtained the first eyewitness account of the Tsar's last days under the Bolsheviks and of his trial and brief farewell to his family, which shows that until his very last hour Nicholas Romanov was intriguing with his military leaders for the restoration of the monarchy, and that it was the discovery of this plot by the Ural District Soviet which caused the order to be given for his execution."
— CARL W. ACKERMAN, The New York Times, 22 December 1918

The many accounts at this time from authors and reporters alike vary so much that it's hard to know with certainty which was the prevailing theory. Sokolov's unfinished book was published in Russian soon after his death but modern experts have commented that there are signs of extensive editing by a third party, begging the question; who edited this important work and more importantly, why? Maybe it was just line editing to prepare the manuscript for publication or perhaps someone had censored it. On his death his research disappeared without a trace which is manna from heaven for a conspiracy theory.

Recovering The Relics

The safe keeping of the Romanov remains and other items from the Sokolov Investigation that left Russia must have been discussed by the principal émigrés in Paris, the de facto headquarters of Russian exiles. For the monarchists these relics of the royal family were as sacred as the Turin shroud to Christians. In the event of a death of one of the custodians such as Sokolov, it is inconceivable that they would not have considered a contingency for the safe keeping of these valued artefacts. When Nikolai Nikolaevich refused to accept the Sokolov Box, Sokolov took it to exiled officials at the Russian Orthodox Church Abroad Memorial of Saint Job in Brussels, where it was gratefully accepted. They also accepted his conclusion that the bodies of the royal family had been disposed of at Ganina Yama and that they now possessed the remains in their entirety. This was the belief until the discovery of the graves many decades later. The Orthodox Church in Russia never acknowledge the remains even then, until the advent of DNA profiling when everything was re-evaluated.

When the church in Brussels was demolished to rebuild a new one in 1938, two containers lined with lead were discovered in a wall. One contained a letter itemising the contents of the boxes and giving the chain of custody from Sokolov, to Prince Alexei Alexandrovich Shirinsky-Shikhmatov (*page 450*) and on his death in 1930 it passed to his son who handed them over to the Russian Orthodox Church Abroad. So this was how in actuality, the Sokolov Box passed from Sokolov to the Russian Orthodox Church Abroad. Sometime after 1930 the relics were placed in lead lined containers and hidden in a wall. It was unfortunate that as soon as 1938, the wall was demolished to reveal the containers. Inside were found glass jars filled with soil and tissue from Ganina Yama, intended for future investigators with better forensic techniques. The contents were kept at a church in Paris until construction was completed in Brussels and then moved back there, where they have remained ever since.

Perhaps the Shirinsky-Shikhmatov's had provided the lead containers but was the need to hide them indicative of a third party actively searching Paris for Romanov artifacts, particularly since Sokolov's mysterious death in 1924 when his documents had disappeared. Was it necessary for the same reason that the flask containing Alexandra Feodorovna's finger was sent to New York. Who knows what became of the chest in the possession of Mikhail Nikolaevich de Giers; more is known about the two wooden boxes.

CHAPTER XXI

De Giers came from a wealthy family of politicians; notably his father Nikolay de Giers had been the Foreign Minister responsible for the Franco-Russian Alliance. Mikhail de Giers was more famed for being the last Russian ambassador in Constantinople but it was after the Russian Revolution 1917 that he really thrived and would form the Council of Ambassadors in Paris as Russia's representation abroad, simultaneously chairing several committees pertaining to Russian interests abroad. Historian Boris Nolde said the following about Mikhail de Giers:

"... his whole approach to life found its expression, inspired by the awareness that the age-long and everlasting interests of Russia, the Russian people and the Russian state, were above any transient forces and even above the regime itself." — BORIS NOLDE, historian

The *Petit Journal* confirmed in December 1930 that General Maurice Janin (Commander of the French Mission in Siberia) had indeed delivered Sokolov's wooden boxes to Mikhail de Giers of whom it's known, kept hold of them until he died in 1932, despite attempts to take them from him by the self-proclaimed Russian Emperor-in-exile Kirill Vladimirovich. After Kirill's proclamation in 1924 that he was the supreme leader of the Romanov family, he approached Nikolai Nikolaevich enquiring about the relics. Nikolai Nikolaevich disliked Kirill intensely and was therefore very uncooperative so Kirill had approached de Giers directly who considered it his solemn duty to guard the relics and declared their location to be a 'state' secret (of the Russian monarchist government abroad,) even from the Romanovs. Could Kirill have been the third party that was searching Europe for Romanov artefacts during the early 1930s, there would appear to be no better candidate. Was it also a coincidence that on Kirill's death in 1938 the relics hidden in the wall were discovered as if there was no longer the need for them to remain hidden.

De Giers outlived Sokolov (d. 1924) and Vladimir Orlov (d. 1927) but not Kirill Vladimirovich. Kirill had been supportive of the Provisional Government in 1917 but during the uprisings that summer he went to Finland before the October Revolution 1917 with his wife Victoria and they escaped in 1920 to Coburg, staying there with Victoria's family for several years. They bought a small estate in Saint Briac, a small fishing village in northwestern France. Kirill settled there and joined the collective of memoir writers in producing his book, *My life in Russia's service* (1939).

When Mikhail Alexandrovich (Nicholas II's brother) was ruled legally dead in a London court in July 1924, Kirill had proclaimed himself as head of the Romanov family and in 1926 elevated himself further to emperor, to the amusement of existing family members such as Maria Feodorovna and Nikolai Nikolaevich, being the root of the present day divisions in the family. Not unsurprisingly, despite Kirill's efforts, when de Giers died in 1932 the wooden boxes passed to the Orlov estate and were inherited by Nikolai Vladimirovich Orlov. Rather interestingly Orlov had written the preface for Sokolov's publication of the Sokolov investigation, first published in Russian as *The Case of Nicholas II's Murder* (1919). The English version (1920), translated by William Sutcliffe, did not contain Orlov's preface. A roughly translated extract from the preface is, "*He* [Sokolov] *decided to announce the truth himself, from himself, and not under the flag of any political party.*" Orlov's wife Princess Nadejda Petrovna when she died in 1988 at ninety years old was for some years the oldest that was deceased of the émigrés that had escaped Russia.

Unlike the many Russian émigrés that sowed permanence in France, Nikolai Orlov went to America working as an United Nations interpreter and was considered to be an active KGB agent. The best explanation for what happened to the wooden boxes is provided by author Victor Alexandrov in his successful book *The End of the Romanovs* (1966) which was lauded for its unique perspective but also criticised for containing wrongly labelled images and other discrepancies. The details are spurious, like the author was providing a theory based on a dubious source that he considered important enough to present in the four page timeline 'Historical Outline' in the front matter. Despite its vagueness it confirmed that Orlov didn't take the wooden boxes to Canada with him because they turned up at the Salle Drouot auction house in Paris and the lots of 'objects, paintings and mementoes.' were all purchased on 9 October 1950 by M. I. Gurvich.

Alexandrov made an entry in the timeline for April 1962 that Orlov died on his estate at Fontainebleau which is when Alexandrov said he visited Gurvich at Val-de-Grâce, a year after Orlov died in May 1961. This reveals that Gurvich was in possession of the auctioned items for eleven years (since 1950) and begs the question why he hadn't revealed the contents sooner knowing of their historical significance. More likely Alexandrov got his dates mixed up and the Orlov estate auctioned the items after Nikolai Orlov died in 1961 and Alexandrov got to hear about it during his research and caught up with Gurvich in 1962. Whatever had been the case, it meant that the Sokolov relics passed from the guardians to private buyers. Alexandrov published his book by claiming to have discovered the wooden boxes in Gurvich's attic and when they passed to him he used sixty photographs from the contents for his book which were seen for the first time; no wonder Victor Alexandrov's book had been a best seller.

Alexandrov described M. I. Gurvich as a Russian antique dealer and bibliophile but could this have actually been the painter Iosif Mikhailovich Gurvich (b. 1907-1993), the 1974 Honoured Artist of the Russian Soviet Federated Socialist Republic (RSFSR), whose paintings still sell at Bonhams and Christies and can be seen at exhibitions and museums in

CHAPTER XXI

Moscow, Kiev, Kaunas, Baku, and at other foreign galleries. A clue that the Paris lot buyer (given as 1950 but was probably in 1961) may have been this artist is in a reference Alexandrov made to paintings he saw at Gurvich's residence at the Val-de-Grâce district of Paris, *"In a corner is a large painting of a man in evening dress, with a black patch over one eye, who seems to stand guard over a pile of cases and paintings."* Amid that pile in the attic were the wooden boxes that Alexandrov claimed to have discovered.

Gurvich grew up living with his father in Odessa where he developed his artistic style, notably a form of expression epitomised by the sculptor Constantin Brancusi, the painter Chaim Soutine, and sculptor and painter Amadeo Modigliani; all living and working in Paris at the time when surrealism was growing throughout the 1920s and 1930s. Gurvich held a passion for the artists Guiseppe Giorgio de Chirico, Paul Delvaux, Salvador Dali, Rene Magritte and particularly the French painters Andre Breton, Pierre-Auguste Renoir, Henri Matisse and Paul Cezanne; so much so, that Gurvich was nicknamed 'the Russian Cezanne'.

After World War II he moved to Moscow and taught children and war invalids. One wonders how Gurvich who lived in Moscow came to be in Paris, buying at auctions and storing his purchases at two nearby premises, Salle Drouot and Val-de-Grâce, being just two and a half miles from each other. Perhaps Val-de-Grâce was his studio and that's where Alexandrov found him. Gurvich must surely have known the significance of the wooden boxes, perhaps he saw them simply as a collection of historical documents from the revolution because Alexandrov described him as a bibliophile and perhaps Alexandrov had persuaded him that they would be better utilised in the hands of a writer.

Alexandrov describes how he was with Gurvich in the attic at Val-de-Grâce searching through documents when they came upon the wooden boxes tucked in a corner. There was an inscription on the inside of the lids, 'N. Sokolov' and in one of them were Sokolov's photographic plates. With the Sokolov Box and the wooden boxes accounted for it left the chest containing the clothing from Ganina Yama still out there. Alexandrov believed the chest, *"containing the relics of the Imperial Romanov family,"* and not just clothes, had been moved to a Paris vault by de Giers and Orlov.

The Paris vault was raided in 1943 by the Gestapo and after the war ended a search was conducted in Paris but nothing was found except that a rumour started that the chest had been taken to New York, possibly to the same bank that was storing other Romanov artefacts, perhaps alongside items being collected by Kirill Vladimirovich. New York was and is also the location of the headquarters of the Russian Orthodox Church Abroad, and where the preserved finger of Alexandra Feodorovna from the relics of the Sokolov Box was kept. There had undoubtedly been a co-ordinated effort between the Church and RECA to collect Romanov artefacts.

Discovering the Graves

The date of discovery of the main grave differs in accounts because of the Soviet secrecy up until the end of the Glasnost period (1986–1991). Some accounts confuse the date the main grave was discovered with the date when the discovery was announced which are many years apart. Nevertheless, the story goes that a team of amateur investigators located the main grave in May 1979 after examining some clues from the Sokolov Investigation dossier, Yurovsky's statement and a book by Pavel Bykov.

In 1926 a Bolshevik official called Pavel Bykov published a diary in Russian called *The Last Days of the Romanovs*. It was published as *The Last Days of Tsardom* in London (1934) and *The Last Days of Tsar Nicholas* in New York (1935). It was the first time a Bolshevik had publicly admitted to the murders of the royal family aside from the public announcement that was made for the execution of Nicholas II. In *Chapter XIII - The execution of the Romanov family* of his book, Bykov described the murders at Ipatiev House, Alapayevsk and Perm and also described the disposal of the bodies of the royal family.

The murders are aptly admitted in one sentence on page 80 of Bykov's account, "... *the Regional Soviet decided to shoot the Romanovs without waiting for a trial.*" This was the Chairman of the Ural Soviet who was revealing that the bodies were buried some distance from the Four Brothers pit at Ganina Yama in an area that Sokolov had searched but not excavated. The book was removed from libraries so that by the early 1940s a copy of it could not be found anywhere in Russia. What stymied a search was that the Church in Brussels already had the remains, as far as they were concerned, and the bodies were therefore already accounted for, albeit without agreement from the Soviet Union or the Orthodox Church in Russia.

> "*A great deal of discussion was caused by the absence of any bodies, in spite of the most careful searches. But, as has been mentioned earlier, what remained of the bodies after burning was taken a considerable distance from the pits and buried in a swamp, in the area where the volunteers and investigators made no excavations. There the bodies remained and by now have rotted away.*"
> — PAVEL BYKOV, The last days of Tsar Nicholas, page 88

In 1976, a thirty-four year old archaeologist Dr Alexander Nikolaevich Avdonin secured a permit to conduct scientific geological research in the Sverdlovsk district, without having disclosed the true nature of his objective. He went with his wife Alexandra Avdonin and four scientific researchers. They were Geli Ryabov, a thirty-eight year old film maker/director for the Ministry of Internal Affairs; a fellow geologist Michael Kochurov; a married

CHAPTER XXI

couple of amateur archaeologists from the Sverdlovsk oblast, and a retired geologist. This team were responsible for locating the main grave.

The Romanov story had intrigued Avdonin and Ryabov for many years. Avdonin came across Sokolov's book in 1948 and decided the best places to search would be areas that had not already been excavated, in accordance with Bykov's theory. Ryabov's role at Internal Affairs gave him access to police files and he started looking for documents at the State Archives in Moscow for clues of possible burial sites and that's how he came across Yurovsky's statement which detailed his preparations and provided the clues that would lead to the discovery of the second grave in 2007. Ryabov was hesitant to reveal this because of the way the Soviet system worked and instead contacted Yurovsky's son Admiral Alexander who had in his possession a copy of his father's report. Ryabov learned from it that the Ekaterinburg prisoners were not taken directly to the forest and killed because Yurovsky feared his men would rape the women and create additional problems that he would be unable to control, and this had been the reason he decided on the place of execution at Ipatiev House as it would be simpler to transport the dead bodies after the deed was done.

Ryabov studied a photograph that Sokolov took of a dirt track going through the forest, running alongside the Koptyaki Road, at a place known as 'Pig's Meadow', (*a similar photograph is on page 391*). This location was just four and a half miles from Ganina Yama, where Yurovsky's truck had been stuck in the mud two days after the murders at Ipatiev House. Avdonin made the arrangements to begin work in the field and his team arrived with all manner of detection instruments. But just as with Sokolov's team, during their extensive search they had not thought to look under the railway sleepers where the grave was actually located.

Ryabov then learned of a railway guard that worked nearby where the road crossed the track who had told Sokolov that some men had required railway sleepers for their truck which had become stuck in the mud. Sokolov estimated the truck and the detail had been at Pig's Meadow between 4.30 am and 9.00 am. Ryabov wondered how a contingent of unruly guards could have been kept occupied for such a long period.

Therefore, in the summer of 1979 Avdonin's team once more visited Pig's Meadow and this time they looked under the railway sleepers and on 30-31 May 1979 they unearthed and removed three skulls from the site. Avdonin and Ryabov again became fearful of the repercussions of not having the proper permissions in place and returned to the track one year later, in the summer of 1980, to rebury the skulls in a box. The box of skulls lay there undisturbed until The Moscow News announced their discovery and revealed the location on 12 April 1989 (or 10 April in another account) because Ryabov had given them a revelation interview, much to the dismay of the rest of the team.

The Soviet authorities were indeed not impressed and all works in the area were stopped. To break the stalemate, in 1990 Avdonin wrote to Boris Yeltsin, then the Chairman of the Supreme Council of Russia, to officially inform him where he had discovered the presumed remains of the royal family and asked for an exhumation, *"to bring them back to history."* On the day following Yeltsin's inauguration as Russia's first President, on 11 July 1991, the Sverdlovsk regional Governor Edvard Rossel sent investigators from Ekaterinburg to the location that Avdonin had given. They excavated parts of skeletons including three children with The Associated Press reporting that Russian researchers had unearthed a grave of nine skeletons.

That same year, the prosecutor's office sent Vladimir Solovyev to the aptly renamed Russian Orthodox Church of the 'New Martyrs' in Brussels (previously the church of Saint Job mentioned on *page 465*) in search of the Sokolov Box. He was informed that it was secretly hidden in a wall but Solovyev did not find anything when he was there. Why Solovyev didn't find it is a mystery and perhaps the Soviet impressed upon him that he was not supposed to find it, or maybe the Church had ensured that he did not find it.

In 1992 two leading DNA scientists met at a scientific conference. Peter Gill was working in the new field of forensic identification using DNA profiling in England and in Russia Pavel Ivanov was examining the remains that Avdonin's team had excavated in 1991. Ivanov asked Gill whether DNA profiling could be used on the Romanov remains considering how degraded the DNA samples were likely to be. The team that led the DNA identification now became Pavel Ivanov of the Engelhardt Institute of Molecular Biology in Moscow, Peter Gill of the Forensic Science Service in Birmingham UK, and a third scientist Michael Coble of the Armed Forces DNA Identification Laboratory in Rockville, Maryland, America.

It was revolutionary science and Gill was enthusiastic when Ivanov arrived at Heathrow Airport with the bone fragments. With any profiling the primary concern is with the chain of custody so the specimens were kept isolated. As expected, only a very small sample of DNA could be extracted from just a few cells but it was sufficient to make a comparison with DNA obtained from Prince Philip (Elizabeth II's consort) in 1993, a direct descendant of Alexandra Feodorovna, with their common ancestor for comparison being Queen Victoria in the maternal line. For the paternal line to compare with Nicholas II's DNA, a sample was used from Princess Xenia Cheremeteff Sfiri, the great-granddaughter of Xenia Alexandrovna.

The scientists found matching samples, considered as incontrovertible proof. Yet the test was scrutinised because of the poor quality of the DNA samples and a tiny section that had not been found an identical match. It should be appreciated that Gill had the foremost laboratory in this field with a particular expertise in analysing degraded samples and his DNA profiling method was later used to set up the UK National DNA Database in 1995.

CHAPTER XXI

Only a few laboratories were able to replicate the results however, because of the rarity of obtaining a sample; one team even exhumed Nicholas II's brother George to obtain a sample.

The scientific community was finally satisfied when laboratories in Russia, England and America independently verified a match. The official Russian inquiry wasn't until 1997 when the remains were examined for mitochondrial DNA and established to an accuracy of 99.9 percent that they were a match for Nicholas II, Alexandra, Olga, Tatiana, Botkin (doctor), Trupp (footman), Kharitonov (cook), Demidova (lady in waiting), and one other, an unidentified young female, thought to be Anastasia at the time. The government commission recognised just five of the nine remains of bone fragments which were taken to St Petersburg by Avdonin. The burial service took place on 17 July 1998 at the state owned Peter and Paul Cathedral where the remains were laid to rest in the crypt alongside other members of the Romanov dynasty.

While the Russian Orthodox Church in Russia was difficult to convince, the Russian Orthodox Church Abroad (ROCA) was more accepting of the authenticity of the remains. A small but highly influential pressure group of non-scientific Russians calling themselves the Russian Expert Committee Abroad (RECA), formed soon after the remains were discovered and quickly allied with ROCA and ever since have continually used the international media to oppose the findings of the scientific community. ROCA and RECA are discussed in more detail in *Chapter XXII*.

In July 2004 Dr Sergey Nikitin and Captain Peter Sarandinaki began the first search for a second grave to the north side of Pig's Meadow, around the location where the main grave had been found. They were looking for Alexei and Anastasia which changed after a time when the missing Romanov daughter was agreed not to be Anastasia but instead, Marie. Nikitin and Sarandinaki reasoned that if the grave had not been located by Sokolov's team over a wide search area then perhaps it was within a closer proximity to the main grave and for three years they searched without success until they started looking on the south side of Pig's Meadow. In 2007, about 320 feet from the main grave and just off the track, they discovered the remains of a 10-13 year old male and an 18-23 year old female, presumed to be Alexei and Marie. There were just forty-four partial bone fragments recovered but they were adequate for DNA testing.

One account tells the story of a forty-six year old builder called Sergei Plotnikov who stumbled on a small hollow covered with nettles and then Russian archaeologists took over and found the grave containing the remains of the two bodies. There are several accounts of the discovery and who can know for sure which are true or fake. One account states that Nicholas II was decapitated after being shot and his head delivered to Moscow to prove that he was dead like in a biblical tale presenting a head on a platter. A replacement head was placed in the grave for any discovery made in the future. This story had not anticipated the advent of DNA technology which had since progressed and identified the skull of Nicholas II with certainty.

In spite of DNA profiling confirming the identities of the remains of the royal family, the Russian Orthodox Church in Russia has never accepted the DNA evidence that would finally put rest to the souls of Alexei and Marie who cannot receive a Christian burial until their remains are confirmed. As it stands, the situation can only progress with the exhumation of the remains, which is granted by the Russian President. In 2018, following the centenary anniversary of the murders, Bishop Tihon Shevkunov requested a fresh investigation in to the murders of the royal family and President Putin ordered a new probe by the SLEDKOM (Russian Federation Investigative Committee) to use its facilities to determine once and for all what had happened in the cellar at Ipatiev House and to the remains of the victims. Until the investigation has concluded, things must continue as they are with Alexei and Marie left without proper religious sanction.

Of course, there is still some conspiratorial belief that their remains can never be accepted because they are not the true remains of the two children, because they had survived. It might be all too easy to dismiss Summers & Mangold if they were not highly experienced researchers with the resources of the BBC for the five years it took to complete their work. They brought alive the possibility of survivors and the book may be contentious, but hardly is the opinion of the then American Secretary of State Henry Kissinger (December 1976) a fair appraisal; when asked to comment on the Romanov females having survived, he said, *"That story is a lot of crap."* In the modern day, their remains deserve to be recognised and left to rest in peace.

"The most rigorous approach to the version of ritual murder, a significant part of the church commission has no doubt that this murder was ritual." — BISHOP TIHON SHEVKUNOV

Bishop Tihon Shevkunov is unlikely to offer any contribution to this century old investigation because his views are more in line with the Bolsheviks. He believes in the ritual killing theory blaming the Jews for the murders, as Dieterichs had done (*page 446*) and notwithstanding that a meeting of the Council of Bishops in 1994 reviewing the canonisation of the royal family, examined and concluded that there was no evidence to support this theory. The Jerusalem Post, 28 November 2017, had this to say about the Russian bishop's comments:

"Claims that Nicholas II was killed by Jews for ritual purposes had been limited before the conference to a fringe of zealous antisemites and promoters of unsophisticated conspiracy theories."

The Romanov Saints, canonised on 14 August 2000

CHAPTER XXII
The Road to Sainthood

CONTROVERSY over the remains of Nicholas II and his immediate family should have been put to rest on 30 January 1998 when the Soviet official Boris Nemtsov officially recognised the excavated bones from Ekaterinburg as belonging to the former Imperial Family and when a month later the authorities issued death certificates for five royal family members, thereby permitting their burial at the Peter and Paul Cathedral, despite objections from the Russian Orthodox Church. The service took place in the presence of the first Russian President Boris Yeltsin on the anniversary date of 17 July 1998, that being exactly eighty years since the murders happened. But instead, a dispute ensued over the authenticity of the bone fragments that had provided the DNA samples used for the tests in 1995 to establish the identities.

By way of a compromise it would seem, between the Church and the government, the remains were not laid in the main chapel as Nicholas II had requested but in an ante room nearby. The DNA profiling was conducted in 1993 by doctors Peter Gill and Pavel Ivanov representing the Forensic Science Services Laboratory in the UK and the Russian Academy of Sciences, respectively (*page 471*). They officially released their findings through the UK Home Office, confirming the remains were authentic, which was immediately contested by RECA, the unqualified group outside of Russia and not representative of any Russian community.

CHAPTER XXII

RECA, having no scientific legitimacy were supported by the Russian Orthodox Church and so the government also had to take heed of RECA who argued that the bone fragments used for the tests were fake and had been planted at the grave in 1979 expectant of the eventuality that they would be found at some future time. They were also suggesting that the excavations in July 1991 had been to prepare the layout for a future discovery. Vladimir Soloviev of the Russian Prosecutor's Office, whose job it was to look in to the claim, believed that it was an unfounded presumption based on no evidence at all. This ruling should have seen the end of RECA as a reputable pressure group.

"The bones were part of a fabricated case concocted by the communist regime and perpetuated by Yeltsin's government ... they created these remains." — PETER KOLTYPIN-WALLOVSKY, RECA

In 1922 the Bolshevik revolutionary Yakov Yurovsky, the man who had planned and carried out the murders at Ipatiev House, wrote an account for his superiors which was one of the documents examined by Avdonin and Ryabov for clues that led them to the discovery of the main grave. RECA asserted that Yurovsky was not sufficiently skilled to have written the report and that his statement was therefore communist disinformation. The conspiracy that RECA alluded to, demonstrated in the quote given above, is an example of how this organisation have been mostly problematic rather than helpful and it has been equally unhelpful for the Russian Orthodox Church in Russia to have sided with them.

Avdonin and Ryabov successfully located the first grave from clues in several documents; not just Yurovsky's account known as the Yurovsky Note. It's known that Yurovsky was illiterate and his account was likely written by the Marxist and Russian historian Mikhail Nikolaevich Pokrovsky during 1922 when Yurovsky was sent by Lenin to take charge of the Central Archives in Moscow. This is the view shared by a modern investigation by Margarita Nelipa and Helen Azar who accept that if Yurovsky was limited by his low education then it was equally plausible that he would have dictated his account to Mikhail Pokrovsky. Irrespective of whomever wrote it, the words were dictated by Yurovsky and the clues ultimately led to the discovery of the location of the first grave. The mystery is why RECA suggested that the Communist authorities in 1979 would plant bones to confirm the identity of the remains and why this would have been done simply to resolve an historic argument.

RECA were attempting to discredit two brilliant scientists in Dr Abramov and Dr Maples who remained adamant that their DNA profiling technique was *"virtually beyond any doubt."* The authentication of the Romanov bone fragments, known as the Macroscopic Examination, began in 1992 when forensic anthropologist Dr Sergei Abramov examined the recovered skulls and confirmed they belonged to Nicholas II, Alexandra Feodorovna, and daughters Olga, Tatiana and Anastasia, albeit his results were not published until 2001 in the scientific international journal *Anatomical Record*.

The first test by Dr Abramov compared cranioscopic characteristics and found remarkable similarities in four of the five skulls. The second test method used photographic superimposition and found that only Nicholas II and Alexandra Feodorovna could be identified to a high degree using both methods. Therefore, Dr Abramov's findings could not be accepted for certain and American forensic anthropologist Dr William Maples was invited to Ekaterinburg to examine the nine skeletal remains (five Romanov and four aides). Much of Dr Maples' investigation was based on assumptions such as the absence of dentition in one of the skulls presumed to be Dr Eugene Botkin and the presence of gold and platinum in dental work that could only have been afforded by the extremely wealthy. In the main, Dr Maples, like Dr Abramov, examined bone structures to determine gender and age. In the absence of conclusive carbon dating and DNA profiling, these macroscopic testing techniques were as good as it got back then and Dr Maples had agreed with the authenticity of the remains.

Uranium-lead dating (U-pb) is a dating method used to estimate the age of geological formations such as rocks that formed between one million to several billion years ago by measuring the radioactive decay of uranium isotopes. Carbon dating had been around since the 1940s for dating the remains of former organic matter but it is only useful for a material that is between 500 and 50,000 years old. The new field of DNA profiling offered the definitive method for conclusive identification. The problem with sampling for DNA testing is that the quality degrades over time as the samples come from bones, hair and teeth; from the mutating mitochondria in organic cells. It was due to the poor nature of the remains that in September 1992, Dr Ivanov had taken samples to Dr Gill in England for profiling because that UK laboratory ran the most sophisticated mitochondrial DNA (mtDNA) testing facility in the world, with a speciality in retrieving information from poor quality samples.

An ancient bone specialist was enlisted in Norwegian Dr Erica Hagelberg to examine everything at the molecular level. A year on, they jointly announced their findings on 29 September 1993 in the journal *Russkaya Meditsinskaya Gazeta* (Russian Medical Gazette), stating that the bone fragments that had been examined at the UK facility had been found to belong to the Romanov family, thereby confirming the identities of the remains. The paternal line had been established but Dr Ivanov wanted to gain further evidence in to the maternal line of mutation because Alexandra Feodorovna and Anastasia, being haemophilic carriers, would possess a rare mutation which could be used to prove a connection with the highest level of certainty. Although

DNA profiling was initially advanced, it was open to challenge because the mitochondrial genome containing 16,569 pairs was not fully mapped until 2003. Dr Ivanov hoped to locate the rare mutation and thereby further cement the identification of the remains.

Meanwhile, to address accusations of overly degraded samples, Ivanov sought permission to exhume Nicholas II's brother, George Alexandrovich, which took the best part of two years because the authorities had to clear the exhumation order with the Russian Orthodox Church. After the exhumation in July 1994, Dr Ivanov had a sample for comparison and together with the fragment remains from Ekaterinburg took them all to a separate facility in America. There he met Dr Thomas Parsons at the US Armed Forces DNA Identification Laboratory, where they worked on the remains between 4 June and 9 September 1995.

The Soloviev Commission (August 1993-1998) headed by Vladimir Soloviev was made up of around one hundred scientific experts, other notables including Dr Avdonin, and Orthodox Church representatives. In July 1994 it permitted RECA to conduct a rival investigative DNA analysis in Canada performed by molecular geneticist Dr Eugene Rogaev. The Commission wanted to consider all the competing evidence before submitting their final report to the Russian President. The purpose of the Commission was to establish the authenticity of the remains so that the royal family could finally be laid to rest with a properly sanctioned religious burial.

In America Dr Ivanov was primarily looking to confirm the paternal line that had been established in the UK in 1993, and was seeking a correlation between the sample from George Alexandrovich and Nicholas II. He used the same bones from the remains of Nicholas II that had provided the mtDNA for the UK profiling and was able to duplicate the results. He achieved it using heteroplasmy, the new technique involving a rare mutation in the presence of organellar inside cells that can be used to diagnose mitochondrial diseases. Dr Ivanov found it in the maternal line of both brothers thus confirming the rare mutation occurring in exactly the same location in their DNA sequences and establishing beyond doubt their molecular connection. The paternal line had thus been established and there was complete certainty that the remains of Nicholas II had been confirmed.

Mrs Kulikovska

In 1996, Dr Ivanov published the results of his American tests in the international journal *Nature Genetics*. He had thought that between the first stage of anthropologic examinations, the second stage of mtDNA tests in England in 1993 and the third stage of mtDNA heteroplasmic results in America in 1995, that the identity of the bones making up the remains of the royal family had been globally settled and accepted. To his dismay it was not and he received criticism from RECA, the Russian Orthodox Church and Mrs Olga Kulikovska who disputed that he had taken the genuine Ekaterinburg remains to England and America for the comparison tests.

Mrs Kulikovska was originally from Yugoslavia and the third wife of Tihon Kulikovsky, the son of Olga Alexandrovna and nephew to Nicholas II. Her maiden name was Olga Pupynin Nikolaevna Burton (1926-2020) and they were married on 8 June 1986 when she became Mrs Kulikovska. After Tihon's death she added the title Princess and the Romanov suffix to her name even though her Romanov connection was by marriage, and she called herself Mrs Olga Nikolaevna Kulikovska-Romanova. Her aim was to debunk the scientific findings thus far presented and she attacked the Soloviev Committee and Dr Ivanov personally, whom she hated intensely, accusing him of having taken two bones from the exhumation of George Alexandrovich for the DNA comparisons and that he had claimed that one of them falsely belonged to Nicholas II from the Ekaterinburg remains.

There was no question of skulduggery as the stringent method used for the testing extruded any possibility of using samples from the same donor. This accusation was quickly ruled out by the Soloviev Commission but there was continual opposition from Tihon and Mrs Kulikovska. Tihon refused to donate blood for a DNA sample largely because he and his wife considered Dr Ivanov to be a Soviet scoundrel and they had, on political grounds they said, chosen to side with RECA.

The UK tests in 1993, for the maternal line compared blood taken from Xenia Sfiris, the great granddaughter of Xenia Alexandrovna, and Prince Philip the Duke of Edinburgh. The accusation was about the UK tests not having established the paternal line, because the samples from Nicholas II and his brother George were both taken from George. However, the UK tests for the paternal line had been done between the samples of Nicholas II and Xenia Sfiris which had been a match. Perhaps they should have avoided Tihon and asked his brother Guri instead whom they may have found more helpful. He was the grandfather of Paul Edward Kulikovsky born in Canada in 1960 who spent some years in Copenhagen, London and Denmark and finally Russia to become the first Romanov to settle in Russia since the revolution. Paul Kulikovsky attended the funeral ceremony in 1998 and helped with the reburial of Maria Feodorovna in 2006 from Roskilde Cathedral to St Petersburg, giving the eulogy on behalf of the Romanov family. Evidently Guri's side were more helpful.

Just before Tihon died in 1993 he finally agreed to give a blood sample, perhaps fearing his own exhumation in a future dispute. Mrs Kulikovska with RECA's support put pressure on Soloviev who permitted her to commission an official test in Canada to be conducted by a scientist of her choosing. Dr Rogaev was from the Toronto Hospital near to where Mrs

Kulikovska lived and in 1994 he used Tihon's blood sample to extract mtDNA to compare with the sequences that had been identified and published by doctors Gill and Ivanov in 1993, and was therefore looking at the disputed paternal line of Nicholas II.

Dr Ivanov's attempt to test the paternal line in America came under attack from Mrs Kulikovska who protested that he and the Soloviev Commission had exhumed Nicholas II's brother in 1994, George Alexandrovich, without inviting a Romanov representative to attend. Dr Ivanov had also taken with him the so-called Ōtsu handkerchief that Nicholas II once used to wipe over a wound on his forehead after a failed assassination attempt during a visit to Ōtsu, Japan in 1891. It was just a piece of cloth that Nicholas had used to put pressure on the wound with hardly any blood or sweat visible, let alone any real possibility of obtaining a DNA sample.

Mrs Kulikovska was none too pleased about the handkerchief and asked why Dr Ivanov was taking specimens abroad when all of the 'Ekaterinburg remains' as they were termed, were kept at the Moscow Forensic Medical Centre and were not permitted to leave Russia. RECA joined the argument saying that because the sample from the handkerchief must have been so small, it highlighted Dr Ivanov's lack of expertise in the expert field of DNA profiling because a viable DNA sample could not have been extracted from it. They also argued that the chain of custody was severely compromised on account that the handkerchief had been handled by so many people since it was acquired.

Then there was the issue about the skull of Nicholas II that became literally a bone of contention. The rumour of decapitation was in fact a serious argument for RECA who believed the head was severed and taken to Yakov Sverdlov in Moscow by Yurovsky, to prove that the ex-tsar was dead and a substitute skull was planted at the burial site. The Soloviev Commission closed down the decapitation argument because there wasn't a shred of evidence to support it. But it did not stop there. Attempting to prove the skull of the Ekaterinburg remains was not Nicholas II, RECA argued that there was no evidence of bone repair from the Ōtsu injury. Nicholas II was attacked with a sword that scraped his forehead and he sustained two wounds, six centimetres and nine centimetres in length. The first wound had cut the vessels of the neck and temporal arteries and the parietal bone lost about a centimetre of periosteum. The peritoneum is a soft protective membrane that surrounds an organ, in this case the cranium, which secretes a lubricant that reduces friction.

A general report of the incident was received by Alexander III on 29 April 1891. It lacked the finer details which were not known for some years until the report was located at the Ōtsu hospital, like which side of the forehead had received the injury for example. The reason that the skull of Nicholas II showed no bone repair was because the lacerations had not been deep enough to scrape the bone. The medical reports stated that both wounds were not, "... *penetrating the whole thickness of the skin down to the bone.*" Furthermore, the small amount of periosteum that was lost is not bone and after eighty years in the ground would have decomposed.

So, the wounds had gone down to the bone with one centimetre of the peritoneum membrane cut away and there had been no cranial damage. After the attack Nicholas II was rushed to the Imperial palace at Kyoto to be treated but his injury was not life threatening and he left that same day without any need for further hospital treatment which is another sign that the injuries were not serious enough to have damaged the skull.

The Soloviev Commission was baffled by RECA's claims. On the one hand they were attempting to prove that the ex-tsar's head had been decapitated and taken to Moscow and therefore that the skull found in the grave did not belong to the ex-tsar and, on the other hand, they were accusing the authorities of tampering with the grave to hide the identity of Nicholas II.

RECA were trying to discredit all of the evidence that could identify the remains and Mrs Kulikovska was allowed to cast a net of doubt over the scientific facts for many years. By suggesting the graves were staged it called in to question the samples used for the paternal line tests where a sample had been used from the skull, but the UK tests of 1993, as discussed, had compared this skull sample with Xenia Sfiris and found a match, therefore proving, at least, that whatever skull it was, was a Romanov one. The real question is why Mrs Kulikovska did not see the contradiction.

In 1995, a year after Dr Rogaev in Canada took up the DNA profiling for Mrs Kulikovska, he announced that his samples were a precise match between Tihon and Nicholas II, which he reported to the Soloviev Commission and later published his findings in 1996. In having independently confirmed a DNA match, in particular in the paternal line. Dr Rogaev had shown that the samples used for the UK profiling must have been done with authentic Romanov samples. Despite this, Mrs Kulikovska reported to the Soloviev Commission that there had been no match found. By now the Commission must have suspected that she was a mite scatty.

Having lost credibility with the Soloviev Commission, Mrs Kulikovska funded an independent investigation in 1997, 'independent' because it is not mentioned in the final Soloviev Commission Report of 1998. Its purpose was to undermine all the previous DNA findings. Dr Vyacheslav Popov, a Soloviev Commission member, was enlisted by Mrs Kulikovska to run it. Dr Popov knew Dr Tatsuo Nagai of the Kitazato University in Tokyo and passed to him the Ōtsu handkerchief which RECA now had in their possession. But Dr Nagai judged it too contaminated (as RECA had previously argued,) and didn't attempt to extract a DNA sample. Dr Popov then sent Dr Nagai a hair from George Alexandrovich which Dr Nagai was able to use. A DNA comparison was made with the data from Dr Ivanov's

CHAPTER XXII

published work of 1996 and no match was found using the hair and the test revealed significant differences between the samples. Finally Mrs Kulikovska had a legitimate argument that the remains were fake.

Dr Nagai next went to Russia to compare the DNA between the bone sample from Nicholas II and samples from Tihon Kulikovsky and George Alexandrovich and he was also unable to find a connection. He even got differing results from the tests he had done previously in Japan. The problem with Dr Nagai's tests was that there was no proper record kept and they loosely followed acceptable protocols. He described the results rather unscientifically as being 'similar' to the results of Dr Gill but without finding the heteroplasmy. The Popov-Nagai work was published in 1999 in an obscure publication that omitted standard notation such as the chain of custody. It was not an officially sanctioned investigation by the Soloviev Commission who had total control over the remains and all samples. Neither had any movement of the remains to Japan been authorised by Russian authorities or requests been received from the Japanese government to seek permission for such work to be performed.

Soloviev insisted on the remains always being kept in the hands of the approved experts so where had Dr Popov obtained the hair sample he claimed was from George Alexandrovich and provided to Dr Nagai. Doubt over the authenticity of the samples provided to Dr Nagai explains why he didn't find a match in his comparison tests. When asked, Dr Nagai said his samples had been provided by Dr Popov who had access to the Ekaterinburg remains and who conveniently attended the exhumation of George Alexandrovich.

The insinuation was of skulduggery which Soloviev described simply as, theft. Dr Popov responded on a radio interview in March 2005 saying that some items had strayed and ended up with the Nicholas II Memorial Foundation and that it was those items that Dr Popov had provided to Dr Nagai. At the Memorial Foundation, Dr Popov had removed some tape that was appended to an exhibit of a coat belonging to Nicholas II which was near a sweat stain. Dr Nagai took it to Japan without declaring it and in so doing disregarded the protocols for controlling the integrity of samples. In simpler terms, the DNA he used could have belonged to anyone having been in contact with the coat.

While the unorthodox Popov-Nagai investigation was unfolding, Dr Rogaev was invited to Russia by Mrs Kulikovska to conduct a second investigation and he arrived in December 1997 at the Psychiatric Health Centre in Moscow. This time he had access to a pristine sample from the bone fragments of Nicholas II, otherwise known as skeleton #4. He found a direct correlation between the samples of skeleton #4 and Tihon's blood sample. For a second time Dr Rogaev reported to the Soloviev Commission, on 29 January 1998, that skeleton #4 was maternally related to Tihon Kulikovsky. Two independent investigations had now confirmed to the Soloviev Commission that Dr Abramov's anthropological study of 1992 and doctors Gill and Ivanov's mtDNA profiling of 1993, were the proof that skeleton #4 was indeed Nicholas II, without any shred of doubt.

Dr Ivanov was the custodian of the remains outside of Russia and Mrs Kulikovska had tried to discredit his work in the UK and America. Finally he had been vindicated and the burials of the Ekaterinburg remains on 17 July 1998 were premised on these findings which enabled death certificates to be issued in spite of the Russian Orthodox Church having taken a back seat on the debate regarding the authenticity of the Ekaterinburg remains. In the near future the Church would claim that their inaction was because the Soloviev Commission had not involved them in any DNA testing albeit they did have official representation within the Committee.

Furthermore, the Church Commission for the Canonisation of Saints had asked ten questions of the Committee, which they said had not been answered, and this was the reason, they said, that they could not officially recognise the Ekaterinburg remains as belonging to the royal family. In spite of the overwhelming evidence that the Ekaterinburg remains belonged to the royal family, strangely the Church remained adamant that there was no convincing evidence that the true location of the remains had ever been found. Responding to the Church stalling, Deputy Russian Prime Minister Boris Nemtsov clarified the position stating that he had personally given the Moscow Patriarch Alexy II a large document containing the answers to the questions the Church had asked.

Nemtsov's answer to them arrived in the form of a collation of the files making up the Commission's final report entitled 'Pokayanie' (Repentance). Nemtsov said about the Committee representatives from the Church, *"They didn't tell us anything, neither at government meetings, nor at commission meetings. But they made a political decision, they didn't want to quarrel with the Church Abroad."* Nemtov went ahead and permitted the burials stating that the forensic investigations in Russia corroborated those carried out in the UK and America and were accurate to 99.9%.

Patriarch Alexy II made his view politically clear by not attending the funeral ceremony. The head of the Romanov family in exile at that time, the assumed Prince Nikolai Romanov, stated that he agreed with the findings of the Soloviev Commission and that even if there was a discrepancy the remains needed to be buried as a symbol to bring closure to the Christian aspect concerning the remains. He also insisted that all remains, not just the royal family but including the four aides from Ipatiev House, be buried together at the Peter and Paul Cathedral out of a joint respect for the martyrs.

The Russian Orthodox Church Abroad glorified the royal family as martyrs in 1981 whilst at the same time not recognising the Ekaterinburg remains still holding to the belief that the bodies had perished at Ganina Yama in line with the conclusion of the Sokolov Investigation. The Russian

CHAPTER XXII

Orthodox Church, that had largely kept out of that debate, eventually sided with Dr Nagai's evidence presented by the Kitazato University which had found no DNA correlations (due to doubt over the samples provided by Dr Popov). It would appear that RECA and Mrs Kulikovska had a measure of success because the Russian Orthodox Church both in Russia and Abroad were refusing to recognise the Ekaterinburg remains. RECA went a step further and petitioned the authorities to have the remains removed from the Peter and Paul Cathedral and returned to Ekaterinburg for long term storage.

Mrs Kulikovska went even a step further in telling the Soloviev Commission before it finally closed in 1998 that only a Russian Orthodox Church Commission was acceptable to her, removing the validity of the Soloviev Commission entirely. It could be assumed that this was the end of the matter but it wasn't. In 2004 American lead scientist Dr Alec Knight of the Stanford Laboratory of Anthropological Sciences in California joined Mrs Kulikovska in challenging the identities attributed to the Ekaterinburg bones by the DNA investigations. In the UK the Home Office defended the robust procedures and quality controls employed by its renowned laboratory in 1993. One of the prominent forensic scientists that had worked there as a DNA testing quality and validation expert called Dr Kevin Sullivan, said, *"We considered the remains authentic because they match DNA samples we obtained from existing relatives of the royal family on the maternal side."* And they had the sample from Xenia Sfiris to confirm the paternal line.

Dr Knight revealed in January 2004 that his laboratory had strong evidence that there was no connection whatsoever between the Ekaterinburg remains and the Romanov family. The inference was that previous forensic tests were inconsistent and therefore inconclusive and the issue became one of a lack of evidence to be able to make a connection between the samples. From the bone fragments unearthed in 1991 that had been taken to the UK, sections of the DNA sequence had been analysed to establish the identities and mtDNA had been analysed for a more detailed multi-generational profile in the maternal line. Everything had matched and the identities of the royal family had been established. Dr Knight believed these results were too convenient and discounted them. He did not accept that such pristine samples could be obtained from the medium of eighty year old bones and stipulated that they were overly tarnished with foreign DNA, thus attacking the science itself and the chain of custody, which Dr Gill rebutted with the following statement, as "... *vindictive and political."*

The UK tests, as discussed, were later corroborated in subsequent third party studies. Yet Hollander Dr Peter de Knijff of the Forensic Laboratory for DNA Research at the Leiden University Medical Centre, Netherlands, agreed with Dr Knight that the Gill-Ivanov study had been too perfect to take seriously and cast suspicion over why the Ōtsu handkerchief had not been tested. This was of course, the cloth that Mrs Kulikovska had already rejected on account that there was no reliable chain of custody and of which she was now saying that Dr Ivanov had declined to use because it was a reliable non-bone medium that contained the blood and sweat of Nicholas II which would have shown different test results to the false bones that Dr Ivanov was using for his tests.

There was a spurious rumour that Dr Knight had entered the Romanov forensic debate because a colleague (a law student) suggested on a whim that they try to replicate the findings of doctors Gill and Ivanov. This seems unlikely and has more to do with the influence from Mrs Kulikovska who was no doubt looking out for scientists to join her cause. A trip to New York was funded by RECA where Dr Knight was provided with a sample taken from the finger of Elizabeth Feodorovna, sister to Alexandra Feodorovna, where it was being preserved by Russian Orthodox Bishop Anthony Grabbe.

Dr Knight compared Elizabeth's and Alexandra's DNA and did not find a match, throwing up a shovel-full of ambiguity over the validity of all the Ekaterinburg evidence. The whole argument over authenticity started with questioning the integrity of the DNA samples taken from the remains that were exposed to the elements for many decades. Forensic scientists that were not in agreement with doctors Knight and Knijff argued that permafrost at the grave site had helped to preserve the bones to a sufficient degree where larger sequences of DNA were stable enough to be recovered and which might have become degraded under normal circumstances over an equivalent time. Frozen DNA is known to be more stable albeit Ekaterinburg has very hot summers during July and August.

As for the Church, the Moscow Patriarch reaffirmed that the authenticity of the buried remains at the Peter and Paul Cathedral were not recognised as belonging to the royal family and refuted the determination of the Soloviev Commission. A press release stated that, "... *the Russian Orthodox Church refrains from final judgement regarding the final characteristics of the so-called Ekaterinburg remains.*" Not only did the Church position itself in opposition to the Soloviev Commission and renowned Russian scientists, but it also stood in direct opposition to the Soviet government maintaining that the Church were not being included nor having their questions answered.

In an interview in 2005 with Russian newspaper *Izvestiya*, the assumed Prince Nikolai Romanov discounted the independent investigations by Mrs Kulikovska and RECA stating that the questions the Russian Orthodox Church asked had been answered, the Soloviev investigations were exhausted, and the findings of the Soloviev Commission had been accepted, "*... and all the technical information which was printed and published. The conclusions were based on proof that was beyond absolute doubt.*"

The government took a neutral view (still in 2005). President Sergey Mironov when asked about the authenticity of the Ekaterinburg remains simply stated that there were many points of view. Dr Alexander Avdonin's statement, the man who discovered the main grave in 1979, deserves to have the final say on this subject:

> *"We are dealing with a single-minded entity (RECA) who under the guise of establishing historical truth, discredit the names of well known Russian politicians and entire government institutions of Russia ... and lead the people of a great nation astray."*
> — DR ALEXANDER AVDONIN

If the Romanovs have not had enough of squabbling, they remain today at odds with each other over who is the rightful heir to the dynasty. There are probably two people left that can claim lineage back to Nicholas II and the rest have to go back to Nicholas I who had four sons that make up the four main branches of the Roman family.

- **The Alexandrovichi** (descendants of Emperor Alexander II) Vladimirovichi, Pavlovichi, Kulikovsky, Brasov, Paley

- **The Konstantinovichi** (descendants of Constantine Nikolaevich) Iskander

- **The Nikolaevichi** (descendants of Nicholas Nikolaevich) Petrovich, Romanovich

- **The Mikhailovichi** (descendants of Michael Nikolaevich) Rostislavovich, Nikitich, Andreevich

The Interminable Debate

In 1918 Ipatiev House became a house of special purpose and after that was repurposed several times by the authorities. For a time it served as a museum with an actual tour incorporating the site of the murders in the cellar. In 1974 it was designated a national monument but unfortunately it became too popular with pilgrims who gathered at the site in increasing numbers each year on the anniversary of the murders (17 July) to pray and light candles; a public practice lamenting the monarchy that was not desirable in Soviet Russia. Therefore, Boris Yeltsin, then the First Secretary of the Sverdlovsk Regional Committee of the Communist Party of the Soviet Union (i.e. the Politburo), decided to demolish it on 22 September 1977 based on its new designation as a building of no architectural significance.

Voznesenskaya Square, Ekaterinburg, 1890s, Ipatiev House is on the left

Ipatiev House Enlargement from image above

"*It was impossible to resist, not to fulfil the Politburo Resolution ... They assembled the equipment and demolished it in one night. If I had refused, I would have been left without work, and the new secretary of the regional committee would have complied with the order anyway.*"
— BORIS YELTSIN, memoirs

CHAPTER XXII

Having become desolate in the hands of the Sverdlovsk Soviet with just a wooden cross marking the spot over the cellar where the killings happened, the Russian Orthodox Church was finally given control of the land (2,760 square metres) following glasnost (roughly translated as meaning openness), on 20 September 1990. With Boris Yeltsin, now the first Russian President, in 1991, it meant that construction could begin to build a memorial church to honour the royal family. The burial service was performed in 1998 in St Petersburg with their elevation to Passion Bearers following in 2000. The Church on Blood in Honour of All Saints Resplendent in the Russian Land (i.e. its official name), was completed in 2003 and consecrated by the Metropolitan Bishop Yuvenaly of Krutitsy and Kolomna, acting as the delegate of the Moscow Patriarch, because His Holiness Alexy II was unwell at that time and was unable to travel and preside over the ceremony.

Boris Nikolaevich Yeltsin was a controversial figure in Russian history serving as president from 1991 to 1999. His tenure began when the Soviet Union (USSR) had fifteen Soviet republics. From the start, he established loose regional connections around Belarus (Viskuli, Białowieża Forest, Minsk) including Crimea, and expanded that to a treaty called the Minsk Agreement, better known as the Belovezha Accords which were signed on 8 December 1991 by Yeltsin, President Kravchuk of Ukraine, and Chairman Shushkevich of Belarus. It brought about the end of the Soviet Union and created the Commonwealth of Independent States (CIS) to recognise the independence of the member states and their respective autonomy.

The CIS was quickly followed by the Almaty accords (or the Alma-Ata Protocol) signed on 21 December 1991, to bring together their shared social, political and economic interests. To achieve this he became unpopular within and repelled the Supreme Soviet of the Russian Federation with military force in the October Coup (better known as the Constitutional Crisis of 1993). His resignation from the Communist Party on 31 December 1999 marked the end of the era that had started with the Bolsheviks and the murders of the royal family in 1917. Yeltsin died of heart failure on 23 April 2007, twelve days after being admitted to the Central Clinical Hospital in Moscow and became the first Russian head of state to be buried in a church ceremony since Alexander III, with President Putin declaring it a day of national mourning.

The Memorial church is slightly raised on a platform and was supposed to cover the original Ipatiev House grounds but the old foundations are slightly to one side situated under the present roadway. This means the altar is also off kilter, intended to sit above the cellar, because consecrated altar stones usually contain relics encased in a cavity (Catholic and Orthodox religions) over which the acts of worship are enacted and in this instance the altar was to be sited above a sacred chamber – except that it wasn't! The exact spot is marked outside just to the side of the church with a Russian wooden double cross.

Church on the Blood, Ekaterinburg, Siberia

Veneration is a pretty simple step to identify a person with a high level of holiness or sanctity. A Passion Bearer in the Orthodox Church is the next step from veneration towards sainthood. The religious status awarded to the royal family differed between the Churches in Russia and Abroad; the former was seen to be restricted by the Soviet regime whereas the latter being more liberal was influenced by the Russian émigrés. The Orthodox Church Abroad therefore has been more proactive and forward thinking than its homeland counterpart, notwithstanding it has had to endure the activities of

CHAPTER XXII

RECA. The difference between the Churches has been evident in the attempts to resolve the identities of the Ekaterinburg remains and with the question of their sainthood which determines their status in religious iconry.

The Russian Orthodox Church in Russia, in 1981, debated Nicholas II, about his weakness and whether his actions had directly caused the deaths of so many people in the revolutions of 1905 and 1917 which ultimately led to the deaths of the Romanov family itself. It would take them almost two decades before the Venerated were made Passion Bearers.

The Russian Orthodox Church Abroad canonised the victims of Ipatiev House and Elizabeth Feodorovna as martyrs on 1 November 1981. The Church asserted that politics was not part of the canonisation process but rather that it was about the way in which someone had died or why they were killed. Passion Bearers do not necessarily die for their faith but from the pain endured in being needlessly killed for their beliefs.

At a meeting in 1994 of the Council of Bishops held inside Russia, their initial goal was to establish the criteria to be used for investigating candidates for canonisation. During the three day event they looked at a detailed analysis of the Romanov family's last days; burdened with severe suffering and their eventual death. The purpose of the gathering was to establish what was known thus far about the royal family and to agree to consider the canonisation of the aides Alois Trupp and Ekaterina Schneider. Martyrdom was rejected because the family's deaths were not religious and whilst it's true that Nicholas II brought about his own downfall, in part due to his weaknesses and because he was responsible for the pogroms, the question asked was, how was it possible for someone directly responsible for so many deaths to become a holy saint.

In fairness to the Orthodox Church in Russia, they were being thorough. Things need to be verified and the issue of whether Nicholas II was approving of mass murder matters when considering whether to elevate him to sainthood. The Council of Bishops looked at Nicholas II's position as head of the Royal Orthodox Church. The eventuality of an abdication was not provided for in the Act of Royal Succession and had been an unprecedented event. And again, it mattered whether Nicholas II was executed for his crimes as tsar or for being the head of the Church. Nicholas II had already abdicated for the good of the people and was not therefore the head of the Orthodox Church at the time of his death; a subtlety that allowed the consideration for his sainthood to proceed.

The abdication was seen as relating to him personally with his decision to abdicate having been influenced by the remarkable circumstances at that time in Russia's history. He was judged to have wholeheartedly believed that his abdication was for the good of Russia and had shown much regret after it was done when he realised the nefarious nature of the Bolsheviks that had seized his power. The Council of Bishops also recognised Nicholas

II's work *"for extensive church construction and new canonisations of saints."* Which included the canonisation of Seraphim of Sarov in 1903 (*Chapter VI*). He was acknowledged for progressing St Theodosius of Chernigov (1896), Holy Princess Anna of Kashin, St Joseph of Belgorod (1911), St Germogen of Moscow (1913), St Pitirim of Tambov (1914) and St John of Tobolsk (1916).

Although it was appreciated that political events and the abdication should not be items considered for the canonisation, it was not the actions of Nicholas II but rather his inaction as head of State and Church that was still the root of a dilemma. By not intervening when he could have done so, he contributed in allowing to be created the inevitability that brought about the revolution of 1905 and in not dealing with Rasputin he had contributed likewise to the revolution of 1917 and the demise of the Imperial Family. In ignoring the advice of both institutions of State and Church, how could he be canonised for having suffered when his fate had come by his own hand.

To progress matters, previously in December 1993 and again in August 1995, the Moscow Metropolitan Chairman of the Holy Synod Commission, Yuvenaly, consulted heads of the St Petersburg and Moscow Theological Academies about the Orthodox view on whether there existed a case for the ritual killings of the royal family. It was another angle for exploration that also revived the Russian nepotism that blamed Jews for almost everything. Mentioned earlier (*page 446*), the source of the ritual killings theory was started in 1919 by General Dieterichs and continued in the Church with Bishop Tihon Shevkunov (*page 473*). But in November 1995 the Moscow Patriarch Yuvenaly received the reply that there was no basis to that theory.

"Not having the means for an independent analysis of all aspects of the Royal Family's murder, and preceding from a presumption of innocence, there is no basis for assuming as proven the version of a ritual murder of what happened at the Ipatiev House."

The report by the Holy Synod Commission on the canonisation of saints of the Russian Orthodox Church had taken a couple of years concluding on 25 September 1996. It had examined a multitude of evidence relating to the holy feats connected to the royal family's martyrdom. Patriarch Yuvenaly sent it to His Holiness Alexei II on 10 October 1996, and touched upon the weaknesses of Nicholas II, apportioning some of the blame on Alexandra and Rasputin in mitigation for Nicholas II's inactions, ironically his weakness worked in his favour for once. Yuvenaly summed it up thus:

"Really, how was it possible that such a figure as Rasputin could have such an influence over the Royal Family and upon Russia's political and governing life of his time? The reason for the Rasputin phenomenon lies

CHAPTER XXII

in the illness of Czarevich Alexei. Although it is evident that the Sovereign repeatedly attempted to get rid of Rasputin, he stepped back each time under the influence of the Empress who found it necessary to resort to Rasputin for the healing of the Heir. It can be said that the Emperor found it impossible to go against Alexandra Feodorovna who was tortured by grief over the Heir's illness and who was under Rasputin's influence in this respect." — MOSCOW PATRIARCH YUVENALY

The Church always has stringent requirements for entry in to the hall of holy martyrs. Sainthood requires evidence of miracles and in 1997 Yuvenaly ruled out sainthood for Nicholas II because there was no such evidence. The Church Abroad had wasted no time in proclaiming the seven members of the Romanov family and Alexandra's sister Elizabeth, as Orthodox martyrs and saints at the assembly of bishops millennium meeting in the newly restored Christ the Saviour Cathedral near the Kremlin in Moscow. In respect of their aides, it was decided that while they would not be elevated to sainthood, they were the victims of circumstances beyond their control and the best way to honour their memory was with their inclusion in historical records relating to the new Romanov saints, where they would be always associated with them and similarly immortalised.

The Russian people conferred upon the martyrs their sainthood anyway, referring to them as saints regardless of the status attributed to them by the Church. Their images were replicated on icons and other religious regalia and crowds made yearly pilgrimage to Ekaterinburg. Despite the devotion demonstrated by the people, the leaders of the Russian Orthodox Church did not attend the burial service at the Peter and Paul Cathedral on 17 July 1998.

"The light of all-conquering Christian faith was seen in the suffering the royal family endured during their incarceration with gentleness, patience, and humility, and in their martyr deaths."
— HIS HOLINESS ALEXY II, Russian Orthodox Church in Russia

In 2000 the Russian Orthodox Church made the royal family members Passion Bearers for the humility and forbearance they had shown in accepting their deaths. It meant that construction could begin on the site of the former Ipatiev House to build the new Church on the Blood. It had taken His Holiness Alexy II four years to make it happen as he had taken care to be thorough so that the decision would not cause dangerous 'schisms' as he termed it, in the community. He said, *"... there are different opinions in the Church as to whether to attach the Tsar's family to the assembly of saints."* It had all whittled down to the inescapable devoutness and humility exemplified by each member of the Romanov family and their aides and the love at the heart of their collective being.

The process to begin building a church on the spot of the former Ipatiev House had taken sixteen years to sort out since the Council of Bishops meeting of 1994. The second grave was discovered on 23 August 2007 and announced on 22 January 2008, the bodies verified by DNA testing on 30 April 2008, this whole process was remarkably fast by Church standards. In 2015 the Church pushed for the Romanov investigation to be re-opened stating they had not been fully involved in the developing discoveries during the pre-glasnost era nor with the scientific processes since used in the DNA testing of the Ekaterinburg remains. Finally the Church was showing an interest and in 2018, on the eve of the anniversary of the murders, the Church announced that the remains of the second grave (Alexei and Marie) were accepted as being Romanov.

The day after His Holiness Alexy II died in December 2008, Bishop Kirill was entrusted 'locum tenens' colloquially the position of acting Patriarch. Kirill had been elevated to Archbishop in 1977 and on 1 February 2009 was elected as the Patriarch of Moscow. On the evening of 16/17 July 2018, the centenary anniversary of the Ekaterinburg murders, Kirill led the only tribute to the Romanov martyrs with a night vigil. A liturgy was held at the Church on the Blood and a procession ensued with Kirill, his bishops and an estimated 100,000 people walking from the city centre to the Monastery of the Holy Royal Martyrs at Ganina Yama (13 miles); the same journey that the corpses had been taken to the first burial site.

Kirill's speech that evening insinuated that all of Russia's ails were due to Western influences that had increasingly arrived in Russia since Peter the Great had opened up the country to foreigners. He suggested that Russians had been decent people until they were corrupted by outside influences.

"What happened to our people? After all, the country was covered with churches and monasteries, an absolute majority of the people were baptized, and the churches were filled with people. Why did it happen? Why did the murderers squeeze the trigger, without trembling at what they were doing? It means not everything was favourable. It means the sunlight reflected in the gilded domes was not always refracted into human hearts to strengthen faith in the Lord in them. And we know how over the course of at least 200 years preceding the tragedy of the Ipatiev House some changes occurred in the people's consciousness that gradually but steadily led many to a departure from God, neglect of the commandments, and a loss of spiritual connection with the Church and the centuries-old spiritual tradition."
— HIS HOLINESS KIRILL

* * *

CHAPTER XXII

NEW YORK: 22 August 2012

Statement from the Synod of Bishops of the Russian Orthodox Church Outside of Russia:

During its regular session on June 14, 2012, the Synod of Bishops of the Russian Orthodox Church Outside of Russia deliberated on the matter of the discovery of the remains and other possessions relating to the martyrdom of the Royal Family which had been hidden in the walls of the Stavropighial Memorial Church in Brussels.

During renovations on St Job the Much-Suffering Church, which is also dedicated to the memory of Holy Royal Martyr Nicholas II, the Royal Family and all those martyred during that time of troubles, a sealed lead cylinder was discovered along with a glass tube with a handwritten document containing an inventory of the contents of the cylinder.

The fact that the Memorial Church contained these remains and other objects connected with the brutal murder of the Royal Family in Ekaterinburg had been known to the Synod of Bishops. It was also known that they were handed over by the investigator of the murder of the Royal Family, NA Sokolov, before his death (November 23, 1924), to Prince Alexei Alexandrovich Shirinsky-Shikhmatov, and in 1940 were given to Metropolitan Seraphim (Lukianov), who at the time headed the Western European Diocese, and that further, on October 1, 1950, when the Memorial Church was consecrated by Metropolitan Anastassy, the First Hierarch of the Russian Orthodox Church Outside of Russia, they were inserted into a sealed lead cylinder and built into the walls of the church.

The Synod of Bishops did not deem it proper to organise a search for the sealed capsule following the death of all the living witnesses, though naturally, over the recent two decades, many people exhibited an active interest in its existence.

Now, after its discovery, in light of the fact that the important question of the remains of the Royal Family is coming to a final conclusion based on new evidence and serious scientific research, and since controversy yet remains, the Synod of Bishops expresses its willingness to cooperate in the further study of this matter on the basis of the discovery together with the Church in Russia. An absolute condition of such research will be a pious attitude towards everything relating to the martyric end of the Royal Family and its faithful servants.

The Synod of Bishops believes and hopes that this will help achieve the final answer to this matter, which is so important to the Russian Orthodox Church.

https://www.russianorthodoxchurch.ws/synod/eng2012/20120822_enstatement.html

THE ROAD TO SAINTHOOD

Under the laws of ascension to the throne, There are no Romanovs today holding a rightful claim as there are only descendants from morganatic marriages; one must marry an equal to qualify for the throne. Dukes and duchesses cannot hold the title today because they must be descendants of the male line of a monarch of which there remain none; the last grand duke Andrei died in 1956 and the last grand duchess Olga died in 1960.

The memorial at Ganina Yama

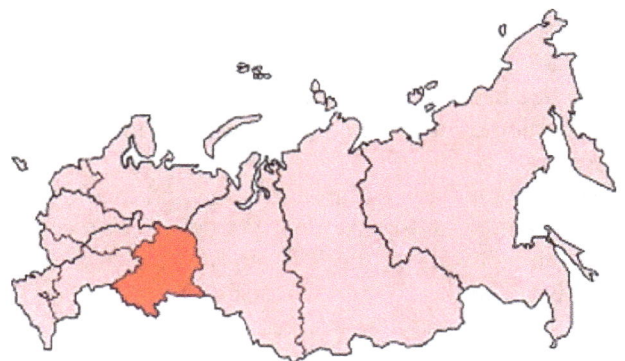

The Soviet Union with the Urals region highlighted

THE END

AFTERWORD

This book comes to an end with a statement by His Holiness Kirill blaming everyone but Russia for their mishaps but in the grand scheme of things his opinion is inconsequential and the absurdity is with a man who lives as a Christian but condones a war. A hundred years ago give or take, Russians and Germans were content to blame the Jews and even today conspiracies run aplenty and are much more of an existential threat to freedoms than ever. First, apocalypse movies, then alien invasions, next big brother and the illusion of democracy and now we face the rise of Artificial Intelligence that supersedes human capability and will ultimately control us.

The same chaos rules today as it always has done and will do tomorrow. The redeeming thing for humans is that sometimes a spontaneous revolution occurs as in Russia during 1905, when the true voice of people is heard for the briefest time. The tragedy is that revolutions rarely bring about change, as we saw in Russia when one revolution was followed by another, followed by seventy years of soviet control and a minor revolution in 1991 which resulted in greater State and religious control. Ultimately the rich and powerful will always do what they want and random revolutions will never change that.

Human history is a saving grace but it is not the definitive or even accurate human story. We see evil where and when we are told to see it, in Mr Putin for example, but did you know that Adolf Hitler was raised in the Catholic Church. In 'Mein Kampf' he did not repudiate the teachings of Christ or religion per se, because it had a great influence on his early education and in his later writings and speeches. But he did make many statements criticising the Catholic and Lutheran churches for their failings to help the people and criticised their meddling in politics. The point is, that even the most hated man in history understood that religion has a cancerous tendency to encroach upon all aspects of life and it is a tool used by the few to control the many. Similarly, Communism may be sound in principle but is flawed in practice because it is a social ideal reliant on controlling human behaviour and ideologies; and ideologies, like religions, are false beliefs and dangerous weapons.

The Russian people have endured religion and ideology for centuries, often led by superstition and corruption, yet they kept a candle alight that we recognise as the tenacity of the Russian in the face of hardship – they can endure anything. In the combined research for this book I came to see the Russian spirit embodied in the lives of five children. That nation is illuminated by their memory. Imagine the children playing and their joy radiating all around them, dancing with their father and praying with their mother, an innocence so cruelly taken - the epitome of sainthood. Their spirits are the true heartbeat of the Russian people. Amen.

APPENDICES

APPENDICE A – Movements under house arrest

KEY DATES

25 March 1917	Placed under house arrest at Tsarskoe Selo. (According to: memories of Count Paul Benckendorff Detained by Eichendorff from 1 March 1917 to 1 August 1917)
31 July 1917	Left Tsarskoe Selo for Tobolsk.
19 August 1917	Arrive at Tobolsk.
25 April 1918	Left Tobolsk for Ekaterinburg (Nicholas, Alexandra, Marie, Dr Botkin, four servants plus aides).
30 April 1918	Arrive at Ekaterinburg (first trip).
23 May 1918	Remaining family arrive from Tobolsk (second trip).
17 July 1918	Official date of the killings (0.15 am).

DURATIONS

22 March 1917 to 31 July 1917	Time at Tsarskoe Selo.
31 July 1917 to 14 August 1917	Travelling to Tobolsk.
14 August 1917 to 25 April 1918	Time spent at Tobolsk.
25 April 1918 to 30 April 1918	Travelling to Ekaterinburg.
30 April 1918 to 17 July 1918	Time spent at Ekaterinburg.

APPENDICE B – Birthdays

1868, 18 May	– Nicholas	Alexander Palace
1872, 6 June	– Alexandra	Neues Palaise
1895, 15 November	– Olga	Alexander Palace
1897, 10 June	– Tatiana	Peterhof Palace
1899, 26 June	– Marie	Peterhof Palace
1901, 18 June	– Anastasia	Peterhof Palace
1904, 12 August	– Alexei	Peterhof Palace

APPENDICES

APPENDICE C – Executions

PERM – 13 JUNE 1918

    Mikhail Alexandrovich (Nicholas' brother, shot in Siberian wood)
    Nicholas Johnson (Mikhail Alexandrovich's secretary)
    Ekaterina Adolfovna Schneider (German tutor) - 4 Sept 1918
    Countess Anastasia Vasilievna Hendrikova - 4 Sept 1918

IPATIEV HOUSE – 17 JULY 1918

    Nicholas Alexandrovich
    Alexandra Feodorovna
    Olga Nikolaevna
    Tatiana Nikolaevna
    Marie Nikolaevna
    Anastasia Nikolaevna
    Alexei Nikolaevich
    Dr Eugene Botkin (court physician)
    Anna Demidova (lady in waiting)
    Alois Yogorovich Trupp (footman)
    Ivan Kharitonov (cook)
    The dogs Jemmy, Ortipo

ALAPAYEVSK – 17/18 JULY 1918 (The 8 coffins taken to Harbin)

    Grand Duchess Elizabeth Feodorovna
        and Sister Varvara Yakovleva from the same convent
    Grand Duke Sergei Mikhailovich of Russia
        and his secretary Fyodor Remez
    Prince Ioann (i.e. John) Konstantinovich of Russia
    Prince Konstantin Konstantinovich of Russia
    Prince Igor Konstantinovich of Russia
    Prince Vladimir Pavlovich Paley

PETER AND PAUL FORTRESS – 28 JANUARY 1919

    Grand Duke Dmitry Konstantinovich (cousin to Nicholas II)
    Grand Duke Nikolai Mikhailovich, (cousin to Nicholas II)
    Grand Duke George Mikhailovich (cousin to Nicholas II)
    Grand Duke Pavel Alexandrovich (uncle to Nicholas II)

ELSEWHERE

    Chemodurov (Tsar's valet)
        3 weeks at Ipatiev House then transferred to prison

    Vasily Alexandrovich Dolgorukov (Court Marshal)
        shot in woods 10 July 1918

K. G. Nagorny (Alexei's sailor nanny)

General Ilya Tatishchev, (Court Marshal – General Adjutant) shot in woods 10 July 1918

I. D. Snedov (Lady in waiting)

A. V. Gendrikova (Court tutor)

Dr Vladimir Derevenko (physician, sailor nanny) executed 1936

SURVIVED

Maria Feodorovna (d. 13 October 1928, Copenhagen)

Grand Duke Nikolai Nikolaevich (d. 5 January 1929, France) and his wife Anastasia of Montenegro (d. 15 November 1935)

Grand Duchess Xenia Alexandrovna (d. 20 April 1960, UK) and her children: Feodor, Nikita, Dmitri, Rostislav and Vassily, son Andrei left Yalta earlier with his father on HMS Forsythe.

Grand Duchess Olga Alexandrovna (d. 24 November 1960, Cooksville, Canada) and her husband and children. The last Romanov to leave Russia, in February 1920.

Dr Derevenko (d. 1936 – executed in the Great Purge)

Sophie Buxhoeveden (d. 26 November 1956, UK)

Charles Sydney Gibbes (d. 24 March 1963, London)

Count Pavel Benckendorff (d. 28 January 1921, Estonia)

Pierre Gilliard (d. 30 May 1962, Switzerland)

Leonid Sednev - kitchen boy (d. 17 July 1942)

Maria Rasputina (d. 27 September 1977, Los Angeles) Prince Felix Yussoupoff (d. 27 September 1967, Paris) and his wife Irina daughter of Xenia Alexandrovna (d. 26 February 1970, Paris)

Elizaveta Nikolaevna Ersberg – maid (d. 12 March 1942, Russia)

Grand Duke Pavel Nikolaevich (d. 17 June 1931) uncle to Nicholas II and his wife Milica of Montenegro (d. 5 September 1951) and their children: Roman, Marina, and Nadejda.

APPENDICES

Princess Helen of Serbia – Montenegro (d. 16 October 1962) the wife of Ioann Konstantinovich who was murdered at Alapayevsk. She was rescued by Norway in December 1918.

Grand Duke Kirill Vladimirovich (d. 12 October 1938, France)

Grand Duchess Elizabeth Mavrikievna (d. 24 March 1927, Leipzig) Mother of the three Konstantinovich brothers murdered at Alapayevsk. She was rescued by Queen Victoria of Sweden in November 1918.

Grand Duchess Olga Konstantinovna (d. 18 June 1926, Rome) Former Queen Olga of Greece and Great grandmother to King Charles III of Britain. Rescued by Denmark in December 1918.

Grand Duke Boris Vladimirovich (d. 9 November 1943, Paris) Cousin to Nicholas II. Escaped from Caucasus in March 1919.

Alexander Mikhailovich (d. 26 February, 1933) husband to Xenia Alexandrovna. And their son Andrei Alexandrovich (d. 8 May 1981). They left Yalta on HMS Forsythe in December 1918.

Grand Duke Andrei Vladimirovich (d. 30 October 1956, Paris) cousin to Nicholas II and his soon wife to be (m. 1921) Mathilde-Marie Kschessinska (d. 6 December 1971, Paris)

THE EXECUTIONERS AT IPATIEV HOUSE

Yakov Yurovsky (the organiser)	S Vaganov
Grigori Nikulin (the assistant)	A Kabanov
P Ermakov (Cheka detachment)	V Netrebin
P Medvedev (head of the guard)	Y Tselms
M Medvedev (aka Kudrin)	

RASPUTIN'S EXECUTIONERS

Prince Felix Yussoupoff (Aristocrat)

Vladimir Purishkevich (Duma member)

Grand Duke Dmitry Pavlovich (Nicholas' cousin)

Dr Stanislaus de Lazovert (Physician/chemist)

Lieutenant Sergei Mikhailovich Sukhotin

APPENDICES

APPENDICE D – Timeline

1861 Emancipation of Russian serfs during the reign of Alexander II.

1861 *14 December* – Prince Albert dies / emancipation of Russian serfs in

1866 *9 November* – Wedding of Alexander of Russia to Princess Dagmar of Denmark. Became, Alexander III and Maria Feodorovna.

1868 *18 May* – Nikolai Alexandrovich (Nicholas II) is born.

1868 *1 July* – Alexander III and family visit UK for two months.

1869 *21 January* – Grigori Efimovich Novykh (Rasputin) is born to Siberian peasants Yefim and Anna in the village of Pokrovskoe on the Tura River.

1871 Creation of the German Empire.

1872 *6 June* – Alix of Hesse and by Rhine (Alexandra) is born.

1881 *13 March* – Assassination of Alexander II, Alexander III becomes Tsar and son Nicholas becomes heir apparent.

1883 *27 May* – Coronation of Alexander III.

1884 *June* – Nicholas 16 and Alix 12 meet for the first time in St Petersburg.

1887 *2 February* – Wedding of Grigori Rasputin to Praskovna Dubrovina. They will have three children that survive birth : Dmitry, Maria, and Varvara. Dmitry dies in infancy.

1887 *8 June* – Russia forms secret Reinsurance Treaty with Germany.

1888 Keiser Wilhelm II becomes German Emperor.

1889 *January* – Alix returns to St Petersburg, Nicholas and Alix fall in love.

1890 *18 March* – Otto von Bismarck is replaced by Leo von Caprivi.

1890 *23 March* – Nicholas begins relationship with Mathilde Kschessinska.

1890 *4 November* – Nicholas is sent on a round the world voyage.

1891 *16 August* – Nicholas returns from world voyage.

1892 Alexandra Feodorovna returns to St Petersburg to visit sister Ella.

1893 *20 June* – Wedding of Duke of York (George V) to Mary of Teck. Nicholas attends representing his parents.

APPENDICES

1894 19 *April* – Wedding of Alix's brother Ernest and Princess Victoria of Edinburgh, in Coburg (becoming Melita of Saxe-Coburg).

1894 20 *April* – Nicholas and Alix announce their engagement.

1894 3 *June* – Nicholas and Alix visit the Prince of Wales in the UK.

1894 6 *August* – Wedding of Princess Xenia Alexandrovna to Grand Duke Alexander Mikhailovich.

1894 21 *October* – Alix arrives at the Russian court, at Livadia, Crimea.

1894 1 *November* – Alexander III dies aged 49, Nicholas II becomes Tsar.

1894 26 *November* – Wedding of Nicholas II and Alexandra Feodorovna.

1895 15 *November* – Olga Nikolaevna is born.

1896 26 *May* – Coronation day.

1896 30 *May* – Khodynka Fields tragedy.

1896 *Summer* – Alexandra suffers a miscarriage a few months after having first daughter Olga.

1896 *September* – State visit to France.

1896 6 *October* – Nicholas and Alexandra arrive in Paris.

1896 19 *October* – Nicholas and Wilhelm II meet in Darmstadt.

1897–1905 Rasputin wanders to holy sites across Russia as a stranniki.

1897 17 *March* – Russia formally demands lease of Port Arthur from China.

1891 *March* – Siberian Railway project begins.

1895 10 *June* – Tatiana Nikolaevna is born.

1898-1904/5 – Nurse/nanny Margaretta Eagar working at Russian court.

1899 26 *June* – Marie Nikolaevna is born.

1900 27 *October* – Nicholas falls ill with typhoid fever at Livadia.

1901 22 *January* – Queen Victoria dies aged 81.

1901 18 *June* – Anastasia Nikolaevna is born.

1901 *January* – Nicholas II and Friedrich Martens nominated for Nobel Peace Prize for convening the Hague Peace Conference.

1901 5 *September* – The Standart arrives at Dunkirk, return visit to France.

1901 19 *September* – Nicholas and Alexandra meet M. Philippe in France.

1902/1903 – Rasputin building good and bad reputation in Kazan.

APPENDICES

1902 *19 August* – Alexandra ends phantom pregnancy with discharge. Publicly announced as miscarriage on 21 August.

1903 *13 February* – Grandest Imperial costume ball ever held.

1903 – Rasputin arrives in St Petersburg.

1903 – First section of the Siberian Railway opens and the first trains run from Moscow to Vladivostok.

1904 *8 February* – Russo-Japanese War begins.

1904 *8 April* – Britain and France form the Entente Cordiale alliance.

1904 *13 April* – Russian flagship Petropavlovsk sinks with 599 lives lost.

1904 *25 August* – Tsarevich Alexei Nikolaevich is born.

1904 – Rasputin goes to the Alexander Nevsky Monastery in St Petersburg and is introduced to Bishop Theophane.

1905 *22 January* – The First Revolution 'Bloody Sunday' starts.

1905 – Anna Taneyeva (Vyrubova) starts as lady in waiting to Alexandra.

1905 – Maria Vishnyakova starts work at court as the girl's governor.

1905 *20 February* – The Battle of Mukden begins in Manchuria. Ends on 10 March 1905 in Japanese victory.

1905 *27/28 May* – Battle of Tsushima ends in Japanese victory.

1905 – 2nd marriage of Princess Victoria-Melita of Saxe-Coburg to Kirill Vladimirovich (becoming Grand Duchess Victoria Feodorovna of Russia).

1905 *2 August* – Master Philippe dies in Lyon.

1905 *5 September* – The Russo-Japanese War ends.

1905 *30 October* – Nicholas issues the October manifesto.

1905 *1 November* – Rasputin is presented to Nicholas and Alexandra for the first time at Peterhof Palace.

1906 *18 July* – Rasputin meets Imperial family a second time at Peterhof Palace.

1906 *21 July* – First Duma is dismissed by Nicholas. Pyotr Stolypin appointed Prime Minister.

1906 *25 August* – Assassination attempt with a bomb on Prime Minister Stolypin at his house, his daughter is badly injured.

1906 *13 October* – Rasputin meets Imperial family for the third time at Peterhof Palace. Meets children for first time.

APPENDICES

1907 – Rasputin is investigated by the church for an alleged connection to the underground sect khlysty.

1907 *20 February* – Second Duma convenes.

1907 *30 April* – Marriage of Anna Taneyeva to Alexander Vyrubov.

1907 *16 June* – Second Duma is dismissed by Stolypin.

1907 *31 August* – The end of the Anglo-Russo Alliance also marks the start of the Triple Entente Alliance between France, Russia and Britain to counter the threat posed by the Triple Alliance of Germany, Italy, and Austria-Hungary

1907 *14 November* – Third Duma convenes.

1908 *9 June* – Nicholas II meets Edward VII off the coast of Reval (now Tallinn, Estonia).

1909 *2 August* – Standart arrives at Isle of Wight for the regatta.

1909 *24 October* – Standart visits Italy for a state visit and to conclude the secret agreement known as the Racconigi Bargain.

1909 *October-November* – Standart calls at Odessa and Sevastopol on return to Crimea from visits to England and Italy.

1909 – The nun Khioniya Berlatskaya from the Tsaritsyn monastery is raped by Rasputin.

1910 *Spring* – The nursery governess Maria Ivanovna Vishnyakova is raped by Rasputin.

1910 *March* – The Moscow Gazette launches the first of many press campaigns against Rasputin.

1910 – Stolypin conducts investigation in to Rasputin's behaviour and expels him from city. He presents the report to Nicholas II who takes no action.

1910 *6 May* – Edward VII dies, Queen Alexandra (Feodorovna of Denmark) becomes Dowager Empress.

1911 *Spring* – Rasputin makes pilgrimage to the Holy Land.

1911 *1 September* – Prime Minister Pyotr Stolypin is shot in a failed assassination but he dies from his injuries four days later.

1912 – Rasputin returns to St Petersburg from exile.

1912 *9 June* – Third Duma completes full five year term.

1912 5 Septem*ber* – Alexei almost dies from haemophilic internal bleeding when he falls out of a boat.

APPENDICES

1912 *15 November* – The members of the third duma re-convene to start the Fourth Duma term.

1913 *Easter* – The last notable lavish great ball is held in St Petersburg.

1913 *24 May* – Nicholas II and George V attend the wedding of Princess Victoria Louise of Prussia (Wilhelm II's daughter,) in Berlin.

1913 The largest party in the Duma, the Octobrists, call for an investigation in to Rasputin's influence over Alexandra.

1914 *28 June* – Archduke Franz Ferdinand (Heir to the Austrian throne) is assassinated with his wife, by Serbian nationalists, starting World War I.

1914 *29 June* – Rasputin is stabbed by Khioniya Guseva outside his home in Pokrovskoe and nearly dies.

1914 *1 August* – Germany declares war on Russia.

1914 *26-30 August* – The Battle of Tannenberg is fought between Russia and Germany. Russia is badly defeated.

1915 *13 March* – First Prime Minister of Russian Empire Sergey Witte dies.

1915 *13 July* – The Great Retreat begins from the Western front.

1915 *9 August* – Russian military field headquarters, the Stavka, is moved to Moghilev in Belarus. Nicholas leaves for the front on 23 August to take control of the army arriving there about five days later.

1915 *10 August* – Winter Palace infirmary opens with 241 staff.

1916 *January–February* – Minister of the Interior Alexei Khvostov plots Rasputin's murder. The plot fails.

1916 *May* – Completion of Siberian Railway.

1916 *7 November* – Grand duke Nikolai Nikolaevich warned Nicholas II of an imminent uprising.

1916 *19 November* – Vladimir Purishkevich makes damning speech in Duma calling ministers marionettes with strings pulled by Rasputin and Alexandra.

1916 *30 December* – Rasputin is murdered at the residence of Felix Yussoupoff.

1917 *2 March* – Fourth Duma ended, formally dissolved on 6 October

1917 – Lili Dehn becomes a lady in waiting to Alexandra.

1917 *7 March* – Nicholas returns to Moghilev from Tsarskoe Selo.

1917 *14 March* – Guard commanded by Colonel Eugene Kobylinsky takes over at Alexander Palace from Imperial Guard.

APPENDICES

1917 *15 March* – Nicholas II abdicates the throne.

1917 *16 March* – Nicholas' brother Mikhail Alexandrovich turns down the throne.

1917 *20 March* – Nicholas placed under arrest at Moghilev.

1917 *25 March* – Imperial family officially under house arrest at Alexander Palace.

1917 *3 April* – Colonel Korovichenko takes over as Commandant at Alexander Palace under house arrest.

1917 *19 August* – Imperial family and servants arrive at Governor's House in Tobolsk.

1917 *September* – Alexander Kerensky proclaims Russia to be a republic.

1917 7 November – October Revolution starts and Bolsheviks overthrow the Provisional Government. Anna Vyrubova is incarcerated in Petrograd.

1918 *13 February* – The Gregorian calendar is adopted in Russia.

1918 *27 February* – Former Imperial Family put on soldiers' rations.

1918 *18 March* – Bolsheviks decide to execute Romanov extended family members at Ay-Todor but they escape to Sevastopol.

1918 *22 April* – Bolshevik Vasily Iakovlev arrives with an armed detachment at Tobolsk, charged with transporting the family and servants to Moscow for trial.

1918 *25 April* – Nicholas, Alexandra, Marie, Dr Botkin and three servants head for Moscow for Nicholas to face trial. The destination is changed to Ekaterinburg.

1918 *30 April* – Nicholas and the others arrive at Ipatiev House in Ekaterinburg.

1918 *17 May* – Commander of the Guard Colonel Kobylinsky is replaced by Commander Rodionov at Ipatiev house.

1918 *23 May* – The rest of the children from Tobolsk arrive at Ipatiev House in Ekaterinburg.

1918 *12 or 13 June* – Grand Duke Mikhail killed in a supposed escape attempt from the Bolsheviks.

1918 *16 June* – Capital punishment introduced.

1918 13 July – Yakov Yurovsky is ordered by Ural Soviet to murder the prisoners at Ipatiev House.

1918 *14 July* – Yakov Yurovsky visits Koptyaki Forest to prepare the grave.

1918 *16 July* – Filipp Goloshchekin arrives at Ipatiev House to oversee the executions. The final confirmation comes to go ahead without delay.

1918 *17 July* – Mass executions at Ipatiev House in the early hours. Corpses buried at the Four Brothers pit at Ganina Yama.

1918 *18 July* – Yurovsky returns to Ganina Yama to recover the remains and rebury them at a copper mine. The plan fails and the graves are made at the Porosyonkov Ravine, 4.5 miles from Ganina Yama.

1918 *19 July* – Filipp Goloshchekin the Bolshevik War Commissar announces that 'Nicholas the Bloody' has been executed and that the rest are being detained indefinitely.

1918 *23 July* – The White Army take control of Ekaterinburg.

1918 *July* – The grave at Ganina Yama is discovered by White Army investigators but no bodies found.

1919 *February* – White Army investigator Nikolai Sokolov visits Porosyonkov Ravine but does not find the two graves there.

1919 *11 April* – HMS Marlborough leaves Crimea with Maria Feodorovna onboard and other Romanovs that are rescued.

1919 *16 April* – The Montenegrin sisters Militza and Anastasia with their husbands board HMS Lord Nelson and complete their escape to Genoa.

1919 *20 April* – Maria Feodorovna and daughter Xenia Alexandrovna and other staff and friends arrive in Malta.

1920 *7 February* – Head of the White Army Admiral Kolchak is executed.

1920 *Good Friday* – Olga Alexandrovna and family arrive in Denmark.

1925 – A vast collection of documents and photographs relating to the Romanov family are transferred to Yale University Archives.

1938 – Josef Stalin officially suppressed discussion of the Romanovs' fate.

1940s – Books referring to 'acts of revolutionary justice' against the Romanovs are taken out of circulation. The executioner Yurovsky's account is removed from display in Moscow's Museum of the Revolution.

1960 24 November – Olga Alexandrovna dies aged 78.

1964 – Anna Vyrubova dies aged 80.

1977 – Ipatiev House is demolished in September as Soviets declare it had no historical value.

1979 *30 May* – The main Romanov burial site is discovered but kept secret until 1991. Three skulls are removed.

1980 – Summer. The skulls and other items are reburied at the Romanov main burial site.

1981 – The Russian Orthodox Church outside of Russia proclaims Nicholas II and his family saints. On the spot that Ipatiev House once stood, the Church on the Blood is built to honour the victims.

1989 *10 April* – The Moscow News reveals the location of the Romanov burial site.

1991 – The remains of Nicholas, Alexandra, Olga, Tatiana, Anastasia, and four of the servants are buried in the Peter and Paul Cathedral in St Petersburg.

1993 – The Romanov remains are identified testing mitochondrial DNA compared to still living descendants of Alexander II. Tests proved they were Romanov remains.

2000 – The Russian Orthodox Church in Russia proclaims Nicholas II and his family saints as Passion Bearers.

2007 *29 July* – The second Romanov grave is discovered at Porosyonkov ravine of two children presumed to be Alexei and Marie.

2007 – Two new Romanov photographs are discovered at the Library of Congress to add to the seven others they had of the Imperial Family.

2008 – American and Russian experts re-affirm the remains unearthed in 1991 belonged to Nicholas II by matching the DNA of skeletal samples with living relatives and from objects such as a blood-stained shirt worn by Nicholas II.

2013 *8 May* – 200 Romanov photographs discovered at the Zlatoust City Museum.

2015 – At the insistence of the Russian Orthodox Church, Russian investigators exhume the bodies of Nicholas II and Alexandra Feodorovna, for additional DNA testing, which re-confirmed the Romanov remains.

2015 – Curator for Russian Art at the Science Museum UK, Natalia Sidlina, discovers 22 albums of Romanov photographs by chance when searching for Russia-related material at the National Science and Media Museum in Bradford.

2018 – Centenary anniversary of the Romanov executions. Over 100,000 pilgrims take part in a procession in Ekaterinburg, from the city centre to a monastery in Ganina Yama. There was no official commemoration.

* * *

APPENDICES

APPENDICE E – Photographs, Prints, Drawings

Attribution where required is given here. Most images are rights free and credit may be given to acknowledge the source.

Emperor Nicholas II, (pd)

APPENDICES

(pd) = Public Domain   (ca) = Colour Added

PAGE

Cover photograph: Nicholas II, (pd), Get Archive LLC
v   Imperial Family portrait, (pd)
1   Banner image: Stavka, Moghilev (pd), Get Archive LLC, edited
2   Queen Victoria with grandchildren, Royal Collection Trust
4   Princess Alice of Great Britain, courtesy of the Getty's Open Content Program
4   Princess Alix, (pd)
6   Chart - British and Russian relationship tree
9   Maria Feodorovna, (pd)
10   Chart – Danish House tree
12   Map of Schleswig, courtesy © Encyclopaedia Britannica, Inc
14   Alexander III & Maria Feodorovna, (pd), (ca)
16   Nicholas & Alix engagement 1894, (pd), Get Archive LLC
18   Print of Nicholas & Alexander wedding 1894, (pd)
19   Drawing of Russian Empire 1900 (pd)
24   Nicholas II reading the morning newspapers (pd)
29   Nicholas & Alexandra 1896, (pd)
31   Danish sisters Queen Alexandra and Maria Feodorovna, (pd)
32   Drawing: The Romanov dynasty tree
32   Drawing: How the cousins are connected tree
34   Print of Nicholas entering Moscow gate, (pd), (ca)
35   Print of Nicholas II at coronation altar
36   The Hessian delegation 1894, (pd)
37   Russian Imperial Crown, (pd)
38   Print of Nicholas II crowning Empress Alexandra 1896 (pd)
40   Print of Emperor and Empress on red steps, 1896, courtesy Penn Museum archives
41   Print of embossed kerchief for coronation 1896, (pd)
42   Coronation biscuit, (pd)
42   Coronation enamel cup, (pd)
45   Khodynka Field 1896, (pd)
47   Visit to Trinity Lavra of St Sergius monastery 1986, (pd)
48   Moscow illumination 1896, (pd)
52   Imperial couple descending red staircase, Moscow, (pd)
53   First Russian automobile (pd), Wikimedia Commons
54   Coronation Fabergé egg, (pd)
55   Drawing of Catherine Palace
56   Drawing of Alexander Palace
58   Fabergé Gatchina Palace egg (pd)

APPENDICES

59	Nicholas II out hunting in Spala, 1875, (pd)
60	Drawing of Anichkov Palace
61	Drawing of Peterhof Palace
62	Drawing of Winter Palace
63	Drawing of Livadia Palace
66	Imperial family portrait on Anastasia's christening day, (pd)
68	Nicholas II & grand duchesses on canon, Peterhof, (pd)
70	Alexandra Feodorovna on bridge at Alexander Palace, (pd)
72	Olga, Mikhail, Xenia Romanov, (pd), Get Archive LLC
77	Dinner at Winter Palace 1873, (pd)
77	Ball at Winter Palace 1873, (pd)
79	Alexandra Feodorovna in brocade gown, 1903, (pd)
82	Tricentenary edition playing cards
83	Carl Faberge portrait
84	Fabergé eggs, (L) The Winter Egg, (R) The Tricentenary Egg
85	Fabergé glass cabinet, (pd), edited
89	King of Siam, Romanov Collection Beinecke Rare Book and Manuscript Library, (pd) (ca)
94	The Montenegrin sisters, (pd)
96	Print by Pavel Piasetsky, Standart at Dunkirk, 1901, (pd), edited
97	Print by Pavel Piasetsky, walking in park, (pd)
100	Letter from Alexandra to Elizabeth, Tony Abbott©2019
101	Master Philippe de Lyon, (pd), (ca)
105	Full portrait of Alexandra by Friedrich Kaulbach, 1903, (pd)
108	Full portrait of Pyotr Badmayev, (pd)
111	Portrait of Sergey Witte, (pd), (ca)
113	Drawing of the Sea of Japan region, (pd)
114	Breaker steamship Baikal, Tyne & Wear Archives, (ca)
114	Transport cars of TSR across Lake Baikal, (pd), (ca)
118	Flagship Petropavlovsk sinking, (pd), (ca)
118	Battle of Mukden, (pd), (ca)
120	Alexandra pregnant, 1904, (pd), (ca)
121	Seraphim procession, (pd), Get Archive LLC
122	Alexandra maternity dress, Tony Abbott©2019
123	Ditto
123	Alexei christening day, 1904, (pd)
124	Alexei christening day family portrait, 1904, (pd), edited
126	Chart of haemophilia, (ca)
128	American newspaper clipping
130	Resident submits petition to Nicholas II, 1904, (pd), (ca)
131	Cossacks on Palace Square, (pd), (ca)
132	Bloody Sunday shootings in Palace Square, 1905, (pd). (ca)
136	The Tauride Palace, building of the State Duma, (pd)

APPENDICES

138	Deputies arrive for opening of the first Duma at Tauride Palace (pd) Get Archive LLC
140	Deputies of first Duma arrive and find Tauride Palace closed, (pd)
142	The fourth duma members (1912-1917), (pd)
146	Drawing of Pokrovskoe rivers, (pd)
150	Rasputin full portrait, (pd), Get Archive LLC
156	Anna Tanyeva's (Vyrubova) house, (pd), (ca)
166	Doctor Eugene Botkin, (pd), edited
167	Doctor Botkin's journal, Tony Abbott©2019
168	Rasputin's salon, St Petersburg, (pd)
168	Portrait of Rasputin by Theodora Krarup, (pd)
170	Girls with pony, (pd), (ca)
172	Alexei on pony, (pd)
173	Alexei and Joy in tree, (pd), Zlatoust City Museum
174	Alexandra in mauve room, (pd), (ca)
175	The maple drawing room at Alexander Palace (pd)
178	(R) Maria Feodorovna with Nicholas II in dress, (pd)
178	(L) Queen Mary with son James, (pd)
179	Eastman Kodak portable cameras, (pd)
182	Anna Vyrubova in cassock with album, (pd)
183	Olga carrying sod, (pd), Library of Congress
183	Governor's Mansion in Tobolsk, (pd), Library of Congress
185	Nicholas II & Anastasia smoking cigarette, (pd), Zlatoust Museum
186	Print of young Tsarevich Nicholas II, (pd), Thormeyer Collection
187	Olga looking through a photograph album, (pd)
190	Standart at shipbuilders, (pd), Peter Lars Elfelt, (ca)
195	Drawing map of north eastern Europe
200	Polar Star leaving Portsmouth 1896, (pd)
202	Print of Nicholas II arriving at Cherbourg 1896, (pd)
204	Print of Nicholas II laying foundation stone, 1896, (pd)
206	Imperial couple riding in carriage, Paris 1896, (pd)
209	Nicholas II inspects troops with President Loubet, 1902 (pd)
210	Marie Antoinette with her children by Élisabeth Vigée, (pd)
211	Sketch of Loubet visiting Imperial Family, 1906, (pd)
214	Standart in bay of Reval, 1908, (pd), Romanov Collection, Beinecke Rare Book and Manuscript Library
215	Nicholas II and Maria Feodorovna greet Edward VII on Standart, (pd), Wikimedia Commons
216	Ladies in white on Standart, (pd), (also Royal Collection RCIN 2917011), edited
218	Sailor nannies (the diadkas), (pd)
220	Dinner onboard Standart, (pd), Get Archive LLC
221	British and Russian royals in Isle of Wight, (pd), Get Archive LLC

APPENDICES

223	Standart at Kiel, (pd)
224	Nicholas with cook, (pd), Get Archive LLC
227	Standart Fabergé egg
227	Standart Fabergé egg surprise
228	Nicholas II and Alexandra Feodorovna smiling on Standart, (pd)
228	Marie and Anastasia reading on deck on Standart, (pd)
229	Nichola reading and Alexandra sewing on the deck of Standart, (pd)
229	Alexei on the deck of Standart with his toy yacht, (pd)
230	The crew of Standart in the ship's mess having dinner, (pd), edited
230	Imperial Family on a launch boat leaving Standart, 1911, (pd)
233	Rasputin, Hermogenes and Iliodor, (pd), edited
240	Rasputin with Ms Vyrubova and Mrs Rodzianko (pd), edited
242	Bishop Theophane, (pd), edited
245	Nicholas II in wheelchair with typhoid fever, 1900, (pd), edited
247	Byelovvyezh hunting lodge, Spala (pd), (ca)
248	Alexandra with Alexei in orthopaedic bed, (pd)
250	Alexandra & Alexei in wheelchairs, (pd)
251	Drawing of Rasputin holding Alexandra, (pd)
256	Drawing of Franz Mesmer, (pd)
261	Nicholas II on the Imperial Train at the Stavka, circa August 1915
263	Nicholas II blessing troops at the western front, (pd)
270	Ambulances at Tsarskoe Selo infirmary, (pd), edited
272	Marie and Anastasia visiting patients, (pd)
272	Alexandra handing instruments to surgeon, (pd), edited
274	Olga & Tatiana dressing a patient, (pd)
275	Olga tending to patient, (pd)
276	Alexandra Feodorovna's dress & apron uniform 1914, (pd)
278	Fabergé red cross portraits egg (pd), edited
284	Telegram from Wilhelm II to Nicholas II
291	Cellar at Yussoupoff Palace, (pd)
293	Newspaper clipping
294	Rasputin's body on the ice, (pd)
295	Rasputin showing bullet hole in head, (pd)
299	Rasputin's daughters, (pd)
302	Nicholas II on balcony of Winter Palace 1914, (pd)
305	Demonstrators in Petrograd scatter 1917, (pd)
313	Anna Vyrubova, courtesy 'The last days of the Romanovs'
316	Drawing of Nicholas II writing in diary, (pd)
327	Newspaper clipping
328	Newspaper clipping
336	Stamps of Nicholas II and George V
341	Extract from Alexandra Feodorovna's diary
345	The governor's mansion, Tobolsk, (pd)

346 Nicholas II & Pierre Gilliard Sawing wood, (pd)
346 Turkeys on animal farm, (pd), edited
349 Last known photograph of Anastasia, (pd)
350 Drawing of Rasputin's house in Pokrovskoe
352 Print of Nicholas II arrival at Ekaterinburg, (pd), (ca)
355 Last photo of Alexei and Olga, (pd), Wikimedia Commons, (pd)
363 Admiral Kolchak inspecting troops of his Volunteer Army
367 Ipatiev House, (pd), Get Archive LLC, edited
367 Ipatiev House postcard, (pd), Get Archive LLC
369 Ipatiev House girls room, (pd)
370 Ipatiev House girls room Murano chandelier, source unknown
371 Ipatiev House, Avdeev's room, (pd)
374 Yakov Yurovsky, (pd)
380 Ipatiev House courtyard inside, (pd)
380 Ipatiev House courtyard inside doors, (pd)
381 Ipatiev House inner doors to basement stairway, (pd)
381 Ipatiev House stairway to basement (pd)
382 Print of Ipatiev House cellar scene before execution, (pd)
383 Print of Ipatiev House cellar scene, unknown source
385 Mauser used by Ermakov, (pd)
385 Ermakov mugshot, (pd)
386 Ipatiev House cellar after search by investigators, (pd)
386 Ipatiev House bullets found in cellar by investigators, (pd)
391 Ermakov at the main grave, (pd)
392 Jewels discovered at Ganina Maya, (pd), Wikimedia Commons
393 Telegram discovered by investigators, (pd)
400 Tatiana and Anastasia with Ortipo, (pd)
424 (L) Alix 6yo, (pd)
424 (R) Marie 13yo, (pd)
430 Maria Feodorovna on HMS Marlborough, (pd), (ca)
432 Danish sisters on balcony at Hvidore, (pd)
434 Olga in nurse uniform, (pd), Get Archive LLC
443 (L) General Dieterichs, (pd)
443 (R) Nikolai Sokolov, (pd), edited
445 Four Brothers pit at Ganina Yama, (pd)
449 Sokolov's wooden boxes, courtesy The End of the Romanovs
450 The Sokolov Box, (pd), edited
475 Print of Imperial Family holy saints, (pd)
487 View of Ipatiev House from Voznesenskaya Square, (pd)
487 View of Ipatiev House from Voznesenskaya Square, enlarged (pd)
489 Church on the Blood, Ekaterinburg, (pd)
495 The Romanov memorial at Ganina Yama, (pd)
495 Drawing map outline of Russia and Urals, Wikipedia

APPENDICE F – Further Reading

Books that are in the public domain (PD) are copyright free, being that 70 years have expired since the death of the author. They can be downloaded from online archives. (* *denotes a particularly interesting read*)

Internet Archive: https://archive.org/
Project Gutenberg: https://gutenberg.org/

Six years at the Russian Court
by Margaret Eagar
Pub: 1906 / PD: Internet Archive

Memoirs of the Russian Court
by Anna Vyroubova
Lady in Waiting to the Tsarina
Pub: 1923 / PD: Internet Archive

The Mad Monk of Russia
by Iliodor
Pub: 1918 / PD: Internet Archive

The Kaiser's Memoirs
by Wilhelm II
(Emperor of Germany 1888-1918)
English translation Pub: 1922
PD: Internet Archive

Confessions of the Czarina
by Count Vassili
(aka Princess Catherine Radziwill)
Pub: 1918 / PD: Project Gutenberg

The Romanovs and Mr Gibbes
by Frances Welch
Pub: 2002
ISBN 10: 190409516X
ISBN 13: 9781904095163

The End of The Romanovs
by Victor Alexandrov
Publisher: Hutchinson & Co Ltd
Pub: 1966

* **The Real Tsaritsa**
by Madame Lili Dehn
Pub: 1922 / PD: Project Gutenberg

The Memoirs of Count Witte
by Count Witte
Pub: 1921 / PD: Internet Archive

From Autocracy to Bolshevism
by Baron P. Graevenitz
Pub: 1918 / PD: Internet Archive

The Last Days of the Romanovs
by George Gustav & Robert Wilton
Pub: 1920 / PD: Project Gutenberg

Once a Grand Duchess
Xenia Sister of Nicholas II
by John Van der Kiste and Coryne Hall
Pub: 2007
ISBN 10: 0750935219
ISBN 13: 9780750935210

The Emperor Nicholas II
as I knew him
by Major-General Sir John Hanbury-Williams
Pub: 1922
PD: Internet Archive

Upheaval by Olga Kleinmichel Woronoff (wife of Pavel Voronov)

APPENDICES

Thirteen Years at the Russian Court
by Pierre Gilliard
Formerly Tutor to the Czarevich
PD: Project Gutenberg

* Rasputin The Untold Story
by Joseph T. Fuhrmann
Pub: 2012
ISBN 10: 1118172760
ISBN 13: 9781118172766

Memories of a Shipwrecked World
Autobiography by Marie Kleinmichel
Translated Pub: 1923

*** Nicholas II
Prisoner of the purple**
By Mohammed Essad-Bay
Pub: 1936 - PD: Internet Archive

* The life and tragedy of Alexandra Feodorovna Empress of Russia A Biography
by Baroness Sophie Buxhoeveden
Pub: 1929 / PD: Internet Archive

At the Court of the Last Tsar
by Alexander Mossolov (Head of the Court Chancellery 1900-1916)
First translation Pub: 1935
PD: Internet Archive

**The reign of Rasputin:
An Empire's Collapse**
by M.V.Rodzianko
Pub: 1927 / PD: Internet Archive

Rasputin: His Malignant Influence and His Assassination
by Felix Youssoupoff
Translated by Oswald Raynor 1955
PD: Internet Archive

* Memories from Moscow to the Black Sea
by Teffi
Translated Pub: 2016
ISBN 13: 9781590179529

Nicholas II
by A.N. Bokhanov's
Pub: 2000
ISBN 10: 5780506353
(Russian version only)

The Murder of Rasputin
by Vladimir Purishkevich
Pub: 1918/1924
Extremely rare collectors item,
(Russian version only)

**H. P. Blavatsky
An outline of her life**
by Herbert White
Pub: 1909 / PD: Internet Archive

**25 Chapters of My Life
The memoirs of Grand Duchess Olga Alexandrovna**
by Paul Kulikovsky, Karen Roth-Nicholls and Sue Woolmans
Pub: 2009
ISBN 10:1906775168
ISBN 13: 9781906775162

**An Ambassador's memoirs
Vol 1 (July 1914-June 2nd, 1915)**
by Maurice Paléologue
(Last French ambassador to the Russian Court)
Pub: 1925 / PD: Internet Archive

**The Last Grand Duchess
Her Imperial Highness Grand Duchess Olga Alexandrovna
1 June 1882–24 November 1960**
by Ian Vorres / Pub: 1964/1965

APPENDICE G – List of Names

TSAR NICHOLAS II

Nikolai Alexandrovich (Nicholas II Tsar of Russia)
Emperor Alexander III (Nicholas II's father)
Dowager Empress Maria Feodorovna (Nicholas II's mother)
Emperor Alexander II (Nicholas II's paternal grandfather)
King Christian IX of Denmark (Nicholas II's maternal grandfather)
Queen Louise of Denmark (Nicholas II's maternal grandmother)
Grand Duke Mikhail Alexandrovich (Nicholas II's brother)
Grand Duchess Olga Alexandrovna (Nicholas II's sister)
Grand Duchess Xenia Alexandrovna (Nicholas II's sister)
Grand Duchess Maria Alexandrovna of Russia (Nicholas II's auntie)
Grand Duke Vladimir Alexandrovich (Nicholas II's uncle)
Grand Duke Pavel Alexandrovich (Nicholas II's uncle)
Grand Duke Sergei Alexandrovich (Nicholas II's uncle, unofficially 'the Duke of Khodynka' and husband to Elizabeth Feodorovna)
Grand Duke Nikolai Nikolaevich (Nicholas II's great uncle, husband to Anastasia of Montenegro)
Grand Duke Constantin Konstantinovich (Nicholas II's cousin)
Grand Duke Alexander Mikhailovich (Nicholas II's first cousin removed)
Grand Duke Peter Nikolaevich (Nicholas II's cousin, husband to Militza)
Grand Duke Andrei Vladimirovich (Included on centenary playing cards as jack of diamonds)

TSARINA ALEXANDRA FEODOROVNA

Alix of Hesse and by Rhine (Alexandra Feodorovna Tsarina of Russia)
Grand Duke Friedrich Ludwig of Hesse and by Rhine (Alix's father, Ludwig IV)
Princess Alice of Great Britain (Alix's mother)
Queen Victoria of the UK and Great Britain and Ireland (Alix's maternal grandmother)
Prince Ernest of Hesse and by Rhine (Alix's brother)
Princess Victoria Melita of Edinburgh (Alix's cousin)
Princess Elizabeth of Hesse and by Rhine (Alix's sister)
Edward VII (Alix's uncle, King of England)
Queen Alexandra (Consort to Edward VII, sister to Maria Feodorovna)
Edward VIII (Alix's first cousin)
George V (Alix's first cousin, Duke of Cornwall and York, later king)
Prince Arthur, Duke of Connaught and Strathearn (Alix's uncle)
Duchess Louise Margaret (Alix's auntie who attended coronation)

APPENDICES

Keiser Wilhelm II (Alix's first cousin, Emperor of Germany)
Princess Elena of Montenegro (Alix's sister, Queen of Italy)
King Victor Emmanuel III (Alix's brother-in-law, King of Italy)
Princess Irene (Alix's sister, wife to Henry of Prussia)
Prince Henry of Prussia (Alix's brother-in-law, married to Irene

COURT MEMBERS

Margaretta Eagar (Children's nurse/nanny 1898 to 1904)
Sophie Tyutcheva (Governess of the Imperial children)
Maria Vishnyakova (Governess of the Imperial children)
Dr Eugene Botkin (court doctor)
Vera Gedroitz (Decorated surgeon and physician to the Imperial Court)
Charles Sydney Gibbes (Children's English language tutor)
Pierre Gilliard (French language tutor)
Alexandra Tegleva (Nurse of Anastasia, wife to Pierre Gilliard)
Mlle Ekaterina Schneider (German language tutor, prisoner separated at Ekaterinburg)
Herbert Galloway Stuart (English tutor to the nephews of Nicholas II 1908-1916)
Countess Anastasia Hendrikova (Lady in waiting, prisoner separated at Ekaterinburg)
Baroness Sophie Buxhoeveden (Lady in waiting from 1913)
Anna Taneyeva (then Anna Vyrubova)
Alexander Vyrubov (Husband to Anna Taneyeva)
Countess Ekaterina Petrovna Kleinmichel (Maid of Honour to Empress Maria Alexandrovna, auntie to Olga Konstantinovna Kleinmichel)
Doctor Girsh (Alexander III and Maria Feodorovna's court physician)
Alexander Mossolov (Head of Chancellery of the Imperial Court Ministry)
Count Pavel Konstantinovich Benckendorff (Grand Marshal of the Imperial Court)
Count Konstantin Ivanovich Palen (Grand Marshal of the Court and former Minister of Justice)
Vasily Aleksandrovich Dolgorukov (Court Marshal)
Count Alexander Konstantinovich Benckendorff (Russian ambassador to England)
Lili Dehn (Alexandra's friend wife of first officer on Standart)
Carl Akimovich von Dehn (Officer on Standart and Lili Dehn's husband)
Grand Duchess Militza (former Princess Milica of Montenegro)
Grand Duchess Anastasia (former Princess Anastasia of Montenegro)
Mr Stcheglov (Nicholas II's librarian)
Dr Kastritzky (court dentist)

Alois Trupp (Nicholas II's footman/valet)
Ivan Ivanovich Tchagine (Captain of the Standart)
Nikolai Pavlovich Sablin (2IC on the Standart)
Dr Vladimir Nikolaevich Derevenko (Physician and Alexei's sailor nanny from 1912)
Klementy Grigorievich Nagorny (Sailor nanny to Alexei)
Adjutant General Tatistchev (Prisoner separated at Ekaterinburg)
Countess Olga Konstantinovna Kleinmichel
Dmitry Malama (Equerry to the Imperial Court)
Vladimir Voeikov (Alexandra Palace head of security 1913)
Count Vladimir Nikolaevich Orlov (Advisor to Alexander III and Nicholas II)
Count Nikolai Vladimirovich Orlov (b. 1891-1961) (Husband to Princess Nadejda Petrovna of Russia)

ARTISANS, ARTISTS, EXPERTS

Carl Faberge (Jeweller)
Mikhail Perkhin (Fabergé workmaster)
Henrik Wigström (Fabergé workmaster)
Mathilde Feliksovna Kschessinska (Prima ballerina, involved with Nicholas II)
Tamara Karsavina (Prima ballerina)
Camille Cerf (Cinematographer)
Vladimir Alekseevich Gilyarovsky (Moscow writer and journalist)
Vasily Safonov (Musician and composer)
Alexander Bokhanov (Russian historian)
Allan Hume (British ornithologist)
Friedrich Kaulbach (court painter to George V)
Pavel Piasetsky (Artist and friend to Nicholas II)
Dmitry Merejkovsky (Russian writer and poet)
Theodora Krarup (Danish court artist, painted 16 portraits of Rasputin)
Sigmund Freud (Neurologist)
J. B. S. Haldane (British Scientist)
Lev Tikhomirov (Editor of the Moscow News)
William Le Queux (Elaborative author of books about Rasputin)
Captain Alexander Mandryka (Investigated Rasputin for the Tsar)
Maxim Gorky (Writer)
Judith Prager (Hypnotherapist)
Professor Dmitry Kossorotov (Did post mortem on Rasputin)
Dr Vladimir Zharov (Russian forensic expert)
Professor Derrick Pounder (Pathologist, head of forensic medicine at Dundee University)

APPENDICES

Lady Colin Campbell (Royal writer)
Eugene Gore Vidal (America writer)
Reverend G.V. Vaughan-James (Chaplain)
David Bullock (Historian)
Ivan Egorovich Plotnikov (Professor of Russian history at Ural State University)
Alexander Avdonin (Discovered Romanov main grave)
Geli Ryabov (Discovered Romanov main grave)
Dmitri Merezhovski (Privy Councillor and one of Nicholas II's favourite authors)
Ferdinand Thrmeyer (French language tutor to Imperial Family)
George William Totten (Photographer at the coronation 1896)
Pavel Mikhailovich Bykov Russian author that wrote the first full account of the fall of the downfall of the Imperial Romanov dynasty
Ivan Starov Russian architect

OCCULTISTS

Madame Helena P. Blavatsky, 1831-1891, (Russian medium, theosophist)
Gérard Anaclet Vincent Encausse (Occultist known as Papus)
Mathilde Theuriet (Wife to Papus)
Master Philippe of Lyon (French healer)
Pyotr Badmayev (Tibetan physician and pharmacist)
Madame Gutjen Sund (Swedish medium)

MINISTERS & OFFICIALS

Prime Minister Pyotr Stolypin (Assassinated 1911)
Prime Minister Kokovtzev
Vyacheslav Plehve (Minister of Interior)
Pyotr Durnovo (Minister of Interior)
Vyacheslav Plehve (Minister of Interior)
Alexei Khvostov (Minister of the Interior that plotted against Rasputin in 1916 and was imprisoned for it)
Pavel Kurlov (Head of the Imperial Security detail and a former Minister of the Interior)
Alexander Isvolsky (Minister of Foreign Affairs)
Pavel Nikolayevich Milyukov (Minister of Foreign Affairs)
Count Sergey Yulyevich Witte (Transport Minister and Interior Minister)
Nikolai Muraviev (Minister of Justice)
General Alexey Kuropatkin (War Minister 1989)
Mikhail Vladimirovich Rodzianko (President of the State Duma)
M. V. Rodzianko (President of the State Duma)
Alexander Kerensky (Duma member, first Prime Minister of the new republic)

APPENDICES

Alexander Vlasovsky (Moscow Chief of Police at Khodynka Field)
Pyotr Rachkovsky (Head of Russian secret police in Paris, the Okhrana)
A. T. Vasiliev (Head of the police department in St Petersburg)
Li-Hung-Chan (Chinese politician and ambassador to Russia)

BRITISH & FRENCH

Lord Kitchener (British Secretary of State for War)
Sir George Buchanan (British ambassador to Russia)
Sir Mansfield Cumming (British naval Captain and founder of secret service SIS)
Major-General Sir John Hanbury-Williams (British army officer at Stavka)
Captain Archibald Campbell (British SIS representative in Russia)
Lieutenant Stephen Alley (British SIS representative in Russia)
Major Cudbert Thornhill (Indian Army officer)
Lieutenant-Colonel Sir Samuel Hoare (Conservative MP, SIS)
Oswald Rayner (SIS agent in Petrograd)
John Scale (SIS agent in Petrograd)
Oliver Locker-Lampson (British MP and SIS who testified in the Yussoupoff case)
Arthur Bigge (First Baron of Stamfordham and secretary to George V)
Governor Methuen (of Malta)
Émile Loubet (Prime Minister of France)
Gustave Lannes de Montebello (French ambassador to Russia)
Maurice Paléologue (French Ambassador to Russia)

RUSSIAN

Filipp Isayevich Goloshchekin (Bolshevik War Commissar, superior of Yankel Yurovsky)
Alexander Avdeev (Commandant at Ipatiev House)
Pavel Medvedev (Assistant to Avdeev)
Alexander Moshkin (Assistant to Avdeev)
Vladimir Lenin (Head Bolshevik revolutionary)
Nikolai Gorbunov (Lenin's secretary)
Yakov Mikhailovich Sverdlov (Bolshevik Chairman of the Central Executive Committee in Moscow)
Alexander Beloborodov (Official at Ural Soviet that sent the coded telegram to telegram to Moscow)
Leon Trotsky (Communist revolutionary)
Vasily Yakovlev (Bolshevik revolutionary)
Pyotr Ermakov (Cheka member and District Commissar and executioner)
Pyotr Voykov (fence for Yurovsky)
Captain de Kotzebue (First Commandant at Alexander Palace house arrest)

APPENDICES

Colonel Korovichenko (Second Commandant at Alexander Palace and Tobolsk house arrests}
Colonel Eugene Kobylinsky (Commander of the Guard at Alexander Palace and Tobolsk under house arrest)
Vasily Yakolev (Bolshevik charged with transporting Romanovs from Tobolsk to Ekaterinburg)
Yakov Mikhailovich Yurovsky (2nd camp commandant at Ipatiev House, Cheka member)
Commissar Rodionov (Bolshevik Commander of the Guard at Ipatiev House from 17 May 1918, took children to Ekaterinburg)
Colonel Pavel Rodzianko (British Expeditionary Force, rescued Joy from Ipatiev House)
Admiral Alexander Kolchak (Established the Sokolov investigation)
Nikolai Sokolov (White Army investigator in to the executions at Ipatiev House)
General Samsonov (World War I, shot himself)
Princess Nadejda Petrovna (third child of Grand Duke Peter Nikolaevich and Princess Milica of Montenegro)

RELIGIOUS

Bishop Theophane (Russian Orthodox priest)
Rasputin (Grigori Efimovich Novykh)
Praskovya Fedorovna Dubrovina (Rasputin's wife)
Aron Simanovich (Rasputin's finance secretary)
Akilina N. Laptinskaya (Rasputin's general secretary)
Maria Grigorovna Rasputina (Rasputin's daughter)
Madame Olga Lochtina (Aristocrat devotee of Rasputin)
Khioniya Berlatskaya (Devotee of Rasputin who accused him of rape)
Father John of Kronstadt (Russian Orthodox Church hiermonk)
Bishop Iliodor (Sergius Mikhailovich Trufanoff, Russian Orthodox priest)
Georgy Gapon (Revolutionary priest that delivered the petition that led to Bloody Sunday 1905)
Bishop Anthony of Tobolsk (member of the Holy Synod 1912-1916)
Bishop Hermogenes of Saratov (Russian Orthodox priest)
Father Aleksei Vasiliev (Priest at Tobolsk)
Vladimir Khlynov (Priest at Tobolsk)

OTHER NOTABLES

Princess Marie Victorovna Bariatinsky (Alexandra's friend)
Kolya Derevenko (Son of Sailor nanny Dr Deverenko and Alexei's friend)
Lieutenant Nikolai Rodionov (Tatiana's favourite officer on the Standart)

APPENDICES

Nikolai Demenkov (Marie's favourite officer on the Standart)
Ekaterina Zborovskaya (Friend of Anastasia that she wrote to when under house arrest)
Lenka Sednev (aka Leonid – Kitchen boy, spared execution by the Bolsheviks)
Prince John Konstantinovich (Suitor of Olga Nikolaevna)
Prince Carol of Romania (Proposed to Marie Nikolaevna)
Prince Felix Yussoupoff (Main conspirator that killed Rasputin)
Irina Yussoupoff (Wife of Prince Felix)
Ivan Kalyaev (Assassinated Grand Duke Sergei Alexandrovich)
Vladimir Purishkevich (Participated in the killing of Rasputin.)
Chionya Guseva (Made failed attempt to kill Rasputin in June 1914)
Colonel Ivan Rodionov (Gave Rasputin a beating at Vasilievsky Island)
Dmitry Kolyaba (Gave Rasputin a beating at Vasilievsky Island)
Franziska Schanzkowska (Imposter of Anastasia)
Dmitry Chudinov (Guard from Ipatiev House that stole photo album)
King Chulalongkorn of Siam (Modern day Thailand)
Empress Eugenie de Montijo (Widow of Napoleon III)
Archduke Franz Ferdinand (Heir to the Austrian throne, assassinated)
Valentina Chebotaryova (Head nurse)
Countess Olga Konstantinovna Kleinmichel (Wife to Pavel Voronov)

NAMES OF DOGS

Joy (Cocker Spaniel belonging to Alexei)
Jemmy (Cavalier King Charles Spaniel belonging to Anastasia)
Ortipo (French bulldog belonging to Tatiana)

NAMES OF PLACES

Moghilev, Poland
Khodynka Field
Tsarskoe Selo
Spala, Poland (Belarus)
Compiègne, France
Pokrovskoe, Siberia
Verkhoturye, Siberia
Ganina Yama, Ekaterinburg
Ay-Todor, Crimea
Racconigi, Italy
Koptyaki Forest, Ekaterinburg
Alapayevsk, Perm
Ivanovskoe Cemetery, Ekaterinburg
Vasilievsky Island, St Petersburg

NAMES OF PALACES

Buckingham Palace (London), ix, 78, 222, 337, 428, 436
Alexander Palace (Imperial Family's preferred residence)
Winter Palace (Official residence)
Livadia Palace (Summer home in Crimea)

Petrovsky Palace (Moscow; official Easter residence), 33-34, 43. 45-46
Peterhof Palace (official summer residence), 30, 61, 64, 66, 120-121, 124, 134, 153-155, 208
Anichkov Palace (on Nevsky Prospect, St Petersburg), 21, 59, 61-62
Apraksin Palace (former part of Winter Palace), 62
Menzikoff Palace (St Petersburg, part of Hermitage museum 1981), 74
Granatov Palace (Moscow), 75
Konstantin Palace (Strelna - Montenegrin sisters), 99
Gatchina Palace (Home of the Dowager Empress), 21, 57, 88, 373
Catherine Palace, 56, 64, 187, 225
The Residential Palace, Darmstadt, 209
Neskoutchnoe Palace, Moscow, 267
Moika Palace (Official name for the Yussoupoff palace), 290
Tauride Palace (Orlov's home and later State Duma), 136-137, 285
Dulber Palace (Yalta, Crimea), 63, 99, 426, 429
Palace of San Antonio (Malta), 431
Amalienborg Palace (Denmark), 431
Fredensborg Palace, Denmark, 431
Biebrich Palace, Wiesbaden, 209
Palace of Versailles, 55, 96, 208, 211
Élysée Palace, 211

VARIOUS NAMES

Putilov Works factory, 110, 129, 321
Mariinsky Imperial Theatre, 81
Uspensky Cathedral, 31
Annunciation Cathedral, 39
Vagankovsky Cemetery, 44
Smolny Institute, St Petersburg, 93
Petropavlovsky Fortress, 102
Balashevskaya Convent (Tsaritsyn), 235, 239
Byelovvyezh hunting lodge (Autumn retreat, Spala, Poland (Belarus), 247
Preobrazhensky Life-Guards Regiment, 8, 49 137, 290
Leub Guard Hussar Regiment, 36

Mariinsky Ballet, 5
Znamensky monastery, 147
Archangels Cathedral, 39
Bolshoi Theatre, 47, 81
Rothney Castle, India, 90
Schlusselburg Fortress, 347

* * *

INDEX OF NAMES

A

Abramov, Dr Sergei, 395, 376-377, 483
Abramov, (Bolshevik), 395,
Ackerman, Carl William, 463-4
Albert, Prince, 1-3
Albert Victor, Prince, 4-5, 13
Alexander III, 4-5, 8, 10, 13-14, 17, 20-21, 23-26, 30, 36, 40, 43, 57, 59, 63-64, 72, 78, 88, 93, 99, 109, 112, 164, 176, 185, 189-191, 205, 211-212, 247, 249, 269, 278, 303, 311, 325, 396, 480, 488
Alexandrovich, Alexei (Romanov), 71
Alexandrovich, George, 478-479, 481-482
Alexandrovich, Pavel, 319-320
Alexandrovich, Sergei, 4, 46, 52, 134, 268, 292, 395, 417
Alexandrovich, Vladimir, 47, 71, 95
Alexandrovna, Olga, 23, 49, 160, 230, 235, 237, 278, 313, 318, 337, 426, 462, 479
Alexandrovna, Xenia, 61, 87, 103, 126, 235, 243, 347, 427, 429, 435, 444, 471, 479
Alexeievna, Empress Elizabeth, 21
Alekseev, General Mikhail Vassilievich, 1, 262, 264-265, 320, 324, 331-332, 334, 360-362, 442
Alexandrov, Victor, x, xiii, 187, 444, 460, 467
Alexy II, His Holiness, 483, 488, 492-493
Alfonso, King, 3, 211, 424-426
Alice, Princess, 2, 4, 14, 21
Alvensleben, General Werner von, 409-410, 413-415
Amfiteatrov, Alexander, 240
Anastasia of Montenegro, 93-94, 97, 259
Anderson, Anna, (see Schanzkowska, Franziska)
Andreyev, Nikolai, 412
Antoinette, Marie, 177, 207-208, 210, 338
Avdonin, Dr Alexander Nikolaevich, 469-472, 476, 478, 485-486
Azar, Helen, 476

B

Badmayev, Pyotr, 99, 107--108, 151, 160, 163-165
Bariatinsky, Princess Leonilla Ivanovna, 225
Bariatinsky, Princess Marie, 87

Basily, Nicolas A. de, 325
Beloborodov, Alexander, 352, 393, 395, 419, 456, 458-460
Benckendorff, Alexander, 184
Benckendorff, Pavel, 67, 184, 282, 287, 328, 338, 497
Beneš, Minister Edvard, 458
Berlatskaya, Khioniya, 234
Bezak, Colonel Fedor Nikolaevich, 414-415
Bigge, Arthur, 337
Birbaum, François, 86
Bismarck, Otto von, 11, 27, 213
Blavatsky, Madame Helena, 89-92, 243
Blyumkin, Yakov, 412-413
Bobrinskaya, Countess Julia Alexeievna, 420
Bokhanov, Alexander, 50
Boodts, Marga, 433
Botkin, Dr Eugene, 107, 159, 165-167, 231, 247-248, 254, 342, 350, 353, 371, 378-379, 383-384, 442, 444, 472, 477
Botkin, Petr S., 421
Brassova, Countess, 373
Brizak, A., 123
Brownell, Frank, 178
Brun, Élisabeth Vigée Le, 210
Brusilov, General alexei, 320, 329, 441
Buchanan, Sir George, 312, 334, 336, 404, 419-420
Buchanan, Merial, 156
Bulygin, 450-451
Buxhoeveden, Sophie, xiii, 80, 154, 157, 160, 207-208, 236, 262, 264, 267-268, 283, 340, 342-343, 354-355, 376, 379, 385, 398, 410-411
Bykov, Pavel Mikhailovich, x, 44, 49, 330, 347, 443, 469-470

C

Carnot, Sadi, 205
Catherine I, 31, 55-56, 73-75
Catherine II (aka the Great), 21, 56, 60-62, 75, 135, 212
Cecil, Robert, 198
Cellarius, Henri, 76
Cerf, Camille, 36, 43, 203

INDEX

Chebotaryova, Valentina Ivanovna, 108, 271, 273
Cheiro (i.e. Louis Hamon), 153-154, 217
Chemodurov, Terenty (valet), 342, 353, 368, 455-456
Chicherin, Georgi, 410, 455
Christian IX, 11, 96, 431, 435
Churchill, Winston, 28, 219, 359, 362, 364-365, 383, 427-428, 454
Corelli, Marie (aka Mary Mackay), 173
Creighton, Bishop Mandell, 45, 50
Crowley, Aleister, 90
Cumming, Sir Mansfield, 401-404, 406, 408
Czerneewski, Waclaw, 271

D

Danilov, General Yuri Nikiforovich, 259, 321-322
Dehn, Carl Akimovich von, 165
Dehn, Lili, 165, 240, 246, 268, 273, 312, 318, 325, 348-349
Demenkov, Nikolai, 224
Demidova, Anna, 342, 353, 366, 379, 384, 390, 472
Derevenko, Kolya, 343, 353, 370-371
Derevenko, Dr Vladimir, 342, 353, 398-399
Dieterichs, Mikhail Konstantinovich, 416, 441, 443, 446, 449, 451-452, 459, 473, 491
Dolgorukov, Vasily Alexandrovich, 67, 282, 334, 342, 344, 353, 355, 374-375, 405, 437
Dominin, Majordomo Parfen Alexievitch, 368, 457, 463-464
Doublier, Francis, 36, 43, 203
Durnovo, Pyotr, 26, 257
Duval, Gabriel Louis, 433
Dzhunkovsky, Vladimir, 462

E

Eastman, George, 178-179
Edward VIII, 15, 217, 221-222, 437
Edward VII, 4, 9, 11, 22, 28, 153-154, 176, 211, 215, 217-222, 238, 308, 385, 431
Elena of Montenegro, Queen, 13, 93, 312, 222, 225, 270, 423
Eliot, Sir Charles, 415-416, 456
Elizabeth I of Russia, 31, 60, 62, 75-76

Elizabeth I of Britain, 402, 435
Ellerik, Gertrude, 433
Encausse, Gérard Anaclet Vincent, (aka Papus), 95, 97, 99-100, 151, 169
Ermakov, Pyotr, x, 378-379, 382-385, 389-390, 460
Ersberg, Elizaveta, 342, 354, 398
Essad-Bey, Mohammed, 264
Eugénie de Montijo, Empress, 219

F

Faberge, Carl, 78, 86
Feodorovna, Alexandra, 1 et al
Feodorovna, Elizabeth, 252, 262, 377, 394-395, 417, 444-445, 452, 459, 485, 490
Feodorovna, Maria, 5 et al
Fersen, Baron, 80
Fonteyn, Dame Margot, 8
Frederiks, Count Adolf, 306, 321-323, 329
Freze, Pyotr, 53
Fuhrmann, Joseph T., 145-147, 298

G

Gapon, Georgy, 111, 129-133, 135
Gedroitz, Vera, 270-272, 274
Gennari, Benedetto (the younger), 178
George V, 5, 15, 22, 30, 88, 176, 192, 221-222, 238, 309, 335-337, 344, 406, 414-416, 419-420, 422-423, 425-426, 428, 434-435, 444
Gibbes, Charles Sydney, 69, 166, 342, 354, 364, 366, 399, 414-416, 447, 451
Giers, Mikhail Nikolaevich de, 453, 462, 465-468
Gilliard, Pierre, 69, 72, 159, 184, 342, 346, 348, 350, 354, 364, 398-399, 414, 447, 451, 453
Gilyarovsky, Vladimir Alekseyevich, 51
Goloshchekin, Filipp, x, 347, 349, 352, 373, 375-377, 381, 384, 390, 392, 398, 405-406, 409-410, 414, 419, 421, 456, 460
Golovin, A, 319
Golytsin, Anna, 297
Goremykin, Ivan, 139
Gorky, Maxim, 240, 268, 407
Grabbe, Count Alexander, 186
Grabbe, Bishop Anthony, 485
Grabbe, Paul, 186

Graffe, Suzanna Catharina de, 434
Grammatikov, Alexander Nikolaevich, 408
Grenfell, Field Marshall Francis, 45
Guchkov, Alexander, 322-325, 331
Gurvich, 467-468
Guseva, Chionya, 286

H

Hagelberg, Dr Erica, 477
Hall, Coryne, 8
Hanbury-Williams, Sir John, 289, 403, 447
Helen of Serbia, Princess, 433
Hélène of Orléans, 4
Hendrikova, Anastasia, 342-343, 353, 355, 396, 398-399
Henry, Prince (of Battenburg/Prussia), 96, 126, 195-196, 223
Hermogenes, Bishop, 148, 158, 232-233, 239, 241-242, 251, 255, 314, 348, 368, 371-372, 395-396
Hoare, Sir Samuel, 364, 403-404
Hume, Allan, 89-91
Hung-Chan, Li, 50

I

Isvolsky, Alexander, 154, 171
Ivanova-Vasilyeva, Nedezhda, 433

J

Janin, General Maurice, 451-452, 466
Josef, Emperor Franz, 64, 194

K

Kalyaev, Ivan, 46
Kannegisser, Leonid, 417
Kaplan, Fanya, 416-418
Karsavina, Tamara, 43
Kastritzky, Dr, 343, 348
Keiser Wilhelm II, 8, 15, 22, 27-28, 49, 96, 141, 192, 194-195, 198-199, 205, 209, 212-213, 215, 257, 269, 281-284, 309, 335, 344-351, 409, 322-423, 426, 433, 461
Kelch, Barbara, 176
Kerensky, Alexander Fyodorovich, 138, 280, 285, 287, 298, 312, 325, 327, 331-332, 334-3366, 338, 345, 347, 358-360, 413, 420-421

Khabarov, Yerofei, 115
Khlynov, Vladimir, 344, 377
Khokhryakovk, Pavel, 396
Khvostov, Alexei, 286
Kissinger, Henry, 473
Kleinmichel, Countess Marie, 49, 70
Kleinmichel, Countess Ekaterina, 225
Kleinmichel, Countess Olga, 225-226
Knijff, Dr Peter de, 484-485
Kochurov, Michael, 469
Kobylinsky, Colonel Eugene, 333, 343-345, 347, 350, 354, 455
Kokovtzev, Vladimir, 244
Kolchak, Admiral, 320, 328, 332, 358-365, 440-441, 448-452, 457, 459
Kolyaba, Dmitry, 241
Kornilov, General Lavr, 332-333, 347, 359-362
Konstantinovich, Konstantin, 103, 395
Konstantinovich, Ioann, 395
Korovichenko, Commandant, 325, 335, 338
Krarup, Theodora, 146, 158, 168
Krasnov, Nikolay, 63
Kreindel, Dr Isaak Solomonovich, 165
Kronstadt, Father John of, 17, 148-149, 169, 239, 314
Krymov, Lieutenant General, 301, 327
Kschessinska, Mathilde Feliksovna, 5, 8, 47, 81, 448
Kulikovska, Mrs Olga, 431, 478-485
Kulikovsky, Tihon, 479, 482, 486
Kurlov, Pavel, 254
Kuropatkin, General, 98

L

Landar, Jeanne Julie, 92
Laptinskaya, Akilina N., 297
Lazovert, Dr Stanislaus de, 290, 292, 296
Lenin, 89, 110, 175, 226, 262, 268, 312-313, 325, 331-332, 347-348, 358, 362-363, 365, 372-373, 375-376, 393, 395, 398, 406-409, 412-413, 416-418, 420-422, 446, 455-457, 461, 476
Lloyd George, David, 334, 337, 406, 427
Lochtina, Madame, 149, 151-152, 157, 239, 242
Lockhart, Sir Robert Bruce, 365, 406-408, 410, 413, 416-418, 428
Lokhvitskaya, Nadezhda, (Teffi) 256, 288

INDEX

Loubet, Émile, 96, 98, 209-211
Louise, Queen of Denmark, 10-11, 65
Louise, Princess Victoria (of Prussia) 22
Ludbrook, Bryan, 35, 181-182
Ludwig, Ernest, 3, 9, 14, 28, 35-36, 209, 432
Ludwig, Friedrich Wilhelm (Ludwig IV), 2-3, 20, 65, 176
Lyandres, Semion 416

M

Malama, Dmitry, 224, 400
Mandryka, Captain, 235
Margaret of Prussia, Princess, 8
Marie, Queen of Romania, 207, 270, 422-424, 427
Mary of Teck, 5, 221, 238, 422
Masaryk, Czech President T.G., 458
Massie, Robert K., 161-162, 181, 207, 453
Maucher, Karl, 433
McDougall, Nadine, 437
Medvedev, Pavel, 366, 378, 383
Melita, Princess Victoria, (See Victoria Malita of Edinburgh), 14, 28
Meltser, Roman, 57
Merejkovsky, Dmitry, 135
Mikhailovich, Alexander, 17, 30, 78, 430, 435-436
Mikhailovich, Sergei, 148, 290, 394-395
Milica of Montenegro, 92-95, 97-99, 120, 153, 156, 430
Miloslayskaya, Maria, 78
Milyukov, Pavel Nikolayevich, 285, 287, 324, 331-332, 334, 419-420
Mniszech, Marina, 74
Mirbach, Count Wilhelm von, 409-410, 412-413, 446, 455, 461
Mitrovich, Giovanni, 91-92
Montebello, Gustave Lannes de, 48, 50-51
Momyakov, Nikolai, 67
Moshkin, Alexander, 366
Mossolov, Alexander, 67, 99, 266, 268, 413-414
Mutnykh, Natalya, 458, 460

N

Nagai, Dr Tatsuo, 481-482, 484
Nagorny, Klementy, 342, 353, 355
Nametkin, Aleksei, 440, 442

Naryshkin, Kiril, 451-453
Nelipa, Margarita, 476
Nikitin, Dr Sergey, 472
Nikolaevich, Nikolai, 71, 97, 106, 135, 259-260, 262-264, 320-321, 323, 430, 452-453, 462, 465-466
Nikolaevich, Pavel, 94-95
Nikolaevna, Anastasia, 93, 126, 431-433
Nikolaevna, Olga, 63, 81, 108, 187, 225, 241, 274, 278, 479
Nikulin, Grigori, 373-374, 378, 380, 384
Nizier, Philippe Anthelme, 92, 95, 97-103, 105-108, 119-120, 151, 153-155, 158, 169, 252

O

Obolensky, A. D., 102
Orlov, Count Grigori Grigoryevich, 57, 420
Orlov, Count Nikolai Vladimirovich, 408, 462, 466-467
Osten-Sacken, Count, 29

P

Palen, Count Konstantin Ivanovich, 46
Paléologue, Maurice, 98, 240, 243, 257, 307, 323, 325
Pankratov, Commissar, 347-348
Papus (see Encausse, Gérard)
Paul I, 27, 30-31, 57, 59
Pavlovna, Elena, 61
Pavlovna, Maria, 278
Perkhin, Mikhail, 58
Peter I, (aka Peter the Great), 21, 23, 26, 36, 40, 55-57, 60, 62, 73-75, 78, 134, 136, 189, 206, 262, 264, 309, 493
Peter III, 57
Petrovna, Princess Nadejda, 462, 467
Philippe, Prince of Paris, 4
Piasetsky, Pavel, 97
Pihl, Alma, 84
Plehve, Vyacheslav, 109, 133, 417
Pokrovsky, Lt general Viktor, 361-362
Pokrovsky, Mikhail Nikolaevich, 462, 476
Prager, Judith, 256
Protopopov, Alexander, 267, 286
Purishkevich, Vladimir, 287-286, 290-292, 296-297, 314, 404
Pustovoitenko, General Mikhail Savvich, 1, 262

INDEX

Q
Queux, William Le, 237

R
Rachkovsky, Pyotr, 98, 102
Radziwill, Princess Catherine, 303
Rasputin, 80 et al
Rastrelli, Francesco Bartolomeo, 60-62
Raumer, Frederich von, 173
Razumovsky, Count Aleksey, 60
Reilly, Sidney, 406, 408, 417-418
Rhodes, Cecil John, 303
Rietzler, Dr, 455
Rinaldi, Antonio, 59
Rodionov, Lieutenant Nikolai, 224, 241, 354
Rodzianka, Anna Nikolaievna (Golytsin), 297
Rodzianka, Tamara Antonovna, 240
Rodzianko, Mikhail Vladimirovich, 80-81, 151, 157, 233, 242, 254-255, 265-268, 286, 302, 304-306, 319-321, 331
Rodzianko, Colonel Pavel, 240, 354, 385, 447
Rogaev, Dr Eugene, 478-479, 481-482
Rossel, Governor Edvard, 471
Royle, Sir Anthony, 453
Rozanov, General Sergey Nikolaevich, 364, 444, 448-449, 451-452
Ruzsky, General Nikolai Vladimirovich, 306-307, 319-324, 331, 360

S
Sablin, Nikolai Pavlovich, 69, 226, 429
Sarandinaki, Captain Peter, 451, 472
Savich, General, 321
Savinkov, Boris, 417-418
Schanzkowska, Franziska, (aka Anna Anderson) 432-434, 458
Schetkivsky, Bishop Chrisanthes, 148
Schneider, Ekaterina Adolfovna, 69, 348, 353, 396-398, 490
Sednev, Ivan, 342, 353, 378
Sednev, Leonid Ivanovich, 342, 353, 377
Seraphim of Sarov, 99, 119-121, 491, 494
Sergeev, Judge Ivan, 421, 440, 442
Sergius, Metropolitan of Moscow, 37, 46-47, 314
Sherekhovsky, Colonel, 440
Shevkunov, Bishop Tihon, 473, 491

Shirinsky-Shikhmatov, Alexei Alexandrovich, 450-451, 465, 494
Shishkin, Oleg, 298
Shulgin, Vasily Vitalyevich, 321-322, 324-325, 331
Shuvalova, Countess Sophie, 184
Simeon of Verkhoturye, 155
Spiridonova, Marje, 373
Sfiri, Princess Xenia Cheremeteff, 471, 479, 481, 484
Simanovich, Aron, 152, 288, 298
Smolskaia, Yulia, 165
Sokolov, Nikolai, xi, 187, 252, 378, 389-390, 398, 419-421, 439-472, 483, 494
Solomko, Sergey, 78
Starov, Ivan, 60-62, 136
Stcheglov, Mr, 172
Stolypin, Pyotr, 67, 140-142, 158, 160, 232, 234, 238-239, 243-244, 254, 315
Stragorodsky, Sergius, 148, 314
Strekotin, Alexander, 381
Sul-Tim-Badma, Dr (Badmayev), 107-108, 160, 163-165
Sund, Madame Gutjen, 99, 153-154, 171, 217
Sverdlov, Yakov Mikhailovich, 375-377, 387, 409, 417, 419, 421, 446, 456, 460, 480

T
Taneyeva, Anna, (see also Vyrubova, Anna), 152, 155-157, 160, 239
Tatishchev, General Adjutant Ilia, 342, 344, 353, 355, 374-375, 405
Tchagine, Ivan Ivanovich, 196, 226
Tchihatcheff, Lieutenant Michael de, 464
Teffi (see Lokhvitskaya, Nadezhda)
Tegleva, Alexandra, 69, 342, 354, 398, 453
Telberg, George Gustav, 444, 448, 461
Theophane, Bishop, 105, 148-149, 151-153, 157, 160, 234-235, 237, 239, 242-243
Thormeyer, Ferdinand, 185-186
Thornhill, Major Cudbert, 403
Tikhomirov, Lev, 237
Totten, George William, 187
Trepoff, General, 325
Trotsky, Leon, 52, 132, 310, 332, 334, 373, 405-406, 413, 416, 418, 425, 455, 460
Trufanoff, Sergei Mikhailovich, 148, 151

INDEX

Trupp, Alois, 342, 353, 379, 383-384, 472, 490
Tuxen, Laurits, 20-21
Tyutcheva, Sophie, 235-236, 242

U

Uritsky, Moisei (Cheka), 417
Urlanis, Boris (demographer), 317

V

Vasiliev, A. T., 239-240
Vasiliev, Father Aleksei, 343, 348
Vassilitchikov, Marie Alexandrovna, 268
Vaughan-James, Reverend G.V., 337
Victoria of Hesse and by Rhine, 13, 28, 422-423, 425
Victoria Melita of Edinburgh, (See Melita))
Victoria, Queen, 1-5, 10-11, 13, 15-16, 20-21, 23, 28, 35, 57, 65, 69, 78, 87, 106, 124, 173, 176, 195-199, 220, 222, 247, 269, 422-424, 436, 471
Vishnyakova, Maria, 236-237
Vladimirovich, Andrei, 448
Vladimirovich, Kirill, 429, 466, 468
Vlasovsky, Alexander, 46
Voeikov, Vladimir, 253
Volkov, Alexei Andreevich, 266, 342, 353, 396-398
Vorontsov-Dashkov, Count Illarion, 36, 46, 91, 303
Vyrubov, Alexander, 152, 157
Vyrubova, Anna, 152, 157-158, 160, 162-163, 165-167, 180-182, 232, 236, 239-240, 242, 244, 246, 249, 253, 268, 270, 272, 274, 289-290, 297-298, 313-314, 318, 325, 335, 399

W

Wigström, Henrik, 227, 278
Wilhelm II (see Keiser)
Wilton, Robert, 409, 448, 450
Witte, Count Sergey Yulyevich, 14, 25-26, 28, 49, 67, 91-92, 98, 102, 106, 111-113, 117, 141, 164, 198-199, 243-244, 257, 267, 269, 286, 308, 310-312, 314-315, 317, 319

Y

Yakovlev, Vasily, x, 329, 350-352, 395
Yakovlev, Evgeniy, 53
Yakovleva, Varvara, 395, 452
Yanushkevich, General Nikolai, 259
Yeltsin, Boris, 299, 471, 475-476, 486, 487-488
Yussoupoff, Felix, xi, 61, 81, 107, 290-292, 297, 299, 337, 378, 404, 429
Yussoupoff, Irina, 61, 81, 290, 292, 348
Yussoupoff, Zinaida, 297
Yussoupoff (s) (generally), vi, 292, 294-295, 306
Yuvenaly, Metropolitan Bishop, 488, 491

Z

Zakveskia, Maria, 407, 418
Zarutsky, Marina, 74-75
Zharov, Dr Vladimir, 296
Zorka of Montenegro, Princess, 92-93, 433

Book Information:

Narrative word count:	163,052
Quotes word count:	13,849
Image text word count:	5,230
Total word count:	182,131
Comparisons:	Ulysses (265, 222)
	Pride and Prejudice (122,685)
Top keywords:	Nicholas (1,009)
	Alexandra (517)
	Russian (497)
	Rasputin (463)
	Royal family (164)
	Ipatiev House (128)

Available in the following formats:

Paperback	-	ISBN: 978-1-80068-965-7 (colour on white paper)
Paperback B&W	-	ISBN: 978-1-80352-799-4 (groundwood paper)
Paperback B&W	-	KDP ISBN: 979-8-85247-188-8 (white paper)
Hardback	-	ISBN: 978-1-80352-695-9 (colour on white paper)
Hardback B&W	-	ISBN: 978-1-80352-911-0 (groundwood, dust jacket)
Hardback B&W	-	KDP ISBN: 979-8-85221-513-0 (cream paper)
Ebook	-	ISBN: 978-1-80352-908-0

Other books by this author:

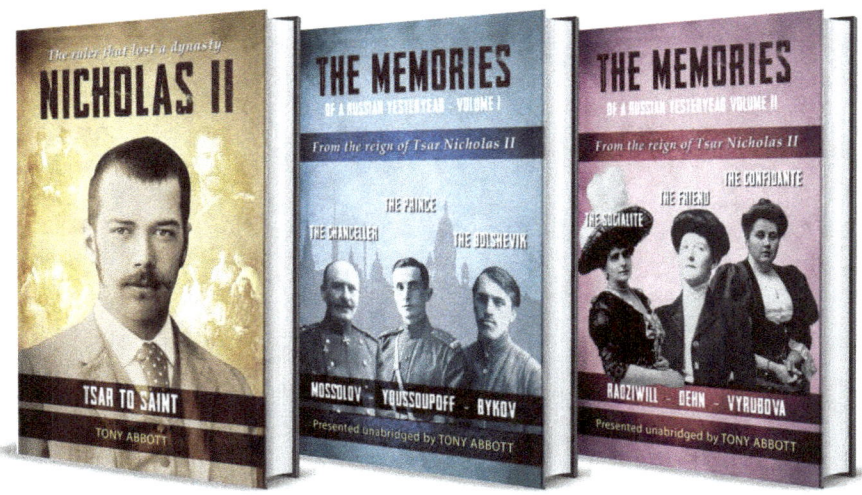

www.ingramcontent.com/pod-product-compliance
Lightning Source LLC
Chambersburg PA
CBHW070054110526
44587CB00013BB/1329